Norway and National Liberation in Southern Africa

Edited by

Tore Linné Eriksen

Nordiska Afrikainstitutet 2000

Indexing terms
Churches
National liberation movements
Trade unions
ANC
FRELIMO
MPLA
SWAPO
Angola
Guinea-Bissau
Mozambique
Namibia
Norway
South Africa
Zimbabwe

Language checking: Elaine Almén

Cover: Adriaan Honcoop

© the authors and Nordiska Afrikainstitutet, 2000

ISBN 91-7106-447-8

Printed in Sweden by Elanders Gotab, Stockholm 2000

Contents

List of Acronyms

AAM	Anti-Apartheid Movement (United Kingdom)
AFL/CIO	American Federation of Labor/Committee for Industrial Organization
AGIS	Africa Groups in Sweden/Afrikagrupperna i Sverige
AIS	Arbeiderbevegelsens Internasjonale Støttekomité (International Solidarity Committee of the Norwegian Labour Movement)
AKP	Arbeidernes Kommunistparti (Workers' Communist Party, Norway)
ANC	African National Congress (South Africa)
ANC	African National Council (Zimbabwe)
AOF	Arbeidernes Opplysningsforbund (Workers' Educational Association)
AUF	Arbeidernes Ungdomsfylking (Labour Party Youth)
BAWU	Black Allied Workers Union
BCM	Black Consciousness Movement
BPC	Black People's Convention
BOSS	Bureau of State Security (South Africa)
CCN	Council of Churches in Namibia
CEIR	Council for Ecumenical and International Relations– Church of Norway (Mellomkirkelig Råd)
CIA	Central Intelligence Agency (United States)
CONCP	Conference of Nationalist Organisations in the Portuguese Colonies /Conferência das Organizações Nacionalistas das Colónias Portuguêsas
COSATU	Congress of South African Trade Unions
CUSA	Council of Unions of South Africa
DANIDA	Danish International Development Assistance
DKK	Danish kroner
DNA	Det Norske Arbeiderparti (Norwegian Labour Party)
DTA	Democratic Turnhalle Alliance
EC	European Community
ECA	United Nations Economic Commission for Africa
EEC	European Economic Commission
EFTA	European Free Trade Association
ELCSA	Evangelical Lutheran Church in South Africa
FAO	Food and Agricultural Organisation
FINNIDA	Finnish International Development Agency
FNLA	National Front for the Liberation of Angola/Frente Nacional de Libertação de Angola
FOSATU	Federation of South African Trade Unions
FRELIMO	Mozambique Liberation Front/Frente de Libertação de Moçambique
FROLIZI	Front for the Liberation of Zimbabwe
ICFTU	International Confederation of Free Trade Unions
ICJ	International Court of Justice
IDAF	International Defence and Aid Fund
IDASA	Institute for Democratic Alternatives in South Africa
ILO	International Labour Organisation
IMF	International Monetary Fund
IOC	International Olympic Committee
IRCOZ	International Refugee Council of Zambia
ISAK	Isolate South Africa Committee (Sweden)
ISC	International Student Conference
IUEF	International University Exchange Fund
LO	Landsorganisasjonen i Norge (Norwegian Confederation of Trade Unions)
LWF	Lutheran World Federation
MK	Umkhonto we Sizwe (South Africa)

MPLA	Popular Movement for the Liberation of Angola/Movimento Popular de Libertação de Angola
MS	Mellemfolkeligt Samvirke (Danish Association for International Co-operation)
MUN	Mineworkers Union of Namibia
MWASA	Media Workers Association of South Africa
NACTU	National Council of Trade Unions
NATO	North Atlantic Treaty Organisation
NAMA	Norsk Aksjon Mot Apartheid (Norwegian Action Against Apartheid)
NCA	Norwegian Church Aid (Kirkens Nødhjelp)
NGO	Non-Governmental Organisation
NEKSA	Norsk ekumenisk komite for det sørlige Afrika (Norwegian Ecumenical Committee for Southern Africa)
NMS	Norwegian Missionary Society
NKIF	Norwegian Union of Chemical Industry Workers (Norsk Kjemisk Industri-arbeiderforening)
NKP	Norway's Communist Party
NOCOSA	Norwegian Council for Southern Africa (Fellesrådet for det sørlige Afrika)
NOK	Norwegian kroner
NORAD	Norwegian Agency for Development Co-operation
NRK	Norsk Rikskringkasting (Norwegian Broadcasting Corporation)
NSA	Norwegian Shipowners Association (Norges Rederiforbund)
NTUC	Nordic Trade Union Council
NPA	Norwegian People's Aid
NUM	National Mineworkers Union
NUNW	National Union of Namibian Workers
NUSAS	National Union of South African Students
OAU	Organisation of African Unity
OD	Operasjon Dagsverk (Operation Day's Work)
OECD	Organisation of Economic Co-operation and Development
OPEC	Organisation of Petroleum Exporting Countries
OPO	Ovamboland's People's Organisation
PAC	Pan-Africanist Congress of Azania (South Africa)
PAIGC	African Party for the Independence of Guinea Bissau and Cape Verde /Partido Africano para a Independência da Guiné e Cabo Verde
PCR	Programme to Combat Racism of WCC
PF	Patriotic Front (Zimbabwe)
PLAN	People's Liberation Army of Namibia
RENAMO	Resistencia Nacional Mocambicana (Mozambique National Resistance)
SACBC	Southern African Catholic Bishops Conference
SACC	South African Council of Churches
SACP	South African Communist Party
SACTU	South African Congress of Trade Unions
SADCC	Southern Africa Development Co-ordination Conference
SADC	Southern Africa Development Community
SAIH	Studentenes og Akademikernes Internasjonale Hjelpefond (Norwegian Students' and Academics' International Assistance Fund)
SASO	South African Students Organisation
SATUCC	Southern African Trade Union Co-ordination Council
SCAT	Social Change Assistance Trust
SEK	Swedish kronor
SIDA	Swedish International Development Co-operation Agency
SOMAFCO	Solomon Mahlangu Freedom College (ANC/Tanzania)
SRB	Shipping Research Bureau
SWANU	South West Africa National Union
SWAPO	South West Africa People's Organisation
SWAPO-D	SWAPO-Democrats
SWC	SWAPO's Women Council

UANC	United African National Council (Zimbabwe)
UDF	United Democratic Front (South Africa)
UDI	Unilateral Declaration of Independence (Rhodesia)
UGEAN	General Union of Students from Black Africa under Portuguese Colonial Domination/União Geral dos Estudantes da África Negra sob Dominação Colónial Portuguêsa
UN	United Nations
UNDP	United Nations Development Programme
UNESCO	United Nations Educational, Scientific and Cultural Organisation
UNHCR	United Nations High Commissioner for Refugees
UNICEF	United Nations Children's Fund
UNIN	United Nations Institute for Namibia
UNITA	National Union for the Total Independence of Angola/União Nacional para a Independência Total de Angola
UNIP	United National Independence Party (Zambia)
UNTAG	United Nations Transitional Assistance Group
USD	US dollar
WAY	World Assembly of Youth
WCC	World Council of Churches
WFTU	World Federation of Trade Unions
WHO	World Health Organisation
WUS	World University Service
ZANU	Zimbabwe African National Union
ZAPU	Zimbabwe African People's Union
ZCTU	Zambian Congress of Trade Unions

An Introductory Note

In August 1994, the Nordic Africa Institute (NAI) in Uppsala initiated a project to document and analyse the involvement of the Nordic countries in the liberation struggles in Southern Africa. This decision coincided with the demise of the apartheid regime in South Africa, which also marked an end to the protracted struggles for national liberation in the Southern African region at large. In this struggle for human rights and national self-determination, Norway and the other Nordic countries rendered diplomatic support and humanitarian assistance to the liberation movements in Angola, Mozambique, Zimbabwe, Namibia and South Africa.

Largely financed through contributions by the Nordic governments, the project on *National Liberation in Southern Africa: The role of the Nordic countries* has been organised as a Nordic undertaking, with national research teams set up in Sweden, Denmark, Finland and Norway. The Norwegian Institute of International Affairs (NUPI) agreed to coordinate the Norwegian part of the project, with Tore Linné Eriksen serving as project leader and Eva Helene Østbye as research fellow. While a more modest and limited work had originally been envisaged, the project soon started to live a life of its own. When it was gradually realised that such a demanding and time-consuming task could not be undertaken by a core team with limited resources, contributions were invited from scholars and activists in order to more fully document the significant role played by the solidarity movements, churches and the trade unions (see chapters 6–9). Although this outside assistance entails some disadvantages in terms of coherence, we trust that it will result in a study that covers wider ground and reflects the importance of popular involvement in the struggle against apartheid and colonialism. Contributions from outside the core team have also made it possible to include a chapter on Rhodesia/Zimbabwe as a diplomatic issue and a chapter concerned with the battle for economic sanctions.

Although our study is broad in scope, it is, of course, far from an all-compassing presentation of the Norwegian involvement in the liberation struggle. We have also had to base the study on the premise that there is a general awareness of the main developments in the Southern African region from 1960 onwards.

Chapters 1–4 focus on the formulation and implementation of official policies, chiefly based on Ministry of Foreign Affairs archives and other unresearched primary sources. Under different circumstances, we would also have liked to look more deeply into the dominant political parties and the mass media. In terms of data collection, a case could also be made for a more systematic use of formal interviews with Norwegian diplomats, politicians, researchers and activists who have been concerned with Southern African issues over the years. While we offer separate chapters on the Namibia Committee at Elverum, the churches, the trade unions and the Norwegian Council for Southern Africa, other important actors—such as the Students' and Academics' Assistance Fund (SAIH), the Norwegian People's Aid and Operation Day's Work (Operasjon Dagsverk)—have only been mentioned in passing. Another aspect that is outside the scope of our study is the substantial economic assistance extended by the Norwegian government to the Frontline States and the Southern African Development Community for regional cooperation.

More importantly, the present study has only to a limited extent been based on Southern African archival material. It is also very unfortunate that a parallel project on the History of the National Liberation Struggles in Southern Africa, to be conducted by the Southern African Regional Institute for Policy Studies in Harare, has not so far materialised. However, in February 1999 our draft manuscript was presented to a conference at Robben Island (*Nordic Solidarity with the Liberation Struggles in Southern Africa and Challenges for Democratic Partnerships into the 21st century*). Since most of the authors of our study were present at this important gathering, we were given the opportunity to exchange views and receive comments and advice from a great number of participants from the Southern African region, many of whom had themselves played prominent roles in the liberation struggles. In addition, we have made use of the unique collection of interviews with representatives from the liberation movements conducted by Tor Sellström. *Liberation in Southern Africa. Regional and Swedish Voices* (Uppsala, Nordic Africa Institute, 1999) is thus to be regarded as a companion volume to our study.

We have over the years contracted many debts. From the very beginning the Norwegian research team has greatly benefited from close cooperation with our Nordic colleagues: Tor Sellström, Christopher Morgenstierne, Iina Soiri and Pekka Peltola. (The titles of the accompanying Nordic studies are listed in the bibliography.) Our special thanks also go to the Nordic Africa Institute, Charlotta Dohlvik and Lennart Wohlgemuth in particular, and to Elaine Almén who language-checked our draft manuscripts. The Norwegian Ministry of Foreign Affairs also deserves our gratitude for their generous funding (and patience!). Although the costs of the project have largely been covered by the Ministry of Foreign Affairs, it goes without saying that we do not intend to present a hagiographic account or a self-congratulatory Festschrift. Finally, it should be noted that each individual author is responsible for his/her contribution to this volume.

Oslo, 15 March, 2000

Tore Linné Eriksen

Chapter I
The Origins of a Special Relationship: Norway and Southern Africa 1960–1975

Tore Linné Eriksen

Introduction[1]

Although the period from 1960 to 1975 only covers fifteen years, it is a period which is marked by great changes in the Norwegian political attitude towards Southern Africa. In the course of these years the Norwegian anti-apartheid movement emerged and saw to it that Southern Africa had its place on the political agenda. It is also in this period that the liberation movements made their first bonds with the Norwegian solidarity organisations and the official authorities in Norway (in that order). The result of this was that in the early 1970s the more sporadic forms of aid extended to refugees and "victims of apartheid" developed into a regular and organised form of support and co-operation. Even though in financial terms the amount of the aid given in this period should not be exaggerated, and although the support given to the liberation movements in Namibia and South Africa in the main belong to the period after 1975,[2] there is no other Western country—apart from Sweden—which had such close relations to the struggle for liberation in Southern Africa. However, in other fields such as the question of economic sanctions, a long period of time was yet to pass before the calls of the liberation movements were complied with. And even then, as we shall see in chapter 5, the sanctions law adopted in 1987 had its loopholes.

The aim of this chapter is to give a sketch of the main features both of the Norwegian official policy and that of the development in the general climate of opinion in Norway. Within the scope of a limited number of pages there will, of course, be many important aspects, actors and nuances which will have to be omitted. Instead of including a little about all sides of

---

[1] Although the author of this chapter is a historian and therefore attempts to adhere to the methodological principles laid down by his profession, it should also be stated—as a matter of transparency—that he has since the middle of the 1960s been closely involved with the Norwegian Council for Southern Africa and other solidarity organisations supporting the liberation struggle.

[2] See chapters 2 and 3.

the subject, only those themes have been chosen which throw interesting light on some of the conflicting choices that had to be made, and on some of the most important changes that took place. For this reason especially much space has been given to the important UN/OAU conference in 1973, which marked a diplomatic breakthrough for the liberation movements on the international level.

As attention is here directed primarily towards the official policy of the Norwegian authorities, with the richly stocked archives of the Ministry of Foreign Affairs as a main source, the reader is recommended to read this presentation together with the chapters dealing with the role of the solidarity movements, the churches and the trade unions (see chapters 6, 7 and 8). As most space is here devoted to *describing* the main developments, one would also refer the reader to the concluding chapter which employs a more analytical and critical approach.

The silent 1950s

Norwegian policies towards South Africa prior to 1960 (including the issue of the legal status of South West Africa/Namibia) were not rooted in any profound interest or involvement in the struggle against racial discrimination and oppression. As is documented in a recent thesis from the University of Oslo, which is concerned with "Norway and the South African issue 1945–1961", the main reason why the question was put on the agenda at all, was the need for the Norway to decide how to cast its vote in the UN General Assembly.[3]

In the Norwegian Parliament, the South African issue was hardly raised when foreign affairs were regularly debated, and as Minister of Foreign Affairs, Halvard Lange, did not take any special interest in questions outside the main Cold War arena.[4] The reports by the Norwegian Consulate General in Pretoria largely reflected the views of the white minority, and did not contribute to any profound understanding of the intensification of the apartheid system and the mass campaigns witnessed by South Africa in the 1950s. Based on a close reading of the consular reports, Ole Kr. Eivindson in his thesis diplomatically concludes that the Consul General in the period 1950–1959 tended to "gloss over the racial issue".[5] (According to the Consul General, the best solution for South Africa would be a kind of "moderate apartheid" rooted in an amalgamation of the Nationalist Party and the

---

[3] Ole Kristian Eivindson, *Norge og raseproblemene i Sør-Afrika, 1945–1961*. Thesis, Department of History, University of Oslo, 1997.

[4] Halvard Lange was—apart from a brief interval in 1963—foreign minister in the Labour Government from 1946 to 1965.

[5] Eivindson, op.cit., p. 19. August Fleischer was the Norwegian Consul General in Cape Town from 1950 to 1959.

United Party.)[6] At the outset of the massive Defiance Campaign in the early 1950s, it was, to give an example, reported that the African majority "is so backward in political development that one does not hear much from them".[7] When a new Consul General was appointed in 1959, he expressed the view that demonstrations and revolts were difficult to explain as "the natives act in a way which seems extremely illogical" and that "demonstrations among culturally backward people give rise to meaningless and hooligan-like forms of expression".[8]

Compared to Sweden, the apartheid system installed in 1948 did not attract any great attention in the Norwegian mass media or among the intelligentsia in the 1950s.[9] There were no prominent public figures and newspaper editors who—like Herbert Tingsten—vigorously dissected the apartheid system and campaigned for the promotion of the human rights of the African majority. Nor were there any well publicised incidents like the "Lidman affair", in which the Swedish novelist Sara Lidman and a young leader from the liberation movement were arrested for contravening the so-called "Immorality Act". Although some church leaders with experience from South Africa voiced their opinion from time to time (see chapter 7), there was no Norwegian to compare with the indefatigable campaigner Gunnar Helander.

Together with the other Nordic countries, Norway had always agreed to put the South Africa issue on the agenda of the United Nations, while South Africa itself argued that the UN—according to Chapter 2, art. 7—had no right to intervene in internal matters. When this issue was raised for the first time in 1946, the Permanent Mission of Norway to the UN—in opposition to the instructions received by the Ministry of Foreign Affairs in Oslo—voted in favour of a resolution stating that the treatment of the Indian minority in South Africa was not consistent with the UN Charter.[10] When the General Assembly in 1952 for the first time discussed the apartheid system in general, Norway strongly argued that South Africa's racial policies were in violation of the UN Charter, and, thus, fell within the competence of the General Assembly. The fact that the United States sided against South Africa and the major colonial powers made the issue much easier for Norway to handle, since it could be regarded as being above the overriding Cold War

---

[6] Memo from August Fleischer to the Ministry of Foreign Affairs, 22 April 1953, quoted by Eivindson, op. cit.

[7] Memo from August Fleischer, 29 March 1952.

[8] Erik Colban was Consul General in the period 1959–1963. The quote is from his memo to the Ministry of Foreign Affairs, 26 August 1959. For another view of the 1950s, see Tom Lodge: *Black politics in South Africa since 1945*. London: Longman, 1983 and Nelson Mandela: *Long Walk to Freedom*. London: Little, Brown and Company, 1994.

[9] The Swedish experience is outlined in great detail by Tor Sellström: *Sweden and National Liberation in Southern Africa. Vol. I: Formation of a Popular Opinion (1950–1970)*. Uppsala: Nordiska Afrikainstitutet, 1999.

[10] Eivindson, op.cit., pp. 39–44.

dividing line which was so influential in determining the foreign policies of Norway. It could even be argued, as Norwegian politicians often did, that it was in fact in the true interest of the West not to confront the new nations by joining forces with colonialism and white supremacy in apartheid South Africa.

With a few nuances, until the late 1950s the Permanent Mission of Norway to the UN followed a consistent line in the 4th Committee and the General Assembly. The general position, which was reflected in the voting pattern, was to avoid denouncing the South African apartheid regime, since this was assumed to make the regime less willing to work with the UN in finding "constructive solutions" to the racial problems. In practice, this led Norway—with the other Nordic countries—to abstain when resolutions containing explicit references to South African discrimination and oppression were introduced. The basic assumption was obviously that the regime itself would only listen to friendly advice as to how to change its policies, and that nothing further than general recommendations to member countries to adhere to the UN charter was acceptable if this strategy of "dialogue" was to yield results. The only noticeable exception was in 1954, when the draft resolution introduced by India deliberately avoided expressing harsh criticism in order to enlist support from the Nordic countries and other Western powers.[11]

By abstaining, it could be argued that Norway was seeking to bridge the gap between the more radical Afro-Asian camp on the one hand and South Africa/the major Western powers on the other. But no initiatives were taken in this early period, and no bridges were actually built. Perhaps passivity (or complacency) seems a more fitting description than active bridge building.

Entering the 1960s: Students, the South Africa Committee and the Nobel Peace Prize

The era of decolonisation

When more attention was focused on South Africa towards the end of the 1950s, the main reason for this was to be found in the interest and commitment shown by more internationally inclined students and other members of the (rather small) academic community. This was followed by the launching of a Norwegian South Africa Committee, the awarding of the Nobel Peace Prize to Albert Luthuli and the convening of an Afro-Scandinavian Youth Congress in Oslo. These years also saw the first consumer boycott of South African goods, initiated by the trade unions and the major youth organisations. In this way, the public opinion and the activities of dedicated anti-apartheid organisations compelled the Norwegian government and the Ministry of Foreign Affairs to formulate a more "activist"

---

[11] Ibid., p. 50.

position in the UN. At a more general level, this observation leads the author of a thesis on Norway and the "racial conflict" in South Africa 1960–1978 to conclude that "my theory is that Norwegian engagement and involvement was the result of pressure from various sources and not that of any direct sense of engagement specifically related to the race conflict in South Africa".[12]

Internationally, this period coincides with the growing isolation of South Africa (especially after the Sharpeville massacre and the South African withdrawal from the Commonwealth) and the strengthening of the Afro-Asian bloc in the UN following African decolonisation around 1960. For the peoples in Southern Africa still living under the yoke of colonialism, the UN Declaration on the Granting of Independence to Colonial Countries and Peoples—adopted in 1960—was a major event. The Declaration called for taking "immediate steps in Trust and Non-Self-Governing Territories or all other Territories which have not yet attained independence, to transfer all powers to the peoples of those territories, without any conditions or reservations, in accordance with their freely expressed will and desire. ..."[13] The refusal of the South African, Rhodesian and Portuguese regimes to comply with the UN Declaration as well as resolutions specifically concerned with apartheid, forced the liberation movements in Namibia, Zimbabwe, Angola, Mozambique and Guinea-Bissau to launch the armed struggle in order to achieve their independence.

Scholarships and the Beukes case

When racial discrimination in higher education was reinforced in South Africa in 1953, the Norwegian National Union of Students (Norsk Studentsamband/Norsk Studentunion) immediately decided to include South African students in exchange programmes with three month scholarships. Although this invitation formed part of a general exchange programme, mainly funded by the Ministry of Foreign Affairs, the move was rightly seen as an act of protest against South African apartheid in education. The International Student Conference (ISC) also urged other countries to follow the Norwegian example. The impact of the programme should, however, not be exaggerated. Until 1959, only two students were invited to Norway under the programme. (One of them, incidentally, was not from South Africa but from Basutoland/Lesotho.)

In 1959 the scholarship system was extended from three months to three years to give the students in question an opportunity to complete their university education in Oslo. The first student to benefit from this extended system was Hans Beukes, who had been invited by the Norwegian National

---

[12] Ragnhild Narum, *Norge og rasekonflikten i Sør-Afrika, 1960–1978*. Thesis, Department of History, University of Oslo, 1998, p. 9.

[13] General Assembly Resolution 1514 (XV), 1960.

Union of Students through the non-racial National Union of South African Students (NUSAS). In addition to a grant received from the Ministry of Foreign Affairs, the scholarship was sponsored by the University of Oslo and the student societies of Oslo, Bergen, Trondheim and Ås. Just before leaving for Oslo, Hans Beukes, a 22 year old law student from Namibia, had his passport and other personal documents confiscated by the South African authorities while in Port Elizabeth waiting to board a Norwegian ship. The reason given was that of "subversive activities" since it had become known that he was to appear before a UN committee concerned with the South West African/Namibian issue. Hans Beukes had also in his home country been involved in political activities associated with the recent formation of SWAPO, the liberation movement of Namibia. In 1960 he was *in absentia* elected to the first national committee of SWAPO.

In the light of the reasons stated by the South African authorities, the Norwegian Ministry of Foreign Affairs saw no legal basis for seeking to influence the South African government to reconsider its decision. The Consulate General in Cape Town was, however, instructed to inform the South African Ministry of Foreign Affairs verbally about the publicity which the incident had caused in Norway, which "has made an extremely negative impression on public opinion in Norway, with a damaging effect on the understanding of the problems facing South Africa."[14]

What was soon known as "the Beukes case" understandably attracted great public attention in Norway, especially within the vocal academic community. Hans Beukes later managed to leave South Africa illegally, and arrived in Oslo on 11 September 1959, carrying a US travel document.[15] Two days later he addressed a prominent debating society, the Norwegian Student Society (Det Norske Studentersamfund), and then immediately left for New York to give testimony to the UN South West Africa Committee. At the student meeting a resolution condemning the apartheid regime was adopted, and the Norwegian National Union of Students/Norwegian Student Society jointly put pressure on the Ministry of Foreign Affairs to bring the Beukes case to the attention of UN 4th Committee as well as the General Assembly.[16] The confiscation of his passport was condemned by the UN, considering it "an act of administration contrary to the mandate for South West Africa".[17] Norway on several occasions appealed to South Africa to grant Hans Beukes a new passport, but to no avail.

As a result of the Beukes case and the increasing interest in South African affairs shown by the student community, the Norwegian represen-

---

[14] Memo, Ministry of Foreign Affairs, 4. Pol. Div., 15 September 1959.

[15] Hans Beukes graduated in 1967 from the University of Oslo with a Master Degree in economics and still resides in Norway.

[16] Stortingsmelding nr. 36, 1959–60, p. 100.

[17] General Assembly Resolution no. 1358(XIV), 17 November 1959.

tatives in the UN 4th Committee and the General Assembly were in the following years especially concerned with the issue of education under apartheid.

The Norwegian South Africa Committee

The initiative to form a South Africa Committee was taken by the Norwegian Students Society. A resolution condemning South African racial policies and calling for international assistance to the victims of apartheid was passed on 12 September 1959, sponsored by representatives from all over the political spectrum. Among the seven sponsors was Tron Gerhardsen, the son of the Norwegian Prime Minister Einar Gerhardsen.[18] The prime movers of the resolution served as the preparatory committee for the Norwegian South Africa Committee, which was based on the following political platform: "1) to organise information activities around South Africa; 2) to internationally oppose the South African government's oppression of the African majority; 3) to organise fund-raising campaigns for the victims of apartheid; 4) to explore the possibilities of a boycott of South African goods".[19]

The committee was launched on 26 October 1959. The invitation was signed by MPs from all political parties and other celebrities, including the Bishop of Oslo (Arne Fjellbu) and the most prominent Norwegian author (Tarjei Vesaas).[20] Among the main speakers at the inaugural meeting was Gunnar Jahn, chairman of the Nobel Peace Prize Committee (and ex-Governor of the Central Bank of Norway), who referred to the leaders of the South African National Party as "nazi-inspired statesmen".[21] The general principles formulated by the preparatory committee were endorsed, and Gunnar Jahn was elected the first chairman of the board, which also consisted of a group of celebrities of high standing in Norwegian society. Among the members of the board were Didrik Arup Seip (Vice-chancellor of the University of Oslo), Johs. Andenæs (professor of law, future Vice-chancellor of the University of Oslo), Albert Nordengen (future mayor of the City of Oslo, Conservative Party), Alette Engelhardt (The Norwegian Housewives' Association), Jacob Sverdrup (future Director of the Nobel Institute in Oslo and professor of history) and Hans Jacob Ustvedt (professor of

---

[18] Among the students actively involved we also find Mariken Vaa (who is today a senior researcher at the Nordic Africa Institute), Torild Skard (later to become MP for the Socialist Left Party, Speaker of the Parliament and Director General in the Ministry for Development Co-operation) and Jan Helge Jansen (future MP for the Conservative party).

[19] Quoted from a letter from Mariken Vaa, Vice-President of the Norwegian National Union of Students, to the Ministry of Foreign Affairs, 24 October 1959.

[20] The invitation was also signed by John Lyng, a Conservative MP who later became Prime Minister (1963) and Minister for Foreign Affairs (1965–1971).

[21] *Dagbladet*, 27 October 1959.

medicine and future Director-General of the Norwegian Broadcasting Corporation).

The Sharpeville massacre

The increasing awareness of the situation in South Africa, which has been documented above, exploded in 1960/61. The Sharpeville massacre of 21 March 1960, in which 69 Africans were killed during a demonstration against the hated Pass Laws, made the international community condemn the South African apartheid regime. For the first time, the Security Council of the UN vehemently denounced the Pretoria regime (France and the United Kingdom abstained). In Norway, the Minister for Foreign Affairs declared that "the heart-rending events which have recently taken place in South Africa have shocked the Norwegian people",[22] and the Ministry of Foreign Affairs received letters from a wide range of Norwegian organisations urging the government to internationally condemn the South African regime. The Norwegian Confederation of Trade Unions (LO) made 28 March 1960—the day for commemorative ceremonies in South Africa—a day of mourning. At many buildings, such as the headquarters of the Norwegian Missionary Society in Stavanger, the flag was flying at half-mast. (Neither the Parliamentary Building nor the Oslo City Hall, however, took part in this symbolic act of solidarity.)[23] Karl Brommeland (MP, The Christian People's Party) wanted the Speakers of the Parliament to express their support to the African population in South Africa, but this initiative did not succeed.[24]

The Nordic Ministers of Foreign Affairs at a joint meeting on 25 April 1960 instructed their diplomats not to attend the official celebrations of the 40th anniversary of the Union of South Africa, a decision that was not well received by the Norwegian Consul General in Cape Town. In his report following the Sharpeville massacre he admitted that the racial policies could give reasons for unrest and protests, but he defended the behaviour of the police at Sharpeville by stating that "when the natives have first been roused and attack the police, they then murder them, unless the police are able to defend themselves adequately". In a later report he added that "there can be no doubt that the activists among the Bantus systematically implement a system of tactical intimidation against their fellowmen. This has been confirmed by our own 'boy' who is himself a Bantu". In an afterthought he conceded that even if the police troops could not be criticised for using their

---

[22] Quoted in Eivindson, op. cit., p. 74.

[23] Ibid., p. 75.

[24] Ibid., p. 74.

guns, the question could be asked if they "... perhaps could have managed with a lesser degree of slaughter ..."[25]

The Nobel Peace Prize to Albert Luthuli[26]

After the banning of the ANC in the aftermath of the Sharpeville massacre, Albert Luthuli was officially nominated as a candidate for the Nobel Peace Prize by 34 members of the Swedish Parliament. The initiative was taken by the Swedish pastor Gunnar Helander, who worked with a British committee led by Ronald Segal. In Norway, the bishop of Rogaland, Fridtjov Birkeli, was one of the most active promoters.[27] Others who supported the candidacy of Albert Luthuli, among them the prominent Norwegian poet, Aslaug Vaa, also emphasised his ideology of non-violence.[28]

As Albert Luthuli was descended from a long line of Zulu chiefs, he in 1935 was called on to assume his functions as a chief in Groutville, Natal. Being on the payroll of the apartheid state, he was in 1952 presented with an ultimatum of either leaving the African National Congress or renounce his position as a chief. When Luthuli was elected President of the ANC in the same year, he was immediately deposed as a chief. As president of the ANC, he was most of the time confined to his place of residence and actually banned from taking part in political meetings and activities. This did not, however, stop him from staying in close touch with the ANC leadership in the formulation of the overall strategy of boycotts, civil disobedience campaigns strikes and other non-violent forms of struggle in the 1950s.

The announcement of the ANC President as prize-winner was very well received in Norway. In the mass media, the decision was even compared with the award of the Prize to Carl von Ossietzky in 1936 for his fight against the Nazi regime in Germany. Most newspapers emphasised his belief in non-violence as well as his strong Christian faith. The focus was mainly concentrated on Albert Luthuli as an outstanding individual and representative of his people, but some newspapers also raised the issue of political measures to be taken against the South African apartheid regime, such as economic sanctions and a possible Norwegian embargo on the supply of oil.[29]

---

[25] See memos from Erik Colban to the Ministry of Foreign Affairs, 28 March 1960, 31 March 1960 and 12 April 1960. In his memo of 14 April 1960 the Consul General concluded that "a very large part of the Bantu population has hardly reached the educational level and the degree of civilisation which must be demanded of a people who are to govern themselves". It was also the opinion of the Consul General that South Africa enjoyed "independent courts of law, with judges who are ingrained with concepts of justice which have an inexpressibly high degree of value in our civilisation. ... The security of justice is enjoyed by all, irrespective of race".

[26] This section draws on a draft prepared by Karin Beate Theodorsen.

[27] *Stavanger Aftenblad*, 25 February 1961.

[28] *Arbeiderbladet*, 16 September 1961.

[29] *Vårt Land*, 5 December 1961.

The fact that the ANC was outlawed and its president was actually under house arrest all made headlines in Norwegian newspapers and raised public awareness about the situation in South Africa. Albert Luthuli was finally granted a passport, but was only allowed to stay in Oslo for eight days.

The news about the Peace Prize was also very well received in other Western Europe countries and in the US. President John F. Kennedy sent his congratulations, and the US Assistant Minister of Foreign Affairs, G. Mennen Williams, urged the South African Government to allow Albert Luthuli to travel to Oslo to receive the Prize. In the Nordic countries, one of the few exceptions was the influential Finnish newspaper, *Helsingin Sanomat*, which carried a critical article arguing that the Nobel Peace Prize to Albert Luthuli was an untimely intervention in a country's internal affairs.[30]

The reactions voiced in South Africa followed—not surprisingly—traditional political lines. Newspapers supporting the Nationalist Party, like *Die Burger* and *Die Transvaaler*, vehemently attacked the Nobel Committee for creating hostility instead of peace, whereas the liberal newspaper *Rand Daily Mail* praised the choice of the committee.[31] The South African Broadcasting Corporation ran a hostile programme about Albert Luthuli, referring to his arrest in 1959 and the charges of high treason brought against him. The minister of "justice", John B. Vorster, even refused to allow him to participate in a reception planned for him in his home area.

During his stay in Oslo, the Church, the trade union movement and the youth organisations, which held a well attended torch parade in his honour, praised Albert Luthuli. He also addressed a service in Oslo Cathedral, encouraging the people assembled to continue their fight against apartheid.[32] When visiting the Norwegian Confederation of Trade Unions headquarters, he was assured of trade union support both in Norway as well as by the International Confederation of Free Trade Unions (ICFTU).

In his speech at the Nobel ceremony, the chairperson of the Nobel Peace Prize Committee—Gunnar Jahn—expressed his conviction that the choice of Albert Luthuli would certainly represent a step forward in bringing about changes in South Africa through non-violent means: "Should the non-white population of South Africa ever rise from their position of humiliation without having to recourse to violence and terror, then this will be due above all to Luthuli, their fearless and incorruptible leader, who, thanks to his noble personal qualities, has rallied his people in support of this policy, a man who throughout his adult life has staked everything and suffered everything without bitterness and without allowing hatred and aggression to oust his abiding love of his follow-men. ... His activity has been characterised by a

---

[30] *Dagbladet*, 24 October 1961.

[31] *Aftenposten*, 4 and 26 October 1961.

[32] *Vårt Land*, 14 December 1961.

firm and unswerving approach: never has he succumbed to the temptation to use violent means in his struggle for his people. Nothing has shaken him from this resolve, so firmly rooted in his conviction that violence and terror must not be resorted to".[33]

The challenge of finding a peaceful solution to the race problem was also the main theme of the Nobel lecture given by Albert Luthuli in the presence of Oliver Tambo and other exiled ANC leaders.[34] The Nobel Peace Award was thus regarded as a "welcome recognition of the role played by the African people during the last fifty years to establish, peacefully, a society in which merit and not race, would fix the position of the individual in the life of the nation". But it was also recognised that "there can be no peace until the forces of oppression are overthrown", and that the basis for peace and brotherhood in Africa was being restored through "the revolutionary stirrings of our continent". In his Nobel lecture, Albert Luthuli also made references to the fight against fascism during the Second World War: "People of Europe formed Resistance Movements that finally helped to break the power of the combination of Nazism and Fascism with their creed of race arrogance and *herrenvolk* mentality". It was also made clear that the freedom struggle, led by the African National Congress, would continue until final victory: "The true patriots of South Africa, for whom I speak, will be satisfied with nothing less than the fullest democratic rights. In government we will not be satisfied with anything less than direct individual adult suffrage and the right to stand for and be elected to all organs of government. In economic matters we will be satisfied with nothing less than equality of opportunity in every sphere, and the enjoyment by all of those heritages which form the resources of the country which up to now have been appropriated on a racial "whites only" basis. In the cultural sphere we will be satisfied with nothing less than the opening of all doors of learning to non-segregatory institutions on the sole criterion of ability. In the social sphere we will be satisfied with nothing less than the abolition of all racial bars. We do not demand these things for people of African descent alone. We demand them for all South Africans, white and black. On these principles we are uncompromising".

Although it was underlined in the Nobel lecture that "freedom cannot come to us as a gift from abroad", Albert Luthuli did also praise the support of the progressive people and governments throughout the world. While he did not go into details as to how this support could be developed and strengthened, the issue of economic sanctions was raised in several news-

---

[33] Address of Gunnar Jahn 10 December 1961. It is, perhaps, somewhat ironic that the ANC a few days later launched its armed struggle, to supplement its political underground activities at home and its diplomatic activities abroad. For a discussion of this debate, see Nelson Mandela: *Long Walk to Freedom*. London: Little, Brown and Company, 1994.

[34] *Africa and Freedom. Nobel lecture delivered in Oslo on 11 December 1961.* (The full text is available at http://www.anc.org.za/ancdocs/history/lutuli.

paper and radio interviews.[35] The subject of sanctions was further elaborated in his autobiography, *Let my people go,* where it was stated that "... I have little doubt that it represents our only chance of a relatively peaceful transition from the present unacceptable type of rule to a system of government which gives us all our rightful voice".[36]

One of the effects of the awarding of the Nobel Peace Prize to Albert Luthuli was that representatives of the South African anti-apartheid opposition approached the Norwegian Consulate General. In this way, the Consulate gained access to new sources of information outside the official and diplomatic circles that generally limited the perspectives of Norwegian diplomats posted in South Africa.[37] In 1963, the Norwegian vice-consul even arranged for a meeting with Albert Luthuli, who was reported to be politically isolated with all his close ANC friends either in prison or in exile. According to the report, Albert Luthuli "had himself regarded it necessary to renounce the ideal principle of 'non-violence' in favour of the principle of 'a minimum of violence'".[38]

At the funeral of Albert Luthuli in Groutville on 30 July 1967 the Scandinavian governments, as well as the Nobel Committee, laid wreaths in their respective national colours. The death of Luthuli also meant that one of the very few channels to ANC inside South Africa was closed for many years.

The Afro-Scandinavian Youth Congress

The Afro-Scandinavian Youth Congress, which was held in Oslo in August 1962, also served to focus more attention on racial oppression and the liberation struggle in Southern Africa.[39] More than one hundred students from all over Africa, representing either student organisations or liberation movements, met for nearly three weeks with two hundred Nordic participants across the political spectrum. Many bonds of friendship between future political leaders in Africa and in the Nordic countries were made, and the importance of the congress has later been emphasised by both parties.[40] The

---

[35] *Aftenposten,* 9 December 1961.

[36] Albert Luthuli: *Let my people go.* London: Fontana Books, 1962, p. 186.

[37] Memo from Erik Colban to the Ministry of Foreign Affairs, 9 January 1962. The practice of not inviting "non-white" guests to official dinners and receptions was, however, not changed for many years.

[38] Report from Jon Aase to the Ministry of Foreign Affairs, 22 October 1963.

[39] In spite of its name, the congress was a joint *Nordic* initiative from students in Norway, Denmark, Sweden, Finland and Iceland.

[40] See, for instance, interview with Joaquim Chissano in Maputo 2 May 1996 in Tor Sellström (ed.): *Liberation in Southern Africa. Regional and Swedish Voices.* Uppsala: Nordiska Afrikainstitutet, 1999. The Mozambican President particularly recalled the discussion about whether to support an armed struggle or not. "It was very interesting because in Mozambique we were still trying to see if we could fight peacefully for independence, although we could already see that the armed struggle was an alternative". The congress is also discussed by Tor Sellström,

congress was also a rare example of bridge building between student organisations that were usually divided according to their Cold War affiliations to the International Union of Students and International Students Conference respectively.

The Southern African region was well represented with 35 delegates and two members of the presidium: Raymond Kunene from the ANC of South Africa and Rupia Banda from UNIP (Northern Rhodesia/Zambia). The General Union of Students from Black Africa Under Portuguese Colonial Domination (UGEAN) sent a particularly strong delegation of nine members, including Joaquim Chissano (future president of Mozambique), Manuel Pinto da Costa (future president of Sao Tomé e Principe) and Henrique "Iko" Carreira (future Angolan Defence Minister). Sympathetic profiles of leading delegates from Angola and Mozambique were also run by the Norwegian press.[41]

When addressing the issue of "Racial problems in Africa", one of the key speakers at the conference, Vice-President Oliver Tambo from the ANC, emphasised the fact that "the core of the race problem that faces Southern Africa, the whole of the continent and, indeed, the whole world, is South Africa".[42] Urging the participants to campaign for economic sanctions against the apartheid, he also stated that "My problem in calling for pressures on South Africa is to convince the youth to convince their governments and people that it is not the South African goods that are cheap, but the forced labour of the Africans (...) The enemies of Africa are those devoted friends of apartheid and racial discrimination—governments, countries and concerns—which have trade agreements with South Africa".[43] The ANC Vice-President made the same appeal for sanctions when the Norwegian Prime Minister, Einar Gerhardsen (Labour), received him—as the first leader of a Southern African liberation movement—on 21 August 1962.[44] (The congress participants were also treated to a reception hosted by King Olav and Crown Prince Harald). From Oslo the ANC leader proceeded to Stockholm and Copenhagen to have talks with the prime ministers of Sweden (Tage Erlander) and Denmark (Viggo Kampmann). In the major Western countries—USA and the United Kingdom—Oliver Tambo was not received at government level until 25 years later.

---

op.cit., pp. 104–111, who underlines the role of the congress in establishing links between future political leaders in Southern Africa and in Sweden.

[41] *Dagbladet*, 18 and 21 August 1962.

[42] Afro-Scandinavian Youth Congress, op.cit., 1962, p. 93.

[43] Ibid., p. 96.

[44] *Aftenposten*, 22 August 1962. See also report from Andreas Andersen, The Prime Minister's Office to the Ministry of Foreign Affairs, 29 August 1962. According to the report, Oliver Tambo expressed his disappointment with the lack of Norwegian support for the initiatives taken at the UN to implement sanctions.

In the Norwegian context, the Youth Congress is also remembered for the ways in which the African participants challenged the Nordic students belonging to the conservative camp. The latter had all assumed that the Congress would restrict itself to the exchanging of views, but the African delegates—with the support of their radical and socialist Nordic colleagues—wanted to pass resolutions condemning apartheid and the major Western powers, asking for economic sanctions and supporting the liberation struggle. The right to adopt resolutions was confirmed with an overwhelming majority (129 votes against 29 and 11 abstentions) during the constituent session, leading the conservative daily, *Aftenposten*, to comment that "the debate revealed very clearly the Africans had not come here to view the Norwegian fjords".[45] The conservative students, who were in the minority, declined to take part in the discussions which aimed at adopting resolutions, and were themselves accused of being paternalistic and undemocratic.[46] Procedural matters also made it necessary for a public rally in Oslo to take place outside the formal structure of the Congress. The rally in the Main Square of Oslo was attended by more than 1000, who listened to speeches by Henrique "Iko" Carreira (Angola), Raymond Kunene (South Africa) and Agrippa Mukahlera (Zimbabwe).[47]

The texts of the resolutions leave little doubt as to the political sympathies of the African delegates and the great majority of their Scandinavian colleagues. Thus, the main resolution on South Africa urged "the Scandinavian Governments to support the struggle for freedom and basic human rights in South Africa by 1) breaking off diplomatic relations with the Union of South Africa, 2) asking the United Nations to organise world-wide economic sanctions against South Africa".[48] In another resolution, the congress called for 1) the abolition of all the oppressive laws designed against the Africans, 2) the immediate granting of democratic rights and release of all political prisoners, 3) the imposition of total economic, diplomatic and cultural sanctions as called for by the African people in the UN, 4) and an unreserved material and moral support for the liberation movements in South Africa".[49] On Rhodesia/Zimbabwe, the Congress condemned "the continuous existence of white supremacy maintained by military force" and called upon Great Britain to "convene a conference with the view of granting a Constitution based on "one man—one vote".[50] The strong presence of stu-

---

[45] *Aftenposten*, 11 August 1962.

[46] The most prominent conservative student leader at the Congress was Fridtjof Frank Gundersen, head of the Organising Committee and future MP for the right-wing Norwegian "Progress Party".

[47] *Dagbladet*, 24 August 1962.

[48] The resolution was adopted with 134 for, 0 against, 8 abstentions and 24 recorded abstentions. See SAYC, op. cit., p. 142.

[49] Ibid., p. 143.

[50] Ibid., p. 145.

dents from the Portuguese colonies was reflected in a resolution that denounced "the military aid given to the fascist government of Portugal by NATO" and appealed "to all progressive organisations in the world, especially UN and the student organisations, to give concrete and effective help to the nationalists in the Portuguese colonies".[51]

To trade or not to trade (1960–64)

The call for a consumer boycott

In the late 1950s, the African National Congress of South Africa (ANC) appealed to the world community to implement consumer boycotts and economic sanctions as a means of putting pressure on the South African regime. The call was first made at the All-African People's Conference in Accra in 1959, and in a letter to the international community signed by Albert Luthuli, G.M. Maicker (South African Indian Congress) and Peter Brown (Liberal Party).[52] In December 1959 this request was supported by the annual conference of the International Confederation of Free Trade Unions, which was particularly concerned with racial discrimination in the labour market.

As early as 20 January 1960, a meeting was convened by the Labour Party and the Oslo women's branch of the trade unions to focus on the threat of racism in general, and on the situation in South Africa in particular. The meeting, which attracted an audience of 350, was addressed by Hans Beukes and Aase Lionæs (Labour MP and later chairperson of the Nobel Peace Prize Committee), who called for a consumer boycott along the lines already initiated by the British Labour Party. This was, according to Aase Lionæs, a form of action in which every single Norwegian housewife could take part: "In this way, we—the peoples who live in the far north (around the polar circle)—can assist the oppressed peoples of South Africa".[53]

Within the trade union movement, a joint decision at the Nordic level was soon made to launch a consumer boycott in the period May–August 1960. The boycott campaign coincided with the great attention devoted to South Africa and apartheid in the aftermath of the Sharpeville massacre. While the expressed solidarity had previously been more or less restricted to the academic community, the boycott campaign and the Labour Day rallies brought the issue of South Africa more directly to a wider public, including the organised labour movement. The Labour Party Norwegian government was, however, cautious not to support the campaign at an official level, and the Norwegian diplomats in South Africa were instructed to make it clear that this was a private action that the government could not influence. There

---

[51] Ibid., p. 147.

[52] *Statement by Albert Luthuli appealing to the British people to boycott South Africa.* The text is available at http://www.anc.org.za/ancdocs/history/lutuli.

[53] *Arbeiderbladet*, 21 January 1960.

was also a fear of retaliatory actions directed against Norwegian exports, which would then have affected the canned fish industry. Then—as later—the fish canning industry warned against economic sanctions and a consumer boycott, and even warned the Norwegian Confederation of Trade Unions that the companies would claim economic compensation for the losses incurred.[54]

Even if the Norwegian government did not want to become officially involved in the campaign, the Labour Party itself expressed its commitment through the 1960 May Day rallies, in which the consumer boycott occupied a central position in the joint Labour Party/Norwegian Confederation of Trade Unions declaration. This declaration, urging the labour movement to take part in the boycott campaign, was co-signed by Prime Minister Einar Gerhardsen and Konrad Nordahl (chairperson of the Norwegian Confederation of Trade Unions).[55] Konrad Nordahl was also a Labour MP, serving on the influential Foreign Affairs Committee of the Parliament. The campaign was fully supported by the daily newspaper *Arbeiderbladet*, which was regarded as being the official mouthpiece of the government. Within the Labour Party, the left-wing opposition (organised around the weekly *Orientering)*, expressed the view that the boycott was primarily of symbolic value only since it was limited to four months, and instead called for a boycott lasting until the apartheid system was crushed.

In his thesis covering Norwegian-South African relations in the period 1945–1961, Jon Kr. Eivindson concludes that the consumer boycott was broadly accepted among the political parties and the Norwegian mass media. The only exceptions were the right-wing newspapers *Morgenbladet* and *Norges Handels og Sjøfartstidende* (today: *Dagens Næringsliv*), which had shipping and export interests close at heart. According to Eivindson, the main parliamentary opposition and the conservative press generally accorded the campaigns their "silent recognition".[56] Berte Rognerud, the most prominent female Conservative MP, supported an appeal from trade union women.

In the period May–August 1960, the import of South African fruit was down by no less than 95%, from NOK 10.9 million to NOK 0.7 million. This compares well with the effect of the campaign in Sweden, where the import of oranges decreased by 25%.[57] There was, however, a major difference since the Norwegian consumers hardly had a choice following the success of the trade unions in persuading the association of wholesalers/importers (Norske Fruktgrossisters Forbund) to cancel all agreements previously en-

---

[54] Eivindson, op.cit., p. 108.

[55] Konrad Nordahl was also a Labour MP, serving on the influential Foreign Affairs Committee.

[56] Eivindson, op.cit., p. 101.

[57] Sellström, op.cit., p. 145.

tered into and desist from importing any South African fruits during the campaign months. It is, therefore, not possible to measure the awareness and commitment of the individual consumers. There is, however, a close parallel to Sweden in the (lack of) long-term effect. According to the official trade figures the boycott lingered on for a few more months, but in 1961 the total amount of imports of fruit from South Africa was back to the 1959 levels, or even slightly higher.[58]

In 1963 a new initiative to launch a consumer boycott was taken by the political youth organisations. It was supported by 48 Members of Parliament (all parties except for the Conservative Party and the Christian People's Party), who signed a petition calling on the government to "... impose an embargo on the import of South African raw materials to our national companies in the same way as the Norwegian Co-operative Society have done. At the same time we appeal to the Norwegian Government to urge importers, retail dealers and consumers not to import, sell or buy South African goods".[59]

The campaign was based on the recommendations from the World Assembly of Youth (WAY) Council meeting in Århus (Denmark) in 1962, as well as the statement by the ANC President that boycott campaigns were the only possible actions to be taken by the international community to avoid a bloodbath. The same argument had been used by ANC leaders meeting with the Norwegian Ministry of Foreign Affairs, or when addressing press conferences and public meetings during visits to Norway. When he was received by the Norwegian Minister of Foreign Affairs on 25 July 1962, Abdul Minty urged Norway to change its position and consider implementing sanctions.[60] This was also the main message of Raymond Kunene (ANC) addressing a Norwegian Action Against Apartheid (NAMA) conference at the Nobel Institute 14 February 1963.[61] At a meeting with the Norwegian Ministry of Foreign Affairs on 9 March 1963 Duma Nokwe (ANC) emphasised that foreign pressure was needed to avoid a disaster, especially in the light of the worsening of the situation in South Africa after the Anti-Terrorism Act had been passed.[62]

"Sympathy is not enough"

In view of the position of Luthuli as a Nobel peace prize laureate, the youth organisations argued strongly that there was a special Norwegian responsibility to adhere to his appeal. This joint effort by the major youth organisa-

---

[58] Eivindson, op. cit., table I, p. 104.

[59] *Aftenposten*, 11 May 1963.

[60] Memo, Arne Arnesen, Ministry of Foreign Affairs, 16 August 1962.

[61] *Dagbladet*, 15 March 1963.

[62] Memo, Ministry of Foreign Affairs, 11 March 1963.

tions (17 in all) led to the formation in early 1963 of Norsk Aksjon mot Apartheid—NAMA (Norwegian Action against Apartheid), since the Norwegian South Africa Committee had chosen not to commit itself on the boycott issue.

This time, the campaign also led to an extensive debate in Parliament following an interpellation by Finn Gustavsen on 11 May 1963. The representative of the small left-wing Socialist People's Party, asked the Government to instruct the state-owned companies (Vinmonopolet and Norsk Jernverk in particular) to stop importing South African goods, and in other ways support the boycott campaign led by Norwegian Action against Apartheid (NAMA). The Foreign Minister, however, argued that Norwegian trade did not amount to more than 0.2% of all South African trade and that the imposition of unilateral Norwegian sanctions "would be a severe blow to the interests of Norwegian enterprises and Norwegian workers."[63] According to Finn Gustavsen, the pleasant words expressed by the Norwegian authorities during the Luthuli visit to Norway were now put to the test. The Norwegian decision to abstain during the vote in the UN General Assembly in 1962 was strongly condemned, and although the resolution adopted by a great majority was not binding in a legal sense, the government was urged to take the necessary measures to implement sanctions. In this regard, the speaker quoted from the address by Oliver Tambo to the Africa Youth Conference in Oslo in 1962: "... The enemies of Africa are those devoted friends of apartheid and racial discrimination—those governments, countries or concerns which have trade agreements with South Africa. ... And who are these? Watch the votes at the next session of the United Nations General Assembly ... and you shall know them. The sun in which the White man has been basking since the dawn of White domination in South Africa is setting ... But no sun can ever set on the African people for no sun has shone on them these last three centuries. We have only dawn and daybreak to look forward to ... The boycott of South African goods, the application of economic and other sanctions on South Africa and the enforcement of a strict embargo on the supply of arms and military weapons and equipment to South Africa, coupled with the unrelenting struggles we are waging in that country, are the kind of pressures which would reduce South Africa's Sabotage Act to a dead letter and confront the Government with a simple choice: to see sense or perish".[64]

In addition to the proposals put forward by the Socialist People's Party (which has worked closely with the anti-apartheid activists and the libera-

---

[63] The calculations were based on a confidential report prepared by the Ministry of Foreign Affairs that estimated the economic losses (including merchant marine) to approximately NOK 150–200 million. "Økonomisk blokade av Sør-Afrika og Portugal", Ministry of Foreign Affairs, 10 September 1962.

[64] The quote from Oliver Tambo is based on the original text in Afro-Scandinavian Youth Congress Report, op.cit., pp. 91–97.

tion movements since the party was established in 1961), calling on the Norwegian consumers to boycott South African goods and urging the Government to implement sanctions, both Reiulf Steen (Labour Party) and Karl J. Brommeland (Christian People's Party) at a more general level requested the Government to consider Norwegian initiatives for international sanctions and other steps towards a solution to the conflict in South Africa.

All three proposals were submitted to the Foreign Affairs Committee of the Parliament, which a month later presented a unanimous report.[65] The report was then debated in a plenary session on 15 June 1963, with more than 20 speakers taking part. The Committee gave full support to the Norwegian position at the United Nations, arguing that resolutions were useless—or indeed harmful—if they did not get the support of the major trading partners of South Africa. On the other hand, it was recognised that sanctions in principle could be a valuable instrument for putting pressure on the South African regime, and that the Government should work within the UN system for a broad acceptance of a more positive attitude to sanctions against South Africa. In order to further this goal, the government was also requested to co-ordinate its further initiatives at the UN with the other Nordic countries. Several speakers supported the idea that Norway—as a member of the Security Council—should introduce a resolution on an arms embargo. On the issue of immediate Norwegian trade sanctions, however, the proposals put forward by Finn Gustavsen only got the two votes of the Socialist People' Party.[66]

Later in the year Norway was indeed instrumental in getting the support of the major Western powers for a limited arms embargo (see below). But—in spite of the wishes of the South African liberation movements and the boycott campaigns initiated by the Norwegian solidarity movement—it took more than 20 years before comprehensive trade sanctions were implemented. As will be shown in chapter 5, neither the Labour Party nor the Conservative/Centre coalition partners were willing to introduce legislation prohibiting Norwegian trade with the apartheid regime until 1986. (And even then, there were many loopholes and exceptions.) In upholding this position, the political leaders of all parties—except for the Socialist People's Party—were supported by the higher echelons of the civil servants in the Ministry of Foreign Affairs/ the Ministry of Commerce and Shipping and the business community at large. The attitude of the Norwegian government

---

[65] Innstilling S. nr. 281 1962/63 (Socialist People's Party had no seat on the Committee).

[66] The proposal included the following paragraphs: "Stortinget [The Norwegian Parliament] expresses its repulsion for the policy of the white minority in South Africa and its sympathy for the struggle of the repressed. ... Stortinget appeals to Norwegian consumers and companies not to buy South African goods. ... Stortinget requests the Government to take all the necessary measures to prevent all import to Norway from South Africa, and if necessary to propose a bill [concerning the matter] for Stortinget ".

was aptly described by Freddy Reddy[67]—a South African student who had arrived in Norway in 1961—when addressing the Labour Party First of May Rally in 1963: "Sympathy is not enough. In the same way as you needed help from without in your fight against Hitler's regime of violence, thus we need support from without in order to fight against Verwoerd's police state. ... What have you done to transform sympathy into action? You have only put forward empty excuses. The business world argues that they cannot implement a boycott [of South Africa] because the Government has not given its agreement to this. The Government says that its approach in the matter is dependent on the action taken by the Great Powers ... All the countries in the world are collectively responsible for the situation in South Africa because they all continue to trade with South Africa and thus keep Verwoerd in power. ... Is large-scale war and massacre necessary to make the countries of the world understand the need to act? Are Ibsen's words still the rule for Norwegians: 'To wish it, to think it, to want it, but to do it ...'?"

Norway in the Security Council 1963–64[68]

Towards a limited arms embargo

While the Norwegian government vehemently decided against implementing economic and diplomatic sanctions against South Africa, for reasons that have been outlined above, the idea of appealing to the UN member states to restrict their supply of arms and military equipment to the apartheid regime seemed more attractive to the governments and its diplomats at the UN headquarters. The issue had been raised during the 17th General Assembly in 1962, when Aase Lionæs (MP, Labour) urged all member countries to stop the supply of arms and other forms of military equipment to South Africa.[69] This initiative had been encouraged by the announcement of the US representative that Washington was considering a ban on all arms which were not meant for "external defence". The Norwegian initiative found its way to the front pages of several South African newspapers, and an editorial in *Die Transvaaler* (which was close to Prime Minister Hendrik Verwoerd) accused Norway of "doing its best to bring about the victory of barbarism over

---

[67] Freddy Reddy had been involved in the establishment of the British Anti-Apartheid Movement (AAM) in London in 1957, and arrived in Norway in 1961 to take up his medical studies. He played an important part in the formation of an anti-apartheid public opinion in Norway, and was much in demand as a public speaker at rallies, conferences and lecture trips sponsored by the Norwegian Action Against Apartheid (NAMA) and the Crisis Fund for Southern Africa (Krisefondet). He was in 1966 elected chairperson of the prestigious Norwegian Students' Society (Det Norske Studentersamfund), a public event which made some people on the far right argue that an African student was not eligible for election to the highest position in a society which—according to its name—was supposed to be a debating society for "Norwegian" students. Specialising as a psychiatrist, Freddy Reddy worked in the ANC refugee settlements in neighbouring countries in the period 1979–1990, and is presently involved in developing "community psychiatry" in a post-apartheid South Africa.

[68] This section draws on Narum, op.cit.

[69] UN, The Special Political Committee, 16 October 1962.

Western civilisation in South Africa".[70] The Consul General in Cape Town reported that several trading partners had cancelled their import orders as an immediate response, and—closer to home—the Norwegian Shipowners' Association warned the Ministry of Foreign Affairs of the negative effects of the exposure given to Norway by the intervention in the UN. A strongly worded letter from the association concluded that "... Against the back-ground of the fact that Norwegian shipping in this connection is especially vulnerable, we wish to underline that all Norwegian statements which serve to put Norway's name in the front line of criticism directed against South Africa, will easily prove to have a damaging effect on Norwegian ship-ping".[71]

The 17th General Assembly (1962) also passed the first UN resolution that appealed directly to all member states to implement economic, military and diplomatic sanctions against South Africa.[72] At the same time, the Spe-cial Committee on the South African Government's Policies of Apartheid Committee ("The Apartheid Committee") was established to closely follow the developments inside South African and to report to the General Assem-bly and the Security Council whenever appropriate. The resolution was adopted with 63 votes against 23 votes, and with all the Nordic countries among the 16 states abstaining. According to the statement of the Norwe-gian Government as expressed by Jens Haugland (Minister of Law) in ex-planation of Norway's abstaining, the Norwegian reservations only applied to the parts of the resolution dealing with economic sanctions and the expul-sion of South Africa from the UN. It was also stated that Norway this time deliberately chose to abstain instead of casting a negative vote: "The change we made in casting our vote is a result of the continued and intensified sup-pression of the African majority during the past year in South Africa. This is in conflict with the appeals which a unanimous world opinion have made through the General Assembly to the South African Government".[73]

The fact that Norway was willing to support the paragraphs concerned with an arms embargo may perhaps seem somewhat inconsistent, since it could also in this case be argued that voting for a proposal not supported by major arms suppliers (France and United Kingdom) would undermine the effectiveness of the UN. In her thesis, Ragnhild Narum explains the differ-ence by pointing out that "the difference for Norway between economic sanctions and an arms embargo lay in the fact that Norway did not export arms to South Africa, but that there were many Norwegian firms that traded

---

[70] *Aftenposten*, 19 October 1962 ("Verwoerd-avis angriper Norge").

[71] Letter from the Norwegian Shipowners Association to the Ministry of Foreign Affairs, 18 October 1962.

[72] General Assembly Resolution 1961 (XVII).

[73] *Dagbladet*, 2 November 1962 ("Kraftig fordømmelse av Sør-Afrika i FN").

with South Africa. In other words, Norway was most positive to sanctions which did not affect its own interests".[74]

Irrespective of the motives of the government, it is a fact that the Norwegian position raised the expectations of the Afro-Asian countries when Norway took its seat in the Security Council for the period 1963–64. Since Norway had always argued that the power to implement sanctions was vested solely in the Security Council, and not in the General Assembly, there were reasons to expect a Norwegian initiative as a Council member when the South Africa issue was put on the agenda in August 1963. The main obstacle was that Norway still did not judge the apartheid regime of South Africa to constitute a threat to international peace and security, which is required in order to adopt mandatory sanctions under Ch. VII of the UN Charter. On the other hand, Chapter VI allows for a resolution that requested all member states to take appropriate measures (including sanctions) in the case of a "disturbance" to peace. After a resolution asking for a comprehensive and mandatory arms embargo had been rejected by USA, France, the United Kingdom, China, Brazil and Norway, a resolution restricting itself to appealing to member states to implement a more limited arms embargo was adopted—against the votes of the United Kingdom and France.[75] The main point of the limited embargo was to block further supplies of equipment for South Africa's own arms industry.

Before leaving the Security Council, Norway played a part in the formulation of Security Council Resolution 5380 (31 July 1963), which requested all states to refrain from offering the Portuguese government assistance enabling it to conduct policies of repression against the peoples of the territories under its administration, and to take measures to prevent the sale and supply to the Portuguese government of arms and military equipment for such purposes. In September 1963, the Norwegian Foreign Minister—together with his Nordic colleagues—also declined an invitation from the South African government to visit South Africa in order to "find the truth". According to the official response, the trip was not seen as serving "the purpose of furthering progress towards a solution in accordance with the principles of the United Nations Charter".[76]

The expert group and the sanctions committee

In preparing for the next round of discussions on South Africa in the Security Council, the aim of the Norwegian government was clearly to avoid an "extreme" resolution from Afro-Asian countries which was totally unacceptable for the major Western Powers. After extensive consultations with

---

[74] Narum, op. cit., p. 46.

[75] Security Council Resolution S/5386, 7 August 1963.

[76] Ministry of Foreign Affairs, 27 September 1963.

all parties concerned, the British UN delegation indicated that it this time would seriously consider supporting a resolution along the same lines as the one rejected in August 1963. The draft resolution presented by the Norwegian government also included the appointment of a UN "Expert Committee", which would be asked to explore all possibilities for finding a peaceful solution to the racial problems of South Africa. The idea was clearly to promote a "dialogue" between South Africa and its main trading partners (United Kingdom and United States of America) as an alternative to sanctions and other form of pressure. The draft resolution was consistent with a proposal introduced to the General Assembly by the Danish Foreign Minister, Per Hækkerup, who acted on behalf of the Nordic countries. The Vice-President of ANC, Oliver Tambo, told the Norwegian Ambassador to the UN that he still considered economic sanctions to be the most effective means to change the situation in South Africa. In his view, a British veto would not necessarily be a bad thing, since it would demonstrate that the Government of Great Britain was isolated. Neither did Oliver Tambo concur with the idea of appointing an expert committee, which he suspected would come up with compromises which did not serve the interests of the African majority. He nevertheless regarded the Norwegian draft resolution as a step forward if it could lead to a unanimous decision in the Security Council.[77] In the debate in the Security Council several countries, among them Ghana and the Soviet Union, asked for more effective measures, such as the implementation of an oil embargo. On the other hand, Great Britain and France made it clear that they did not intend to stop supplying South Africa with arms for "external defence". In the end the Norwegian proposal was unanimously adopted, and Alva Myrdal from Sweden was appointed head of the Expert Committee.[78]

The Expert Committee submitted its report in April 1964. The main proposal was to invite all sections of the South African society to a "national convention", with the aim of creating a new system based on equal rights for all. If this proposal was not accepted by the South African regime before a fixed date, the time according to the Committee would have come for implementing more comprehensive sanctions. The Norwegian delegation to the UN was not particularly happy with the report, and once again made it clear that it was not ready to apply the sanctions weapon against the wishes of South Africa's major economic collaborators. In consultation with the US, Norway was instrumental in getting a resolution accepted calling for a "national convention", the granting of amnesty to members of the opposition facing death sentences during the Rivonia Trial and the appointment of a "Sanctions Committee".

---

[77] Memo from the Permanent Mission of Norway to the UN to the Norwegian Ministry of Foreign Affairs, 22 November 1963.

[78] For a more extensive of the Nordic UN initiative, see Tor Sellström, op.cit., pp. 198–201 and Ragnhild Narum, op.cit., pp. 66–74.

The Sanctions Committee was appointed from among members of the Security Council. It was thus working in close conjunction with the major Western Powers, was mainly concerned with technical issues and served to delay the debate until 1965, that is after the US presidential elections. In a report from the Norwegian delegation to the UN, it was clearly stated that "as is known, the main reason for appointing the committee was to gain time so as to make room for the British and American elections, and for our part, to ensure that we were not confronted by the question of sanctions while Norway was a member of the Security Council".[79] When its final report was presented, it was widely regarded in South Africa as a victory over the most vocal proponents of comprehensive sanctions.[80] The report was never seriously discussed, nor was South Africa to be placed on the agenda of the Security Council until 1970. Once again, South Africa's major trading partners could be relied upon to prevent meaningful sanctions. More than 20 years would elapse before the UN Security Council took firmer action.

Humanitarian action: Legal assistance and support for refugees

The Norwegian Crisis Fund/International Defence and Aid Fund

The Defence and Aid Fund was formed in London in 1959 as a successor to the Treason Trial Defence Fund, established by Christian Action in 1956 to assist in providing legal defence, bail for the accused and maintenance to the families of the accused. The provision of adequate legal defence for the accused led to the collapse of the South African Government's case after more than four years of trial proceedings. The origins may be traced even further back in history; as early as in 1953 Christian Aid—led by Canon John Collins—had collected large sums from the public for assistance to families of those imprisoned in the "Campaign of Defiance of Unjust Laws".

In South Africa, local branches of the Defence and Aid Fund (with varying degrees of formal links to the British DAF) were formed in Cape Town and Johannesburg in the aftermath of the 1960 Sharpeville massacre. While several prominent leaders of the Defence and Aid Fund were banned from the early 1960s, the South African branches were allowed to exist until they were forced to dissolve in 1966.

In 1963 the UN General Assembly appealed to all member states to support internationally recognised organisations involved in providing funds for legal defence and the maintenance of the families of defendants and prisoners in South Africa. Among the organisations singled out in the General Assembly resolutions for this purpose were the Defence and Aid Fund, Amnesty International and the World Council of Churches.[81] (In 1964 the

---

[79] Letter from Sivert A. Nielsen to the Ministry of Foreign Affairs, 17 December 1964. ("Apartheid. Sikkerhetsrådets ekspertkomite").

[80] Narum, op.cit., pp. 78–79.

[81] General Assembly Resolution 1978 B (XVIII), 16 December 1963.

UN Apartheid Committee made the same recommendations.) Just a few days before the UN resolution was passed, on 10 December 1963—the 15th anniversary of the Declaration of Human Rights)—Krisefondet for Sør-Africa (The Crisis Fund for South Africa) was launched in Oslo. One of the main purposes was to serve as a Norwegian branch of the Defence and Aid Fund. The initiative to the Fund was taken by Dr. Fred Lange-Nielsen, who was elected the first chairman. The Fund was based on an impressive range of member organisations: The Norwegian South Africa Committee, The Norwegian UN Association, Amnesty International, The Norwegian Students' and Academics' International Assistance Fund (SAIH), Caritas-Oslo, The Norwegian Refugee Council, The African Students Association, The Norwegian Students Society (Det Norske Studentersamfund), World Federalists (En Verden), youth organisations of all political parties, The Norwegian Students Christian Movement, Jewish Youth Association etc. Among the individual sponsors were the chairmen of both the Norwegian Confederation of Trade Unions (LO) and the Norwegian Employers Association, the vice-chancellor of the University of Oslo, the Speaker of the Parliament and MPs from all political parties represented in the national assembly.

In 1964 DAF was reconstituted as *The International Defence and Aid Fund for Southern Africa (IDAF)*, in order to include legal and other forms of assistance in Southern Rhodesia (Zimbabwe) and other territories in the region as a whole. In addition to the British Defence and Aid Fund, national branches from Norway, Denmark and Sweden were also present at the first annual conference. Fred Lange-Nielsen was elected vice-president of IDAF.

As a response to the UN appeal (see above), the Swedish government in 1965 made its first contribution—USD 100,000—to IDAF, together with a similar amount to the World Council of Churches. This was the first step, which eventually was to lead to a total grant of SEK 800 million before the winding up of IDAF in 1991.[82] In the same year the Dutch Parliament gave its first grant to IDAF, a decision which caused great uproar in South Africa as well as among the (not so few) Dutch friends of the apartheid regime. In 1965 IDAF received its first contribution from Denmark (DKK 200,000), India and Pakistan. The need for assistance also increased as a result of mounting suppression and the very broad definition of "sabotage" contained in the Sabotage Act of 1962.

Compared to its Scandinavian counterparts, the Norwegian Ministry of Foreign Affairs was far more reluctant to develop close links to IDAF. During his stay in Oslo in July 1965, Barnie Desai, a South African in exile working for IDAF in London, was able to brief the Ministry about the financial

---

[82] According to Tor Sellström, op. cit., p. 140, of the approximately £100 million which were channelled into South Africa through IDAF from 1964 to 1991 not less than 70 million came from Swedish sources. A secret network of private correspondents was also set up to write letters and forward money to the families concerned. From the Norwegian side, Kari Storhaug was involved in these activities from the mid-1960s.

support received from other countries, as well as the legal assistance rendered inside South Africa. He also conducted a press conference that was given broad coverage in the Norwegian press. In the same month, the National Council of the Young Conservatives (the youth organisation of the Conservative Party) urged the Norwegian government to make funds available to the International Defence and Aid Fund through its Norwegian branch, the Crisis Fund (Krisefondet). In November the same year, Dr. Lange Nilsen presented the activities—and the financial needs—of the organisation at a meeting with the Norwegian Minister of Foreign Affairs.[83] The chairperson of the Crisis Fund put emphasis on the relevant UN resolutions as well as the fact that funds had already been made available from other Scandinavian countries. On behalf of International Defence and Aid Fund, the Crisis Fund a year later presented the Ministry of Foreign Affairs with a formal application for £ 5,000 (NOK 100,000), while at the same time expressing the hope for significantly higher contributions from future budgets. In early 1967 the Government accepted to grant £ 1,500 (NOK 30,000) to IDAF, to be channelled through the Crisis Fund. (As of April 1967, the total contributions by Sweden were £ 17,859 and by Denmark £ 5,174.)[84]

In early autumn 1967, the Crisis Fund (Krisefondet) applied for a contribution of NOK 200,000 on behalf of IDAF. The application was less than enthusiastically received by the Ministry of Foreign Affairs, where the prevailing position favoured channelling assistance through the UN Trust Fund. But it was noted by the civil servants who were dealing with the application that both the then Prime Minister (Per Borten, Centre Party) and the Foreign Minister (John Lyng, Conservative Party) had been among the initial sponsors of the Crisis Fund. In order to show at least some goodwill towards "a worthy cause" it was proposed to grant NOK 50,000.[85] (The grants from Sweden and Denmark for 1968 were, respectively, NOK 350,000 and 550,000.) This proposal was accepted by the Government as the grant for 1968. In the meantime the Crisis Fund had been dissolved and merged with Norwegian Action against Apartheid (Norsk Aksjon mot Apartheid-NAMA) to form the Norwegian Council for Southern Africa (Fellesrådet for det sørlige Africa).[86] Since the Council took over the function as the Norwegian branch of IDAF, the NOK 50,000 were channelled to IDAF through the Council for 1968.

On several occasions, the Council for Southern Africa complained about the lack of interest shown in the activities of the IDAF by the Norwegian government. For instance, the Norwegian embassy in London did not attend the reception following the annual conference of IDAF in April 1968, while

---

[83] Memo, 1. Pol. Div., 18 November 1965.

[84] Memo, 1. Pol. Div., 27 September 1967 ("Bidrag til International Defence and Aid Fund").

[85] Ibid.

[86] See chapter 6.

the Swedish and Danish embassies were represented. Nor had the IDAF invitation to mark the Human Rights Year and the South African Freedom Day in the Albert Hall on 26 June led to any response from the embassy.[87] This complaint by the Norwegian Council for Southern Africa fits well into a more general pattern; the Norwegian ambassador to Great Britain (Arne Skaug) even declined an invitation from the ANC to address a memorial service in London in August 1967 to honour Albert Luthuli, the winner of the Nobel Peace Prize. The decision was made after consultations with the British Foreign Office, which "advised all foreign embassies against contacts with the ANC", which not only had been outlawed in South Africa, but allegedly was under Communist influence.[88] Similarly, the secretary-general of the British Anti-Apartheid Movement, Abdul Minty, also complained that the AAM enjoyed cordial relations with many foreign embassies in London, but that there were hardly any relations at all with Norway.[89]

For 1969 the IDAF asked for £ 12,000 directly from its London headquarters. It received £ 8,000 (NOK 137,000), while no funds at all were made available for 1970. The stated reason was that all funds had been spent in Nigeria as a consequence of the civil war, since the IDAF grant had been taken from the budget item covering "Natural disaster and humanitarian assistance". In 1971, however, two grants of NOK 150,000 each were made to IDAF, followed by NOK 200,000 in 1972. The extraordinary grant of NOK 150,000 in 1971 came about as a result of a meeting between Abdul Minty of the Anti-Apartheid Movement and Secretary of State for Foreign Affairs, Thorvald Stoltenberg, in Oslo.[90] For the period 1973–1975, the annual grant was—to the great disappointment of IDAF as well as the Norwegian Council for Southern Africa—kept at the same level of NOK 300,000. A major step forward was taken in 1976, when the amount was increased to NOK 1,000,000. The activities of the IDAF had now been broadened to include an Information and Research Department, which published books, reports and the bulletin *Focus on Repression*, while the demand for legal assistance to Namibia and Zimbabwe had increased dramatically over the years.[91] With a Labour Party/Socialist Left Party majority in Parliament, there was in the mid-1970s a strong political backing for the substantial increase.

---

[87] Letter from Lars Borge-Andersen, chairperson of the Norwegian Council for Southern Africa, to the Ministry of Foreign Affairs 16 June 1968.

[88] Memo from the Norwegian Embassy in London to the Ministry of Foreign Affairs, 29 July 1967.

[89] Arne Skaug to the Ministry of Foreign Affairs, 18 February 1966.

[90] Memo, 1. Pol. Div., 24 September 1971 ("Besøk i Utenriksdepartementet av herr Abdul Minty, London").

[91] There are reasons to believe that the formal and informal links after 1973 between Abdul Minty and the Ministry of Foreign Affairs under the Labour government were instrumental in securing this substantial increase. See report from a meeting between Abdul Minty and Secretary of State for Foreign Affairs, Arne Arnesen, Ministry of Foreign Affairs, 19 August 1975.

The Special Committee for Refugees from Southern Africa

Apart from the funds granted for legal assistance inside South Africa, the main attention of the Norwegian authorities was focused on refugees from South Africa and other territories in the region, with special emphasis on education for young refugees. A large share of this support was channelled through the UN system. The Nordic countries were the principal contributors to various UN funds for education and training programmes for refugees from South West Africa/Namibia, the Portuguese colonies and South Africa, which were set up in the 1960s. At the initiative of the Nordic countries, in 1967 the funds were consolidated into the United Nations Education and Training Programme for Southern Africa, which also benefited Zimbabweans. If grants to the UN Trust Fund for South Africa, which was mainly concerned with legal assistance, are included, the Norwegian government from 1965 to 1973 contributed approximately NOK 9 million to these funds.[92] In addition, smaller amounts were given to the Christian Institute in South Africa and the World Council of Churches' Programme to Combat Racism (PCR) from 1972 onwards (see chapter 7).

The Special Committee on Refugees from Southern Africa played the key role in channelling official funds for educational purposes, disposing of approximately NOK 20 million in the period 1963–1976. The Special Committee had its origins in a unique initiative taken by the Foreign Affairs Committee of the Norwegian Parliament in June 1963. (It should be noted, especially for those interested in inter-Nordic rivalries, that Norway in this regard was ahead of Sweden.)[93] Independent of the budget proposals presented by the Norwegian government, the Foreign Affairs Committee unanimously granted NOK 250,000 to activities in support of young refugees from South Africa (later Southern Africa). The initiative was taken by Aase Lionæs (Labour MP), who had served as a member of the Norwegian UN Mission which a few years earlier had been particularly concerned with the issue of education under apartheid, and was met with support from all political parties represented in the Parliament. It was also suggested that an independent committee should be established to decide on how to distribute the funds, consisting of three members representing a) the Norwegian Refugee Council, b) the University of Oslo and c) the Norwegian South Africa Committee. The amount of NOK 250,000 for 1963 was later in the same year increased to 500,000, while a new budget line (Ch. 143–Aid to South African refugees), was established for this purpose. Aid to refugees was at this time not a part of the ordinary budget for development assis-

---

[92] The figure is calculated on the basis of information given by Olav Stokke in his "Norsk støtte til frigjøringsbevegelsene", *Norsk Utenrikspolitisk Årbok 1973*. Oslo: Norwegian Institute of International Affairs, 1973, p. 58.

[93] The Swedish "refugee million" emerged from the Budget Proposals for the financial year 1964/65. The proposals were submitted in January 1964, and came into force from 1 July 1964. See Tor Sellström, op. cit., pp. 70–71.

tance, and was consequently not administered by the Norwegian aid agency (Norsk Utviklingshjelp).[94]

The Special Committee was expected to work in close consultation with the Ministry of Foreign Affairs, while the Norwegian Refugee Council was asked to serve as the secretariat. This construction largely survived until the Special Committee (also known as the Committee of Three) was dissolved in 1982, although the secretariat was moved to the Ministry of Foreign Affairs in 1972. Thus, the administrative set-up was from the beginning to differ from the procedures chosen in Sweden and Denmark in 1963/64, where the parallel activities right from the beginning were to be more firmly situated within the aid agency/Ministry of Foreign Affairs.[95] Consisting of seven members, the Swedish Consultative Committee on Education Support to African Refugee Youth also reflected popular movements and the anti-apartheid public opinion to a larger extent. Although the Norwegian South Africa Committee was already defunct in 1963, and had been replaced by Norwegian Action against Apartheid /The Crisis Fund (later to merge as the Norwegian Council for Southern Africa) as the leading anti-apartheid movement, it was represented on the Special Committee by Lauritz Johnson until its final days in 1982.[96] The fact that no representative associated with the Norwegian Council of Southern Africa was ever invited to join, served to keep the Committee isolated from the solidarity movements and grassroots activities. In striking contrast to Sweden few links to the liberation movements were developed. When direct support to liberation movements was institutionalised in Sweden in 1969, the Consultative Committee discussed the allocation of grants.[97] According to the guidelines, scholarships for studies in Sweden should as far as possible be restricted to persons with a particular connection to African liberation movements.[98] This fact also partly explains why there was a vocal community of Southern African students who acted as spokespersons of the liberation movements, while this was—with a few notable exceptions—strikingly lacking in Norway. Direct Norwegian support to the liberation movements was never handled by the Special Committee, but was kept strictly within the domain of the Ministry of Foreign Affairs and NORAD (after 1973).

[94] Its name was changed to Norwegian Agency for International Development (NORAD) in 1967 and to *Norwegian Agency for Development Co-operation* in 1998.

[95] See Tor Sellström, op. cit., pp. 70–79 and Christian Morgenstierne, *Denmark: A flexible response—humanitarian and political.* Uppsala: Nordiska Afrikainstitutet, 1999 (draft).

[96] Lauritz Johnson was a highly respected public figure, especially known for his radio programmes for children and younger listeners.

[97] Its name was, consequently, changed to the Consultative Committee on Education Support and Humanitarian Assistance to African Refugees and *National Liberation Movements* (emphasis added). Its mandate was enlarged in 1978, and the Committee was later to be known as the Consultative Committee on Humanitarian Assistance.

[98] Tor Sellström, op.cit., p. 478.

Until the early 1970s, the Special Committee more or less lived its own life, with little public interest and even less control or evaluation of its activities. For practical purposes, it can also in this period more or less be regarded as an offshoot of the International University Exchange Fund (IUEF).[99] In the period 1967–72, the secretary of the Committee was Øystein Opdahl, who had been the first executive director of the IUEF up to 1966 and later was appointed to the IUEF board. Øystein Opdahl had also served as a consultant to the Special Committee while heading the IUEF Secretariat, working closely with Dr. Cato Aall who for the first two years was serving on the Special Committee as the representative of the Norwegian South Africa Committee.[100]

The Special Committee for Refugees from Southern Africa 1963–1975

Year	NOK	
1963	500 000	
1964	–	
1965	500 000	
1966	500 000	
1967	500 000	
1968	1 600 000	
1969	1 650 000	
1970	1 650 000	
1971	1 900 000	(+ 700 000 to the Mozambique Institute)
1972	2 300 000	
1973	2 500 000	
1974	3 500 000	
1975	3 600 000	

The two main activities funded during the first years were educational institutions in Africa (mainly secondary schools in Botswana, Lesotho and Swaziland that catered for South African students) and scholarship programmes administered by the IUEF.[101] In the period 1964–66 the Special Committee was closely involved with the International Refugee Council of Zambia, of which Cato Aall served as secretary. The activities of IRCOZ was mainly in favour of refugees from Zimbabwe. A limited number of South

---

[99] The IUEF was established in 1961 in Leiden by the International Student Conference, and continued its work after the ISC was closed down in 1967 when its involvement with the CIA had been exposed.

[100] Cato Aall also took the initiative to Norske Skolers Afrikakomité, an organisation that collected funds and made "twinning" links between Norwegian secondary schools and secondary schools in Southern and Eastern Africa. The Committee was close to the solidarity movement, and contributed in the mid-1960s to an understanding of the struggle against apartheid and colonialism among the Norwegian youth.

[101] A major part of the support to education institutions in Africa, such as Ephesus House in Swaziland, was also channelled through IUEF.

African students in Norway benefited from the funds made available through the Special Committee.[102]

As referred to above, there was little direct involvement with the activities administered by the liberation movements themselves. The only major exception is the single case of channelling two grants to the Mozambique Institute in Dar es Salaam in 1969 and 1971 (see below). This was however mainly a matter of procedure, since the grant was given by the Parliament in addition to the regular budget of the Committee and earmarked for this purpose. The first direct grant from the Committee itself to a liberation movement seems to be a small amount of NOK 10,000 to a UNITA seminar in 1970.[103] In 1972, the Committee paid the expenses of an ANC delegation visiting Oslo, led by Oliver Tambo. The Committee was presented with an ANC Vocational Training Programme for South African refugees in Tanzania and Zambia, but nothing came out of the visit.[104] With the addition of scholarship programmes, vocational training and other activities administered by the UN High Commissioner for Refugees, the pattern set in the first years was to endure through the whole life span of the Committee. There was also a high degree of continuity in the composition of the Committee, with Sigurd Halvorsen of the Norwegian Refugee Council serving as the only chairman. In 1965 Lauritz Johnson replaced Cato Aall as a representative of the already defunct Norwegian South Africa Committee, while the University of Oslo was represented by Bjarne Waaler (1963–67), Torkel Opsahl (1967–74) and Asbjørn Eide (1974–82).

In 1971 the Foreign Affairs Committee of the Norwegian Parliament expressed the view that a closer Ministry of Foreign Affairs involvement was needed in the work of the Special Committee. From 1970 the Ministry had an observer at all Committee meetings, and in 1972 the secretariat of the Committee was moved to the Ministry. The secretary appointed from within the regular staff of the Ministry made the preparations for the committee meetings, including the presentation of the applications and the preliminary assessments. (As from 1973 NORAD was also represented by an observer.) This coincided with a growing scepticism in all the Scandinavian countries

---

[102] Among the South African students were Isaac Mgemane, Zanele Sidzumo Mokgoatsane and Maxwell Mlonyeni.

[103] This decision originated from Øystein Opdahl, and was accepted by the three members outside normal procedure. UNITA was at the time the only Angolan movement which was not recognised by the OAU. Several UNITA leaders, among them Jonas Savimbi, Jorge Valentim and Jorge Sangumba, are known to have had close links to the International Student Conference/IUEF while Øystein Opdahl was Secretary General in the early 1960s. At that time they belonged to the UPA/FNLA, which was affiliated to the ISC. Øystein Opdahl introduced Jorge Valentim to the Scandinavian countries, and in 1968 IUEF assisted Jonas Savimbi in returning to Angola. The UNITA/IUEF/Swedish connections are discussed in Tor Sellström, op.cit., pp. 196–398. See also the interview with Jorge Valentim in Tor Sellström (ed.), op. cit., p. 35.

[104] A member of the ANC delegation, Martin Legassick, was invited for dinner at the residence of the Crown Prince of Norway—the present King Harald—with whom he had made friends during their student days in Oxford.

concerning the role of the *International University Exchange Fund (IUEF)*, as expressed at common Nordic meetings discussing aid to refugees and liberation movements. While it was recognised that the organisation had unquestionable competence in the field of scholarships, the highly ambitious move into new avenues (competing with ILO, UNDP, FAO and other development agencies) was met with mounting resistance among the Scandinavian aid agencies.[105]

Under the new administrative regime, the budget at the disposal of the Committee increased from NOK 1.6 million in 1970 to NOK 3.5 million in 1975. At the same time, a significant degree of Nordic co-ordination was institutionalised through regular meetings and exchange of reports. A system of "framework agreements" with UNHCR and IEUF was also developed, although individual project proposals still had to be worked out and presented for consideration. In 1975 out a total budget of NOK 3.5 million each of the two organisations had approximately NOK 1.4 million at their disposal.

After the "take-over" by the Ministry of Foreign Affairs, the Norwegian Students' and Academics' International Assistance Fund (SAIH)—with close links to the solidarity movements—was also accepted as a channel of funds to Southern Africa, albeit at a modest level. SAIH had for many years been involved in fund-raising activities and campaigns to raise the awareness of the liberation struggle. It also had a long-standing working relationship with Swaneng Hill School in Botswana, led by Patrick van Rensburg. Apart from channelling a grant of NOK 170,000 from the Special Committee to Swaneng Hill School in 1972, to be followed up in the following years, SAIH also received smaller amounts to be distributed to organisations inside South Africa itself: South African Students Organisation (SASO), Black People's Convention (BPC), Black Allied Workers Union (BAWU), all linked in one way or another to the black consciousness tendency within the liberation struggle. Through SAIH the Special Committee also gave a small amount of NOK 60,000 to the SWAPO farm in Zambia. An application for NOK 120,000 for an ANC Research Centre in Dar es Salaam was, however, turned down by the Committee.

Following a decision by the Parliament to give direct assistance to the development activities of FRELIMO, MPLA and PAIGC in 1973 (see below), one could perhaps have expected the Special Committee to develop closer links with the other movements in the region, in particular the ANC of South Africa and SWAPO of Namibia. In 1975 it was agreed to set aside NOK 300,000 for scholarships to SWAPO students, to be channelled through the Lutheran World Federation, but the Committee did not receive the required information. The same amount was, therefore, transferred to the re-

---

[105] Bjørnar Utheim, Ministry of Foreign Affairs, 18 February 1975 ("Report from visit to UNHCR and IUEF").

cently established UN Institute for Namibia (UNIN) in Lusaka. Direct links to the ANC were never developed, except for a small grant of NOK 100,000 in 1975 for educational activities of the Luthuli Memorial Fund of South Africa. The Fund was set up by the National Executive Committee of the ANC in Addis Ababa in the late 1960s, and had already received financial contributions from Sweden and Finland. In an information leaflet enclosing the application to the Special Committee, it was emphasised "... that the humanitarian aid programmes of the Fund are directly related to the liberation struggle of our people. ... Consequently, support for these programmes is support for our freedom struggle".[106]

The Special Committee more or less followed the established procedures and priorities in its remaining years until 1982, when assistance to refugees was integrated into the regular activities of the Ministry of Foreign Affairs. The annual grants had increased from NOK 4 millions in 1976 to 9 million in 1982. At this stage, the assistance given to refugees through the Special Committee was much less controversial and much easier to handle than the substantial support given directly to the liberation movements, and the Ministry of Foreign Affairs saw no reason why a separate administrative and decision-making structure should be maintained.

FRELIMO, Eduardo Mondlane and the Mozambique Institute: 1965–71

In her thesis on Norwegian-South African relations in the 1960s and 1970s, Ragnhild Narum convincingly argues that the years 1963/64, when Norway was a member of the UN Security Council, were followed by a "re-active" period in which far less interest in the South African issue was expressed by the Norwegian government and the Ministry of Foreign Affairs.[107] To a large extent, this also goes for the solidarity movements. The campaign for sanctions was running out of steam with the negative vote in the Norwegian Parliament in 1963/64, and the liberation struggle in South Africa itself entered a dark period after the outlawing of PAC and ANC and the crushing of the opposition. Within the anti-imperialist sections of the youth of Norway, the focus clearly shifted to other areas: Latin America, Indochina and the Middle East. Unlike in many other Western countries, the Vietnam solidarity movement was never allowed to completely overshadow the involvement with the struggle in Southern Africa. Likewise, the fact that the Norwegian Council for Southern Africa was mainly based on member organisations instead of individual members, also served to keep it intact as a broad, non-sectarian movement at a time when other progressive organisations in the early 1970s were more or less taken over by activists associated with a "marxist-leninist-maoist" line.

---

[106] *Luthuli Memorial Fund Appeal*, p. 1. It should be noted that one half of the grant was for a kindergarten project inside South Africa itself.

[107] Narum, op.cit., ch. 5: "Passive years".

The only part of Southern Africa that succeeded in attracting a substantial degree of attention was the Portuguese colonies: Angola, Mozambique and Guinea-Bissau. The liberation movements themselves could claim a not insignificant success on the ground, and the involvement of the NATO and EFTA countries as backers of Portuguese colonialism understandably caught the attention of many Norwegians. In the second half of the 1960s, FRELIMO of Mozambique—under the able leadership of Eduardo Mondlane—came to symbolise the struggle against racism, colonialism and social injustice. As we shall see, the modest financial support given to the Mozambique Institute was an important step along the road to a more extended co-operation with the liberation movements in the 1970s. The case of FRELIMO also illustrates the fact that the relations between the Norwegian government and the liberation movements—without exception—were initiated by the movements themselves, often acting in close co-operation with the Norwegian anti-apartheid and solidarity organisations. The traditionally conservative diplomats, whether based in Norway or in Portugal/South Africa, showed—at best—little interest. In many cases the liberation movements were met with outright hostility.

The first visit of Eduardo Mondlane to Norway took place in September 1965 as part of a Scandinavian tour sponsored by the World Assembly of Youth. He had been elected President of FRELIMO at the inaugurating congress in 1962, and also enjoyed an international reputation on the basis of his academic merits as a university anthropologist in the United States and as a UN official working for the Trusteeship Council. Although FRELIMO was established in 1962, and the armed struggle was launched two years later in the Cabo Delgado province bordering Tanzania, it is fair to describe the struggles in the Portuguese colonies as "the unknown wars" as far as the Norwegian public opinion was concerned in the mid-sixties.[108] During his brief stay in Norway in 1965, however, Eduardo Mondlane met with representatives for youth organisations, the Norwegian Refugee Council, the Crisis Fund for Southern Africa and the Council for Ecumenical and International Relations of the Norwegian Church (Mellomkirkelig Råd). He was also received at the Ministry of Foreign Affairs at a rather junior level. The fact that Mondlane was president of FRELIMO seemed to be unknown in the Ministry. In the report written after his visit, it is stated that it was not clear which position he held in the movement, but that it seemed as if he was in charge of external affairs and "did a lot of travelling".[109] The FRELIMO president also appeared on television and gave several interviews to the national press. In contrast to the visit to Sweden, however, he was neither received by cabinet members nor invited to lecture at the universities.

---

[108] Tore Linné Eriksen: "Glemmer vi de portugisiske koloniene?", *Arbeiderbladet*, 24 March 1966.

[109] Memo from a meeting with Eduardo Mondlane, written by Kaare Sandegren, Ministry of Foreign Affairs, 10 September 1965. According to the report, Mondlane "made a very favourable impression".

(The visit coincided with the final days of the Norwegian election campaign, which led to a change in government from the Labour Party to a coalition of the four "non-socialist" parties.)

According to the press reports, the FRELIMO president was far from impressed by the Norwegian stand on Portuguese colonialism, which he suspected was a consequence of Norway and Portugal being members of the same military alliance. At the same time, it was emphasised that the membership of NATO gave Norway an opportunity to raise the issue from within the military alliance. Responding to the unavoidable question as to the sources of their military equipment, Mondlane made it clear that he welcomed support from all quarters: "We prefer West European arms, since our soldiers then can use the bullets confiscated from the Portuguese".[110]

Through the visit of Eduardo Mondlane, the Norwegian authorities as well as the general public were also informed about the recent advances on the battlefield and the need for material support for the education and health projects inside Mozambique as well as in neighbouring Tanzania. ("When the country is liberated after three to four years, we will have enough skilled manpower to take over the administration".)[111] The more specific needs in the field of education and health services were also presented to the Ministry of Foreign Affairs, with special emphasis on the Mozambique Institute in Dar es Salaam, which was headed by Janet Mondlane. However, when the Portuguese Ambassador to Norway later approached the Norwegian Ministry of Foreign Affairs to ascertain whether the FRELIMO president had asked for assistance, the answer was negative.[112]

Two years later, in October 1967, the next visit by Mondlane attracted much wider attention. This may be seen as a reflection of a mounting solidarity campaign in Norway, which, of course, was not unrelated to a more general radicalisation among youth organisations. *Afrika Dialog*, which was the magazine published by the Norwegian Action against Apartheid (NAMA) had also recently released a special issue on the Portuguese colonies and the complacency of the Norwegian government, as witnessed by the abstention in the UN General Assembly when a resolution condemning Portugal and calling for an arms embargo and economic sanctions was adopted during the 1966 session. The Minister of Foreign Affairs had bluntly refused to answer questions—in writing—put to him by the NAMA magazine, and had also made it clear that he did not want to instruct his Secretary of State or any high-ranking civil servants to grant interviews.[113]

---

[110] *Aftenposten*, 9 September 1965.

[111] *Dagbladet*, 6 September 1965.

[112] Memo, Ministry of Foreign Affairs, Einar Ansteensen, 13 September 1965. The Portuguese Ambassador also deplored the fact that a representative of a "terrorist" movement, backed by China, had been received by the Ministry.

[113] Letter from Kjell Colding, the Secretariat of the Minister for Foreign Affairs, 8 April 1967.

This time the president of FRELIMO was invited to address a public meeting, which attracted an audience of more than 200 on a Saturday evening. It was organised by an ad hoc committee—*Møte med den tredje verden* (Encounter with the Third World)—which consisted of fifteen political and cultural youth organisations, supported by the Trade Union Council of Oslo. The committee was set up for the occasion, with the chairperson of the Norwegian Action against Apartheid—Lars Alldén—as the prime mover (see chapter 6). The address was followed by a panel discussion, with prominent journalists, researchers and solidarity activists serving on the panel. Several MPs were invited to take part, but the only one to accept was Finn Gustavsen, Socialist People's Party. Secretary of State for Foreign Affairs, Frithjof Jacobsen (Conservative Party), declined an invitation, without stating any reason.[114] During his brief visit to Oslo, the FRELIMO president also addressed the annual conference of the Socialist Youth League, the youth organisation of the Socialist People's Party.

The FRELIMO president was once more received at the level of civil servants at the Ministry of Foreign Affairs.[115] According to the report, he particularly raised the issue of material support to the activities of the Mozambique Institute in Dar es Salaam, which at the time was already receiving support from Sweden, Denmark and Finland.[116] The request for assistance was also one of the main points made in the address to the public meeting the same evening, in which detailed information about the role of the primary schools in the context of an economic and social transformation of the liberated areas was given. The need for textbooks and medicine was also stressed when Eduardo Mondlane met with a group of Labour MPs.

As can be expected, the emphasis put by Mondlane on the links between the Portuguese membership in NATO and its capacity to conduct wars in three African territories, as well as the responsibility of Norway as a NATO and EFTA member, was not favourably received by the political establishment. Neither was his argument that Portugal was certainly encouraged in its colonial wars by the voting patterns of Norway at the United Nations.[117] The insistence of the Norwegian government that no such links existed, as well as the general tendency to situate the liberation struggle in the Portuguese colonies in a Cold War perspective, were recurrent themes in the public debate. The press reports from the solidarity meeting also made the highest ranking official in the Ministry of Foreign Affairs state in a brief note

---

[114] Letter from Frithjof Jacobsen, Ministry of Foreign Affairs, 30 August 1965.

[115] Memo, 1. Pol. Div., 13 October 1967. See also the extensive report of the Eduardo Mondlane address, written by Sverre Bergh-Johansen, Ministry of Foreign Affairs, 13 October 1967.

[116] The Institute had, for instance, received SEK 150,000 from the Swedish "refugee million" in 1965. In the 1965–68 period, SEK 1,7 million had been disbursed. The early Sweden-FRELIMO relations are covered in detail by Tor Sellström, op.cit., pp. 439–472. See also Iina Soiri and Pekka Peltola: *Finland and National Liberation in Southern Africa*. Uppsala: Nordiska Afrikainstitutet, 1999.

[117] *Arbeiderbladet*, 9 October 1967.

that what was reported from the address of the FRELIMO president "has strengthened my doubts as to whether it is wise to receive representatives of rebel movements in the Ministry".[118]

In retrospect, the two visits by Eduardo Mondlane in 1965 and 1967 respectively, must be regarded as the opening of a new chapter in the history of the Norwegian support to the liberation struggle in Southern Africa. In 1969, the Mozambique Institute received NOK 200,000 through the Special Committee for Support to Refugees from Southern Africa, following the example set by Sweden four years earlier. This was the first time public funds were granted directly to a liberation movement, although the Institute was a separate legal entity.[119] The Foreign Affairs Committee in Parliament had already in late 1967 proposed a grant to the Mozambique Institute,[120] but during 1968 the activities of the Institute was seriously affected by internal rivalry.

In 1971, the Parliament made a decision to grant NOK 700,000 to the Mozambique Institute by adding this amount to the budget of the Special Committee. The decision was unanimous, and the recommendations from the Parliamentary Committee on Foreign Affairs clearly indicated that the support to the Mozambique Institute this time went beyond educational assistance to refugees: "The committee has also noticed that the Institute has now widened its activities to include the liberated areas of Mozambique. ... The committee assumes that the activities in the liberated areas will necessarily be more difficult and more expensive to maintain than outside Mozambique, and will underline the importance of Norwegian support to the Institute being upheld and of the aid being increased under the changed conditions".[121] The actual transfer was delayed for a year due to the internal problems affecting FRELIMO in the aftermath of the assassination of Eduardo Mondlane in early 1969. (These problems did, however, not restrict the Swedish and Danish government from resuming their financial support to the Institute in 1971.) During a visit by Janet Mondlane to Oslo in March 1972, the decision was made that the procurement of goods to be supplied should be handled by the Norwegian Council for Southern Africa.

---

[118] Memo, Ministry of Foreign Affairs, Thore Boye, 18 October 1965.

[119] FRELIMO consistently maintained a critical stance towards the separation between humanitarian assistance and the armed struggle, but taking into account the insistence by many donors, FRELIMO had deliberately chosen to run the Institute's education and health activities as an independent unit. See interview with Janet Mondlane in Tor Sellström (ed.), op. cit., pp. 41–45.

[120] Budsjettinnstilling S. No. 204, 1967/68.

[121] Innstilling S.20, 20 October 1971. See also the debate in Parliament 2 November 1971 (*Stortingsforhandlingene*, 2 November 1971, pp. 586–588).

Lisbon—1971: A lonely voice in Nato?[122]

According to the standard academic texts on the history of the post-war
Norwegian foreign policies, a recurrent theme in the 1950s and 1960s was
the conflict between the UN principles of decolonisation on the one hand
and the expression of solidarity with Norway's partners in NATO on the
other.[123] In the 1950s, these conflicting interests came to the surface as a result of the French colonial wars in Indochina and Algeria, while the US war
against the peoples of Indochina and the Portuguese colonial wars in Africa
were among the most contentious issues during the 1960s and early 1970s.
Apart from being partners in NATO from 1949, Norway and Portugal were
also both founding members of the European Free Trade Association (EFTA)
in 1960. Since the principles of the UN Charter were frequently referred to as
a cornerstone in Norwegian foreign policies, the flagrant Portuguese rejection of the 1960 UN Declaration on Decolonisation was met with sharp criticism and outright condemnation from most Norwegian political parties.

In the United Nations itself, the Afro-Asian countries came to constitute
a majority of the members as a result of the decolonisation process. Following the uprising and the Portuguese massacres in Angola in 1961, "the Portuguese question" (as it was often euphemistically called) formed an important part of the UN agenda, and resolutions calling for African independence and strong measures to be taken to force Portugal to stop its colonial
wars were introduced to every single General Assembly. With some modifi-
cations, the Norwegian position did not substantially change during the
1960s. Norwegian governments, irrespective of their political colours, did
not accept resolutions that called for economic sanctions, which were regarded to run contrary to the principles of EFTA membership. Norway,
therefore, routinely abstained when the Afro-Asian countries introduced
resolutions at the UN that were passed with a large majority.[124] It was also
totally unacceptable to a Norwegian government to support resolutions that
implied a NATO responsibility for the colonial wars or called for a military
embargo. From a Norwegian point of view, it was important to block any
measures that could make it difficult for Portugal to secure the necessary
equipment for the country to fulfil its obligations within the NATO collective security framework. A change took place in 1968, when the Permanent
Mission of Norway to the UN decided to vote in favour of a Afro-Asian

---

[122] Apart from the Ministry of Foreign Affairs archives, this section is largely based on Jan E.
Grøndahl, *Portugal-saken. Norge og Portugals kolonipolitikk 1961–1974*. Thesis, Department of History, University of Oslo, 1997.

[123] Knut Einar Eriksen/Helge Øystein Pharo: *Kald krig og internasjonalisering 1945–1965. Norsk
utenrikspolitikks historie, bind 5*. Oslo: Universitetsforlaget, 1997.

[124] Portugal did not expect active support from countries like Norway for its colonial wars. But,
as it was put by Foreign Minister Franco Nogueira to his friend the Norwegian Ambassador
(Reusch): "We do not ask for your support, but we ask for your passivity". Quoted in Grøndahl, op.cit., p. 17.

draft resolution in order not to part from the other Nordic countries and Canada. (The Ministry of Foreign Affairs in Oslo, on the other hand, had originally found it "very unfortunate" to give its support to the resolution.)[125]

During the 1960s, neither the Labour Party government nor the Conservative/Centre coalition (1965–71) raised the Portuguese colonial issue at NATO or EFTA council meetings, and it was officially stated on many occasions that the UN was the only appropriate forum. The change of policy at the official level did not take place until the beginning of the 1970s. In his thesis on "The Portugal question 1960–1974", Grøndahl is especially concerned with the way in which this "move to the left", especially among the youth, in the end also came to be reflected within the Labour Party while in opposition from 1965 to 1971. Seen in this perspective, which is also shared by other recent studies of Norwegian foreign policies in the same period, the shift towards a more hostile attitude to the regime in Lisbon was consistent with a more strongly pronounced anti-colonial and anti-imperialist opinion (Vietnam) and a mounting criticism of NATO partners on issues involving democracy and human rights (Turkey, Greece).[126] The question of the Portuguese colonial wars combined the two issues. A detailed investigation of the deliberations at the Labour party annual conferences and the minutes of the Party Committee on international affairs, also reveals that the more "conservative" sections of the Labour Party were increasingly worried that the Portuguese colonial policy would increasingly become a liability to the alliance, and that the frequent attacks on Portugal in the Norwegian mass media might weaken the support enjoyed by the NATO alliance as such. It is also reasonable to assume that the Labour Party wanted to attract younger and more radical voters after losing the general elections in 1969.[127] The need for reformulating the party position, therefore, was inspired by moral challenges as well as by more opportunistic reasoning.

The breakthrough for a more "activist" position took place in 1970/71. During the general debate on Norwegian foreign policy in Parliament in late autumn 1970, prominent spokesmen from the Labour party urged the Conservative Foreign Minister (John Lyng) to raise the issue of the colonial wars in NATO and EFTA. In late 1970 the Foreign Affairs Committee of the Norwegian Parliament unanimously adopted the same position.[128] This debate coincided with a visit to Norway by the FRELIMO leader, Joaquim

---

[125] Grøndahl, op.cit., pp. 36–37.

[126] The standard text is Rolf Tamnes: *Oljealder, 1965–1995. Norsk utenrikspolitikks historie, bind 6.* Oslo: Universitetsforlaget, 1997.

[127] Grøndahl, op.cit., pp. 156–160.

[128] Innstilling S. 126 (1970/71), 24 November 1970.

Chissano, who publicly criticised the Norwegian position at the UN.[129] Before the Parliament debated the issue in a plenary session on 22 April 1971, a split in the conservative coalition over the European Common Market issue led to a change in government. The Labour party urge for a more radical line to be taken by the Norwegian Minister of Foreign Affairs within NATO and EFTA was then accepted by all parties in Parliament, and had now to be followed up in practice by the incoming Labour party government itself.

The first occasion was to be the NATO Ministerial Council meeting in early June 1971, which—incidentally—was held in Lisbon. The Norwegian decision to take this opportunity to appeal to the Portuguese government to change its colonial policies, was—to put it mildly—met with little understanding among the other NATO partners. Apart from differing opinions held on the matter, the Norwegian intervention was widely regarded within the alliance as a hostile act and an insult to the host nation. In order to soften the reactions, the Ministry of Foreign Affairs made bilateral contacts with all major NATO partners before the meeting to explain its position more fully. Apart from underlining the universal principle of the right of all peoples to self-determination, a major point in these talks was the need for the Norwegian Foreign Minister to voice his opinion in order to show the Norwegian public that being a member of NATO did not preclude the right to hold independent positions. It was also reiterated that the colonial wars could jeopardise the support for NATO in Norway as well as damage the standing of the Western powers in the Third World in general.[130]

At the Lisbon Ministerial Council meeting, the Norwegian Foreign Minister, Andreas Cappelen, ended his general intervention by asking the Portuguese government "to reconsider its colonial policies". Since this did not come as a surprise to the other NATO partners, it was hardly commented upon by other speakers. The speech was, however, given broad coverage by the Norwegian mass media. Internationally, especially among the Afro-Asian countries, the speech was hailed as a most courageous action. As we will see below, a high-level OAU delegation visiting the Nordic countries in the following autumn expressed its gratitude to the Norwegian government.

Seen in retrospect, the Norwegian effort to influence its major NATO partners can hardly be described as a success. In the Kissinger/US National Security Council Memorandum on Southern Africa (January 1970), it was argued that the whites were destined to stay and that access to Angolan and Mozambican ports was important in the name of "global realism" and US strategic interests.[131] In a recent study of the decolonisation process it is

---

[129] "To abstain from voting over resolutions against the colonial policies of Portugal is equivalent to casting one's vote for Portugal. All talk of formalities to excuse one's vote cannot help us", *Arbeiderbladet*, 18 November 1970.

[130] Grøndahl, op.cit., pp. 66–72.

[131] The National Security Study Memorandum 39 was later published as *The Kissinger Study on Southern Africa*. Nottingham: Spokesman Books, 1975.

maintained that from 1970 until the collapse of the Lisbon regime in April 1974 the United States aided the Portuguese colonial war by the supply of aircraft, ammunition and defoliants and with the training of troops in counter-insurgency techniques in US army camps in the Panama Canal Zone. It is also concluded that "Western pressure on Portugal in the last decade of the empire was most sustained among those with least leverage, most notably Sweden and other Nordic countries. Those with greater potential influence in Lisbon showed no obvious inclination to use it over Africa".[132]

Support for national and social popular movements: The making of a principle

As we have observed, government funds had since 1963 been made available for refugees from Southern Africa, later to be followed by funds for legal assistance to the victims of apartheid. These activities were, however, undertaken outside the aid budgets and outside the regular channels for development co-operation. This was also the case when NOK 200,000 was given to the Mozambique Institute in 1969. We have also seen that the calls for humanitarian assistance and direct aid to the liberation movements were made by the solidarity organisations around 1967/68. The debate was triggered off by the visits of Eduardo Mondlane and other prominent representatives of the liberation movements in the Portuguese colonies, and was in the beginning mainly expressed through the Norwegian Council for Southern Africa. In the autumn of 1968, Norway—together with Sweden and Denmark—voted in the UN General Assembly for a resolution which called on all member states to give assistance to the liberation movements in the Portuguese colonies.[133]

White Papers—known in Norway as Parliamentary Reports (*Stortingsmeldinger*)—are instruments used by the government to introduce changes in the principles guiding major policy areas. In the field of development assistance, the Parliamentary Reports presented to the Parliament in the 1960s were both formulated before the issues of development assistance to—or channelled through—liberation movements had been raised. At the turn of the decade, however, mounting pressure for aid to liberation movements combined with administrative needs for effective guidelines served to put the question firmly on the political agenda. The first opportunity emerged when the Council of the Norwegian Agency for International Development (NORAD) in 1969 was asked to prepare an extensive statement on the principles guiding Norwegian aid policies. The process has been recorded in

---

[132] Norrie MacQueen: *The Decolonisation of Portuguese Africa. Metropolitan Revolution and the Dissolution of Empire.* London: Longman, 1997, p. 55.

[133] General Assembly Resolution 2395 (XXIII),"Question of Territories under Portuguese administration". A resolution to the same effect was passed by the General Assembly in 1969: General Assembly Resolution 2507 (XXIV). The Norwegian position is explained in *Stortingsmelding nr. 27 (1969–70)*, pp. 108–11.

great detail and analysed by Olav Stokke, who himself played a prominent role as a member of the draft committee.[134] The final statement, which was passed after a heated debate on 13 April 1970, did to some extent reflect the radicalisation of thinking about Third World issues and development assistance which had taken place since the mid-1960s. The principles outlined by the NORAD council have generally had a profound impact on Norwegian aid policies, but what is important for our purpose is the fact that the statement includes the following section: "The council is (... also) of the opinion that support given to educational measures, etc. for citizens from countries that have not yet gained their independence, or refugees from other countries, must be given a flexible and workable form. The council maintains that Norway ought to give active support to such measures, as has earlier been done in the case of Norwegian support to FRELIMO's Mozambique Institute in Tanzania".[135] This paragraph was unanimously accepted. Although the recipients for such assistance are defined as citizens and refugees, the explicit reference to the Mozambique Institute clearly gives an opening for aid to be channelled through liberation movements.

In addition, a more controversial paragraph (carried by a majority of 8 to 5) states that "formal demands (... that as a main principle aid must go to a public authority in the receiver country) must not prevent Norway, as a part of its development policy, from giving support to projects launched by large popular organisations and movements working for national and social liberation". Since this paragraph did not specify that these popular movements were restricted to countries which had not achieved independence, it could be interpreted as favouring support to the development activities of movements involved in a struggle against their own governments. The minority members of the Council regarded this as a contravention of the principle of non-interference, a principle that however did not prohibit support to liberation movements in non-independent nations.

The increased support for the principle of giving aid directly to the liberation movements was also expressed through left-wing representatives of the Labour Party while in opposition after the 1969 elections. Arne Kielland (Labour MP) raised the issue in the Parliament on 19 June 1970 as well as in several newspaper articles.[136] In the period 1969–73, in which the Socialist People's Party was without any seat in Parliament, the Norwegian Council of Southern Africa could always count on Arne Kielland. Apart from promoting the interests of the liberation movements and the Norwe-

---

[134] Olav Stokke: "Utviklingsbistand og frigjøringsbevegelser", *Internasjonal Politikk*, no. 4, 1970. Olav Stokke, who has written extensively on Norwegian aid policies in the capacity of Senior Research Fellow at the Norwegian Institute for International Affairs, was as the time a member of the NORAD Council. The other members of the Draft Committee were Finn Moe (Labour MP), Sissel Rønbeck (chairperson of the Norwegian Labour Youth-AUF) and Rolf Roem Nielsen (The Federation of Industrial Employers).

[135] Ibid., p. 400.

[136] "Frigjøringsorganisasjoner", *Arbeiderbladet*, 10 July 1970.

gian anti-apartheid public opinion, he also took part in the delegation of the Council to the Rome 1970 Conference on support to the liberation movements in the Portuguese colonies.[137]

In August 1970, the statement by the NORAD Council was discussed by the NORAD Board of Directors, which noted—rightly so—that it contained certain new principles, *in passu* support to social and national liberation movements. Since it was not a prerogative of NORAD to decide on the main principles for Norwegian assistance, the Board emphasised that changes had to be made by the Parliament, following proposals for new guidelines formulated by the Government.

The ball was now firmly set in motion, and the Ministry of Foreign Affairs soon started its preparations for a report to the Parliament. In the Parliamentary Report no. 30 (1970–71)—*Certain questions of a principle nature related to Norway's development aid*—the Centre/Conservative coalition government in principle accepted the recommendations of the NORAD Council, but deliberately chose a quite narrow interpretation by restricting the assistance to "humanitarian aid".[138] In other words, regular development assistance directly to the liberation movements in control of liberated areas was rejected. The Parliamentary Report was never discussed by the Parliament until the incoming Labour Party government introduced another Report: *On certain key topics relevant to Norway's co-operation with the developing countries—Report no. 29 (1971–72).*[139] The new White Paper addressed itself to several important issues, such as the selection of the main recipients of Norwegian assistance ("partners in development"), the role to be played by the private enterprise sector, the choice of different forms of assistance (multilateral vs. bilateral aid) etc. While all these issues had also been discussed at earlier stages in the development of Norwegian aid policies, the questions related to the support for national and social popular movements were for the first time brought up in a Parliamentary Report. The extensive discussion of this new principle was deemed to be necessary by the Labour party minority government in order to anchor the decision in a broad consensus. The Ministry of Foreign Affairs, therefore, took as its point of departure a wide range of resolutions adopted by the UN General Assembly and the Security Council. Particular emphasis was put on the General Assembly Resolution 1514, which was unanimously adopted in 1960. (There were, however, nine abstentions, among them South Africa, Portugal, France, United Kingdom and the United States of America.) Containing the *Declaration on the Granting of Independence to Colonial Countries and Peoples*, this resolution lays down that the subjection of peoples to alien domination consti-

---

[137] After the European Community referendum in 1972, Arne Kielland "crossed the floor" to join the Socialist People's Party, and was in 1973 elected MP for the Socialist Left Party.

[138] Parliamentary Report no. 30 (1970–71), pp. 4–5.

[139] The report was translated into English and published by NORAD, Oslo, 1973.

tutes an infringement of human rights, is in conflict with the UN Charter and impedes the development of peace and co-operation in the world. The "Decolonisation Declaration" also requires that immediate steps should be taken to transfer all powers—without any conditions or reservations—to the peoples in the areas in question.

The basis for the recommendation to make available "both humanitarian and other forms of financial assistance to the peoples in dependent areas struggling to achieve national liberation", is also found in the General Assembly resolutions urging member countries to provide moral and material support for the peoples and the liberation movements. It is, furthermore, emphasised that the UN, as well as the individual UN member countries, has a special responsibility with regard to the situation in the remaining Portuguese colonies, Rhodesia and Namibia. The fact was also mentioned that Norway at the UN 24th General Assembly in 1969 had voted in favour of a resolution which contained an appeal to the member countries "to increase their moral support and material assistance to the people in the territories under Portuguese domination who are struggling for their freedom and independence". Similar resolutions on Namibia had also been supported following the decision by the UN in 1966 to revoke South Africa's mandate and to transfer direct responsibility for the administration of the area to the United Nations. With regard to the illegal Ian Smith regime in Rhodesia, Norway had both adhered to the Security Council mandatory sanctions and supported resolutions urging member states to give material and moral support to the liberation movements.

Since no references were made to the Republic of South Africa, the country was obviously not included in the category of "dependent areas". This was later assumed to be the main reason why assistance to the ANC was not introduced until 1977 (see chapter 3). This is in marked contrast to the 1969 principles guiding Swedish assistance to the liberation movements, which had included assistance to "the victims of the policy of apartheid, stating that such support could *inter alia* be motivated by the explicit condemnation by the United Nations of South Africa's policy".[140]

Calling attention to the strict rules guiding the export of Norwegian arms and military equipment, the Parliamentary Report also confirmed the principle that support by way of arms or financing of armed warfare was excluded from any Norwegian assistance. It was, at the same time, made clear that no requests to this effect had been received from the liberation movements in question.

With regard to projects initiated by liberation movements outside their own countries' borders, with the consent of the host country and primarily intended for refugees, the Parliamentary Report stated that such support

---

[140] See Statement no. 82/1969 by the Appropriations Committee of the Swedish Parliament, pp. 23–24.

had already been given to refugees from Southern Africa through the relevant UN institutions as well as through the Special Committee for Aid to Refugees from Southern Africa. Following the recommendations passed by the NORAD Council, a special reference was also made to the aid which had already been given to FRELIMO's Mozambique Institute in Tanzania. According to the Government, the question of channelling humanitarian aid to national and social popular movements in dependent areas should, therefore, not be regarded as a new principle: "It must be seen as a normal internationally accepted duty for the world outside, on a humanitarian basis, to give various forms of help if the aim is to ameliorate need and human suffering. Humanitarian aid to national and social popular movements is in keeping with the general view expressed on the part of Norway in recent years in relation to the development of international humanitarian rules of law. ... In the light of this, it seems clear that aid for humanitarian ends (in the widest sense), such as medicine, health care, clothing, food, educational measures etc., is in accordance with our UN obligations and our view of the principles of humanitarian assistance".[141] A reference is also made to the initiative taken on a former occasion by Norway in the UN and in the International Red Cross with the aim of ensuring that humanitarian aid should be extended to civilian populations experiencing need and suffering as a result of war, internal conflict and natural catastrophes. This initiative was later carried further in the UN. As to the question of other forms of economic assistance than strictly humanitarian aid and support for refugees, it is argued that there is no clear division between development assistance and humanitarian aid: "Whether the aid has a short-term emergency aid objective or a more long-term objective aimed at promoting development, this cannot be said to make any difference to the fundamentals of the case".[142]

As regards the question of whether assistance should be given *directly* to the liberation movements' own institutions or through multilateral channels (for instance the UN or the OAU), the government was of the opinion that this must be deliberated in each separate instance. While UN programmes are primarily intended to cover refugees from the territories in question, the liberation movements themselves had requested assistance for social and humanitarian programmes in the liberated parts of their territories. For practical reasons—and to avoid aid being used for other ends than what was intended—it was argued for assistance in kind (food, clothing, medicine, and educational material). This did not, however, mean that the Government wanted to exclude more direct development aid where organised administrative authority was exercised.

As to the choice between several areas and "possibly also between several liberation movements", the most suitable course would, according to

---

[141] *Parliamentary Report no. 29 (1971–72)*, op.cit., p. 25.
[142] Ibid., p. 25.

the Report, be to base the choice on organisations which were recognised by the OAU. This question had already been cleared with an OAU delegation visiting Norway in the autumn of 1971 (see below).

Before Report no. 29 was debated in Parliament a new change in government took place, as Prime Minister Trygve Bratteli had announced that he would resign if a majority voted against Norway entering the European Community in the referendum in September 1972. A new minority government was formed, consisting of the Liberal Party, the Centre Party and the Christian People's Party. The new government accepted the Report of its predecessor as the basis for the discussion in the Parliament on the future guidelines for development assistance.

The normal procedure is for a Parliamentary report from the government to be subjected to an extensive discussion in the Foreign Affairs Committee of the Parliament, which then presents a recommendation to be debated by a plenary session. Thus, the *Recommendation to Parliament No. 135 for 1972–1973* is to be regarded as an authoritative document.[143] While the members of the Committee were split according to party lines on several issues—such as the long-term target for aid budgets, a unanimous Committee gave support to the idea of extending assistance to "popular movements operating in dependent areas struggling for national liberation". With reference to the grant to FRELIMO's Mozambique Institute, the Committee as a whole expressed its wish "that this form of support should be continued and expanded, where there is sufficient justification, e.g. in recommendations from competent UN agencies, as was so in the case in question". While confirming the principle that support cannot be given in the form or arms, or the financing of armed struggle, it is maintained that these provisions are no obstacles to support being given on humanitarian grounds to the population in countries or areas under any foreign administration. It was further stated that "The Committee feels that assistance of this kind has the backing of large sections of the Norwegian population". The Committee also recognised that it is extremely difficult to draw up more definite lines of policy for Norwegian aid, when it comes to direct support to national popular movements. Such assistance must, therefore, largely be based on actual case-by-case appraisals. "A prerequisite is that some form of organised administrative authority must be exercised in the liberated area and that this authority should seem stable, be capable of upholding law and order and able to assist in the implementation of the projects".

While forming part of a broad consensus, the three Committee members representing the Conservative Party also included a separate paragraph on the issue of liberation movements in their more general minority observations. It was underlined that a necessary condition for assisting the popula-

---

[143] This document is translated into English: *Recommendation from the Foreign Affairs and Constitutional Committee on certain key topics relevant to Norway's co-operation with the developing countries.*

tion in areas under foreign administration was that it was in accordance with international law. While stating that "much could be said for channelling aid via the UN, the Red Cross and the Norwegian Church Relief (AID)", the Conservative MPs were also open for providing aid through movements working for national and social liberation. "This must be restricted, however, to humanitarian relief, aid to refugees and aid within the sectors of education and social welfare. By means of special scrutiny arrangements, Norway must see that this aid is used for the purposes for which it is intended. The said members attach paramount importance to relief being made available in answer to the need for aid, and not according to political criteria".[144]

The positions held by the parties in the Foreign Affairs Committee were confirmed during the debate in Parliament on 8 February 1973. The two parties not represented in the Committee—the Liberal Party and the Socialist People's Party—were both strong proponents of the idea of supporting the liberation movements. When the government two months later presented its general long-term programme, outlining the main political principles guiding its activities for the coming four years, development assistance to the liberation movements occupied a prominent position. The new principle for development assistance even figured in the introduction as one of a few selected "political pillars".[145]

The new guidelines for assisting the liberation movements were at the time hailed as "a radical renewal in the Norwegian policy of development aid and its general foreign policy in relation to developing countries".[146] While the liberation movements' demand for independence had been recognised long ago, the launching of the armed struggle was a more complicated issue for the Norwegian public opinion. The move from humanitarian assistance through the UN and the Special Committee for Refugees to supporting economic and social activities inside the liberated areas, might be seen a further step towards a firm commitment to the liberation struggle. The new guidelines have also been characterised as being "tailor-made" for the Portuguese colonies.[147] This commitment by the government and the Parliament to assist liberation movements in the Portuguese colonies was also a far cry from the position held by the Norwegian ambassador to Lisbon, which was very close to the corporate nationalism and the imperial

---

[144] Ibid., p. 63. In spite of these reservations, the Norwegian Conservative Party departed from its Swedish sister party, which at the time asserted in the Standing Committee of Foreign Affairs that "... to actively support revolutionary movements (...) is not in agreement with international legal principles nor with the Swedish policy of neutrality". The statement is quoted in Tor Sellström: *Sweden and National Liberation in Southern Africa. Vol. II.* Uppsala: Nordiska Afrikainstitutet (forthcoming).

[145] Parliamentary Report no. 71 (1972–73), Ministry of Finance, p. 3.

[146] Olav Stokke (1973), op.cit., p. 55.

[147] Jon Bech: *Norsk bistand til frigjøringsbevegelsene i det sørlige Afrika.* Oslo: Norsk Utenrikspolitisk Institutt, 1978, p. 10. (*Forum for Utviklingsstudier*, nr. 10, 1978).

celebrations of the *Estado Novo*. In reports to the Norwegian Ministry of Foreign Affairs in the late 1960s and early 1970s it was consistently reported that "the terrorists" did not have any support from the local population, that there was no such thing as a liberation struggle or a rebellion, and that no signs of oppression or discrimination could be found in the "overseas provinces" of Portugal.[148] That the UN Charter on decolonisation had confirmed that "all peoples have their right to self-determination" seemed to be of no concern to the ambassador.

The UN/OAU conference in Oslo in April 1973: A watershed

The OAU initiative

During a goodwill mission to the Nordic countries in October 1971, a high-level delegation of the Organisation of African Unity (OAU)—headed by President Ould Daddah of Mauretania—expressed their general appreciation for Norwegian support in the UN on issues relating to decolonisation and apartheid. In particular, the delegation noted with thanks the Norwegian stand against Portugal's colonial policies, as expressed during the 1971 NATO summit in Lisbon. Norway was also asked to increase its pressure on the NATO partners supplying arms to Portugal, as these supplies—according to the OAU delegation—made it possible to free other weapons for use in the colonies. Similarly, the hope was also expressed that Norway would urge the United Kingdom to remain firm on the Rhodesia issue. It was also highly appreciated that Norway intended to increase its humanitarian support and other forms of economic assistance to the African liberation movements. [149]

Three months before the OAU visit to Oslo took place, the Norwegian Ministry of Foreign Affairs had—via its UN Mission—received a request from the OAU to host a World Conference for Support of Victims of Apartheid and Colonialism in Southern Africa. The initiative had been taken

---

[148] See for instance an extensive memo of 6 April 1971 from the Norwegian Embassy in Lisbon, in which the Ambassador (J. Finne-Grønn) surveys the recent history of the "overseas provinces" from the first "outburst of terrorism" in 1961 to the recent UN resolutions. It is difficult to imagine how an official propaganda pamphlet produced by the fascist regime itself would have treated the subject in a different manner. (The leader of MPLA, Dr. Agostinho Neto is described as a traditional healer ("medisinmann"). The memorandum concludes that "the real difficulty which faces the Portuguese is not the 'terrorists' or the 'liberation movements'. Neither is it the dissatisfaction of the African population in Angola or Mozambique. There is no 'suppression' of the native population, who are not the object of any form of discrimination, nor is there any form of rebellion. The difficulty is the official attitude common to the countries of the Western world, whose publicity media support the abolition of European rule over other races. The 'war' has gone on for ten years without the attackers having made any progress. Portugal is prepared to continue its defence not only in the ten coming years, but for as long as is necessary. For the Portuguese the defence of their provinces in Africa has become part of their everyday burden. In spite of this, quick progress is being made, both in continental Portugal as well as in the areas overseas". See also his enthusiastic report on the visit by President Caetano to the African colonies (29 April 1969).

[149] Memo, Ministry of Foreign Affairs, 2. Pol. Div., 10 October 1971 ("Utenriksminister Cappelens samtaler med delegasjonen fra OAU").

by President Kenneth Kaunda in early 1970, and then supported by the OAU Summit later in the same year. The main purpose of the conference was to formulate a programme of action to hasten the process of decolonisation and the abolishment of apartheid in Southern Africa, with a special emphasis on co-ordinated and effective assistance to the liberation movements. The focus on liberation movements clearly reflected the need for a new strategy since Western resistance had made comprehensive sanctions an unrealistic option. African countries were also anxious that world opinion should not forget Southern Africa. In order to inform Europeans about the situation in Southern Africa, and to raise awareness of colonialism and apartheid as a moral problem for the whole of mankind, the decision was made to hold the conference in Europe. It seems as if Sweden was the first choice for such a conference, but OAU was told that Sweden was already busy preparing for the UN Environmental Conference in 1972, and that Norway would probably be a better idea.[150]

The OAU request of 21 July 1971 had not been formally answered when the visit to Oslo took place, although the Permanent Mission to the UN had noted in a report that "it seems difficult to say no to Norway's being the host country, since in the OAU, expectations have already been created for holding the conference in Oslo".[151] During the meeting with the OAU delegation, the Norwegian Minister of Foreign Affairs—Andreas Cappelen—restricted himself to asking for further information about the purpose and format of the conference. There were obviously many practical and political issues to be discussed, and it was still unclear what role Norway and the other Nordic countries were expected to play. At this stage, the Norwegian government and Parliament were still considering what position to take on direct support (aid and other economic assistance) to the liberation movements, although a grant to the Mozambique Institute had already been made.

In accordance with established procedure among the Nordic countries, the Norwegian Ministry of Foreign Affairs wanted to involve the other Nordic countries before a final decision to host the conference was made. The issue was first raised at a Nordic joint consultation in November 1971. At this stage no final decision had been reached, and the OAU request of July was still unanswered. According to the presentation by the Norwegian officials at the meeting, it was to be an OAU conference with no Norwegian official participation in the preparations. Apart from a potential financial

---

[150] Memo from a meeting with Mahmoud Sahnoun (Deputy Secretary-General of OAU) in Geneva 4 December 1971, written by Arne Arnesen and Tom Vraalsen.

[151] Arne Arnesen, Ministry of Foreign Affairs to Ketil Børde at the Permanent Mission of Norway to the UN Delegation, 8 October 1971. The memo also states that "the reality of the matter is that we can hardly avoid hosting the conference, but there can be no question of the Government being its sponsor".

contribution and providing a technical secretariat, no further involvement was envisaged.[152]

Officials from all the Nordic foreign ministries discussed the issue again in Copenhagen in late January 1972.[153] According to the reports from the meeting, neither Denmark nor Finland showed any great enthusiasm for the whole venture. They, therefore, did not want to commit themselves to any Nordic participation *en bloc,* although this was clearly assumed by the OAU. While Norway and Sweden had already decided to take part, the decision would be taken at a later stage in Denmark and Finland. Norway wanted full participation by the other Nordic countries not only in the Conference itself, but also in the work of the Organising Committee to be appointed. The reason was, according to the Norwegian report from the Copenhagen meeting "to get control of the preparations and to prevent the conference from getting out of course from the start, to promote "constructive solutions", and to "avoid the bombastic". A more substantial involvement in the preparations was rejected by Denmark and Finland, and was met with great scepticism even from Sweden. The official from the Danish Ministry of Foreign Affairs warned that militant groups could dominate the conference, while the Nordic countries were described as being "neither reactionary nor militant".

Preparing for the conference

In the months following the OAU visit to Oslo, several meetings took place between officials of the OAU (led by Mahmoud Sahnoun, Deputy Secretary-General) and the Norwegian Ministry of Foreign Affairs for further exchange of views.[154] In accordance with the wishes of the Norwegian representatives, it was finally agreed that the conference should be based on experts in individual capacities. Norway also wanted a stronger UN involvement, and in February 1972 the UN Association of Norway agreed to serve as the Technical Secretariat. The major political and practical arrangements were finalised at a meeting to coincide with the OAU Heads of State Summit in Rabat in June 1972.[155] A formal organising committee was also set up to deal with all remaining issues, consisting of representatives from the OAU, the UN, the Norwegian Ministry of Foreign Affairs and the liberation movements.

As to budget matters, it was indicated that Norway was willing to consider covering the expenses of the participants from the liberation move-

---

[152] Memo, 1. Pol. Div., 10 November 1971 ("Referat fra Samrådingsmøte 8. November 1971").

[153] "Referat af det nordiske FN-kontorchefmøde den 25.–26. Januar 1972 i København". Ministry of Foreign Affairs, 25 9/12.

[154] See reports in the Ministry of Foreign Affairs archives (25 9/12) from meetings held in Geneva 4 December 1971; Oslo 14 April 1972 and Addis Ababa, 9–10 May 1972.

[155] Memo, 1. Pol. Div., 19 June 1972 ("OAU-konferansen i Oslo, mai 1973").

ments, possibly in co-operation with other Nordic countries. OAU was expected to cover its own costs, while the UN and other governments should be approached for further financial contributions. In discussing the agenda of the conference, the point was stressed by Amilcar Cabral—President of the liberation movement of Guinea-Bissau (PAIGC)—that the conference should concentrate on political and diplomatic issues ("la bataille diplomatique et politique") in addition to humanitarian assistance, while it should be left to the individual governments to consider the issue of military support. The fact that this position, aiming at achieving "realism" instead of wasting time on fierce polemics, was taken by the representative of the liberation movements obviously was received with great enthusiasm by the Norwegian participants. Amilcar Cabral also wanted a stronger Norwegian involvement, for instance in sending invitations, so that it would be clear that it was more than an ordinary OAU conference. From the Norwegian side, there was at this stage still a great reluctance to go beyond providing the technical secretariat.

The Rabat meeting succeeded in drafting the two-fold agenda of (a) assessing the current situation in the various fields of assistance (direct material and humanitarian), diplomatic actions, political actions, legal actions as well as actions vis-à-vis public opinion and (b) discussing future actions to be taken by the UN, OAU, governments, non-governmental organisations and liberation movements in support of victims of colonialism and apartheid. It was also agreed that the Organising Committee should decide on the papers and documentation to be commissioned for the conference, and which organisations and individual experts were to be invited. It was also confirmed that the conference should be organised as a meeting of experts, and not as a formal conference between government representatives. Invitations should be extended to member states of the Security Council, the UN Special Committee on Decolonisation, the UN Special Committee on Apartheid and the UN Council for Namibia, the Nordic countries, the UN specialised agencies (UNESCO, WHO, FAO and ILO), members of the OAU Liberation Committee and the nine African liberation movements recognised by the OAU. The two representatives from each of the 65 countries invited were expected to participate in their personal capacities as "experts".

Among experts to be invited were also individuals associated with organisations like the World Council of Churches, the British Anti-Apartheid Movement, International Defence and Aid Fund, the (Holland) Angola Committee, the UK Committee for Freedom in Mozambique, Guinea-Bissau and Angola as well as the International University Exchange Fund (IUEF).

As mentioned above, Norway had at an early stage of the preparations argued that it would be highly desirable to obtain a larger measure of support and involvement on the part of the UN. This coincided with the wish of the OAU to assure the liberation movements a higher degree of international legitimacy. A major step in this direction had already been taken in 1970, when the UN General Assembly adopted a "Programme of Action for the full implementation of the Declaration on the Granting of Independence to Colonial Peoples and Countries".[156] The Programme of Action confirmed "the inherent right of colonial peoples to struggle by all necessary means at their disposal against colonial Powers which suppress their aspiration for freedom and independence". The same principle, with particular reference to Southern Africa, was affirmed in the General Assembly Resolution 1287 (XXVI) in December 1971. When the UN Security Council met in Addis Ababa in February 1972, the resolution related to the Portuguese Territories also recognised the legitimacy of the struggle of the liberation movements in Angola, Mozambique and Guinea (Bissau) and called on Portugal to transfer power to political institutions freely elected and representative of the peoples.[157] In 1972, the Council for Namibia agreed to a request from the South West African People's Organisation (SWAPO) to attend the meetings of the Council in an observer capacity. In a resolution adopted by the General Assembly in the same year, the Assembly noted the fact that, in consultation with the OAU and through it, representatives of the national liberation movements in Angola, Guinea-Bissau) and Mozambique, had been invited to participate in an observer capacity at its considerations of these territories.[158] The Assembly also reaffirmed that national liberation movements were the authentic representatives of the true aspirations of the peoples of those Territories, and that all governments, the specialised agencies and other organisations within the UN system and the UN bodies concerned should, when dealing with matters pertaining to the territories, ensure the representation of these Territories by the liberation movements in an appropriate capacity and in consultation with the OAU. Along similar lines, the resolutions passed by the General Assembly and the Security Council relating to Southern Africa stated that any settlement in Southern Rhodesia must be worked out with the full participation of the genuine political leaders representing the majority.[159] While the Security Council recognised the legitimacy of the struggle of the people of Southern Rhodesia to secure the enjoyment of their inalienable rights to self-determination and independence, the General Assembly resolution accordingly requested all Governments, the specialised agencies and other organisations within the UN system to extend all moral and material assistance to the people of Zimbabwe.

During the autumn of 1972 the conference was transformed into a UN/OAU conference, a fact which also served to strengthen the commitment of Norway and the other Nordic countries. While the General Assem-

---

[156] General Assembly Resolution 2621 (XXV), 1970.

[157] Security Council Resolution 312, 1972.

[158] General Assembly Resolution 2918 (XXVII), 1972.

[159] General Assembly Resolution 2945 (XXVII) and the Security Council Resolution 328, 1972.

bly previously had noted—in passing—that OAU intended to convene a conference in Oslo, a resolution introduced by Sweden in early November 1972 requested the UN, in co-operation with the OAU, to organise the planned UN/OAU Conference of Experts for the Support of Victims of Colonialism and Apartheid in Southern Africa.[160] Portugal and South Africa voted against, with 7 abstentions (France, United Kingdom, United States, Spain, Costa Rica, Brazil and Malawi).

All remaining issues were resolved during Organising Committee meetings in New York in December 1972 and in Oslo in January 1973.[161] As representative of the liberation movements, Amilcar Cabral was expected to take part in the organising committee meeting in Oslo, but was killed a few days before.[162] It was also confirmed that no resolutions should be adopted at the conference, but that an agreed summary report should be presented to the UN General Assembly 28th Session later in the year. The invitation to the Norwegian ambassador to the UN, Ole Ålgård, to serve as the President of the conference strengthened the direct Norwegian involvement. The choice of Ambassador Ole Ålgård reflected the wish of the OAU to demonstrate that the conference was of concern to the world community. From a Norwegian point of view it was also argued that a "realistic" conference was more likely to result if Norway was in a position to influence the deliberations of the conference through the presidency.[163]

As the host nation of the Conference, Norway strongly appealed to all permanent members of the Security Council to attend. This turned out to be an uphill struggle, since in the end the United States, United Kingdom and France declined the invitation. Apart from abstaining when the resolution on the conference was passed by the UN General Assembly, the US had also recently withdrawn from the UN Special Committee on Decolonisation. During meetings with US diplomats in Oslo, New York and Washington, representatives of the Norwegian Ministry of Foreign Affairs argued strongly that the presence of all Security Council members would "create the necessary balance", and that it might be useful for the US to attend in order to make sure that unfounded accusations and misrepresentation of the United States position should not be left unanswered.[164] When the US chargé d'affaires in Oslo expressed his opinion that "it was hardly desirable that a NATO country should in this way be put on trial within another

---

[160] General Assembly Resolution 2910 (XXVII), 1972.

[161] Meeting of the Organising Committee in Oslo January 225, 1973. Agreed summary of conclusions. (Ministry of Foreign Affairs Archives, 25 9/12b).

[162] It has later been suggested that the timing of the killing of Amilcar Cabral can be related to the fact that he was expected to be appointed President of the conference. (Information from Abdul Minty, Pretoria 16 July 1998.)

[163] Memo, 1. Pol. Div., 11 January 1973.

[164] Memo from the Norwegian Ministry of Foreign Affairs to the Norwegian Embassy in Washington, 23 January 1973.

NATO country's territory", he was reminded that the proposal to convene an *expert conference* was deliberately put forward by Norway in order to create "an atmosphere that was sane and reasonable, and make it easier for a country like the USA to take part".[165]

When the Norwegian Ministry of Foreign Affairs was informed about the final decision not to attend, the reasons stated by US diplomats in Oslo were that the conference as then planned would adopt unacceptable reports and recommendations, be contentious and duplicative of UN proceedings and give new impetus to unacceptable status for liberation movements in the international community and be an unhealthy precedent for the UN to sponsor one-sided discussion". The last point referred to the fact that neither South Africa nor Portugal had been invited to send "experts".[166] However, the chairperson of the US House of Representatives Foreign Affairs Sub-Committee on African Affairs, Charles Diggs Jr., had already been invited as an individual expert. In his statement at the Conference, he made an explicit reference to the US decision not to attend: "I think that it is particularly significant that the Conference had decided that its site be in Oslo because of the implications of our presence in a NATO country as it relates to United States involvement with Portugal. Little wonder our mission here, among other components of the American government, was opposed to this as a site".[167]

The conference

While the first Norwegian involvement in the UN/OAU Conference took place under a Labour Party Government, the three-party coalition government of the Liberal Party, the Centre Party and the Christian People's Party—formed in October 1972—upheld the commitment, and made a contribution of US 31,500 towards meeting the expenses and travel costs of the representatives of the liberation movements. (Altogether the Nordic countries made available US 79,500 for this purpose.) A change in government was of less importance, since at this stage a more understanding position vis-à-vis the liberation movements had developed inside the Ministry of Foreign Affairs. A new—and less conservative—generation of diplomats had slowly made its impact. This was particularly noticeable among the personnel who had taken part in the preparations for the UN/OAU Conference,

---

[165] Transmission ("Utgående melding") to the Permanent Mission of Norway to the UN, 12 January 1973.

[166] Transmission ("Utgående melding") to the Permanent Mission of Norway to the UN, 16 March 1973. The reference to the US position is based on "talking points" made available to the Ministry by a US diplomat in Oslo.

[167] Olav Stokke/Carl Widstrand (eds.): *Southern Africa. The UN-OAU Conference, Oslo 9–14 1973. Vol. 1, Programme of Action and Conference Proceedings.* Uppsala: Scandinavian Institute of African Studies, 1973, p. 230.

and who were also more sensitive to the Norwegian opinion and to public debate outside the corridors of the Ministry of Foreign Affairs.[168]

Although Norway deliberately chose not to be represented by high-ranking civil servants, Arne Arnesen—who now took part in the capacity of a journalist with the social democratic *Arbeiderbladet*—had as a civil servant in the Ministry of Foreign Affairs been intimately involved with the Organising Committee.[169] The other Norwegian "individual expert" was Gunnar Stålsett, the Secretary-General of the Council of Ecumenical and International Relations of the Norwegian Church (Mellomkirkelig Råd). Being a prominent member of the Centre Party, he was at the time of the conference Secretary of State for Education, Church and Culture.

The conference, which was the first OAU conference held outside the continent of Africa, was officially opened by the Norwegian Minister of Foreign Affairs, Dagfinn Vårvik on April 9 1973. In his opening address he confirmed the Norwegian commitment to the liberation struggle: "The Norwegian government by hosting the conference, wanted to express once more its full support for the peoples of southern Africa who were struggling for their liberation and against *apartheid*".[170] The first day of the conference happened to be a day loaded with heavy symbolism in Norwegian history because of the German invasion on April 9 1940, a fact which was reflected in the editorial comments in several newspapers.[171]

By focusing on the liberation movements and the need for humanitarian assistance and other forms of support, the UN/OAU Conference made a significant contribution to the struggle against apartheid and colonialism. This is reflected in the two-volume report—*Southern Africa. The UN-OAU Conference*—that gave prominence to the points put forward by the representatives of the liberation movements.[172] The change of focus initiated by the Oslo conference was aptly summed up by Abdul Minty of the British Anti-Apartheid Movement in his paper: "Almost since its inception the United Nations has been concerned with the problem of *apartheid* and white domination. Over the years the subject has been discussed and debated repeatedly and more resolutions have been drafted and adopted on this question than on any other single issue. Initially the resolutions concentrated

---

[168] Arne Arnesen, Tom Vraalsen and Ketil Børde were among the diplomats who in the 1970s played a prominent role in forging links with the liberation movements.

[169] Arne Arnesen was appointed Secretary of State for Foreign Affairs in the Labour Party government which took power later in the same year.

[170] Olav Stokke/Carl Gösta Widstrand, op.cit., vol. 1, p. 41.

[171] According to the Christian daily *Vårt Land* "some African countries were still occupied, and the task of Norway should therefore be to contribute to the liberation of Southern Africa— partly by supporting the liberation movements and partly by making it clear to the present rulers that they sooner or later have to lose" *Vårt Land*, 9 April 1973.

[172] Olav Stokke/Carl Widstrand (eds.): *Southern Africa. The UN-OAU Conference, Oslo 9–14 April 1973, Vol. 1: Programme of Action and Conference Proceedings; Vol. 2: Papers and Documents.* Uppsala: Scandinavian Institute of African Studies, 1973.

on making calls and appeals to the white rulers to heed international public opinion and abandon the policy of *apartheid*: only to be rejected by the Pretoria regime. Later, with more African States joining the United Nations they began to demand international boycott action against the *apartheid* State and all its institutions, and more recently there are trends towards recognising the legitimacy of the African liberation struggle and providing international political and material support for it".[173]

Based on this understanding of the new stage in the struggle, several speakers expressed their reservations that the title of the conference should describe it as being in support of the "victims of colonialism and apartheid", while support for those struggling against colonialism and apartheid would have been more appropriate. As argued by Baldwin Sjollema, World Council of Churches: "First, should we speak about 'support to victims of *apartheid* and colonialism' as the title of this conference reads? Haven't we finally passed that stage? Are we not here with the representatives of the liberation movements and those who are already responsible *de facto* for the well-being of millions of people in liberated territories?"[174] The same point was made by Oliver Tambo, who stated in his address that "we should rise above the relationship of victims and supporters and combine at a new level of joint action against a common foe".[175] In reality, however, the conference emphasised and generally accepted the paramount role of the liberation struggle, while all forms of collaboration with the apartheid regime, the Portuguese colonial government and the illegal regime of Ian Smith in Southern Rhodesia were vehemently denounced. This development of the conference led to the following concluding remarks by Herbert Chitepo of the Zimbabwe African National Union: "When the meeting started, there was some apprehension among some that the Conference would not succeed. In the liberation movements, we feared that a meeting sponsored by the United Nations, an organisation committed to the search for peaceful solutions of international disputes, might underplay or endeavour to shift us from our commitment to armed struggle. To us in the liberation movements, one of the cardinal successes of this Conference has been its acceptance of the inevitability of armed struggle and its support for that struggle".[176]

Several background papers by the liberation movements in Mozambique, Angola and Guinea-Bissau brought to the conference information about their recent military advances, the organisation of liberated areas and need for development assistance for projects within the fields of education, health and agriculture. FRELIMO claimed to have liberated more than one-fourth of the country in the years following the launching of the armed

---

[173] Ibid., vol. 2, p. 9.

[174] Ibid., vol. 1, pp. 235–236.

[175] Ibid., vol. 1, p. 14.

[176] Ibid., vol. 1, p. 69.

struggle in 1964, and thus carried the responsibility for catering to the needs of one million people, in addition to the educational programmes set up in the neighbouring country of Tanzania. Representatives of the OAU Liberation Committee, who had recently visited the liberated areas, testified that FRELIMO enjoyed the full support and confidence of the people in the liberated areas. This was also confirmed by Lord Gifford in his address to the Conference, based on his travelling around for two weeks inside Tete province.[177]

While thousands of Africans in the 1960s had to flee their home countries because of persecution or in search of education, the concept of "liberated zones" in Mozambique, Angola and Guinea-Bissau later obliged the liberation movements to provide food, salt, soap, cloth etc., to establish health and educational services and to have to arrange for the growing of crops as well as for economic and social development in general. In addition to presenting these needs to the international community, many speakers also stressed that "support to development programmes in liberated territory is only possible because of the armed struggle which preceded the liberation of an area".[178]

The Oslo Conference also gave a voice to the liberation movements from other territories than the Portuguese colonies. Several papers, reports and interventions by representatives from the ANC and the PAC told the story of mounting black resistance inside South Africa itself, such as a storm of student protests and industrial strikes bringing Durban to a near standstill in early 1973.[179] Many speakers deplored the fact that the impression was often given that the apartheid regime was unshakeable and would remain so forever. In his address to the conference, the ANC president Oliver Tambo argued that "We have suffered from a feeling that because South Africa is so powerful, we should wait until all the enemies around South Africa have been eliminated. In the meantime South Africa is using precisely that period of waiting to consolidate its internal position to build up their armaments ... consolidate its position in Namibia etc.[180]

Another significant feature of the conference was the attention devoted to the activities and impact of the non-governmental organisations in North America and Western Europe. Several speakers and papers highlighted the seminal role of the solidarity movements and support groups in disseminating information, raising funds, collecting food, clothing and medicine as well as establishing contacts between the liberation movements and

---

[177] Ibid., vol. 1, pp. 89–96.

[178] Baldwin Sjollema, World Council of Churches, ibid., vol. 1, pp. 235–236.

[179] Among the ANC participants was Chris Hani, later to become Commander of Umkhonto we Sizwe and Secretary-General of the South African Communist Party. He was, however, not registered under his real name, but appeared as Zenzile Msethu. See Vladimir Shubin: *ANC: A view from Moscow.* Cape Town: Mayibuye Publishers, 1999 and Tor Sellström, op.cit., Vol. II.

[180] Ibid., vol. 1, p. 145.

prospective donors. It was also noted that in countries whose Governments provided assistance to the liberation movements, the work of support groups appeared to have encouraged increases in amounts of aid. Among the groups and international organisations represented at the Conference were International Defence and Aid Fund (Canon L. John Collins), the British Anti-Apartheid Movement (Abdul Minty), International Exchange University Fund (Lars-Gunnar Eriksson), World Council of Churches/ Program to Combat Racism (Baldwin Sjollema), The Dutch Angola Committee (Sietse Bosgra) and the UK Committee for Freedom in Mozambique, Guinea-Bissau and Angola (Lord Gifford).[181] A conference in 1974 was also proposed in order for the anti-apartheid and other similar groups to discuss public action in Western Europe and North America.[182]

Representatives of the non-governmental organisations were among the most vocal critics of the role played by the Western powers as the major trading partners of South Africa and suppliers of arms to Portugal. The point was also often made that some Western powers were violating the UN arm embargo, which was considered to be the most far-reaching decision of the Security Council on the question of apartheid. Non-governmental organisations were also asked to publicise the activities of companies involved in southern Africa and organise public campaigns for their withdrawal.

The Programme of Action

As mentioned above, in working out the procedures of the conference it had been agreed not to adopt any resolutions, but to "highlight" proposals and recommendations in a report to be presented to the UN 28th General Assembly for consideration. The recommendations were formulated to constitute a Programme of Action which established that the struggle of the peoples of Southern Africa "is entirely just and legitimate, deserving the complete support of the world community" and that it is "the solemn duty of international organisations, Governments and peoples to accelerate the isolation of the colonial and apartheid regimes and channel massive assistance to the liberation movements".[183] Apart from denouncing the colonial and apartheid regimes as well as "the collaboration of certain Governments and major economic interests", the Programme of Action also contained recommendations pertaining to diplomatic activities and implementation of

---

[181] Conspicuously lacking from this list is the Norwegian Council for Southern Africa, which as the leading solidarity organisation of the host country was not officially involved with the conference at any stage.

[182] Abdul Minty in Stokke/Widstrand, op.cit., vol. 2, p. 16. No such conference was held, but a seminar hosted by IUEF and the Norwegian National Union of Students was held in Oslo 24 February–2 March 1974. The purpose of the seminar, which was directed by Mahmoud Sahnoun, was to improve the planning and co-ordination of assistance to the liberation movements.

[183] The Programme of Action is published *in extenso* in Stokke/Widstrand, op. cit., vol. 1, pp. 17–39.

PROGRAMME OF ACTION

(75) Action should be taken by all United Nations bodies, the organisations of the United Nations system, the specialised agencies and other international organisations to ensure full representation and participation by liberation movements as the authentic representatives of their peoples and countries.

(76) All Governments and organisations should deal directly with the liberation movements recognised by the Organisation of African Unity on all questions concerning their countries.

(78) The right of the peoples of southern Africa to strive for their liberation by all appropriate means, including armed struggle against the oppression and brutality of the colonial and racist regimes, should be fully recognised and supported.

(90) The struggle for the people of southern Africa for freedom and independence is a legitimate struggle, and the international community has a duty to provide moral and material assistance to the liberation movements recognised by the Organisation of African Unity.

(92) The colonial and racist regimes could not have continued to defy United Nations resolutions and world opinion but for the attitude of some Governments allied to them, which prevent effective international action and assist these regimes. Foreign economic interests, in their exploitation of the resources of southern Africa, continue to assist these regimes and profit from the oppression of the African peoples. It is, therefore, imperative that African peoples of these Territories receive all necessary assistance to the liberation movements in their just struggle, including armed struggle.

(95) There is increasing need for direct assistance to the oppressed peoples in southern Africa and their liberation movements in order to support the movements in the conduct of their legitimate struggle for freedom, to help in the reconstruction of the liberated areas and to alleviate the suffering occurring in the course of their struggle.

(98) At this stage, greater moral and material assistance to the liberation movements is among the most effective ways to secure peace in the region by hastening the completion of the process of decolonisation and elimination of *apartheid*.

(99) In providing assistance to the oppressed peoples in southern Africa and their liberation movements, it should be recognised that this is not charity but an act of solidarity with peoples engaged in a just struggle.

(101) Governments and organisations providing assistance to liberation movements should avoid paternalism. They should, as far as possible, provide direct assistance to the liberation movements to be administered by the movements themselves as the authentic representatives of the people of these Territories.

(102) The needs of the liberation movements vary from territory to territory, depending on the stage and the nature of the struggle. Nevertheless, increased assistance should be provided to the liberation movements as their struggles are complementary and are all developing further.

(103) Special reference should be made to the large-scale needs in the liberated areas for the provision of essential supplies for the populations and for national reconstruction. Military, medical and school supplies, food, clothing, farm implements, means of transport and printing facilities are urgently required on a much larger scale.

sanctions. A number of operative paragraphs also dealt explicitly with ways and means of supporting the struggle of the liberation movements and channelling assistance to their humanitarian and developmental activities. All governments were also called upon to give financial support to non-governmental action groups working for the support of liberation movements in southern Africa.

Outside the conference hall

Although the major part of the conference was conducted behind closed doors, the presence in Oslo of prominent leaders of the liberation movements and a wide range of individual experts did not go unnoticed by the mass media and the general public. Never before had the liberation movements received such a broad—and generally sympathetic—coverage. Even if the Norwegian solidarity movement, the Norwegian Council for Southern Africa, was not invited to officially take part in the conference, it was actively involved in a "solidarity week" all over the country. Apart from supporting the liberation struggle, the Council during its campaign also focused on the responsibility of the NATO countries for the colonial wars, the role of multinational corporations and the Norwegian trade and shipping links with the apartheid regime. On the opening day of 9 April, a well-attended public rally was addressed by Marcelino dos Santos (FRELIMO), Vasco Cabral (PAIGC) and Mahmoud Sahnoun (Political Secretary of the Conference).[184] Two days later the Peace Research Institute of Oslo (PRIO) hosted a conference on the South African military machine, addressed *inter alia* by Abdul Minty. Together with other public meetings and exhibitions, the activities of the Norwegian Council for Southern Africa were highly instrumental in bridging the gap between the expert conference and the wider Norwegian public. This was reflected in the reports from the conference published in the *United Nations Secretariat News:* "The Conference appeared to be supported by all segments of Norwegian society. The young people of Oslo organised a multi-media exhibition and held seminars and lectures on the liberation struggle in southern Africa at the University. Labour groups also organised discussions on southern Africa at which liberation leaders were invited to speak. (The Conference itself was held in the Trade Union Hall.) There were daily programmes on Norwegian television and radio relating to the themes of the Conference. The press coverage of the Conference was outstanding—almost 300 representatives from the mass media attended the Conference. The liberation movement leaders were in constant demand for interviews and speaking engagements and are truly popular figures in the Scandinavian countries. One evening during the

---

[184] The rally was met with a counter-demonstration by a handful of members of the neo-fascist National Youth League, handing out leaflets proclaiming "solidarity with our white kinsmen in Southern Africa", *Nationen*, 10 April 1974.

Conference, a mass demonstration in support of the liberation movements took place that was also attended by many participants from the Conference. A movie theatre in Oslo devoted a week to showing films relating to the plight of the oppressed peoples in southern Africa. The prestigious Nobel Institute also held a panel discussion on southern Africa. These activities were not limited to Oslo, as lectures, films and manifestations of solidarity were held in other Norwegian towns including Trondheim and Tromsø".[185]

The conference was well covered by the Norwegian mass media, since this was the first major UN conference to be held in Oslo. Generally, the conference was regarded as a breakthrough for the legitimisation of the liberation movements in the eyes of the Western public opinion. The editorial comments, however, largely reflected the political position of the newspapers. On the far right, the *Morgenbladet* vehemently condemned the conference for being a propaganda show directed against NATO, while the conservative *Aftenposten* expressed its sympathy with the US decision not to attend. In a less than enthusiastic editorial *Aftenposten* warned against "the danger of the conference ending as a propaganda show, which in the long run will not serve the interests of the worthy cause". The editorial of Aftenposten also deplored the fact that Portugal and South Africa were not present to defend themselves, and criticised the conference for not discussing racial discrimination in other parts of Africa" (Uganda/Burundi). In a similar vein, *Verdens Gang* emphasised that it was important for the host country to avoid "a politicising assembly", as if the liberation of Southern Africa was a technical issue to be solved by objective experts. On the other hand, Christian, liberal and social democratic newspapers fully supported the aim of the conference. Based on a cursory reading of the national press, it is impossible not to conclude that a growing understanding of the liberation struggle—in all its manifestations—evolved during the conference week. Even if the belief in peaceful solutions and UN negotiations is an important part of the Norwegian official *credo*, it was increasingly realised that these alternatives were blocked by the colonial and racist regimes. This political understanding undoubtedly improved the basis in Norway for an increased material support for the liberation movements in the years to come. A growing consensus in the host country itself seemed to be fully expressed—although in a cautious and diplomatic way—by Ambassador Ole Ålgård in his concluding address: "A peaceful solution to the problems of southern Africa would be in the true interests of all concerned. Because of the intransigent policies of the oppressive minority regimes, the peoples in southern Africa have been compelled to take up arms in their struggle for liberation. Taking this into consideration it has been emphasised that humanitarian, material and eco-

---

[185] *United Nations Secretariat News*, 31 May 1973, p. 6.

nomic assistance to liberation movements must be based on the clear understanding of and moral support for the cause for which they are fighting".[186]

After the conference

At the OAU Council Meeting 17–23 May 1973 in Addis Ababa, the recommendations of the Oslo Conference were endorsed as "constructive and important contributions in the struggle for the liberation of the Territories
under colonial and racist domination".[187] It was also noted with satisfaction
that representatives of the liberation movements participated on an equal
footing with the OAU and UN member states. The OAU Council further
"expressed its profound appreciation and gratitude to the Governments of
the Scandinavian countries and in particular to the Government of Norway
for hosting the conference and creating the necessary conditions conducive
to the successful outcome of its deliberations".

The importance of the Oslo Conference was also emphasised by several
speakers when the UN "Special Committee of 24" met on 13 June 1973. The
FRELIMO representative, Jorge Rebelo, expressed his appreciation for the
role that was played by the Nordic countries: "There is nothing strange in
this—as Sweden, Norway, Denmark and Finland have been consistently
supporting our struggle. But we consider that the new approach they are
taking—now supporting us politically and not only on a humanitarian basis
is an important development".[188] In his statement, Jorge Rebelo also pointed
to the fact that the conference was not just a talking shop, "but a working
meeting from which concrete programmes of action emerged, which if fully
and properly implemented will provide the liberation movements with the
means for their fight and the total isolation of Portugal".

In its assessment of the conference, the Ministry of Foreign Affairs emphasised the contributions made by the representatives of the liberation
movements in achieving a "realistic attitude", resulting in a conference that
had been "less propagandistic than often was the case in the context of the
UN".[189] In preparing for the UN General Assembly, it was however evident
that the Programme of Action adopted by the conference contained several
important points which were regarded by the Nordic governments as being
totally unacceptable.[190] Among them were formulations that could imply
that NATO as an organisation supported the colonial wars. It was also clear

---

[186] Stokke/Widstrand, op.cit., vol. 1, p. 73

[187] OAU CM/Res. 304. Resolution on the Oslo International Conference in Support of Victims
of Colonialism and Apartheid.

[188] Statement by Mr. Jorge Rebelo (FRELIMO) at the 915th meeting of the Special Committee of
24, on 13 June 1973.

[189] Memo, Norwegian Ministry of Foreign Affairs, 6 June 1973.

[190] Transmission ("Utgående melding") from the Norwegian Ministry of Foreign Affairs to the
Permanent Mission of Norway to the UN, 10 July 1973. 1010 5D. See also Memo, 1. Pol. Div., 16
August 1973.

that NATO as an organisation supported the colonial wars. It was also clear that the Nordic countries still did not want to be fully associated with the armed struggle, and that they could not go along with the formulation that "support should be given to the liberation movements ... to enable them to carry out their armed struggle". They also maintained that all questions relating to sanctions were to be left to the Security Council. The question of the participation of the liberation movements as observers in the UN was still an intricate one. During the 27th Assembly (1972), the Nordic countries had abstained on the vote concerning the status of the liberation movements, while a large majority voted to allow them the status of observers on questions relating to Southern Africa. To grant the liberation movements "full diplomatic recognition", as called for in the Programme of Action, went far beyond what was regarded as acceptable, although the question of observer status in the 4th Committee and the right to speak in other committees and during plenary sessions on an *ad hoc* basis was to be considered. On the other hand, it was obvious that the Nordic countries after the Oslo Conference wanted a more flexible position than at previous General Assemblies, and that they therefore were open to compromises acceptable to the African member states.

The joint Nordic strategy, which eventually was to succeed, was to avoid a detailed discussion of the Programme of Action in the General Assembly. The preferred alternative was to support a resolution restricting itself to "take note of" the UN/OAU Programme of Action, in the same vein as the Lusaka Manifesto was treated by the UN General Assembly in 1969. The more contentious issues—as seen from a Nordic point of view—would then be left to the more concrete resolutions relating to Portuguese territories, Southern Rhodesia and South Africa later in the 28th Assembly. Bearing in mind the high expectations from the African countries and the special responsibility Norway carried as host nation, it was of utmost importance to avoid a resolution which the delegation could not support, or—alternatively—which compelled Norway to make substantial reservations in explanation of the vote it cast. It was also deemed to be in the "pragmatic and realistic" spirit of the Oslo conference itself to adopt a resolution with wide acceptance.

In late September the OAU presented a draft resolution, which was immediately met by strong objections from the Nordic countries. Through extensive and private consultations with the African states involved, Norway presented an alternative operating paragraph, restricting itself to "commending the Programme of Action highlighted by the Conference to the attention of UN organs, the organisations within the UN system and the OAU, as well as of Governments, NGO's and the public." If this was accepted, Norway indicated its willingness—together with other Nordic

countries—to sponsor the resolution.[191] The final outcome was to be a resolution with these exact formulations in the operative paragraph, and the
resolution concerned with the UN/OAU conference was accordingly introduced to the General Assembly by Ole Ålgård on behalf of Norway,
Sweden, Denmark, Finland, Iceland, Nigeria, Tanzania and Zambia. A confrontation was avoided, and the resolution was passed against the lonely
votes of South Africa and Portugal.

Towards the end of the Portuguese empire (1972–75)

The first steps: Guinea-Bissau

Apart from the two modest grants to FRELIMO's Mozambique Institute in
Dar es Salaam (see above), it was the increasingly close links with the
PAIGC—the liberation movement in Guinea-Bissau—which paved the way
for official assistance to the liberation movements. PAIGC was the all dominant movement, and—in marked contrast to Angola and Mozambique—the
situation was not complicated by any significant settler dimension. Before he
was assassinated in January 1973, Amilcar Cabral had as President of
PAIGC developed cordial relations to Norwegian—as well as other
Nordic—politicians and diplomats. This was particularly the case during the
preparations for the UN/OAU Conference in Oslo.[192]

As was often the case, the ground had been prepared by the Swedish
grants to PAIGC and the experience gained by Sweden in assisting the education and health services of the liberation movement since 1969.[193] The
major part of the funds raised by Operation Day's Work in 1971 and 1972
was also channelled through PAIGC, mainly for the payment of textbooks
printed in Sweden. This annual campaign among secondary school students
was instrumental in raising funds as well as the awareness of large sections
of the Norwegian youth, following in the footsteps of similar campaigns in
Sweden and Finland.[194] The Operation Day's Work formed part of the activities of the Norwegian Association for Secondary Schools Students (NGS),
which was supported by all political youth organisations. During the campaign all Norwegian secondary school students were granted a day off from
school in order to work in companies, public institutions etc., and were also

---

[191] Memo from the Ministry of Foreign Affairs to the Permanent Mission of Norway to the UN, 28 September 1973.

[192] In 1972 Amilcar Cabral was invited to address the UN General Assembly on behalf of the liberation movements in the Portuguese colonies, but declined the offer when he was told that the Nordic ambassadors were "very unhappy". According to Salim Ahmed Salim, who at the time was chairman of the UN Decolonisation Committee, Amilcar Cabral did not want to embarrass the Nordic countries. See interview with Salim in Tor Sellström (ed.), op.cit, pp. 244–245.

[193] Tor Sellström: *Sweden and National Liberation in Southern Africa, Vol. II.* Uppsala: Nordiska Afrikainstitutet (forthcoming).

[194] The fund-raising campaign in Finland, which mainly focused on Mozambique, is treated in great detail in Iina Soiri/Pekka Peltola, op.cit., pp. 34–43.

involved in an International Week focusing on education for development and general North/South issues. In 1971 and 1972 the campaign managed to raise NOK 1. 25 million for MPLA, FRELIMO and PAIGC.[195] In conjunction with the campaign, prominent representatives of the liberation movements—among them Armando Panguene and Janet Mondlane from FRELIMO—toured Norwegian secondary schools and gave press interviews in local newspapers.[196] (Janet Mondlane later described the Operation Day's work in the Nordic countries as an exercise in "moral education".)[197] The campaign was also an important channel for disseminating information about the liberation struggle through pamphlets and magazines. The Norwegian edition of *The Struggle for Mozambique*, written by Eduardo Mondlane and published after his death, also contributed to a deeper understanding of the struggle against Portuguese colonialism.[198]

The decision to campaign for the liberation movements was a highly controversial one, although the point was repeatedly made that the funds collected were earmarked for humanitarian assistance and activities within the fields of education and health. Several Norwegian newspapers—among them *Verdens Gang*—opened their pages for conservative attacks on the Operation Day's Work (OD).[199] In Bærum, a county outside Oslo, the students split away from the central campaign and concentrated their efforts on raising funds for the Mozambique Institute, since the Institute was formally regarded as an independent institution and thus more acceptable for a conservative public.

The PAIGC representative to the Scandinavian countries, Onésimo Silveira, frequently paid visits to Norway, and developed cordial relations with the Norwegian Council for Africa as well as with Labour Party politicians. The writings of Amilcar Cabral were easily available in Swedish and English in the early 1970s, and were widely read among solidarity activists involved in the campaign for the liberation movements. A selection of Cabral's articles and speeches was also translated into Norwegian in 1973.[200] Serving as the representative of the liberation movements in the preparatory

---

[195] Stokke/Widstrand, op.cit., vol. 2, p. 40. The major part—NOK 800,000—went to PAIGC.

[196] See for instance an extensive interview with Armando Panguene in *Vårt Land*, 15 October 1971.

[197] Interview with the present author, Oslo, 18 October 1997. See also interviews with Janet Mondlane in Tor Sellström (ed.), op. cit., pp. 41–45 and in Iina Sori/Pekka Peltola, op. cit. pp. 198–205. Interestingly, this popular support through OD took place at a time when the official aid to the Mozambique Institute was suspended.

[198] *Kampen for Moçambique*, Oslo, Gyldendal, 1970. The Norwegian edition contained an introduction by Tore Linné Eriksen urging the readers to contribute to the FRELIMO fund-raising campaign run by the Norwegian Council for Southern Africa.

[199] *Verdens Gang*, 17 September 1971.

[200] *Frigjøringskamp i teori og praksis*, Oslo: NOVUS, 1973. Selection, translation and introduction by Johan Thorud. See also Tore Linné Eriksen: "Amilcar Cabral og Guinea-Bissau: En frigjøringsleder og en utviklingsmodell", *Kirke og Kultur*, no. 2, 1973:86–98.

committee of the UN/OAU Conference until his tragic death in January 1973, Amilcar Cabral had also impressed the civil servants of the Norwegian Ministry of Foreign Affairs.

The PAIGC representative to the Scandinavian countries also extended an invitation to a Norwegian journalist specialising on African issues, Johan Thorud, who was then able to visit liberated areas of Guinea-Bissau in late 1971 together with two Swedish journalists (Jean Hermansson and Anders Ehnmark). His extensive reports were published in *Arbeiderbladet* (the main organ of the Labour Party), and later formed the basis for his book *Geriljasamfunnet*.[201] Johan Thorud also presented a report to the NORAD administration, and served in a working group appointed by the Labour Party to recommend future policies with regard to the liberation movements. It is difficult to overestimate the importance of the writings (and lobbying activities) of Johan Thorud, who, after all, was the only Norwegian to visit the liberated areas of Guinea-Bissau and who was able to reach a wide audience through newspapers, books and radio/television interviews. In 1973 he also visited the liberated areas in northern Mozambique. As a former solidarity activist and a leading spokesperson of the Norwegian Action against Apartheid (NAMA) and the Crisis Fund for Southern Africa (Krisefondet), Johan Thorud was also in close touch with the Norwegian Council for Southern Africa after the two organisations joined forces in 1967.

The first application for a grant to PAIGC , to be used for food, clothing and medical equipment, had been presented to the Ministry of Foreign Affairs as early as March 1970.[202] At this time, the liberation movement had already been given assistance from the Swedish government, amounting to SEK 1 million in 1969. No formal response was given until the Labour Party replaced the Centre/Conservative government in April 1971. Secretary of State for Foreign Affairs, Thorvald Stoltenberg, then indicated his positive attitude at a more general level, but it took another year before the Ministry of Foreign Affairs proposed a grant of NOK 1 million. From the archival sources it seems as if the planned visit by Onésimo Silveira to Oslo on March 16 1972 was the triggering factor, as the Ministry of Foreign Affairs wanted to break the good news when the PAIGC representative was received by the Secretary of State for Foreign Affairs. Anticipating the outcome of the general debate in the Norwegian Parliament on support to the liberation movements, the Ministry of Foreign Affairs had in February 1972 worked out the general rules guiding future Norwegian aid co-operation. Based on these guidelines, the Ministry easily accepted the PAIGC proposals for

---

[201] Johan Thorud: *Geriljasamfunnet. Guinea-Bissaus kamp mot Portugal.* Oslo: Tiden, 1972.

[202] Letter to the Norwegian Ministry of Foreign Affairs from Onésimo Silveira 6 March 1970. As often was the case, the visit of the PAIGC representative to the Ministry of Foreign Affairs was followed by another visit by the Portuguese Ambassador, who wanted to know at what level the PAIGC representative had been received, the response given to his request for humanitarian assistance etc. (Memo from Kjeld Vibe, Ministry of Foreign Affairs, 10 March 1970.)

health and education projects inside liberated areas in Guinea-Bissau as well as in the neighbouring countries of Guinea and Senegal. After consultation with the PAIGC Office in Conakry, it was later decided to earmark the first Norwegian grant for food supplies and five ambulances. A high-level NORAD delegation visited the PAIGC headquarters in Conakry in October 1972, and was also able to visit hospitals and schools close to the border to Guinea-Bissau.[203] The delegation was led by Eskild Jensen, who praised the liberation movement and its capacity for handling assistance in his final report as well as in newspaper interviews. ("Of all the organisations and institutions I have been in contact with, there are none that have made such an immediately positive impression on me as the liberation movement PAIGC".)[204]

For 1973, the amount of aid channelled to PAIGC was increased from NOK 1 million to 1.5 million, and the co-operation with the liberation movement was further developed at the political and administrative level. In May 1973 a Norwegian delegation again visited the PAIGC headquarters in Conakry. Among the members of the delegation was Tor Oftedal, Labour MP and a prominent party spokesperson on international affairs. The NORAD programme officer in charge of the assistance to PAIGC, Helge Svendsen, later wrote an enthusiastic report for the NORAD magazine, outlining the history of PAIGC, the current stage of the struggle and the very impressive achievements in the field of education and health services.[205]

The regularisation of a special relationship

Following the Parliamentary Report (no. 29 1971–72) concerning North/South-policies, in which the Labour Party government proposed to make assistance to liberation movements a regular feature of Norwegian aid, which was later adopted by the Parliament in February 1973, a new budget line was initiated. For 1973 the Parliament set aside NOK 5 million to the liberation movements in Southern Africa (Guinea-Bissau included), leaving to the Ministry of Foreign Affairs the task of dividing the total amount between the liberation movements. The fact that the day-to-day administration of the assistance was moved from the Ministry of Foreign Affairs to NORAD, reflects the entering of a new phase of *development co-operation*. An early decision was made to allocate NOK 1.5 million to each of the three movements struggling against Portuguese rule, and which—in one way or another—had already received Norwegian assistance in 1972: FRELIMO, PAIGC and MPLA. A smaller part of the grant of 5 million was also used for covering the costs of inviting delegations from the liberation movements to

---

[203] *Rapport fra besøk til PAIGC i Guinea-Bissau 2–6 oktober 1972.* NORAD, Eskild Jensen, 18 October 1972.

[204] Interview with Eskild Jensen, *Arbeiderbladet*, 11 November 1972.

[205] *NOR-KONTAKT*, no. 3, 1973.

take part in the OAU/UN Conference in Oslo in April 1973. SWAPO of Namibia and ZAPU/ZANU of Zimbabwe were supposed to share the remaining 400,000, but in the end, not more than 200,000 was set aside for this purpose. ANC of South Africa was not expected to receive any aid at all through this new budget post, which was to be used for movements in territories not yet independent.

Of the total grant of NOK 5 million for 1973, not more than 2 million was eventually spent according to the guidelines. While PAIGC was able to fully utilise its grant, which was largely based on the priorities already accepted in 1972, the task of agreeing on procedures and conducting negotiations with FRELIMO and MPLA turned out to be so complicated, bureaucratic (from all sides!) and time-consuming that very little money was actually spent before the end of the year. (FRELIMO did not receive a single cent, while the recorded disbursement to MPLA amounted to NOK 280,000.)[206] Since the administrative procedures did not allow for transferring the grants to the liberation movements from one year to another, a substantial amount was thus actually lost. This obviously came as a shock to the movements, which had been under the impression that the grants could be spent in 1974.

For 1974, the budget proposals agreed upon were only marginally increased to NOK 6.5 million. Later in the year, however, the Labour party government (which came to power following the September 1973 elections), presented a revised budget which increased the total amount available for the liberation movements to NOK 12 million.[207] While all practical matters were to be taken care of by the NORAD administration, the power to decide on the allocations still rested with the Ministry of Foreign Affairs. For 1974 the decision was made to allocate NOK 5 million to PAIGC and FRELIMO respectively, NOK 1.25 million to MPLA, 300,000 to SWAPO and 100,000 to each of the two Zimbabwean liberation movements (ZANU and ZAPU). If the grants made available to refugees from Southern Africa—through UN Funds and the Special Committee—are added, the total amount for 1974 was in the range of NOK 16.5 million. As we will see below, with the exception of the blocking of the grant to MPLA, the assistance set aside for 1974 was largely spent according to the plans.

For 1975, the direct aid to the liberation movements was further increased to NOK 15 million. The increase was largely to benefit FRELIMO (NOK 7 million), as against 5 million to PAIGC, 1.5 million to MPLA and 1.5 million to be divided between SWAPO and the African National Council of

---

[206] Bech, op.cit., p. 10.

[207] Stortingsproposisjon nr. 1, tillegg 6 (1973–74). After a visit to Conakry, Lusaka and Dar es Salaam in March 1974, the Secretary of State for Foreign Affairs (Arne Arnesen) wanted to add another NOK 3 million—which had been "lost" in 1973—to cater for the documented needs of the liberation movements. (See his memo to the Minister for Foreign Affairs, 29 March 1974). In the end, however, the Ministry decided against his proposal.

Zimbabwe, which was supposed to serve as an umbrella organisation for aid which had previously been channelled to ZAPU and ZANU respectively (see chapter 4). In addition, NOK 3 million was set aside for UNHCR Programmes for repatriating refugees from Guinea-Bissau and Mozambique.[208] As we will see below, the funds allocated to MPLA for 1974 were withheld by the Ministry of Foreign Affairs. The actual funds disbursed to SWAPO and the liberation movements of Zimbabwe were also less than originally planned for.

FRELIMO and MPLA

After several difficult years which were characterised by defections and political rivalries following the assassination of Eduardo Mondlane, FRELIMO was consolidated in 1970 as a unified movement and was able to extend its military struggle and political activities into the more heavily populated provinces of Tete, Manica and Sofala.[209] The Portuguese propaganda efforts in the aftermath of the Kavandame defection in 1969 met with considerable success in the Western press, including the Norwegian newspaper *Aftenposten*.[210] Exercising control over extensive areas, FRELIMO was also involved in building a new society in the liberated zones. A "development plan" for the liberated zones had been drafted in 1970, and in Norway was presented to the Ministry of Foreign Affairs via the Norwegian Council for Southern Africa.[211] In 1970 the Mozambique Institute was again functioning, and could present prospective donors with wide-ranging plans for increased activities within the field of education (Dar es Salaam and Bagamoyo), training of nurses and other health personnel (Dr. Américo Boavide Hospital in Mtwara) and the administration of refugee settlements (Tunduru).[212] Under the directorship of Janet Mondlane, who was a frequent and popular visitor to the Nordic countries, the Mozambique Institute in practice was to serve as an aid co-ordination unit for FRELIMO.[213] The fact

[208] This amount was taken from the special budget vote for international humanitarian assistance, Ch. 198.

[209] The development of the liberation struggle is outlined in David Birmingham: *Frontline Nationalism in Angola and Mozambique*. London: James Currey, 1991 and Allan Isaacman/ Barbara Isaacman: *Mozambique: From Colonialism to Revolution*. Boulder, CO: Westview Press, 1983.

[210] In an article in *Aftenposten* (10 April 1969) it was maintained that the defection of Kavandame was a turning point in the war, and that he "defected with 60,000 (sic) well equipped guerrilla fighters". Interestingly, this piece of Portuguese government propaganda was "lifted" from *Aftenposten* word for word—without giving a source—and presented as an internal Ministry of Foreign Affairs memo, signed by LE (24 April 1969).

[211] For an outline and analysis of the programme in Norwegian, see Tore Linné Eriksen: "FRELIMO's program for utvikling", *Samtiden*, no. 8, 1970.

[212] These activities were witnessed by the author during a visit to Tanzania in May–July 1972. See Tore Linné Eriksen: "FRELIMO—Militær og sosial framgang", *Dagbladet*, 8 August 1972.

[213] At independence in 1975, Janet Mondlane was appointed head of the section for development co-operation in the Ministry for Economic Affairs and Planning.

that it was situated in Dar es Salaam, made possible more regular—and friendly—contact with the NORAD office and the great number of Norwegians (journalists, scholars and representatives of NGOs etc.) flocking to Tanzania in the early 1970s. In the Nordic countries, FRELIMO and the Mozambique Institute also benefited from being associated with the Government of Tanzania and Julius Nyerere himself.

While previous grants had been earmarked for the Mozambique Institute within the special budget post for refugees from Southern Africa in 1969 and 1971, the acceptance of the Government Parliamentary Paper (no. 29 1971–72) opened up for direct support to FRELIMO's educational and health activities in general. According to a letter from Janet Mondlane to the NORAD office in Dar es Salaam, "the aid given to FRELIMO has taken on a new form which has a more positive political significance than that of previous years".[214] For 1973, FRELIMO was allocated NOK 1.5 million out of the total amount of 5 million set aside for assistance to the liberation movements. Although several meeting were held between NORAD officials and representatives of FRELIMO, and written requests for goods to be purchased were presented to NORAD in June, the lack of established procedures and an extremely cautious scrutinising by the Ministry of Foreign Affairs of all supplies ordered made it impossible to make use of the 1973 grant until it was too late. The first year of direct co-operation between FRELIMO and the Norwegian Government could, therefore, hardly be described as a success. On various occasions, Janet Mondlane made it clear to the NORAD office in Dar es Salaam that FRELIMO would have preferred more simplified procedures in order to make use of the funds more smoothly and quickly.[215]

The lesson was learnt, and the major part of the NOK 5 million allocated for 1974 was spent in time according to the requests from FRELIMO. In addition to paying for clothing (mainly from India), local food supplies and the import of education material and equipment for health centres and hospitals, NORAD agreed to co-finance the recurrent expenditure for the secondary school in Bagamoyo. Out of the total grant, 10% was paid to FRELIMO in cash for covering local transport and administrative costs. Since the standard procedure was 5%, this decision can be seen as an indication of the trust with which FRELIMO was met by the Norwegian aid authorities.

Compared to Mozambique and Guinea-Bissau, the struggle in Angola was at the beginning of the 1970s less known in Norway. No Norwegians had ever visited the liberated areas inside Angola, and there were no books or extensive reports on Angola available in Norwegian. However, a brief article appeared in the NORAD magazine in late 1973, outlining the

---

[214] Letter of 25 June 1973 from Janet Mondlane to the NORAD office in Dar es Salaam.
[215] Ibid.

progress made by MPLA in running schools and hospitals in liberated areas in Eastern Angola.[216] The fact that more than one movement claimed to be the leading force fighting the Portuguese colonial regime also complicated the issue, although neither the Norwegian Council for Southern Africa nor the Norwegian government ever seriously considered supporting any other movement than MPLA. The President of MPLA, Agostinho Neto, paid his first visit to Norway in 1970, arriving directly from an International Conference in Rome in support of the struggle in the Portuguese colonies. The fact that the Angolan leader—together with Amilcar Cabral (PAIGC) and Marcelino dos Santos (FRELIMO)—had obtained an audience with the Pope, undoubtedly contributed to the mass media interest. Being a guest of the Nordic Social Democratic Parties, the MPLA president was received by the Ministry of Foreign Affairs at the level of civil servants.[217] (A Centre/ Conservative coalition government was then in power.) During his visit, Agostinho Neto also held meetings with the Norwegian Council for Southern Africa, the Norwegian Confederation of Trade Unions and the Norwegian Refugee Council. A detailed request for humanitarian assistance, however, did not yield any concrete results. The Angolan leader also had to leave empty-handed after his next visit to Oslo in March 1972, when he—as the first president of a liberation movement in Lusophone Africa—was received by the Labour Party Prime Minister, Trygve Bratteli.

MPLA was the only one of the three Angolan movements that succeeded in developing links to Norwegian political parties and solidarity organisations, and clearly benefited from its close links with PAIGC and FRELIMO and membership in the CONCP alliance.[218] Unlike in Sweden, the question whether to support FNLA or UNITA before 1974 did not occupy a prominent place in the Norwegian debate. UNITA was for a brief period in the mid-1970s enjoying a constituency within "marxist-leninist-maoist" circles because of its pro-Chinese and anti-Soviet rhetoric, but Jonas Savimbi was never able to attract any support from the Norwegian Council for Southern Africa. At an official level, the Norwegian Ministry of Foreign Affairs stuck to its principle of only considering support to movements recognised by the OAU Liberation Committee, which did not accept UNITA as a member until after the coup d'état in Portugal in 1974. On the other hand, Holden Roberto's FNLA was recognised by the OAU, but it was mainly regarded as an ethnically-based Bakongo movement. Although of Angolan nationality, Holden Roberto spent most of his life in Zaire, and FNLA never achieved a multiethnic national identity. The warm relations

---

[216] Knut Andreassen, *NOR-KONTAKT*, no. 6, 1973.

[217] Memo, 1. Pol. Div., 9. July 1970. ("Samtale med lederen for MPLA, Agostinho Neto").

[218] CONCP (Conferência das Organizacoes Nacionalistas das Colónias Portuguêsas) was established in April 1961 to co-ordinate the struggle in all Portuguese colonies in Africa and Asia.

enjoyed by FNLA with prominent members of the Swedish Liberal Party did not take root in Norway.

In August 1972, Norway agreed to contribute USD 50,000 to the building of a simple boarding school catering for 200 orphaned Angolan refugees under MPLA's care in Sikongo in the Western Province of Zambia.[219] The application for financial support had been discussed with the Norwegian Minister of Foreign Affairs, Andreas Cappelen, during his visit to Tanzania in May 1972. The request was strongly supported by the NORAD office in Lusaka, which urged the Norwegian government to decide on the issue in a matter of weeks because of the approaching rainy season that would make the transportation to the site virtually impossible.[220] The decision was facilitated by the fact that the Norwegian head of the Zambia Christian Refugee Council, Øystein Tveter, agreed to be in charge of the construction work in close co-operation with the NORAD office in Lusaka and two construction engineers working for the Danish Churchaid. This extraordinary grant was made from the budget line for "Humanitarian assistance and natural catastrophes".

The boarding school for children was followed up in early 1973 with a grant of another USD 50,000 for a similar school in Chavumu in the North-Western Province of Zambia. The project was this time funded from the first regular grant to MPLA. In May 1973 the NORAD office in Lusaka received a document from MPLA, signed by President Agostinho Neto, which contained a detailed list of projects.[221] Among the projects proposed by the MPLA were two buildings in Dar es Salaam for storing non-military supplies, installations for an offset print-shop in Lusaka and a special fund for buying petrol for the transportation of goods from Lusaka to the Angolan. However, the process of finalising the aid programme was extremely time-consuming, and contrary to the assumptions of the MPLA as well as the NORAD representative in Lusaka, the funds not actually spent before the end of the year were lost forever. In practice, this meant that only approx. NOK 280,000 out of 1,5 million had been spent by the MPLA before the end of the year. The situation was further complicated by the fact that MPLA severely suffered from internal rivalries (see below).

The years of transition (1974–75)

With the political changes taking place in Portugal in April 1974 (the "carnation revolution"), which partly came about as a result of the advancing liberation struggles in Guinea-Bissau, Mozambique and Angola, the co-operation between the Norwegian government and the liberation move-

---

[219] Kongelig Resolusjon, 25 August 1972.

[220] Letter from Halldor Heldal (NORAD, Lusaka) to the Ministry of Foreign Affairs, 6 July 1972.

[221] Letter of 23 May 1973 from Agostinho Neto to the NORAD Office in Lusaka.

ments entered a new stage. PAIGC was then already in control over the major part of Guinea-Bissau, and in September 1973 declared Guinea-Bissau "a sovereign, republican, democratic, anti-colonialist and anti-imperialist state". In November 1973 Guinea-Bissau was formally accepted as the forty-second member of the Organisation of African Unity (OAU). PAIGC would most probably have been immediately recognised by the new regime in Portugal as the government of an independent Guinea-Bissau if it had not been for the precedence this could set for the two other territories.

In the months following the collapse of the fascist regime in Lisbon, the new rulers did not agree upon the strategy to be followed for Mozambique and Angola.[222] In talks with the Norwegian Minister of Finance in July 1974, the Social Democratic Minister of Foreign Affairs, Mario Soares, had indicated a transitional period of 1–2 years for Mozambique and 2–3 years for Angola. (He also added that it would be a relief for Portugal to get rid of the burden of Mozambique, which was described as a "deficit area".)[223] Because of its cordial relations with the Socialist Party of Portugal, the Norwegian Labour Party government chose to co-ordinate its policies closely with the Portuguese government. Consequently, Mario Soares was assured that Norway would refrain from any decision that might complicate the Portuguese efforts to resolve "the colonial question" through negotiations.[224] This is the reason why Norway did not grant Guinea-Bissau diplomatic recognition until September 1974, when it was already clear that an agreement had been reached between Portugal and the PAIGC.

In Mozambique FRELIMO saw little to negotiate beyond a date for the formal transfer of power.[225] In early September 1974 an agreement between FRELIMO and Portugal was signed in Lusaka, which resulted in the establishment of a government of transition aiming at full independence on 25 June 1975. According to the Lusaka agreement, FRELIMO was given six of the nine members comprising the provisional government. This fact led Norway to enter into aid negotiations with FRELIMO more or less in accordance with the procedures developed for independent countries. The assistance to FRELIMO was still handled by the Mozambique Institute under the directorship of Janet Mondlane.

In April 1975, a seven-person FRELIMO delegation visited Oslo, headed by Marcelino dos Santos, the Vice-President of FRELIMO and the future

---

[222] See MacQueen, op.cit.

[223] Per Kleppe, Memo after a visit to Portugal 7–10 July 1974.

[224] Memo, 1. Pol. Div., 5 July 1974. See also Memo, , Pol. Div., 21 June 1974, based on the talks between Foreign Minister Knut Frydenlund and Foreign Minister Mario Soares during the NATO Council Meeting in Ottawa, 18–19 June 1974.

[225] See the Executive Committee of FRELIMO resolution of 27 April 1974: "We cannot accept that democracy for the Portuguese people should serve as a cover to impede the independence of our people. Just as the Caetano period demonstrated plainly that there was no such thing as liberal fascism, it must clearly understood that there is no such thing as democratic colonialism", quoted in MacQueen, op. cit., p. 126.

Minister for Economic Affairs and Planning. While previous FRELIMO visits to Oslo had been hosted by the Norwegian Council for Southern Africa, the delegation was this time invited by the Ministry of Foreign Affairs and received more or less with the same protocol as a government delegation from an independent country.[226] Talks with the Prime Minister and the Foreign Minister were for the first time included in the programme, which primarily focused on future development co-operation. (An informal supper with solidarity and student organisations, who had on previous occasions acted as hosts to FRELIMO delegations, was at the last minute called off by the Protocol Service of the Ministry of Foreign Affairs.)

It was agreed during the FRELIMO visit to establish diplomatic relations immediately upon Mozambique's independence, and dos Santos extended his invitation to the Norwegian government to take part in the celebrations in Maputo on the 25 June.[227] The wish was also expressed that the support given during the liberation struggle would be developed further, the close links between Tanzania and Norway obviously serving as a model.

During the question hour in the Norwegian Parliament on 23 April 1975, on the very day the high-level FRELIMO delegation was arriving in Oslo, Arne Kielland (MP, Socialist Left Party) wanted to know what steps the Government had taken to ensure that the support to FRELIMO would be further developed and intensified after independence. The MP argued strongly for including Mozambique in the select group of major recipients of Norwegian assistance ("hovedsamarbeidsland"), making an explicit reference to the Swedish decision to increase its support from SEK 15 million to FRELIMO to 50 million to an independent Mozambique. The Minister of Foreign Affairs, Knut Frydenlund, confirmed that NOK 7 million (out of a total grant of 15 million to the liberation movements) was to be utilised by FRELIMO before 25 June or by the Government after independence. The intention of the government was clearly to increase the support further, but the Minister deliberately refrained from making any firm commitment to grant Mozambique privileged status as one of the core "programme countries".

In his message to the nation on Independence Day, President Samora Machel singled out Scandinavia, Finland and the Netherlands as being among the Western countries which had given support during the liberation struggle. President Samora Machel also paid an official state visit to the Nordic countries in April/May 1997.

In the first period after independence Norway was reluctant to commit itself to an extensive aid programme that would have included the opening of a NORAD office in Maputo. For 1976 the assistance (NOK 15 million) was

---

[226] Memo, 1. Pol. Div., 24 May 1975.

[227] Norway was eventually represented by the Minister for Foreign Trade, Einar Magnussen, and the Ambassador to Tanzania (and Mozambique), Per Th. Nævdal.

mainly concentrated on a joint Nordic agricultural programme (MONAP) to be administered by SIDA, the Swedish aid agency. In 1977, however, the Labour Party government proposed to add Sri Lanka and Mozambique to the list of "major partners in development". The proposal was eventually accepted with the support of the votes of the Socialist Left Party and the Centre Party, while the Christian People's Party, the Conservative Party and the right wing Progress Party voted against including Mozambique. The transformation of FRELIMO from a liberation movement into a Marxist-Leninist party, as well as the general tendency to apply a Cold War perspective to Third World issues, had obviously made development co-operation with Mozambique a highly contentious issue.

While the independence of Mozambique was achieved through a negotiated settlement with FRELIMO being the only liberation movement, Angola in 1974–76 witnessed fierce competition between three movements, a heavy South African invasion and substantial involvement of the USA, Soviet Union and Cuba.[228]

As we have seen, only a small part of the 1973 Norwegian grant to MPLA was actually spent. The Ministry for Foreign Affairs had for 1974 set aside NOK 1.25 million for MPLA, but apart from a small amount used for completing the boarding school project in Zambia and paying for a truck, the funds were not made available. At the end of the year, MPLA had to accept the transfer of approximately NOK 1 million to a UNHCR programme under preparation. The main reason for the Norwegian reluctance to work with MPLA in dispersing the 1974 grant was the high degree of internal rivalry in the movement, which meant that the leadership of Agostinho Neto was being seriously challenged by the Active Revolt (Joaquim Pinto de Andrade) and the Eastern Revolt (Daniel Chipenda). The problems were frankly discussed by Agostinho Neto when meeting the NORAD representative in Lusaka in late January 1974. According to the MPLA president, the very grave situation made it impossible for the Norwegian-funded school in Sikongo to function properly, as this area was largely out of reach of MPLA. The NORAD representative was also informed about the decision by the Zambian authorities to suspend all assistance to MPLA, while China stepped up its support to UNITA and FNLA retained its close links to the US and Zaire.[229] It is also a fact that the Zambian government advised the NORAD office in Lusaka to channel the aid programme through the OAU Liberation Committee sub-regional office in Lusaka, a step which would unquestionably have brought the programme more under Zambian control. These proposals were, on the other hand,

---

[228] The complicated story is outlined by David Birmingham: *Frontline Nationalism in Angola and Mozambique*. London: James Currey, 1992. See also MacQueen, op. cit.

[229] Letter from Ola Dørum (NORAD, Lusaka) to the Ministry of Foreign Affairs, 15 February 1974. The report is based on a meeting with Agostinho Neto on 30 January 1974.

firmly rejected by the MPLA president in a meeting with the NORAD Resident Representative in September 1974.[230]

From other sources, it is known that the lack of progress in the disbursement of the 1974 grant to MPLA was a cause of disappointment to the MPLA president. An example of this is found in a letter to Tom Vraalsen (then Head of Division) from Øystein Tveter, who as Lutheran World Federation representative in Lusaka and Dar es Salaam was in close touch with the liberation movements. His letter, which was based on a meeting with Agostinho Neto in Dar es Salaam on 11 July 1974, clearly reflects the considerable disappointment after the promising overtures which had been made during a visit by Tom Vraalsen and Secretary of State for Foreign Affairs (Arne Arnesen) to Conakry, Lusaka and Dar es Salaam in March/ April 1974.[231] According to the letter, it was difficult for MPLA to maintain the human infrastructure and the support and trust of the people when Zambia obstructed transports and the Scandinavian countries were holding back on their aid. The letter concluded that "Whatever the reason is, the delay is likely to have considerable effect on the development of the struggle in Angola".[232]

Based on archival sources in the Norwegian Ministry of Foreign Affairs, it is difficult not to conclude that the headquarters in Oslo—not to speak of the Norwegian Embassy in Lisbon—expressed a much more reluctant (if not outright hostile) attitude towards MPLA than what was reflected in the reports from the NORAD representative Ola Dørum on the ground in Lusaka. The strained relations between MPLA and Norway became even more obvious after the signing of the tri-partite Alvor Agreement between MPLA, FNLA and UNITA in January 1975. The decision to effectively freeze all further assistance to MPLA seems to have been taken by the Ministry of Foreign Affairs in early 1975,[233] but was never openly communicated directly to the MPLA. Neither were the NORAD officials in Lusaka properly informed about the decision. The NORAD office in Lusaka repeatedly complained to the Ministry of Foreign Affairs that no guidelines as to the aid programme with MPLA had been issued.[234]

While Norway and Sweden had more or less adopted the same position vis-à-vis MPLA in 1973/74, their policies in the critical year of 1975 were poles apart. SIDA had in December 1974 reached an understanding with MPLA about the allocations of the aid programme, and—more significantly—this agreement was endorsed by the Swedish Cabinet after the

---

[230] Letter from Ola Dørum to the Ministry of Foreign Affairs, 24 September 1974.

[231] See note 206.

[232] The letter of 11 July 1974 is filed in the Ministry of Foreign Affairs Archives, 25 4/93.

[233] Memo, 1. Pol. Div., 18 March 1975.

[234] See, for instance, letters from the NORAD office in Lusaka 30 April 1975 and 21 May 1975. The letters were written by Agnete Eriksen, who had been appointed programme officer for co-operation with the liberation movements.

Alvor Agreement had been signed in January 1975. While the NORAD office in Lusaka had frozen all relations with MPLA, representatives of the Swedish Embassy in the Zambian capital were busy preparing for the implementation of the humanitarian assistance programme to MPLA. There were even formal consultations with the MPLA headquarters in Luanda on several occasions, *inter alia* to sort out problems concerned with local procurement of commodities. In October 1975 Paulo Jorge—the future Foreign Minister of Angola—attended the annual conference of the Swedish Social Democratic Party on behalf of MPLA. Later in the same month the Swedish Minister for Development Co-operation, Gertrud Sigurdsen, publicly declared that the "Swedish government will fulfil its undertakings to the MPLA liberation movement in Angola".[235] According to Tor Sellström, the official aid relationship—although never significant in quantitative terms—did amount to a *de facto* recognition of MPLA as Angola's "government-in-waiting". This is also how it was understood by MPLA, not to speak of the competing FNLA and UNITA movements.[236]

While MPLA had seen major military advances in August/September 1975, exercising control in 12 of 16 provinces, in the weeks preceding the Independence Day, South African military forces and UNITA troops marched northwards towards Luanda, while FNLA troops, heavily supported by Zairian invading forces with US equipment, were approaching the capital from the north. When the colonial power left the country on 11 November 1975, MPLA did not control much of the country apart from Luanda, its immediate surroundings, some coastal enclaves and inland corridors. MPLA in the end prevailed with the assistance of Soviet arms and Cuban troops, that had arrived in early November.

Since the MPLA government did not effectively control any substantial part of the Angolan territory on 11 November 1975, the Norwegian Ministry of Foreign Affairs argued that the standard criteria for recognition were not fulfilled. The call for recognition from the Norwegian Council for Southern Africa, the Socialist Left Party and the youth league of the Labour Party, was answered in the negative by the Foreign Minister on 13 November. After an extensive review of all diplomatic and legal aspects involved, it was even decided that the receipt of Christmas greetings from Foreign Minister José Eduardo dos Santos should not be acknowledged. (It was argued that even if this did not amount to a formal recognition, it could be regarded as "a political act".)[237] The Norwegian Minister of Foreign Affairs in early February once more explicitly rejected the call for diplomatic recognition.[238] In

---

[235] Quoted in Tor Sellström, Vol. II, op. cit., forthcoming.

[236] Ibid.

[237] Memo, 1. Pol. Div., 6 January 1976.

[238] This came as a response to a question put forward in Parliament by Finn Gustavsen (Socialist Left Party) on 4 February 1976. This was at the time also the position of the Swedish government, but the Foreign Minister—Sten Andersson—added that "The government's view

mid-February 1976, however, the situation had significantly changed with the defeat of the South African troops and the MPLA gaining military control over the major part of the country. The MPLA government had then also been recognised by Portugal itself and the majority of African states, and had been accepted into the OAU. According to an internal Ministry of Foreign Affairs memorandum, it was argued that recognition by Norway and other Western countries could serve to counterbalance the influence of the Soviet Union and Cuba. The point was also made that Norway after all had always regarded MPLA as the main movement and the only movement qualified for receiving Norwegian assistance and that to withhold recognition at this stage would constitute "an act of obvious diplomatic hostility".[239]

On 18 February 1976 a message from Foreign Minister Knut Frydenlund was transmitted to the Angolan Foreign Minister proposing that diplomatic relations be established between Norway and Angola. As no response was given, a new cable renewing the message was sent in late September. The Angolan government was also requested to make proposals as to how to make use of the NOK 1.5 million allocated to MPLA for 1975. (The grant was, in the same way as in 1974, eventually transferred to the United Nations High Commissioner for Refugees to be spent on repatriation and rehabilitation.) In the following month the Angolan chargé d'affaires in Stockholm, Maria Jesus de Haller, paid a visit to Oslo as a guest of the Norwegian Council for Southern Africa. According to remarks made by the Angolan representative to the mass media, she seemed not to be fully informed about the attempts by the Norwegian government to establish diplomatic links.[240] In a meeting with the Secretary of State for Foreign Affairs, Thorvald Stoltenberg, she was also told that the Ministry of Foreign Affairs was more than willing to host a visit by the Angolan chargé d'affaires at any time.[241]

Diplomatic relations were not formally entered into until 31 October 1977 through the Angolan ambassador to the United Nations. At this time, Sweden had already opened an Embassy in Luanda and established a significant aid programme, while the Danish Minister of Foreign Affairs had paid a state visit to Luanda. The Norwegian Labour Party government was much less enthusiastic about giving aid to Angola, and obviously feared a hostile public opinion mainly concerned with the Cuban issue with strong Cold War overtones. (All political parties in parliament, except for the Socialist

---

is that MPLA is the political movement (which has) roots among the people (and) has combined the struggle for independence with efforts to establish social and economic justice in Angola." Quoted in Tor Sellström, Vol. II, op.cit, forthcoming.

[239] Memo, Ministry of Foreign Affairs, Kjeld Vibe, 16 February 1976.

[240] *Dagbladet*, 3 October 1976.

[241] Memo, Ministry of Foreign Affairs, 11 October 1976. ("Samtale mellom statssekretær Thorvald Stoltenberg og Angolas chargé d'affaires i Stockholm, Maria Jesus de Haller".)

Left Party, later agreed to bring the development co-operation with Cuba to a halt as punishment for the country's assistance to the MPLA government in Angola.)[242] After the establishment of diplomatic relations in 1977, it would take five more years before a Norwegian ambassador paid a visit to Luanda to present his credentials. A Norwegian aid office and Consulate was not opened in Luanda until 1986.

The independence of the Portuguese colonies closed the first chapter in the history of the Norwegian support to the liberation struggles in Southern Africa. The time had now come for the liberation movements in Zimbabwe, Namibia and South Africa itself to attract the attention of the Norwegian public and the Norwegian authorities. In terms of actual money granted to the movements, the late 1970s and the 1980s would see a much more substantial contribution from the Norwegian government, as will be described and discussed in subsequent chapters.[243]

---

[242] The first call for an "aid blockade" had already been made in parliament on January 21, 1976 by a pro-South African MP from the right-wing "Progress Party" (Erik Gjems-Onstad).

[243] See also the Statistical Appendix.

Chapter 2

The Namibian Liberation Struggle: Direct Norwegian Support to SWAPO

Eva Helene Østbye

Introduction

Namibia's struggle for freedom was long. It began during the German colonisation, which from its start in 1884 had disastrous consequences for the Namibian people. The suppression of the inhabitants and the plundering of the natural resources continued throughout the years of South African occupation that followed from 1915. In 1921 South Africa was entrusted by the League of Nations to administer Namibia as a mandatory area, but violated the trust from the outset. The terms of the mandate stated that the administration should "promote to the utmost the material and moral well-being, and the social progress of the inhabitants".[1] After the Second World War, Pretoria demanded that Namibia be included in South Africa, but this was opposed by the United Nations. However, as a result of the Nationalist Party's victory in the South African elections in 1948, apartheid was strengthened in the two countries.

In 1966, the UN General Assembly brought South Africa's mandate to an end. Instead, at a special session in 1967 the world organisation established a Council for Namibia as the highest authority for the territory. The council should lead the territory to national independence. The implementing and administrative functions were at the same time transferred to a Commissioner. By establishing that South Africa no longer had any legal rights over Namibia, in 1969 the UN Security Council also recognised its responsibility towards the Namibian people. Finally, the verdict by the International Court of Justice in The Hague in June 1971, which declared the South African presence in Namibia as illegal, confirmed that formal responsibility over the territory was in the hands of the world community.

As South Africa neither respected the UN decisions, nor the verdict of the international court in The Hague, the Namibian liberation struggle against Pretoria's occupation intensified and received growing international

---

[1] Peter H. Katjavivi: *A History of Resistance in Namibia*. London, 1988, p. 13.

attention. However, despite the fact that more than a thousand statements and initiatives to promote national independence were made by different UN bodies up to 1990, getting the international community to extend material support for the struggle proved more difficult. The liberation movements were looked upon with suspicion by the leading Western powers. Their main supporters outside of the Afro-Asian group were the Soviet Union and the other socialist countries. However, in the humanitarian field the Nordic countries were to support the nationalist movement with considerable resources, both at the official and at the non-official level.

This chapter will discuss the assistance given to SWAPO by the government of Norway. Presentations of the support given through other Norwegian channels are discussed elsewhere in this study. The direct official support was substantial: from the first allocation in 1974 until independence in 1990 it amounted in total to around NOK 225 million.[2] Why was this support given? What was the money used for? What was the character of the co-operation between the Norwegian government and SWAPO? A chronological presentation will serve as the basis for this discussion.[3]

How it all started

Parliamentary decision; principles and priorities

The liberation struggle in Namibia was not conducted by the UN or other international organisations, but by the Namibians themselves. In 1959, the South West African National Union, SWANU, was established as a nationalist organisation based on different elements of the anti-colonial resistance. However, due to internal differences SWANU was unable to remain united, and the following year the South West Africa People's Organisation, SWAPO, was formed by members of the Ovamboland's People's Organisation, OPO. SWAPO's main objective was the establishment of a free, democratic government in independent Namibia.[4] Both SWANU and SWAPO were recognised in 1963 by the Organisation of African Unity, OAU. However, SWANU lost this recognition in 1965, mainly due to the lack of a military strategy for the liberation struggle. As the only Namibian liberation movement recognised by the OAU, and from 1976 declared by the UN General Assembly as the "sole and authentic representative of the Namibian people",[5] SWAPO's leading role in the liberation struggle was unchallenged. Following the UN resolutions and OAU decisions, Norway de facto also

---

[2] A table of the disbursements is found in Appendix 1.

[3] For the support through the churches, trade unions, the Norwegian Council for Southern Africa and the Namibia Association, see chapters 6–9.

[4] Katjavivi, op.cit., p. 45.

[5] Ibid., p. 100.

recognised SWAPO as the legitimate Namibian liberation movement, and initiated exclusive co-operation with the organisation.[6]

Until the end of the 1950s, Norwegian contacts with Namibia had mainly been through the whaling and fishing industry. Norwegian whaling companies had for decades been established in Walvis Bay when in 1959 the Namibian student Hans Beukes was given a scholarship to study in Norway. Beukes' passport was, however, confiscated by the South African authorities and the Norwegian Foreign Ministry brought the case to the attention of the UN Fourth Committee and the General Assembly. The "Beukes case" contributed to a growing awareness of the political situation in Namibia and to Norwegian support for Namibia's independence at the UN in the early 1960s. When the Norwegian government in 1964 received a first request for direct aid from SWAPO, it was thus against the background of "the action it took in connection with the case of South West Africa in the United Nations."[7] Nevertheless, it would take ten years from the first request until any direct support was given to SWAPO.[8]

After years of debate in the Norwegian Ministry of Foreign Affairs[9] and the Norwegian Agency for International Development, NORAD, the government proposed in February 1973 to grant direct humanitarian assistance to the liberation movements in Southern Africa. When the Parliament later in the same month endorsed the proposal, it confirmed a practice that was about to become established. Support from the Norwegian Foreign Ministry to the oppressed peoples of the region had been granted since 1964 through the Special Committee for Refugees from Southern Africa. This committee was set up in 1963 by the Norwegian Parliament to administer the distribution of funds granted over the national budget. By 1974, NOK 20 million had thus been channelled to institutions such as the International University Exchange Fund (IUEF), the Lutheran World Federation (LWF), the International Refugee Council of Zambia and FRELIMO's Mozambique Institute.[10] In addition, Norway had supported UN programmes for Southern Africa, such as the UN Education and Training Programme for South West Africa

---

[6] However, this did not entirely exclude humanitarian support to Namibian refugees outside SWAPO's care. In 1976, the Special Committee for Refugees from Southern Africa allocated an amount of NOK 50,000 earmarked for SWANU (via the UNHCR). Memorandum. Samtale med representanter for South West African National Union (Consultation with representatives for SWANU), 1 Political Affairs Division, 10 November 1976, Archives of the Norwegian Ministry of Foreign Affairs (in the following referred to as MFA) 77 9/5 XII.

[7] Letter from the Vice President of SWAPO, Louis Nelengani, to the Norwegian Ambassador in the UAR, Cairo, 31 March 1964, MFA 77 9/5 I.

[8] For the official policy up to 1975, see chapter 1.

[9] For the sake of convenience, the Norwegian Ministry of Foreign Affairs will be referred to as the Foreign Ministry.

[10] See chapter 1.

(Namibia) which was founded in 1961 and was incorporated into the UN Education and Training Programme for Southern Africa in 1967.[11]

Giving support directly to the liberation movements required clear guidelines. An absolute prerequisite was that the support be solely humanitarian. For this reason Norwegian official support primarily went to the work SWAPO was carrying out in favour of Namibian refugees in the neighbouring countries. In addition, only movements recognised by the OAU and fighting for national liberation in what were termed "dependent areas", were to receive support.

Besides the prerequisite that the assistance should be based on UN decisions, it also had to be in accordance with the priorities of the Co-ordination Committee for the Liberation of Africa, set up by the OAU to ensure the most efficient strategy for doing away with dependence and apartheid. This implied that the resources in the first phase were primarily to be concentrated to the Portuguese-occupied territories, where the liberation movements were perceived as having the best organisational set-up and, therefore could most efficiently make use of the aid.[12] After the liberation of Guinea-Bissau, Angola and Mozambique, the main focus would then shift to the liberation of Zimbabwe, with Namibia and South Africa following in that order.[13] The extent to which these priorities were respected can be seen by studying the allocations for the various movements. In 1973, the first year of direct support from Norway to the liberation movements in Southern Africa, NOK 3.75 million out of the NOK 4.5 million allocated for this purpose went to the liberation movements in the Portuguese colonies. In 1974, the corresponding figures were 11.25 out of 12 million, and in 1975 the liberation movements in these countries received 14.5 out of a total allocation of NOK 15 million.[14]

Keeping in line with the OAU strategy for liberation, while at the same time acknowledging the role played by the liberation movements outside the Portuguese colonies, the Norwegian Foreign Ministry decided in January 1974 that it would increasingly seek to meet the requirements of the latter.[15]

---

[11] Ibid.

[12] 1 Political Affairs Division, 2 September 1974, MFA 34 9/5 III.

[13] See e.g., Memorandum. Støtte til frigjøringsbevegelser (Support to Liberation Movements), 1 Political Affairs Division, 29 August 1973, MFA 34 9/5 II; Foredrag til Statsråd for Kgl. res. (Draft to the King in Council for Royal Decree), 3 November 1978, both in MFA 34 9/5 VIII.

[14] It should be noted that these are the sums allocated. The sums actually disbursed, were not identical. The contribution to PAIGC in Guinea-Bissau was also included in this allocation, with NOK 5 million both in 1974 and 1975. See chapter 1. For figures actually disbursed, see table in Appendix 1.

[15] Memorandum. Nordisk bistandssjefsmøte (Meeting of the Nordic directors for development co-operation), Oslo, 7 January 1974, 1 Political Affairs Division, MFA 34 9/5 II.

Getting acquainted: The 1973 UN/OAU Conference in Oslo

Hosting the UN/OAU Conference of Experts for the Support of Victims of Colonialism and Apartheid in Southern Africa in Oslo 9–14 April 1973, the Norwegian Government achieved a deeper understanding of the situation in Southern Africa and also got to know the liberation movements better.[16] At this conference, the leaders of the liberation movements were received as legitimate representatives of their countries, and a new foundation was laid for direct contacts between the Norwegian Government and SWAPO. According to President Sam Nujoma, the conference also made a strong impact on public opinion in the Western world.[17] The SWAPO delegates Andreas Shipanga and Ben Amathila, respectively Secretary for Information and SWAPO representative to the Nordic countries, discussed with the Norwegian Foreign Ministry the arrest of 85 Namibians in Windhoek the previous month. Shortly after the conference, the Foreign Ministry received a request from SWAPO for USD 25,000 to engage lawyers for those arrested and provide maintenance to their dependants. The money was to be sent to the Lutheran World Federation (LWF), and earmarked for SWAPO.[18] While the Norwegian authorities were considering the application, Moses Garoeb, the Secretary General of SWAPO, visited the Norwegian embassy in Bonn with the information that a new wave of unrest and arrests in Windhoek had made the need for legal aid even more acute.[19] Against this background, in 1973 the Foreign Ministry decided to make NOK 100,000 available to SWAPO, to be transferred via the LWF as earlier requested. The support opened up "the possibility for more direct support in the future", just as Carl-Johan Hellberg, Africa Secretary at the LWF, in a letter to Sam Nujoma had suggested that it might.[20] The following year, SWAPO thus requested, and was granted, NOK 200,000 for legal aid via the LWF, but also NOK 100,000 as direct assistance to SWAPO's humanitarian work for Namibian refugees. To establish a framework for the co-operation between Norway and SWAPO, annual bilateral discussions would from then on take place between the parties.

---

[16] See chapter 1.

[17] Sam Nujoma in Memorandum. Besøk i Oslo 21.–22. februar 1978 av SWAPO-delegasjon (Visit to Oslo 21 and 22 February of a delegation from SWAPO), 1 Political Affairs Division, 27 February 1978, MFA 34 9/5 V.

[18] Letter from Ben Amathila, SWAPO representative to the Nordic countries, to MFA, 22 May 1973, MFA 34 9/5 II.

[19] Memorandum. Søknad fra SWAPO om norsk bidrag til rettshjelp ... (Application from SWAPO for Norwegian contribution to legal aid ...), 1 Political Affairs Division, 18 September 1973, MFA 34 9/5 II.

[20] Carl-J. Hellberg, LWF, to Sam Nujoma, 20 June 1974, MFA 34 9/5 II.

Seeing is believing

Against the background of a proposed increase in the Norwegian allocation to the Southern African liberation movements, the Foreign Ministry needed to acquire a deeper understanding of the situation in the region. In March 1974, an official delegation went to Southern Africa to visit the refugee camps and discuss the situation with the leaders of the liberation movements. The delegation, led by State Secretary Arne Arnesen, became convinced of the great need for humanitarian support in the region and was impressed by the liberation movements' work for the refugees. After the visit, Arnesen concluded that the registered needs and the requests for aid made it necessary to further increase the Norwegian support for 1974 from the proposed NOK 12 million to NOK 15 million. Although this did not happen, the proposal is an expression of a new awareness of the situation in Southern Africa.

Based on the discussions with the Norwegian delegation visiting Lusaka, SWAPO submitted a detailed request for food, medicines and office equipment for the humanitarian work carried out for the Namibian refugees in Zambia, adding up to a total of NOK 100,000.[21] The request was granted, and although the amount did not represent a great proportion of the total Norwegian allocation for 1974, it was significant in that it was the first direct official allocation by Norway to SWAPO. The agreement that was subsequently signed in December 1974 thus marks the beginning of the direct co-operation between the government of Norway and SWAPO. [22]

Over the following years, Norway would receive a number of visits where SWAPO representatives informed officials about SWAPO's refugee projects and the general political situation. They also discussed the strategy for the struggle and the role Norway could play.[23] In these meetings, SWAPO not only asked for financial assistance, but also for political support to increase the pressure of the world opinion and isolate South Africa.[24] In particular, SWAPO urged Norway to help persuade the Western countries to observe the UN arms embargo, implement an investment ban and declare a trade boycott against South Africa.[25]

---

[21] Arne Arnesen/Tom Vraalsen, MFA, to NORAD, 25 March 1974, MFA 34 9/5 II.

[22] The proposal for an agreement was sent on 16 December and the reply from SWAPO on 20 December 1974, MFA 34 9/5 III.

[23] Memorandum. Samtale i UD med representanter for SWAPO (Consultations in MFA with representatives from SWAPO), 21 January 1975, MFA 34 9/5 III.

[24] See e.g., Samtale i UD med representanter for SWAPO (Consultations in MFA with representatives of SWAPO), 4 April 1975, MFA 34 9/5 III.

[25] Memorandum. Samtale med representanter for den namibiske frigjøringsorganisasjon SWAPO hos Statssekretæren (Consultation with representatives from the Namibian Liberation Movement SWAPO in the office of the State Secretary), 12 October 1977, MFA 34 9/5 VII. From SWAPO: Peter Katjavivi and T. Hishongwa. Norwegian representatives: Secretary of State for Foreign Affairs Thorvald Stoltenberg, Political Adviser Leonard Larsen and Executive Officer Jon Bech.

With the strong emphasis on the support to the struggles in the Portuguese colonies, the liberation of Guinea-Bissau, Mozambique and Angola in 1974/75 led to a reorientation of the Norwegian support. In Zimbabwe, Namibia and South Africa the struggles continued. It was not, however, until 1977 that the Norwegian Parliament agreed to give direct support to the South African liberation movements, as South Africa was not considered a "dependent area" (see chapter 3). Besides the Portuguese colonies, it was thus only Namibia and Zimbabwe that were receiving direct support. In 1975, however, the aid granted to the African National Council of Zimbabwe was found difficult to implement due to the divisions between the member movements.[26] The Norwegian consulate in Lusaka reported that it was "relatively hard to find out what [was] going on inside Rhodesia".[27] This situation left SWAPO as the only liberation organisation receiving Norwegian support seen by the Norwegian aid administration to have had "a normal year" in 1975.[28] It also contributed to giving a stronger focus in Norway on the liberation struggle in Namibia.

Establishing a co-operative framework and administrative routines

As Norway started to give direct support to SWAPO, a framework for the co-operation and procedures for the annual allocations were established in close co-operation with the SWAPO headquarters in Lusaka.

The Foreign Ministry administered the support to the liberation movements, and made annual proposals regarding the total allocation for these, which after having been accepted by the Norwegian Parliament formed the foundation for the negotiations regarding the support. The implementation of the aid was the responsibility of NORAD, whose resident representatives in Lusaka (later also in Harare and Luanda) were in close contact with the SWAPO leadership. Following detailed discussions between SWAPO and NORAD regarding the utilisation of the allocation, the requests were forwarded to the Foreign Ministry in Oslo. Based on the Ministry's own discussions with the leaders of the liberation movements and assessment of the situation, the Foreign Ministry then made a proposal regarding the total size and distribution of the allocation for the liberation movements. Only after this had been approved by the government could the grant be released.

Within the general humanitarian framework, there were no strings attached. The fact that SWAPO was free to buy the items needed wherever it saw fit was greatly appreciated.[29] When required, NORAD's procurement

---

[26] PM. Bistand via frigjøringsbevegelser 1975 (Support through Liberation Movements 1975), Vice-Consul Agnete Eriksen, the Consulate in Lusaka, 28 November 1975, MFA 34 9/5 IV.

[27] Øivind Lyng, the Consulate in Lusaka, to MFA, 21 January 1976, MFA 34 9/5 IV.

[28] Head of Division Svennevig, NORAD, to MFA, 12 March 1976, MFA 34 9/5 IV.

[29] Referat fra samtale mellom utenriksminister Frydenlund og SWAPO's president Sam Nujoma (Report from a consultation between the Minister of Foreign Affairs Frydenlund and the President of SWAPO Sam Nujoma), New York, 30 September 1976, MFA 34 9/5 IV.

office offered assistance for non-local purchases. A certain percentage, varying from 5 to 12, was given to SWAPO in cash to cover administrative expenses.

Giving direct assistance to the liberation movements was a new experience to the Norwegian Foreign Ministry. The framework and routines established for bilateral foreign aid did not prove entirely suitable for this kind of support. Lessons had to be learned. Norway also had to get to know the recipients; the leaders of the liberation movements and partners in the negotiations. The first five years of the co-operation—until 1980—became a time of adjustment. Administrative procedures had to be worked out to ensure that everything was done in accordance with established principles. This was a time-consuming task. In addition, the Parliamentary decision was often made late in the year, which meant that the actual disbursements for a given financial year were made far into the following year—and sometimes even later.[30] Any delay in the process led to frustrations and contradictions, whether it was Norway that spent a long time in processing the requests, or SWAPO that was late in presenting its submissions. Examples of both will follow below. As the co-operation became more established and predictable, the system was made more flexible, leading to earlier decisions and subsequent disbursements.

There was a sincere willingness in the Norwegian Foreign Ministry to assist the liberation movements, but the implementation in the early years was hampered by a lack of established personal contacts and of procedures that still needed adjusting to function well. At the same time, SWAPO had internal problems that it did not communicate to its co-operation partner to the necessary extent.

When the Norwegian government towards the mid-1970s started to give aid to SWAPO, it also received applications from Norwegian solidarity organisations to fund planned projects for Namibian refugees in co-operation with SWAPO. At the end of 1975, these requests were rejected by the Foreign Ministry, the explanation being that SWAPO "had problems in finding acceptable use of the funds already made available to them".[31] Nevertheless, at the end of 1975, SWAPO was seen as the only liberation movement receiving Norwegian support that was capable of conducting concrete aid negotiations and the only one that could be expected to utilise the contributions efficiently.[32]

---

[30] In Norway, the financial year corresponds to the calendar year.

[31] Memorandum. Bistand til frigjøringsbevegelser—private organisasjoners rolle (Support to Liberation Movements—the role of NGOs), 1 Political Affairs Division, 28 October 1975, MFA 34 9/5 IV.

[32] Memorandum. Norsk støtte til frigjøringsbevegelser i Afrika (Norwegian support to the Liberation Movements in Africa), 1 Political Affairs Division, 17 June 1975, MFA 34 9/5 II.

Co-operation in the 1970s

Internal SWAPO conflicts—Norwegian apprehensions

If 1975 had been "normal" for SWAPO, this could certainly not be said for the following year. When Agnete Eriksen, vice consul in Lusaka and programme officer for the support to liberation movements, learned that hundreds of SWAPO members had been taken prisoner by the Zambian government on the instructions of the SWAPO leadership, she discussed the matter with Vice President Mishake Muyongo and Richard Kapelwa, Deputy Secretary of Defence and responsible for procurements under the NORAD aid programme. They explained that the "so-called 'rebels'", led by Andreas Shipanga, had tried to cause a split within SWAPO which would enable them to go back to Namibia and join the South African sponsored constitutional negotiations that SWAPO was boycotting. "It was therefore necessary to keep these people detained to avoid that they corrupted others."[33] When the NORAD representative communicated that the situation could affect the Norwegian aid, it "was seen as extortion". Eriksen, however, argued that "a certain amount of trust [had] to exist if support for the liberation movements was still to be accepted in Norway".[34]

In a report to the Foreign Ministry, the Norwegian consulate in Lusaka asked for advice on how to deal with the situation. As long as new developments did not take place, it recommended that the support should not be cut off, as this could lead to a break in the contacts with the SWAPO leaders. Funds remaining from the 1975 allocation were considered too small to justify a break, and it was seen as important to keep the communication lines open. At the time, SWAPO had already been informed that Norway had allocated NOK 1.5 million for 1976, and was in the process of making a request for the utilisation of that amount. The consulate was waiting for SWAPO's proposal, but did not recommend the signing of a new agreement for 1976 until it knew more about the direction in which SWAPO was heading: "SWAPO's reasons for keeping some of its members detained do not seem quite convincing", Eriksen reported to Oslo, explaining that it "might be the start of a major political purge within SWAPO that had to come sooner or later".[35] Without control over any liberated areas, SWAPO had until then appeared more as a liberation front than a political party, but the NORAD representative in Lusaka saw the internal conflicts as possibly being part of a change in this respect.[36]

---

[33] Memorandum. Situasjonen i SWAPO (The situation within SWAPO), Vice Consul Agnete Eriksen, the Consulate in Lusaka, 26 May 1976, MFA 34 9/5 IV.

[34] Ibid.

[35] Ibid.

[36] Ibid.

Soon thereafter the Foreign Ministry interpreted the arrests as a reaction provoked by dissatisfaction by one group within SWAPO against an undemocratic leadership.[37]

While the NORAD office in Lusaka recommended that the finalisation of the 1976 agreement should be postponed until the situation was clarified, the Foreign Ministry did not regard the situation inside SWAPO serious enough to justify going back on existing commitments. However, the possibility remained, they argued, not to accept SWAPO's proposed distribution between posts. For example, SWAPO had clearly stated that it did not want part of the 1976 allocation to be used for legal aid to prisoners through the Lutheran World Federation unless additional funds were made available to the organisation. The Ministry suggested that this should be done anyway.[38] SWAPO had earlier been informed that Norway planned to give 10% of the 1976 allocation in cash, which was a higher percentage than any other liberation movement had received. The argument had been that SWAPO needed the cash contribution to cover its administrative expenses, and that it did not constitute a problem as the organisation seemed to function in an efficient and united way.[39] As unity within SWAPO now was called into question, it was proposed that the cash contribution be cut down to 5%. The remaining 5% could instead be spent on legal aid and channelled through the LWF.[40]

The Foreign Ministry left it to the representation in Lusaka to assess whether the developments within SWAPO required that the disbursements be held back.

The Ministry was also interested in knowing how the Zambian government, which had been operative in detaining the SWAPO opposition, viewed the situation. The following month, the representation reported that the Zambian authorities had handed over the prisoners to SWAPO, whose leadership had their full support.[41]

In order to get guidance on how to deal with the situation, the other Nordic countries were consulted for advice. The Swedish aid agency, SIDA, reported that it did not consider the disagreements within SWAPO serious enough to affect the Swedish support. On the contrary, the allocation for

---

[37] Memorandum. Bistand til frigjøringsbevegelsen SWAPO (Support to the Liberation Movement SWAPO), 1 Political Affairs Division, 12 June 1976, MFA 34 9/5 IV.

[38] Memorandum. Bistand til frigjøringsbevegelsen SWAPO i 1976 (Support to the Liberation Movement SWAPO in 1976), 1 Political Affairs Division, 12 July 1976, MFA 34 9/5 IV.

[39] Assistant Director General Arnfinn Sørensen, NORAD, to MFA, 23 June 1976, MFA 34 9/5 IV.

[40] Memorandum. Bistand til frigjøringsbevegelsen SWAPO i 1976 (Support to the Liberation Movement SWAPO for 1976), 1 Political Affairs Division, 12 July 1976, MFA 34 9/5 IV.

[41] Øivind Lyng, the Consulate in Lusaka, to the Embassy in Dar es Salaam, 6 August 1976, MFA 34 9/5 IV.

SWAPO had been considerably increased from 1975/76 to 1976/77, and the allocated SEK 5 million was about to be disbursed.[42] Norway still hesitated.

Sweden not only increased its allocation; it also ignored the Zambian request to channel the support through the host government and continued to transfer the money directly to SWAPO. [43] The situation was similar in Finland: the internal struggles did not have any impact on the aid, and the money would be disbursed as SWAPO wished. Denmark did not give direct support to SWAPO.

The Swedish and Finnish reactions contributed to the recommendation by the Norwegian representation in Lusaka to release that part of the proposed allocation which covered food supplies. It did, however, also suggest that the amount allocated for transport expenses be held back until the situation within SWAPO was clarified.

More alarming news: Norway is not reassured

The arrests of the SWAPO dissidents had taken place in April 1976, and the discussions within the Norwegian authorities went on during the following months. Maybe the whole situation would calm down? In that predicament, it could not have been reassuring for the Lusaka representation to read in the local newspapers at the beginning of August that the Zambian government had handed the prisoners over to SWAPO. A small group, including Andreas Shipanga, had been sent to Tanzania. In addition, SWAPO's central committee was reported to have "set up a military tribunal where the dissidents possibly faced death by firing squad".[44]

The consulate could have been informed by SWAPO that the situation was not quite so dramatic. Instead SWAPO contributed to the uncertainty by not keeping in contact, despite the fact that "both Dr. [Libertine] Amathila and Secretary for Economic Affairs Mr. Kapelwa a long time ago [had] announced that they would come to discuss the use of the rest of the allocation for 1975 and the budget for 1976".[45] The NORAD office in Lusaka asked the Foreign Ministry in Oslo to consider when to release the remaining funds in light of the fact that they "for the time being [did] not know anything about what [was] actually going on within the movement".[46]

When the SWAPO representatives contrary to agreements did not visit the Norwegian consulate, it was seen as an indication of a lack of unity within the movement, in spite of what the SWAPO leadership publicly was

---

[42] Letter from Øivind Lyng, the Consulate in Lusaka, to NORAD, 11 August 1976, MFA 34 9/5 IV.

[43] Ibid.

[44] *Times of Zambia*, 6 August 1976.

[45] Øivind Lyng, the Consulate in Lusaka, to the Embassy in Dar es Salaam, 6 August 1976, MFA 34 9/5 IV.

[46] Ibid.

stating.[47] The NORAD office in Lusaka was not at all assured that the unity of SWAPO had been re-established. Against that background, the Foreign Ministry agreed in the beginning of September to hold back a part of the disbursements until the picture was clearer.[48] However, the funds for legal aid, earmarked for Namibian prisoners and their dependants, were transferred via the Lutheran World Federation, and the allocation for food together with the 5% cash contribution was also disbursed. The rest of the allocation, mainly consisting of funds to cover transport expenses, was withheld.[49]

A meeting in New York

At the same time, SWAPO was given contradictory signals from the highest level of the Norwegian Government. Thus, at the end of September 1976, a meeting was held between the SWAPO President Sam Nujoma and Norwegian Foreign Minister Knut Frydenlund in New York, where the situation in Southern Africa and the co-operation between Norway and SWAPO was discussed. According to the Norwegian minutes from the meeting, not a word was then said about the internal SWAPO situation. Instead, Frydenlund informed Nujoma that "a substantial increase in the support for SWAPO" was being prepared. Furthermore, he advised SWAPO to "concretely tell the representation in Dar es Salaam or Lusaka what kind of support SWAPO would like".[50]

Did the one Norwegian hand not know what the other was doing, or did this reflect that Norway had adopted some new strategy in relation to the internal SWAPO struggle? It must be remembered that it was not just Norway and SWAPO that were involved in this situation. Norway's relations with both Kenneth Kaunda and the Zambian authorities and Julius Nyerere and those of Tanzania were very good. The SWAPO rebels were detained in these countries, with the help of the governments who supported the SWAPO leadership. To the Norwegian government these must have been important factors when deciding on the financial support for SWAPO.

The Foreign Ministry staff, however, still needed information about what was going on within SWAPO and asked SWAPO's representative to the Nordic countries, Ben Amathila for an explanation at a meeting in Oslo in October 1976. Was it true that nearly a thousand people had been detained because "they by their well-founded complaints about corruption etc.

---

[47] Øivind Lyng, the Consulate in Lusaka, to NORAD, 11 August 1976, MFA 34 9/5 IV.

[48] Tore Toreng, MFA, to NORAD, 1 September 1976, MFA 34 9/5 IV.

[49] Jan E. Nyheim, MFA, to NORAD, 1 September 1976, MFA 34 9/5 IV.

[50] Referat fra samtale mellom utenriksminister Frydenlund og SWAPO's president Sam Nujoma (Report from a consultation between the Minister of Foreign Affairs Frydenlund and the President of SWAPO Sam Nujoma), New York, 30 September 1976, MFA 34 9/5 IV.

represented a threat to the present leadership"?[51] The minutes from the meeting reveal that Amathila's explanation of the situation within SWAPO was not entirely clarifying. According to the minutes, he characterised "the last months' development as very unfortunate for SWAPO, which by now had managed to avoid a split". He did, however characterise the crisis as a split, and viewed the timing of the split as "most unfortunate".[52] According to the SWAPO representative, of the 500 detainees, 450 were expected to be released after questioning and around 50 were expected to be exposed as South African collaborators. "10–12 of the assumed leaders" of the opposition" were—"for their own safety's sake, and to cut off possible communication with South Africa"—transferred to Tanzania. According to Amathila, responsibility for the split rested with South Africa, which had managed to use "the bad lines of communication within the liberation movement— between leadership and cadres—(...) to exploit a genuine dissatisfaction".[53] The Foreign Ministry's officials at the meeting nevertheless assured Ben Amathila that the rest of the allocated contribution for 1976 would be disbursed before the end of the year.

In December 1976, the government decided that the allocation for 1976 should be increased from NOK 1.5 million to 2.5 million,[54] to be used according to SWAPO's plans. The Foreign Ministry did, however, "against the background of the accusations raised against the SWAPO leadership of misuse of grants" instruct the Norwegian Consulate in Lusaka, to "aim at the Norwegian funds being utilised in areas where a certain control could be enforced".[55] Large, unspecified posts should be avoided. If SWAPO, however, insisted on its original request, it should be accepted.

As it turned out, the Foreign Ministry not only increased the 1976 allocation with an extra million NOK, but it also fully accepted SWAPO's proposal for the use of the grant. All that was left of the Norwegian reaction to the 1976 incidents within SWAPO was to earmark NOK 150,000 via the LWF for legal aid and to decrease the cash contribution from 10% to 5%,[56] contrary to the expressed priorities of SWAPO.[57]

---

[51] Memorandum. Møte med SWAPO's representant i Skandinavia, Ben Amathila (Meeting with the representative of SWAPO in Scandinavia, Ben Amathila), 20 October 1976, 1 Political Affairs Division, MFA 34 9/5 IV.

[52] Ibid.

[53] Ibid.

[54] Royal Decree, 17 December 1976, MFA 34 9/5 V.

[55] Telegram from MFA to the Consulate in Lusaka, 17 December 1976, MFA 34 9/5 V.

[56] Letter from Jan E. Nyheim, MFA, to the Consulate in Lusaka, 24 February 1977, MFA 34 9/5 IV.

[57] SWAPO vice-president Mishake Muyongo to the Consulate in Lusaka, 12 January 1977, MFA 34 9/5 V.

Without any further comments on the internal strife within SWAPO, the Foreign Ministry in December 1976 proposed a further increase up to NOK 4 million in the support for 1977.[58]

The Norwegian relationship with Kaunda and Nyerere, and the consultations with the other Nordic countries, are only part of the explanation why the so-called "Shipanga affair" did not influence the Norwegian support. The background to this, and a more pressing reason, was that the need for humanitarian aid grew stronger and more acute with the increasing number of Namibian refugees as a result of intensified South African repression. Humanitarian—not primarily political—concerns were in fact decisive.

1976 not only saw internal problems develop within SWAPO, but it was also a year of dramatic developments in the region as a whole. After the Soweto uprising thousands of South African and Namibian youths sought refuge in the neighbouring countries. The pressure on the Frontline States intensified and South African attacks became more frequent. At the beginning of 1976, SWAPO faced serious problems with providing the increasing number of refugees with food. The rapid increase in the number of refugees in the region pouring into Angola, Mozambique, Botswana, Lesotho, Swaziland, Zambia and Tanzania—countries which already received substantial Norwegian and/or international aid to provide for their own citizens—also made the need to increase the general humanitarian support acute.

These developments overshadowed the hesitation that SWAPO's internal problems had evoked in Norway. The fact that Swedish and Finnish aid was not affected was also important for the Norwegian stance. In retrospect, it should be noted that their reasons did not necessarily apply to Norway. Sweden had through early contacts, built communications with the leaders of SWAPO that were based on trust and accepted their decisions.[59] Finland, on the other hand, in 1976 did not channel any funds to SWAPO in Southern Africa, but spent its entire allocation to SWAPO on Namibian students in Finland.[60] In comparison, Norway's apprehension appears as fully understandable. Nevertheless, the critical situation in Southern Africa heavily influenced the Norwegian government to disregard the "Shipanga affair". This not only led to an increase in the support for SWAPO, but also for the liberation movements that Norway supported in Zimbabwe.[61] In 1977, Norway also started to support the OAU-recognised liberation movements of South Africa, ANC and PAC.[62] From 1977 to 1978, the Norwegian alloca-

---

[58] Telegram from MFA to the Consulate in Lusaka, 17 December 1976, 34 9/5 V.

[59] Tor Sellström: *Sweden and National Liberation in Southern Africa. Vol. II.* Uppsala: Nordiska Afrikainstitutet (forthcoming).

[60] Iina Soiri and Pekka Peltola: *Finland and National Liberation in Southern Africa.* Uppsala: Nordiska Afrikainstitutet, 1999.

[61] See chapter 4.

[62] See chapter 3.

tion for humanitarian aid to the liberation movements in the region again increased substantially, from NOK 12 million to NOK 22 million.

The increased Norwegian allocations for humanitarian support were followed by political assurances in various meetings with the leaders of SWAPO that Norway would stand behind their liberation efforts until Namibia was free.[63]

Towards consolidation of the co-operation

As the support increased, it also became vital that the procedures functioned as well as possible. Although some years would lapse before the co-operation was consolidated, by 1976–1977 the general framework had been established: every year SWAPO was informed about the size of the Norwegian allocation; after discussions with NORAD in Lusaka, a request was sent to the Foreign Ministry in Oslo for acceptance; when approved, and endorsed by the government, the money was released. NORAD's resident representatives in Southern Africa carried out disbursements and control. The direct support to SWAPO was only in the form of humanitarian aid to Namibian refugees. In the 1970s, it went to food, transport, medical supplies, social welfare, agriculture and administration. In 1980, when the balance of forces in Southern Africa changed with the liberation of Zimbabwe, NOK 8 million was allocated for these purposes.

The contacts between Norway and SWAPO increased during these years. At the same time as both SWAPO and Norway tried to establish procedures that could facilitate the implementation of the support, a trust based on personal relationships was gradually built up. In addition to recurrent meetings between SWAPO and the local representatives of NORAD, delegations from the Foreign Ministry regularly visited SWAPO and the Namibian refugee camps. Every year, SWAPO delegations also visited Oslo for discussions with the Foreign Ministry, NORAD and the Norwegian non-governmental organisations (NGOs). Central during SWAPO's visits were discussions about the political situation aimed at securing further Norwegian support.

The co-operation had been resumed after the 1976 crisis, but the Foreign Ministry made it a prerequisite for continued aid that its representatives were given an opportunity to visit the SWAPO centres in the Western Province of Zambia.[64] It was not sufficient that a SWAPO delegation in the autumn of the same year again explained to the Foreign Ministry that the

---

[63] E.g., Memorandum to the Minister of Foreign Affairs. Samtale mandag 16. mai (...) med Sam Nujoma (Consultation Monday 16 May (...) with Sam Nujoma), 11 May 1983, MFA 34 9/5 C IV; Memorandum. Samtale 16 May 1983 med Sam Nujoma (Consultation 16 May 1983 with Sam Nujoma), 1 Political Affairs Division, 11 May 1983, MFA 34 9/5 C IV.

[64] Telegram from MFA to the Consulates in Gaborone and Lusaka: Reise til Botswana og Zambia—konsulent Sverre Bergh-Johansen, mai 1977 (Official trip to Botswana and Zambia—Executive Officer Sverre Bergh-Johansen, May 1977), 9 May 1977, MFA 34 9/5 V.

internal differences, described as "normal in the liberation movements", had been solved and that everything was "functioning as before".[65] The major purpose of the official Norwegian visits to the refugee camps was to obtain a deeper insight into the humanitarian requirements. They also made it possible to ensure that the support was used as agreed. This was certainly the case in the spring of 1977, at a time when the waves caused by the crisis within SWAPO started to calm down.

SWAPO's headquarters move from Zambia to Angola

As the Norwegian authorities towards the end of 1977 got a more satisfactory grasp of the situation, it again started to change. At the beginning of 1978, SWAPO had relocated most of its headquarters from Lusaka—where Norway had a NORAD office serving as the Consulate—to Luanda, where the Norwegian representatives even had trouble in getting visas.[66] An internal opposition to the move from Zambia to Angola was reflected in SWAPO's communications with Norway. However, in a situation where SWAPO in addition to sorting out its own internal problems faced an increasing number of refugees and the escalation of South African repression and warfare, the organisation did not make time to keep Norway sufficiently informed. This left Norway—although genuinely interested in supporting SWAPO's struggle—with some uncertainty regarding the implementation of the support. The SWAPO request for 1978 can serve as an example of this.

During a visit to Norway in February 1978, the SWAPO President Sam Nujoma presented a request for Norwegian support to a number of SWAPO projects inside Namibia, concerning education, health, agriculture and SWAPO's administration in Windhoek. The projects were regarded as being important for the liberation struggle and it was "clear from Nujoma's account that SWAPO preferred support for projects inside Namibia".[67] When asked whether SWAPO was capable of implementing the projects, Nujoma replied that it was possible, but that it had to take place under cover.[68]

To inform a possible decision on support to projects inside Namibia, the Foreign Ministry asked the Norwegian embassy in Dar es Salaam and the

---

[65] Samtale med representanter for den namibiske frigjøringsorganisasjonen SWAPO hos Statssekretæren (Consultations with representatives for the Namibian Liberation Movement SWAPO in the office of the State Secretary), 12 October 1977, MFA 34 9/5 VII.

[66] Utbetaling til frigjøringsbevegelsen SWAPO (Support to the Liberation Movement SWAPO), 2 Political Affairs Division, 29 August 1980, MFA 34 9/5 XII; Memorandum. Utbetaling til frigjøringsbevegelsen SWAPO (Support to the Liberation Movement SWAPO), 1 Political Affairs Division, 29 August 1980, MFA 34 9/5 XII.

[67] Memorandum. Besøk i Oslo 21.–22. februar 1978 av SWAPO-delegasjon (Visit to Oslo 21–22 February 1978 of a delegation from SWAPO), 1 Political Affairs Division, 27 February 1978, MFA 34 9/5 V.

[68] Ibid.

representations in Lusaka, Maputo and Gaborone for advice. It also raised the question with the UN Commissioner for Namibia, Martti Ahtisaari. Without explicitly rejecting the idea, Ahtisaari "was sceptical about the thought of changing the channels of support for SWAPO at that given time".[69] The Norwegian representatives at the UN shared this view, as the tension in Namibia had increased. Many SWAPO members were reported to have been arrested and a number of high-ranking internal leaders had fled the country. It would also be difficult to control the way in which the money would actually be used inside Namibia.[70]

After repeated reminders to SWAPO by the NORAD representative in Lusaka, the organisation submitted a formal request for 1978 in April of the same year.[71] It only referred to projects outside Namibia while the projects that had been presented by President Nujoma in Oslo some months earlier were not mentioned. The request for these projects, NORAD was told, had instead been sent to Sweden.[72]

Norway did not want to make a decision regarding the new request until a visit to SWAPO and the SWAPO camps had been arranged. In June 1978, two representatives of the Foreign Ministry, Knut Thommessen and Bjørnar Utheim, finally went to the SWAPO camp at Nyango in Western Zambia. Here, they were reassured that the Norwegian support had been used according to agreements, as well as convinced about the need for increased aid to the 4–5,000 refugees assembled there. The lack of medicines and the fact that daily meals had been cut down from two to one a day made a particularly strong impression on the delegation.[73] By this time, however, SWAPO had already started to move most of its activities to Angola.

The need for aid to the refugee camps was confirmed in discussions with the SWAPO representation in Lusaka, where Vice President Muyongo "agreed that one for the time being should not give support to projects inside Namibia."[74]

No decision on the allocation of support was however taken. The Norwegian uncertainty in this regard was further confirmed when Sam Nujoma himself some months later—in November 1978—requested that the entire

---

[69] Report from the Permanent Norwegian Mission to the United Nations. SWAPO. Kanalisering av bistand i 1978 (SWAPO. Channelling of Support for 1978), 14 April 1978, MFA 34 9/5 V.

[70] Ibid.

[71] SWAPO: NORAD support to (...) SWAPO. Proposed expenditure, 17 April 1978, MFA 34 9/5 VII.

[72] Letter from Consul Per Tobiesen, the Consulate in Lusaka, to MFA, 21 April 1978, MFA 34 9/5 VII.

[73] Memorandum. Thommessen og Utheims reise til Lusaka, Botswana, Mozambique og Tanzania 21. mai til 3. juni 1978 (Thommessen and Utheim's trip to Lusaka, Botswana, Mozambique and Tanzania 21 May to 3 June 1978), 13 June 1978, MFA 34 9/5 VII.

[74] Ibid.

1978 allocation be channelled to SWAPO inside Namibia through the Lutheran World Federation in Geneva.[75]

Again the general situation in Southern Africa can provide part of the explanation: in late 1977, South Africa adopted as its official policy the so-called "total strategy", implying a mobilisation of all available resources in defence of the apartheid state. The immediate consequences of this were an enormous military build-up and increased repression, with assassinations, arrests and torture inside Namibia. This made it extremely difficult for SWAPO to operate within Namibia, and also led to a massive increase in the number of refugees. Most of them went to Angola. In April 1978, SWAPO informed the Norwegian government that it was responsible for 16 500 refugees in Angola and 5,000 in Zambia.[76]

Meanwhile, South Africa was taking part in negotiations between the Contact Group (the five Western members of the Security Council: USA, Great Britain, France West Germany and Canada), the Frontline States and SWAPO, regarding a peaceful settlement in Namibia. The negotiations broke down after South African forces on 4 May 1978 attacked SWAPO's refugee camp at Kassinga, Angola, where they killed over 600, mostly women and children, and wounded many hundreds more.[77]

The new situation worked both ways regarding the Norwegian support. On the one hand, it was obvious that the need for support was increasing. After Kassinga, the Norwegian UN representation in New York urged the Foreign Ministry to release the 1978 allocation, while the negotiations at the UN were in intermission. If Norway waited until the negotiations were resumed —and new problems arose —both SWAPO and the Contact Group, as well as the Norwegian opinion, could interpret the Norwegian support as being used deliberately to influence the negotiations. On the other hand, "a quick disbursement of the allocation could more easily be tied directly to the actual humanitarian needs without being set into the political context of the negotiations".[78] Even if SWAPO had not suggested anything of the sort, a further postponement of the disbursement could, similarly, be taken as pressure on SWAPO in the negotiations. Out of consideration to the continued contacts with SWAPO, the Norwegian UN delegation in New York was of the opinion that SWAPO might listen more to the Norwegian views if the grant for 1978 had already been disbursed.[79]

---

[75] Letter from Sam Nujoma to the Norwegian Minister of Foreign Affairs, 4 November 1978, MFA 34 9/5 VIII.

[76] SWAPO: NORAD support to (...) SWAPO. Proposed expenditure, 17 April 1978, MFA 34 9/5 VII.

[77] Mvula ya Nangolo and Tor Sellström: *Kassinga: A Story Untold*. Windhoek: NBDC, 1995.

[78] Report from the Permanent Norwegian Mission to the United Nations to MFA, 12 May 1978, MFA 34 9/5 VII.

[79] Ibid.

The situation was indeed difficult. The most prominent SWAPO leaders like President Nujoma and Vice President Muyongo were not co-ordinated regarding their requests and the Norwegian consulate in Lusaka could not easily get in touch with the SWAPO leaders. It was, in addition, difficult to understand SWAPO's needs, as these were changing with the move not just of the headquarters, but also of the majority of the refugees, from Zambia to Angola.

At the same time, the negotiations at the UN were resumed. In September 1978 the Security Council adopted Resolution 435 for a solution to the Namibian question based on a proposal by the Contact Group. This created a fragile, but widely shared hope of Namibia becoming free in the not too distant future. But as it became clear that South Africa showed no real willingness to negotiate, the hope of an imminent solution was again lost.

Norwegian considerations regarding the support

The Norwegian Parliament did not make a decision regarding the 1978 allocation for SWAPO until November of the same year. The Norwegian representation in Lusaka reported in February 1979 that SWAPO was in a financially difficult situation; the allocation from Swedish SIDA had been spent, and the organisation had unpaid bills to honour. The consulate strongly appealed to the Foreign Ministry to accept SWAPO's budget and disburse the support: "SWAPO cannot understand the drawn out treatment of this question."[80]

Over a month later—at the end of March 1979—the Ministry in Oslo replied, stating that the proposed distribution was acceptable and that disbursements of the 1978 allocation could take place.[81] Part of the 1978 allocation was for vehicles that would be delivered to SWAPO as the Japanese manufacturer received payment from Norway. In May 1979, this had still not happened. The NORAD resident representative in Lusaka, Tor Elden, then stated in a letter to the Foreign Ministry that the "way we have treated SWAPO, with the late acceptance of the budget by the Foreign Ministry, and now the delay in the payment for the cars, has made SWAPO wonder if Norway is in the process of cutting them out."[82] A couple of weeks later the vehicles were paid for. Elden wrote to Oslo that although the representation would "try to mend the relationship with SWAPO through a luncheon", he thought that if there were more delays, "SWAPO would seriously start doubting Norway's ability to handle even simple matters."[83]

---

[80] Telex from Consul Per Tobiesen, the Consulate in Lusaka, to MFA, 14 GFebruary 1979, MFA 34 9/5 IX.

[81] Bjørnar Utheim, MFA, to the Consulate in Lusaka, 28 March 1979, MFA 34 9/5 IX.

[82] Telex from Tor Elden, the NORAD resident representative in Lusaka, to MFA/NORAD, 21 May 1979, MFA 34 9/5 XII.

[83] Telex from Tor Elden, the NORAD resident representative in Lusaka, to MFA, 4 June 1979, MFA 34 9/5 XII.

The 1979 allocation did not prove any easier. Partly because of the late release of the 1978 support—and partly because SWAPO had been busy sorting out other urgent matters—the request for 1979 was not submitted until March 1980.[84] The resident representative in Lusaka, however, found it difficult to advise the Foreign Ministry on the matter, as both SWAPO's administrative headquarters and the refugees in the Nyango camp were being moved to Angola. He therefore planned a visit to the new SWAPO camps in Kwanza Sul, Angola, before giving recommendations regarding the request.[85]

Discussing the Norwegian support with President Nujoma the following month, Elden was invited to Kwanza Sul. Nujoma assured him that the practical arrangements would not be a problem. The Norwegian resident representative to Zambia was, however, denied a visa for Angola.[86] By this time, Norway had recognised Angola, but no diplomatic representation had been established.

New uncertainties arose when news reached the Lusaka consulate that Vice President Mishake Muyongo "seemed to have" resigned, thus creating a split in SWAPO. The background "was supposed to have been" that "Muyongo refused to move from Lusaka".[87] A couple of months later, Elden was informed by SWAPO's representative in Lusaka, Hifikepunye Pohamba, that Muyongo was accused of wanting to establish his own nation in Caprivi, and thus contributing to the South African plans for an apartheid "internal solution".[88] Pohamba stated that Muyongo still was the Vice President of SWAPO, but that he had refused to move to Luanda, where he feared that he would be assassinated. Elden believed that there were indications that Muyongo had challenged the leadership of Sam Nujoma.[89] Later in the same month, Muyongo was actually expelled from SWAPO.

This confusion contributed to a long delay in the disbursement of the support and to the fact that the allocation for 1980 was not being increased from the previous year. Instead, it was even discussed in the Norwegian

---

[84] SWAPO's forslag for 1979 (SWAPO. Proposed expenditures 1979), 19 March 1980, MFA 34 9/5 XI.

[85] Tor Elden, the NORAD resident representative in Lusaka, to MFA, 21 March 1980, MFA 34 9/5 X.

[86] Utbetaling til frigjøringsbevegelsen SWAPO (Disbursements to the Liberation Movement SWAPO), 2 Political Affairs Division, 29 August 1980; Memorandum. Utbetaling til frigjøringsbevegelsen SWAPO (Disbursements to the Liberation Movement SWAPO), 1 Political Affairs Division, 29 August 1980, both documents in MFA 34 9/5 XII.

[87] Tor Elden, the NORAD Resident representative in Lusaka to MFA, 9 May 1980, MFA 34 9/5 XI.

[88] Tor Elden, the NORAD Resident representative in Lusaka to MFA, 4 July 1980, MFA 34 9/5 XII.

[89] Ibid.

Foreign Ministry whether to use part of the allocated SWAPO funds for other purposes, as was suggested by Knut Thommessen.[90]

In August 1980, Knut Thommessen raised the issue that part of the SWAPO allocation for 1978 and most of the allocation for 1979, had still not been used. In his opinion, this was due to the fact that "consul Elden has not been able to arrange a meeting with the SWAPO leadership, which is now in Angola". Furthermore, he doubted if SWAPO really could make use of the financial support: "Our aid is for food, medicines, clothes and transport, and it has simply not been possible for these people to spend all the money given to them for these purposes."[91]

Thommessen therefore found it "meaningless" to withhold the funds allocated for SWAPO, while the UNHCR was in urgent need of money. He recommended the Foreign Ministry to reduce the already agreed 1980 allocation for SWAPO, and to disburse the remaining amount only after SWAPO had given a proper account of how the support for 1979 had been spent. The balance, he argued, could be given to the UNHCR.[92]

The Foreign Ministry in Oslo did not agree, emphasising that the responsibility for the unused allocated funds for 1978 and 1979 largely fell on Norway. In both cases, the decision regarding the support had been taken late in the year, implying that the release of the funds could only take place in the following year. SWAPO could not be blamed for this. Nor was it SWAPO's responsibility that the Norwegian representative was not issued a visa for Angola. In addition, the Ministry did not doubt that SWAPO's running of its refugee projects was efficient and well administered.[93]

The Ministry was also of the opinion that it would be politically unfortunate—both towards the liberation movements and the domestic opinion—if allocations already given were to be withdrawn. Furthermore, it would contradict the repeated Norwegian assurance of support for the Southern African liberation movements. Internal opposition in the liberation movements was unfortunate, but—the Ministry argued—the delay was to a large extent due to Norwegian conditions and a reduction of the support would be in direct opposition to the declared official Norwegian policy. Instead, the allocated support should go in its entirety to SWAPO.[94]

---

[90] Knut Thommessen was at the time so-called Ambassador 1, to be used for special commissions.

[91] Tor Elden, the NORAD Resident representative in Lusaka to MFA, 4 July 1980, MFA 34 9/5 XII.

[92] Memorandum to the Minister of Foreign Affairs, Knut Thommessen, 27 August 1980, MFA 34 9/5 XII.

[93] Memorandum. Utbetaling til frigjøringsbevegelsen SWAPO (Disbursements to the Liberation Movement SWAPO), 2 Political Affairs Division, 29 August 1980, MFA 34 9/5 XII.

[94] Memorandum. Utbetaling til frigjøringsbevegelsen SWAPO (Disbursements to the Liberation Movement SWAPO), 1 Political Affairs Division, 29 August 1980, MFA 34 9/5 XII.

Visit to Kwanza Sul: Contacts re-established

By this time the problems encountered between Norway and SWAPO were starting to be resolved. The SWAPO leadership was finally settled in Luanda and appeared united and ready to resume contacts with Norway. In September 1980, a delegation of prominent SWAPO leaders, led by Sam Nujoma, visited Oslo for consultations with the Foreign Ministry. Here the situation within SWAPO, the political situation in Southern Africa and the Norwegian support were again discussed in detail. The new possibility for an open dialogue created a better understanding of the other's views and paved the way for the close co-operation that was to follow in the 1980s.[95] Shortly after the consultations, representatives of the Foreign Ministry were, finally, also able to visit Kwanza Sul. Through this visit, what can be called the "running-in phase" of the co-operation between Norway and SWAPO ended. As with the visit to Nyango two years earlier, the representatives of the Foreign Ministry, Knut Thommessen and Tor Elden, were reassured by what they saw in the refugee camps. Although becoming aware of the great needs, they were impressed with SWAPO's administration of Kwanza Sul, the close relations between the leadership and the ordinary members and with what they described as high moral standards in the camps.[96] SWAPO submitted a revised request for the financial year 1979, reflecting the changed requirements following the move to Angola and the increase in the number of refugees that had taken place since their last request was submitted.

On SWAPO's request and the recommendation of the resident representative in Lusaka, the delayed part of the humanitarian support for 1979 was finally disbursed, with NOK 1 million in cash for administration and NOK 7 million for food and transport in the Nyango and Kwanza Sul camps.[97] In October 1980, SWAPO also requested that the support for the financial year 1980 should be used for a project planned by SIDA regarding the building of a school and a medical clinic in Kwanza Sul. The resident representative Elden supported the request. As Norway did not have a diplomatic representation in Luanda, it would, however, be difficult to follow up the use of the funds.[98] Nevertheless, by making the building of the school and the

---

[95] Samtaler i UD 3. september med delegasjon fra SWAPO (Consultations in MFA 3 September 1980, with a delegation from SWAPO). The SWAPO delegation: President Sam Nujoma, Secretary of Foreign Relations Peter Mueshihange, Secretary to the President Kapuka Nauyala, the representative of SWAPO to the Nordic Countries, Hadino Hishongwa, 1 Political Affairs Division, 9 September 1980, MFA 34 9/5 XII.

[96] Memorandum. Støtte til SWAPO for 1979 og 1980 (SWAPO. Support for 1979 and 1980), Lusaka, 7 October 1980, MFA 34 9/5 XII.

[97] National Treasurer in SWAPO Hifikepunye L. Pohamba to the Consulate in Lusaka, Re-Financial Contribution by the Royal Norwegian Government to SWAPO for Fiscal Year 1979, 22 October 1980; Elden to MFA, Støtte til SWAPO 1979 (SWAPO. Support for 1979), 27 October 1980, both documents in MFA 34 9/5 XIII.

[98] Tor Elden to MFA, 27 October 1980, MFA 34 9/5 XIII.

clinic a joint Swedish/Norwegian project, the administration of the 1980 allocation would be taken away from Norway. SIDA's representative in Luanda would then be responsible for the project. As this was also SWAPO's wish, the Foreign Ministry soon decided to recommend the request, and in December 1980 this was accepted by the government. In this way, the accumulated balances from earlier years were committed and the planning brought up to date. From 1981, this enabled both SWAPO and Norway to deal with the support within the year for which it was actually granted.

In the late 1970s, personal contacts and administrative routines were thus established which in the 1980s facilitated the implementation of the Norwegian support to SWAPO.

The 1980s: Close and consolidated co-operation

Broad political support

The political climate in Southern Africa became harder in the 1980s. An un-compromising apartheid regime in an increasingly militarised South Africa was responsible for numerous military attacks in attempts to destabilise the Frontline States. Pretoria's establishment of a Council of Ministers in Wind-hoek in July 1980 and the setting up of an "interim government" in June 1985 confirmed that South Africa was not trying to advance an internation-ally acceptable, but an "internal solution". The hope that existed in the late 1970s of liberation in a "not too distant future" faded away, making a longer perspective of the planning of the Norwegian support necessary. At the United Nations, negotiations continued, but they were constantly obstructed by South Africa's repeated invasions of Angola. The diplomatic offensive by the US President Ronald Reagan, linking the withdrawal of Cuban troops from Angola to South Africa's withdrawal from Namibia, led to a stalemate in the Namibia negotiations for most of the 1980s. At the same time, the number of Namibian refugees under SWAPO's care grew steadily.

At the end of 1980, Norwegian aid authorities estimated that SWAPO had more than 40,000 refugees in Angola.[99] Out of these, 25–30,000, mostly women and children, were estimated to be staying in Kwanza Sul, and at least 10,000 reported refugees were staying in other camps in Angola. In addition, there was a large number of SWAPO freedom fighters, which was rising with young men fleeing from the introduction of compulsory military service in Namibia from the beginning of 1981. Only some 2,000 civilian refugees were still in Nyango. By 1985, SWAPO was reported to have 75,000 refugees under its care, of whom 70,000 were in Angola and 5,000 in Zambia.[100]

---

[99] Foredrag til Statsråd (Draft to the Council of State), November 1980, MFA 34 9/5 XIII.

[100] Request from SWAPO for 1985. Attachment to a letter to Bjarne Lindstrøm, 28 February 1985, MFA 34 9/5 C XIII.

The character of the co-operation between Norway and SWAPO changed from 1980. With personal relations and administrative routines suitable for humanitarian assistance to a liberation movement established, the Norwegian government was from the early 1980s in a better position to implement the support. The internal SWAPO conflicts, which had negatively influenced the movement's capacity to administer the support, as well as to maintain a fruitful dialogue with Norway, were at the same time resolved. At both the donor's and the recipient's end, conditions were thus in place for a more consolidated co-operation.

Throughout the 1980s, the Norwegian direct support to SWAPO steadily increased, irrespective of the political colours of the governments in power. It also broadened, from consisting mainly of payments for items required by SWAPO, to assuming a character of fully-fledged mutual co-operation. NGOs representing different sections of the Norwegian civil society, such as the church, the labour movement, the students and solidarity organisations were engaged as operating partners, reflecting that the assistance to SWAPO enjoyed broad political support in Norway. This was also made explicit by the Conservative government that was elected after continuous Social Democratic rule since Norway started the direct support to SWAPO. Shortly after its formation in October 1981, the new government confirmed during the apartheid debate in the UN General Assembly that it would continue to support the refugees in Southern Africa through humanitarian assistance. During the Namibia debate, it likewise announced that it would increase the support for the Namibian refugees. This was followed up by increased allocations both for SWAPO and the liberation movements in South Africa, and for projects for Namibian refugees implemented by the UN and various NGOs.

The situation of the 1970s, with under-utilisation of the annual grants, and large carry-overs into the following years, changed in the 1980s to more planned priorities and systematic use. The contact was closer, the predictability larger, the routines better, both from Norway's side and from SWAPO's. The decisions regarding the size of the allocations were taken earlier in the year, and the requests from SWAPO could therefore be submitted within the first months. As a rule, the allocations were disbursed before the end of the year. (Exceptions to this rule, were the allocations for the SWAPO secondary school in Loudima, which in the first years were allocated, but not disbursed as no other donors pledged support.) The negotiations regarding the support took place in Lusaka until 1986, when they on SWAPO's request were moved to Luanda. From then on, they also had the same character as Norway's regular country programme negotiations with independent governments.

As seen elsewhere in this study, a major part of the official support was in the 1980s channelled to extensive projects, implemented in co-operation with other agencies and organisations. The direct support, however, basically consisted of meeting SWAPO's requests for humanitarian assistance. NORAD implemented the support, except for the support given to SWAPO in Harare in 1988 and 1989, where the Norwegian Save the Children was responsible for taking care of the procurements.

In the implementation of one specific project, however, SWAPO requested the Namibia Association to act on its behalf, thereby providing a channel for the Norwegian Government's direct support to SWAPO.[101] A presentation of the development of the construction and running of the Namibia Secondary Technical School in Congo, can therefore serve both as an example of a project initiated by a Norwegian NGO to SWAPO, and as an expression of the direct support rendered for SWAPO by the Foreign Ministry.

The Namibia Secondary Technical School in Loudima

Throughout the 1980s, by far the largest project in the Norwegian support for SWAPO, was the planning, constructing and running of the Namibia Secondary Technical School in Loudima, Congo. The size of the project did not just relate to the costs—although these were considerable, with around NOK 50 million for the construction, and NOK 10 million annually for the running of the school. The physical size of the school was also large: 8000 square metres of buildings were erected on an area of 750 square kilometres. 3 kilometres of access roads were built, in addition to the roads on campus. The significance of the school lies primarily, however, in its role as a pilot project. In addition to providing Namibian students in exile with a secondary education, it provided SWAPO with very valuable experience for the building up of a secondary education in Namibia after liberation. In close co-operation with the Namibia Association, and with the Foreign Ministry as main donor, SWAPO proved to the sceptics that it was able to lead both the building and the running of this school. The political importance of the Loudima school also lies in the fact that at Loudima, curricula and syllabi for Namibian secondary schools were developed. The ideas on which the Congo school was based, have been realised in Namibia in the development of the school system in democratic Namibia.

The request

During discussions with SWAPO in Luanda in March 1982, the Norwegian Foreign Ministry was requested to grant financial support to the building of a school centre planned near Loudima in the People's Republic of Congo, where a site had been allocated by the Congolese government.[102] A formal

---

[101] For more on the Namibia Association, see chapter 9.

[102] Kristian F. Petersen and Leif Sauvik, Lusaka, to MFA. Rapport fra en tjenestereise til Angola i forbindelse med norsk bistand til SWAPO (Report from an official trip to Angola in connection with Norwegian support to SWAPO), 9 March 1982, MFA 34 9/5 C II.

request regarding the implementation of this project had already been sent to the Namibia Association in Norway, which promptly started a preliminary survey including discussions with SWAPO and a visit to Loudima in March.[103] The need for a secondary school for Namibian pupils was undisputed: secondary education was available to less than 1% of all those starting primary school in Namibia and SWAPO's facilities for secondary education for the increasing number of school children and students under its care were very poor.[104] By building and running the Loudima school, SWAPO sought to create a comprehensive institution capable of providing a five-year programme of general education, as well as programmes concerning science, technology, agriculture and polytechnics, combining theory and practice. Agricultural production was also included in the plans for the school. In addition to providing the pupils with teaching and homes, the school would also serve as a prototype for the future secondary school system in a free Namibia—whenever that might be. SWAPO was willing to build the school despite the uncertainties regarding the time of liberation, as the potential gains would be important. The organisation wished that the school would start with already 270 students at the end of 1982, and to be gradually expanded until 1,000 students could be enrolled.

The project was planned in two phases, the first consisting of the actual building of the centre and the provision of water. The second phase was to be concerned with the running of the school: working out curricula, providing the school materials, engaging teachers etc. SWAPO hoped that UNESCO and UNHCR would grant considerable support to the school.[105]

Discussing Norwegian support for the school

The Foreign Ministry regarded the project as "undoubtedly worthy of support", but needed clarification regarding the agreement with the Congolese authorities, the total costs and the participation of other donors before any decision could be made.[106] In discussions with Senior Executive Officer Knut Vollebæk, SWAPO's Secretary of Education, Nahas Angula, asked if Norway could lead the building phase and, if necessary, get in touch with donors such as SIDA and DANIDA for co-operation.[107]

---

[103] The Namibia Association to MFA, attachment: Namibia Secondary Technical School. SWAPO, January 1982, 10 February 1982, MFA 34 9/5 C II.

[104] Spørsmål om norsk støtte til SWAPO's skoleprosjekt i Kongo (Question of Norwegian support to the school project of SWAPO in Congo), Knut Vollebæk, 12 May 1982, MFA 34 9/5 C I.

[105] Memorandum. SWAPO. Etablering av en "Secondary Technical School" i Loudima, Congo SWAPO (The foundation of a Secondary Technical School in Loudima, Congo, Knut Vollebæk, Brazzaville, 10 May 1982, MFA 34 9/5 C II.

[106] Ibid.

[107] Spørsmål om norsk støtte til SWAPO's skoleprosjekt i Kongo (Question of Norwegian support to the school project of SWAPO in Congo), Knut Vollebæk, 12 May 1982, MFA 34 9/5 C I.

While the UNHCR did not have any funds for the construction phase and other donors hesitated, the Norwegian Foreign Ministry after a visit to the site in May 1982 decided not to let the uncertainties regarding the time of Namibia's liberation prevent the building of a secondary school which was so urgently needed. It would, under any circumstances, be important as a forerunner to the new school system in a free Namibia. The repatriation of the large number of Namibia's refugees was also likely to take years. The MPLA school in Congo had been used for six years after the independence of Angola and the UN Institute for Namibia in Lusaka planned to continue teaching for five years after independence. In the Foreign Ministry support to the Loudima school was described as "politically safe". Support to the liberation movements enjoyed broad political support and the use of the grants for educational purposes was "right on target" regarding the purpose of the allocations for humanitarian support.[108]

In 1982, the Foreign Ministry therefore allocated NOK 4 million for the construction of the Loudima school, provided that the plans for the implementation were accepted. Before a release of the grant could take place, an agreement between Congo and SWAPO also had to be signed, giving SWAPO the right to the area of the building site. Support for the running of the school had, in addition, to be guaranteed by UNESCO or other relevant organisations.[109]

The planning of the educational and technical aspects of the school advanced well during 1982. In May, representatives of i.a. UNESCO and ILO recommended the project in a UN inter-agency report after a visit to the area and a study of the plans. In June, SWAPO submitted an education plan and in August an agreement was signed between Congo and SWAPO. A project document with plans for the building of the school was at the same time presented by the Namibia Association, which had also recruited technical and administrative advisers for the implementation of the project.[110]

With regard to financial planning, the pace was, however, slower. The lack of sponsors became evident at an informal meeting arranged by the UN Namibia Council to discuss the financing of the Loudima school in October 1982, in connection with the UNHCR Executive Committee meeting in Geneva. The representatives of SWAPO, UNHCR, Denmark, Finland, Sweden, the Netherlands and Norway, as well as those of the Council attended the meeting. SWAPO emphasised the high priority of the project, but no

---

[108] Memorandum. SWAPO. Kontakt med Namibiaforeningen og brevveksling vedrørende oppføring og drift av Loudima-skolen i Kongo (SWAPO. Contact with the Namibia Assosiation and correspondence concerning building and running of the Loudima-school in Congo), 1 Political Affairs Division, 12 December 1984, MFA 34 9/5 C VII.

[109] Memorandum. SWAPO. Etablering av en "Secondary Technical School" i Loudima, Congo (SWAPO. Foundation of a Secondary Technical School in Loudima, Congo, Knut Vollebæk, Brazzaville, 10 May 1982, MFA 34 9/5 C II.

[110] MFA 34 9/5 C III.

commitments were made and no conclusions reached.[111] Although a number of possible sponsors approached by SWAPO in principle agreed on the importance of the school, by the end of the year no one had pledged concrete support. As Norway would not disburse the grant for the building of the school until the running costs had been covered, the 1982 allocation was reallocated to Kwanza Sul to avoid carry-overs.[112] In the 1983 budget, however, a new allocation of NOK 4 million was reserved for the school, to be released as soon as support for the second phase was secured.[113]

Although recognising economic difficulties within the UN system as the reason for the delays, Sam Nujoma nevertheless expressed dissatisfaction with the restrictive Norwegian attitude in a meeting with the Norwegian Foreign Minister in Oslo May 1983.[114] Nujoma was informed that a recent decision made by the UN Council for Namibia to allocate 250,000 USD for the running of the school had brought a financial solution closer and promised to actively work for the start-up of the project. This was followed up by engaging the Namibia Association to make a time-plan for the construction phase and estimates of the total costs, and to start working out the educational plans. As the Ministry was not confident that this small and young NGO had the necessary competence to carry out the construction works, as SWAPO had requested, it also engaged the private Norwegian consultancy firm NORPLAN, later to be in charge of the construction, to make qualified estimates of the design and scope.[115]

Although no formal decision on support to the Loudima school had been taken, plans were thus developed both with regard to the building and running of the school.

Developing a school plan

The objectives and overall guidelines for the school were set by SWAPO. The preparations for the curricula were carried out in close contact between the Namibia Association and SWAPO, on the basis of SWAPO's educational policy and philosophy. A first conference in this respect was held at the United Nations Institute of Namibia in Lusaka in September 1982, and in October 1983 the first proposal for the educational structure was accepted

---

[111] Telex. The Norwegian UN-delegation in Geneva to MFA, 19 October 1982, MFA 34 9/5 C III.

[112] Sam Nujoma, in a telex to Foreign Minister Svenn Stray, John Vea, Norwegian Embassy in Stockholm to MFA, 5 November 1982, MFA 34 9/5 C IV.

[113] B. Lindstrøm, Lusaka, to K. Vollebæk, MFA 34 9/5 C IV.

[114] Memorandum. SWAPOs president Sam Nujoma's besøk i Norge. Samtale med utenriksministeren (The visit of the President of SWAPO Sam Nujoma to Norway. Consultation with the Minister of Foreign Affairs), 14–17 May 1983, 1 Political Affairs Division, 20 May 1983, MFA 34 9/5 C IV.

[115] Memorandum. Besøk i Norge av SWAPO's president dr. Sam Nujoma, 14.–17. mai 1983 (The visit of the President of SWAPO Sam Nujoma to Norway 14–17 May 1983), MFA 34 9/5 C IV.

and an agreement in principle reached regarding the school curricula. The Namibia Association was asked to continue the curriculum planning and prepare guidelines for the syllabi.[116]

With the support of the Foreign Ministry, the Namibia Association in September 1984 arranged a conference at Lillehammer, Norway, where a general policy and a guiding curriculum were defined. A more specific framework for each syllabus for the first three years was also developed. The work was led by SWAPO's Secretary for Education and Culture, Nahas Angula, who described the conference as "a milestone in the march towards a free Namibia and a new example of the practical support Norway was willing to give in order to achieve justice, freedom and independence for a colonised people which had endured such heavy ordeals".[117] Having laid the foundation for the curricula, the Namibia Association continued the work on the details. After a revision by SWAPO's Education Department, a workshop would finalise the preparations of the curricula and syllabi in time for the opening of the school.[118] This workshop was arranged jointly by the Namibia Association and SWAPO in Lusaka in January 1986. The syllabi and curricula were continuously developed during the years the Loudima school was operating, based on the experiences acquired and with the aim of making them suitable also for the schools in Namibia after independence. Specialists from SWAPO, Zimbabwe, Zambia and other co-operating partners participated at workshops regularly arranged by the school. The school adopted the British school system from Form 1 to Form 5, and co-operated closely with Zambia and Zimbabwe. The Namibian students sat for the Cambridge International General Certificate of Senior Education, IGCSE, examination, arranged in co-operation with the examination boards of Zambia and Zimbabwe, as well as the University of Cambridge.

Norway becomes committed

After the discussions held with SWAPO in Lusaka in October 1983 regarding the plans for the Loudima school, on SWAPO's request NORPLAN continued the planning of the building programme, leading to a presentation of a proposal for the construction in April 1984. The costs were estimated as NOK 51–66 million. The Namibia Association, however, reacted against what it saw as planning for a too advanced school. NORAD supported this view and the building plans were made simpler, cutting the costs down to NOK 40 million. The Namibia Association estimated the running costs to

---

[116] Minutes of Meeting. SWAPO. Namibia Secondary Technical School, Loudia. Meeting on Educational Planning, Lusaka, 291083. Tore Johnsen, NORPLAN, 14 November 1983, MFA 34 9/5 V.

[117] Lillehammer Tilskuer, 8 September 1984.

[118] The Namibia Association. Oppsummering fra fagplanseminar. Lillehammer 6.–9. september 1984 (Sum up from a professional seminar at Lillehammer 6–9 September 1984), Elverum 12 September 1984, MFA 34 9/5 C VII.

NOK 10 million per year. On NORAD's suggestion, a group was subsequently appointed to secure continuous steering and supervise the development of the project. The group was mandated to make binding decisions regarding the implementation of the project, within the framework set by the Ministry.[119] It consisted of the Namibia Association, representing SWAPO; NORAD as adviser and the Foreign Ministry, as responsible for the support to SWAPO. At the first meeting of the steering group in August 1984, the Namibia Association was authorised to start the necessary layout work at the project area, financed by the general SWAPO allocation for 1984.[120]

Although no formal decision had yet been taken, the Norwegian Government had become committed through all the preparatory work conducted and the positive signals sent to SWAPO. When the formal decision to finance the construction of the Loudima school was finally made in September 1984, the project was thus well planned. The Namibia Association had managed to assure the Foreign Ministry that it could handle the responsibility for the implementation of the investments and the construction of the school, while NORPLAN was contracted to advise the Namibia Association during the building process. This turned out to be a less than fortunate arrangement. The disagreements between the organisations remained, ending with the Namibia Association cancelling the contract with NORPLAN in October 1987 and winning a law suit against the firm, demanding compensation for extra costs as a result of NORPLAN's calculations.[121]

At the end of 1984, Sam Nujoma was informed by Foreign Minister Svenn Stray that the Norwegian government had decided to allocate up to NOK 40 million for the construction of the school, as well as NOK 5 million annually for five years after completion of the project to cover part of the operational costs. The money would, as SWAPO had suggested, be channelled through the Namibia Association of Norway, acting on behalf of the liberation movement.[122]

The costs for the school would be taken from the annual allocations for SWAPO. These were, however, substantially increased in the following years, thus avoiding that the decision would lead to serious cuts in other activities. The already established humanitarian assistance to the refugees in Zambia and Angola continued as before.

---

[119] Contract between the Royal Norwegian Ministry of Foreign Affairs and the Namibia Association regarding Construction of the Namibia Secondary Technical School in Loudima, Congo, MFA 34 9/5 C VII.

[120] Report. Videregående skole for Namibiske flyktninger i Loudima, Congo. Første møte i styringskomiteen (Secondary school for Namibian refugees in Loudima, Congo. First meeting in the steering committee), 1 Political Affairs Division, 5 September 1984, MFA 34 9/5 C VII.

[121] Letter to NORPLAN from the Lawyers Næss and Sanderud, 26 October 1987, MFA 34 9/5 C XII.

[122] Svenn Stray to SWAPO President Sam Nujoma, 20 December 1984, MFA 34 9/5 C VII.

Securing further support

Following the decisions by the two major donors of the Loudima school, Congo and Norway, the UN Commissioner for Namibia, Brajesh C. Mishra, worked on the financing of the running of the school. At an informal round table meeting in October 1984, which the Commissioner organised jointly with the UNHCR, SWAPO presented the project and the requirements to the representatives of a number of governments, as well as of the OAU, UNESCO, UNICEF, WHO and UNDP, to assess what further support could be expected. Another meeting with the same objective was arranged with representatives of various NGOs. At both meetings, Mr. Mishra stated that "the long overdue school" would also need support from other sources than Congo, which had allocated the land, and Norway, which would cover the costs for the preparation of the physical infrastructure, including furnished buildings.[123]

Through these meetings, the Namibia Secondary Technical School in Loudima was widely presented. Potential donors were informed that SWAPO was the implementing agency for a school that would both meet the acute needs for secondary education and serve as a prototype in a free Namibia. The curricula of the school were presented: the subjects, examination principles and the underlying pedagogic philosophy of 'combining hands and head', or "to foster the relationship between school and community, theory and practice and study and work".[124] At the meetings the representative of the Norwegian government explained that although Norway would sponsor the construction and part of the running costs, it was evident that only one agency or government could not bear the whole financial burden for the school. Positive indications of further support were also given.

In 1985, Norwegian NGOs also decided to support the school. Operation Day's Work, the annual solidarity campaign where secondary students spend a day raising funds for educational projects in poorer parts of the world, brought in NOK 15 million for the students at the Loudima School. NOK 12.5 million was also given to the Loudima school from a yearly fundraising campaign arranged by the Norwegian Broadcasting Corporation. In the UN International Youth Year 1985 this was arranged in favour of Norwegian youth organisations working with information on the north/south conflict, engaging young people in practical solidarity work, and getting funds for development projects. The Namibia Association was one of the organisations co-operating on this fundraising campaign. During the following years, the school was in addition sponsored by various UN

---

[123] The Namibia Technical Secondary School, Donors Informal Round Table, Geneva, Palais des Nations, 10 October 1984, MFA 34 9/5 C VII.

[124] Nahas Angula: "The Relationship between Education and Society: Namibia in the conditions of National Liberation Struggle and after Independence", p 5. Paper presented at the "SWAPO seminar on Education and Culture for Liberation", Lusaka, 1982, Nordkvelle, 34 9/5 C XIV.

agencies; WUS, Denmark; TSL-Finland (The Finnish Social Democrats' organisation for education and international support); Overseas Service Bureau, Australia; the University of Bremen, the Federal Republic of Germany and the British Council and Namibia Refugee Project in England. The school was also supported by the Finnish and Swedish governments, through FINNIDA and SIDA, respectively.

Life at the school

The first pupils arrived at Loudima in June 1986, when 113 girls and 8 boys from SWAPO's educational centres in Zambia and Angola started an intensive course in English in preparation for the school year that began in September 1986. Five years of schooling would then prepare the students, aged 13–25 years, for further studies at university level, or for work. The teaching was organised through departments for Science, Languages, Social Sciences and Pre-vocational training. The programme consisted of three years of junior secondary education, with theoretical and pre-vocational training, and two years of senior secondary education, with the possibility of entering a vocational training scheme. The different backgrounds from previous schooling was a problem. 'Bridging courses' were therefore established to prepare the students for Form 1.

When the school was officially opened on SWAPO's Women's Day, 10 December 1986, it had a Namibian principal, and teachers and other staff from Namibia, Denmark and Norway. Later, teachers from Finland, Great Britain and Australia were also recruited. Congolese citizens were also engaged in various positions.

The board of the school was led by Nahas Angula and composed of representatives from SWAPO, Congo, the UN, the Norwegian Foreign Ministry, the Namibia Association, and the UN Institute for Namibia and WUS Denmark. At its regular meetings in December 1987, 1988, 1989 and 1990, the board was informed by the school director on the daily running of the school, the building leaders' reports on the construction works, accounting and budgets for the building and running of the school etc. School regulations, administrative plans and staff rules were also discussed.

By the end of 1988, there were around 500 people living in the small English-speaking community that developed at Loudima. Of these, 368 were students. The rest were Namibian and non-Namibian teachers, staff and children. The teaching of the various subjects was divided between the organisations that were represented with teachers at the school, although all teachers helped out in other fields when necessary. Pre-vocational training was mainly taken care of by Finnish teachers, while the agricultural department was administered by WUS, Denmark, and the Danish teachers taught farming and life sciences. The teachers recruited by the Namibia Association were mainly concentrated on physical sciences, maths and language, while the Namibian teachers were responsible for social sciences and co-responsible for a number of other subjects.[125]

The students were comprehensively organised to compensate for the lack of normal family contacts. In each class, a leading student was appointed to take care of the students' contacts with the school and each of the student houses had a committee of adults, with a housemaster as head of the committee, to help the students with their daily routines or to deal with more serious problems. Leisure time activities were also encouraged and helped to ensure companionship at the school—through political groups such as the SWAPO Youth or the SWAPO Women's League, disco nights, video shows and sports. One example of the latter was that the school volleyball team took part in local tournaments.

In the summer of 1989, the first group of students sat for examinations after a three-year course at junior secondary level.

Yngve Nordkvelle, a Norwegian researcher in international education, concluded in a report after fieldwork at the Loudima school in October and November 1987, that "according to the objectives of the school set out in several documents since 1982, all the main goals have been achieved".[126] After it had been running for almost one and a half years he described the school as well functioning, the teaching and syllabi being developed in a constructive way, and the buildings serving their purpose. Although there was a lack of teaching materials, such as suitable textbooks, he stated that "except for the students, there was nothing particularly African about the school".[127] These, on the other hand, were described in various documents through the years as very highly motivated and hard working.[128]

Namibian liberation—the school closes down

At an extra-ordinary board meeting in March 1989, the future of the school was discussed in the light of the new political situation, with planned Namibian elections in November of the same year and independence from 1 April 1990. It was, according to SWAPO's priorities, agreed that the students at Loudima should continue there until they had completed their secondary education, but that new intake of students should be discouraged.[129] This meant that the last group of students for the five-year educational programme would be enrolled in August 1989. The building

---

[125] Life Science, Domestic Science, Typing, French, Physical Education, Physical Science, Metal Work, Sewing, Social Science, Maths, Woodwork, English and Political Education.

[126] Yngve Nordkvelle: *Code and context in the making of a curriculum for liberation and self-reliance.* Report from fieldwork at "The Namibia Secondary Technical School" in Loudima, People's Republic of Congo, preliminary version, MFA 34 9/5 C XIV.

[127] Ibid., p. 14.

[128] The Namibia Association of Norway: *Annual report 1987,* p. 23.

[129] Namibia Secondary School. Extraordinary Board Meeting, 13 March 1989, MFA 34 9/5 C XVII.

programme was to be phased out and SWAPO's properties were to be transferred to Namibia. At the meeting, the representative of the Norwegian Foreign Ministry pledged continued support after independence, but in which form and for how long would have to be discussed after the elections, when the future situation and the bilateral Norwegian aid to Namibia had become clearer.[130] As the school was to run for at least five more years, the board decided to invest NOK 4.5 million in a powerline to connect it to the Congolese electric power and telecommunications network.

In December 1990, however, the board decided to close the school by the end of 1991. The students were to be repatriated to Namibia. A team consisting of one representative of the new Namibian Ministry for Education and three Norwegian consultants was appointed to assess the possibilities existing in Namibia for students that had not been able to finish their education in Loudima. The report submitted by the team in March 1991, "Learning by Production", was criticised in Namibia, and an additional report was submitted by Namibian authorities in May.

In June 1991 plans for the closing of the school were drawn up at a board meeting. The Namibia Association was entrusted with overall responsibility for the whole operation, including chartering of three passenger and two cargo planes. The reception in Namibia of the students and the equipment was the responsibility of the Namibian government.

In December 1991, the school was handed over to the Congolese state. For some years, it was run by the Roman Catholic Church for Congolese students, with the Namibia Association as a consultant during a transition period.

In independent Namibia, the pedagogics developed at the Loudima school, has strongly influenced the building up of a school system in the 1990s.

Nordic co-operation

Norway and her Nordic neighbours co-operated closely regarding the policy of support for the liberation struggles in Southern Africa. For example, at the level of international organisations, such as the UN, the Nordic countries often co-ordinated their positions, usually appearing as a group. In addition, in 1978, the Foreign Ministers of Denmark, Finland, Iceland, Norway and Sweden agreed on a Joint Nordic Programme of Action against Apartheid, which was reviewed in 1985 and updated in 1988 following Nordic sanctions against South Africa. In the 1980s, regular meetings between the Foreign Ministers of the Nordic countries and their colleagues in the Frontline

---

[130] Memorandum. SWAPO. Ekstaordinært styremøte Namibia-skolen (SWAPO. Extraordinary Board Meeting the Namibia School), Loudima, Congo, 13–14 March 1989, Mette Ravn, 20 March 1989, MFA 34 9/5 C XV.

States were also arranged to discuss the situation in Southern Africa and Nordic assistance to the region.[131]

Consultative meetings were also instituted from 1984 to strengthen the Nordic co-ordination with regard to the implementation in the field of the humanitarian assistance to SWAPO, as overlaps between different activities were taking place.[132] SWAPO's responsibilities and workload increased with the growing number of refugees. As the Nordic countries were among its largest donors, it was important that they kept each other informed of ongoing and planned activities. By exchanging views and experiences, the overlaps could thus be avoided and the support made more efficient.

The Norwegian and Swedish support programmes were in their basic outlines very similar, while the Danish and Finnish support was of a somewhat different character. This was reflected in close co-operation between Norway and Sweden regarding the practical, operative implementation of the assistance in the field.[133] Direct consultations between Norway and Sweden on the practical co-operation therefore took place on a number of occasions, while the discussions between the Norwegian aid administration and those of Denmark or Finland were less frequent and of a more general character.

The close relationship between Norway and Sweden was also manifested in continuous contacts between the Norwegian and Swedish representatives in the field. In particular, this was of great importance after the move of SWAPO's headquarters to Luanda, when the Swedish aid agency SIDA assisted as problems arose in the implementation of the Norwegian support in Angola. This lasted until 1986, when a Norwegian consulate was established in the Angolan capital. At the project level, this co-operation was also expressed with regard to the recruiting of experts and in the implementation of the actual projects. In 1978, for example, Sweden forwarded a request from SWAPO to Norway for SEK 2 million for the purchase and transport of food and medicines to Angola, where 15,000 Namibian refugees were in a very difficult situation.[134] Norway allocated the money and SIDA took care of the logistics. The school and hospital in Kwanza Sul is another example, where the Norwegian Foreign Ministry from 1980 agreed to support a project that SIDA had developed with SWAPO, making it possible to cover part of the vast needs for education and medical services in the camp. While Norway gave considerable financial support, SIDA remained the im-

---

[131] See Tor Sellström: *Sweden and National Liberation in Southern Africa. Vol. II.* Uppsala: Nordiska Afrikainstitutet (forthcoming).

[132] Minnesanteckningar från möte om Nordiskt bistånd till SWAPO (Report from a meeting according Nordic support to SWAPO), 28 November 1984, MFA 34 9/5 C.

[133] The Swedish support for the liberation movements in Southern Africa was more extensive than the Norwegian, this was also reflected in the administrative resources spent on it in the two countries, in 1986 being three man-labour years in Sweden and one third in Norway.

[134] Memorandum. Anmodning om bistand til SWAPO (Request for support to SWAPO), 9 February 1978, MFA 34 9/5 VII.

plementing partner, being responsible for the administrative aspects of the project.

Towards independence: From support for the liberation struggle to bilateral development aid

New guidelines for the transition period

An agreement based on the UN Security Council Resolution 435 regarding independence for Namibia was signed between South Africa, Angola and Cuba on 22 December 1988, to be implemented from 1 April 1989. This dramatically changed the situation and thus the basis for the Norwegian support. SWAPO would, naturally, run for the democratic elections in Namibia. As the UN presupposed impartiality towards the political parties in Namibia during the transition period, the Norwegian Government had to consider the implications regarding continued Norwegian support to SWAPO. Although South Africa would still administer Namibia during the transition period, a UN civilian and military contingent, UNTAG, would for twelve months from 1 April 1989 monitor and guarantee the preparations for the elections, as well as the takeover by a democratically elected new Namibian government.

Guidelines were laid down by the UN regarding international aid during the transition period. It would, obviously, be unreasonable to suddenly cut off the support to SWAPO's humanitarian work for the Namibian refugees in exile. Existing humanitarian aid programmes (that did not include cash payments) could thus continue without causing problems. New programmes, of which there was a great need in view of the return of the refugees to Namibia, were only acceptable if they were deemed to be impartial.

Adhering to these guidelines was voluntary, but participation in UNTAG would be impossible for those supporting SWAPO as a political party. The Norwegian Foreign Ministry also argued that violations to this impartiality should be avoided, as it could be used by South Africa to undermine the process.[135] According to the Ministry, being present in Namibia in the transition period was the best way the Nordic countries could support the development in Namibia, and thereby SWAPO. Only through being there, could Norway assist in preventing harassment to repatriated refugees, and election fraud.[136]

As South Africa did not accept Swedish military participation in UNTAG, and the role of Denmark was not yet defined, the Ministry argued

---

[135] Memorandum. Namibia. Spørsmål om støtte til SWAPO i overgangsfasen til selvstendighet (Namibia. Questions regarding support for SWAPO in the transitional period to independence.) 1 Political Division, 2 February 1989, MFA 34 9/5 C XV.

[136] Memorandum to the Minister of Foreign Affairs. UNTAG-operasjonen og spørsmålet om norsk støtte til SWAPO (The UNTAG-operation and the question of Norwegian support to SWAPO), 1 Political Affairs Division, 10 February 1989, MFA 34 9/5 C XV.

that it might be left to Norway and Finland to secure the Nordic presence. The Norwegian Foreign Ministry therefore emphasised the importance of not jeopardising the Norwegian participation in UNTAG. Finland was expected to be part of the military contingent, while Norway was supposed to become part of the civilian.

The Norwegian Minister for Development Co-operation, Kirsti Kolle Grøndahl, was of a somewhat different opinion: as South Africa was trying to undermine the independence process by training assassins, building up terror groups, engaging in scaremongering and preparing for election fraud, she maintained that SWAPO should receive Norwegian aid for the election campaign.[137]

These two positions can be seen as a prelude to the changes that were taking place in the Norwegian aid administration with regard to independent Namibia. The building up of the bilateral aid co-operation, which was administered by the Norwegian Ministry for Development Co-operation, ran parallel to the phasing out of the support that had been given to SWAPO by the Foreign Ministry. This was a gradual process, and it was the position held by the Foreign Ministry that was decisive regarding the character of the support during the transition period in Namibia. Norway was very careful not to give support that SWAPO could use for its election campaign. Nevertheless, this did not prevent the Foreign Ministry from financing the move of SWAPO's print-shop from Zambia to Namibia, although post facto. The print-shop, which Norway had funded since its start in 1982, was of great significance during the election campaign.[138] When requested to finance the move of the print-shop, the Ministry found it reasonable to support the move. "This support should, however, not be disbursed until after the elections in November."[139] The Namibia Association thus had the NOK 830,000 it spent on moving the print-shop and investing in some new equipment, refunded after the elections.[140]

Norwegian private organisations were, of course, free to use their own funds to support SWAPO—or any other party. NGOs were also used by the Foreign Ministry to channel funds for projects considered as impartial, such as church schools, inside Namibia. The Norwegian Church Aid, for example, received substantial funding from the Foreign Ministry for its support to the work of the Repatriation, Rehabilitation and Rebuilding Committee. The official Norwegian support for ongoing SWAPO projects outside Namibia continued.

South Africa's role as the administrating power during the transition period did, however, rule out any development co-operation with

---

[137] *Arbeiderbladet*, 7 February 1989.

[138] See chapter 9.

[139] Telex from the consulate in Windhoek to MFA, 17 October 1989, MFA 34 9/5 C XVII.

[140] Telex to the consulate in Windhoek from MFA, 11 December 1989, MFA 34 9/5 XVII.

Namibia's administration in this period, as that would have served to give legitimacy to this role. Political parties could not be used as channels, on account of the impartiality principle. Official Norwegian support to projects inside Namibia could, however, be transferred through Norwegian and Namibian private organisations to carry on existing projects and to efforts run by UN organisations. Support could also be granted for preliminary surveys for trade and industry, to prepare for a possible commercial co-operation between Namibian and Norwegian companies in the future. As SWAPO had asked for a strong international presence in the transition period, the policy of banning private visits by Norwegian aid personnel was also lifted.

An example of the kind of new project to which Norway could give direct support, even if the project was initiated by SWAPO, was the preparation of a new legal system in Namibia. Norway allocated USD 100,000 for a seminar series that SWAPO implemented together with Sweden, which had the aim to help to develop the legal system for independent Namibia. Norway and Sweden supported a group of seven researchers and lawyers, of whom three were from SWAPO, who would produce draft legislation for independent Namibia. As the UN Institute for Namibia had agreed to lead the project, it was not seen as colliding with the impartiality principle.[141]

Norway also supported a conference arranged by SWAPO in Harare in 1989, which had the aim of bringing together the internal and external leadership to ensure that they had established a common platform regarding strategy for when Security Council Resolution 435 was implemented. By sharing the experiences of ZANU at the independence elections in Zimbabwe in 1980, SWAPO would be better prepared for the future process in Namibia.

It led to great difficulties for SWAPO that Norway and other donors to a large degree cut off their support in the transition period. Ongoing projects had to be terminated, often at short notice. Sweden did not follow this strategy, but continued giving support to SWAPO's projects as before.

Norway did become a member of the civilian part of UNTAG, as did Sweden. Denmark and Finland also formed part of the military contingent.

From humanitarian assistance to development co-operation

The Norwegian government's support for the liberation struggle was followed by co-operation regarding bilateral aid. Namibia was geographically situated in the main region for Norwegian aid, and giving aid to independent Namibia would be a continuation of the support given to SWAPO through the years. Norway gave substantial support to the countries in Southern Africa, not least through SADCC, which Namibia would join

---

[141] Memorandum. SWAPO. Bistand til lovgivningsprosjekt (SWAPO. Support to a legislation project), 1 Political Affairs Division, 27 April 1989, MFA 34 9/5 C XV.

shortly after independence, to help reduce the member countries' dependence on South Africa. Plans were made between the Nordic countries for the bilateral aid, based on consultations with SWAPO. The shaping of the aid naturally had later to be discussed with the new government after independence, and be in accordance with its priorities. The large needs that would come into existence following independence would have to be met to avoid a breakdown of existing institutions. It was therefore important to secure continuity.

In a meeting between the Nordic Ministers of Development Co-operation at the end of August 1989, it was decided to appoint a Nordic working group to plan and co-ordinate the Nordic support for Namibia after independence. The group submitted a report in December the same year, emphasising the importance of co-ordination, but ruling out the need to develop specific methods or build up specific administrative structures for Nordic co-operation.[142]

SWAPO requested the Nordic countries to concentrate their aid efforts on different areas; that Denmark primarily would give aid to agriculture, Finland to forestry and water supplies, Sweden to transport and finance, while Norway, together with Iceland, was requested to support the development of the oil and fishery industries. This included research on resources, coast guard surveillance of Namibian waters, and development of legislation, notably the "Sea Fisheries' Act".

Promises of aid for independent Namibia were not empty words: in 1990 the size of the Norwegian foreign aid for Namibia was NOK 65 million, rising to NOK 85 million the following year. In addition to education, Norway concentrated its efforts on fisheries and energy as requested.[143]

The nature of the co-operation: "As good friends"

The relationship between SWAPO and the Nordic countries was described in 1986 by SWAPO's Foreign Secretary, Theo-Ben Gurirab, as that of good friends: together it was possible to discuss views on the co-operation and frustrations over the lack of progress on the Namibia question.[144] This is a good description. Concerning the relationship between Norway and SWAPO, once these friends got to know each other well, they developed a profound mutual respect. This, in turn, made it possible to have frank and open discussions, also regarding difficult cases where their views differed.

---

[142] Utvecklingssamarbetet mellan Namibia och de Nordiska länderna: Förslag till samarbete och samordning (The Development co-operation between Namibia and the Nordic countries. Proposal for co-operation and co-ordination) December 1988. Library of the Norwegian Institute of International Affairs, Oslo.

[143] White Paper No. 49, 1990–91, p. 50; White Paper No. 66, 1991–92, p. 62.

[144] Memorandum. Det sørlige Afrika. Statssekretær Frøysnes' samtale med SWAPO-delegasjon (Southern Africa. State secretary Frøysnes consultation with a SWAPO-delegation), 4 March 1986, MFA 34 9/5 C X.

The support extended to SWAPO by the Norwegian government was rooted in broad segments of the Norwegian people.[145] The grants given to the struggle, both directly and via international and local organisations, rose steadily irrespective of whether the government in power was left or right. The common experience of being a small country occupied by a large, fascist power was used on a number of occasions, both by Norwegians and by SWAPO, to strengthen this solidarity. The major Christian newspaper in Norway, "Vårt Land" already in 1978 drew the parallel between Namibia's situation and that of Norway during the Second World War, to mobilise its readers for solidarity with Namibia.[146] In the same spirit, the mayor of Elverum in 1986 encouraged SWAPO's Secretary General Toivo ya Toivo to "fight for freedom in Namibia like we fought for freedom in Norway during the Second World War."[147] Sam Nujoma, likewise, very often reflected on this in his consultations with the government and in his speeches given in Norway. Sometimes this was done very explicitly, as when he in an interview stated that "the same nazis, who were in Norway during the war, [were] taking part in the occupation of Namibia."[148]

On a personal level, President Nujoma's contacts with the Norwegians went back to his childhood days, when he worked as a handyman at a shipyard for whaling boats in Walvis Bay. Later he was office assistant to the head of the Norwegian whaling station there. In a conversation with the Norwegian representative in Lusaka, Nujoma remarked that he had the best of memories from that time.[149] On one of his many visits to Norway, in 1987, President Nujoma spent a day at sea, fishing with an old friend from these early years.[150]

Good friends can argue. The close personal relations established during the struggle, the regular consultations and the mutual insights into the respective situations, also made it possible to disagree. Discussions regarding the family reunion of SWAPO dissident Andreas Tankeni-Nuukuawos can serve as an example. Tankeni-Nuukuawos and his wife had been given political asylum in Norway in 1978, but their children were kept in Zambia by SWAPO. Raising this sensitive question with President Nujoma, representatives of the Norwegian Foreign Ministry tried to persuade SWAPO to release the children, while Nujoma argued for SWAPO's right to deal with

---

[145] How this solidarity was mobilised can i.a. be seen in the chapter on the Namibia Association (Chapter 9).

[146] *Vårt Land*, 23 November 1978.

[147] The Namibia Association, *Annual report 1986*, p. 13.

[148] *Hamar Arbeiderblad*, 15 May 1987.

[149] Memorandum. Samtale med representanter for den namibiske frigjøringsorganisasjonen ... SWAPO i Lusaka (Consultation with representatives from the Namibian Liberation Movement ... SWAPO in Lusaka), 27 May 1977, MFA, 34 9/5 VI.

[150] Letter from Knut Johannesen to MFA, 27 August 1987, MFA 34 9/5 C XII.

the case as it saw fit.[151] There were also times when the Norwegian Foreign Ministry disagreed with SWAPO on the strategy for gaining independence. In February 1978, for example, a SWAPO delegation discussing the political situation and the Norwegian aid, stated in Oslo that the necessity of the retreat of the South African troops and the inclusion of Walvis Bay into independent Namibia were non-negotiable. Director General Torbjørn Christiansen, who led the meeting, however, "indirectly appealed to SWAPO to show a will to compromise and to avoid locked-up situations", to make it possible for the ongoing negotiations to lead to a peaceful transfer to independence within the stipulated time frame.[152] To this, Nujoma replied that it was not just a question of achieving independence before a certain date, but also of what kind of independence it would be.

In the same year, 1978, when the structures for the co-operation were still being established, the Foreign Ministry received a visit from Lars Gunnar Eriksson and Craig Williamson, who requested Norwegian support for the International University Exchange Fund's planned assistance for SWAPO's administration, and for the election campaign in Namibia. This was turned down, as the Ministry "saw no reason to take an indirect way via organisations, when [it] had as direct and good contact with the recipient as was the case with SWAPO".[153] This was not only an expression of the wish to develop the relations with SWAPO—it was also very fortunate, as Craig Williamson was exposed two years later as being a high-ranking South African spy.

Did Norway in its support actually meet SWAPO's needs? It is important to bear in mind that SWAPO, being aware of the restrictions laid down by the Parliament for the Norwegian support, did not ask for aid outside these frames. The fact that SWAPO—for example—never asked Norway for arms reflects SWAPO's awareness that such a request would have been turned down.

In addition to material aid, SWAPO also wanted Norway and the other Nordic countries to give political aid: to put pressure on other Western Countries to support the struggle and to vote in favour of SWAPO's views in the UN General Assembly. Although SWAPO could state that the "people of Norway have demonstrated their support time and time again in forums like the United Nations"[154], Norway and the other Nordic countries

---

[151] Memorandum to the Political Department. Besøk av SWAPO delegasjonen i Norge (Visit of a SWAPO delegation to Norway), 1 Political Affairs Division, 9 September 1980, MFA 34 9/5 XII; Tor Elden, the NORAD resident representative in Lusaka, to Ambassador Thommessen, 31 October 1980, MFA 34 9/5 XIII.

[152] Memorandum. Besøk i Oslo 21.–22. februar 1978 av SWAPO-delegasjon (Visit to Oslo 21–22 February 1978 of a SWAPO delegation), 1 Political Affairs Division, 27 February 1978, MFA 34 9/5 VII.

[153] Memorandum, Leonard Larsen, 6 September 1978, MFA 34 9/5 VII.

[154] Attachment to letter from Mishake Muyongo to the Consulate in Lusaka, 12 January 1977, MFA 34 9/5 V.

did, however, often vote contrary to SWAPO's wishes, on principled grounds regarding the role of the UN as a peace promoting institution, open to all countries in the world. They could therefore never vote in favour of the use of arms, nor of excluding South Africa. SWAPO also often asked for Norway and Denmark to request the other NATO members to stop supplying South Africa with arms—which was contrary to the UN arms embargo.[155] SWAPO also regularly asked Norway to introduce economic sanctions and to stop transporting goods, such as oil, to South Africa.[156] SWAPO had to wait until March 1987 until a comprehensive boycott was imposed.[157]

But there was never any doubt on whose side Norway was. The message to the South African authorities was clear, like the sharp reaction when the South African Foreign Ministry complained about the contents of a schoolbook for Namibian students that had been written and produced in Norway, with funding from the Ministry. The Department of Foreign Affairs in South Africa found it "regrettable" that the Foreign Ministry had financed what it viewed as "propaganda for SWAPO under the guise of a 'textbook'".[158] In his answer, the Norwegian Consul in Cape Town stated that: "The refugees receiving the assistance in question are not residing on South African territory and, equally pertinent, come from an area over which South African authority was decided as terminated 20 years ago by the competent International Organisation."[159]

Sam Nujoma often stated in meetings that the Norwegian support, both politically and otherwise, had been of great importance, not least because it started at a relatively early stage: "The material and moral support given from Norway (...) went back to the time when SWAPO did not receive notable support in the Western world".[160] Following the difficult period where Norway and SWAPO were building up their relationship, Sam Nujoma was in 1980 invited to Norway for consultations. According to Hadino Hishongwa, SWAPO representative to the Nordic countries, this visit "came at a very crucial stage of our struggle for national independence,

---

[155] In particular France and the United Kingdom, as for example referred to by the chairman of the Apartheid Committee, Nigerian Ambassador Mr. Ogbu, in his account to the 29th UN General Assembly.

[156] As in: Samtaler i UD 3. september med delegasjon fra SWAPO (Consultations in MFA 3 September with a delegation from SWAPO), 1 Political Affairs Division, 9 September 1980, MFA 34 9/5 XII. In a consultation with Svenn Stray, Minister for Foreign Affairs, in May 1983 Nujoma again asked for sanctions, MFA 34 9/5 C IV.

[157] The sanctions issue is covered in chapter 5.

[158] The Department of Foreign Affairs, Pretoria, to the Consulate-General of Norway, Cape Town, 12 March 1986, MFA 34 9/5 C X.

[159] Bjarne Lindstrøm to MFA, 19 March 1986, MFA 34 9/5 C X.

[160] Memorandum. Samtale med representanter for den namibiske frigjøringsbevegelsen ... (Talks with representatives of the Namibian liberation movement ...), Lusaka, 27 May 1977, 1 Political Affairs Division, 8 June 1977, MFA 34 9/5 VII.

[and] enabled SWAPO to meet the Government, NORAD and various important personalities, political parties, trade unions, churches, youth organisations and solidarity groups. It also made it possible to once more explain our policy and political stand in the crises of our country, as well as to express our appreciation to the Norwegian Government, the Norwegian people and NORAD for their unwavering commitment to support our just struggle."[161]

The support from the Nordic countries to the liberation struggle also contradicted the South African propaganda that the anti-apartheid struggle was an East-West issue. The Nordic countries were not a part of the eastern bloc—on the contrary, Norway and Denmark were members of NATO, and Denmark was also a member of the EEC. By supporting the liberation in Southern Africa, the Nordic countries contributed to making the question of liberation in Southern Africa a question of justice and human rights, not of increasing communist influence.

The substantial direct support of NOK 225 million from the Norwegian government to SWAPO was complemented by support given to non-governmental and various UN organisations working for the liberation of Namibia.

After the "running-in phase of the co-operation, where the Norwegian aid authorities and SWAPO got to know each other and developed well-functioning structures for the implementation of the support, the relations between the two were very good. With few exceptions, the implementation of the co-operation was satisfactory to both parties. The Norwegian government knew that it could trust SWAPO to use the support according to agreements, and SWAPO knew it could rely on continued Norwegian support.[162]

---

[161] Hadino Hishongwa to Knut Frydenlund, 30 September 1980, MFA 34 9/5 XII.

[162] For representative remarks e.g., Memorandum. Disponering av Norges bidrag til frigjøringsbevegelsen SWAPO i 1977 (Disposal of the Norwegian contribution to the Liberation Movement SWAPO in 1977), 1 Political Affairs Division, 16 June 1977, MFA 34 9/5 V; Memorandum. Norges støtte til frigjøringsorganisasjonen SWAPO i 1978 (Norwegian support to the Liberation movement SWAPO in 1978), 1 Political Affairs Division, 20 February 1979, MFA 34 9/5 VII.

Chapter 3
The South African Liberation Struggle: Official Norwegian Support[1]

Eva Helene Østbye

Introduction

When the Norwegian parliament in 1973 decided to support the liberation movements in Southern Africa, it defined the recipients as "the peoples in dependent areas struggling to achieve national liberation". The South African liberation movements were thereby left out.[2] In doing so, the parliament sought to be on the safe side of the limitations in international law with regard to interference in the internal matters of independent countries. This restriction was then part of the framework of the Norwegian support programme for liberation movements, and only a new parliamentary decision could change this to include South Africa.

In the years that followed, changes took place which made the Norwegian Ministry of Foreign Affairs[3] propose that this restriction be reconsidered, and on 6 June 1977 the parliament decided to also extend direct support to the African National Congress (ANC) and the Pan-Africanist Congress of Azania (PAC).

This chapter will discuss the direct, official Norwegian support for the liberation struggle in South Africa; why it was excluded from the decision in 1973 and what it was that brought about the change in this in 1977. The character of the support for the ANC and the PAC will then be outlined. Finally, other aspects of official Norwegian support for democracy in the country will be briefly touched upon.

---

[1] This chapter is primarily based on documents from the archives of the Ministry of Foreign Affairs, which have been opened for the period up to 1990. As the account given for 1990–1994 is based on open sources only, it is of a different character.

[2] See chapter 1.

[3] For the sake of convenience, the Norwegian Ministry of Foreign Affairs will be referred to as the Foreign Ministry, and the abbreviation MFA will be used in the footnotes as reference to these archives.

The beginnings of direct support to the liberation movements

Why not earlier?

Although the decision to give direct support to ANC and PAC in 1977 was early in comparison to the rest of the Western countries, it was late compared with Norway's other support programmes for the liberation movements in Southern Africa. Norway's closest neighbour, Sweden, with whom the situation in Southern Africa was constantly discussed, and who had a similar, although more substantial support programme for the liberation movements, had already started supporting the ANC in 1973. That same year Norway also received a request from the ANC for financial support for a vocational training programme for refugees.[4] Why did the Foreign Ministry wait until 1977 to recommend to parliament that direct support should also be extended to liberation movements from South Africa itself?

There were reasons other than the fear of breaking international law that led to the support for liberation movements in South Africa not starting before it did. The support was only to be used for humanitarian work for refugees, and the number of South African refugees under the care of the liberation movements was very small. While large groups by 1973 had fled from the four other countries in the region fighting for their independence, refugees from South Africa had left individually. Up to 1976, there were very few South African refugees in the neighbouring countries, and the need for assistance to these was small, compared to those of Angola, Mozambique, Zimbabwe[5] and Namibia.

In addition, the Foreign Ministry had decided to follow the strategy for the liberation of Southern Africa adopted by the OAU. In short, this implied attacking most strongly the weakest links in the chain, which were viewed to be the Portuguese colonies, then Zimbabwe and Namibia, before finally concentrating on the liberation of South Africa. This was seen as being the most effective way of fighting colonialism and apartheid, and a decision to postpone giving support to South Africa and instead concentrate efforts on the other countries could be justified by this "domino theory".[6] As in Sweden, however, the objections might have been overcome if the Foreign Ministry in 1973 had been more reassured about the work the ANC and the PAC were conducting. In fact, at this time it did not know the movements, or their need for support, at all well. When considering whether to recommend

---

[4] Letter to the Norwegian embassies in London and Nairobi, and to the consulates in Cape Town and Lusaka: Besøk i Norge av representanter for frigjøringsbevegelse for Sør-Afrika, African National Congress (ANC). Anmodning om norsk støtte (Visit to Norway by representatives of liberation movement in South Africa, ANC. Request for Norwegian support), 1. Political Affairs Division, 16 January 1973, MFA 77 9/5 VIII.

[5] The name Zimbabwe will be used, also when applied to the time when the country was called Rhodesia.

[6] For more on the OAU strategy, see Tor Sellström: *Sweden and National Liberation in Southern Africa. Vol. II.* Uppsala: Nordiska Afrikainstitutet (forthcoming).

that they be included, the Ministry at the beginning of 1973 therefore sent out enquiries to Norwegian missions in various countries, asking for information and opinions.[7] The responses were very reserved.

The Norwegian embassy in London replied to Oslo that the ANC was regarded as being "a little obscure. The intelligentsia has been living in London for ten years and has spent the time writing political manifestos". According to Olav Sole at the embassy in London, as far as the mission knew, the ANC was not involved in guerrilla actions. The British Foreign Office, which had been consulted on the question, "thought it knew" that the ANC had an office in Lusaka. It did not believe that the organisation was engaged in humanitarian work for refugees from South Africa, of which there were not believed to be many in Zambia and Tanzania. Instead, the ANC's "activities possibly took place to a larger extent in London than in Africa".[8]

NORAD's resident representative in Lusaka, consul Ola Dørum, discussed the matter with the ANC's Chief Representative in Lusaka, Thomas Nkobi, before reporting back to the Ministry that the organisation took care of 75–80 refugees in Zambia, and around 200 in Tanzania. Although the level of activities was thus modest, it wanted support to create income generating opportunities for the refugees by establishing a farm in Zambia, near Livingstone. The ANC did not receive support from the UNHCR, since they as "freedom fighters fell outside of the mandate". According to Dørum, the presence of the ANC was not much more than tolerated by the Zambian authorities, and Dørum recommended that Norway at least give the ANC a "token" allocation. This would be "highly appreciated as moral support to an under the circumstances not much acknowledged liberation movement, which both materially and politically is in a particularly difficult situation".[9]

Olav Myklebust at the Norwegian consulate in Tanzania confirmed that the refugees under the ANC's care were in need of support. According to the ANC itself, the number of refugees was 200, but representatives of the OAU Liberation Committee that the consulate had consulted estimated it to be closer to 100. He confirmed that these did not receive support from the UN, as they were not defined as refugees by the UNHCR. With regard to ANC activities, "one could register a common sense of scepticism. It seems to be a widespread opinion that the organisation does not have good lines of communication with South Africa and that it does little besides taking care of the interests of its members in exile and spreading information to other countries".[10]

---

[7] See footnote 4.

[8] Letter from the embassy in London to the MFA, 5 February 1973, MFA 34 9/4 II.

[9] Dørum, Lusaka, to the MFA, 31 January 1973, MFA 34 9/4 II.

[10] Letter: ANC-anmodning om norsk støtte (The ANC-request for Norwegian support), Olav Myklebust, 4 April 1973, MFA 34 9/4 II.

According to representatives of the OAU Liberation Committee, neither the ANC nor the PAC was active inside South Africa: "When the OAU has recognised these, it is due to the lack of better organisations".[11] A prerequisite for granting support had to be that competent persons assessed the ANC's plans thoroughly, as they seemed to be overdimensioned and unrealistic, the Ministry was informed.

These responses came too late to influence the parliamentary decision, which was taken on 8 February 1973. They did however, reflect the attitude of the diplomatic corps, which it is safe to assume influenced the decision to exclude South Africa from the support programme. The question was, however, constantly reconsidered.

South African oppression and increased international awareness

In South Africa oppression increased from the mid-1970s. Demonstrations were brutally crushed, and in 1976 the Soweto massacre shook the whole world, thus becoming a crucial moment in the resistance to apartheid. A process followed which culminated in October 1977, when 18 organisations working for liberation, democracy and human rights were banned and their leaders arrested. Among these organisations were trade unions, newspapers, black consciousness organisations and the Christian Institute, which had been receiving support from the Norwegian Missionary Society from the late 1960s and from the Church of Norway through its Council on Ecumenical and International Relations from 1971.[12] In fact, the Norwegian Consul in Cape Town Egil Winsnes was present when South African security police raided the Institute's office on 19 October 1977, and shortly thereafter requested the Ministry for funds to support people there who had lost their jobs.[13]

At the United Nations, the situation in South Africa was regularly discussed, and a number of resolutions condemning the policies of the apartheid regime adopted. The tone in these intensified after the Soweto massacre, as expressed in UN Security Council Resolution 392 (1976), which reaffirmed that "the policy of apartheid is a crime against the conscience and dignity of mankind and seriously disturbs international peace and security". Furthermore, the resolution recognised the "legitimacy of the struggle of the South African people for the elimination of apartheid and racial discrimination".[14] In October 1977 the UN Security Council requested all governments

---

[11] Ibid.

[12] The close and extensive co-operation between the Norwegian Church and the Christian Institute is discussed in chapter 7.

[13] Ragnhild Narum: *Norge og rasekonflikten i Sør-Afrika 1960–1978 (Norway and the racial conflict in South Africa 1960–1978)*. Oslo: University of Oslo, 1998, p. 130.

[14] United Nations: *The United Nations and Apartheid 1948–1994*. The United Nations Blue Books Series, Vol. I, 1994. New York: Department of Public Information, United Nations.

and organisations to take appropriate measures to secure that South Africa abandoned the policy of apartheid and ensured majority rule based on justice and equality. This included demands that South Africa cease violence and repression against the black people and other opponents of apartheid, release the political prisoners, abrogate the bans on organisations and the news media opposed to apartheid, abolish the policy of bantustanisation, the bantu education system and all other measures of apartheid and racial discrimination. Later in 1977, the Security Council adopted for the first time binding sanctions against a member country, when in November it declared a mandatory arms embargo against South Africa.[15]

Pressure from civil society and the cold war question

In Norway too, public awareness about the situation in Southern Africa grew, and as everywhere else, the Soweto massacre was an eye-opener. The Foreign Ministry had, however, been giving support, although modest, to church, trade union and student organisations in South Africa engaged in the struggle against apartheid politics since 1963, through the Special Committee for Refugees from Southern Africa.[16] In the spring of 1976, this Committee had also granted NOK 66,000 to the ANC Women's Section for a literacy project for refugees in Zambia.[17] The same year, the Norwegian government banned currency licences and export credits. This was the first piece of sanctions legislation against South Africa passed by any Nordic country.

In the UN, Norway had long before the mid-1970s been a strong opponent of South African apartheid politics, advocating increased international pressure on the Pretoria government. This had been followed up by humanitarian and economic support via the UN and other international organisations. The pressure for stronger, more committed efforts to support the democratic forces in South Africa did, however, increase, as did the level of activity regarding the question in the Norwegian non-governmental organisations (NGO).

In 1976 the Norwegian Confederation of Trade Unions (LO) in close cooperation with the Norwegian labour movement as a whole, launched a broad campaign against apartheid. The campaign had two major objectives. One was to summon support in Norwegian public opinion for stronger economic sanctions against South Africa. The other was to raise funds for democratic forces in Southern Africa, such as liberation movements and trade unions, and for humanitarian assistance to refugees. A consumer boycott was initiated, where the Norwegian Consumers Co-operative stopped

---

[15] UN Security Council Resolutions 417 (1977) and 418 (1977).

[16] See chapter 1.

[17] Minutes from meeting of the Special Committee for Refugees from Southern Africa, 31 May 1976, MFA 77 9/5 XI.

all imports from South Africa for a year, and the trade unions of the state wine monopoly prevented any South African wine or brandy from being imported to Norway from 1977 to 1994.[18] The Church of Norway started supporting the Christian Institute in South Africa in 1973, with money allocated by the Foreign Ministry, and became increasingly involved in the anti-apartheid struggle. This was reflected both in the local congregations and in the communication with the Foreign Ministry.[19] The Council for Southern Africa continuously campaigned for Norway to start granting direct support to the liberation movement in South Africa, both publicly and directly to the Foreign Ministry and parliament.[20] The Students' and Academics' International Assistance Fund (SAIH) supported South African refugees, primarily in the field of education, as well as informing the Norwegian public, students in particular, about apartheid.[21] A number of smaller NGOs initiated projects and local trade unions sent letters to the Foreign Ministry, asking for direct support to South African liberation movements to be initiated.[22] The pressure from civil society was vital in bringing about the decision to start giving direct assistance to the ANC and the PAC.

It falls outside the frames of this study to give an account of the motions and processes in parliament. It should, however, be mentioned that the Socialist Left Party, which had two members in the parliamentary Foreign Affairs Committee from 1973 to 1977, also put considerable pressure on the labour government to start supporting the liberation movement in South Africa.

There was also a fear in the Foreign Ministry that the situation in Southern Africa would develop into an East-West conflict. Labour Party Prime Minister Odvar Nordli thus stated in a speech in March 1976 that if there was to be any hope of contributing to hatred from colonial times being replaced with understanding and co-operation, it was important to have the African reality as a point of departure. According to Nordli, the ideological fight between democracy and communism had its roots in countries outside the African continent. The Western world should not leave it to the communist countries to side with the liberation movements: it was the West itself that had to see to it that the new states in Africa were not dominated by communist powers in other parts of the world. This could only be achieved through sensible conduct. It was therefore more important to listen to the opinion of the African population itself regarding how they wanted to shape

---

[18] See chapter 8.

[19] See chapter 7.

[20] For more, see chapter 6.

[21] Vesla Vetlesen: *Frihet for Sør Afrika. LO og kampen mot apartheid.* Oslo: Tiden Norsk Forlag, 1998, pp. 43–45. See also Inger A. Heldal (ed.): *From Cape to Cape against Apartheid.* Mayibuye History and Literature Series No 61, 1996. Cape Town: Mayibuye Books.

[22] For example: Letter from Elverum Faglige Samorganisasjon to the MFA, 4 April 1977, MFA 34 9/4 III.

their own future than to export our ideals and principles to Africa, he argued.[23]

At the United Nations' International Conference in Support of the Peoples of Zimbabwe and Namibia in Maputo in May 1977—the month before the Norwegian decision to start supporting liberation movements in South Africa—Under-Secretary of State Thorvald Stoltenberg warned against foreign intervention in Southern Africa. It was obvious, he stated, that the alternative to some form of negotiated settlement in the area would be a continuing and intensifying conflict whose repercussions would be felt far beyond the area itself. The effects this could have on world peace dictated that efforts for peaceful solutions were immediately made.[24]

Proposal for support

Through its co-operation with the liberation movements in Mozambique, Angola, Zimbabwe and Namibia, the Foreign Ministry had since 1973 considerably increased its understanding of the situation in the region and the activities of the liberation movements. The Ministry had also established routines for co-operation with liberation movements from other countries in Southern Africa.

As the major part of the Norwegian allocation for liberation movements had been reserved for the Portuguese colonies, the administrative capacity in the Foreign Ministry for support to the liberation movements in Southern Africa increased after these were liberated in 1974/75. The new situation in Southern Africa, which emerged after the liberation of Mozambique and Angola, and the increase in the number of refugees in the region which resulted from the intensified conflict in South Africa in 1976, strongly motivated that a revision of the Norwegian decision was carried out. It was also fundamentally important that a decision to start giving such support, could be based on the yearly appeals by the UN General Assembly to all member countries to give assistance to the recognised liberation movements in South Africa, thus rendering it a basis in international law. Furthermore, a decision could be motivated by reports from the Swedish Foreign Ministry, stating that it was satisfied with the co-operation with the ANC. The requests submitted by the liberation movement to Sweden were well prepared and the use of the allocations was well accounted for. [25]

---

[23] Speech in the Vestfold Labour Party 20 March 1976. Ref. Jon Bech: *Norsk bistand til frigjørings-bevegelsene i det sørlige Afrika*. Forum for Utviklingsstudier, No. 10, 1978. Oslo: Norsk Utenrikspolitisk Institutt.

[24] Statement by Mr. Thorvald Stoltenberg, Under-Secretary of State, Norway, at the Maputo Conference on May 18, 1977. In *Nordic Statements on Apartheid, Supplement*, 1978, pp. 19–24. Uppsala and New York: Scandinavian Institute of African Studies and the UN Centre Against Apartheid.

[25] See Tor Sellström: *Sweden and National Liberation in Southern Africa, Vol. II*. Uppsala: Nordiska Afrikainstitutet (forthcoming).

The Foreign Ministry[26] at the beginning of 1977 found that all this had made the time ripe for recommending that Norway start extending direct humanitarian support to the liberation movement in South Africa.

The question of Norway's relations with South Africa was discussed at a governmental conference on 24 January 1977, as a direct response to a call from the International Solidarity Committee of the Norwegian Labour Movement for increased pressure on South Africa.[27] The government here decided to follow the advice from the Foreign Ministry and propose that Norway should oppose the IMF granting support and loans to South Africa, that the consulate general in Cape Town should become more active in the humanitarian field—and that Norway start supporting the internationally recognised liberation movements in South Africa. This was formally proposed to parliament in March 1977, although the only liberation movement mentioned by name, was the ANC. It was also proposed to include the legal black consciousness movement in the direct support programme.[28]

Parliamentary decision

The then Secretary of the Norwegian Council for Southern Africa, Øystein Gudim, followed up the proposal in a letter to the parliamentary Foreign Affairs Committee, which was preparing the matter for decision by parliament. He argued that Norway should take the consequences of support given to UN resolutions against the apartheid regime in South Africa, and meet the UN appeals to its member countries to support the liberation movements in exile by giving material assistance to the liberation movement. The Council for Southern Africa saw South Africa as a dependent region with regard to international law, in the same way as Zimbabwe. There could therefore be no objection in principle against granting support to national liberation movements in their struggle for self-determination for the majority of the people in South Africa. Gudim was pleased to learn that such support was now being proposed, and hoped that in the future this support would increase.[29]

With reference to UN recommendations, the parliamentary Committee for Foreign Affairs decided to accept that Norway should start giving humanitarian support for South African refugees through the liberation movements. The representatives of the Conservative Party, which was in a minority in the Committee, made it an absolute prerequisite that the support was only given as humanitarian assistance for South African refugees in

---

[26] In the Foreign Ministry, the 1. Political Affairs Division handled the support for liberation movements.

[27] Narum, op. cit., p. 126.

[28] St. prp. nr. 138 (1976–77), March 1977.

[29] Letter from Øystein Gudim to the parliamentary Foreign Affairs Committee, 25 April 1977, MFA 34 9/5 V. For more on the Council for Southern Africa, see chapter 6.

exile, so as not to be in contravention of the principle of non-intervention.[30] Although it was in favour of giving support to the ANC also inside South Africa, the government saw it as important to maintain the broad political unity that existed in Norway regarding the support to the liberation movements in Southern Africa. The conditions presented by the Conservative Party were respected.[31]

When the proposition was discussed in parliament on 6 June, Foreign Minister Knut Frydenlund referred to the post-apartheid situation to motivate support: "From Norway's side we have also seen the contact with the liberation movements in Southern Africa as an important part of Western countries' co-operation with the future Black majority regimes in the areas." The proposition was adopted. The decision to start granting direct support to the liberation movements in South Africa, was thus well prepared.

Against the background of the position of the Foreign Affairs Committee, the Foreign Ministry would have as a guideline that the support for South African liberation movements had to be concentrated on their work for refugees. The parliamentary decision was also interpreted as prohibiting that funds were used for illegal activities inside South Africa.[32] As the Ministry increasingly came to support church organisations and other parts of the legal resistance movement, the demand that the support was only given to refugees outside South Africa was again discussed in 1981. The Labour government had recently been replaced with a Conservative government and the new Foreign Minister, Svenn Stray, gave the green light for the internal support to continue.[33]

By Royal Decree of 22 July 1977, the Foreign Ministry was finally given the authority to use the allocation, which was raised from NOK 5 to NOK 12 million for humanitarian work for refugees carried out by the liberation movements in Zimbabwe, Namibia and South Africa. The allocation was to be equally shared between the three countries and be spent on items such as transport, food, medicine and education. The Foreign Ministry would also channel part of the support via the legal black consciousness movement in South Africa. The detailed distribution was left to the Ministry.

[30] Innstilling S.nr. 334 (1976–77).

[31] Bech, p. 15.

[32] Memorandum. Norsk støtte til frigjøringsbevegelsene i et sørlige Afrika. (Norwegian support for the liberation movements in Southern Africa), 1. Political Affairs Division, 5 July 1977, MFA 34 9/5 V.

[33] Utdrag referat fra avdelingssjefsmøte. Prinsippspørsmål om fortsatt humanitær bistand til Sør-Afrika (Excerpts from meeting with heads of departments. Questions of principle regarding continued humanitarian support for South Africa), 26 November 1981, MFA 34 9/4 V.

The co-operation with the ANC

The first contact

The granting of the Nobel Peace Prize to the ANC President-General Albert Luthuli in December 1961 made the ANC's struggle against apartheid widely known in Norway, not least within the church, where Luthuli through Norwegian missionaries in Natal enjoyed broad support. In connection with the Afro-Scandinavian Youth Congress in Oslo, Oliver Tambo—who had accompanied Luthuli to the Nobel ceremonies—returned to the Norwegian capital in August 1962. During his stay, he was received by Prime Minister Einar Gerhardsen, establishing direct contacts between the ANC and the Norwegian government.[34]

After the banning of the ANC in April 1960, the Nationalist Party government stopped at nothing to crush the organisation. In the ANC's own words, by mid-1965 "the ANC had effectively been destroyed within South Africa. It was to be another eight years before there was significant reconstruction of an ANC underground, and eleven years before the resumption of armed activity inside South Africa".[35]

In this period, up to 1973, contact between the Norwegian government and the ANC was very modest. When Norwegian diplomats in 1973 informed the Ministry about the ANC, they were not mistaken in saying that as an organisation the ANC was not active inside South Africa. But this did not reflect the fact that the majority of the ANC leaders, who had not been killed or imprisoned, had had to escape, and that the repression had been so hard that the organisation needed to rebuild itself.

In January 1973, Oliver Tambo again resumed contact with Norway, when he visited Oslo together with Masizi Kunene and Martin Legassick. (As a friend of the Norwegian Crown Prince Harald from student days in Oxford, Legassick was also invited home to the Crown Prince for a private dinner.) The delegation was hosted by the Norwegian Council for Southern Africa, and was also received by the Foreign Ministry for political talks. The Ministry stated that "for reasons of principle" it could not cover the ANC's expenses in connection with the visit.[36] Against the background of the reception given in Sweden, where travel costs and accommodation had been paid, the Foreign Ministry did, however, decide to arrange a lunch for the delegation.[37] In addition to discussions with the Foreign Ministry on the situation in South Africa and the activities of the ANC, the delegation also

---

[34] See chapter 1.

[35] African National Congress: Statement to the Truth and Reconciliation Commission, p. 47. August 1996.

[36] Memorandum. Henvendelse fra den sør-afrikanske organisasjon African National Congress (ANC) om besøk i Norge" (Communication from the South African organisation ANC), 1. Political Affairs Division, 2 January 1973, MFA 34 9/4 II.

[37] Besøk i Oslo av representanter for den sør-afrikanske organisasjon ANC (Visit to Oslo from representatives of the South African organisation ANC), 5 January 1973, MFA 34 9/4 II.

visited the Nobel Institute and the Norwegian Confederation of Trade Unions (LO), where they met the International Secretary Thorvald Stoltenberg, who later in 1987 became Foreign Minister. Only three months later, Tambo again visited Oslo, as a participant at the OAU/UN Conference of Experts for the Support of Victims of Colonialism and Apartheid in Southern Africa.[38] In the meantime the decision not to support the ANC directly had been made.

As South Africa was excluded from the support programme, and the Ministry was busy administering support for the liberation movements in the other Southern African countries, contact between the Norwegian Foreign Ministry and the ANC over the following years was neither close nor frequent. When the ANC representative to Scandinavia, Sobizana Mngqikana visited Norway in November 1976, it was his first visit to Norway in two years. [39]

The main purpose of Mngqikana's visit was to find out whether Norway would be willing to join Sweden in a project to help the new wave of refugees fleeing from South Africa. This was after the Soweto massacre, and thousands of radicalised schoolchildren and students were pouring into South Africa's neighbouring countries. Many of these were sent on to Tanzania, where a camp was being set up in Mazimbu, in the Morogoro region, to take care of the young refugees. This was where the Solomon Mahlangu Freedom College (SOMAFCO), which was to receive substantial Norwegian support, was established.

When he was told that the request could only be met after a new parliamentary decision, the ANC representative declared that he had problems understanding the Norwegian distinction between the different liberation movements that till then had excluded the ANC from receiving support. None of these movements regarded South Africa as an independent state. The ANC representative saw it as totally unrealistic to base a stand against the racist regime on resolutions adopted by the UN Security Council, as the interests of the Western powers in South Africa would block any constructive decisions. If the political will was there, Mngqikana maintained that the many resolutions adopted by the UN General Assembly could form a basis for a decision to support the South African people and their representatives. He also could not understand the logic in a number of other organisations working against the oppression inside South Africa receiving Norwegian support, while the liberation movement could not be used as a channel for humanitarian assistance efforts.[40]

---

[38] See chapter 1.

[39] Memorandum. Samtale med representant for African National Congress (Consultation with representative of ANC), 23 November 1976, MFA 34 9/5 IV.

[40] Ibid.

The project that Mngqikana had come to discuss was, however, to be the first ANC project to receive Norwegian support. The Swedish Foreign Ministry had already requested the Norwegian Foreign Ministry for co-funding for this project, which consisted in providing transport and subsistence for South African refugees under the care of the ANC. As the number of South African refugees in 1976 –77 suddenly rose by thousands, the need for assistance became acute. This situation had arisen very fast, and the request had been sent to Sweden in addition to the already negotiated support. When Sweden then allocated SEK 2.1 million, the money available for 1976/77 had already been spent. Therefore Sweden approached Norway for co-operation on this project, which was found to be very worthy of support.[41]

The Foreign Ministry agreed that this would be well suited for Norwegian support: "By joining Sweden one would also benefit from the good contacts Swedish authorities have already established with the ANC in Lusaka—which would facilitate later co-operation with the liberation movement." However, before giving a response to Sweden, a general decision on direct support for the liberation movements in South Africa had to be taken. As this was such a worthy project, the Ministry argued that it could be used to convince parliament to start supporting the ANC, and suggested that it could serve this purpose when the Foreign Minister was to discuss the matter with the government and Foreign Affairs Committee in parliament.[42]

In March 1977 the ANC sought a reaction to the request, but was told to wait for parliament to decide later in the spring session on the principle of support for South Africa.[43] At the end of May 1977, representatives of the Foreign Ministry met the ANC leadership in Lusaka where they were given a detailed orientation of the ANC's activities in the past and present by Secretary General Alfred Nzo. With reference to the early contact between Norway and the ANC, especially through Oliver Tambo, a renewal of this relationship was also discussed. Although this was nearly two weeks before the decision in principle was taken on support for the South African liberation movement, it was expected that this would be positive. Therefore the Ministry could also discuss with the ANC what kind of support the ANC would want from Norway for 1977.[44] The ANC after the consultations submitted a detailed request for support to the SOMAFCO school project, as

[41] Memorandum. Spørsmålet om norsk bistand til frigjøringsbevegelsene i Sør-Afrika. Svensk henvendelse om eventuell fellesfinansiering av ANC prosjekt (The question of Norwegian support for liberation movements in South Africa. Swedish enquiry regarding possible joint financing), 1. Political Affairs Division, 11 November 1976, MFA 34 9/5 IV.

[42] Ibid.

[43] Memorandum. Møte med representant for SACTU (Meeting with a representative for SACTU), 1. Political Affairs Division, 23 March 1977, MFA 34 9/5 V.

[44] Memorandum. Samtale med representanter for ANC i Lusaka (Consultation with representatives of the ANC in Lusaka), 27 May 1977, 1. Political Affairs Division, 8 June 1977, MFA 34 9/5 V.

well as for the transportation/subsistence project which SIDA was already supporting.[45]

When the decision was finally taken in the beginning of June, it did not take long before the ANC received a reaction to the request. As the project had been thoroughly assessed and was supported by Sweden, the Norwegian Foreign Ministry did not consider it necessary to make a detailed investigation of the project. In the middle of August the ANC was informed that the Foreign Ministry had allocated NOK 2 million for 1977 for the requested projects.[46]

Framework and procedures for the co-operation

After the decision to support the ANC had been made, a framework and procedures for the co-operation had to be developed. Through frequent meetings between the ANC and the Norwegian Foreign Ministry the two parties developed a close relationship. The experience Norway had gained through co-operation with other liberation movements, on the one hand, and the competence and professionalism of the ANC, on the other, contributed to making this an—in the circumstances—remarkably smooth process.

The assistance was based on annual negotiations between the ANC and the Foreign Ministry. Every year representatives of the Foreign Ministry visited Southern Africa and discussed strategy and requirements with the ANC's representatives and leadership. The Ministry was also kept informed about the co-operation through reports from the Norwegian resident representatives in Frontline States such as Zambia, Tanzania and Botswana, responsible for the implementation of the support. In the Foreign Ministry, it was the 1. Political Affairs Division, which administered the co-operation, and which considered the formal request before advising parliament on approval. ANC leaders also regularly visited the Foreign Ministry in Oslo for consultations.

In August 1977, the ANC suggested that the annual allocations be divided into quarterly payments in advance. When the support had been negotiated, and agreement reached on how to distribute the funds between the countries where the ANC took care of refugees, and for what purposes, the first tranche was to be released. The next would be released after the consulate in Lusaka or embassy in Dar es Salaam had received and approved the account of the utilisation of the money, together with vouchers. Revised audits for the whole year would also be presented. This system had been developed in co-operation with Sweden, whose experience with it

---

[45] Memorandum of the African National Congress of South Africa submitted to the Royal Norwegian government on 30 May, 1977 in Lusaka, Zambia. MFA 34 9/5 V.

[46] Res. rep. Per Tobiesen, Lusaka, to the ANC, 12 August 1977, MFA 34 9/5 VIII.

was good.[47] It was therefore also accepted by Norway for local procurements. The system for disbursements in countries where Norway did not have representation, like Swaziland and Botswana, was initially more complicated, as there Norway wanted pro forma vouchers from retailers before releasing the grant. This did, however, change after some years, as it proved to be too time-consuming and complicated.

It is an indication that Norway trusted the ANC to use the grants as agreed that the Foreign Ministry accepted the introduction of this system right from the start. None of the other liberation movements already receiving support from Norway received quarterly payments in advance in 1977.[48] With the ANC, this system worked relatively well through all the years of assistance, with only a few exceptions to confirm the rule. In some cases, for instance, vouchers disappeared after South African raids against ANC offices. In 1981 the ANC representative in Swaziland Stanley Mabizela, was arrested and put in jail by Swazi police, and accounting to NORAD suffered.

The Norwegian consul in Maputo, Arne Dahlen, pointed out later the same year that Norway had very little control over the use of the disbursements in Swaziland, and raised the question of whether Norwegian money could have been used for weapons, ammunition etc.[49] This worry was taken very seriously by the Foreign Ministry, whose representatives discussed the matter with the Swedish embassy in Maputo and representatives of the UNHCR, as well as with the ANC representations in Zambia, Tanzania, Mozambique and Swaziland. The allegations were categorically repudiated by the ANC Treasurer General, Thomas Nkobi, and nothing was found that could substantiate them. For one thing, Nkobi said, the ANC did not need to use Norwegian money for arms, as they were getting all the arms they needed from the Soviet Union and other socialist countries. Besides, the humanitarian support from Norway was of such vital importance, that the ANC would in no way risk doing anything that could jeopardise future assistance. South Africa would plant rumours of misuse, but they were untrue, Nkobi stated. After investigating the matter, the Foreign Ministry concluded that there was no reason to mistrust the ANC's use of the Norwegian financial support.[50] On a few later occasions in the 17 years of co-operation, worry was expressed over the accounting. In 1987, the person dealing with the ANC's accounts in Botswana was deported when he had a large number

---

[47] Tobiesen, Lusaka, to the MFA. ANC (SA) Anvendelse av norsk støtte for 1978 (The utilisation of Norwegian support for 1978), 22 November 1978, MFA, 34 9/5 XIII.

[48] Bjarte Erdal. Møte på representasjonens kontor (Meeting at the NORAD office), 30 August 1977, MFA 34 9/5 VII.

[49] Arne Dahlen to MFA, 171 December 1981, MFA 34 9/5 B II.

[50] Norwegian contribution to the ANC-Swaziland in 1981. Question of misuse of the funds (Norsk bidrag til ANC-Swaziland 1981. Spørsmål om misbruk av midlene), Bjarne Lindstrøm, 1. Political Affairs Division, MFA, 22 February 1982, MFA 34 9/5 B II.

of receipts in his possession.[51] In Maputo in 1988, the ANC was poorly staffed, and accounting suffered.[52] And in January 1989, the Foreign Ministry informed the ANC representative in Maputo that it was "becoming increasingly concerned with the manner in which the ANC is treating the financial book-keeping and planning".[53] Therefore no further payments could be made until satisfactory records of expenditures were presented. When the accounts were presented, they were of such a nature that it created a discussion in the Foreign Ministry on the difficulties of having thorough control of the use of the funds. Misuse was, however, not discovered.

The Foreign Ministry did take some important precautions regarding the disbursements. The parliamentary decision still prevented Norway from giving support to the ANC inside South Africa for "home front activities", despite repeated requests for such assistance. It would also have been very difficult to control the use of funds disbursed in South Africa. In addition to this restriction, the Ministry decided that the international procurements had to be handled through NORAD in Oslo, and not, as the ANC wished, through its own office in London.[54] Sweden accepted that the ANC itself administered the buying of items internationally, and had no serious problems with documentation and control of the purchases.[55] Because of this, the Norwegian consulate in Lusaka also recommended that Norway follow the same principle. The Ministry, however, decided against this, to be on the safe side with regard to control routines.[56]

The allocation for 1977 was planned to be divided equally between the SOMAFCO school project in Mazimbu and transport and subsistence for refugees.[57] Due to considerable delays in the Mazimbu project, the ANC had problems using the allocated funds for 1977, 1978 and 1979 as agreed. It is a sign of the good relations that developed that this did not lead the Foreign Ministry to recommend that the allocation for the ANC be cut down. It just stated that the money should be used "within reasonable time".[58] The diffi-

---

[51] ANC Botswana, to NORAD, Gaborone, 5 October 1987, MFA 34 9/5 B 23.

[52] Arthus Sydnes, the Norwegian consulate in Maputo to MFA, MFA 34 9/5 B 26.

[53] NORAD representative Nils Vogt to Kingsley Xuma, 27 January 1998, MFA 34 9/5 B 29.

[54] Niels L. Dahl to MFA. Møte med ANC (SA)-ledelsen (Meeting with the ANC (SA)-leadership), 23 March 1979, MFA 34 9/5 IX.

[55] Interview with Roland Axelsson in Tor Sellström (ed.): *Liberation in Southern Africa. Regional and Swedish Voices*. Uppsala: Nordiska Afrikainstitutet, 1999.

[56] Memorandum. Norsk støtte til frigjøringsorganisasjonen ANC (S-A) (Norwegian support to the Liberation Movement ANC (S-A)), 1. Political Affairs Division, MFA, 9 January 1979, MFA 34 9/5 IX.

[57] As discussed 300877 with Secretary General Alfred Nzo, Treasurer General Thomas Nkobi, Project Secretary Mohammed Moosajee and Project Co-ordinator Jimmy Phambo.

[58] Memorandum. Norsk bistand til frigjøringsbevegelsene i det sørlige Afrika for 1979 (Norwegian support for the liberation movements in Southern Africa 1979), 1. Political Affairs Division, MFA, 20 July 1979, MFA 34 9/5 X.

culties in implementing the Mazimbu project stemmed from construction
and supply problems, as well as adverse climatic conditions. To help in carrying out the plans for Mazimbu, the ANC requested Norway for expert
assistance for this project, in addition to the financial assistance.[59]

Despite the ANC having problems with the implementation in
Mazimbu, the Ministry argued that it would be politically unfortunate to cut
down the allocation, as the ANC's activities were increasing with rising ten-
sions in South Africa. But as there were delays in getting the SOMAFCO
project started, the Ministry could on the other hand not recommend an increase in the allocations. In addition to the direct support, the ANC was also
receiving support which was allocated by the Ministry, but implemented by
Norwegian NGOs.[60]

During the first years of support, the framework and routines for the co-
operation were established, and the relationship between Norway and the
ANC became close. The Ministry was satisfied with the ANC's administration, as is shown by the comment after having received the request for 1983
that it "as usual" was "well-documented and clearly set out".[61] Discussions
between the two were open and frank, and the system with payments in advance functioned well. The Foreign Ministry was kept well informed by the
ANC both regarding the strategy for the struggle and the plans for taking
care of the refugees. Over the years, some problems naturally arose in the
co-operation. In the late 1980s, the administrative capacity of the ANC got
strained, and communications with Norway suffered. And the ANC was not
happy about Norway ending the co-operation with the private Norwegian
consultancy firm NORPLAN. Still it is safe to say, that bearing in mind the
difficulties facing the co-operation, in general it was very close and well
functioning.

The Norwegians appreciated the co-operation with the ANC, and vice
versa. The ANC also valued the "all-round assistance" the Norwegian government was "consistently" giving "in the international community, particularly in the United Nations".[62]

---

[59] Tor Elden, Lusaka to the embassy in Dar es Salaam, 26 March 1979, MFA 34 9/5 IX.

[60] Memorandum. Fordeling av bistand til frigjøringsbevegelsene i det sørlige Afrika for 1980
(Distribution of support to the liberation movements in Southern Africa), 1. Political Affairs
Division, 21 August 1980, MFA 34 9/5 XII.

[61] Memorandum. Humanitær bistand til Frigjøringsbevegelsene i det sørlige Afrika. Fordeling
av 1983-bevilgningene (Humanitarian support for the liberation movements in Southern Africa.
Distribution of the 1983 allocations), 28 February 1983, 1. Political Affairs Division, MFA 34 9/5
B IV.

[62] Treasurer General T.T. Nkobi to Res. Rep. Tor Elden, Lusaka, 11 December 1980, MFA 34 9/5
XIII. The Norwegian support given in the international community, such as the UN, will only
be discussed to a small extent in the present study.

Maintenance of refugees

In large, the financial assistance was divided between providing daily necessities for refugees under the care of the ANC and in the planning, construction and maintenance of the refugee settlements in Mazimbu and Dakawa. In total, the direct support from Norway to the ANC amounted to more than NOK 400 million.[63] The majority of this, went to the development and maintenance of Mazimbu and Dakawa.

The assistance for the upkeep of refugees involved providing necessities such as food, clothes, medicines and transport for people under the care of the ANC in Angola, Botswana, Lesotho, Mozambique, Swaziland, Tanzania, Zambia and Zimbabwe.

Up to 1986, the negotiations regarding the support were held in the beginning of the year for which it was to be allocated. The time it then took for the ANC to submit the request, for the Foreign Ministry to consider it and the parliament to approve of the general size of the grant, had as a result that the funds were not ready to be disbursed before March or April in the year for which they were allocated. As the budget year coincided with the calendar year, this delay led to difficulties. The Ministry therefore changed this in 1986 so that the negotiations were held in the autumn of the year preceeding the year under discussion, to make it possible to deal with the request in time for the funds to be disbursed from the beginning of the year.

The Norwegian embassies and consulates in Southern Africa were responsible for approval of external orders before these were forwarded to the Ministry in Oslo. As the number of refugees, and the size of the support, grew, the administration of procurements became too extensive for the Norwegian representatives. In 1985, the chargé d'affaires in Harare, Knut Vollebæk, therefore suggested that the Ministry engaged a non-governmental organisation, such as the Norwegian People's Aid, NPA, to take care of the practicalities in connection with the procurements.[64]

The idea was accepted by the Ministry, but instead of the NPA it engaged the consultancy firm NORPLAN to administer the non-local procurements for refugees in Tanzania. NORPLAN had already been engaged in 1978 as consultant in the planning and construction of Mazimbu, and in 1983 was engaged directly by the Foreign Ministry to implement planned projects. NORPLAN administered and led the construction works of infrastructure such as roads, water and electricity. From the beginning of 1984, NORPLAN also became involved in the planning of Dakawa, and from the beginning of 1986 was also engaged by the Ministry to administer non-local

[63] See Statistical Appendix for details.
[64] Knut Vollebæk , Harare, to the MFA, 29 October 1985, MFA 34 9/5 B XV.

procurements, both equipment for the building and construction, and "daily necessities" for the refugees.[65]

The lists of items to be procured still had to be approved by the embassy in Dar es Salaam. Through NORPLAN, the Ministry also funded technical expertise for planning, supervising and co-ordinating the construction works in the settlements.[66]

As a result of disagreements with the Foreign Ministry, NORPLANs contract was terminated at the end of 1987. Instead a comprehensive co-operation agreement was signed with the Norwegian People's Aid, NPA, where the NPA from January 1988 took over responsibility for the implementation of the Norwegian direct assistance to the ANC (and the PAC) in Tanzania, Zimbabwe and other countries, as and when requested by the ANC. The Ministry still conducted annual negotiations with the ANC and prepared the guidelines concerning the funds. It was then the responsibility of the NPA to observe these. As executing agency in the implementation of the support, the NPA acted on behalf of the Ministry, setting up the yearly budget, preparing time schedules for procurements and payments, conducting negotiations and signing agreements with contractors for building projects. The NPA was chosen for this, as it already had an established relationship with the ANC. From 1979 it had carried out health training courses for students coming from the ANC and SWAPO. Based on this experience, the NPA built up a health training centre in Viana, Angola. With support from the Foreign Ministry, and in co-operation with the ANC, in 1986 the NPA engaged an administrator for the health division of the Viana transit camp. The NPA involvement in the health sector also included providing a health training instructor for Viana and support for the ANC's Health Department, as well as supplying the ANC with ambulances in Angola and Zambia. From 1985, the NPA also started constructing emergency houses in Dakawa.

The ANC still protested against NORPLAN's role being reduced, and the NPA becoming executing agency in the Norwegian assistance to the development of Mazimbu and Dakawa and in the procurement of equipment and commodities in general. The ANC felt that the NPA "lacked the necessary experience, and tended to sacrifice speed and efficiency in a misplaced wish to source materials locally".[67] The ANC was afraid that the NPA lacked the wide range of expertise needed for overall guidance of the infrastructural development.[68]

---

[65] Tore Johnsen, NORPLAN, 28 October 1988, Summary of history (Historisk sammendrag). MFA 34 9/5 B 27.

[66] MFA/ NPA/ ANC workshop "ANC development centre, Dakawa" 27–28 April. ANC Submission, s. 6. MFA 34 9/5 B 29.

[67] Sean Morrow: "Dakawa Development Centre: an African National Congress settlement in Tanzania, 1982–1992", *African Affairs*, No. 389, 1998, p. 518.

[68] MFA/ NPA/ ANC workshop "ANC development centre, Dakawa" 27–28 April. ANC Submission, s. 6. MFA 34 9/5 B 29.

After a year as executing agency, the NPA was of the opinion that the relationship and co-operation between the NPA and the ANC was very good. Despite some different points of view regarding the various projects, agreement had been reached on the final solutions.[69] It did, however, point at difficulties stemming from the fact that the ANC was "not primarily developed to work with technical matters" and felt that "the ANC must try get a more stable workforce and fill vacant positions in the administration in Dakawa with qualified personnel".[70] The Norwegian Ambassador in Dar es Salaam, Gunnar Garbo, in 1989 also expressed concern about the administration of the settlements. According to agreements, it was the ANC's responsibility to organise the maintenance of these. If they were unable to organise it themselves, then they were responsible for requesting external assistance. The embassy was worried that this was not being done.[71]

As a consequence of the close co-operation with the NPA from 1988, the ANC to a much larger degree than before also received administrative and management training.[72] This was needed especially as the growth in the number of refugees and the complexity of the projects from the mid-1980s strained the administrative capacity of the ANC.

Towards the end of the 1980s, Norway also directly supported the ANC administration, through funding the ANC office in Norway and participating in funding of the ANC office in Dar es Salaam. Assistance was also given for fellowships and scholarships and for cultural activities and the Department of Information and Publicity.[73]

Mazimbu and SOMAFCO

In exile large numbers of young people who had fled South Africa contacted the ANC for support and training. In Mazimbu the ANC developed a settlement where children and youth received education at the Solomon Mahlangu Freedom College (SOMAFCO) in preparation for returning to a democratic South Africa. SOMAFCO was a response to the need for providing them with education to "create skilled and politically conscious people who would move into crucial positions in a future liberated South Africa and infuse the country with the ideas of the Freedom Charter."[74]

---

[69] Norwegian People's Aid-Tanzania: *Annual Report 1988.*

[70] Secretary General Odd Wivegh and Project Officer Svein O. Lie to 1. Political Affairs Division, 13 September 1989, MFA 34 9/5 B 30.

[71] Gunnar Garbo to the MFA, 8 February 1989. MFA, 34 9/5 28.

[72] Annual consultations Royal Norwegian government /NPA and the ANC, 18 November 1987. The Mayibuye archives: ANC-Lusaka Secretary General, Office of the Treasurer General 1984–1991 (60.1–60.5).

[73] Agreed minutes between the African National Congress (ANC) and the Norwegian Ministry of Foreign Affairs (MFA) held in Oslo 17 October 1989. MFA 34 9/5 B 30.

[74] Sean Morrow, op.cit., p. 499.

After the initial problems, the development of SOMAFCO and the Mazimbu settlement went well. With the help of foreign donors, the ANC in Mazimbu also created institutions such as a large farm, a hospital, kindergarten, and primary and nursery schools. The settlement at Mazimbu also included agricultural projects, cultural and sports facilities, production of furniture and clothes, as well as extensive housing. Ultimately, the South African population in Mazimbu numbered around 3 500 people.[75]

From 1977, the first year of Norwegian support, a large part of the allocation was ear-marked for Mazimbu. Over the following years, Norway played a major role in the development of the settlement, being responsible for planning and building constructions such as a children's centre, primary school, hospital and administration block, as well as infrastructure such as water and sewage systems, and roads and bridges. Norway also provided part of the running expenses for Mazimbu.

Norway gave such substantial support to the Mazimbu settlement, as it was well organised and clearly covered a need. The growing number of refugees also increased the need for the settlement. These projects were seen as being "politically safe"; education was "right on target" for the Norwegian humanitarian support for the liberation movements. In addition to this, the danger of misuse of funds was minimal, as it was Norwegian firms that planned and implemented most of the projects.[76] In 1981, the total assistance to the ANC was NOK 3.5 million. Of this, NOK 2 million went to SOMAFCO, while NOK 500,000 went to care and maintenance of refugees in Botswana, and the same amount for refugees in Swaziland and Zambia. In the beginning of 1982, senior executive officer Bjarne Lindstrøm visited Mazimbu, and was impressed with what he described as "more of a well adjusted village" than a camp. He was convinced that the need for support was great, especially for materials for the construction and teachers and educational material for the schools.

When considering a request for NOK 7.1 for providing water and sewage systems in the settlement, in 1982 the Ministry stated that the "ANC's Morogoro project undoubtedly is the most successful project that the liberation movements in Southern Africa have implemented." As this "model project" to a large extent was planned and designed by Nordic architects and engineers, was run in an excellent way, and the carrying out would be left to a Norwegian entrepreneur firm with experience from Tanzania, Noremco, the request was granted.[77]

---

[75] Ibid.

[76] Memorandum. ANC Tanzania. Besøk i Mazimbu og Dakawa (Visit to Mazimbu and Dakawa), Bjarne Lindstrøm, 31 January 1984, MFA 34 9/5 B VII.

[77] Memorandum. The ANC's Morogoro-project in Tanzania. Sewage and water supply (ANCs Morogoro-prosjekt i Tanzania. Vannforsyning og kloakkavløp), 21 December 1982, 1. Political Affairs Division, MFA 34 9/5 B IV.

This good impression was confirmed when Gisle Mjaugedal from NORAD's representation in Tanzania visited the settlement in 1984. "Skilful, well-informed and hard working" people were running a "model project, marked by order, diligence and beauty". The efforts made by the refugees themselves, who numbered 1 500 at the time of the visit, were especially appreciated.[78]

People were working everywhere, trees were being planted along good roads, simple, but solid houses had been planned and built by the ANC themselves. The schools were busy, a library and an assembly hall were under construction. In the carpentry and sewing workshops people were busy, and in the agricultural projects chickens and eggs, pigs and crops were produced. Machines and equipment were well maintained, and water and electricity were in working order. Mjaugedal reported to the Foreign Ministry that he was impressed with the ANC's ability to run a refugee camp and make good use of the support.[79]

Some critical voices were, however, also raised about the way Mazimbu developed. The resident representative of the Norwegian Refugee Council in Nairobi, Thor Stegne, raised the question of whether it was wise to isolate the ANC refugees in a model town removed from the realities in the host country. Was this a good way to prepare them for the society they would meet when returning to South Africa?[80] To this, the Ministry replied that the main reason why Mazimbu was functioning so well, was largely due to the ability of the ANC refugees to plan and carry out their projects themselves.[81] Stegne responded that considering the size of the investments, and the fact that the projects were led by a strong, experienced organisation such as the ANC, he did not find it surprising that the result was good. That was exactly why the country giving asylum ought to benefit more. In Mazimbu, the ANC refugees had a higher standard of living than the Tanzanians, and this led to conflicts, Stegne argued. This was especially critical in a country where equality was a leading political objective.[82] The Mazimbu complex relied heavily on Tanzanian labour, and Stegne criticised the degree to which Tanzanians were engaged to do large parts of the productive work. He was not alone in raising this question. ANC's Treasurer General Thomas Nkobi in 1983 firmly stated that Dakawa should not become like Mazimbu, where "80% of the people actively engaged in developing the complex are Tanzanians. This is not acceptable."[83]

---

[78] Memorandum. Fra besøk i ANC's flyktningeleirer ... (From a visit to the ANC's refugee camps in Mazimbu and Dakawa), Gisle Mjaugedal, 18 December 1984, MFA 34 9/5 B XII.

[79] Ibid.

[80] Thor Stegne to the Norwegian Refugee Council, 24 May 1985, MFA 34 9/5 B XII.

[81] Bjarne Lindstrøm to the Norwegian Refugee Council, 26 April 1985, MFA 34 9/5 B XII.

[82] Thor Stegne to the Norwegian Refugee Council, 24 May 1985, MFA 34 9/5 B XII.

[83] As quoted in Sean Morrow: op. cit., p. 507.

In addition to the critique regarding the lack of integration of refugees into the Tanzanian society, Stegne also criticised the use of resources and technology chosen by NORPLAN. The Ministry's response to this was that it was the ANC which had requested the consultancy of NORPLAN, and that the plans for the camp had been made in close co-operation with the ANC.

Two Norwegian volunteers in 1988 also criticised the fact that the refugees in the ANC settlements had a much higher standard of living than the Tanzanians surrounding the camps, and that they were not encouraged to do their own productive work. In their opinion, the nine donor countries represented in Mazimbu had to take part of the responsibility for not adequately co-ordinating their support. More attention should be given to developing the leadership of the settlement, and less to providing basic necessities, they argued.[84]

SOMAFCO was formally opened in August 1985, and played a very important role in taking care of young South Africans, and providing them with education.

Dakawa Development Centre

Before the Mazimbu settlement had been completed, it became clear that it could not provide room for all the ANC refugees that were coming to Tanzania. In 1982 a site of 2 800 hectares was allocated by the Tanzanian government in Dakawa, 60 km away from Mazimbu, to meet the increasing need for providing the growing exiled community of South Africans with accommodation, as well as educational, health, cultural and recreational facilities. The Dakawa Development Centre was conceived as a model that would serve as an example for community development projects in democratic South Africa.

The centre also covered the need for a place where newly arrived young people could stay until they could be enrolled in school classes at SOMAFCO. The ANC decided to enrol students in classes at SOMAFCO only at the beginning of each school year, to avoid disrupting the ongoing school programme. At Dakawa, the Ruth First Education Orientation Centre was established to cater for those who came during the school year, until they could start their schooling at SOMAFCO. A Vocational Training Centre was also set up in Dakawa, and institutions that could provide for those newcomers that were not students, were established. Agricultural and small industry projects were initiated.

The development of Dakawa had very high priority for the ANC, and it was important to the ANC that Dakawa should be seen as a separate entity from Mazimbu. From 1984 it requested that the Norwegian assistance should be concentrated on the construction of this settlement. First of all, it

---

[84] Rune Bergh and Inger Eggen: Rapport om forholdene i Mazimbu (Report on the conditions in Mazimbu), 15 August 1988, MFA 34 9/5 B 27.

was imperative to the ANC that a proper, detailed feasibility study for Dakawa was made, to avoid "some of the deficiencies in planning we encountered in Mazimbu where we overlooked the necessity for such a study."[85] As the ANC was very content with NORPLAN's work, in 1984 it requested the Foreign Ministry to provide the funds for NORPLAN to carry out this study.[86]

NORPLAN produced a Development Plan for the Dakawa project, which covered all aspects of the settlement. This plan was adopted by the ANC with only minor alterations early in 1984. The ANC also wanted NORPLAN to make regulation plans for four villages, try out biological toilets, make plans for the school structure at the Dakawa project, and propose an organisational plan for the settlement. Especially the latter two were seen as interesting, as they would give Norway a chance to exercise considerable influence over the future modelling of the Dakawa project. It was anyhow noted that it could be seen as a vote of confidence that the ANC turned to Norway for such a vital task, rather than to countries in Eastern Europe.[87]

Thor Stegne was also critical of NORPLAN for designing Dakawa as an isolated urban community, with no exchange with the surrounding communities.[88] Although the embassy in Dar es Salaam saw it as important to respect the ANC's decisions with regard to defining what would ensure that exile became as meaningful as possible for the refugees, it also expressed the need for keeping an eye on the costs and choice of technology for Dakawa.[89]

From 1983 to 1987, NORPLAN was appointed overall consultant for the development of Dakawa. The construction works were carried out by the Norwegian/Tanzanian firm Noremco. A substantial amount of work was carried out by contractors, donor agencies and the ANC itself.

When the NPA took over the responsibility in January 1988, it chose to continue using NORPLAN as consultants. As the development of Mazimbu was seen as having been successful, it was also easier to find other interested donors for the implementation of projects in Dakawa than it had initially been for Mazimbu.

Dakawa was planned for a population of 5,000, but did not grow to the dimensions envisaged. In 1990 the South Africans there numbered approximately 1,200. Despite this, and despite everything not working out as planned with regard to construction and maintenance, "the building of a

---

[85] Thomas T. Nkobi to Foreign Minister S. Stray, 29 September 1983, MFA 34 9/5 B VII.

[86] Ibid.

[87] Memorandum. Bistand til ANC (Support for the ANC), 1. Political Affairs Division, MFA, 18 April 1984, MFA 34 9/5 B VIII.

[88] Thor Stegne to the Norwegian Refugee Council, 24 May 1985, MFA 34 9/5 B XII.

[89] Ola Dørum to MFA, 9 May 1985, MFA 34 9/5 B XII.

functioning settlement in this very difficult environment was a remarkable achievement."[90]

The Dakawa Art and Craft Project was transferred from Tanzania to Grahamstown, South Africa, in October 1992. In his opening speech Deputy President in the ANC Walter Sisulu said that the "Dakawa Art and Craft Project is in its own right (...) a monument to the close ties of friendship and solidarity between the peoples of Sweden, Norway, Tanzania and South Africa. It is a symbol of our common hatred for the system of apartheid." The project, which had been established in Tanzania to provide stimulation and creative activity for ANC exiles in that country, was now meant to provide badly needed skills in an area where unemployment was rife and thus epitomise the ANC's desire to democratise its culture.[91]

The ANC conference at Gran, Hadeland

The National Executive Committee of the ANC arranged in March 1989 a strategy meeting for the ANC diplomatic service (chief representatives and regional treasurers), to review the situation in South and Southern Africa and assess its implications for the international diplomatic and political work of the ANC. The conference took place at Gran, not far from Oslo. It was hosted by the International Solidarity Committee of the Norwegian Labour Movement and the Norwegian government, and opened by the Foreign Minister Thorvald Stoltenberg. The Norwegian assistance for the meeting was described by Secretary General Alfred Nzo as being "yet another milestone in the development of our relations".[92] In a closing address the representative of the Foreign Ministry, Øystein Mjaaland, stated that the privilege of having been included in the ANC's internal deliberations was regarded by the Ministry as "a sign of friendship, and we want to be your friends."[93]

To conclude this brief overview, the South African Minister of Housing, ANC's Sankie Mthembi-Mahanyele could be quoted. In an interview in 1995 she said:

> They believed in us and we really appreciated that. After the unbanning of ANC, we were also lucky to receive some diplomatic training in Norway. A group of us went there to be exposed to foreign affairs' issues, because at that time we were running ANC missions all over the world. We were taken for a special course, funded by the Nordic countries, but led by the Norwegian government. (...)We were now operating at a different level, because we were getting into things like Norwegian trade, foreign policy options for Norway, NATO and the future vision of Norway towards the European continent. We

---

[90] Sean Morrow: op. cit., p. 502.

[91] *Eastern Province Herald*, 19 October 1992.

[92] Report from the conference. Mayibuye archives: ANC–Lusaka Secretary General, Office of the Treasurer General 1984–1991 (60.1–60.5).

[93] Ibid.

were engaging at a different level. We were dealing with policy issues. It was not just humanitarian assistance, but a package of how to move forward, getting exposure to how governments work and run their business. We had done a similar course at the European Union, but there was something specific that we received from Norway, namely aspects of communication. It was because of our close friendship with that country. [94]

The Co-operation with the PAC

The reasons for support

It was obvious that if support was to be given to a South African liberation movement, it should be given to the ANC, as this was the South African peoples' leading organisation and well respected internationally. It is not quite as easy to understand why Norway also decided to support the PAC. In the end of the 1970s, the PAC was torn by internal problems, questions were raised about its ideology being anti-white, the organisation only took care of a small number of refugees, and it had little support internationally. The ANC repeatedly argued against Norwegian support for the PAC, disputing both its strategy and representativity. In the democratic elections in South Africa in 1994 and 1999 the PAC received 1.25% and 0.71 % of the votes. What motivated the Norwegian government to support this movement?

As part of the considerations on whether to propose that Norway start supporting liberation movements in South Africa, NORAD, at the request of the Foreign Ministry, in 1975 asked the embassy in Dar es Salaam for information. Having started by enquiring about the ANC, NORAD continued: "We know less about the other large resistance movement in South Africa, Pan Africanist Movement (sic.)"[95]—proving its point by exposing that it was not even quite sure about the name of the organisation. The gathering of information was not to be carried out in such a way that it could lead to expectations about support within the two movements.[96]

In September 1976, the 1. Political Affairs Division at the Foreign Ministry recommended that Norway in 1977 should start supporting the ANC, because of the ANC's broad base and the good Swedish experiences with the organisation.[97] It did not suggest that Norway start supporting the PAC.[98] A year later it did. What motivated this change?

---

[94] Sankie Mthembi-Mahanyele (aka Rebecca Matlou), ANC-administrative officer at the ANC mission to Sweden and the Nordic countries in Tor Sellström (ed.): *Liberation in Southern Africa. Regional and Swedish Voices*. Uppsala: Nordiska Afrikainstitutet, 1999.

[95] Svennevig to the Norwegian embassy, Dar es Salaam, 14 November 1975, MFA 34 9/5 IV.

[96] Svennevig to the Norwegian embassy, Dar es Salaam, 25 November 1975, MFA 34 9/5 IV.

[97] Norges bistand til frigjøringsbevegelsene i det sørlige Afrika. Disponeringsforslag for 1977 (Norway's support for liberation movements in Southern Africa. Proposal for 1977), 1. Political Affairs Division, 16 September 1976, MFA 34 9/5 VIII.

[98] Ibid.

In October 1976, PAC visited the Foreign Ministry, at the same time up-dating the Ministry on the organisation and requesting future Norwegian support. The PAC was informed about the restrictions in Norwegian policy, which at this time still excluded support for the South African liberation movements.[99] To more systematically prepare for a decision when these re-strictions were lifted, the Foreign Ministry started collecting information about the PAC. The need to know was further strengthened after the PAC submitted a formal request in May 1977, regarding support for a transit- and rehabilitation centre to be established in Tanzania.[100] Initially the Ministry was of the opinion that support for the PAC should be postponed until it had a better impression of the PAC's humanitarian work, but again turned to the embassy in Tanzania for information. It was particularly interested in learning how the government of Tanzania, the OAU Liberation Committee and the Swedish embassy in Tanzania viewed the PAC and the proposed project.[101]

Ambassador Per Nævdal gave an enthusiastic response to the Ministry: both the Tanzanian Foreign Ministry and the OAU Liberation Committee "were very positive" to the planned transit- and rehabilitation centre, which they thought was urgently needed. The UNHCR office in Dar es Salaam had visited the project together with a representative of the OAU Liberation Committee, and shared the view that it was well worth supporting. Accord-ing to Nævdal, the Swedish embassy had recommended Swedish support for the PAC centre.[102] Because of Sweden's long-established relations with the ANC, it was unlikely that the Swedish government would support the PAC in the foreseeable future. SIDA, however, did not rule out the possibility of a small amount being granted to the PAC already in 1977.[103] Through a copy of a letter from the Swedish embassy in Tanzania to the Foreign Ministry in Stockholm, the Norwegian Foreign Ministry learned that it "seemed to be obvious" that the PAC was making a "valuable contribution for South African nationalists in Tanzania", and that their financial responsibility had increased. The UNHCR also found their need for

---

[99] Samtale med representanter for den sør-afrikanske frigjøringsbeveglesen (Consultations with representatives for the South African liberation movement) Pan Africanist Congress of Azania (PAC), 1. Political Affairs Division, 13 October 1976, MFA 34 9/5 IV.

[100] Acting Treasurer General Mfanasekaya P. Gqobose to the Foreign Ministry, 3 May 1977, MFA 34 9/5 V.

[101] Tore H. Toreng to the embassy in Dar es Salaam. Søknad om støtte fra den sør-afrikanske frigjøringsbevegelse PAC (Request for support from the South African liberation movement PAC), 31 May 1977, MFA 34 9/5 V.

[102] Per Nævdal, Dar es Salaam to MFA. (Søknad om støtte fra den sør-afrikanske frigjørings-bevegelsen PAC) Request for support from (...) PAC, 10 June 1977, MFA 34 9/5 V.

[103] Memorandum. Norsk støtte i 1977 til frigjøringsbevegelsen i Sør-Afrika (Norwegian support for the liberation movement in South Africa), 5 July 1977, MFA 34 9/5 V. On Sweden, the ANC and the PAC, see Tor Sellström: *Sweden and National Liberation in Southern Africa. Vol. I: Formation of a Popular Opinion 1950–1970*, pp. 169–175 and 244–255. Uppsala: Nordiska Afrikainstitutet, 1999.

funding legitimate as they were taking care of 175 refugees in Tanzania. Although the ANC was better established, the PAC was also recognised by the OAU and it was "not ruled out that some kind of assistance to the PAC would contribute positively to the liberation of South Africa". The embassy recommended that assistance be given to the PAC—if not for anything else, to get to know the movement better.[104]

After having discussed the matter with the Tanzanian Foreign Ministry, the OAU Liberation Committee, the UNHCR and the Swedish embassy, Per Nævdal had "no scruples about recommending Norwegian support for the project."[105]

Against this background, the Ministry changed its position regarding support for the PAC in 1977, and recommended that the planned rehabilitation and transit centre in Tanzania should receive NOK 650,000. Due to the methodical and effective oppression of the South African regime, the Ministry found it hard to form a well-founded opinion of what role the PAC was playing in South Africa, but it did have reason to believe that its position as an organisation was weak. The Ministry did, however, believe that both the ANC and the PAC held a strong position in the hearts and minds of the African population in South Africa.[106] The humanitarian work the PAC was doing for South African refugees in Tanzania was in any case seen as valuable.

The first years of support: internal strife

The PAC benefited from the trust the Foreign Ministry had in the ANC by being granted the same kind of disbursement system as the ANC: quarterly payments in advance. In 1977, however, as decisions were taken late in the year, the whole allocation was disbursed at once. The planned centre in Tanzania then turned out to be delayed. The original plan had been to place this centre in Morogoro, near the ANC settlement. Due to disagreements between the PAC and the ANC, however, the Tanzanian government preferred to change the site. The centre was instead going to be put up in Pongwe, near Bagamoyo, where a site was put at the PAC's disposal at the beginning of 1978.

This not only postponed the PAC's plans, but also made the planned transit and rehabilitation centre three times as expensive—the Foreign Ministry was informed when Treasurer General and member of the Central Committee of the PAC, Mfanasekaya P. Gqobose, visited the Ministry in

---

[104] Per Lindström to the Swedish Foreign Ministry, 14 February 1977, MFA 34 9/5 V.

[105] Per Nævdal, Dar es Salaam to MFA. Søknad om støtte fra den sør-afrikanske frigjøringsbevegelsen PAC (Request for support from the South African Liberation Movement PAC), 10 June 1977, MFA 34 9/5 V.

[106] Memorandum. Pan-Africanist Congress (PAC), 1. Political Affairs Division, 4 October 1977, MFA 34 9/5 VII.

February 1978. The increased costs were also due to the building materials having to be imported, and to the fact that it was no longer planned to use the free labour of the PAC members. Norway was therefore requested to increase its support. To strengthen the application, the PAC informed the Ministry that the Students' and Academics' International Assistance Fund (SAIH) had agreed to contribute NOK 10,000 to this new project, which would take care of all South African refugees under the PAC's care in Tanzania, from 50 to 300 at a time.[107]

Shortly after the decision to grant the PAC support had been made, it became clear that there was increasing unrest within the organisation. At a meeting with Anna Runeborg from SIDA and Chargé d'Affaires Rolf W. Hansen at the Norwegian Embassy in Tanzania, Acting President Potlako Leballo confirmed that the PAC had great disciplinary problems with members in Dar es Salaam who had not been given grants to study in other countries, or been chosen for military training "in China and other African countries".[108] Leballo further argued that the problems stemmed from the lack of facilities to teach and train the refugees, who were young, bitter and frustrated about not being equipped and trained for fighting in South Africa. According to Leballo, theoretical training was needed, if these young people were to avoid "aimless terror actions, which would further polarise the situation and lead to a danger of a bloodbath in South Africa". Violent acts were not to be directed against white civilians, maintained Leballo, who was reported to have "made a good impression" on the Norwegian Chargé d'Affaires, who informed the Foreign Ministry in Oslo that Norwegian support to a transit- and rehabilitation centre could serve as a sensible contribution towards defusing disagreements.[109] According to Rolf W. Hansen in March 1978, there was "no doubt that the planned rehabilitation centre (would) be able to fill an important role for South African refugees in Tanzania." Norway's positive attitude should therefore be maintained.[110] On account of the doubts that had been raised about the PAC from the OAU Liberation Committee and others, it was, however, important to avoid Norway ending up as the only contributor to the centre. Too much money should in any case not be committed to the project for 1978, as it was uncertain when the projecting implementation could start. The Chargé d'Affaires instead suggested that the support for Namibia and Zimbabwe be

[107] Memorandum. Besøk i Oslo 23. februar av PAC-representant (Visit in Oslo 23 February by PAC representative), 27 February 1978, MFA 34 9/5 VII. SAIH was founded in 1961. Under the motto "education for liberation", it was closely involved with support to the anti-apartheid struggle from the early 1960s.

[108] Rolf W. Hansen, Chargé d'Affaires, Dar es Salaam to the MFA. Samtale med fungerende president i (Consultations with acting President of) the Pan African Congress, Potlako Leballo, 2 February 1978, MFA 34 9/5 VI.

[109] Ibid.

[110] Rolf W. Hansen, Chargé d'Affaires to the MFA, 14 March1978, MFA 34 9/5 VII.

increased.[111] This was supported by Ambassador Knut Thommessen [112] who argued that the liberation movements in Zimbabwe should have priority before those in South Africa. Of these, the ANC should be given much more than the PAC, which had had 35 persons in the camp when he had visited in June 1978 and did not, in his opinion, deserve particular support.[113]

The reason why there were so few PAC members in Tanzania at the time of Thommessen's visit was that most of the 500 refugees that allegedly had been under the care of the PAC early in the year had been sent out of the country, and new intakes had been stopped.[114] The reason for this, the embassy in Dar es Salaam was informed in March, was that what the PAC could offer the refugees was not satisfactory. Now there were only 60 refugees left in Tanzania under the care of the PAC and the internal strife had abated. The situation was under control. [115] This proved to be not quite the case. Accused of corruption, undemocratic leadership and of having built up his own private army, Leballo was one of those excluded by the PAC Central Committee in June 1978. The army was not brought under control, and the crisis culminated with the murder of the PAC's Director of Foreign Affairs David Sibeko in June 1979.

The way the organisation was functioning, together with accusations of misuse of NORAD funds and lack of proper accounting for the grants, made NORAD change the disbursement routines and introduce stricter control mechanisms in 1979. The allocations were no longer disbursed directly to the PAC, but to the suppliers, and only after pro forma vouchers had been presented.[116] Despite this, and the PAC not being able to use the whole grant for 1978, the support was not cut off, as it was still recognised by the OAU Liberation Committee. It was, however, halved from NOK 1 million in 1978 to NOK 500,000 in 1979. The PAC was informed that Norwegian support in the future depended on whether the organisation managed to get its problems sorted out, as well as the need for support.[117]

Norway gave the PAC initial help to start the transit and rehabilitation centre in Pongwe.[118] Visiting the Norwegian embassy in Dar es Salaam in January 1980, the PAC Chairman Vusile L. Make regretted that the grant

---

[111] Ibid.

[112] Knut Thommessen was Ambassador 1, at the disposal of the MFA for special commissions.

[113] Memorandum. Norsk hjelp til frigjøringsbevegelsene (Norwegian support for liberation movements), Knut Thommessen, 14 June 1978, MFA 34 9/4 VII.

[114] Memorandum. Besøk i Olso 23. februar av PAC representant (Visit in Oslo 23 February by representative of PAC), 1. Political Affairs Division, 27 February 1978, MFA 34 9/5 VII.

[115] Rolf W. Hansen, Chargé d'Affaires to MFA, 14 March 1978, MFA 34 9/5 VII.

[116] Memorandum. Norsk bistand til PAC for 1979 (Norwegian support for PAC in 1979), 1. Political Affairs Division, 12 September 1979, MFA 34 9/5 X.

[117] Ibid.

[118] Telex from the Norwegian delegation to the UN, 13 November 1978, with an account from a letter from Sibeko, MFA 34 9/5 VII.

from Norway had been reduced, but could understand the Norwegian authorities' need to see how the organisation was developing. The PAC was now on the right track, he said, and would soon regain the force and the international recognition that had been lost as a result of the showdown with Leballo and his supporters. As the PAC would now become more militarily active inside South Africa, their need for support would rise. And so, they hoped, would the Norwegian allocations. [119]

Information office in Oslo

In August 1977, the PAC had already opened an information office for the Nordic countries in Oslo, and at the same time similar offices were opened in Canada and Liberia. This was part of a strategy to strengthen the diplomatic part of the liberation struggle, which had been given urgency after Soweto. The first representative in the Nordic countries, Count Pietersen, and the PAC were happy about the "excellent reception" he had been given.[120] In a meeting with State Secretary Eskild Jensen at the Prime Minister's Office he was assured that the Norwegian authorities were happy about the establishment of the information office, which the Ministry hoped would contribute to greater understanding about the liberation movements in Africa.[121] To help find office premises, the Norwegian Foreign Ministry on the PAC's request also wrote a statement saying that Norway, like the OAU and the UN, acknowledged the PAC as a true representative of the South African people. [122] The other liberation movements in Southern Africa were already established in Stockholm. Pietersen also submitted a request to the Ministry for NOK 305,000 for the information office, and the PAC's Director of Foreign Affairs David Sibeko had in a letter to the Ministry confirmed that the Central Committee of the PAC supported the request.[123] It was, however, turned down. The PAC, like all the liberation movements, was given a part of the allocation in cash for administrative purposes. For 1978, this was 5%, or NOK 50,000, and this was used for the information office.

The PAC's internal problems and bad lines of communication are reflected in the requests for the information office in Oslo. According to

---

[119] Niels L. Dahl to MFA. Støtte til frigjøringsbevegelser. PAC (Support for liberation movements. PAC), 7 January 1980, MFA 94 9/5 XI.

[120] PAC to MFA, 8 November 1977, MFA 34 9/5 VII.

[121] Memorandum. Delegasjon fra den sør-afrikanske frigjøringsorganisasjonen PAC ... (Delegation from the South African liberation organisation PAC ...), Leonard Larsen, 5 October 1977, MFA 34 9/5 VII.

[122] Memorandum. Etablering av informasjonskontor for Norden i Oslo (Establishment of information office for the Nordic countries in Oslo), 1. Political Affairs Division, MFA, 24 August 1977, MFA, 34 9/5 VII.

[123] Telegram from Bjørnar Utheim, MFA to the Norwegian embassy in Dar es Salaam, 23 November 1978, MFA 34 9/5 VIII.

Mogale Mokgoatsane and Erret Radebe, responsible for respectively administration and finance at the PAC office in Dar es Salaam, Pietersen had never been authorised by the PAC to request the 305,000 for the Oslo office.[124] In 1979, the PAC closed the office.

The cold war context

The ANC received support from the Soviet Union, while the PAC was backed by China. This, of course, was the source of controversies of various kinds. Among Norway's allies in NATO and in conservative circles in Norway, there were those who believed in the allegations put forward by the apartheid regime, that the ANC was a pawn in the Soviet Union's fight for influence in Africa. Did Norway start supporting the PAC to be able to "prove" to these critics that the cold war context did not influence the choice of which liberation movements to support? By supporting both movements, it would be easier to focus on the ANC and the PAC being *nationalist* movements.

This might have been part of the consideration. But, in the late seventies, the Norwegian political party that caused the most concern to the political establishment was the Maoist *Arbeidernes Kommunistparti (m-l)* (The Workers' Communist Party) (AKP), while the Soviet-backed *Norges Kommunistiske Parti* (Norway's Communist Party) (NKP) had little support or influence. Through trade unions and other organisations, AKP achieved a far greater influence than their modest showing at the elections would imply. The party was, however, seen as being so extremist that very few in the political establishment would be associated with it. Doing anything that might be interpreted as support for the AKP would be extremely difficult for the Ministry. This can be illustrated by a handwritten note by State Secretary Thorvald Stoltenberg in connection with a visit by a PAC delegation in October 1977, just a few months after the decision to grant support had been made: if he and a colleague took the PAC delegation out for an informal dinner, he wrote, they could "manage to physically keep them away" from the AKP representatives until the programme and press conference were over.[125]

This was such a serious issue that Leballo the following summer assured representatives of the Ministry that Count Pietersen had been ordered not to "associate with" the AKP. [126]

---

[124] Rolf W. Hansen, Chargé d'Affaires, Dar es Salaam to MFA, 5 November 1978, MFA 34 9/5 VIII.

[125] Attachment to memorandum: Program for besøk i Norge av delegasjon fra Pan-Africanist Congress (Programme for visit by PAC delegation in Norway), 4–6 October 1977, MFA 34 9/5 VII.

[126] Memorandum. Thommessen og Utheims reise til (Thommessen and Utheim's trip to) Lusaka, Botswana, Mozambique og Tanzania ..., 21 May to 3 June 1978, MFA 34 9/5 VII.

The PAC regularly used the fact that the ANC received support from the Soviet Union as an argument against the organisation. To the Charge d'Affaires in Dar es Salaam, Leballo regretted the interference by the superpowers in African politics, which was expressed in the Soviet Union supporting the ANC, and China the PAC. The PAC would accept support from wherever it could get it, but did not want to be subject to any other regime, nor use them as models for the future South Africa. [127]

These assertions might have contributed to the good impression made on the embassy. Visiting the Foreign Ministry in February 1978, Treasurer General Mfanasekaya P. Gqobose assured the Ministry that the PAC was freer in its relationship with China than the ANC was with the Soviet Union. What the PAC wanted, he stated, was to build up an egalitarian society with the same possibilities and rights for all, irrespective of race.[128] When he was asked about the PAC's relationship with China, Gqobose answered that China did not wish to make the PAC a lackey, at the same time suggesting that the ANC was a tool for Soviet interests.[129] Or, as Leballo once put it: "The PAC believes in socialism, not in communism like the ANC does".[130]

There is nothing in the available material to substantiate that the cold war context was part of the consideration in the Ministry regarding whom to support in South Africa. The figures for the support given to the ANC and the PAC from 1977 and all through the 1980s, more than indicate that the Ministry did not worry about the Soviet support for the ANC. The ANC, however, took seriously the question of repudiating allegations that it was a Marxist organisation controlled by the Soviet Union. Being a NATO member, this certainly would have made it very difficult for Norway to give its support. However, the ANC observer delegate to the UN, Johnny Makatini can be said to have presented a rather special interpretation when he assured the Norwegian ambassador Ålgård that "the support received from the Soviet Union was minimal compared to the support that was received from Norway and other Western countries".[131] He might, however, have referred to the fact that the support from the Nordic countries significantly contributed to repudiating the claim that the liberation struggle was an East-West issue, when he also stated that "the Norwegian contribution was of essential political significance". [132]

---

[127] Rolf W. Hansen. Chargé d'Affaires, Dar es Salaam to MFA. Samtale med fungerende president i (Consultations with acting President in) Pan Africanist Congress, Potlako Leballo, 2 February 1978, MFA 34 9/5 VI.

[128] Memorandum. Besøk i Oslo 23. februar av PAC representant (Visit to Oslo 23 February by PAC representative), 1. Political Affairs Division, 27 February 1978, MFA 34 9/5 VII.

[129] Ibid.

[130] Memorandum. Thommessen og Utheims reise til (Thommessen and Utheim's trip to) Lusaka, Botswana, Mozambique og Tanzania ..., 21 May to 3 June 1978, MFA 34 9/5 VII.

[131] Nordun, telex to the MFA, 8 November 1978, MFA 34 9/5 VII.

[132] Ibid.

The decision to also grant support to the PAC seems to have been the result of a combination of limited knowledge, positive recommendations received for the PAC project from the embassy in Tanzania, and Norway choosing to be on the safe side by supporting both organisations that were recognised by the OAU and the UN.

Reactions to the PAC support

It was not just the PAC that unfavourably characterised the ANC. It was also the other way round. The ANC was outspoken on the question of Norwegian support for the PAC, and regularly recommended the Foreign Ministry to cut this off.[133]

A week after the PAC had been in Norway with a delegation in October 1977 Sobizana Mngqikana and Indres Naidoo visited the Ministry and informed them about ANC activities outside and inside South Africa. At the same time they categorically repudiated the claim that the PAC was actively engaged in political or refugee work. Instead various factions within the PAC were opposing each other. In Africa, only Tanzania had recognised the PAC, they declared. The ANC saw the struggle not as being between black and white, but between oppressor and oppressed, and was recognised by all the frontline states.[134] The PAC, on the other hand, was said to have "a touch of racism".[135]

In addition, the ANC in March 1979 informed the Foreign Ministry that they viewed the PAC leadership as "corrupt and without support in South Africa", and that the money was not used according to agreements. Norway should therefore not support the PAC.[136]

The ANC kept up its critique of the PAC until the democratic elections in 1994. In 1988, Oliver Tambo was interviewed by Norway's major conservative newspaper, *Aftenposten* (where the trade union in 1984 received two ANC students for four months of graphic training). Being otherwise very positive to the Norwegian contribution to the liberation struggle, he raised one single criticism: Norwegian support for the PAC.[137]

While the PAC's major criticism of the ANC was that it had a close relationship to the Soviet Union, the ANC criticised the PAC for what it was and

---

[133] Memorandum. Norsk støtte til frigjøringsorganisasjonen (Norwegian support for the liberation movement) ANC (S-A), 1. Political Affairs Division, MFA, 9 January 1979, MFA 34 9/5 IX.

[134] Notat. Samtale med representanter for den sør-afrikanske frigjøringsorganisasjonen ANC hos statssekretæren (Memorandum. Consultations with representatives of the South African liberation organisation ANC at the office of the State Secretary), 12 October 1977, 1. Political Affairs Division, 31 October 1977, MFA 34 9/5 VII.

[135] Reddy Mazimba to R.W. Hansen. Chargé d'Affaires, Dar es Salaam, 6 February 1978, MFA 34 9/5 VI.

[136] Niels L. Dahl to MFA. Møte med ANC (SA) ledelsen (Meeting with the ANC leadership), 23 March 1979, MFA 34 9/5 IX.

[137] *Aftenposten*, 17 March 1988.

was not doing. In the 1980s, the PAC only rarely criticised the ANC in meetings with the Foreign Ministry. Instead, in a number of meetings with the Ministry it expressed the hope that the two organisations would co-operate, but this was met with little interest from the ANC.

The crisis in the PAC in the late 1970s further weakened its position. From various quarters, the organisation was accused of misuse of funds, lack of strategy for the struggle for a democratic South Africa, and lack of activity inside the country. At the beginning of 1978, SIDA programme officer Anna Runeborg informed the Norwegian embassy in Dar es Salaam that Laban Oyaka, Assistant Executive Secretary in the OAU Liberation Committee, was negative towards the PAC. When Oyaka had "learnt that Norway had granted 650,000 to the PAC's transit centre, he expressed worry over this" because of the PAC's internal conflicts. Chargé d'Affaires Rolf W. Hansen at the Norwegian embassy defended the PAC: the OAU criticism lacked nuance, as it did not take into consideration the fact that the PAC, contrary to the ANC, up till then had not had a reception centre for their members in Tanzania: "It seems to be a fact that the bad offer that the PAC members have so far had in Tanzania has been a major cause for the internal conflicts that have occurred".[138] After a consultation with director Mwasakafyuka in the Tanzanian Foreign Ministry a couple of months later, Hansen did, however, report back to Oslo that Mwasakafyuka advised Norway to choose a very careful line and preferably refrain from extending direct support to the PAC until the situation became clearer.[139]

In March 1979, Ambassador Niels L. Dahl reported to Oslo that he had meetings with UNHCR's resident representative in Dar es Salaam, Mr. Chefeke, who had lost confidence in the PAC. Many of the best people there had been excluded in 1978. Chefeke regretted that in 1977 Norway transferred funds directly to the PAC, such that control opportunities were lost. The former Treasurer General in the PAC, Mfanasekaya P. Gqobose, who according to Chefeke was an honest person, had disagreed with Leballo and other leaders on using the Norwegian grant for 1977 earmarked for Pongwe for other purposes, and had therefore been excluded. One result of this would be that it would be very difficult to find out what the allocation had actually been used for. The UNHCR representative stressed that it was important not to give the PAC money directly, but give it to suppliers against pro forma invoices.[140]

Leballo was removed from office in May 1979, and the strong internal controversies continued. Both from Sweden and from the UNHCR, the Ministry was warned against extending direct support to the PAC. Yet Norway

---

[138] Rolf W. Hansen, Chargé d'Affaires, Dar es Salaam to MFA: Synspunkter på PAC fra OAUs frigjøringskomite (Views on PAC from the OAU Liberation Committee), 7 February 1978, MFA 34 9/5 VII.

[139] Rolf W. Hansen to MFA, 4 May 1978, MFA 34 9/5 VII.

[140] Niels L. Dahl to MFA, 14 March 1979, MFA 34 9/5 IX.

was not alone in its support: the Dutch, the UNDP, and UNHCR had also allocated funds for the transit and rehabilitation camp in Pongwe.[141]

The uncertainties with regard to the PAC were also confirmed by a "high level" representative in the Tanzanian Foreign Ministry, who, according to Ambassador Dahl, had not minced his words in his criticism of the PAC leadership: "They are all a bunch of crooks who think of nothing else than how to enrich themselves."[142] The source at the embassy had "carefully suggested" that Norway perhaps should reconsider its support for the PAC.[143]

After a couple of years of co-operation with the PAC, the Foreign Ministry in August 1980 had its doubts about whether it was right to support the organisation. As in the year before, internal conflicts in the organisation led the Ministry to consider cutting off support. This was, however, found to be too "politically unfortunate". The Ministry therefore recommended that the allocation be kept at the same level as 1979, NOK 500,000, in the hope that the active work that Tanzania's government was doing to re-establish the PAC as a serious organisation would succeed.[144]

The relationships between the Norwegian Foreign Ministry and the two South African liberation movements supported at the beginning of the 1980s were thus very different. When they started, the Ministry did not know either very well, but chose to share the recognition given to both by the OAU and the UN. In the first three years of co-operation, the Ministry had lost most of its faith in the PAC. The level of support had decreased and strict disbursement and control routines were established. At the beginning of the 1980s, uncertainty marked the relationship between the PAC and the Norwegian Foreign Ministry.

The 1980s: maintenance of refugees and a road to Ruwu

After John Pokella had become Chairman of the PAC in 1981, internal conflicts in the organisation no longer caused serious problems for the co-operation with Norway. When Pokella died in 1985, Johnson Mlambo was unanimously elected new Chairman by the PAC Central Committee. Although the Norwegian support was very small compared to that for SWAPO or the ANC, it was important to the PAC, both financially and politically, as it was

---

[141] Notat. Norsk bistand til frigjøringsbevegelsene i det sørlige Afrika for 1979 (Memorandum. Norwegian support for the liberation movements in Southern Africa for 1979), 1. Political Affairs Division, MFA, 20 July 1979, MFA 34 9/5 X.

[142] Niels L. Dahl to MFA, 31 July 1979, MFA, 34 9/5 X.

[143] Ibid.

[144] Notat. Fordeling av bistand til frigjøringsbevegelsene i det sørlige Afrika for 1980 (Memorandum. Distribution of support to liberation movements in Southern Africa for 1980), 1. Political Affairs Division, MFA, 21 August 1980, MFA, 34 9/5 XII.

the only support that was received on a regular basis.[145] In total, it amounted to less than NOK 25 million from 1977 to 1990.[146] Other governments that gave direct support, although irregularly, were Yugoslavia, China and Finland, the PAC informed Norwegian Chargé d'Affaires Dag Mjaaland in 1985.[147]

Norwegian support for the maintenance of refugees under the care of the PAC was used for items such as food, soap, medicine and transport, supplied under strict control, and to a large extent bought through NORAD's procurement office in Oslo. In 1984, the PAC requested that a part of the allocation be paid in cash, to make it possible to buy food close to a settlement in Kitonga. As the Norwegian Ambassador Ola Dørum in Dar es Salaam found the request reasonable and the co-operation by then was running well, this was granted. Dørum did not suspect that this would lead to misuse. Instead of paying the suppliers directly, 25–30% of the monthly grant was paid directly to the PAC in cash, on demand of receipts.[148]

It was primarily refugees in Tanzania that received the support, but a small part also went to maintenance of PAC refugees in Botswana and Zimbabwe. In 1988, Norway also gave 200,000 for medical treatment to the PAC President Zephania Mothopeng in London and 100,000 for a PAC women's conference.

In addition to daily necessities for refugees, Norway implemented one major project for the PAC: a road to Ruwu, Kitonga. The Tanzanian government had granted land and property there for a settlement for the PAC, and also prepared a plan for the development of the site. Although Norway did not believe the PAC's information that they were responsible for over 700 refugees, as the PAC had earlier given "totally unrealistic figures", the number of refugees was large enough to justify developing a settlement. And for this, a road would be necessary.[149] It was important for a positive decision that the Ministry had been informed that the UNDP had allocated around USD 250,000 and the UNHCR about USD 100,000 for the development of the settlement, and that the Tanzanian government had given assurances that the project would be integrated into the development plans of the region.[150] According to the PAC, in the end the settlement also re-

---

[145] Chief representative in Harare, Waters Toboti in February, 17 February 1986, MFA 34 9/5 D II.

[146] See appendix for details.

[147] Charge d'Affaires Dag Mjaaland Dar es Salaam, 20 November 1985 to MFA. Sør Afrika. Samtale med presidenten for PAC (South Africa. Consultations with the president of the PAC), MFA 34 9/5 II.

[148] Ola Dørum, Dar es Salaam to MFA, 18 April 1984, MFA 34 9/5 D I.

[149] Notat. PAC. Økonomisk behov i 1984 (The PAC. Financial requirements for 1984), Bjarne Lindstrøm, 19 January 1984, MFA 34 9/5 D I.

[150] Dørum, ambassador in Dar es Salaam to MFA, 10 January 1984, MFA 34 9/4 D I.

ceived support from the Tanganikya Christian Refugee Service, the governments of the Netherlands and Nigeria, as well as Norway.[151]

The Ministry was not convinced that the PAC would manage to build the Kitonga settlement. The need for this was increasing with the number of refugees, and the Ministry decided to contribute to its development by building a 14 km road. Norway contracted the consultancy firm NORPLAN, and after some discussion regarding the cost and necessary standard, NORPLAN planned and supervised the construction of the road. The PAC would take over responsibility for the maintenance of the road, and equipment was granted for this. Kitonga was to be the centre for all PAC refugees in Tanzania, and with a road that could be used all year round, the potential for food production could be utilised. A community did develop at Ruwu, which provided a safe refuge for the modest number of refugees that stayed there.

From January 1988, the Norwegian People's Aid (NPA) was given responsibility for implementation of the direct support for the PAC and the ANC. It had become too complicated and time-consuming for the embassy to follow up project agreements, both with regard to the direct procurements and the building projects. The NPA by then already had a close relationship with the ANC. The co-operation with the PAC was also going well, and Secretary General Odd Wivegh reported towards the end of 1989 that it was the impression of the NPA that the funds made available to the PAC were "used with great care. The members themselves [were] working hard to stretch the money with their own manpower". The co-operation with external contractors and consultants also seemed to be good.[152] When NPA took over the maintenance of the road from NORPLAN, routines were changed which cut costs considerably and made it possible to further upgrade the road.

The question of whether Norway should stop supporting the PAC was regularly considered. The support was, however, maintained, as the internal situation improved and the PAC was covering a humanitarian need for the refugees. It was decisive that the OAU did not withdraw its recognition. In 1986, Johnson Mlambo informed the Norwegian State Secretary in the Foreign Ministry that the PAC was working for "an Africanist, socialist and democratic South Africa which takes care of the material, mental and psychological needs of individuals".[153]

In 1992 it became obvious that this did not necessarily mean all individuals: in reaction to an attack on a golf course by members of the PAC, the

---

[151] Brochure: *Masuguru—Ruwu, A Pan Africanist Congress (PAC) of Azania Refugee Settlement*, PAC 1989. MFA 34 9/5 D III.

[152] Secretary General Odd Wivegh to MFA, 28 September 1989, MFA 34 9/5 D II.

[153] Memorandum. South Africa. Statssekretær Frøysnes' samtale med lederen for PAC, Mr. Johnson Mlambo (Consultation between State Secretary Frøysnes and the PAC Chairman, Johnson Mlambo), 1. Political Affairs Division, 6 May 1986, MFA 349/5 D II.

support was cut off. In the words of the then Secretary of Foreign Affairs in the PAC, Gora Ebrahim, what happened was that

> in 1992 we went with a delegation to Norway where assistance of about 200,000 US Dollars was promised. But there was an incident that occurred in 1992, known as the King Williamstown attack on a golf course. The Norwegians then decided to suspend all assistance to us. We went into the election campaign without any assistance from any source.[154]

Other official Norwegian support

In addition to the direct support for the ANC and the PAC, there are a number of other aspects of the official Norwegian policy with regard to the liberation struggle in South Africa that deserve mentioning here: the Nordic co-operation, the Nobel Peace Prize to Desmond Tutu, the special kind of diplomacy shown by Norway with regard to the South African regime, the opening of a South African consulate in Oslo, and support through other channels.

Nordic co-operation

At a meeting of the Nordic Foreign Ministers in Helsinki in September 1977, a decision was made to appoint a working group to appraise common Nordic efforts against South Africa. The working group submitted its report in March the following year, and it was discussed by the Nordic Foreign Ministers at a meeting in Oslo later the same month. A Joint Nordic Programme of Action was then adopted. The South African government's policy of apartheid remained the principal cause of the racial conflict in Southern Africa, it stated, and international pressure against the apartheid regime had to be increased. The so-called Oslo Plan, which was expected to be gradually extended to include new measures, included the following points:

- prohibition or discouragement of new investments in South Africa;
- negotiations with Nordic companies with a view to restricting their production in South Africa;
- a recommendation that contacts with the apartheid regime in South Africa in the field of sport and culture be discontinued;
- increased Nordic support to refugees, liberation movements, victims of apartheid etc.

Later in 1978, the Nordic countries also agreed to introduce visa requirements for South African citizens.

---

[154] Gora Ebrahim, Secretary of Foreign Affairs in PAC, Member of the National Assembly in democratic South Africa in Tor Sellström (ed.): *Liberation in Southern Africa. Regional and Swedish Voices.* Uppsala: Nordiska Afrikainstitutet, 1999.

In addition to these unilateral Nordic measures, it was also agreed that the Nordic countries in the UN should work for:

- the adoption of resolutions in the Security Council against new investments in South Africa;
- proposals in the Security Council which could result in binding resolutions against trade with South Africa;
- ensuring strict observance of the Security Council's resolutions on the arms embargo against South Africa.

The Nordic Foreign Ministers also appointed a permanent working group with representatives from the Nordic Foreign Ministries to see to it that the Programme of Action was observed, and to consider new measures against South Africa, including sanctions. Visiting Oslo in March 1978, Oliver Tambo expressed approval of the Joint Nordic Programme of Action in a meeting with Foreign Minister Knut Frydenlund, in the sense that it expressed a wish to put condemnation into action. He did, however, hope that it would be extended to include a comprehensive boycott of South Africa.[155] As can be seen in chapter 5, it would, however, take almost a decade until a comprehensive Norwegian sanctions law was finally adopted by the parliament on 20 March 1987.

An extension of the Programme was adopted in October 1985 and revised in March 1988 when all the Nordic countries had introduced prohibitions on investments in and trade with South Africa and Namibia. Again stating that they viewed the apartheid policy as a serious threat to peace, the Nordic Foreign Ministers encouraged other countries to take initiatives to increase and make more effective the international pressure against South Africa in addition to imposing sanctions. This included support to South Africa's neighbouring countries to relieve the effects of the destabilisation policy and reduce their dependency on South Africa. (The Nordic countries increased their co-operation with the SADCC countries. The total Nordic assistance to the Frontline States from 1978 to 1987 amounted to USD 4.6 billion.)[156]

The extended Joint Nordic Programme of Action also stated that the Nordic countries would work internationally for the liberation of Namibia, for effective boycott of South Africa including oil and air traffic, for increased information on the apartheid policy and for increased support to the opponents and victims of the apartheid system.

The Nordic countries also co-operated in the field. Denmark, Finland, Norway and Sweden were all involved in the development of the ANC's

---

[155] Memorandum. Besøk i Oslo 14–16 mars 1978 av ANC delegasjon. Møte med utenriksminister Frydenlund. (Visit to Oslo by ANC delegation 14–16 March 1978. Consultations with Foreign Minister Frydenlund), 1. Political Affairs Division, 29 March 1978, MFA 34 9/5 VII.

[156] *Norsk Utenrikspolitisk Årbok* (Yearbook of Norwegian Foreign Policy) 1988, NUPI, Oslo.

settlements in Dakawa. The co-operation was particularly close between Norway and Sweden, who planned, negotiated and carried out the assistance in similar ways. For example, the Swedish representation assisted Norway in implementing support for the ANC in countries where Norway did not have an embassy or consulate. Although Norway did not support the ANC inside South Africa, and Sweden was not as heavily involved in the development of Mazimbu and Dakawa as Norway, the support programmes of the two countries were similar. Every year annual negotiations were held with representatives of the Foreign Ministries and the ANC leadership, which resulted in agreed minutes regarding the support. The support was de facto to a large degree co-ordinated. It could, for instance, be agreed in one of the countries where South African refugees received support that Norway would provide one kind of items and Sweden another, in the most optimal way. Swedish representatives proposed in 1988 that Norway should administer Sweden's support for agriculture in Mazimbu, as Sweden's administrative capacity in Dar es Salaam was not dimensioned for this, while Sweden could take care of the implementation of Norway's support for the ANC's agricultural projects in Zambia.[157] This did not materialise as the Norwegians wanted to be present in both places to keep a broad contact with the ANC, but it is an expression of the close relations between the two donors. Both Norway and Sweden applied the same disbursement system and this also required co-operation to avoid duplication and render the assistance more efficient.[158]

The Nobel Peace Prize to Desmond Tutu 1984

Although the Nobel Committee is independent, the whole Nobel ceremony has such strong Norwegian official participation that it should be mentioned, if only briefly.[159] The prize has been awarded three times to South Africans for their work against the apartheid system: to Albert Luthuli in 1961, to Desmond Tutu in 1984—and to Nelson Mandela and Frederik de Klerk in 1993. Here, it is the prize for Desmond Tutu that will be briefly touched upon, as it was awarded in the time period discussed in this chapter.

After being nominated for the Nobel Peace Prize several times, Desmond Tutu was awarded the prize in 1984, 23 years after Albert Luthuli.[160]

---

[157] Telex from the Norwegian embassy in Dar es Salaam to MFA. ANC: norsk og svensk samarbeid om prosjekter. (The ANC: Norwegian and Swedish support on projects), 30 November 1988, MFA 34 9/5 B 27.

[158] Interview with Roland Axelsson in Tor Sellström (ed.): *Liberation in Southern Africa. Regional and Swedish Voices*. Uppsala: Nordiska Afrikainstitutet, 1999.

[159] The Nobel Peace Prize for Albert Luthuli in 1961 is discussed in chapter 1.

[160] The author wishes to thank Karin Beate Theodorsen for providing the material on the Peace Prize.

In his speech to the Nobel laureate, the Chairman of the Norwegian Nobel Committee, Egil Aarvik, said that it was "the Committee's wish that [the] award should be seen as a renewed recognition of the courage and heroic patience shown by black South Africans in their use of peaceful means to oppose the apartheid system".

Reactions in Norway to the award were predominantly positive. But the question of sanctions was also raised in a number of newspaper articles and in statements from the Church, the trade union movement, the Council for Southern Africa and others.[161] It was emphasised that it was a paradox to award the Peace Prize to a person who was continuously calling for trade sanctions against South Africa, while Norwegian trade with the country was increasing. The Peace Prize also contributed to the pressure that led the government to impose sanctions at a later stage.

The granting of the Nobel Peace Prize to Desmond Tutu led to increased attention on the South African struggle against apartheid, both in Norway and internationally. Information was spread, and anti-apartheid campaigns were launched all over the world. The award to Desmond Tutu made it even more difficult for the South African propaganda to describe the liberation struggle as terrorism, or to justify the apartheid policy in any way.

"... on the brink of normal diplomatic activities"

In 1976, the government decided that the Norwegian consulate general in Cape Town should become more active in humanitarian work. A process was initiated which was to end with the consulate becoming heavily engaged in what Foreign Minister Knut Vollebæk in 1998 euphemistically characterised as being "on the brink of normal diplomatic activities".[162] In 1985, the consulate co-operated with the Norwegian Church in setting up the Social Change Assistance Trust, which distributed money to a large number of grassroots organisations in the Cape Town area.[163] In 1986, the apartheid regime declared a nation-wide state of emergency, which made the situation for the opponents of the regime even more difficult. At the same time, it made the need for support inside the country more urgent.

Norway did not support the activities of the liberation movements inside South Africa, as the parliament had decided that only legal activities were to be supported inside the country. The definition of what was legal was stretched in the second half of the 1980s, when from January 1986 the Norwegian consul Bjarne Lindstrøm started his diplomatic activities. These were carried out in close co-operation with Knut Vollebæk, who in 1986 re-

---

[161] E.g., *NTB*, 16 October 1984; *Stavanger Aftenblad*, 17 October 1984; *Nationen*, 18 October 1984; *Aftenposten*, 22 October 1984; and *Vårt Land*, 23 October 1984.

[162] Radio programme: The history of South Africa, part 3, Norwegian Broadcasting Corporation 16 November 1998. Reporter: Tomm Kristiansen.

[163] For the co-operation with the Church, see chapter 7.

turned to Oslo from the embassy in Harare to become Head of the 1. Political Affairs Division at the Foreign Ministry, and Trond Bakkevig, Secretary General of the Church of Norway Council on Ecumenical and International Relations (CEIR).

Primarily, this involved the channelling of money via the Norwegian representation directly to people working for democracy in South Africa. It was not a practice started by the Cape Town consulate, but the dimensions of this practice became extraordinary there. In Santiago de Chile too, Norwegian diplomats had earlier had at their disposal a sum of money to be used for instant humanitarian assistance, when other aid channels were impossible. In 1979, the resident representative of NORAD in Gaborone, Øystein Tveter, similarly requested the Foreign Ministry in Oslo for a sum for this purpose. As post, telephone and telegraph services were monitored by the South African police in Botswana, not all requests could be sent to Oslo. The Nigerian representative in Gaborone had a sum of money at his disposal, to be used in emergencies, while Tveter had to use other sources to cover this kind of expense. The Foreign Ministry saw the need for this, and also felt that it could contribute to the consulate making useful contacts with, for instance, representatives of the Black Consciousness Movement inside South Africa. It therefore allocated NOK 10,000 for these purposes in Botswana in 1979.[164] The same year NOK 50,000 was allocated for the consulate general in Cape Town. The money could be used for purposes approved by the Consul, without too many questions being asked from Oslo. The Ministry was of the opinion that this would be tolerated by the South African authorities, as they were not interested in the number of diplomatic stations being reduced further than it was already. However, the Ministry preferred that the money be channelled to the legal opposition in other ways than through the diplomats, as it would not serve the cause to have diplomats expelled on account of having transferred too large contributions to the opposition. [165]

The practice of having money to spend for immediate purposes was thus not new when Bjarne Lindstrøm became Consul General in Cape Town. But the extent to which he was using the facility was quite unnormal. In addition to the "local emergency fund" allocation being raised to NOK 100,000 in the 1980s, the Ministry in total channelled around NOK 25 millions through CEIR, transferred via banks or carried into South Africa by Trond Bakkevig, to be distributed by Bjarne Lindstrøm to grassroots organisations.

---

[164] Memorandum. NORADs stedlige representasjon i Gaborone, Botswana. Spørsmål om "håndpenger" (Question of "petty cash"), 1. Political Affairs Division, 6 February 1979, MFA 34 9/5 IX.

[165] Memorandum: Support for liberation movements in South Africa 1981, 1. Political Affairs Division , 9 April 1981, MFA 34 9/5 B II.

The trust between the main Norwegian actors and between the Norwegians and people working for liberation and democracy in South Africa was decisive for this practice. According to Vollebæk, the time it took to process a request could sometimes be down to twenty minutes. Most of this activity is, naturally, not reflected in the Ministry's archives. Bakkevig, Lindstrøm and Vollebæk have, however, given information about this in various interviews. In a programme on Norwegian radio in November 1998, Lindstrøm said that this support went to various kinds of activities all over South Africa and aimed at bringing people together to give them a chance to organise against the apartheid regime.[166] This involved "clubs for black children, community houses, libraries, print-shops, agricultural projects and art centres. It could also be institutions such as advisory offices in black townships, where people, after having been exposed to police brutality, for example, could get advice on what doctor to see. They needed doctors that they could rely on and that they knew would not pass information on to the police".

One of the ways in which the apartheid regime tried to suppress the opposition was to prevent it having offices with telephones, prevent communication, transport etc. What the consulate tried to do, according to Lindstrøm, was to help provide opposition groups with a place to meet and work from in a decent degree of safety, like the Community House in Cape Town (which, however, was opened on a Monday and partly destroyed by a bomb the following Friday. It was rebuilt with Norwegian support).

When asked by radio reporter Tomm Kristiansen whether the diplomats considered this activity in accordance with Norwegian foreign policy, Vollebæk replied that they of course "realised that it was political work, but the underlying humanitarian aspect was so dominant that (they) did not think very much about the political side of it. (...) There was no room for normal diplomatic relations between the Republic of South Africa and Norway. The expressed opinion of the Norwegian government, supported by an overwhelming majority of the Norwegian parliament, was that Norway should contribute to abolishing the apartheid system."[167]

At times, the consul let people whom the police were looking for stay in his house together with his family. In his own words: "you couldn't suddenly say 'I don't know you' when a co-operation partner got into trouble". If he had asked the Ministry in Oslo for instructions, he would have received a negative reply. Therefore he did not ask.

---

[166] Radio programme: The history of South Africa, part 3, Norwegian Broadcasting Corporation 16 November 1998. Reporter: Tomm Kristiansen. The theme is also discussed in Tomm Kristiansen: *Mandelas land*. Oslo: Cappelen, 1995 and in Trond Bakkevig: *Den norske Kirke og kampen mot apartheid*. Oslo: Mellomkirkelig Råd, 1995. See also the interview with Knut Vollebæk in Tomm Kristiansen/Aud-Lise Norheim (eds.): *Høvdingen*. Oslo: Cappelen, 1999.

[167] Ibid.

The active role played by the consulate general was in accordance with the decision of 1976 that the consulate should become more active in humanitarian work. As long as it was not used for illegal activities, it did not contradict the parliamentary decision. Whether it was, or was not, is not an issue in this connection. The Ministry felt sure that the money was used according to the rules laid down.

Was this arrangement established to compensate for the decision not to support the ANC inside the country? The sums distributed by the Norwegian Consulate were small compared to what Sweden channelled into South Africa, where only through the ANC SEK 200 million were channelled inside the country for homefront activities.[168] Norway did, however, support other legal anti-apartheid activities within South Africa, through various NGOs. In addition to this, it was, in any case, probably close to as much as the Foreign Ministry could do in carrying out its commitment to the anti-apartheid struggle inside South Africa, given the guidelines set by the Norwegian parliament.

South African and ANC representations in Oslo

In April 1988, the Norwegian government decided to let South Africa open a consulate general in Oslo. The South African authorities had during the previous months started to make conditions more difficult for the Norwegian consulate general in Cape Town and for the representatives of other countries in South Africa. According to *Aftenposten*, "what the government in Pretoria particularly disliked, was the diplomats' extensive contacts with the opposition, often including the handing over of money. South Africa interpreted this as subversive activity".[169] While Norway had maintained diplomatic representation in South Africa since 1906, South Africa had until 1988 not had corresponding representation in Norway. To take care of its interests in the Nordic countries, South Africa had had legations in Sweden and Finland and a consulate general in Denmark. If South Africa was not allowed to open a consulate in Oslo, they threatened to close the Norwegian consulate in Cape Town.

As can be seen in chapter 6, the anti-apartheid opinion in Norway strongly objected to a South African consulate being opened in Oslo. Numerous demonstrations were arranged and information distributed through pamphlets and medias.

Despite this, Willem Bosman came to Norway as apartheid South Africa's Consul in October 1988. By agreeing to a South African consulate being established in Oslo, the Norwegian government acted contrary to the ANC's boycott policy. How could the Norwegian government, which had

---

[168] See Tor Sellström: *Sweden and National Liberation in Southern Africa, Vol. II*. Uppsala: Nordiska Afrikainstitutet (forthcoming).

[169] *Aftenposten*, 16 October 1988.

called so strongly for sanctions against South Africa in international fora and had such close contacts with the ANC, decide to go against their own call for diplomatic isolation? In November 1998 Foreign Minister Vollebæk explained the decision thus:

> What we did was to consult with the ANC. I went to Zambia on a one-day visit (...) to talk with Oliver Tambo, to get his approval to let South Africa open a consulate in Oslo. We did not call it "approval", but it was clear that his answer would be decisive. Even then we were thinking that this was quite unique, that an independent nation felt that it needed to consult the liberation movement in a far-off country over a decision that it could make on its own. We did not want to do something that could disturb the work we were doing. The signals we got back were clear: We should let South Africa open the consulate, because our presence inside South Africa was so important. But Tambo also said: "I cannot publicly confirm this, I might even criticise you for it. But you must do it".[170]

Vollebæk informed the press of his consultations with Oliver Tambo in 1988.[171] These were neither confirmed nor denied by the ANC.

In October 1986, the ANC had established an office in Oslo, with Raymond Mokoena as resident representative. (The ANC activities in Norway had previously been undertaken by the Nordic representative based in Stockholm.) The main task of the Oslo office was to inform about the struggle, advocate sanctions and further develop the co-operation with the Norwegian government and NGOs. In July 1988, the ANC informed the Ministry that as a result of a decision by the National Executive Committee of the ANC, he would be replaced by Thandie Rankoe.[172] In this way, the representation would be "be better equipped in meeting the growing challenges of our struggle in the international arena."[173] A year later, the ANC office was further strengthened when Delukufa Sandlwana was appointed as Deputy Chief Representative in Norway.[174] It is reasonable to see the strengthening of the ANC office in Oslo partly as a reaction to the establishment of the South African Consulate.

Whatever the case may be, the decision to let South Africa open an official representative's office in Norway was in violation of the ANC's policy for diplomatic boycott. It does not, however, seem to have led to the ANC mistrusting the Norwegian government. The close contacts and co-operation continued as before. As discussed earlier, the following year the ANC entrusted Norway with providing security, premises and general support for a

---

[170] Radio programme 16 November 1998: *The history of South Africa*, part 3, Norwegian Broadcasting Corporation.

[171] E.g., *Aftenposten*, 16 December 1988.

[172] Thandie Rankoe had worked for Norwegian People's Aid in Gaborone and Harare.

[173] Alfred Nzo to the Norwegian Foreign Minister, 28 July 1988, 34 9/5 B 27.

[174] Thandie Rankoe to the MFA, 11 December 1989, MFA 34 9/5 B 30.

major conference of chief representatives and regional treasurers held in Norway in March 1989.

A relationship from people to people

The direct co-operation between Norway and the liberation movements in South Africa was primarily concerned with humanitarian support for refugees. It started at a later stage than the Norwegian support for the liberation movements in Angola, Mozambique, Zimbabwe and Namibia. On the other hand, the support for the ANC was far larger than that given to any of any of these—in total it amounted to more than 400 million NOK in the period from 1977 to 1990. The PAC received less than 25 million NOK.

Pressure from civil society was vital in bringing about the decision to start the direct assistance, and the support from the Norwegian government was likewise sustained and supported by broad groups of the Norwegian society. As can be seen elsewhere in this study, the official support can not be seen in isolation from the various efforts made by different groups in the Norwegian society. A number of Norwegian NGOs were directly involved in supporting the struggle. And all over the country, local arrangements were initiated to inform about apartheid and collect money for the struggle.

This was strongly emphasised by Thabo Mbeki in February 1999, when he opened a conference in Cape Town regarding the role of the Nordic countries in the Southern African liberation struggle. He there stated that it was

> important that the relationships that developed in the end between the peoples of Southern Africa and the peoples of the Nordic Countries, encompassed entire societies. Among the Nordic countries it was entire peoples who got involved in the struggle for emancipation of the peoples of Southern Africa. What developed, was a relationship from people to people. (...) It would seem to me, that if we build on this extraordinary thing that happened as we united in this common struggle for national liberation, and united as people to people, and united now—basing ourselves on that experience, basing ourselves on the relationships that have been built and say here's a new strategic challenge, let us once more co-operate from people to people to meet these challenges together—it would seem to me that if we did that—and I'm sure we can do that—this remarkable relationship between the Nordic countries and the countries of Southern Africa would still have something new to teach the rest of the world for the future.[175]

---

[175] Video recording from the conference *Nordic Solidarity with the Liberation Struggles in Southern Africa, and Challenges for Democratic Partnerships into the 21st Century*, 11 February 1999.

Chapter 4
Norway and "Rhodesia": 1965–1980[1]

Wolf Lorenz

Introduction

This chapter will examine what has been called "the Rhodesia issue" in the years between 1965 and 1980. The emphasis will be on Norwegian diplomatic history and to a lesser extent on humanitarian assistance to the liberation movements and popular involvement as manifested in the work of Norwegian NGOs. I have for reasons of convenience chosen to call the territory concerned *Rhodesia*. Its official name was Southern Rhodesia, in Norway "Rhodesia" was the most commonly used term, although "Southern Rhodesia" was frequently used during the 1960s. "Zimbabwe" was little used except by the liberation movements themselves and the political left and the solidarity organisations in the 1970s. Rhodesia was the term used by the territory's white leader Ian Smith, and it consequently became widely used. Since Northern Rhodesia changed its name to Zambia at independence in 1964, there was no practical reason to distinguish between Northern and Southern Rhodesia.

Northern Rhodesia (Zambia) and Nyasaland (Malawi) gained independence from Britain in 1964, and were thus admitted to UN membership. Southern Rhodesia, under the leadership of a white minority never exceeding 5% of the total population, was unable to negotiate independence from Britain because of the unwillingness of the regime to award equal political rights to the territory's African majority. As more and more of the former colonies achieved their independence in the 1960s, the problems in Southern Rhodesia attracted great international attention, and when Ian Smith unilaterally declared Rhodesia independent in November 1965, this action was widely condemned as an illegal act. In the years to follow, the UN Security

---

[1] The following chapter is based on my thesis *Norge og Rhodesia-spørsmålet, 1965–79* (Norway and the Case of Rhodesia, 1965–79), completed at the University of Oslo. The thesis examines Norway's involvement with the situation that arose after Ian Smith's unilateral declaration of independence for Rhodesia in 1965. The main aim is to examine diplomatic history based on the archives of the Norwegian Ministry of Foreign Affairs, and the Norwegian Ministry of Trade and Shipping on the treatment of the issue in the National Assembly, in the archives of the Norwegian Shipowners' Association, as well as in the archives of involved NGOs. Little or no research has been done on the period up to 1965.

Council imposed a range of mandatory sanctions on Rhodesia. The sanctions were, however, not able to topple the regime, as some countries covertly disregarded the sanctions, and others, namely Portugal and South Africa, openly ignored them. Since sanctions largely failed and the British government had vehemently rejected military intervention, the illegal regime was able to hold on to power. The prospects for the African majority, severely controlled, poorly organised and politically divided, seemed bleak. It was only the fall of the dictatorship in Portugal in 1974, and the subsequent independence of its African colonies, most importantly Angola and Mozambique, that altered the stalemate in Southern Africa. With South Africa its only ally, and a hostile regime installed in the renamed Mozambican capital of Maputo, Rhodesia was soon to find herself in dire straits.

In a military sense, the liberation movements had up to this time not constituted any major challenge to the Smith regime, whose armed forces were well equipped. Liberation movements in Rhodesia were generally characterised by shifting alliances and internal problems. These divisions were actively exploited by the Rhodesian government in their policy of divide and rule. Successive nationalist movements had been banned, bishop Abel Muzorewa's African National Council (ANC) being the only organisation to be allowed a certain freedom by the regime. The white population regarded the ANC as "moderate" and of little consequence because it possessed no military strength. Two important organisations had been banned: the Zimbabwe African People's Union (ZAPU), led by Joshua Nkomo, and the Zimbabwe African National Union (ZANU), led initially by Ndabaningi Sithole and later by Robert Mugabe. Mainly for strengthening their position in international negotiations, ZANU and ZAPU were later to form the Patriotic Front (PF). Their guerrilla armies as well as their political organisations were, however, kept intact. The white minority sought co-operation with Muzorewa in the "internal solution" in 1978, which produced multiracial elections from which the PF was excluded. A Muzorewa-led government was the result. In the first *free* elections in 1980 ZANU won a landslide victory.

Norway and Rhodesia had few links, and from a Norwegian point of view, the problems in Rhodesia did not touch upon traditionally sensitive foreign policy issues such as security and European integration.

As Norwegian trade interests in Rhodesia were limited to the import of tobacco and sugar, and exports were limited to urea (fertiliser), fish produce, paper and cardboard, trade interests between the countries were not significant. In 1965, Norway imported Rhodesian goods for 12.2 million Norwegian kroner, while exports ran at 10.9 million NOK.[2] Norwegian multinational companies like Norsk Hydro and Elkem dominated this trade, as did Rhodesian tobacco. Norwegian shipping interests, with one of the largest

---

[2] *Norwegian Yearbook of Statistics*, 1966.

merchant fleets in the world, not least oil tankers, were affected however by the sanctions imposed by the UN Security Council. It was inconceivable that the Norwegian Shipowners' Association would dispute the decision of the UN Security Council. Another matter was what one tried to accomplish within the law, or at the side of the law. In some isolated instances Norway violated UN sanctions. Norway was able to terminate trade with Rhodesia relatively quickly, but compared to Sweden's abrupt cessation of trade, Norwegian trade continued for a long time. In 1965 and 1966, before full and mandatory sanctions had been imposed, the conservative Minister of Trade and Shipping, Kåre Willoch, was quite liberal in granting licenses for exports to Rhodesia. Imports, on the other hand, were quickly banned. Many Western countries actually *increased* trade with Rhodesia in these early years.[3]

The early years

Contact between the Rhodesian liberation movements and the Norwegian authorities had been made even before Rhodesia's unilateral declaration of independence (UDI) in 1965, similarly links between these movements and the Norwegian NGO Norwegian Action against Apartheid (NAMA) had been established. The contact was however sporadic, and there is no evidence that Norwegian authorities, i.e. the Norwegian Embassy in London or the Ministry of Foreign Affairs in Oslo, regarded the exchange of information with the liberation movements as particularly interesting.

From an official Norwegian point of view the Rhodesian issue could primarily be viewed as a symbolic question up to the mid-seventies, and, had it been given, Norwegian humanitarian support to the liberation movements would probably not have been opposed by her allies. However, the liberal-conservative government that ruled Norway from 1965 to 1971 showed little interest in the issue. There was a feeling that sanctions needed time and full implementation to yield definite results, and that patience was vital. Besides, Norway's primary concern was her own role in Europe, and compared to the wars in Vietnam and Biafra, the situation in Southern Africa was of minor interest. This was to change, albeit not in any revolutionary fashion (see chapter 1).

Politicians taking an interest in Rhodesia were mainly to be found on the far right and among socialists; on the far right the *Anders Lange's Party*, formed in 1973 was alone in its wish to abandon sanctions, backed by its political sympathy for the Smith regime and by the *laissez-faire* view that

---

[3] UD 25 4/25 B, 11, memorandum First Political Division. According to the Ministry of Foreign Affairs, several countries had increased their exports to Rhodesia: France by 200% , Portugal by 350%, the FRG by 64% , the Netherlands by 49% and Japan by 38% .

trade should not be restricted in any way. [4] This argument was raised when the United States unilaterally lifted its sanctions on Rhodesian chrome ore in 1973. On the other side of the political spectrum, Finn Gustavsen, representing the *Socialist People's Party*, was the single most important proponent of majority rule in Rhodesia. His party took a strong anti-imperialist stance. From time to time he raised the issue in the National Assembly, *Stortinget*, while also co-operating with the Norwegian Action against Apartheid, and later with its successor organisation, the Norwegian Council for Southern Africa.

These two parties were the only parties represented in the Norwegian parliament not to be part of any government during the 14 years of illegal rule in Rhodesia.[5] As the other parties largely ignored the question, all the more influence was left to the senior civil servants of the Ministry of Foreign Affairs, UD. Few of these took any interest in the question at an early stage, with one important exception; Secretary General Boye, ranked first in the Ministry of Foreign Affairs. His personal views are among the very few discernible up to 1973, and they were manifested on various occasions. When Ian Smith had unilaterally declared Rhodesia independent in 1965, many countries, such as Sweden and Finland immediately broke off their diplomatic ties with Salisbury. Norway and Denmark, however, took their time. While Denmark maintained representation in Salisbury and Bulawayo, Norway maintained her honorary consulate in Salisbury. Not until Smith declared Rhodesia a republic in 1970 were these relations broken off, even then against the strong and repeated advice of Boye. On one occasion he argued that the consulate should be kept open because any concession made to "our sunburnt friends in Africa" would only lead to further demands.[6]

A similar question was raised at the same time. According to the UN sanctions so-called *interline agreements* between Air Rhodesia and other airlines were not allowed. Scandinavian Airlines System, SAS, jointly owned by the three Scandinavian governments, claimed they were the only airline observing the sanctions, and informed Boye that they no longer wished to honour the sanctions. Boye acquiesced and noted that there were no such sanctions anyway. South African Airways was to represent SAS in Salisbury.[7]

---

[4] Anders Lange's Party was the forerunner of the right-wing "Progress Party" (Fremskrittspartiet).

[5] During the 14 years of illegal government in Rhodesia, the following parties were in power in Norway: 1) 1965–71 a coalition of the Conservative Party, the Liberal Party, the Centre Party and the Christian People's Party, 2) 1971–72 Labour government, 3) 1972–73 a coalition of the Liberal Party, the Centre Party and the Christian People's Party, 4) 1973–76 and 1976–81 Labour governments.

[6] UD 25 4/25, 28, memorandum Boye, 30 August 1968.

[7] UD 25 4/25 B, 16, memorandum Boye, 18 December 1969.

Boye had, incidentally, served six years on the SAS board, a fact that may have influenced his judgement. In the end, his views were disregarded, as it would have been somewhat difficult to sell such arguments to the Norwegian public. As his views were not accepted, there were clearly other civil servants opposing him, but his high rank probably forced them to use all their diplomatic skills in doing so. The relative power of the civil servants was most likely made possible by the indifference of the politicians; it seems unlikely that a more concerned political leadership would have approved of such views.

Norwegian foreign policy in relation to the Third World has rarely led to severe disputes between the major political parties, and this also held true for Rhodesia, for a long time anyway. The forces that brought about a change can be situated both in a geopolitical context as well as on the domestic Norwegian scene. The larger part of the seventies, in the aftermath of the referendum in which a majority voted against Norway joining the EEC, was characterised by a political move to the left. Only late in the decade did the political pendulum swing to the right again.[8] This of course also relates to changes in geopolitics where a brief *rapprochement* between the East and the West was followed by renewed hostilities, often fought by proxy in the Third World. Southern Africa became a part of the cold war, and consequently the great powers invested new interest in the region.

1973–78

From the early seventies, a change in Norwegian policy is detectable. After the referendum on Norwegian EEC-membership in 1972, there was a turn to the left in Norway, from which a stronger interest in relations between North and South arose. The political left, as represented by the Socialist People's Party and later the Socialist Left Party had no representatives in parliament in 1969–73, but had a vocal large group of representatives in 1973–77. Changes in Norway's policy on the region stem both from structural changes as well as from the role of individuals. The lack of concerned politicians and civil servants came to an end in the early seventies as new actors entered the scene. They represented a longstanding tradition in Norway based on a combination of social democratic values of solidarity and similar Christian, humanitarian values. In one of the world's richest countries, free from a colonial past that damaged so many Western countries' reputation in the Third World, many felt that small Western countries held special responsibilities for bridging gaps in the Third World.[9]

These views, coupled with a more principled anti-imperialist attitude, were very strong in the Socialist Left Party, successor of the Socialist Peo-

---

[8] Berge Furre: *Norsk historie 1905–1990: vårt hundreår.* Oslo: Samlaget, 1993:346.

[9] Stokke, Olav: "Utviklingsbistand og frigjøringsbevegelser" in *Internasjonal politikk* 4/70, 1970; Stokke, Olav: "Norsk støtte til frigjøringsbevegelser" in *Norsk Utenrikspolitisk Årbok 1973.*

ple's Party. They were also represented in the Norwegian Labour Party, but such views were not restricted to the political left, representatives of the Christian People's Party to a certain extent also reflected such attitudes. Ministers of Foreign Affairs Dagfinn Vårvik (Centre Party), Andreas Cappelen (Labour) and later Knut Frydenlund (Labour) took great interest in the question, as did the State Secretaries Thorvald Stoltenberg and Arne Arnesen. Cappelen was a vocal opponent of Portuguese colonial rule in Africa, and his criticism of Portugal, presented in NATO as it was (see chapter 1), can be viewed as particularly important because Portugal and Norway were militarily allied through NATO and economically allied in the European Free Trade Association (EFTA). Indeed, combined with Norwegian efforts in the UN, it must have been a determining factor in the OAU's decision to hold its conference on the African liberation struggle in 1973, its first conference ever held on non-African soil, in Oslo. (The UN/OAU Conference in 1973 is treated in greater detail in chapter 1). At this landmark conference Rhodesia was represented by ZANU and ZAPU, but the liberation of Rhodesia was not put as high on the agenda as the liberation of the Portuguese colonies. Importantly however, contact and trust were deepened. Norwegian authorities had worked hard to secure the participation of government representatives from Western countries, but with little success. The other Scandinavian countries were represented, so were Australia and Austria, but Norwegian efforts to secure the participation of countries such as Britain, France and the United States came to naught, as these countries did not wish to endanger their relationships with the governments in Lisbon and Pretoria.

Norway had a similar experience in 1977, with a different outcome, when a major conference on the liberation of Namibia and Rhodesia was held in Maputo. Again, the Scandinavian countries were active, and since Norway was a member of the organising committee, the Norwegian representatives worked hard to secure the participation of the major Western countries. Again it was strenuous work, but this time their efforts were not futile; wide participation was secured and Norwegian solidarity with Southern Africa had again been proven.

Norwegian financial assistance to the liberation movements had been initiated at the time of the UN/OAU conference in Oslo in 1973. (See chapter 1.) It had been made clear to the movements that applications for such assistance would be considered positively, but it was also made clear that aid in the form of arms was incompatible with Norwegian policy. Indeed, Norwegian officials never ceased to stress the importance of finding peaceful solutions for Rhodesia. The first applications for aid were received in 1973 but arrived too late to be considered. From 1974, Norway supported the liberation movements not only in word, but also in deed.

In 1974, through NORAD, the Ministry of Foreign Affairs chose to create a post whose exclusive duty would be to maintain day to day contact with the liberation movements. This contact point was housed at the Norwegian consulate in Zambia, Lusaka. This action indicated a strong element of recognition.

At the UN Assembly in 1972, Minister of Foreign Affairs Vårvik found it frustrating to vote for weak UN resolutions regarding Rhodesia, and had urged the other Nordic governments to vote in favour even of resolutions asking Britain to bring the Rhodesian rebellion to an end "by all means possible" and similar wordings. In doing so, Vårvik followed in the footsteps of Finn Gustavsen's argument presented years earlier, that one should not only vote for what seemed *realistic*, sometimes one ought to vote simply to be *heard*. Norway did not want to legitimise the use of violence, but sought to establish the liberation movements' right to *fight* for their cause, very much in the same way it had been a moral imperative to fight the German occupation of Norway during World War II. The other Nordic countries, Iceland excluded, were however most unwilling to change their positions in 1973. Not only did Norway face strong, Nordic resistance, Norwegian views were, not surprisingly, opposed by the British delegation at the UN. Under this combined pressure, Norway gave in and resumed to the traditional position of abstention on these resolutions. This is one of the rare cases in this period where Norway went further than the other Nordic countries. Over the years though, this changed, and in the late seventies the Nordic countries abstained or voted in favour of such resolutions.

In addition to these diplomatic efforts, the Norwegian government extended humanitarian assistance to the liberation movements. While a touch of Cold War in Southern Africa was felt more strongly in many Western capitals, the Labour Party government from 1973 and the Ministry of Foreign Affairs argued that the escalating hostilities should not be seen in such a context. The liberation movements should not be labelled "communist" or "non-communist", they were *nationalists* fighting for their right to rule their country.[10] The funds allocated to the liberation movements rose steadily from a mere NOK 200,000 in 1974 to NOK 8 million in 1979. With the exception of a single grant to the Muzorewa-led United African National Council in 1977, the funds were equally divided between ZANU and ZAPU.[11] In the period 1977–1979 NOK 20 million was extended in direct support to ZAPU and ZANU. As shown in tables VI and X in Appendix 1, substantial amounts were also channelled through the Botswana Refugee Council and other organisations catering for refugees from Zimbabwe.

---

[10] UD 25 425, 39, memorandum First Political Division, 18 May 1976; for similar assessments prior to NATO's Ministerial Meeting in December 1976, see UD 25 9/24, 2, memorandum First Political Division, 6 December 1976; unsigned memorandum, 21 December 1976; *ibid.*, 3. Memorandum First Political Division, 18 October 1977.

[11] UANC received NOK 380,000 for its activities inside Rhodesia and NOK 70,000 for its office in Stockholm. See Jon Bech: *Norsk bistand til frigjøringsbevegelsene i det sørlige Afrika.* Forum for Utviklingsstudier, no. 10/78. Oslo: Norsk Utenrikspolitisk Institutt, 1978. Further details on the support to ZANU and ZAPU are given in the Statistical Appendix: Table VI.

The lack of unity in the liberation struggle was not only a Rhodesian problem. Viewed from afar, these divisions were not easily understood, and caused general frustration among donors. While ZAPU and ZANU both had their roots in the early 1960s, the African National Council—led by bishop Abel Muzorewa—was formed in the early 1970s to oppose an Anglo-Rhodesian settlement proposal which was regarded by the African majority as being totally unacceptable. The early 1970s also saw the establishment of a small splinter group called Front for the Liberation of Zimbabwe (FROLIZI). Obviously frustrated by the lack of progress in the liberation struggle, in December 1974 Kenneth Kaunda and Julius Nyerere urged the four movements—ZAPU, ZANU, FROLIZI and ANC—to sign the so-called Lusaka Unity Accord. The Unity Accord, which later was endorsed by the OAU Liberation Committee—was signed with the purpose of joining forces under the umbrella of the African National Council (ANC), but personal, ideological and ethnic differences were soon to paralyse the umbrella organisation. In terms of humanitarian assistance, the open rivalries made it extremely difficult both for Norway and Sweden to enter into agreements and make use of the funds allocated in 1974–1976. In 1975 ZANU also suffered from internal problems in the aftermath of the assassination of its acting leader, Herbert Chitepo, and the following clampdown on ZANU members by the Zambian authorities.

In 1975 the situation was further complicated when Joshua Nkomo returned to Rhodesia with the intention of entering into negotiations with Ian Smith. This, to put it mildly, met with little approval from the other liberation movements, and signalled the final blow to the Unity Accord. The negotiations never yielded any results, and ZANU soon relaunched its armed struggle. ZAPU had won the support of Zambia's president Kenneth Kaunda and was able to operate from bases in Zambia. After a fierce struggle for leadership in ZANU, Ndabaningi Sithole was replaced with Robert Mugabe in the driver's seat. ZANU was now able to operate out of Mozambique, where FRELIMO had opened a front in the province of Tete as early as in 1968. The independence of Mozambique in 1975 obviously represented a watershed in the struggle for majority rule in Rhodesia.

For the purpose of presenting a common front during the Geneva Conference in October–December 1976, ZAPU and ZANU formed a unity pact under the name of the Patriotic Front (PF). The two movements largely carried on their struggle on the ground as separate armies and kept their organisational structures intact. The two PF partners were able to resume links with Norway during the Geneva Conference. They were also recognised by the OAU and the Frontline States as being the only genuine liberation movements. Lacking armed forces and being marginalised during the Geneva Conference, Abel Muzorewa reconstituted his movement as the United African National Council (UANC) and soon opened negotiations with Ian Smith's Rhodesian Front. In March 1978 he—together with Ndabaningi

Sithole—joined the Smith government as a junior partner in the non-recognised internal dispensation.

The final years

Outside Scandinavia, the policy of extending support to the liberation movements was, however, not shared by many in the West in the late seventies. To an increasing extent the choice of which movements to support also became a contentious issue in Norway. The Christian People's Party and the Conservative Party strongly criticised the Labour government's proposition to cancel the support given to the UANC, once Muzorewa and Smith had agreed on the so-called internal solution in March 1978.[12] The internal solution did indeed result in some Africans taking part in a new government, but both ZANU and ZAPU, at that time trying to co-operate in the *Patriotic Front*, opposed this as a "sell-out". The United Nations was not consulted, and the internal solution was widely rejected. Norway condemned the solution and the following elections in the UN, and Minister of Foreign Affairs, Knut Frydenlund condemned the solution at the bi-annual meeting with his Nordic colleagues.[13]

The deterioration in the relationship between Norway and the UANC had started earlier. The understanding had to a large extent been based on two factors: one was the sympathy for the peaceful solution advocated by Muzorewa; unnecessary bloodshed, after all, was not wanted. A second factor was the fact that Muzorewa had a Norwegian assistant, the Methodist missionary Kåre Eriksson, through whom the Ministry of Foreign Affairs had gained sympathy for the UANC. Muzorewa later chose to expel his Norwegian assistant, who had raised some critical questions. This did not increase Muzorewa's support in the Ministry of Foreign Affairs in Oslo.

Norwegian politicians and senior civil servants must sometimes have experienced minor cultural shocks in dealing with low rank representatives of the liberation movements. They had very different modes of expression and did not always know how to communicate with Norwegian officials. Some of the UANC representatives, including the head of the Stockholm office, Joyce Mutasa, had a perception of language that differed from the Norwegian one. Words like "liar" or "quisling" were not uncommon terms used by the UANC representatives to characterise members of the other liberation movements. This was quite unlike the language normally used in the Ministry of Foreign Affairs in Oslo. An UANC representative of Norwegian origin, Rolf Lind, had also done much harm to the reputation of the

---

[12] The "internal solution" was illegal by international law, and was not recognised by any country at all.

[13] UD 25 3/87, bulletin from the Nordic Foreign Ministers' Meeting, 20 February 1978; UD-info 8/79; UD 25 3/89, bulletin from the Nordic Foreign Ministers' Meeting, 30 March 1979.

UANC by his greatly over-simplified description of the fight against communism in Rhodesia.[14]

As Muzorewa had chosen to be part of a solution unacceptable to almost everyone, and as the internal solution brought everything but peace to Rhodesia, the Labour government proposed to withdraw all Norwegian support to the UANC. There was support for this proposition in the National Assembly, Labour and the Socialist Left Party, having a majority of one, but it met with strong opposition from the Conservative Party and from the Christian People's Party. These parties argued that it was unwise to continue to support the Patriotic Front as long as it sought a military solution and as long as a peaceful alternative existed, i.e., the UANC. They never proposed outright the recognition of the internal solution or the elections held by the Muzorewa/Smith regime, of which the Christian People's Party was the strongest proponent. This party, driven by feelings of religious brotherhood and by its Danish sister party, was very careful in how it phrased its support for Muzorewa, always taking care to leave backdoors open in its wording. The words "recognise the regime" were not heard, instead there was loose talk about "not losing opportunities" etc.[15]

It is not easy to assess why the non-Socialist parties did not reject the internal solution more decisively. For the Christian People's Party, the reasons given above were important. The Conservative Party, by far the largest of the non-Socialist parties, was more careful, and their support for the internal solution, if there indeed was such support, was never openly uttered. They were careful to emphasise their support for peaceful solutions, but who would not support a peaceful solution, were it only realistic?

Norway's largest newspaper, the conservative *Aftenposten*, was, excluding the ultra-conservative *Morgenbladet*, Muzorewa's strongest advocate in Norway. On repeated occasions Aftenposten's editorials gave support to the internal solution and to Muzorewa. Aftenposten's treatment of the case of Rhodesia has been thoroughly examined by researcher Tore Linné Eriksen and the chairperson of the Norwegian Council for Southern Africa, Øystein Gudim.[16] Their conclusion, in a conference paper in 1979, was that the paper was very pro-Muzorewa, and that its coverage was very much presented within a cold war context, mainly based on sources close to the illegal regime in Salisbury. Aftenposten was often viewed as a mouthpiece of the

---

[14] UD 25 4/25, 42, memorandum, First Political Division, 17 March 1977.

[15] UD 25 4/25, 50, Kåre Kristiansen of the Christian People's Party to the Labour government, 9 June 1979.

[16] Eriksen and Gudim: "Solid bakgrunn for egne meninger?" Aftenpostens dekning av konflikten i Rhodesia (Zimbabwe) 1977–1979, sakspapir til seminaret "Massmediarapporteringen i Norden om konfrontationen i södra Afrika", ("Sound foundation for opinion?" Aftenposten's coverage of the conflict in Rhodesia (Zimbabwe) 1977–1979, document for the seminar "Nordic mass media reports on the confrontation in Southern Africa"), held in Kungälv, Sweden, 28–30 May 1979, arranged by Nordiska Afrikainstitutet, Uppsala.

Conservative Party, but in this case, it seems as if the newspaper went further than did the Conservative Party itself.

Local elections were scheduled for the autumn of 1979 in Norway, and the non-socialist parties had had encouraging polls. It is possible to view their repeated emphasis on "peaceful solutions" in the context of some of these parties wanting to profile themselves.

Then, there were the developments in Rhodesia itself. Muzorewa had, when joining Smith's government, promised to bring peace to a wartorn Rhodesia. This promise proved empty. On the contrary, the liberation struggle advanced, the difference being that Rhodesia now had a black prime minister; Abel Muzorewa. This did not go down well with his supporters in the Western world. Repeated Rhodesian air strikes against camps in neighbouring Zambia and Mozambique caused deep consternation in Norway. So did alleged PF-massacres of white nuns and of the white survivors of a plane crash in Rhodesia. There was a war on the battlefield and there was a propaganda war fought in the Western media. Both sides had difficulty in winning the latter. Norwegians, in spite of the experience of German occupation during the Second World War, were quite unaccustomed to war, and the atrocities in Rhodesia made it difficult for some of the Norwegian supporters of the respective parties concerned.

During the Rhodesian government's desperate warfare in 1978, Muzorewa was invited to Norway by the Christian People's Party. Seen from Norway, the conflict in Rhodesia had in many ways lacked the *symbols* that can be so important when trying to arouse attention for a cause. In the South African case, such symbols existed; the import of oranges from *Outspan*, Cape Brandy, oil carried by Norwegian supertankers, the maintenance of a Norwegian consulate in Cape Town or the opening of a South African representation in Oslo etc. Muzorewa was now to fulfil this role for Rhodesia. He was attacked in several newspaper articles and the Norwegian Council for Southern Africa organised demonstrations during his visit. In the Ministry of Foreign Affairs, there was a debate about whether he should be received at all. Foreign Minister Knut Frydenlund feared reprisals by the conservative press and the opposition if Muzorewa was not received, in the end they had a private meeting and Frydenlund took great care in stressing that Muzorewa was not received as a representative of a legitimate government, but as a representative of the UANC. In the internal discussion in the ministry it was emphasised that there was a tradition of receiving anyone who wanted to be received. Renewed economic assistance was however out of the question. The air strikes against Zambia and Mozambique made Muzorewa lose sympathy in Norway, and his support within the non-Socialist parties was faltering.

It is difficult to assess the importance of the NGOs such as the Norwegian Action Against Apartheid and the Norwegian Council for Southern Africa, parts of their archives may have been lost, and naturally such organisations do not work on a very systematic basis. It appears that there was only a small number of people taking active part in their work. That is not to say they were not influential; their representatives were clearly competent in their use of the media, study groups, demonstrations etc. They issued several publications about the situation in Rhodesia, providing an alternative source of information on the conflict. In 1977 the Norwegian Council for Southern Africa organised a large hearing about Southern Africa that brought awareness about the situation to the public and credibility to the organisation.

Rhodesia was but one of the questions these NGOs were concerned with, and only in 1978 and 1979 was Rhodesia the most important of these. Angola and Mozambique were important both before and after their liberation, and South Africa was always regarded as the key problem. Rhodesia was certainly important to them, but it is questionable whether they had any real influence on Norwegian foreign policy. Their support of the liberation movements was strong, but they had less to say about how the government should treat the case of Rhodesia, apart from increasing financial support to ZANU and ZAPU. Their main merit was the public interest they were able to prompt through the media, demonstrations, their information service, and their ability to raise public awareness about the situation in the region as a whole.

With the decreasing importance of the dissenting voices, opposition against the government's continued support for the two PF-partners (ZANU and ZAPU) in late 1978 and 1979 was mainly restricted to Aftenposten. The Christian newspaper *Vårt Land* had severely criticised the non-Socialist parties for not condemning Muzorewa and the elections of 1979.[17]

As war dragged on in Rhodesia it became clear that it was only a question of time before the internal solution was to collapse. In spite of the Norwegian non-Socialist parties' efforts to redirect support to ZANU and ZAPU to the UNHCR or the International Red Cross, Norway had continued to give direct support to these two liberation movements. There had been repeated Norwegian signs of frustration regarding the liberation movements inability to *unite* in their fight for majority rule. Viewed from one of the world's most homogeneous societies it was difficult to understand why ZANU and ZAPU could not better co-ordinate their efforts to overthrow the Smith regime. Indeed, there had been Norwegian threats to cut off support if the movements not able to stop fighting each other.[18]

There are several factors that make Norway's role in the final stages of the Rhodesian drama interesting. Apart from the other Nordic countries, there was little support for the liberation movements by the Western gov-

---

[17] *Vårt Land* launched a comparison of Ian Smith and the South African PM John Vorster with Adolf Hitler and his German commissioner in Norway, Josef Terboven, 23 November 1978.

[18] UD 25 4/25, 40, memorandum talks Stoltenberg and Muzorewa, 2 September 1976.

ernments. Some financial aid did trickle in from Holland and from West Germany, but the main support came from Norway and Sweden. Norway was a member of NATO and depended totally on her allies for her security needs. Traditionally, Britain had been the single most important guarantor of Norwegian security, although this role was perhaps taken over by the US and West Germany in the late seventies. As mentioned above, the Labour government refused to see the situation in Southern Africa as solely an East/West conflict, and clearly intended to demonstrate to the African countries that at least some Western countries were trustworthy. On repeated occasions, but not with great success, Norway tried to drive this point home with Britain and her other allies.

Another fact that put Norway in an interesting position in 1979 was the election to the UN Security Council. Norway's membership at the time that the case of Rhodesia was actually solved, was of course partly coincidental. On the other hand it was in harmony with the more ambitious foreign policy initiated by Minister of Foreign Affairs Knut Frydenlund in the late seventies. This development took place as other important political changes happened in the West. In the US, the Carter administration had greater respect for the integrity of small countries than some of the preceding administrations. A much stronger emphasis was placed on human rights, and the US ambassador to the UN, the African-American Andrew Young, took profound interest in finding a solution for Rhodesia.

In Britain, the Tories under their new leader Margaret Thatcher resumed power in May 1979. Lord Carrington, the new Foreign Secretary, was in the words of the British Permanent Representative to the UN, Anthony Parsons "determined to shed the albatross of Rhodesia from the neck of British foreign policy".[19] Norway would have to find a balance between the more liberally inclined US government and the expected pro-Muzorewa line of Mrs. Thatcher. As a member of the Security Council, Norway was seated at a most important table, together with her Western allies France, the USA, Britain and Portugal. Norway's powerful neighbour, the Soviet Union was also represented, as were important African nations like Zambia and Nigeria.

The membership of this selected circle made Norway a most interesting interlocutor in 1979. In this last year of Rhodesia's existence, Norway was heavily involved in the "diplomats' liberation" of Southern Africa. Knut Frydenlund, State Secretary Thorvald Stoltenberg and special adviser in Security Council matters, Tom Vraalsen, were leading figures in the Norwegian diplomatic efforts. On several occasions they met with the PF leaders Joshua Nkomo and Robert Mugabe, while contact with Muzorewa had ceased in the second half of 1979. There were also repeated meetings with

---

[19] Neil Parsons: *The new history of Southern Africa*. London: Macmillan, 1995, p.131.

Andrew Young and Lord Carrington as well as with US vice-president Walter Mondale.

One point Norwegian officials always stressed in their talks with British representatives was the importance of finding a solution that was acceptable to *all* parties concerned. In talking with the British, that meant a solution not excluding the PF. The British were frustrated by what they perceived as the PF's lack of interest in real negotiations about Rhodesia's future. Indeed, the liberation movements had two interests in these final stages of liberation; majority rule, of course, was one. However, differences between the two organisations comprising PF, ZANU and ZAPU, were great and mutual trust was limited. Both movements, accordingly, sought the best possible basis to negotiate from, which meant securing as much as possible through military strength. After all, negotiations with Smith had failed numerous times, trust in him was non-existent, and victory on the battlefield was coming closer. Over and over again, the point of including all parties was made by the Norwegians. The British were not uncomprehending, and knowing the liberation movements' respect for Nordic views, British officials worked to persuade their Norwegian colleagues to seek to moderate the PF's demands. This was a repeated pattern in both the negotiations in Geneva in 1976 and later in connection with the final talks at the Lancaster House conference in London in 1979.

Norway had a tight rope to balance as the case of Rhodesia came closer to a settlement, for what kind of settlement would it be? On the one hand, Britain was Norway's chief trading partner and a prominent ally. There were indications that the British government was heading for a solution unacceptable to PF, the OAU and to the Frontline States. On the other hand, Norway had strongly advocated majority rule in Southern Africa, and the country's political credibility was at stake. The ties with the liberation movements had grown strong, so had the ties with the Frontline States, Norway had repeatedly supported Zambia in the UN, and president Julius Nyerere in Tanzania was also regarded as a friend and ally.

What then was to be done? As some sort of end dragged near, the main worry of the Ministry of Foreign Affairs in Oslo was that a solution unacceptable to the PF was going to be reached. This explains the increased diplomatic efforts made by Norwegian officials in 1979, they did not wish to make a choice between such parties. Secretly though, a choice was prepared by State Secretary Johan Jørgen Holst of the Labour Party. There was an obvious frustration over what was deemed a British lack of flexibility, and Norway worked hard to avoid a choice. At the end of the day, however, Holst drafted a memorandum to Frydenlund, in which he argued that if a choice *had to be made*, the relationship with Britain had to prevail. This was based on the long-time ties between Britain and Norway. Holst stressed that this choice would have to be made in a manner not jeopardising the relationship with Third World countries, but was unable to explain just how.[20]

Luckily however, this option was never tested. An agreement *was* reached at Lancaster House 24 December 1979, paving the way for democratic elections and independence in 1980. The one subject of negotiation identified by Holst, the length of the period of transition, was solved by the parties. The fact that Norway would have chosen solidarity with Britain if forced to, must not obscure the fact that repeated efforts were made to *avoid* such a choice. Indeed, the Britons had emphasised their displeasure at the very pro-African stance of the Norwegian government. More than once there had been warnings from the British ambassador and from the British delegation to the UN. It had been made clear that Mrs. Thatcher would be "very cross", should the Norwegian representative in the Security Council cause any difficulties. On one occasion Lord Carrington told the lawyers of the Norwegian Ministry of Foreign Affairs, sensing their search attempt to hide in judicial questions, plainly to "go to hell".[21]

In supporting the cause of the liberation movements in the Security Council, Norway was in the fortunate position of not being the only small, Western member. There was also Portugal, slowly trying to rebuild her reputation in Africa. Only few years after ceasing to be a colonial power in Africa, Portugal had been able to restore some respect in Southern Africa. Needless to say, Portugal had a lot to lose from once again letting a African majority down. So to some extent, Norway and Portugal had concurrent interests in Southern Africa, and the two countries were able to work together on several occasions in the Security Council, making it easier to disagree with Britain.

Conclusion

Norway was but a minor player in the liberation of Southern Africa, but her role should still not be trivialised. Lasting support for African liberation movements was rare in the West, and it was even rarer among NATO members. There was a strong altruistic element in this support. For long, the political costs of this support had been limited, but as the political costs were rising, support continued. In the Third World, the Western powers were often regarded as supporters of the white suppresser regimes in Southern Africa, and Nordic efforts were made to show that strong forces in the West did in fact support majority rule.

The Nordic countries are small and the funds they could provide were limited. This support had a moral side and an economic side. It filled a moral void that other Western countries had been unwilling or unable to fill.

---

[20] UD 25 4/25 B, 29, memorandum Holst, 13 November 1979.

[21] UD 25 4/25, 51, Norwegian Embassy in London to the Ministry of Foreign Affairs, Oslo, 20 November 1979.

Few, if any strings were attached to this aid. There had been statements that aid might be restricted if the liberation movements were not able to unite. Norway to a certain degree also tried to influence her major ally in Africa, Tanzania, to pressure the PF to accept a settlement. Separate letters were sent from Norwegian prime minister Nordli and the Danish prime minister Anker Jørgensen, in which Julius Nyerere was urged to use his influence, at the same time as Norway and Denmark were to put pressure on Britain.[22] If this yielded any results may be an open question, but an effort was clearly made. There were never any threats, though, to cut development aid. Largely, the Norwegian aid was given without ulterior motives. It was self-serving only in the sense that it would promote peaceful relations in international politics—an important point in a small NATO country sharing a border with the Soviet Union.

---

[22] UD 25 4/25, 51, Confidential memorandum Vraalsen, 6 November 1979.

Chapter 5

"Fuelling the Apartheid War Machine": A Case Study of Shipowners, Sanctions and Solidarity Movements

Tore Linné Eriksen and Anita Kristensen Krokan

Introduction[1]

The supply of crude oil was vital for the survival of the apartheid economy and the South African war machine. It is, therefore, not difficult to understand why the African National Congress (ANC) and the international anti-apartheid movement singled out oil as a critical issue in the struggle for sanctions against the South African minority regime. While the Norwegian trade with South Africa was rather modest in terms of commodities (see table 1), Norwegian shipowners in the tankers market occupied a prominent position as transporters of crude oil and oil products. The main focus of this chapter will, therefore, be on the shipping of crude oil by Norwegian tankers. (For a further discussion of the Norwegian debate on sanctions, see chapters 1, 6 and 7). The idea is to take a closer look at how the Norwegian shipowners, the anti-apartheid movement, the main political parties and the successive governments responded to the ANC call for oil and transport sanctions as a step towards ending apartheid. The period in question spans from the early 1980s to the adoption of the Norwegian sanction laws in 1987.

As is evident from other parts of this study, the sanctions issue is only one element in the Norwegian policies towards Southern Africa. There are, however, several reasons why the role of the Norwegian shipping industry merits special treatment as a case study. The most important reason is the fact that the support to the liberation movements and the Frontline States was accepted across the political spectrum, while the deliveries of oil to the apartheid regime turned out to be a highly contentious issue.

---

[1] This case study is largely based on Anita Kristensen: *Norske myndigheter og boikotten av Sør-Afrika*. Thesis, University of Oslo, 1996; R. Hengevold/J. Rodenburg (eds.): *Embargo. Apartheid's Oil Secrets Revealed*. Amsterdam: Amsterdam University Press, 1996 and Tore Linné Eriksen: "Norge, sanksjoner og Sør-Afrika" ("Norway, sanctions and South Africa") pp. 83–112 in *Norsk Utenrikspolitisk Årbok 1985*. Oslo: Norwegian Institute of International Affairs, 1986. The authors also thank Karin Beate Theodorsen for her generous assistance during the initial phase of this project.

Background: Norwegian official policy until 1984

During the Labour Party minority government (1973–1981) Norway imposed various unilateral sanctions against South Africa, such as prohibiting
new bank loans, investments and export credit insurances. At the same time,
sports and cultural links were kept at a minimum. Apart from these actions,
Norway—together with the other Nordic countries—was consistently calling for mandatory sanctions within the UN system. From the late 1970s the
official Norwegian policy also stated that there was to be no sale to South
Africa of oil produced from the North Sea oil fields.[2] This position resulted
from a "gentlemen's agreement" between the Norwegian government and
the companies exporting Norwegian oil. There were, however, no legal restrictions on Norwegian tankers transporting oil originating from other
countries to South Africa. This seemingly inconsistent attitude was dramatically exposed at the beginning of the 1980s, mainly as a result of the concerted efforts of the Norwegian Council for Southern Africa (NOCOSA) and
the Shipping Research Bureau (SRB). While NOCOSA had been formed in
1967 (see chapter 6) as an umbrella anti-apartheid movement, SRB was set
up in Amsterdam in 1980 to monitor and make public the involvement of
shipping companies in supplying oil to South Africa.[3] According to SRB, the
first aim was

> ... the publication of comprehensive lists of oil tankers which had visited African
> ports during at least 24 hours in 1979 and 1980, together with their owners, flags
> and cargo capacities; the publication of a black list of shipping companies and
> ships (especially those of the major oil companies) which had made themselves
> guilty of shipping oil to South Africa; the extension of this basic data with the
> "voyage histories" of the tankers in question, with the specific goal of determin-
> ing whether a pattern of any kind could be elucidated from the data respecting
> the origin of the oil and the various detours and tricks of the embargo-breaking
> trade by means of which oil eventually wound up in South Africa (swap
> arrangements, transhipments in Rotterdam, the Netherlands Antilles, Singa-
> pore).[4]

The first publication produced by the SRB was a special report on Norway,
presented in Oslo on 3 December 1980. This report especially featured the

---

[2] Stortingsmelding nr. 26 (1985–86): *Om norske tiltak mot Sør-Afrika*, p. 9.

[3] According to Øystein Gudim: "A defeat for the shipping lobby? The Norwegian experience"
in R. Hengevold/J. Rodenburg (eds.), op.cit., there was a distinct Norwegian input to the establishment of The Shipping Research Bureau. In late 1979, the left wing weekly *Ny Tid* (New
Times) carried a story about Norwegian oil tankers from the Bergesen Group delivering crude
oil to South Africa in June and July in the same year. The source for this piece of information
was a report to the Ministry of Foreign Affairs from the General-Consulate in Cape Town.
While other newspapers paid little attention to the story, the issue was brought up at the UN-
sponsored International Seminar on the Role of Transnational Corporations in South Africa,
held in London in early December 1979. Øystein Gudim, who attended the conference, explains
how some of the first informal contacts on the oil sanctions issue were made during the course
of this conference.

[4] R. Hengevold/J. Rodenburg, op.cit., p. 59.

history and movements of the Norwegian tanker "Havdrott", which according to public reports had made two trips to South Africa between January 1979 and October 1980. Investigations by the SRB showed, however, that possibly 12 trips had been undertaken during this period, without having been disclosed to the international shipping press (read: Lloyd's).[5]

Based on the 1980 report issued by the SRB, the shipowners were criticised for sabotaging resolutions by the OPEC countries to not supply South Africa with oil, as well as neglecting resolutions passed by the UN General Assembly calling for a mandatory oil embargo on South Africa. Anti-apartheid activists in Norway, as well as the mass media, showed a keen interest in the material provided by the SRB. Close links were also developed with the ANC London Office, where Frene Ginwala on many occasions showed great interest in exposing the role that was played by a large number of Norwegian tankers.

Following extensive mass media coverage of the documentation provided by NOCOSA/SRB about the heavy involvement of Norwegian tankers in transporting crude oil to South Africa, the shipowners were met by strong moral reactions from broad sections of the political establishment as well as the general public. Even if the oil transports were not prohibited in a legal sense, they were considered morally and politically unacceptable. The shipowners began to censor the information they regularly provided to the business newspaper "Norges Handels- og Sjøfartstidende".[6] In the weekly "Shipping List" they would no longer include Cape Town and Durban as destinations for tankers, and they were trying their best to camouflage trips to South Africa.[7]

The public pressure for oil and shipping sanctions was increasing in line with the general acceptance of the need for trade sanctions as a means of fighting apartheid. In the question hour in Parliament in January 1983, Bjarne Ytterhorn from the rightwing "Progress Party" wanted to know if the Conservative Party minority government agreed to the proposal from Kaci Kullman Five (MP, Conservative) to instruct the shipping companies to report all calls at South African harbours to the Norwegian authorities. Even if the Minister assured the questioner that no actions to restrict the shipping companies would be taken, his answer reflected the anxiety shared by representatives from most political parties, the Conservative Party included, about the need for actions of some kind against Norwegian shipping companies involved in trading with South Africa.

This anxiety was becoming more pronounced when the conservative minority government, headed by Kåre Willoch, was succeeded in June 1983 by a coalition which also included the Centre Party as well as the Christian

---

[5] Ibid., p. 62. The case of "Havdrott" had already been exposed by Norwegian newspapers, see for instance a front page report in the liberal newspaper *Dagbladet*, 12 April 1980.

[6] The newspaper has since changed its name to *Dagens Næringsliv* (Daily Business).

[7] Gudim, op.cit., p. 282–283.

People's Party. The latter was well known for having strong anti-apartheid activists as members, and the Church of Norway played a prominent role in the anti-apartheid movement (see chapter 7). It is also worth noting that the Minister for Commerce and Shipping, Asbjørn Haugstvedt, belonged to the Christian People's Party. The anti-apartheid organisations, as well as the Church, expected him to stop the shipping companies from transporting crude oil to the racist regime, whereas his fellow conservative members of government were far more reluctant to interfere with the commercial interests of the shipowners community. The Norwegian Shipowners Association (NSA) had historically developed close links with the government, irrespective of its political colours, and the Ministry of Commerce and Shipping in particular, and was used to getting their way. The NSA was, consequently, prepared to fight to continue their traditional relationship with South Africa and to avoid any kind of restrictions or sanctions. As we will see, the NSA also had a well functioning lobby system that could easily be mobilised for this purpose.

When Bishop Desmond Tutu was awarded the Nobel Peace Prize in October 1984, the banning of Norwegian oil transports to South Africa became an even hotter political issue. A call for sanctions had been made by Desmond Tutu earlier in the same year when addressing a hearing on South Africa's aggression against its neighbouring countries, which was hosted by NOCOSA in Oslo (see chapter 6). Researchers and activists associated with the anti-apartheid movement contributed several newspaper articles focusing on Desmond Tutu's strong request for economic sanctions against the apartheid regime. A recurrent theme was the inconsistent behaviour of giving the Peace Prize to Bishop Tutu while simultaneously allowing Norwegian ships to oiling the war machine. It was also claimed that as much as one third of the South African oil import was delivered by Norwegian tankers, and that South Africa was storing oil and securing enough deliveries to continue the illegal occupation of Namibia.[8]

Registration of oil transports

As a step towards a more comprehensive sanctions law, the NOCOSA in the early 1980s consistently argued for a system of registration of oil transports to South Africa. The aim was to identify the number of shipping calls to South African harbours and to increase transparency concerning these calls. In making this call for registration, the NOCOSA also hoped to avoid being accused by the NSA of publishing exaggerated estimates of the volume of oil deliveries to South Africa by Norwegian tankers. The proposals were promptly and vehemently rejected by the NSA, which were not used to public investigation of this kind.

---

[8] Tore Linné Eriksen: "Fredspris og oljefrakt", Norwegian Institute for International Affairs, Pressetjeneste, 23 October 1984.

The files of the NSA from 1984 to 1987 concerning this issue reflect the great resistance within the shipping community towards any measures to be taken to reduce the involvement in transporting oil to South Africa. In particular,-the NSA—not surprisingly—strongly objected to the principles of making information about each individual call public and to including Norwegian-owned ships flying under foreign flags. The wide range of letters and memoranda sent to the Parliament, to the political parties, to the civil service, to the government as well as to high-ranking and influential individuals clearly demonstrate how much was considered to be at stake.[9] The number of newspaper articles, the frequent correspondence with the shipping companies as well as other organisations within the shipping industry, in addition to the co-operation with the other Nordic shipowners' associations, also indicate that any effective measures to limit the deliveries of oil to the apartheid regime were regarded as a serious threat to the Norwegian shipping industry. The tone of voice in the correspondence, including the hidden and more open "warnings" from the shipowners about the economic consequences for the country of any limitations or banning legislation being introduced, also add to this viewpoint.

On 15 March 1984 the NSA responded to an inquiry from the Ministry of Oil and Energy concerning statistics from the Shipping Research Bureau, showing that from 1981/82 thirty-four Norwegian tankers called at ports in South Africa for possible oil deliveries. In their reply the NSA did not deny that oil may have been delivered by Norwegian registered tankers, but instead chose to focus mainly on the origin of the oil, concluding that it must have been loaded in one of the Arab states. This may have been the case, due to the complicated and less transparent ways in which contracts were entered into. Most shipowners involved with oil transports operate in the spot market, which means that the ships are rented to contractors for a certain period of time without the owner having information about the final call of the ship.

In response to her call for an embargo on oil transport to South Africa, the leader of the opposition—Gro Harlem Brundtland (MP, Labour)—also received a personal letter and a lengthy statement on the various aspects of oil deliveries to South Africa, in which the NSA reiterated that shipowners exercised limited control in deciding the destination of oil deliveries. Apart from emphasising the point that oil cargoes on board tankers might be sold a number of times before being unloaded, the NSA argued that unilateral regulations omitting certain harbours might destroy the possibility for Norwegian shipowners to compete in the international market. According to NSA the main actors in the international oil market were the oil-exporting countries and the major oil companies, while the transporting companies played a modest role. The NSA also pointed to the possible effect the pro-

---

[9] What was at stake did not necessarily have to be in terms of lost income. It could just as well be the fear of losing a market position.

posed system of registration might have on employment, concluding that restrictions on transports of oil to South Africa was only acceptable as a part of a broader agreement between the major shipping countries, preferably within the framework of United Nations.

The NSA provided the Ministry of Foreign Affairs with the same arguments, adding that out of a total yearly freight income of NOK 750 million on transports to and from South Africa, the income on transport of oil did not amount to more than approximately NOK 70 million.[10] In the same letter, the NSA also questioned the allegations by the Shipping Research Bureau that Norwegian tankers delivered about 35% of the total South African oil import. Furthermore, the NSA rejected claims that Norwegian tankers had been concealing their identity or destinations when involved in the transport of oil.[11] This conclusion left no doubt that any unilateral restrictions on Norwegian shipping companies were totally unacceptable.

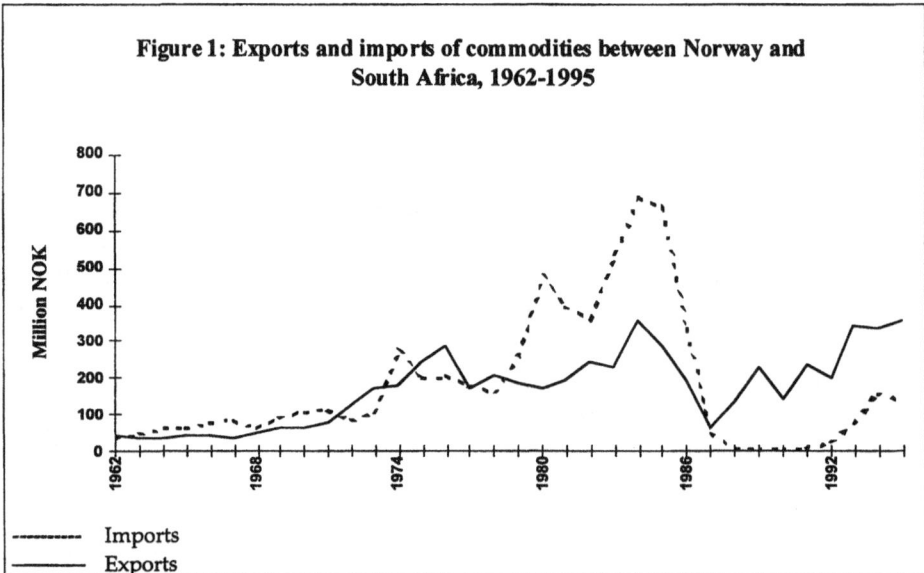

Figure 1: Exports and imports of commodities between Norway and South Africa, 1962-1995

---------- Imports
———— Exports

Source: Kristensen (1996) based on Historical Statistics, Statistics Norway, Oslo–Kongsvinger, 1995.

1985/86: Increasing pressure for sanctions against South Africa

During 1985 the struggle for international sanctions against the apartheid regime was intensified in Norway as well as in the international community at large. As is shown in chapter 6, NOCOSA was also very active lobbying local authorities to support and implement sanctions. This campaign also resulted in harbour authorities boycotting ships that made trips to and from

---

[10] NSA letter to the Ministry of Foreign Affairs, 11 July 1984.

[11] Several examples were given by Norwegian newspapers during 1985, see for instance *Arbeiderbladet*, 11 July 1985 and *Dagbladet*, 12 and 17 July 1985.

South Africa. At the same time, the trade figures graphically documented that the trade with South Africa, which had always been at a fairly low level, significantly picked up in the years up to 1984. (See figure 1.) The intensification of the debate on sanctions also reflected the mounting resistance towards the South African apartheid regime, as witnessed by the resurgence of mass protests led by the United Democratic Front. In addition to the ANC call for sanctions, which had been consistently made since the late 1950s, the same request came from the UDF, the trade unions (COSATU) and the South African Council of Churches. In Norway, the debate was particularly linked to the increasing trade figures, which peaked in 1984, and the fact that Norwegian tankers were involved in transporting a substantial part of the oil needed by South Africa. Desmond Tutu had also called for oil sanctions during his visit to Norway to receive the Nobel Peace Prize in December 1984. In Lusaka in March 1985 ANC and SWAPO issued a joint "Call for an Oil Embargo", signed by Oliver Tambo and Sam Nujoma. The call was accompanied by an ANC press statement entitled *Oil Fuels Apartheid*, which included a black list of "shipping companies and traders known to have been involved in supply and transport of oil to South Africa since 1979".[12]

In January 1985 discussions had already opened between the Ministry of Commerce and Shipping and the shipowners, based on a set of proposals submitted by NOCOSA a few months earlier and supported by the trade unions, requesting public registration of all ship calls on South Africa. The NSA still strongly argued against any public registration of Norwegian ships, and warned that even modest measures might have serious consequences. In a letter to the Minister for Commerce and Shipping in February 1985 it was also warned that any negative effects from preventing Norwegian ships calling at South African harbours would be followed by demands for economic compensation.

27 March 1985 the Minister for Commerce and Shipping, Asbjørn Haugstvedt (Christian People's Party) presented a programme of action, containing some rather modest proposals on the oil issue.[13] The Parliament was also informed that the Ministry of Justice was considering, in co-operation with all parties concerned, a ban on the *sale* of Norwegian crude oil to South Africa. As for the registration of ships calling at South African harbours, the Minister announced that a voluntary system would be established in co-operation with the NSA, whereby the NSA would provide quarterly reports to the Ministry of Commerce and Shipping about the number of Norwegian-*registered* tankers which had delivered crude oil to South Africa as well as the quantity in question. According to the proposal, no names of ships or shipping companies were to be mentioned. It can only be specu-

---

[12] ANC/SWAPO: *A call for sanctions*. London, 7 August 1985; Frene Ginwala (ANC): "A question of political will", *The Observer*, 25 August 1985 and R. Hengevold/J. Rodenburg, op.cit., p. 105.

[13] Stortingsforhandlingene 27 March 1985.

lated to what extent the Ministry had been influenced by its high-ranking civil servants, who were generally known to echo the views of the NSA.

When debating the programme of action in early June 1985, the Foreign Affairs Committee of the Parliament called for more comprehensive and strict measures to be taken.[14] The committee unanimously asked for a system of registration that included all Norwegian-*owned* ships—not only oil tankers—including those registered under a "flag of convenience". It even went further and recommended that the registrations should be carried out by a government body (The Ministry of Commerce and Shipping) instead of by the NSA, and that the lists of names of the ships be made publicly available. The Foreign Affairs Committee was at this time headed by Jakob Aano (Christian People's Party), who was known for his interest in Third World issues and for his longstanding involvement with the liberation struggle in Southern Africa. Together with other prominent MPs, the chairperson of the committee also served on the parliamentary "contact group" which had been established by NOCOSA (see chapter 6).

During the plenary debate in Parliament on 7 June 1985, the recommendations made by the Committee on Foreign Affairs were supported by all the parties except for the right wing "Progressive People's Party", which objected to any actions being taken against the South African regime. On the other hand, the Socialist Left Party favoured a sanctions law banning all trade and shipping links with South Africa.

The activist position taken by the Parliament came as a great surprise to the NSA, which now had to conclude that a system of registration could not be avoided. The lobbying activities of the NSA, consequently, were aimed at a system of registration to be undertaken by NSA itself on a voluntary basis. In addition, an internal memorandum reveals that the strategy chosen included efforts to postpone the final political decision[15]. When approaching the Ministry of Commerce and Shipping, the NSA also favoured a method of registration that did not include Norwegian-owned ships flying foreign flags. In a comprehensive memorandum to the Ministry, prepared in early September, it was argued that publication of the names of the ships could violate confidentiality clauses in contracts, thereby resulting in their cancellation altogether. This could, furthermore, lead to the shipowners being forced to sell their ships, which in this case might result in loss of employment opportunities for Norwegian seamen. The NSA memorandum also estimated that gross income of the 20 calls to South Africa by Norwegian-registered oil tankers amounted to NOK 50–80 million, while other earnings from the South African shipping links—bulk cargo (coal, iron ores) and special tankers transporting chemicals—were estimated to NOK 700–800 million.

---

[14] Innstilling S. Nr. 284 (1984–85), 4 June 1985.

[15] Executive meeting of the NSA, 28 August 1985.

According to the minutes from an NSA executive meeting on 25 September 1985, the NSA had already received the draft registration law from the Ministry for comments. The Minister for Commerce and Industry had also indicated at a meeting with the NSA that he would have preferred a voluntary agreement, but that he felt obliged by the recommendations by the Foreign Affairs Committee. The draft proposals, therefore, included three points that were completely unacceptable to the NSA:

– The registration was to include all ships calling at South African ports.

– The arrangement would also include Norwegian ships flying foreign flags.

– The information about the ship calls was to be made public.

In order to strengthen its case against the draft proposals, the NSA decided to ask the renowned Boston consultancy firm, Arthur D. Little Inc. to prepare a report on the consequences for Norwegian shipping of the various systems of registration or a banning of all ship calls at South African ports. Enclosed with the request was an English version of the comprehensive NSA memorandum presented to the Ministry of Commerce and Shipping on 2 September 1985. The Arthur D. Little report was based on interviews with 32 brokers, charterers and representatives from other organisations within the shipping industry, and was presented at a press conference on 4 November 1985.[16] The conclusions of the report were partly related to the general situation in the international shipping market, which was described as being depressed and overtonnaged. Concerning the consequences of a public registration of Norwegian ships, the report stated that: "The official publication of the names of Norwegian ships calling at South African ports could be as damaging to owners as a total ban, regardless of whether the name of the charterer is also identified".[17]

When presenting the Little Report, the managing director of the NSA, David Vikøren, estimated that if adopted the proposed law on registration might mean a loss of approximately 5–10% of their share in the international shipping market for Norwegian shipowners. He also stated that previous estimates indicating losses of approximately 200–300 jobs and an income of NOK 700–900 million were too conservative, and that the consequences would be considerably larger.[18] It was also argued that the publication of the names of the ships calling at South African ports constituted a violation of South African laws, which made all information concerning imports of chemical and oil products illegal. According to David Vikøren, the consul-

---

[16] Arthur D. Little: *Impact on Norwegian shipowners' charter prospects of possible government legislation on calls to South African ports. Report to The Norwegian Shipowners' Association.* November 1985.

[17] Ibid., p. 18.

[18] These figures obviously include indirect costs and the loss of income from all shipping links with South Africa.

tancy report concluded that the proposed arrangement of registration would represent nothing less than the closing down of the Norwegian shipping industry altogether.[19]

The NSA intensified their lobbying activities throughout the autumn. Apart from distributing the Arthur D. Little report to various seamen and sea officers' organisations, the relevant Parliamentary committees and the most influential newspapers, the press at large was provided with a great number of press releases and articles describing the possible damage for the shipping industry if the proposed law were to be adopted by the Parliament. In a letter to the Prime Minister Kåre Willoch, it was reiterated that Norway would lose between 10–20% of its total shipping market if the law was adopted.[20] The Prime Minister, who was known for having shipping interests close at heart, was asked to adhere to the original agreement between the Ministry of Commerce and Shipping and the NSA to introduce a voluntary registration without revealing the names of the ships or shipping companies.[21]

The lobbying activities of the NSA during the autumn of 1985 turned out to be highly successful in forcing the government to reconsider its position. When the Ministry of Commerce and Shipping announced the Government proposals on economic measures against apartheid in December 1985, the methods of registration were quite different from the ones recommended by the overwhelming majority in Parliament. According to the proposals, the arrangement for registration did not include Norwegian-owned ships flying foreign flags, the registration was to be undertaken by the NSA and only the number of calls and the total tonnage were to be made available to the general public. The Government also requested the shipowners not to enter into contracts specifically designed for deliveries of crude oil to South Africa.[22] In addition, the Ministry gave notice that they would propose a law enforcing total sanctions on sale of Norwegian crude oil to South Africa.

When the limited economic actions to be taken against South Africa were presented, not only the Labour Party and the Socialist Left Party but also the three centre-liberal parties represented in the coalition government expressed their disappointment with the weak measures concerning registration of ships transporting oil to South Africa. This strong reaction should also be understood as a response to the SRB report on the Bergesen d.y. & Co shipping company, which maintained that the major Norwegian company was most probably the world's foremost transporter of crude oil to

---

[19] Introduction by David Vikøren 4 November 1985 upon presenting the Arthur D. Little report.

[20] Letter from NSA to Kåre Willoch 4 November 1985.

[21] While serving as a member of Parliament, Kåre Willoch had additional income from the business lobby, including the NSA. See Gudim, op.cit., p. 284.

[22] NSA press release 18 December 1985.

South Africa in the 1979–1985 period.[23] Even the primate of the Church of Norway, bishop Andreas Aarflot of Oslo, reacted strongly. In his New Year Message delivered on January 1 1986, he criticised both the Government and the shipowners and called for a total oil embargo against South Africa. Both parties reacted vehemently, and the managing director of the NSA wrote a personal letter to the bishop explaining the consequences of a total ban on Norwegian transport of oil to South Africa.[24] Andreas Aarflot was also criticised by members of the government representing the Christian People's Party, among them the Minister for Church and Education, Kjell Magne Bondevik. On the other hand, he was fully supported by the Secretary-General of the Lutheran World Federation (Gunnar Stålsett) and the Secretary-General of the South African Council of Churches (Beyers Naudé).[25]

The Government White Paper presented in January 1986 was clearly a compromise between the interests of the NSA and the viewpoints of the Church, NOCOSA and other anti-apartheid organisations.[26] The Government had obviously been caught in the crossfire between contending forces that had employed effective lobbying methods. The decision was eventually made to include all Norwegian-owned ships, whether they were registered in Norway or abroad. On the other hand, only tankers involved in transport of crude oil would be part of the arrangement. From the NSA point of view, it was also noted with satisfaction that only quarterly statistics of calls and the volume would be made public. The implication of this was that the names of the ships and shipping companies involved were not to be disclosed. According to the guidelines introduced by the Government, the shipowners were expected to gradually reduce their deliveries of crude oil to South Africa. If not, the threat of a legal ban was kept in reserve.

A press statement from the Managing Director of the NSA, David Vikøren, shows that the compromise introduced had already been accepted by the NSA as the lesser of two evils. In this statement, it was emphasised that the final proposals from the Government would cause far less damage than the ones proposed by the broad majority in the Parliament. Even if the NSA still objected to unilateral measures, the registration in question would only affect parts of Norwegian shipping , and would allow time for re-arrangements. In addition the NSA noted that Norway—together with the

---

[23] The Shipping Research Bureau: *Oil shipments to South Africa by tankers owned and managed by Sig. Bergesen d.y. & Co of Norway, January 1979–January 1985 (Amsterdam: SRB, 1985).* This report followed on a similar study on A/S Thor Dahl: *Oil shipment to South Africa by the tankers Thorsaga, Thorshavet and Thorsholm, owned by A/S Thor Dahl of Norway 1981–1984* (1984). See also SRB: *West European involvement in breaking the oil embargo against South Africa* (1985).

[24] Letters to Andreas Aarflot from the managing director of the NSA, David Vikøren, 3 January 1986 and 13 January 1986.

[25] The debate following the intervention by bishop Andreas Aarflot is covered more fully by Tore Linné Eriksen, op.cit., p. 104–108. See also chapter 7.

[26] Stortingsmelding nr. 26 (1985–86), 31 January 1986.

other Nordic countries—was committed to working for comprehensive and binding UN Security Council sanctions against South Africa.[27]

The system of registration and publication related to transport of crude oil to South Africa was operational from 1 April 1986 to 30 June 1987, when it was superseded by a sanctions law banning such transport. Table 1 shows the deliveries as reported by the NSA in this period. Table 2 shows the deliveries as reported by the SRB.

Table 1. *Deliveries by Norwegian-owned tankers during the voluntary registration system*

Quarter	Number of deliveries	Flag:		Tons of crude oil
		Norwegian	Other	
1986 Apr–June	4	2	2	926,438
1986 July–Sept	2	1	1	527,466
1986 Oct–Dec	1	-	1	250,000
1987 Jan–Mach	0	-	-	0
1987 Apr–June	4	3	1	1,200,000

Source: NSA in letters: 7/7–86, 14/10–86, 23/6–87, 21/4–87, 7/7–87

Towards a crude oil embargo

As in all Western countries, calls for comprehensive sanctions and other actions to be taken against the apartheid regime were made by broad sections of the Norwegian society in 1986. This development made the limited measures—based on the compromise which was described in the previous section—seem far too cautious and out of touch with the public opinion. The NSA, now enforcing the system of registration, was undoubtedly aware that proposals for a total ban on transport of oil to South Africa might well be raised once again, and that the NSA and the shipowners were continuously being questioned on their willingness to register ships transporting crude oil. In a circular distributed to member companies on May 29 1986 it was noted that an arrangement for full publication of names of tankers calling at South African ports might well be around the corner.[28] The NSA were also concerned by the fact that the Ministry of Commerce and Shipping was considering a law banning all economic relations with South Africa. A step in that direction was taken when the Parliament in June 1986 passed legislation that banned the sale of Norwegian crude oil. The law was in the following month extended to include refined oil and gas products from the North Sea fields.[29]

---

[27] NSA Circular no. 3, 3 February 1986.

[28] NSA Circular, 29 May 1986.

[29] Although the Ministry of Oil and Energy had notified all companies operating in the North Sea fields that it disapproved of the sale of Norwegian oil to South Africa, small quantities had found their way to South Africa. A report to this effect had been published by the SRB during the NOCOSA hearing on South Africa's Aggression against Neighbouring Countries, held in Oslo in March 1984. See Gudim op.cit., p. 283.

Table 2. *Deliveries by Norwegian-owned tankers during the voluntary registration system(1986–87). Registrations are by the Shipping Research Bureau. The list includes ships that were less than 50% Norwegian-owned.*

Sailed to South Africa from	Shipping company	Owner of oil cargo	Month in South Africa	Dwt. Tonnage
Quatar/UAE/Oman	Periscopus Norman Intern.	-	Mars/Apr-86	224,607
UAE/Oman	Mosvold	-	Apr-86	274,938
Pers. G.	Ugland	-	Apr-86	230,683
Iran/UAE	Bergesen	Marimpex	Apr-86	230,683
Saudi-A/Pers. G.	Bergesen	-	May-86	284,919
UAE/Oman	Bergesen	-	May-86	284,522
Bahrain	John Frederiksen	Marimpex	May-86	103,332
South Yemen	Ugland	-	May/June-86	54,626
UAE Norman Intern.	Periscopus June-86	224,607		
UAE	Mosvold	Marc Rich	June/July-86	274,938
UAE/Oman	Bergesen	Marimpex	July-86	289,981
Pers. G	Bergesen	Marc Rich	July-86	284,522
Pers. G	John Frederiksen	Marc Rich	Aug/Sept-86	218,035
UAE	Bergesen	-	Oct-86	284,522
UAE	Mosvold	-	Des-86	274,938
Iran	Bergesen	Marc Rich	Mars-87	284,507
Oman	Bergesen	Transvorld Oil	Apr-87	289,981
Saudi-A/UAE/Quatar	Bergesen	Marimpex/Mark Wolman	Apr-87	360,700
Iran	Bergesen	Marimpex	Apr-87	284,522
France	Andreas Ugland	AOT Ltd.	Apr-87	54,500
Iran/Pers. G	Mosvold	Marimpex	May-87	274,938
UEA/Oman	Bergesen	Transworld Oil	June-87	360,700
Saudi-A/Pers. G	Bergesen	-	June-87	284,522

Source: Shipping Research Bureau; Hengevold/Rodenburg, 1995.

The pressure for comprehensive sanctions reached a peak when the Government White Paper was debated in Parliament in June 1986. The debate, which coincided with the tenth anniversary of the Soweto uprising, followed a change in government from a conservative/centre coalition to a Labour Party minority government headed by Gro Harlem Brundtland. During the debate, representatives of the Labour Party strongly indicated that the new government intended to introduce comprehensive sanctions—including a ban on all transport of crude oil—in the immediate future.[30]

Throughout the summer and autumn of 1986 the NSA were actively lobbying against unilateral Norwegian shipping sanctions. This time, the other Nordic shipowners' associations were called on to write identical

---

[30] Innstilling S. Nr. 227 (1985–86).

letters to their governments advocating that Nordic shipping sanctions alone would have no effect on the South African regime unless forming part of a UN embargo.[31] The member companies were also asked to approach the Ministry of Shipping and Commerce explaining the severe consequences for Norwegian shipping if further steps were taken to limit their international market competitiveness.[32] A detailed and comprehensive paper was also presented to the Parliament, to the Prime Minister and to trade unions within the shipping industry. The letter pointed very specifically to the loss of income for the Norwegian shipping industry, as well as the great number of employees affected, if a boycott law against South Africa was introduced. Compared to previous figures presented by the NSA, it was now argued that the indirect losses might amount to NOK 4 billion and that 1,000–1,200 Norwegian crew members might lose their jobs with immediate effect. The NSA also warned that many shipping companies would be forced to close their businesses in Norway and move abroad. If this were the case, no less than 90,000 jobs within the shipping business were said to be in danger. As part of their lobbying activities directed towards the government, the political parties and the public opinion, the NSA also argued that there was no need for legal sanctions as the published figures showed that only two Norwegian-owned tankers had unloaded crude oil in South Africa in the period 1 July–30 September.

At this point the NSA strategy was obviously to postpone any legal sanctions, arguing, *inter alia*, that it was reasonable to wait for a proper evaluation of the arrangement of registration. In a paper presented to the Foreign Affairs Committee on August 7 1986, it was, however, indicated that the NSA might consider legal sanctions if they only applied to the transport of crude oil. The NSA probably recognised that legal sanctions of some kind or another were inevitable, and that the most successful strategy would be to restrict them to sectors where they would have the least economic effects. Correspondence with the shipping and brokers' companies clearly indicates that the NSA was well informed about the ongoing work in the Ministry of Commerce and Shipping and in the Foreign Affairs Committee.[33]

The Labour Party government eventually introduced its sanctions law on 14 November 1986.[34] As expected it put less severe restrictions on the shipping industry than on most other industries. The sanctions were limited

---

[31] Letters sent to the shipowners' associations in Denmark, Sweden and Finland, 4 August 1986.

[32] Letter to the NSA members, 7 August 1986.

[33] Circular sent to shipping and brokers' companies 30 October 1986. That the NSA had access to privileged information is also indicated in a letter to Kaci Kullman Five (MP, Conservative) on 23 December 1986, signed by Arild Wegner. In the letter, which expresses disappointment as to statements made by Kjell Magne Bondevik (Christian People's Party), Kaci Kullmann Five is asked whether "we may reveal what we know without causing you trouble" (authors translation).

[34] Ot.prp. nr. 14 (1986–87). *Om lov om økonomisk boikott av Sør-Afrika og Namibia for å bekjempe apartheid.*

to a ban on transport of crude oil only, while refined oil products could still be shipped to South Africa. Neither were general cargo, bulk and chemicals transport in cross-trading for other countries banned. It was also stated that a delivery of crude oil would not constitute a violation of the sanctions law if the Norwegian company in question could not reasonably have known that the cargo was destined for South Africa. Since the sanctions law also opened for exemptions in other vital areas, such as manganese ore import, it has aptly been described as a "Swiss cheese", full of holes (see chapter 6). The exemptions made for manganese ore explain why Norwegian import from South Africa actually increased in the 1987–88 period. Several violations of the sanctions law were also reported without any action being taken by the proper authorities.[35]

In accordance with estimates presented by the NSA itself, it can safely be concluded that the most profitable parts of the shipping links with South Africa were not affected by the legislation. In a circular informing the shipowners about the law, the NSA made a point of confirming that the Government had taken into account the warning that severe consequences would follow if more extensive limitations were to be introduced.[36] In fact, selected parts of the law proposal were a direct copy of the text that had been contained in the letters from the NSA.

The NSA, however, were not satisfied with the term "Norwegian ships" and called on experts at the Faculty of Law in Oslo to present their views on whether the law could be applied to Norwegian ships flying foreign flags.[37] They were also trying to convince members of Parliament, and the members of the Foreign Relations Committee in particular, that applying sanctions on an industry as international as the shipping industry would imply economic as well as psychological consequences. The correspondence with key MPs, among them Kjell Magne Bondevik (Christian People's Party) and Kaci Kullman Five (Conservative Party) shows that the NSA were now worried that the Committee would consider additional measures affecting the shipping industry, i.e. including the deliveries of refined oil and gas products as well.[38]

When the Foreign Affairs Committee finally presented its recommendations in February 1987, the NSA seemed to be relieved that they largely corresponded with the government proposals[39]. Most importantly, the law was limited to transport of crude oil only, and this did not apply to the transport of oil products or any other goods. In a circular to their members, the NSA referred to the political pressure for stronger sanctions, even voiced from

---

[35] *AFRIKA-Informasjon*, nr. 5, 1989, p. 5–9.

[36] NSA Circular to shipowners, 14 November 1986.

[37] Letters to Finn Seyersted (21 November 1986) and Eivind Smith (4 December 1986).

[38] Letters to Kaci Kullman Five (23 December 1986) and Kjell Magne Bondevik (5 January 1987).

[39] Innstilling O. Nr. 29 (1986–87). *Innstilling fra utenriks- og konstitusjonskomiteen om lov om økonomisk boikott av Sør-Afrika og Namibia for å bekjempe apartheid.*

time to time by the Prime Minister herself, and concluded that "compared to the political opinions expressed, the arguments from the shipping industry have no doubt been taken into consideration".[40] Regarding the contested issue whether sanctions adopted by Parliament could legally be applied to Norwegian-owned ships flying foreign flags, the NSA seemed satisfied with the interpretation given by the Ministry of Foreign Affairs, stating that in such cases the law was not to be applied.

The sanctions law was finally debated in Parliament on 16 March and 19 March 1987, and came into effect from 20 March.[41] The Minister of Commerce and Shipping at the time, Kurt Mosbakk, has later revealed that there were differing opinions in the Labour Party on the issue, but that those who found the law to be too weak lost out in the end.[42]

Conclusions

As we have seen above, NSA to a certain extent succeeded in their lobbying activities. No efforts seemed to have been spared to put pressure on the government, the political parties, the Church as well as the general public. The correspondence shows particularly strong ties between the NSA and the Ministry of Commerce and Shipping. The arguments employed were of a rather dramatic kind, based on figures and presenting conclusions exaggerating the consequences of unilateral sanctions against South Africa. Much money was also spent on the campaign. (The Arthur D. Little report commissioned to support the case of NSA, for instance, cost NOK 350,000).[43]

When the Norwegian government initially suggested a registration of tankers transporting crude oil to South Africa, the proposals coincided with a difficult period in the international tanker market.[44] While it is reasonable to believe the NSA recognised that one kind of restriction or another was unavoidable, the intensive lobbying activities were aimed at delaying a ban on oil transports in order to await the developments in the tanker market. While the first calls for a ban was made in the early 1980s, the law was eventually not implemented until 1987. It is fair to conclude that the campaign of the shipowners significantly contributed to the postponement and

---

[40] Circular to shipowners, 17 February 1987.

[41] 20 March 1987, no. 15 1987: *Lov om økonomisk boikott av Sør-Afrika og Namibia for å bekjempe apartheid.*

[42] Gudim, op. cit., p. 292.

[43] NSA, internal letter, 25 September 1985.

[44] The 1979 Iran Revolution and the temporary cessation of Iranian oil exports precipitated a major increase in the price of crude oil. This increase is referred to as "the 2nd tank-ship crisis" (Victor Norman and Tor Wergeland ,1981): *Stortankmarkedet frem til 1985: En analyse av markedet for tankskip over 200.000 dwt. Skipsfartsøkonomisk markedsforskning.* Senter for anvendt forskning. Norges Handelshøyskole, Rapport nr. 5/1981). The first tank-ship crisis came in 1974, and was partly a result of a decrease in demand of transport and an increase in supply of tonnage. The second crisis had significant repercussions for the world economy in general and especially for the shipping market (Martin Stopford: *Maritime Economics.* London: HarperCollins Academic, 1992, p. 72.).

that they, therefore, succeeded in one of their main aims. Since all products other than crude oil were exempted from the transport ban, the profitability of the Norwegian shipowners was not severely affected. The transport of refined oil products did continue, although it was heavily criticised by the broad anti-apartheid movement. The ban on crude oil transport also came at a fortunate time for the shipowners. With a booming international tanker market, the consequences of the restrictions imposed on shipping links with South Africa were rather limited.

On the other hand, Norway in the end was the first major shipping nation to impose a legal ban on crude oil transports to South Africa. Neither is there any doubt that even the limited measures introduced by the Norwegian government went far beyond what the NSA had originally wanted. For the first time, the Norwegian shipowners experienced that their economic and juridical arguments lost to the political and moral arguments. The question, therefore, has to be asked: How could the anti-apartheid forces of Norway, with limited resources, fight such an influential business group with enormous resources at its disposal?

In his contribution to the Shipping Research Bureau study on the history of oil transports and sanctions, Øystein Gudim of the Norwegian Council for Southern Africa (NOCOSA) points especially to the close co-operation between anti-apartheid activists and the mass media press in disclosing the transport of oil to South Africa and in raising public awareness on the issue. In this respect, the importance of the reliable information from the SRB cannot be overestimated. In spite of its limited resources and its close ties to the ANC and the anti-apartheid movement, the Bureau was often referred to by the Norwegian press as a "well-respected research institute". When explaining why the oil transports could become such an important public issue in Norway, Øystein Gudim also emphasises that the shipowners were a visible target and "enemy" easy to identify and attack.[45] Whereas the NSA were used to economic and legal arguments, they now had to enter the terrain of moral and political arguments. In this new terrain, an alliance of the Church, the trade unions and the anti-apartheid activists dominated.[46] This alliance seemed to be strengthened when the Christian People's Party entered the centre-conservative government in 1983. The fact that the Ministry for Commerce and Shipping was led by a representative of a party hosting many anti-apartheid activists, especially made the government more open to

---

[45] "Some people found it easier to engage themselves in the struggle for freedom in South Africa when there was a target within Norway to protest against. The shipowners transporting oil to South Africa became an ideal target for anti-apartheid activists from diverging backgrounds. NOCOSA's membership grew thanks to Bergesen, Mosvold and other shipowners. 'The enemy' was no longer a white regime far away but its friends in Norway", Gudim, op. cit., p. 283.

[46] This alliance included several trade unions, although it should be noted that the Seamen's Union mainly restricted itself to demanding public registration. Unlike its counterparts in Denmark and Great Britain, it decided against joining the Maritime Union against Apartheid when it was established in 1983. See Gudim, op. cit., p. 289 and chapter 8 in this study.

pressure from the Church. With the Christian People's Party back in opposition again in May 1986, the party could more freely pursue a policy of requesting a ban on all oil transports. At the same time, the change in government obliged the Labour Party to stand by at least some of its promises from their days in opposition. This development made the NSA reluctantly to reconcile themselves to the political realities.

When explaining the outcome of the struggle for sanctions, it should also be emphasised that the demands were not formed in isolation, but were part of an international pressure building up against South Africa. In the mid-1980s, the attention of the mass media was also focused on the aggression of the apartheid regime against the black majority as well as against neighbouring countries. The pressure was increased when the state of emergency was declared in South Africa in 1985 and more countries, especially the US, were seriously considering sanctions. It, therefore, made sense to describe oil as a strategic product of utmost importance for the apartheid regime. This was, as we have seen, also the way in which oil transport was being regarded by the ANC and SWAPO of Namibia. The fact that the apartheid regime itself also looked upon oil as a strategic product, was evident from the legislation which made it a criminal offence to disclose any information about the import, distribution and storing of oil.

Although Øystein Gudim argues that "the shipping industry managed to protect most of its interests and probably the most important part of the trade" and that "crude oil transports were sacrificed in order to be able to maintain the other shipping links with South Africa"[47], he nevertheless claims that the sanctions law was a moral victory for the solidarity movement and a political defeat for the NSA. With limited resources at their disposal, he also maintains that it was probably a wise decision for the anti-apartheid forces to concentrate on certain areas, in this case sanctions of crude oil transports, and to get as much publicity as possible on that particular issue. It is also a fact that stronger ties were developed between NOCOSA, the trade unions, the churches and sections of the mass media, and that this broad alliance—as has been shown in chapter 6—was of critical importance in the final years of the struggle against apartheid. Thus, the lesson has been aptly summed up: "If David is to beat Goliath, it is important to create strategic alliances".[48]

---

[47] Gudim, op.cit., p. 292.

[48] Ibid., p. 294.

Chapter 6
The Norwegian Council for Southern Africa (NOCOSA): A Study in Solidarity and Activism[1]

Nina Drolsum

Introduction

Madserud Tennis Club, Oslo, 1964. A Davis Cup tie, South Africa vs. Norway, where tennis is known as the "white sport". Demonstrations against the South African players are forbidden. On the spectator stands sit 200 anti-apartheid demonstrators who have bought tickets for the opening match. The match is in progress, and the demonstrators get up from their seats and start throwing black tennis balls onto the court, then quickly invade the court and sit down, linking themselves together and holding onto the net. The police have great difficulty in carrying the demonstrators out, and the match has to be abandoned for the day. Next day no tickets were available to the public.

The demonstrations at Madserud attracted attention in both the Norwegian and international press. The Oslo national daily, Aftenposten, was indignant; the demonstrators wore jeans and other suspect articles of clothing, and the males had beards. The demonstrators, however, came from all the political parties and organisations which formed part of *Norwegian Action Against Apartheid*, and wanted to ensure that the Norwegian Sports Association's urgent request that the match not be played was complied with.

The history of this and other similar events dating from the early 1960s resulting in ultimately significant information activities and effective political approaches to the Norwegian authorities, is an important but relatively unknown aspect of Norwegian support for the liberation of Southern Africa. This chapter aims at presenting the most important events in, and results of, the history of the *Norwegian Council for Southern Africa—NOCOSA*, from its inception in 1967 and until the first universal elections were held in South Africa in 1994.

NOCOSA's solidarity work cannot first and foremost be measured in terms of money. Although the funds collected by the Council were trans-

[1] For a more extensive discussion of the role of the Norwegian Council for Southern Africa, see Nina Drolsum: *For et fritt Afrika*. Oslo: Fellesrådet for Afrika/Solidaritet Forlag, 1999.

ferred without deduction to the liberation movements, they were merely symbolic in comparison with the amounts channelled to the liberation movements by the Norwegian Government via the Norwegian Church and the Norwegian Confederation of Trade Unions (LO). The mainspring of NOCOSA's involvement was idealistic and its principle objective was to keep a close watch on and to influence Norway's official policies towards the freedom struggle in Southern Africa. The Council's efforts in creating public awareness, influencing attitudes and providing information, came to represent an important contribution to the shaping of Norwegian foreign policy towards the apartheid regime in South Africa and indeed liberation movements throughout Southern Africa. These efforts were above all significant in constantly directing attention towards the problems caused by apartheid at times when there was no clear Norwegian political policy. Awareness and knowledge of these issues among politicians and the general public remained comparatively insignificant for a long time. It was therefore especially important for the Council to invite representatives of the liberation movements in Southern Africa to Norway and to acquaint the Norwegian authorities with their struggle. These efforts were an important contribution to establishing connections between the liberation movements and the Norwegian Government and to promoting Norwegian involvement.

The Council was also characterised by an activist approach to a greater extent than other organisations engaged in anti-apartheid activities, for instance the Norwegian Church's Council on Ecumenical and International Relations (CEIR) and the labour movement. It was a matter of active intervention, both in involving the grass roots and in participating in information work. The number of demonstrations and events organised by the Council, the stands, "Action Weeks", the exhibitions, the campaigns, participation in debates in the news media, and the issuing of press statements, was extensive. Initiatives were also taken in connection with a number of fund-raising events on behalf of the liberation movements. The magazine *Afrika Dialog* (1967–68) and later *Afrika Informasjon* with four annual issues commencing in 1978, were the only publications of their kind in Norway. NOCOSA also produced several study booklets, information bulletins, pamphlets and leaflets in the interests of informing the public.

The study booklets were an important feature of the Council's production. In these, the apartheid system and the conflicts in each of the countries in Southern Africa were described and discussed in depth. The most important current events were taken up, contributing to issues being placed on the political agenda and the Norwegian position being debated. Many of these booklets were written by Norway's foremost researchers in the field of African studies: Tore Linné Eriksen, Arne Tostensen and Elling Njål Tjønneland, who were or had themselves been, active participants in NOCOSA.

The mobilisation of the grass roots was one of the Council's foremost objectives. Broad public support was important in attempts to prompt the

Norwegian authorities into putting increased political pressure on South Africa directly or through international involvement. Schools, colleges and universities were among the major arenas chosen for this work. The activists also to a large degree consisted of committed students and pupils. The ultimately large number of local branches scattered around the country followed up centrally planned arrangements or took their own initiatives.

Through daily efforts over a lengthy period, the follow-up of specific cases, contact with political organs, the writing of articles and the issuing of press statements, NOCOSA built up an action-oriented apparatus and a significant network of contacts embracing Parliament, the Ministry of Foreign Affairs, and the press. Though there were periods when intensity may have seemed to diminish, the daily work for, and involvement in, solidarity with the freedom struggle in Southern Africa was consistently present to a high degree. While the Council's level of activity and impact were stronger in some periods than in others, such variation was particularly associated with international events which stimulated intensified effort and afforded the Council increased attention on the part of authorities and the mass media.

NOCOSA's strength has in particular been in its impact on and through the media. The reason for this was firstly that the injustices of the apartheid system have always made good copy. But it is also significant that NOCOSA has itself had competent media people, and through them enjoyed excellent contact with the newspapers. Revelations concerning violations by Norwegian shipping companies of the international oil-boycott resulted in the apartheid issue acquiring a Norwegian dimension, and additional impact. The Council also often felt that correctives to Norwegian mass media coverage of Southern Africa were called for.[2]

The Council's appointment of a special information worker in 1984 resulted in this aspect of the work being professionalised. Through the introduction of a special information strategy and by integrating its use of the media with its political activities, NOCOSA itself could often set the agenda for the debate on Southern Africa.

A progressive tightening of media censorship in South Africa in the 1980s made it difficult to obtain reliable news and information from South Africa. The Council was anxious lest this resulted in news coverage on South Africa drying up and that the world would forget South Africa in the shadow of press censorship, which moreover probably was the apartheid regime's objective. At the same time the South African authorities engaged in propaganda activities in order to delude the world with the message that the unrest in South Africa had quietened down and that the situation was not nearly as bad as some were making it out to be. NOCOSA therefore re-

[2] In 1979 Tore Linné Eriksen and Øystein Gudim presented a paper at a mass media conference at the Nordic Africa Institute on *Aftenposten's* coverage of the final days of the illegal settler regime in Zimbabwe, concluding that it had been pervasively negative throughout its discussion of the liberation movements. See chapter 4.

garded information gathering as of paramount importance, as also the possession of adequate knowledge of the situation prevailing in the whole of Southern Africa; moreover the mediation of such information to the press was coupled with participation in public information campaigns through holding lectures and making presentations. News was constantly coming from South Africa of the killing of whites by blacks and of the fear under which the whites were living because of the unrest in the country. It was thus important for NOCOSA members to speak up and remind the public of the historical background to the armed freedom struggle: the use of violence during the Sharpeville massacre in 1960, the banning of the ANC, and the impossibility of making headway through non-violent means. In 1988, the Council launched *Nytt fra Det sørlige Afrika*, a small newspaper presenting news derived from independent news agencies which could serve as a corrective to the propaganda and the censored news emanating from South Africa.

During the first few years of its existence, NOCOSA's activities were performed by a few enthusiastic souls, but the expertise acquired by the organisation in the process resulted in the authorities gradually turning to it for information and consultation. It is a measure of the Council's strength that its critics often complained that Norwegian foreign policy was governed by NOCOSA rather than by the elected political organs. Naturally this was not so, as in reality the policies implemented were far from those wished for by the Council. Indeed it was precisely in this circumstance that its significance as a promoter and provider of information lay.

The Council comes into being

As a result of the Sharpeville massacre in March 1960 and the award of the Nobel Peace Prize to Albert Luthuli of the ANC the same year, the early Norwegian anti-apartheid involvement became consolidated in organised forms. *Norwegian Action Against Apartheid (NAMA)* saw the light of day in February 1963 to promote the isolation of, and sanctions against, the South African apartheid regime. *The Crisis Fund for South Africa* was started in December the same year, in order to provide legal support for political prisoners and their families in South Africa, the fund being established as a sister organisation to the British *International Defence and Aid Fund* which had been in existence since 1959.[3] Both NAMA and the Crisis Fund were umbrella organisations with largely overlapping membership. Since the same persons were often involved in both organisations, it was deemed appropriate to merge the two into one and the same organisation. There was, moreover, a need for a broadening of public awareness so as also to encompass the entire region of Southern Africa, not least because of both Mozambique's and Angola's freedom struggles, and to create a joint council for all of

---

[3] For more on the Crisis Fund and IDAF, see chapter 1.

Southern Africa. The new Council became more than merely a combination of the two previous organisations. The area of involvement came to embrace the whole of Southern Africa and—to a lesser degree—the Portuguese colonies of Guinea-Bissau, the Cape Verde Islands, and Sao Tome and Principe. The idea was to exercise active political pressure on the basis of the broad support enjoyed by NOCOSA among its member organisations.

In this manner, the Council was launched in 1967, founded on the same kind of organisational structure as the two former organisations. Initially there were approximately 20, most of them political and other youth organisations. Gradually, trade unions and teachers' and students' unions joined NOCOSA, as well as organisations engaged in international development and other solidarity work. In 1976, the Council was opened up to individual membership, and several local branches were formed. At its maximum, the Council embraced 44 organisations, over 2,000 individual members, and 18 local branches.

The umbrella organisational model turned out to be both an asset and a liability in the performance of the Council's work. A joint organisation could not be dominated by a particular political direction, as was the case with many other solidarity organisations at that time. On the other hand, this could present difficulties in mobilising activists. Its compass was nevertheless significant for political impact. The scope of the member organisations also facilitated reaching a large number of people with information through annual meetings and conferences. Several of them were sizeable youth organisations such as *The Norwegian Youth League* and *The Norwegian Rural Youth*. This avenue of disseminating information would not have been possible if NOCOSA had been a single, independent organisation. At the same time, the active members who kept the Council going had to create internal credibility and have the support of all the member organisations in all its activities, and this often represented an additional workload.

During the initial period of the Council's existence, it remained, as had been the case prior to 1967, only a small group of people worked on a voluntary basis, with no permanent office staff. Public subsidies covering running costs gradually increased, starting with support for purely informational activities in the early 1970s, later increasing also to cover recurrent expenditures. This enabled the Council in 1976 to engage a secretary on a half-day basis. Towards the end of the 1980s, the Council had 8–9 fulltime workers, including two conscientious objectors (as an alternative to military service).

1967–1981: The initial period

During the initial period, the Council's activities to put the struggles of the liberation movements in Southern Africa on the agenda was for a long time overshadowed by other events such as the Vietnam war and Norway's EEC referendum in 1972. The transformation came about as the result of dramatic events such as the military coup in Portugal in 1974, which set in train the decolonisation of Portugal's overseas possessions, South Africa's war against Angola in 1975, and the Cuban military support to Angola's liberation movement, MPLA. These events engaged the press, providing fresh impetus to the work of the Council. There was an increase in its activities, particularly in 1976 following the Soweto uprising, which aroused enormous international attention, prompting many to become actively involved in the work of the Council.

An important task during the initial years was arranging contacts between the liberation movements and the Norwegian authorities, knocking on office doors, accompanying visitors to meetings and keeping the press informed. In this manner, interest in the liberation of Southern Africa was kept alive. The attitude of Norwegian authorities toward the wars of liberation and the struggle for a democratic and non-racial South Africa up to the beginning of the 1970s was, as has already been mentioned, reserved, and at best marked by uncertainty and ignorance.[4]

Activities associated with the spreading of information were particularly directed at schools and youth organisations, through lectures and the distribution of information material. In 1969, the Council opened special bank accounts on behalf of Angola's liberation movement MPLA, Mozambique's FRELIMO, and Guinea-Bissau's PAIGC, while simultaneously encouraging institutions and organisations to contribute funds to the movements. In addition, Members of parliament were requested to donate funds to the work of the respective liberation movements in the liberated territories.[5] For a long time (and right up to 1973) support of any significance was provided by Norwegian authorities only to refugees and not directly to the liberation movements. (See chapter 1.)

From 1973 on, NOCOSA organised nearly annual so-called Africa Weeks. The first of these came in connection with a conference held in Oslo under the auspices of the United Nations and the *Organisation of African Unity* (OAU). These Africa Weeks had as their main objective to convey to the general public information on conditions in Southern Africa. During the first few years (apart from 1973 when there were also events in Bergen, Trondheim and Tromsø), the Africa Weeks were held in Oslo and its surroundings, but gradually they came to be spread all over the country.

Many of the Africa Weeks were held jointly with other organisations, frequently in co-operation with *The Norwegian Students' and Academics' International Assistance Fund (SAIH)*, which was also actively involved in the anti-apartheid struggle. The Africa Weeks always demanded a great deal of time and effort on the part of the Council's members, and mobilised many who were not otherwise active.

---

[4] See Ole Kristian Eivindsson: *Norge og raseproblemene i Sør-Afrika, 1845–1961*. Thesis, Department of History, University of Oslo, 1997; Ragnhild Narum: *Norge og rasekonflikten i Sør-Afrika*. Thesis, Department of History, University of Oslo, 1998.

[5] Executive Committee's Activity Report for the period 16 June to 9 November 1970.

NOCOSA's first international contacts came about first and foremost through its membership of the *International Defence and Aid Fund—IDAF*, which it had taken over from the old *Crisis Fund for South Africa*. IDAF was an international organisation based in London, in which several of the members were South Africans living in exile. The organisation raised funds for the legal defence of political prisoners in Southern Africa, and the support of their families. The Council channelled funds from the Ministry of Foreign Affairs through IDAF for this purpose until such time as direct connection had been established between Norwegian authorities and IDAF in the 1970s. NOCOSA's chairperson in 1969, Bjørg Ofstad, was for a while Vice-President of the organisation and in this way contact was established with other British organisations. During this period there was also frequent contact with the Angola Committee in Amsterdam as well as with other Dutch anti-apartheid organisations. The activities in Holland were intensive and information acquired from this source was important for the Council. However, much of the information was obtained directly through the news bulletins produced by the liberation movements themselves.

In Sweden, The Swedish Committee for Isolation of South Africa (ISAK) and The Africa Groups of Sweden (AGIS)were involved in anti-apartheid activities, and in Denmark there was The Danish Association for International Co-operation (MS). Contact with these organisations, and in particular the Swedish ones, was of importance for the exchange of information and for co-operation on various events. Visits by representatives of the liberation movements were frequently co-ordinated by the Nordic organisations.

The Council rings the doorbell

Before the Council came into being, there had already been a considerable amount of contact with the liberation movements, and several of their representatives had visited Norway. This contact continued, and from 1967 NOCOSA frequently played host to these visitors. The Council's most important role was to establish contacts between representatives of the liberation movements and Norwegian authorities, in particular the Ministry of Foreign Affairs, political parties and trade unions. Press coverage was also arranged during their visits. Leaders of liberation movements regarded the Scandinavian countries as their most important supporting players in the Western world and were themselves eager to establish fruitful contact. Such visits thus often came about through the offices of the liberation movements in Sweden and London, or they were mediated through the British Anti-Apartheid Movement. The Council itself often invited important persons to their own events or arranged itineraries for such visitors in order to meet people outside Oslo. Such round trips entailed a number of lectures at regional colleges and folk colleges all over Norway. The informational value was clear, as NOCOSA was often approached for information following such visits.

The visit of the leader of the Mozambican liberation movement immediately prior to the establishment of NOCOSA in 1967 was a special occasion. Awareness in Norway of Portuguese colonial policies had increased in concert with the radicalisation of the Norwegian youth and student environment. Thus Eduardo Mondlane received a warm welcome by a specially created committee consisting of 15 political and cultural youth organisations, headed by the chairperson of the Norwegian Action Against Apartheid, Lars Alldén. Norwegian activists were familiar with some of Eduardo Mondlane's writings and speeches, and his charismatic personality inspired and motivated NOCOSA, which was established shortly after Mondlane's visit, to continue its efforts. His book, *The Struggle for Mozambique*, was later translated into Norwegian.[6] Mondlane's attack on Portugal and in this connection also on NATO, was fierce, making it difficult both for the conservative Norwegian government and Members of Parliament from other parties, apart from the Socialist People's Party, to meet him. The invitation for the Ministry of Foreign Affairs to be represented on a debating panel with Eduardo Mondlane was rejected without any reason being given (see chapter 1). At a public meeting attended by over 300 persons, Mondlane underlined the importance of supporting the Mozambique Institute in Dar es Salaam, which provided schooling and training for Mozambican refugees. Press coverage of Mondlane's visit was comprehensive, with banner headlines and editorials both before and after his visit.

Another important visitor to Norway in this period was the leader of the Angolan liberation movement MPLA, and subsequently Angolan President, Agostinho Neto. On this occasion, (which took place in 1970), NOCOSA together with the Labour Party (which at that time was in parliamentary opposition), acted as hosts. Agostinho Neto received a great deal of attention from the press, was interviewed on radio and television, and had meetings with several political parties.

In 1971, Sam Nujoma, the leader of Namibia's liberation movement, SWAPO, paid his first visit to Norway. He met the Norwegian Prime Minister Trygve Bratteli. This was the first time Nujoma was received by a Prime Minister from any of the Western countries. Relationships with SWAPO, however, were of a rather different character as Namibia was a country under occupation and the liberation movement was in a way seen to be more legitimate than for example ANC of South Africa.[7]

One year after Nujoma's visit, the Council also received the leader of Guinea-Bissau's liberation movement, Amilcar Cabral. Through the visits of these prominent liberation leaders, as well as a number of other representatives from the liberation movements, the Council hoped to be able to per-

---

[6] Eduardo Mondlane: *Kampen om Mocambique*. Oslo: Gyldendal 1970.

[7] However, ANC's Oliver Tambo had met with Prime Minister Einar Gerhardsen as early as in 1962 (see chapter 1), but this connection was not followed up.

suade the authorities to make public contributions to their struggle for freedom. Moreover, issues related to the liberation of Southern Africa were
given prominence as a result of these visits i.a. through the mass media, and
Parliament could no longer side-step them in foreign policy debates.[8]

The transition to recognition of the liberation movements on the part of
Norwegian authorities was gradual. Both the Norwegian Confederation of
Trade Unions (LO) and, as we have seen, the Ministry of Foreign Affairs,
hesitated for some time to meet with liberation movement representatives
who were visiting Norway. As far as representatives of ANC were concerned, the difficulties were partly associated with the close connection
between the apartheid-regime and Great Britain, France, the USA as well as
other NATO-partners, while ANC by many Western observers were seen to
be close to "the other side" during the Cold War. Within the NATO alliance,
there were a strong desire for close direct links between South Africa and
NATO. South Africa, desiring close links with the Western military apparatus, played up the spectre of communism and maintained that the apartheid
regime was an important bastion against communism. These factors had
certainly influenced internal attitudes in the Ministry of Foreign Affairs for
some time. As for leaders of the liberation movements from the Portuguese
colonies, it was not without problems for Norwegian authorities to receive
them in order to discuss Portugal's warfare, with which Norway was in
alliance through its membership of NATO. Diplomats from the Portuguese
Embassy usually turned up at the Ministry of Foreign Affairs shortly after
meetings with liberation movements to enquire as to what had been said
and whether the visitors were still in the country.

Thus leaders and representatives of the liberation movements were up
to the early 1970s mainly confined to meeting Norwegian officials through
the UN office of the Ministry of Foreign Affairs'. Often the meetings took
place in town or at NOCOSA's office. This hesitant attitude was replaced by
intensified interest, as the conflicts in Southern Africa were often debated at
the United Nations, and it was important for the Norwegian Ministry of
Foreign Affairs to keep itself informed. After the Council had drawn a large
number of leaders of liberation movements to the offices of politicians and
civil servants. Norwegian authorities must gradually have felt themselves
under a certain amount of pressure to establish direct contact with the
liberation movements. This applied in the first instance to liberation move-

---

[8] In the course of succeeding years, NOCOSA received visits from i.a., Peter Katjavivi (1969 and
1971), Uazuvara Katjivena (1971) and Ben Amathila (1971 and 1972), all of SWAPO; Raymond
Kunene and Tany Mlobiso (1969) of ANC; George Peake (1968) of PAC; Henry Hamadziripi
and Richard Hove of ZANU; Kotsho Duve (1969) of ZAPU; Janet Mondlane (1969 and 1971),
Armando Panguene (1972) and Marcelino dos Santos of FRELIMO; Antonio Neto (1971, 1972
and 1973), Saydi Mingas (1973) and Dr. d'Almeida (1972) of MPLA; Onésimo Silveira (1971 and
1972), Aristides Pereira and Gil Fernandez (1974) of PAIGC. Also Denis Brutus (1969), South
African poet and activist who, as leader of SAN-ROC (South African Non-Racial Olympic
Committee) campaigned to have South Africa excluded from international sports arrangements.

ment leaders in the Portuguese colonies, and to the Namibian liberation movement, SWAPO.

Areas of involvement: NOCOSA at the crossroads

The Council's strategy was initially to concentrate its work in areas where the potential for achieving results was optimal. At that time, the Council undoubtedly regarded the Portuguese colonies as more vulnerable than the regimes in South Africa and Zimbabwe. The priority given to the struggle in the Portuguese colonies had broad support among the member organisations, although Portugal was a member of NATO and thus an ally of Norway. In political milieus, however, it was precisely the fact that Portugal and Norway were members of the same military alliance that constituted an important element in the resistance to a weapons boycott of Portugal. The Council did not neglect the proffered opportunity to express fierce criticism of NATO. In 1971, a study booklet on "Portugal and NATO" was produced in which Portugal's economic and military oppression of its colonies was described, as well as the country's economic and military agreements which underpinned the support of Portugal's colonial wars on the part of several NATO-countries. NOCOSA's criticism of NATO was not unproblematic internally in the organisation either. The Young Conservatives could not accept this criticism and after a while withdrew their membership of the Council.[9] Some members of the Young Conservatives nevertheless from time to time participated in the work of the Council.

When, in the spring of 1971, Parliament was to debate for the first time a proposition drafted by the Foreign Relations Committee concerning Portugal's colonial policies in Africa, NOCOSA made a direct approach to the government and to other Members of Parliament relating to the deployment of jet fighters in the Portuguese colonies, which previously had been used in the Norwegian Air Force. The Council tried on several occasions to direct public attention to Portugal's brutal colonial wars in Mozambique, Angola and Guinea-Bissau, and NATO's involvement in these wars. This activity continued at the meeting of NATO Ministers in Lisbon in June 1971 (see chapter 1) and in Copenhagen the following year, as appropriate occasions for once more drawing attention to the matter. Meetings of both NATO's Council of Ministers and of the Nordic Foreign Ministers were always closely followed up, and the Council encouraged its member organisations and other sympathisers to hold meetings and engage in political activities related to these meetings.

---

[9] When Willy Brandt, who was a popular figure in Norway, received the Nobel Peace Prize in 1971, NOCOSA organised a demonstration protesting against West Germany's military support of Portugal. Young Conservatives dissociated themselves from this demonstration, feeling that it was out of place and unsuitable as an instrument for promoting liberation of the Portuguese colonies (letter to the Council from Young Conservatives dated 6 December 1971, signed by Helge Ole Bergesen).

Seminars and study circles were organised, and great efforts were made to raise public awareness concerning Portugal's military offensives and the African liberation struggles. NOCOSA's study booklet on Portugal and NATO was sent to members of Parliament. The Minister of Foreign Affairs received open letters questioning NATO's role, and these were also published in the press. As a result of addressing itself to members of Parliament, the Council on several occasions found that important issues were taken up in Parliament, either during foreign affairs debates or during question time. This applied i.a. to demands that the government raise the matter of Portugal's colonial policies with NATO, that it should dissuade member countries providing military and economic succour to Portugal from continuing such support, and that Norway should use its veto rights in connection with the provision of NATO-weapons to Portugal.

The matter of development assistance to the liberation movements had regularly been raised since the beginning of the 1970s. It was first through Parliamentary White Paper No. 29 (1971–72)—*Concerning Certain Topics Relevant to Norway's Co-operation with Developing Countries*, which was debated in 1973, that the way was opened for providing direct support to the liberation movements (see chapter 1). It was, however, a matter of humanitarian assistance in the form of commodities and not of the transfer of funds. NOCOSA demanded direct financial assistance and much larger sums than the total of NOK 5 million which in 1973 had been allocated to PAIGC, MPLA and FRELIMO together. The Council was nevertheless pleased that assistance was now being provided and felt that it was an important step in the right direction.

The Council also launched a campaign to get Norway to recognise Guinea-Bissau as an independent state. This had been recommended by 65 countries at the UN General Assembly in 1973. 93 countries voted for, 7 voted against and 30 abstained from voting, among them Norway and several other Western European nations. The Council felt that the government had not made sufficiently clear representations on the matter and therefore challenged the Foreign Minister in an open letter to provide concrete and precise answers to a number of questions. Clarification was requested as to which liberation movements the government regarded as legitimate representatives of the people in the three Portuguese colonies, and, viewed against the background of innumerable resolutions at the United Nations and the fact that Norway had in recent years given both material and political support to PAIGC, whether the government did not feel itself politically obliged to recognise Guinea-Bissau.[10]

During the liberation war in Angola and following independence in 1975, the Council had been in little doubt that it was MPLA which represented the people and were leading the struggle for the independence of

---

[10] Open letter from NOCOSA to the Minister of Foreign Affairs (undated and unsigned).

Angola.[11] In 1975, efforts in support of MPLA and attempts at providing a truer picture of Angola in the Norwegian mass media laid claim to a great deal of the Council's attention. On repeated occasions, the Council pressed the Norwegian authorities to declare Angola a main partner country for Norwegian development co-operation, but never succeeded in having this accepted. The effort to get Mozambique adopted as a main development co-operation partner country was, however, crowned with success in 1977.

Towards the end of the 1970s, Zimbabwe had naturally enough become a principle area of involvement for the Council. Relationships with the two liberation movements *Zimbabwe African National Union (ZANU)*, and *Zimbabwe African People's Union (ZAPU)* became a topic of debate at NOCOSA's annual general meetings. There was no essential disagreement within the Council that ZANU was the most representative liberation movement. Many of the Council's representatives wanted its support to be exclusively concentrated on ZANU, while the majority felt that there was no reason to choose sides before the elections in 1980. Support was therefore concentrated on the Patriotic Front, the political organisation, which had been set up jointly by ZANU and ZAPU in connection with negotiations held in Geneva in 1976.[12]

Upon Zimbabwe achieving its independence in 1980 following an overwhelming election victory for ZANU under the leadership of Robert Mugabe, the question arose as to NOCOSA's role vis-à-vis Zimbabwe as a liberated and independent state. The Council's chief areas of involvement would from now on be Namibia and South Africa. It was nevertheless regarded as important to support the reconstruction of Zimbabwe, and co-operation with the Norwegian Students' and Academics' International Assistance Fund (SAIH) in sending a medical team to the country was initiated. This was followed by an educational project with a total of seven Norwegian teachers working in Zimbabwean secondary schools. The proceeds of fund-raising campaigns were additional to the support provided by NORAD and later also the Operation Day's Work (OD).[13] Zimbabwe was thought to be the only country in Southern Africa capable of withstanding pressure from South Africa, and which could contribute to making the entire region less dependent on its apartheid neighbour. It was therefore important for NOCOSA to continue focusing on Zimbabwe for several years after the country had achieved independence. At the same time, the Council wanted

---

[11] In some of the member organisations there were discussions as to whether one should not also support FNLA, but there was no official disagreement that MPLA was the most representative organisation.

[12] See chapter 4.

[13] The Norwegian Schools' own annual solidarity campaign. In 1971 and 1972 the proceeds went to liberation movements in Angola, Mozambique and Guinea-Bissau. In 1982 it went to Zimbabwe. In 1985 there was a joint Nordic solidarity campaign for Southern Africa. In 1988 the money raised through this campaign again went to educational activities in Southern Africa (see p. 234), and in 1994 to education for liberation in South Africa.

Norway, in conjunction with the other Nordic countries, to follow up the agreement on co-operation with the SADCC-countries[14] more comprehensively than had originally been planned.

New fund-raising approaches were devised in financing projects in Zimbabwe. One proposal was to introduce a solidarity tax. All NOCOSA members were requested to contribute a small sum through giro transfers every second month. Another method was to encourage project sponsorship, requiring three annual payments of NOK 500 over three years. In return, sponsors received regular reports from project workers in Zimbabwe. Since a large number of sponsors were teachers, this information was also used as teaching material in the schools.

The UN/OAU Conference in Oslo, 1973

The cautious diplomatic approach of the authorities in the 1960s underwent some change during the early 1970s. The breakthrough came when Norway hosted the OAU/United Nations *World Conference for Support of Victims of Apartheid and Colonialism in Southern Africa* in 1973. At the conference, the liberation movements and their leaders were acknowledged, and political leaders from Southern Africa met their political counterparts in Norway.

However, NOCOSA was not pleased with the arrangements at the conference, fearing that diplomatic manoeuvres might shift the focus to the victims of apartheid and colonialism at the expense of support given to the liberation struggle.[15] In a letter to the Ministry of Foreign Affairs, the Council requested to be allowed to participate at the conference in line with other solidarity organisations and experts who had been invited to attend. The Council felt that the host country's own solidarity organisation should have an automatic right of participation at the conference, not least on account of the continued supportive solidarity work remaining to be done in Norway. They therefore hoped for an official invitation, but had to be satisfied with an offer of observer status on one of the conference days.

In its activities NOCOSA felt a strong need to focus on crucial problems which the organisers of the conference either were unwilling or unable to deal with. This applied in particular to NATO's role and to foreign (including Norwegian) capital investment and trade with the oppressors in Southern Africa. The Council therefore proposed that an alternative Africa Week be held during the OAU conference. It was organised in co-operation with the Peace Research Institute in Oslo, PRIO. The Norwegian solidarity endeavours on behalf of the liberation movements were presented in their full breadth. The statement released by the Council had the following text:

---

[14] Southern Africa Development Co-ordination Conference (today; Southern African Development Community).

[15] The conference, however, turned out to be more along the lines that NOCOSA (and the liberation movements themselves) had wanted, see chapter 1.

> The aim of the Africa Week is to provide information to the public in order to acquaint people with the themes to be discussed at the conference. Solidarity work on behalf of the liberation movements must be organised in Norway, and we wish to involve people in active participation against oppression and for liberation. So information is important. But there is a danger that the conference may come to be of a closed nature, concerning itself with technical discussions.[16]

The Council concentrated on these topics: the responsibilities of NATO's member countries and the role of multinational capital in the areas of conflict in Southern Africa; Norway's responsibility imposed by its membership in NATO and the relationship between the European Free Trade Association (EFTA) and Portugal. The increased trade and shipping with South Africa were also discussed. Among innumerable activities during the Africa Week were a photo exhibition, films, stands, news sheets, demonstrations, meetings with leaders of liberation movements and separate seminars in Oslo, Bergen, Trondheim and Tromsø. A wide range of information material on the various liberation movements and their struggle for independence, on apartheid, and on the wars of liberation, was made available. Representatives of the liberation movements, as well as other participants at the OAU conference, participated at activities organised by the Council, thus making the liberation movements also known outside the conference halls. MPLA's leader, Agostinho Neto, who participated at the conference, called on the Council and opened a meeting at the Nobel Institute.

PAIGC's, MPLA's and FRELIMO's flags were carried in processions during demonstrations, and it was demanded that Norway, should increase its aid to the liberation movements to at least NOK 50 million as the next step. "Should one compare the support provided (to liberation movements) with Norway's trade with the colonial powers and the apartheid regime, it becomes apparent how pathetically little we have contributed to the liberation struggle so far", said NOCOSA's chairperson Stig Utnem in his appeal on behalf of NOCOSA.

NOCOSA's Hearing on South Africa, 1977

While the OAU/UN-conference in 1973 was organised by the Norwegian Government, the next conference on South Africa was set up by NOCOSA in Oslo in the autumn of 1977. The hearing was an important step forward in bringing the conflicts in Southern Africa into focus. It was a major event, with extensive participation and broad press coverage. The immediate background to the hearing was the recent Soweto uprising and the increasing tension in South Africa which had once more made the international community turn a spotlight on the brutal oppression of the people by the apartheid regime. Such an arrangement was at the same time important in

---

[16] Press statement by NOCOSA, 30 March 1973.

stimulating the Norwegian anti-apartheid movement into stronger commitment and an intensification of its activities.

The objective of the hearing was to reveal the true nature of the apartheid system and at the same time contribute to increased sympathy and support for the liberation struggle in Southern Africa. The idea was that persons who had suffered directly under the oppression inflicted by the South African regime should appear as witnesses. Centrally placed representatives of the ANC, the South African Congress of Trade Unions (SACTU), South African church organisations, student and other movements, as well as prominent experts and relevant witnesses, made statements. Selection of experts and witnesses was made in conjunction with the International Defence and Aid Fund, the British Anti-Apartheid Movement, and the ANC-offices in London and Stockholm. In addition, representatives of SWAPO and the Patriotic Front of Zimbabwe were present. Statements made by witnesses and their credentials presented during the hearing were to be assessed by an Investigative Commission and included in a report, together with a communiqué on South Africa. The Commission consisted of 25 persons and had broad representation; leaders of political parties, trade union spokespersons, representatives of religious and humanitarian organisations, lawyers, scholars, journalists and others. Egil Olsen, today best known as "Drillo" and for many years manager of the Norwegian national football team, at that time politically involved as an active radical, was also included in the panel. The Labour Movement's International Solidarity Committee, AIS, at first declined to participate, as they at that time were accustomed to doing when approached by NOCOSA for support or participation. However, after consideration, AIS nevertheless attended. The Norwegian Foreign Minister, Knut Frydenlund, opened the hearing.

The official communiqué issued after the hearing took as its starting point the 1976 UN *Programme of Action against Apartheid*, the Lagos Declaration from the UN Conference in Nigeria (August 1977), and a number of other articles, declarations and UN reports which were presented to the hearing as background material. Witnesses' reports on imprisonment, torture and killings made a strong impression on those assembled and confirmed that conditions in South Africa were steadily worsening. A representative of SACTU requested the trade unions in the Nordic countries to organise boycotts and to exert pressure on the authorities to stop all trade and other economic collaboration with South Africa. Against this background, the Investigative Commission fully endorsed the descriptions of conditions in South Africa set forth in the UN Programme of Action, and the Lagos Declaration:

> We express our support for the legitimate struggle being waged in Southern Africa against apartheid and oppression. We support the international campaign to isolate the present South African regime. We regard the fact that South Africa is able to construct an extensive modern military machine as extremely serious.

This represents a direct threat to other African states as well. It necessitates a compulsory weapons embargo and sanctions in accordance with Chapter 7 of the UN Charter. Norway must give added support to those African states subject to South African aggression. We further demand that the Norwegian Government begin an official investigation into, and charting of, the military connections between members of NATO and South Africa. Norway must do its utmost to prevent South Africa from, directly or indirectly, being incorporated into NATO's projects, if such projects involving South Africa exist.[17]

Through this Declaration, the participants at the hearing expressed their support for the UN Programme of Action (see box). Norway, as the only one of the Nordic countries which had voted for this UN Resolution, was requested to implement the boycott with immediate effect and not to wait until broader international agreement had been reached. Norway was also asked to co-ordinate sanctions, not least within the Nordic countries.

The investigating committee regarded the hearing as a significant step in the direction of increased attention to the conflicts in Southern Africa, both in the mass media, in the labour unions, among the churches and in political and other organisations. According to the Declaration, there was also a hope that the hearing would generate stronger public reaction to, and consequently increased pressure on, political organs to implement the UN programme.

The hearing marked a turning point for NOCOSA. From being a small, Oslo-based anti-apartheid group, it became a major, countrywide grass roots movement. The member organisations were drawn more actively into the Council's activities, which afforded it increased impact, both politically and in public opinion.[18]

1981–1990: Expansion, co-operation and struggle

The struggle for a democratic and non-racial South Africa was always fundamental to NOCOSA's commitment. After both the Portuguese colonies and Zimbabwe had become independent states, the struggle against the apartheid regime occupied centre-stage once more. There had been tendencies in some solidarity environments, including the Norwegian Students' and Academics' International Assistance Fund (SAIH), to prefer supporting the *Black Consciousness Movement (BCM)*, which was a mass movement but lacking in effective organisation. There were, however, no strong political divergence between the Black Consciousness Movement and the ANC, although some, for a variety of reasons, wanted to build up an alternative to ANC. NOCOSA produced a booklet in 1978, "The Liberation Struggle" as part of a series under the title *South Africa in Focus*, in which it was clearly

---

[17] Declaration from the hearing on South Africa in Oslo, 12 and 13 October 1977, p. 4.
[18] Interview with Elling Njål Tjønneland, chairperson of NOCOSA in 1977, 9 June 1998.

emphasised that ANC was the organisation which had the necessary organisational strength to lead the liberation struggle.[19]

We see the UN Programme of Action as a natural point of departure for a strengthened struggle against South Africa's apartheid regime, and against South African occupation of Namibia and their aggression against other African states such as Angola and Zambia. We particularly want to draw attention to the following section of the programme, which calls upon all governments to:

Terminate all economic collaboration with South Africa, and in particular refrain from extending loans, investments and technical assistance to the racist regime of South Africa and companies registered in South Africa;

Implement fully the arms embargo against South Africa without any exceptions or reservations;

Prohibit airlines and shipping lines registered in their countries from providing services to and from South Africa;

Suspend cultural, educational, sporting and other exchanges with the racist regime of South Africa;

Provide financial and material assistance, directly or through the Organisation of African Unity, to the liberation movements recognised by that organisation;

Encourage the activity of anti-apartheid and solidarity movements and other organisations engaged in political and material assistance to the victims of apartheid, and to the South African liberation movement;

Ensure, in co-operation with the UN and the South African liberation movements, the widest possible dissemination of information on apartheid and on the struggle for liberation in South Africa.

We stress that these recommendations are made to the Norwegian Government as well, as there are still many sections it has done nothing about. We particularly want to deplore that Norwegian trade with South Africa has increased sharply in recent years, in addition to the co-operation, which exists concerning shipping. The authorities must guarantee that individual sectors and places of work do not suffer unilaterally due to the ending of economic links with South Africa.

In order to strengthen and effectuate its work, NOCOSA in 1981 established a number of special committees: a South Africa Committee, a Zimbabwe Committee, a Namibia Committee, and a Boycott Committee, so that each group could concentrate on specific tasks. In this manner it became easier for NOCOSA to devote itself to several tasks simultaneously, and it was also easier to involve a larger number of its members at the same time. Political goals were defined, such as bringing the trade unions and the churches into closer co-operation with NOCOSA and gaining access to Parliament more readily. Through a Trade Union Committee created in order to co-ordinate more closely the work of the various labour unions and the Norwegian Con-

---

[19] Elling Njål Tjønneland: *Kampen for frigjering*. Oslo: Norwegian Council for Southern Africa, 1978.

federation of Trade Unions (LO), there came gradually to be built up a relationship of trust towards the trade unions and the international trade union
offices. Through the establishment of a *Parliamentary Contact Group for Southern Africa*, co-operation with Members of Parliament became more firmly
established. The new strategy proved effective and gave NOCOSA the lift it
needed to be able to meet the challenges of the 1980s. Asbjørn Eidhammer
headed NOCOSA from 1981 to 1984 and played a crucial role in strengthening the Council. At the annual meeting in 1985, the previous year was
summed up as a year of breakthrough for the anti-apartheid movement in
Norway. The intensification of the mass struggle in South Africa itself and
the award of the Nobel Peace prize to Desmond Tutu in 1984 were deemed
to have been part of the reasons for this. However, NOCOSA also regarded
the increased co-operation with parliamentarians via the Contact Group and
with representatives of the labour unions as important factors.

During the early 1980s, South Africa came to feature firmly on the political agenda in Norway. The pressure generated by the solidarity organisations, Members of Parliament, the labour movement and the church organisations, had grown so strong that the authorities were compelled to take
action, i.a. in order to give sanctions against South Africa renewed consideration. The Norwegian attitude towards sanctions had until then been too
confined to getting a binding resolution passed by the United Nations, arguing that a boycott would be ineffective if implemented solely by Norway.
The Council nevertheless at that time felt that Southern Africa was being
given far too little attention by the Norwegian government, and that the
political leadership in the Ministry of Foreign Affairs hesitated to express an
opinion or to participate in public discourse.[20] NOCOSA's letters and requests often received evasive replies. One case confirming perceptions regarding the lack of involvement on the part of the authorities was that Norway neglected to react when the IMF granted loans to South Africa. The
Council moreover felt that Norwegian support for the victims of apartheid
was of little value as long as Norwegian commerce and industry, and in
particular the transport of oil, made it possible for South African aircraft to
bomb Namibian refugees in Angola and to destroy villages in Mozambique.
That the Norwegian government in 1982 readily acceded to Great Britain's
request to introduce sanctions against Argentina during the Falkland Island
conflict, made the Council enquire as to why the government could not do
the same in the case of South Africa whose occupation of Namibia was illegal, and whether Norwegian jobs were not of equal importance when seen
in relation to Argentina as in relation to South Africa.[21]

---

[20] Between 1981 and 1983, Norway had a Conservative Party government, while from 1983 to
1986 there was a coalition made up of the Conservative Party, the Christian People's Party and
the Centre Party. Svenn Stray from the Conservative Party was Foreign Minister for the whole
period.

[21] *Aftenposten*, 28 April 1982.

It was not only NOCOSA which felt that the involvement of the Norwegian authorities towards Southern Africa was lukewarm. In 1983, the Ministry of Foreign Affairs refused to continue supporting the *World Campaign against Nuclear and Military Collaboration with South Africa*, which Norway had supported since the beginning of 1979. This triggered disillusionment and the Council argued strongly for the Ministry of Foreign Affairs to reverse their decision. The Norwegian authorities had supported the establishment of the World Campaign, as had the Swedish Prime Minister, the Frontline heads of government, and the leadership of ANC and SWAPO. The aim of the campaign was to launch an effective weapons embargo against South Africa. Abdul Minty, who directed the campaign, opened an office in Oslo and carried out exhaustive investigations, in co-operation with, among others, the United Nations, into weapons supplies to South Africa, and into the country's nuclear capabilities.[22]

Southern Africa hearing in 1984

In order to put Southern Africa on the agenda and to acquaint public opinion with the aggression of the apartheid regime and with the sufferings of the peoples of the region, NOCOSA in 1984 organised a new international hearing on *South Africa's Military Aggression against Neighbouring States*. The setting for the hearing was a situation becoming steadily more acute in Southern Africa resulting from repeated military assaults and threats against its neighbours. It was important for the apartheid regime that the Frontline States should not become so strong that they could provide direct support for the ANC's freedom struggle. It was also of great importance for Botha's regime that Angola, Mozambique and Zimbabwe did not succeed in their policies so that South African propaganda on dissolution, chaos and decline as a result of black majority government could continue. Seen as a whole, South Africa, in collaboration with terrorist groups, conducted destabilisation policies through military aggression, economic blackmail and sabotage. South Africa's brutal attacks and terrorist activities particularly seriously affected Mozambique and Angola. Namibia was caught in a grip of steel and in 1984, nearly 20 years after the UN deprived South Africa of the right to administer the territory, there were few prospects of change.

The idea of a new hearing came into being in 1982 after a successful Africa Week (then known as *Action against Apartheid*) in which most of the active members, both locally and centrally, had participated, so that it could by now justifiably be described as nation-wide. Twenty of NOCOSA's member organisations participated and there were activities in 30 places scattered throughout the country. The media coverage was extremely posi-

---

[22] Background Memorandum on the World Campaign against Military and Nuclear Collaboration with South Africa, NOCOSA, 1983. Abdul Minty is today Deputy Director-General, Ministry of Foreign Affairs, South Africa.

tive and provided a broad, strengthened foundation upon which anti-apartheid activities could in future be built.[23]

One of the reasons for the success of the 1982 campaign was the co-operation with the Namibia Association in Elverum, which had been established after a major Namibia campaign in 1980 (see chapter 9). The Namibia Association had an approach to mobilisation of local support, which was altogether different from NOCOSA's. The Namibia Association directed its efforts at all manner of associations and organisations; schools, colleges, housewives' associations, trade unions, sports clubs and missionary societies, to name a few. This modus operandi was highly instructive for the Council. The Namibia Association, led by the enthusiastic Dag Hareide, thought more expansively than NOCOSA was used to, and this co-operation resulted in a higher level of ambition on the part of the Council.[24]

Ambitions to hold a large international hearing developed into a joint effort involving NOCOSA, the Africa Groups of Sweden, and the Danish Association for International Co-operation, resulting in an event which had a lot of impact in Norway. Key figures in the Ministry of Foreign Affairs, the trade union movement and church circles, were invited to participate. Funds for the arrangement started rolling in, most of them from the Ministry of Foreign Affairs. Support from participants, audiences and the press, was extensive, and a total of between two and three thousand persons participated in the hearing. The final session, at which the well-known historian Basil Davidson was the main speaker, drew 1,200 people. Among specially invited speakers were Archbishop Desmond Tutu, who was awarded the Nobel Peace Prize later the same year, and Archbishop Trevor Huddlestone (who as a priest in the Johannesburg slums had drawn international attention to the injustices of apartheid through his book *Naught For Your Comfort*, and who now headed the anti-apartheid movement in Britain). Among other prominent guests was Thabo Mbeki from the ANC. In addition, representatives from Angola, Mozambique, Zimbabwe, Lesotho, Zambia, Botswana, Tanzania and Nigeria participated.

Besides focusing on South Africa's military aggression against neighbouring states, the hearing also intended to debate the role of the Nordic countries in Southern Africa. South Africa's military aggression was confirmed through eyewitness accounts, videos and the presentation of research reports. A multi-media presentation by the photographers Aslak Aarhus and Ole Bernt Frøshaug, *White Shadows*, illuminated both the master-servant relationship between whites and blacks in South Africa and the aggression of the apartheid regime against its neighbours. The presentation was an important documentation, which was later widely used by other organisations

---

[23] Annual Report 1981–82.

[24] Interview with Asbjørn Eidhammer, NOCOSA's chairperson between 1981 and 1984, 19 September 1997.

as well as by the NORAD Information Division. The hearing lasted all of three days and resulted in a declaration by the Panel, which summed up matters and made recommendations in respect of Nordic action vis-à-vis Southern Africa. On the Panel sat Members of Parliament from Norway, Sweden and Denmark, researchers and representatives from trade unions and the churches. The declaration confirmed that the hearing had produced proof of "the build-up of the South African war economy and war-machine since the 1960s, facilitated by deliveries of weapons, technology and oil from—in particular—Western countries, where also the Nordic countries have participated".[25]

The Panel also established that there could be no lasting peace in the region as long as the apartheid regime continued to exist. It was therefore the duty of the Nordic governments, for the trade union movement, the churches and other political organisations, to do their utmost to eliminate apartheid, to assist Namibia to achieve independence and to establish peace in the region.

Raising support and activism

A great deal of the work consisted of involving others in active support for the liberation movements. Labour unions and clubs at the workplace were important in this connection. The Council solicited support for its endeavours for direct financial support to ANC. Information was provided in the form of lectures at annual meetings, articles in technical journals, and the dissemination of general information at meetings and rallies. In 1986, an agreement was worked out with Norges Bank (The Bank of Norway) for fellowships of 6-months' duration for ANC-trainees. Two members of the South African labour organisation, SACTU, received practical training at Aftenposten's printing works and two others commenced training as electricians at Sogn High School in Oslo.

Many trade unions collected equipment of various kinds, which was sent to ANC's refugee camps at Mazimbu and Dakawa in Tanzania. Magnor Glass Works were about to celebrate their centenary and wanted to combine this with practical support for the causes championed by NOCOSA. This took the form of casting a crystal block with a "Biko" motif, and the profits were sent to a school for children in Mazimbu. The project realised NOK 70,250. In a postcard campaign under the motto "Set the Children Free", 100,000 postcards were sent to the country's primary and secondary schools all over the country. The cards were intended to be posted direct to the South African President P.W. Botha, demanding that all children and young people held in South Africa's prisons for political activities be freed.

---

[25] Declaration of the Panel in the report from the International Hearing on South African Aggression Against Neighbouring States, Oslo, 1984.

The declaration of the Panel asked the Nordic Governments to:

Increase their support to the liberation movements in South Africa (ANC and SWAPO), as well as to the independent trade unions, the church organisations and to other forces ... struggling for national independence, democracy and a non-racist society;

Substantially increase the assistance to the Frontline States and to their organisation of economic co-operation, SADCC, in order both to assist in reconstruction after the massive South African destruction and to enable them to resist South African economic and military pressure in the future ...;

intensify efforts to secure full implementation of the arms embargo against South Africa, and to oppose all forms of nuclear and military co-operation in the future ... An important contribution to the effort to supervise the arms embargo and to disclose any military collaboration between South Africa and other states, is to provide support to the World Campaign against Nuclear and Military Collaboration with South Africa;

strengthen the efforts to obtain binding international sanctions against South Africa. Until such sanctions are adopted by the UN Security Council, the Nordic governments must halt the increase during recent years in trade and transport services ...;

instruct Nordic representatives to the World Bank and the International Monetary Fund (IMF) consistently to oppose any credit facilities to South Africa;

enact national legislation prohibiting any involvement in extraction of natural resources in Namibia as well as import, transport and sale of such resources as long as that country is occupied by South Africa;

provide increased support to the solidarity organisations and anti-apartheid movements in our part of the world which carry out valuable work to disseminate information about the conditions in Southern Africa, and which mobilise political, material and moral support to the Frontline States and the liberation movements.

NOCOSA also published the book *Ingen tårer. Vår framtid er lys.* (*Cry no tears. Our future is bright),* written by Tore Linné Eriksen.[26] The book, which was mainly directed to younger readers, told the story of Nelson Mandela and Winnie Mandela in the South African struggle for liberation. (It was later translated into Danish and published by the Danish Association for International Co-operation—MS).

The political pressure on the Norwegian authorities to embark on a full boycott campaign against the apartheid regime occupied much of the Council's energies. Included in this was the task of influencing public opinion. Campaigns against those who traded with South Africa increased in frequency, and the Shell boycott in particular attracted a great deal of countrywide attention. This is further discussed below.

NOCOSA had long wanted ANC to open an office in Oslo. This finally took place in 1986 and was welcomed by the Norwegian anti-apartheid movement. Raymond Mokoena ran the office for the first few years. Later

---

[26] Eriksen, Tore Linné: *Ingen tårer. Vår framtid er lys.* Oslo: Gyldendal Norsk Forlag and NOCOSA, 1988 .

Thandie Rankoe (now South African Ambassador to Tanzania) took over. The ANC office was a tower of strength to the anti-apartheid movement in Norway through expanded co-operation between the two bodies and the potential for increased information on the freedom struggle, as well as direct knowledge of what was happening in South Africa. In a press release by NOCOSA, Raymond Mokoena underscored that the establishment of ANC's office was an expression of a desire for increased co-operation with the Norwegian authorities and the non-governmental organisations (NGOs). While praising the important task, which Norway had taken upon itself in connection with the boycott campaign, he called for even stronger international pressure to be brought to bear on the apartheid regime. He felt that one of the most important contributions Norway could make would be to introduce a ban on all transport of oil and petroleum products to South Africa by Norwegian owned tankers.[27]

Mozambique in focus

In 1987 and 1988, Mozambique's problems came to occupy the foreground in the Council's work. The country was being attacked by the South African-supported terrorist organisation RENAMO, while drought and famine were simultaneously afflicting parts of the country. At the beginning of 1988, an estimated 4 million people were threatened with starvation, and 2 million became internal refugees in their own country. Health posts, schools and development projects, were burnt to the ground and destroyed by RENAMO, and the civilian population was under constant threat of attack and of being massacred.

In 1987, NORAD and the Mozambique-Norway Friendship Association, in close co-operation with the Council, organised a cultural event, *The Mozambique Manifestation*. This consisted of a major art and culture exhibition, film shows, a multi-media presentation of Mozambique, lectures, seminars, and exhibitions of traditional dances and songs by the *Companhia Nacional de Canto e Danca*. The Council's main responsibility was to produce and distribute information material and to arrange a two-day seminar on Mozambique, concentrating on South Africa's destabilisation and military aggression against Mozambique and how Norway could best support the country. The Mozambique Manifestation was well attended and received a great deal of positive attention in the press and through radio and television.

This laid a solid foundation for starting a campaign in 1988 for support to Mozambique. The aim of the campaign was to inform the public on conditions prevailing in the country and to bring pressure to bear on the Norwegian authorities so that they would allocate Norwegian development aid funds to be used in the defence of Mozambique. During the February press conference at which the campaign was presented, the Council's chairperson,

[27] Press communiqué by NOCOSA, 21 October 1986.

Reidar Andestad, demanded that the government present a proposition to Parliament to ensure that additional funds for civil military equipment for Mozambique, such as communications equipment and trucks, be made available. This gave rise to a debate in the press, and *Arbeiderbladet*, *Verdens Gang* and *Dagbladet*, three of the largest national daily newspapers, supported NOCOSA's demands in editorials. The Norwegian Agency for Development Co-operation, NORAD, recommended that *support be provided for passive protective measures at Norwegian development projects where this was deemed necessary for security*.[28] This met the Council's demands only to a limited degree, and efforts were continued to persuade the Norwegian authorities to provide direct civil military support.

The promotion of cultural activities and fund-raising on behalf of Mozambique were two other important tasks associated with the Mozambique campaign. NOCOSA launched a nation-wide fundraising campaign jointly with the Norwegian Students' and Academics' International Assistance Fund (SAIH) and invited the Mozambique Radio Orchestra, *Marrabenta*, together with dancers, to do a tour of Norway. The previous year's successful visit by the Mozambique National Dance Ensemble had demonstrated that cultural arrangements represent an excellent vehicle for the mediation of information, and Marrabenta's countrywide tour was the highlight of the campaign. Money collected through the fundraising campaign and resulting from Marrabenta's tour were used for the provision of warning equipment (requested by the Mozambique government for a particular district) so that the population could seek refuge against imminent attack, as well as for a more long-term school rehabilitation project in Maputo.[29]

The final years of the 1980s

During the final years of the 1980s and at the commencement of the 1990s, the Council could view with satisfaction the increased scope of activities against apartheid. Operation Day's Work (OD), the Norwegian Schools' own annual solidarity campaign, launched their 1988 campaign under the slogan "Education against Apartheid". NOK 5 million was collected, and the money was devoted to the upgrading of schools in Mozambique, education of SWAPO refugees in Angola, SAIH's alternative educational programmes in South African townships, and the continuation of NOCOSA's teacher projects in Zimbabwe. The Council was responsible for much of the preparatory work associated with Operation Day's Work, and i.a. led OD's study tour of the region. A great deal of the work consisted of providing information material for the schools. OD was immediately succeeded by the *Schools against Apartheid* campaign run by the Norwegian Union of School

---

[28] Annual Report, 1988–89.

[29] Annual Report, 1988–89.

Employees, one of NOCOSA's member organisations. This campaign was carried out jointly with the Norwegian Ministry of Church and Education, as well as a number of teacher and pupil organisations and NGOs. Once more the Council provided information material and, not least, speakers. In connection with the campaign, NOCOSA produced the booklet "Amandla— South Africa in the 1980s", which was distributed as class sets to the schools. A booklet from NOCOSA written by Tore Linné Eriksen; "Den brutale naboen" ("The brutal neighbour"), which in detail described the involvement of the South African apartheid regime in regional warfare and destabilisation, was also used in the lessons at school.

In 1989, *Women Together* was the motto of the Norwegian television campaign, and the Council was involved in its promotion. The funds raised were used i.a. on the construction of a women's centre in Katutura in Namibia. In 1990, a similar centre for ANC-women was constructed inside South Africa.

Upon attaining independence in 1990, Namibia was given the highest priority by NOCOSA in a similar manner to Zimbabwe when it had achieved independence ten years earlier. The spreading of information was of great importance, and a study tour to the country was given wide coverage by newspapers and magazines. A major hearing on Namibia was arranged specially for journalists and organisations. A fundraising activity in connection with SWAPO's election campaign and the Namibian trade unions realised NOK 340,000. After the elections, NOCOSA arranged a visit to Namibia (financed by the Ministry of Foreign Affairs) for a delegation comprising Young Conservatives, The Norwegian Young Christian Democrats, The Norwegian Labour Youth, and Socialist Youth League of Norway. It also participated in an initiative for a similar visit (financed by NORAD) by a delegation of journalists.

The Council's co-operation with the labour movement

There was a great deal of sympathy for the struggle against apartheid at all levels of the labour movement, and its own organisations were involved in supporting liberation movements and refugees from South Africa and Namibia. Nevertheless, NOCOSA still felt that the political pressure exerted by the labour movement was limited. For instance, the labour movement had not pressed the Norwegian authorities with a key demand to implement a boycott of South Africa. At the same time, the labour movement provided an important channel for exercising political influence.

The need for overtures towards the Norwegian labour movement became especially strong at the beginning of the 1980s. Throughout the 1970s, relations between NOCOSA and the labour movement had been strained as the latter's International Solidarity Committee (AIS) was not only sceptical towards the ANC, but also refused to recognise its trade union, SACTU. Among other reasons, this was because SACTU was affiliated to the communist dominated World Federation of Trade Unions (WFTU) (see chapter 9). The Council felt the decision by the AIS/The Norwegian Federation of Trade Unions–LO to be one-sided, with potentially unfortunate consequences. It thus became increasingly important for the Council to have the necessary perspective and knowledge as a corrective and counterbalance to the labour movement's approach. For its part, LO regarded the Council's insistence on LO-recognition of, and financial support to, SACTU as "interference with LO's internal affairs".[30]

As part of its endeavours to involve the labour movement in joint efforts, the Council in 1981 invited Andrew Molotsane to inform the Norwegian labour movement on SACTU's work. Molotsane's meetings with the trade unions were very successful. Everywhere he went interested audiences received him, and he inspired confidence and sympathy. The meeting between Molotsane and the Norwegian Graphical Union resulted in the latter expressing a positive attitude toward both SACTU and the Council, and an interest in supporting boycott efforts. One proposal was to provide financial assistance to refugees from Southern Africa by arranging for them to be trained in graphics. This idea became reality when *Aftenposten*'s printing works hosted two youths from SACTU.

In Bergen, a meeting was held with the Bergen Council of Trade Unions, which wanted to start a local NOCOSA branch. It also desired improved relations between LO/AIS and the Council, and disagreed with LO's attitude towards the Council. Many of the groups with whom Molotsane met expressed similar sentiments as well as an interest in joining efforts aiming at the introduction of a boycott. The Council had not expected such a warm response and felt encouraged to increase its efforts in relation to the labour movement.[31]

In the early 1980s, the Council initiated the preparation of a report on Norwegian trade with South Africa and the consequences a boycott might have for Norwegian jobs. As we shall see later, efforts to implement a boycott had gained momentum through numerous campaigns and demonstrations, as well as through systematic efforts to prevent Norwegian contacts with South Africa. The report was produced by Norwegian economists at the Norwegian School of Economic and Business Administration, establishing NOCOSA as an organisation with more to offer than merely calling for boycotts. It provided a detailed overview over Norwegian trade with South Africa, the number of workplaces involved, and what it would cost to maintain them in the event of a boycott.

In the foreword to the report, which became known as the Bergen Report, the Council borrowed Julius Nyerere's words:

---

[30] Vesla Vetlesen: *Frihet for Sør-Afrika. LO og kampen mot apartheid.* Oslo: Tiden Norsk Forlag, 1998, p. 42.

[31] Report on Moletsane's visit to Norway, 15–23 November 1981.

Those who invest in South Africa, and those who trade with the country, help to pay the costs of apartheid. They contribute to the growth of the apartheid economy while profiting from it themselves. In this process, they themselves become a corrupt part of apartheid. They are participants in the process, no matter how far away they live or how free they may be of racial prejudice at the personal level... Those who are opponents of racism as an ideology and way of life can make no other honest choice than to isolate the current government of South Africa.[32]

The report was presented during the inauguration of the Council's campaign "Action against Apartheid" in 1982. To coincide with the campaign, a report arguing the case of sanctions was prepared by Tore Linné Eriksen.[33]

The Bergen report was presented to the Ministry of Foreign Affairs as well as a number of trade unions. Together with the Bergen Council of Trade Unions, NOCOSA later that year held a labour conference on South Africa, attended by shop stewards from all the unions. The Bergen report was presented, and the following statement was adopted and issued by the conference:

The conference holds that a total embargo of oil is the most effective tool in the struggle against the apartheid regime, and we are alarmed by the fact that 20–25% of South Africa's import of oil is carried on Norwegian ships. We feel that Norway can play a pivotal role in this area, and we call on the Norwegian government to take immediate steps to effect a boycott of oil transport in accordance with the resolution of the Bergen Council of Trade Unions at its annual meeting on 25th March this year... In keeping with the UN resolution which Norway supported, we must take steps toward a total economic boycott of South Africa... A number of jobs in certain areas of industry are currently dependent on trade with South Africa. We call on LO and the government to follow up the resolutions made in the Bergen Report in order to reduce this dependence.[34]

At this point, NOCOSA's work in respect to trade unions was making headway. There was strong motivation to continue the work, and in the following years this was given priority by the Council. A Trade Union Committee consisting of representatives and members of a large number of unions was established in 1983. Ellen Stensrud from the Oslo section of the Iron and Metal Workers Union chaired the committee, with Gunnar Myrvang from the Norwegian Union of Chemical Industry Workers as deputy. The Committee was to involve trade unions in organised and systematic solidarity activities, and not least, to get trade unions and organisations to throw their weight behind a call for a boycott of South Africa. It became es-

---

[32] Ø. Gladsøe, E. Holm, O. Norderhaug, A. Ofstad, H.K. Voldstad: "Norske arbeidsplassers avhengighet av handelen med Sør-Afrika" ("Norwegian workplaces dependent on trade with South Africa"), Bergen, March 1982.

[33] Tore Linné Eriksen, "Sanksjoner, Sør-Afrika og Norge" ("Sanctions, South Africa and Norway"), NUPI-memorandum No. 239, Norwegian Institute of International Affairs, March 1982.

[34] Statement adopted at labour union conference on South Africa, Bergen 27 March 1982.

pecially important to get local clubs and unions to raise the issue of trade with South Africa with management.

This labour bore fruit. Norsk Kabelfabrikk (producing cables) stopped its export to South Africa as a result of pressure from the local trade union club. In a letter to the club, the Council congratulated it on the success of its efforts and informed members that it was inspiring to those who worked with these issues on a daily basis to see local branches beginning to raise such issues.[35] The Council encouraged the local branch to exhort colleagues in the same field to follow its example by exerting pressure within their companies. In the autumn of 1985, Elkem Aluminium at Lista stopped its import of South African manganese, and the management admitted that it had been under heavy pressure from the local branch to do so.

As in Bergen, the labour movement in Tromsø instituted co-operation with the local branch of the Council and with the United Nations Association in Norway. Their joint efforts were based on the labour movement's desire to lend its weight to anti-apartheid endeavours, as well as to utilise the resources available in the two organisations.

Since many of the politically influential persons in the labour movement were sceptical towards the Council's boycott efforts, much of the involvement took place at the local level. At local annual meetings, a large number of resolutions were adopted, calling on LO's central administration and individual unions to implement a total boycott of South Africa. In 1985, for instance, the local Trade Union of Vinmonopolet (the Norwegian state monopoly selling wine and spirits) adopted the following statement: "The grass roots must be activated by union and local club involvement, but LO centrally should retain the main responsibility and be in charge of co-ordination".[36] The Council wrote to all the trade unions in the country, inviting them to join. Following this, many unions did become members and every year small and large contributions came into the Council's coffers for information and campaign work.

Relations with the LO's central administration improved. As a result, LO, the Church of Norway and NOCOSA arranged a joint activity in connection with the Nobel Peace Prize award to Bishop Desmond Tutu in 1984. This was the first time the Church of Norway and LO engaged in a joint event, and the Council's contacts with both bodies played a significant role in furthering their co-operation.

In 1985, the following trade unions were represented on the Council's trade union committee: the Norwegian Iron and Metal Workers Union, the Norwegian Union of Chemical Industry Workers, the Norwegian Civil Service Union, the Norwegian Union of School Employees, the Norwegian

---

[35] Letter from NOCOSA (Asbjørn Eidhammer) to the Iron & Metal Workers' local branch at Norsk Kabelfabrikk, 1 January 1984.

[36] Letter from Vinmonopolets Arbeiderforening to NOCOSA, 7 March 1985.

Graphical Union, the Norwegian Union of Railway Workers and the Norwegian Union of Building Industry Workers, as well as a representative of the Oslo branch of the Labour Party. Not all of these were appointed by their trade unions as official representatives, some having agreed to participate at the request of the Council which was continuously seeking to increase the breadth of representation and invited the Norwegian Union of Transport Workers to be represented on the committee. The Norwegian Seamen's Union declined a similar invitation.

The Council and the Norwegian Union of Chemical Industry Workers (NKIF)

The Council's relationship with the Norwegian Union of Chemical Industry Workers (NKIF) was particularly close. At its annual meeting in 1984, NKIF passed a resolution in favour of boycotting South Africa and at the same time granted NOK 50,000 each to ANC and SWAPO. Representatives from the two liberation organisations were invited to keep NOCOSA informed of conditions in Southern Africa and to participate at a press conference organised in co-operation with the Council. Given the fact that major Norwegian ferro-manganese corporations considered that they were dependent on manganese imports from South Africa, the annual meeting's resolution was sensational: NKIF will together with the Norwegian Council for Southern Africa and LO, strive to find alternatives to the current trade between the chemical industry in Norway and South Africa.[37]

It was in particular the chairperson of the union, Arthur Svensson, who established contacts and made the union's policy known. In February of 1985, the Council and NKIF arranged a two-day conference on the Norwegian chemical industry and trade with South Africa. NKIF's deputy leader, Olav Støylen, included the following in his opening remarks at the conference:

> The union has joined the Council in organising this conference as it is an organisation enjoying broad support within the Norwegian community, and because it has managed through its work to make South Africa a more burning issue for the Norwegian public than it might otherwise have been.[38]

At the conference the Council also presented a report revealing that Norwegian trade with South Africa had increased by 37% over the preceding year, and that it was larger than it had been for many years.

For NKIF, a total boycott of South Africa was a difficult matter because it would adversely affect many workplaces in Norway's industrial sector. NKIF nevertheless wished to tackle the problem head on, and in co-opera-

---

[37] The Norwegian Union of Chemical Industry Workers (NKIF)/NOCOSA: "Norsk kjemisk industri og handelen med Sør-Afrika" ("The Norwegian Chemical Industry and the Trade with South Africa"), report from a conference at Leangkollen, 19–20 February, 1985, p. 3.

[38] Ibid.

tion with NOCOSA, called a meeting to examine the scope of the Bergen report and to examine whether there might be alternative high quality sources of manganese to replace imports from South Africa. Both shop stewards and company management involved in export to, or import from, South Africa attended the seminar, together with a representative from LO. Parliament had recently passed legislation to reduce trade with South Africa. This led participants to agree to work together on following up the new bill. The meeting agreed to promote with renewed vigour a proposal to Norwegian authorities to create a transitional fund for Norwegian industries and businesses that might be affected by restrictions on trade with South Africa. These lobbying efforts were primarily to be directed at the Ministry of Trade and the Cabinet. NKIF was to approach the aluminium industry, i.e. Årdal og Sunndal Verk, Elkem and Norsk Hydro, to review the import of manganese and ferro-manganese, and to approach Norsk Hydro in order to terminate phosphate imports from South Africa.[39]

At a conference which shop stewards at the Sunndal section of NKIF, the Årdalstangen section of NKIF and the Høyanger section of NKIF held, the stewards demanded that Årdal og Sunndal Verk (ÅSV) should find suppliers in other countries than South Africa:

> ÅSV currently imports large quantities of electrolytic manganese from South Africa. We request ÅSV to put a stop to this trade. ÅSV must therefore find suppliers in other countries... If ÅSV does not intensify its efforts, we will have to consider measures for stopping trade with the racist regime.[40]

NKIF's involvement may be surprising, since many jobs would have been endangered by a full embargo.[41] In her book, *Frihet for Sør-Afrika. LO og kampen mot apartheid* (Freedom for South Africa. LO (Norwegian Confederation of Trade Unions) and the Struggle against Apartheid), Vesla Vetlesen writes about LO's co-operation with the Council and suggests that NKIF's involvement was not merely a result of idealism:

> Nevertheless, the above-mentioned areas of conflict, ... did not prevent the development of an improved climate of co-operation between the Council and LO/AIS. The Council's efforts deserved respect, and LO had to take the organisation seriously. One organisation, NKIF, decided it would be expedient to appoint a representative to the Council as an insider in order to exert influence. As Olav Støylen, at the time NKIF deputy leader, argued, "If you can't beat them, join them![42]

---

[39] Minutes of meeting on chemical industry and trade with South Africa, 17 June 1985.

[40] Statement from conference of representatives, Spåtind, 23–26 October 1985.

[41] Approximately 4–5,000 Norwegians worked with the manganese imported from South Africa.

[42] Vesla Vetlesen: *Frihet for Sør-Afrika. LO og kampen mot apartheid*. Oslo: Tiden Norsk Forlag, 1988, see p. 43.

However, Arthur Svensson, who for many years was chairperson of NKIF, repudiates this: "We became involved first and foremost because of the ANC and SWAPO, and our participation in the labour union committee had nothing to do with protecting Norwegian workplaces. Even though more than 1,000 jobs were in jeopardy, we felt that a boycott was the correct line of action".[43]

The struggle for sanctions

Boycott of South Africa was an important part of the struggle against apartheid right from the beginning, when Norwegian Action Against Apartheid and the Crisis Fund for Southern Africa were established in the early 1960s. When on behalf of ANC the Nobel Peace Prize winner Albert Luthuli in 1960 called for a full boycott of South Africa, it became an important motivation for the anti-apartheid movement. It was nonetheless heavy going, possibly because the level of public awareness concerning apartheid was low. The Council's information campaigns contributed strongly toward raising such awareness, and, following the Soweto uprising in 1976, it became easier to gain public support for the Council's efforts.

It was only at the beginning of the 1980s that efforts in this direction began to take form. The Council's boycott committee, established in 1982, worked on cases referred to it and also raised issues at its own discretion. There were two avenues of attack: the first of these involved campaigns at the local level in order to promote grass roots public involvement. A "boycott package" was put together and mailed to all NOCOSA's local branches and to others showing interest. The package contained background information and practical hints on areas in which the Council felt it possible to achieve results. A municipal boycott campaign launched in the late 1970s only really started paying off in the mid-1980s. The other main avenue of approach was at the highest political level, with special emphasis on efforts to end exports of oil and weapons to South Africa.

The main argument against boycott as a weapon in the struggle against the apartheid regime was that it would prove futile if Norway were the only country to implement the policy. Consequences for South Africa would be negligible, but for Norwegian industry and jobs they could be severe. Although the Council was convinced that a boycott would eventually yield results, an equally important argument was that the liberation movements themselves had repeatedly called for Norway to boycott South Africa. In the opinion of the Council the main concern was to support the liberation movements' plea for a boycott of the apartheid regime, primarily because their leaders themselves had faith in boycott as an effective means of forcing

---

[43] Interview with Arthur Svensson, 17 June 1998.

the regime into submission.[44] But in Norway, as in the rest of the world, economic interest was often the weightiest consideration.

In many instances, NOCOSA won through with their pleas for a boycott. Following an appeal from the Council, the University of Oslo requested its employees not to participate in scientific and cultural events at which South Africa was represented. South African participants were barred from attending numerous conferences, seminars, etc. in Norway. The Norwegian Mountain Touring Association stopped selling canned goods from South Africa at its hostels and tourist cabins. The Norwegian Dairies ceased exporting cheese to South Africa. Two Norwegian banks, (The Norwegian Bank and Kristiania Bank) had also decided to stop selling Kruger Rands. Representatives of the Norwegian Agency for Development Co-operation (NORAD) no longer travelled via Johannesburg with Scandinavian Airlines (SAS), and SAS eventually for a variety of reasons discontinued flying to South Africa. In the autumn of 1986, The Norwegian Union of Postal Workers joined an international trade union campaign to boycott South Africa and refused to handle post to South Africa for the remainder of the year.

Other issues were more complex and, despite concerted efforts on the part of NOCOSA, were less successful. This was especially true of deliveries of oil and petroleum products by Norwegian tankers to South Africa (see chapter 5). The Council was unsuccessful in stopping the sale of SWAKARA furs from Namibia, which even the Norwegian Red Cross used as prizes in its lotteries. The Norwegian Red Cross was unwilling to discuss the issue. The local Oslo NOCOSA branch ran a campaign against all the shops in Oslo which sold SWAKARA furs. Activists handed out pamphlets and informed the public that the shops were selling stolen goods (on the strength of UN Decree No. 1, which decrees that it is illegal to remove or participate in the removal of natural resources from Namibia). The police, however, interrupted the peaceful information campaign and arrested eight of the activists.

In January 1986, the Norwegian government introduced a "sanctions package" aimed against the apartheid regime in South Africa. Licenses were now mandatory for all trade with South Africa, and all Norwegian transportation of oil to South Africa was to be registered. It had originally been proposed that vessels transporting oil to South Africa would be identified by name but the government later backed away from this provision.[45] The Council was not satisfied with these measures and felt that the government had bowed its knee to shipping interests despite the fact that the Norwegian public, through its support of municipal boycotts, had clearly indicated that it was ready for a total embargo of the apartheid state.

---

[44] See Tore Linné Eriksen, "Sanctions, South Africa and Norway", Norwegian Institute of International Affairs, 1982.

[45] See chapter 5.

In October 1986, NOCOSA brought to light the fact that the Labour Party government had, in contravention of the above-mentioned UN decree, granted Norsk Hydro a license to continue the export of explosives to Namibia. The explosives were used for extraction of uranium. Moreover, the license was granted after the Norwegian parliament imposed restrictions on trade with Namibia and had introduced license requirements. This case became a serious embarrassment to the Brundtland government. Reidar Andestad, then chairperson of the Council, told the press that it was a political scandal and a crass example of the gap between Norwegian rhetoric and practice in relation to South Africa. A seriously aggravating consideration was that it was widely assumed that Namibian uranium was being used in the manufacture of nuclear weapons in South Africa. Minister of Trade, Kurt Mosbakk, regretted the sale, but claimed in an interview with the left-wing newspaper *Klassekampen* that there was no legal basis for denying Norsk Hydro a license for this trade. Nevertheless, this incident led to hectic meetings in the Ministry and the sale immediately fell through, the management of Norsk Hydro having at their own discretion decided to discontinue deliveries. Herøya Trade Union (a local branch) had already declared that it would under no circumstances continue to load calcium nitrate onto ships bound for Namibia.

In addition to all the efforts aimed directly at those involved in Norwegian trade or co-operation with South Africa and at putting pressure on Norwegian authorities, much of the Council's activity took the form of organising demonstrations. Many of these were staged in connection with demands for a total embargo of South Africa, and NOCOSA could not complain about the level of participation. On 11 October 1985, the UN-declared *Day of Solidarity* with political prisoners in South Africa, events were staged all over Norway, with town-square meetings and torchlight parades in many of the largest cities. Norwegian transport of oil was the focus of attention. In Oslo alone there were over 1,600 demonstrators. Jostein Nesvåg, the pastor of Bøler Lutheran parish, and Frene Ginwala of the ANC, both made public appeals.

On 13 June 1986, while the Norwegian parliament was considering new boycott measures, a joint demonstration was arranged by NOCOSA, the Oslo Council of Trade Unions, The Norwegian Students' and Academics' International Assistance Fund, the Council on Ecumenical and International Relations, calling for a total boycott of South Africa. Two thousand demonstrators shouted "Full boycott of South Africa NOW" so loudly outside Parliament that several MPs went to the windows to see what was going on. A few days later, on 16 June, a number of events were planned to commemorate the 10th anniversary of the Soweto uprising. Pioneer Mogale of the ANC addressed the gathering in Oslo and called upon the authorities to stop oil and petroleum trade with South Africa, because "This oil lubricates the weapons that kill in South Africa". He had himself been a part of the

Soweto uprising in which a lot of youths were killed. Memorial meetings and demonstrations were held all over Norway to commemorate the day. The Norwegian Students Christian Movement, the Norwegian Youth Council and NOCOSA arranged a spontaneous vigil in Stavanger Cathedral, with prayers, hymns and information about the situation in South Africa. This was the first time a vigil was spontaneously arranged in a cathedral on the basis of a political situation.

The consumer boycott

The UN sanctions resolution, which was passed in the early 1960s, was primarily aimed at sports events and the arms trade with the apartheid regime. The consumer boycott was initiated by the Norwegian labour movement and political youth parties, which got their own boycott campaigns going in the early 1960s (see chapters 1 and 8). From the mid-1970s, a number of boycott campaigns against shops selling South African products were organised, primary targets being Del Monte canned food and Cape grapes. The Council produced a list of all South African trademarks being imported and sold, and local branches contacted wholesalers and shops and held frequent demonstrations protesting against shops selling such "forbidden fruit". The Socialist Youth League of Norway, student groups and other local activist organisations also arranged regular protests.

It was not until January 1986 that the Norwegian parliament passed legislation requiring licenses for all trade with South Africa. At that point, only a few shops still carried South African products and some factories and shops, which had imported cheap fruit, were stuck with large surplus stocks. The Heistad factories in Telemark, for instance, were stuck with 20,000 cans of fruit when the ban on imports was imposed. In order to dispose of the fruit, the county administration offered to buy the entire stock for NOK 60,000, provided that a third of the money was donated direct to the liberation struggle in South Africa. The basis for the agreement was Heistad's desire to deal with the fruit in a morally acceptable way. Because of this, the Administrator of Telemark County, the factory manager and NOCOSA signed a contract. The fruit was distributed and served as dessert at the more than 30 retirement homes and other institutions in the county.

The municipal boycott

Although a number of contacts between Norway and South Africa were severed as results of the Council's boycott efforts, it proved impossible, at least for a long period, to achieve unified policies at the national level. Thus towards the end of the 1970s, the idea of a municipal boycott emerged. In 1977, Målselv Municipality in Troms began boycotting South African products, setting an example to the rest of the country. There were at that time a number of "nuclear free zones" around the country, and it is possible that municipal boycotts of South Africa took their inspiration from this concept.

The idea was to encourage involvement at the local level, thereby generating public opinion, which would force the government and parliament to take action. The scope of the campaign was extensive—and labour-intensive! In May of 1978, the Council sent a letter to all the municipal councils in Norway calling on the business community and the citizenry not to purchase South African products:

> On behalf of the African people, we hope for a favourable and timely response from the municipal council, and that Norway might set an example for the rest of the Western world as the first country to adopt a boycott of South African products. This may become a concrete symbol of the Norwegian people's solidarity with the oppressed black majority in South Africa.[46]

The petition was supported by prominent politicians from most of the leading Norwegian parties. The chairman of the Norwegian Confederation of Trade Unions (LO) was asked to sign it, but brusquely refused the request. To cite LO's reply: "In connection with the above-mentioned petition we would again like to remind you that LO *runs its own* solidarity efforts through the International Solidarity Committee, AIS. LO has no intention of changing this practice".[47]

The Council hoped that the municipal campaign would reinvigorate the debate concerning trade with the apartheid regime. Norwegian trade with South Africa increased in 1978 despite the anti-apartheid year of 1977. Many local councils were quick to follow up NOCOSA's request by approving boycott measures. Others felt that it was not up to municipalities to become involved in foreign policy issues and decided "on principle" not to deal with the issue. By July of the same year (1979), 39 (out of 454) municipalities had voted to follow the Council's request.

In 1985, after some years with little activity in the area of municipal boycotts, the Council made renewed concerted efforts to involve the municipalities, which until then had not passed any resolution on a boycott of South Africa. Once more all the municipalities were contacted, and by 1986 nearly 80% of Norway's municipalities had approved anti-apartheid boycotts. In October 1985, Telemark became the first county in which every municipality had introduced boycotts against South Africa. In all, ten county councils (out of twenty) passed resolutions supporting the boycott. Public interest had by now reached a higher pitch of intensity, and the most recent boycott cam-

---

[46] Letter from NOCOSA to the county's local administrations, 9 May 1979.

[47] Letter from LO signed by Thor Andreassen and Kaare Sandegren, 3 April 1978.

paign put South Africa on the agenda in numerous circles and sparked debate in the local media.[48]

Oslo was one of the municipalities that by 1979 had petitioned the administration to adopt boycott measures against South Africa. In 1985, Oslo Municipality followed up their boycott policy by proposing a number of new measures. One such measure was to chart producers, exporters and transports of Norwegian products to South Africa, as well as to boycott artists and performers who had appeared in South Africa and consequently appeared on the UN "black"-list.

The exertions on the part of NOCOSA in addition to the multitude of activities initiated by local branches throughout Norway contributed to heightening the population's awareness and deepening its concern for these issues. At the same time, the Council made strenuous efforts to get the government to adopt a total trade embargo of South Africa and to introduce boycott legislation. For many a long year the municipalities were well ahead of the government in this respect.

The culture and sports boycott

The Council entreated the Norwegian Confederation of Sports and the Norwegian Gymnastics Federation not to participate in a gymnastics event in South Africa in 1970. This was one of the first boycott incidents since the Madserud demonstrations in 1964 to attract public attention. No Norwegian athlete had competed in South Africa for a long time. The Council now called on sports organisations to take steps to have South Africa excluded from the International Gymnastics Federation. Athletes, team managers, individuals and youth organisations supported the campaign, but this was not enough to keep the Norwegian gymnasts at home. The campaign obtained broad coverage both in the newspapers and on television, thus providing a welcome opportunity for the Council to draw the public's attention to conditions in South Africa. It was also hoped that this and similar campaigns in other countries might lead the International Olympic Committee (IOC) and other sports organisers to exclude South Africa from all international sports events.[49]

The IOC had for many years attracted attention because of its dithering approach to South African participation in the Olympic Games. In 1968 it was decided that South Africa would be permitted to participate in the Summer Games in Mexico City because the apartheid regime had agreed to send a mixed team. The Olympic Committee voting procedures allow for secret ballots, and the Norwegian representative on the committee, Jan

---

[48] This strategy for creating debate was welcomed by many local politicians who were concerned with international issues but without any possibility of discussing foreign affairs with local administrations. A form of alliance between solidarity movements and local politicians thus came into being.

[49] Activity Report from the board for the period 16 June 1969–9 November 1970.

Staubo, did not disclose how he had voted, but he never repudiated the assumption that he had voted in favour of South African participation. The Council felt that it was in any event "quite incredibly hypocritical" of Staubo to say that the IOC's decision was a victory for black athletes in South Africa.[50]

In 1981, NOCOSA vehemently protested a South African scout group's participation at the Norwegian Guide and Scout Association's jamboree held in Norway. This was in clear violation of the UN call for a cultural boycott of South Africa, especially since the South African scouting movement operated within the apartheid system and the leaders had shown no involvement in relation to apartheid politics. The Council stated in a press release that if the South African flag were flown at the scout camp, it would be a disgrace to the Norwegian scouting movement. The Council sent a letter to the Norwegian Guide and Scout Association informing it about South Africa's apartheid policy and calling on it to exclude South Africa from the international scouting movement.

In 1984, the Council requested the Norwegian Musicians' Union to promote an artistic boycott of South Africa. The issue was of current interest as a Norwegian pianist had recently performed in that country. At the very least, the Council called on the Musicians' Union to inform its members on apartheid issues and to encourage them not to visit South Africa.[51] The Union, which was not in a position to make a decision before its annual meeting in 1986, agreed that it was important to keep members informed and requested information material from the Council. The Musicians' Union raised the issue with the Norwegian Artists' Council, an umbrella organisation for all Norwegian artists associations, which requested each of its member organisations to deal with the issue.[52]

Little by little the Council's boycott efforts paid off. In the autumn of 1985, Bergen Philharmonic Orchestra reported that musicians who performed in South Africa would no longer be allowed to stand on their stage.[53] The television-division of the Norwegian Broadcasting Corporation (NRK) decided to boycott South Africa in compliance with UN guidelines, while NRK's radio division decided to leave the decision up to individual radio journalists. All local radio stations in Oslo decided to heed the Council's request to boycott artists who had performed in South Africa. In situations where there was ambiguity concerning a guest's relationship to South Africa, NOCOSA was consulted.

---

[50] Lars Borge-Andersen: "Today we continue speaking about South Africa and IOC", from a debate 1 March 1968.

[51] Letter from NOCOSA to Norsk Musikerforbund, 16 October 1984.

[52] Letter from Norsk Musikerforbund to NOCOSA, 22 October 1984.

[53] *Nationen*, 12 October 1985.

Two incidents in particular threw the spotlight on the Norwegian culture and sports boycott. The first was the South African runner Zola Budd's invitation to participate in an important Oslo road-race in 1984. The following year it was the invitation to two British singers, Cliff Richard and Shirley Bassey, to perform at the Momarkedet summer concert, an annual televised event arranged by the Norwegian Red Cross. The latter were on the UN list of artists who had performed in South Africa, thereby violating the cultural boycott of that country.

Zola Budd had in 1984 assumed British citizenship in order to make it possible for her to participate in the Olympic Games that year. However, South African newspapers still spoke of her as a representative of their country, and the Council felt she was being exploited in South African propaganda tactics. The South African Minister of the Interior confirmed that she still held a South African passport in addition to her British one.[54] When NOCOSA first heard about the situation, Zola Budd was relatively unknown and the Council felt that it was unlikely that protests would be staged. The Oslo race-committee interpreted this to mean that the Council welcomed her to Norway. When this was publicised in the Norwegian media and also in Britain, the Council felt compelled to make it clear that Zola Budd was unwelcome unless and until she denounced apartheid and renounced her association with her native country's apartheid policy. On the day of the race, a flock of journalists turned up as did a large number of protesters armed with banners, one Council representative following Budd across the finishing line sporting a large poster with the accusation "Zola Budd—There's no running away from apartheid". This incident generated wide newspaper coverage and the picture of Zola Budd and the poster-bearer appeared in print all over the world.

Some of the Council's leaders asked themselves in retrospect to what extent Zola Budd could be held responsible for government policy of her country. She had become a means of attracting attention to the situation in South Africa, but was also a victim of political tactics. It had been the first boycott protest to gain such prominence in media coverage in a long time, and the Council's gain was that the UN's cultural boycott of South Africa had become well publicised.

Zola Budd may have been a victim, but one could hardly say the same about Cliff Richard and Shirley Bassey and the fuss surrounding their performance at the Norwegian Red Cross concert. Artists who had performed in South Africa had themselves decided to do so, and it would be a conscious decision with known consequences. When the Council learned that the two artists would in August 1985 be performing at the concert, it immediately informed the organisers that the performers were on the UN blacklist

---

[54] Press release by NOCOSA, 2 May 1984.

and that they had not expressed any regrets regarding their visits to South Africa.

The Council nevertheless agreed not to stage protests against these concerts, primarily because the UN boycott list was not sufficiently well known, and because the organiser was a humanitarian organisation.[55] Arne Skouen of the daily *Dagbladet* telephoned the Council and reprimanded it for not protesting against the concerts. In his column "Plain talk", he wrote that the Council had failed in its duties as watchdog. A protest was nevertheless staged at Momarkedet when a group of demonstrators from the Socialist Youth League appeared to protest at the holding of the concert. The organisers had hired military police to stand guard at the concert, and fierce altercations arose between the demonstrators and the soldiers. Joakim Winters, then chairman of NOCOSA, strongly criticised the Defence Ministry in a press release. He claimed that it had allowed soldiers to intervene in a civilian demonstration:

> Nothing like this has happened in Norway since Prime Minister Kolstad and Minister of Defence Quisling sent in soldiers in the battle of Menstad in 1931.[56]

> It is especially shocking that the military are employed against people who are demonstrating against, among other things, the use of soldiers against civilians in the racist nation of South Africa. This is no less than a national disgrace.[57]

The Council demanded an immediate and unreserved apology from Prime Minister Kåre Willoch. These statements were perhaps crass and somewhat ill considered, but in situations like these there is little time for reflection, and the situation was serious enough. The press showed tremendous interest in the issue and ran several stories while Winters was interviewed on television. There was no response from Willoch and the Council had to be satisfied with a statement from the Ministry of Defence, which could be interpreted as an apology.[58]

What was sensational about this incident was that NRK, which every year broadcasts this concert live, decided to boycott it. Swedish television was also supposed to have broadcast the concert but decided to follow suit.

Norwegian transport of oil to South Africa

One of the Council's most important areas of interest, moreover calling for substantial resources, was to prevent Norwegian shipping from transporting

---

[55] Press releases by NOCOSA, 18 June 1985 and 23 August 1985.

[56] The Battle of Menstad was the result of one of the largest labour conflicts in Norwegian history. After workers at Norsk Hydro had been on strike for six months, the authorities sent in the police to end the strike. The police were chased away, however, and soldiers were then sent into action against the strikers.

[57] Press release by NOCOSA, 25 August 1985.

[58] Interview with Joakim Winters, 27 April 1998.

oil to South Africa. The Council repeatedly called for Norwegian legislation against such transport to the apartheid regime. Press releases were sent out untiringly and endless press conferences were held. Occasionally the Council only learned of oil deliveries by reading the newspapers, but more frequently it was the Council that informed the press. This gradually became popular media material and led to major stories in all the country's newspapers. Co-operation with the Dutch organisation, Shipping Research Bureau (SRB), which was established in 1979, was of great importance. SRB kept track of all shipments of oil to South Africa and its reports clearly demonstrated that Norway was responsible for the major share of oil deliveries to the apartheid regime. There was extensive exchange of information between SRB and NOCOSA, Øystein Gudim being an indefatigable anchorman in this tug-of-war between NOCOSA and the shipping companies.[59] A joint NOCOSA-SRB report published in 1982 received a great deal of media coverage, both at home and abroad.

In 1982, the Council had a meeting with the Secretary of State for Foreign Affairs, Eivinn Berg of the Conservative Party, to discuss Norwegian trade with and transport of oil to South Africa. The Council referred to SRB's report and demanded legislation to prohibit the continuation of this activity. The Council also asked the Ministry of Foreign Affairs to consider the proposals contained in the report for the reduction of trade with South Africa, and to write to companies trading with that country, informing them of Norwegian policies relating to such trade. During the meeting with Mr. Berg, the Council further requested that Norway play a more active role in the planning of an international conference on the shipment of oil to South Africa, and that Norway initiate the establishment of a group of experts to work on preparations for the conference.

At the meeting, Eivinn Berg rejected a unilateral boycott out of hand, whether in the area of trade or the shipment of oil. The reason for this refusal was the argument that a unilateral Norwegian boycott would have minimal effect on South Africa but have potentially serious consequences for Norwegian companies. The government saw no reason for intervening in Norwegian transport of oil to South Africa so long as there was no binding resolution by the UN Security Council to that effect. His position was that if Norway implemented such a decision on its own, Norwegian transport would be taken over by other shipping companies, with consequently unacceptable financial losses in an already difficult market. For the same reason, Norway wanted the focus at the UN conference to be on export, not the transport, of oil. However, Berg said that a law against Norwegian oil trans-

---

[59] See chapter 5 and Øystein Gudim: "A defeat for the shipping lobby? The Norwegian experience", in R. Hengevold/J. Rodenburg: *Embargo. Apartheid's Oil Secrets Revealed*. Amsterdam: Amsterdam University Press, 1996.

ports might be possible provided the political will was there, but felt that this was not the case at that time.[60]

During the international hearing on South Africa's military action against neighbouring countries (held in Oslo in March of 1984), the Shipping Research Bureau (SRB) not only documented that Norwegian oil transports were continuing, but also presented evidence that Norwegian North Sea oil had found its way to South Africa. Almost all the political groups represented at the conference condemned this state of affairs so that the government had to promise to increase its efforts to ensure that Norwegian oil did not benefit the apartheid regime.

The potential economic consequences of a boycott could be serious for shipping companies, and they therefore tried to keep their oil deliveries literally under cover by covering the name painted on the ship's side and lowering the flag upon entering harbour, common practices in attempts to prevent the vessels from being identified. In addition, ships made arrangements with harbour authorities to use code- and not ship-names. Also ship radios were kept as silent as possible on entering South African harbours.

In 1986, the Shipping Research Bureau (SRB) presented a new report disclosing that Norwegian ships and owner interests were involved in 51 of 83 oil shipments to South Africa. This demonstrated that parliament's call for Norwegian shipping companies to voluntarily boycott South Africa had had no effect. In an interview with the daily newspaper *Arbeiderbladet*, the head of LO's international division, Kaare Sandegren, declared the numbers to be shocking. The Council remarked that the SRB figures revealed that Norwegian shipping companies were the leading transporters of oil to South Africa. At a press conference, NOCOSA's chairperson, Reidar Andestad, said: "Norway's South Africa policy will remain a bluff until the government introduces a law prohibiting transport of oil on Norwegian keels".[61]

In order to demonstrate that the Norwegian public was opposed to Norway's role as supplier of oil to the apartheid regime, the Council initiated a postcard campaign. This formed part of *Campaign Against Apartheid–86*, and letters were sent to all NOCOSA's member organisations, local branches and individual members, to mobilise them in the collection of signatures. The postcards had the inscription: "Contribute to making this a good year for more people: Prohibit Norwegian oil transport to South Africa", and were to be addressed to the Minister of Foreign Affairs.[62]

In June 1986, a UN oil boycott conference was held in Oslo, and another conference on South Africa was held in Paris later that summer, providing unique opportunities for Norway to take a leading role on the boycott issue.

---

[60] NOCOSA's record of a meeting with Eivinn Berg at the Ministry of Foreign Affairs, 22 September 1982.

[61] *Nytt fra Norge* (News from Norway), 22 September 1986.

[62] Press release, NOCOSA, 11 February 1986.

"When Norway argues that a total embargo of South Africa would cost too much, it gives countries with even closer economic ties with that country an even better excuse. There is no excuse for supporting the apartheid regime in Pretoria. What are we waiting for?" asked Reidar Andestad, chairperson of the Council, at a press conference in Oslo in June of 1986, the day before the above-mentioned oil embargo conference in Oslo. He praised the Norwegian Union of Railway Workers which, along with the Union of Transport Workers, had voted to boycott South African shipments. "The next step must be for the Norwegian authorities to demand that oil companies seeking concessions for exploration or operation in the North Sea, cut out their activities in South Africa in order to continue their activities in Norway", said Andestad.[63]

Sanctions legislation

NOCOSA's painstaking boycott efforts contributed towards the organisation gaining a stamp of quality. The Council's constant pressure on the authorities through boycott activities, the municipal boycott and co-operation with Members of Parliament, trade union representatives, church members and others, was undoubtedly one of the contributing factors in the government's decision to propose boycott legislation in late 1986 (see chapter 5). It is also important to see this work as forming part of international co-operation in which impulses and ideas from an international anti-apartheid movement, and especially Britain, the Netherlands and the USA, were followed up in Norway. Pressure created by the international boycott became more and more noticeable in South Africa. The oil embargo made it increasingly expensive for the apartheid regime to procure this important commodity. At the same time, a bank and finance boycott threatened the regime's renewal of loans. The culture and sports boycott struck individuals especially hard, particularly as this was the boycott that was most consistently enforced.

Another four years passed following the Council's meeting with Secretary of State for Foreign Affairs (Eivinn Berg) before Norway, with Knut Frydenlund (Labour) as Minister of Foreign Affairs, mended its ways in respect of the boycott issue.[64] At that time, Denmark had introduced a trade boycott and legislation against tankers delivering oil to South Africa. At a UN conference on economic sanctions in Paris during the summer of 1986, Frydenlund stated that the government had previously regarded a unilateral boycott as pointless because it would not have had any effect. Now, however, the government was willing to put into effect binding sanctions against South Africa, irrespective of how few other countries were prepared to do

---

[63] Press release by NOCOSA, 3 June 1986.

[64] It would perhaps not be correct to say that the government mended its ways. The boycott legislation was initiated by the Conservative/Centre coalition which was in power from 1983 to 1986, but adopted by the Labour government in 1987.

the same. "Because one country sets an example for others", he explained. NOCOSA's head of the boycott committee, Øystein Gudim, rebuked Norway in no uncertain manner for its double standards when in a later speech he had to apologise on behalf of Norway for supporting the apartheid regime in a number of ways:

> Although Norway conducts a better policy than many other Western countries do ... Norway must be judged not only by what it says, but also what it does. This is especially true of the transport of oil to South Africa ... Approximately one third of South Africa's oil imports are transported on Norwegian owned tank ships. This has been the case for more than seven years. Norwegian shipping companies earn blood money by transporting oil to the war machine in South Africa and Namibia.[65]

In the boycott legislation enacted in February of 1987, a full year after the majority of Members of Parliament had indicated they were in favour, transport of unrefined oil remained the weak link (see chapter 5). At the same time, the boycott law provided dispensations for Norwegian companies importing manganese ore and other minerals. Such loopholes in the law provoked the Council into making a number of statements and into taking fresh initiatives. A "doughnut campaign" was staged outside the Parliament to symbolically illustrate the Council's views on legislation, which was full of holes.

The import of manganese ore represented another major problem for the Norwegian boycott of South Africa. Norway was the world's largest producer of manganese alloys for the global steel industry, and South Africa provided 40%–50% of the manganese ore imported by Norway. This manganese was especially important because of its low phosphate content, and it was feared that a Norwegian boycott would instantly affect the entire production at Elkem in Sauda and Elkem in Porsgrunn. The Council felt that it was time to reorganise production and that government funds should be made available for this purpose in order to minimise the detrimental effects of the boycott. To the Council's undisguised dismay, the ferro-alloy industry was given dispensations from the boycott year after year. And as if that was not enough, the companies used their dispensation to purchase and build up large surplus stocks in anticipation of possible tightening of such regulations. Imports increased rapidly immediately after the Act had been passed. In 1988, imports from South Africa more than doubled in relation to the preceding year.

The Council repeatedly reported violations of boycott legislation to the police, but almost all such cases were rapidly laid aside, either because of the inadequate nature of the evidence or as a result of lack of policing resources.

---

[65] *Klassekampen*, 19 June 1986.

The Shell Boycott

Besides exposing Norwegian transport of oil to South Africa, the Council's work in connection with a boycott directed at the Shell Oil Company was the issue that attracted most attention and demanded the hardest work and level of involvement from NOCOSA. In 1986, a united international anti-apartheid movement made the international Shell Company its main target for boycott activities. This was a determining factor for the Council's decision to implement a boycott of Shell in Norway. Protests had been staged in several Western countries: Great Britain, the USA, Sweden, Australia and the Netherlands. The reason for selecting Shell as a main target was that the company delivered much of South Africa's oil and was the largest investor in a number of South African industries, including mining and chemicals. While other companies were disinvesting and pulling out of South Africa, Shell continued to increase its investments.

The boycott was a twin-stage affair in which NOCOSA first approached municipalities, large companies and institutions to ask them to boycott Shell. The intention was to strike against Norwegian Shell and not against individual filling station owners who were distributors for Shell. At that time, almost 80% of Norway's municipalities were supporting the Shell boycott, and there was reason to hope that it would be effective. Should this persuade Shell to terminate its involvement in South Africa, it was probable that it might induce other companies to follow suit.

At first, the Council limited the boycott to nine companies wholly owned by Shell. Local Shell distributors in privately owned petrol stations were merely requested to display a poster showing that they had dissociated themselves from Shell's investments in South Africa and to send a letter to Shell International protesting against Shell's activities in the country. Should these measures not have the desired effect, a more comprehensive consumer boycott would be started. In the course of 1988, Shell lost 1.7% of its national market share in Norway, while in the northern part of Norway, the decrease was up to 3.3%. In an article in the magazine for the motor industry *Motorbransjen*, a Shell representative said that Shell's involvement in South Africa was a negative factor for the company.[66]

An important aspect of the boycott was to make repeated requests to Shell in Norway to pressure the parent company to withdraw from South Africa. Shell Norway invited NOCOSA to a meeting at which it tried to persuade the Council to call off its boycott. Neither party was willing to budge: Shell in Norway would not take any initiative by way of asking Shell International to pull out of South Africa, and the Council vowed to continue its boycott.[67]

---

[66] *Motorbransjen*, No. 3 1989.

[67] NOCOSA press release, 24 November 1986.

There were mixed reactions to the Shell boycott with some name-calling. The Norwegian Shell immediately reacted by dubbing the campaign political terrorism.[68] The Norwegian Association of Motor Car Dealers and Service Organisations called it a harassment campaign. Petrol distributors themselves felt that the campaign was unfair and incomprehensible. But many of the privately owned petrol stations that distributed Shell products followed NOCOSA's request and asked Shell to pull out of South Africa. By the end of 1986, 475 of almost 500 petrol stations had protested against Shell's involvement in the apartheid state and committed themselves to displaying posters at filling stations to this effect. Roughly 25 filling stations wholly owned by Shell were, however, subject to boycotts and demonstrations.

The Council requested municipalities to go a step beyond the municipal boycott already in effect by approving a boycott of Shell products. Several municipalities approved such actions, including the city of Oslo, which was a large consumer of Shell's furnace oil.

When the City Recorder ("Namsretten") in Oslo during the autumn of 1987 judged the boycott of Shell to be illegal unless all petroleum companies in the same situation were treated equally, the Council expanded its boycott to include BP, Total, Mobil, Chevron and Texaco. Nevertheless Shell retained top priority. The municipality of Oslo among several others followed up with a general boycott of all companies involved in South Africa. They acquired their information from the Council.

As sponsor, Shell was involved in many sectors and the boycott therefore affected more people than those who merely bought or sold Shell products. Many sports teams had to turn down sponsorship agreements with Shell besides having problems with other oil companies which the NOCOSA encouraged them to boycott. At the University of Tromsø, students had long had to put up with poor housing conditions, and in the autumn of 1987 the oil company Total offered to donate NOK 5 million towards new student accommodation. At a meeting of the student body, a large majority voted against receiving what they referred to as "blood money" from Total. The oil company had 700 petrol stations in South Africa and had been singled out as the prime target of a French boycott campaign. It was a very tough decision indeed for students who would have to sacrifice sorely needed housing.[69] Shortly after the refusal to accept money from Total, the University of Tromsø became the centre of another red-hot issue; this time it was Shell that wanted to finance a project involving medical research under Arctic conditions. However, the University did not want to be associated with

---

[68] *Norges Handels og Sjøfartstidende*, 12 November 1986.

[69] *Finnmarken*, 19 November 1987 and *NTB*, 20 November 1987.

Shell, especially after the controversy involving Total and the students at the same University.[70]

The Shell boycott was followed up by the Council's special committee, Artists Against Apartheid, which asked all artists organisations in Norway to encourage their members to turn down financial support from Shell, as well as to refuse to enter into agreements with institutions receiving financial support from that company. The Harstad Music Festival followed this up by withdrawing from a sponsorship agreement with Shell.

Publicity surrounding the Shell boycott and the Council reached new heights towards the end of 1988 and at the beginning of 1989. This was evident from NOCOSA's news-clippings-file of articles in which it featured. In 1987, the Council scored 767 press mentions, and the following year this number had increased to over 1,300. Shell felt pressured to respond to the bad publicity resulting from the boycott, and countered this through advertising campaigns costing millions of Norwegian kroner.

Most turbulence surrounded the Norwegian Football Association's negotiations with Norske Shell concerning a multimillion (Norwegian kroner) contract, which would make Norway's premier division central to Shell's marketing strategy. The Council immediately requested a meeting with the Football Association to inform them of the background to the Shell boycott. Eivind Arnevåg, captain of Vålerenga, one of Norway's most popular football teams, and also a member of the Council, warned that he would not play in the premier division if Shell were to become a major sponsor, and the Norwegian Football Association decided to cancel its contract with Shell. In the wake of this incident, discussion arose concerning other cultural and sports organisations sponsored by Shell. The Council participated in a number of panel debates and gave lectures at the request of organisations and trade unions. The leader of the South African National Union of Mineworkers, Cyril Ramaphosa, contributed to the boycott campaign by visiting Oslo. During press conferences and on television news, he denounced Shell's activities in South Africa, particularly in the mining sector. He reported i.a. that in mines of which Shell was a joint owner, security guards shot at strikers, and that workers were dismissed for joining the trade union.[71]

Relations with Norwegian authorities, particularly the Ministry of Foreign Affairs, were somewhat touchy for a while. The Shell boycott and demonstrations against the establishment of a South African consulate in Oslo were contributing factors. At a meeting with the Council, Knut Vollebæk, who at the time dealt with matters affecting NOCOSA at the Ministry, begged the Council to show more understanding and to be team players

---

[70] *Nordlys*, 1 December 1987.

[71] Letter from NOCOSA's Runar Malkenes to Knut Vollebæk at the Ministry of Foreign Affairs, 10 January 1989.

with the Ministry of Foreign Affairs. Sjurd Tveit, NOCOSA's chairperson at the time, replied that they were indeed on the same team, but that the Council was a striker while the Ministry of Foreign Affairs was in the defence line-up.

The consular issue

The establishment of a South African consulate in Norway in 1988 gave rise to a great deal of activity and public debate. The Ministry of Foreign Affairs explained to NOCOSA the importance of the Norwegian consulate in South Africa as it was being used to channel funds to the organisations involved in the struggle against apartheid, and that there was a risk of it being closed if Norway refused to allow a reciprocal South African consulate to be established in Norway. While the Council had some sympathy for this position, it was committed to severing all ties with South Africa and could make no exception in this case. The issue had great symbolic value and the Council protested the establishment of the consulate and recommended that the South African Consul, Wilhelm Bosman, be isolated. As a result, a number of demonstrations and protests were organised.

At first Bosman had great difficulties in renting suitable premises for the consulate. The Council had written to all of Oslo's real-estate agents requesting them not to assist Bosman with finding a home or offices. All the same, Bosman obtained a lease in Bærum after an individual homeowner contacted Bosman to offer him his villa.

From his very first night at the SAS hotel in Oslo, everywhere Bosman went demonstrators were sure to go. In October and continuing well into the onset of winter in December, the Council initiated a "demonstration relay" in front of the consul's house in the Oslo suburb of Jar. Every day, a different member organisation of the Council marked its protest against his presence in Norway. The demonstrations were legal, but activists from *Blitz* (a controversial sub-culture of youth living on the margins of society) sometimes took over with rather more forceful demonstrations against the South African consul, leading to violent clashes with the police. After a number of such confrontations, Bosman's neighbours insisted on the consulate being moved. The relay concluded with a demonstration in the centre of Oslo with approximately 700 participants.

NOCOSA further highlighted the boycott by consistently refusing all requests to participate on panels and in meetings attended by the South African consul. Amnesty International in Norway, however, chose to seek Bosman out and have a direct confrontation with him concerning the Consulate's views on the apartheid regime. According to the Council, this tactic was a blind alley. "Bosman will not allow himself to be influenced. He is a representative of the worst regime in the world and must be isolated",[72] said

---

[72] *Arbeiderbladet*, 20 February 1989.

Jørn Riise to *Arbeiderbladet*. During his meeting with Amnesty, Bosman had stated that claims of racial discrimination, torture and abuse were mere propaganda.

In connection with the campaign *Schools Against Apartheid* in 1989, Wilhelm Bosman wrote a booklet about South Africa which he sent to all the upper secondary schools in Norway. The packages had no return address and the book identified neither author nor publisher. The only identifying feature was Oscars gate 15, Bosman's home address. The book was considered a whitewash portraying South African authorities in a favourable light, which Bosman tried to sneak into the schools. This incident attracted a lot of attention, especially because Bosman's foreword characterised the book as a contribution to the campaign supported by the Ministry of Church and Education, NOCOSA, and several teachers' unions.[73]

When Bosman was to return to South Africa on 25 November 1992, he held a farewell party at the South African consulate. As a memorial to all the victims of apartheid, the Council had every day since All Saints day on 1 November laid wreaths, flowers or mourning bands outside the consulate. During the farewell party, fliers were handed out to all arriving guests. On 19 November, a brief commemorative service for the victims of apartheid (arranged jointly by the Norwegian Students' Christian Movement and NOCOSA) was also held outside the consulate. The service was led by the Students' Christian Movement's secretary general, Trygve Natvig, and university chaplain Anne Hege Grung, and eleven ANC-representatives from all over the world attending a course held by the Ministry of Foreign Affairs participated.

Cultural activities

The cultural dimension of the Council's work has played its part in making the organisation into more than a conventional solidarity organisation. By organising tours and festivals for African artists, musicians, dancers, actors and poets, NOCOSA has succeeded in conveying African culture directly to the Norwegian public. Through art sorrow, joy, war and oppression, daily life, love and sensuality were expressed in a manner which won respect and sympathy for the freedom struggles of the African people. Icy Norwegian winters were warmed by an explosion of colourful dancers, fiery rhythms and the joys of music. In this way, NOCOSA's endeavours were not confined to politics and censure, but also engaged in cultural mediation which lent a positive spirit to the important cause for which it was fighting. In addition to being a positive counterbalance to the negative image of Africa often created by the media, the Council could in this way reach out to a wider audience than those already involved in solidarity work.

---

[73] *Adresseavisen*, 15 March 1989.

A cultural activity especially worthy of mention was ANC's *Amandla Cultural Group* which visited Norway in 1980, holding concerts in Oslo, Lillehammer, Elverum and Kristiansand. NOCOSA thus realised for the first time that through this kind of approach it was easier to reach people who would otherwise not have become particularly involved in Southern Africa. In 1986, a record, *Amandla*, featuring both Norwegian and African musicians, was produced. The Council, as already mentioned, was now in 1987 focusing on Mozambique, so it was fitting that a Mozambique Manifestation consisting of cultural events and seminars, was held between 22 April and 6 May. The greatest attraction was *Companhia Nacional de Canto e Danca*, Mozambique's national dance group. People had to queue up to get hold of tickets for their performances, and the public was taken by storm. In the same year, a *"South Africa Festival"* was held. Cultural groups with over 40 artists from the ANC, SWAPO, and others drawn from Angola, Mozambique, Tanzania, Zambia and Zimbabwe, toured Sweden, Denmark and Norway. The aim was to share with Scandinavian audiences a fragment of African culture through song, dance and drama. Mozambique's radio orchestra, *Marrabenta*, accompanied by four dancers, toured Norway for three weeks in 1988 to enthusiastic acclaim. The dance ensemble from Mozambique and the *Bagamoyo Dancers* from Tanzania toured Norway for ten days in 1990, a cultural fireworks display with 50 dancers, musicians and actors. Also worthy of mention was the Soweto poet Mzwakhe Mbuli and the band, *The Equals*, who in November 1990 toured Norway with performances of music, dance and poetry.

The cultural dimension was also encompassed by many Norwegian artists who engaged in anti-apartheid work, and who lent a hand at many of the Council's arrangements. After the Norwegian Association of Musicians had become involved in the boycott issue in 1984, the Association encouraged its members to make an appearance at the Council's anti-apartheid activities. This resulted in *Artists Against Apartheid* being established by the Council in 1989 as a separate committee. Artists Against Apartheid co-operated with the Council on joint actions and special artists' performances, and efforts were made to discourage artists from performing in South Africa. Some of the events in which Artists Against Apartheid participated were: "Soweto Day" on which occasion the inhabitants of this South African city were celebrated in the foyer of Det Norske Teater (The Norwegian Theatre, Oslo) with the exhibition *Pictures from Soweto*, as well as with cultural events accompanied by political appeals; upon Mandela's 70th birthday in 1988 he was honoured by Norwegian rock-artists performing gratis at the Rockefeller music hall, a festival which lasted a full 24 hours; ANC's 77th birthday was marked by a major performance at the National Theatre at which a number of actors participated and at which NOCOSA and ANC made appeals; a large Soweto-event in 1990, again in the centre of Oslo; and the solidarity presentation "Skjebnetime" (The Hour of Fate) on behalf of the

ANC, held at the Norwegian Opera, also in 1990. In connection with an art lottery in 1988, Artists Against Apartheid mediated contacts with Norwegian painters, resulting in the donation of paintings to a value of NOK 150,000.

Artists Against Apartheid also followed up the initiative "The Freedom Pledge", by Little Steven and Harry Bellafonte. All Norwegian artists were requested to sign a pledge in which they undertook once a year to donate to the anti-apartheid campaign the income from a concert, exhibition or some other artistic arrangement.

In 1988, NOCOSA got its own choir *Inkululeko* (meaning "freedom" in Zulu and Xhosa) launched by the Council's Oslo group. The idea was to use the force of the freedom songs in the liberation struggle in South Africa to inspire and lend colour to anti-apartheid arrangements in Norway. Inkululeko chose to be an independent choral group, but according to its statutes, the choir has all along been "a cultural group supporting NOCOSA's political platform". The choir has performed on innumerable occasions, at rallies, arrangements, seminars, conferences, and at schools. When it was at its most active, Inkululeko gave over a hundred performances per year. In 1991, Inkululeko produced a successful cassette and accompanying booklet with songs, and these have been used a great deal in schools and by other choirs.

Inkululeko also performed before many legendary anti-apartheid figures such as Frank Chikane in 1989, Walter Sisulu and Govan Mbeki in 1990, Alfred Nzo in 1992, and also Nelson Mandela and F.W. de Klerk in connection with the Nobel Peace Prize award ceremony in 1993. In 1995, the choir finally had the opportunity of visiting South Africa and among other events performed in several townships.

1990–1994: The final years before democratic elections in South Africa

The announcement of the release of Nelson Mandela and the unbanning of ANC on 2 February 1990 were experienced as a victory for all who had been actively involved in the anti-apartheid struggle. In Norway, a *Release Nelson Mandela Reception Committee* was established. Such committees were simultaneously created in a number of countries, at the initiative of Archbishop Trevor Huddleston in England. The Norwegian committee, which consisted of representatives from NOCOSA, several of the largest aid organisations together with the local ANC office, was to celebrate Mandela's release and at the same time direct attention to the remaining work to be done. The media event represented by Mandela's release was also to draw attention to the plight of other political prisoners. The committee organised a reception on 5 March 1990 and a festival on 11 March in honour of Nelson Mandela.[74]

However, the guest of honour did not come to Norway before 1992. Mandela had been invited by the Norwegian government as its guest, and

---

[74] Annual Report 1989–1990, *Klassekampen*, 9 December 1993.

the visit took place from 17 to 19 May. Under the leadership of Thandie Rankoe at the ANC-office in Oslo, NOCOSA, in co-operation with Artists Against Apartheid, the Council on Ecumenical and International Relations and the Labour Movement's International Solidarity Committee (AIS), planned a festival with many artistic presentations and speeches in honour of Nelson Mandela. This event coincided with the celebration of Norway's Constitution Day, the 17 May. The festival was highly successful with a full house and excellent media coverage. Constitution Day was strongly marked by the presence of the renowned guest, and the school bands taking part in the street procession played "Nkosi Sikelel'i Afrika" in his honour.

The Nobel Peace Prize had been awarded jointly to Nelson Mandela and Frederik de Klerk in 1993 for the peaceful dismantling of the apartheid regime and for having laid the foundation for a new democratic South Africa. NOCOSA had mixed feelings about the dual award but decided not to criticise it as it was hoped that the award would promote the democratisation process in South Africa. Nelson Mandela himself stated that he was willing to share the Peace Prize with de Klerk. The Council emphasised that it did not feel that the award had been made to two equal parties, and many felt that the prize should have gone to Mandela alone. During the final three years of the apartheid regime, 11,000 people had been killed, with de Klerk's complicity. However, in order to ensure that the elections could be implemented, the Council concluded that political realities dictated the necessity of co-operating with de Klerk.

Despite scepticism towards the shared award, Mandela's visit to Norway turned into a renewed popular celebration. Artists Against Apartheid were invited by the ANC-office to hold a celebratory breakfast at the Grand Hotel in honour of the distinguished guest and his delegation, and it was indeed a grand occasion. Folksinger Lars Klevstrand sang "Velkomna med æra" (Welcome in honour) and Mandela clearly appreciated being lionised. "I want to thank you for all your support, and to tell you that our victory is your victory", he said.[75]

A cheering procession of nearly 2,000 honoured Nelson Mandela with song, torches, ANC flags, and posters portraying Mandela as they marched in procession down Karl Johan (Oslo's main street) on the evening after the award ceremony. Frederik de Klerk was not mentioned with a single word in the appeals, which were held before the procession started. Outside the Grand Hotel the procession halted and, led by Inkululeko, ANC's national anthem resounded rhythmically as Mandela and his daughter stood together with de Klerk and his wife on the balcony and received the enthusiastic acclaim of the multitude. Just before the prize-winners withdrew from the balcony, 20 or so demonstrators arrived on the scene and shouted slogans such as "Kverk de Klerk" (Choke de Klerk), and "de Klerk is a

---

[75] *Klassekampen,* 9 December 1993.

racist",[76] and removed all doubt as to who they felt the peace prize should really have been awarded to by the Norwegian people.

Negotiations between the ANC and the de Klerk government continued for three years before agreement on transition to a democratic system of government was signed in November 1993. The negotiations were complicated and often ground to a halt, as in 1992 when Africans were massacred in the Ciskei "homeland". The assassination of Chris Hani at Easter in 1993 nearly destroyed the entire process and also gave rise to strong feelings of desperation and sorrow in the Norwegian solidarity movement. There was real anxiety that people would be too scared to participate in the elections planned for April 1994. There was particular fear that Nelson Mandela might become the victim of assassination, as there was no reason to believe that the extreme right wing would accept democratic elections.[77]

In order to contribute towards the democratisation process, NOCOSA co-operated with the Council on Ecumenical and International Relations, the Norwegian Ecumenical Committee for Southern Africa, AIS, Norwegian People's Aid, the Norwegian Students' and Academics' International Assistance Fund (SAIH) and the Norwegian Church Aid on a campaign "Democracy for South Africa". The campaign was launched in connection with the Nobel award to Mandela and de Klerk in 1993. Nelson Mandela had requested continued international assistance in the final act of the liberation struggle leading up to South Africa's first free elections. It was the first time that 17–18 million South Africans were to participate in elections, the majority of them could neither read nor write, and political violence at times made it difficult to engage in electioneering. The campaign was an information and enlightenment campaign, and was simultaneously to raise funds for ANC's election preparations.

Continuation of the boycott?

When the Transitional Council in South Africa was established, the Council released the following statement:

> This is a day of joy, a day for which we have longed for many years. The establishment of a transitional electoral council (TEC) in South Africa sends the signal that economic sanctions against South Africa can be dismantled. ... The Boycott has worked. ... It is apparent that we would not have come this far in the democratisation process in South Africa without sanctions. The challenge for Norway and the rest of the world is now to contribute towards ensuring that the construction of the South African economy does not consolidate an economic apartheid system.[78]

---

[76] *Arbeiderbladet*, 11 December 1993.

[77] Article in *Folkets Framtid* (The People's Future) by Øystein Gudim, 7 July 1993.

[78] Press release by NOCOSA, 24 September 1993.

It was ANC which had called for the establishment of a Transitional Council as one of the conditions for lifting sanctions against South Africa. Another condition was the fixing of the date of free elections. The Transitional Council was established on 23 September 1993, and ANC instantly cancelled its demand for sanctions. Norway had six months previously declared that Norwegian sanctions should be lifted as from 15 March 1993. The Council was in strong disagreement concerning this. In an appeal at a memorial for Chris Hani on 19 April, Hege Hertzberg, at that time NOCOSA's chairperson, regretted that "the Norwegian government had renounced its responsibility as the former most prominent opponent of apartheid by terminating the boycott, without there being any (safeguarding) clause on real negotiations".[79] When Norway decided to lift sanctions in March, the government had clearly hoped that a multi-party conference in South Africa that same month would have led to the establishment of an interim government as well as setting a date for the holding of free elections. The conference did not produce the hoped for results, and the Council proved right in its pronouncement that Norway already prior to the conference had sold its chickens before they were hatched.[80] It might appear that NOCOSA was "more Catholic than the Pope" at a time when relations with South Africa were slowly but surely being normalised. But the Council feared that the negotiations in South Africa would fail, and in common with the ANC, wanted international pressure to continue until there remained no alternative to a democratic system of government.

Valediction

> Say not the struggle naught availeth,
> The labour and the wounds are vain,
> The enemy faints not, nor faileth,
> And as things have been, things remain.
> *Arthur Hugh Clough, 1819–1861*

With the success of the South African people in their struggle to dismantle apartheid as a political system, the goals of the Norwegian Council for Southern Africa had been reached. At the same time, its members could look back on an eventful involvement which had mobilised all kind of people from school children to pensioned members of Parliament, from all trade categories and political parties (except the right-wing Progress Party). Certainly the Council had had many curses heaped upon its head, particularly from the conservative end of the political spectrum. Such characterisations as "self-constituted power group", "unscrupulous activists", "leftist guerrillas" and "amateur terrorists", often scorched the air in heated debate or singed the pages of the conservative press. The Council could, however,

---

[79] Press release by NOCOSA, 19 April 1993.

[80] Press release by NOCOSA, 23 February 1993.

strike back by saying that its credentials were in order, the organisation represented all political youth organisations (again with the exception of the Progress Party Youth), received financial support from three ministries, and had been consulted by the Norwegian Ministry of Foreign Affairs on specific issues.

The non-sectarian position and the support from members from all over the political spectrum contributed to the strength of NOCOSA. There were also close bonds between the Council's leadership and important organisations such as the Council on Ecumenical and International Relations, SAIH, prominent scholars and gradually also with sections of the trade union movement. Many major arrangements came into being as a result of joint efforts from among them, and several of those who wore their rompers in the NOCOSA nursery are to be found today as journalists, researchers, workers in large and small organisations, or at the Ministry of Foreign Affairs.

Another important aspect of NOCOSA's work was that it managed to involve people in thinking globally but acting locally. Information from the organisation reached even the remotest corners of this far-flung country, into every tiny local newspaper editorial management, into schools, colleges, universities and halls of informal learning. The presentation of the struggle of the liberation movements to ordinary Norwegians was strongly emphasised, resulting in several countrywide tours being arranged for their representatives from abroad to every region of the country. At the same time its approach was goal-oriented in order to influence Norwegian policies in areas such as economic assistance to the liberation struggle or isolation of the apartheid regime.

The mass media were an important and forceful instrument in the performance of these tasks. The Council managed to gain a foothold in the media, thanks to both contacts with press circles and its own production of articles, contributions to debates, and commentaries on current events. The scope and extent of press attention related to the Council's activities was at its widest towards the end of the 1980s.

The results of the kind of solidarity work engaged in by the Council are not immediately apparent. It is nevertheless obvious that by seeing to it that the public had constant access to and was supplied with a steady stream of information, NOCOSA played its part in ensuring that Southern Africa was prominent on the agendas of Parliament and other Norwegian institutions of governance and authority. In doing so it kept alive the interest of the mass media in the freedom struggle, and NOCOSA's information activities were of great significance. As an ancient Norwegian proverb has it, many streams makes a mighty torrent ("Mange bekker små blir til en stor å"), and the pressure put on the Norwegian authorities applied by the many who were actively involved, ultimately contributed to a change in policies. The Council had served as an important instrument for some 40 popular organisations joined together in the common cause of supporting the struggle against apartheid and colonialism.

Instead of dissolving the organisation immediately after South Africa had finally held free elections in 1994, the Norwegian Council for Southern Africa reorganised itself as *The Norwegian Council for Africa*. Its political sphere of interest would henceforth embrace all African countries south of the Sahara. South Africa nevertheless continues to be central to the Council's work, as Zimbabwe and Namibia had been during the years immediately after attaining their independence. Above all, the Council has—within its admittedly limited resources- continued to provide support for people-centred participation in the construction of a democratic South Africa.

Chapter 7

The Freedom Struggle in Southern Africa:
The Role of the Norwegian Churches 1948–1994

Berit Hagen Agøy

I visited South Africa for the first time, as a student, in 1986. On 17 May, Norway's Constitution Day, I went to the Norwegian Seamen's Mission Church in Durban to take part in the celebrations. A lot of people were gathered, mostly descendants of Norwegian traders and missionaries who arrived in South Africa more than a century ago. Others were newcomers working for The Norwegian Missionary Society for a short period. My host was one of these, a Norwegian pastor working for the Evangelical Lutheran Church in South Africa. Some months earlier he had, as one of very few Lutherans, signed the *Kairos Document*, and he was known to be a committed anti-apartheid activist. He had introduced me to some of his South African friends, people whose Christian faith had inspired them to take an active part in the struggle against the racist regime. I was now looking forward to meeting Norwegians living in the Durban area, hoping to find more of these dedicated freedom-fighters. After a while, an elderly lady came towards me and gave me a small leaflet which read "Let us pray that Mandela must be kept in prison until he is saved". I was taken by surprise, and asked what it meant. Her reply was: "Don't you know that Mandela is a Communist and a terrorist and that the ANC is fighting against all Christians?" When I carefully tried to dispute this, I was for the first time in my life told I could not be a true Christian.

On 17 May, six years later, I was sitting in the Oslo Cathedral listening to the "terrorist" standing at the pulpit reading from the Bible. Nelson Mandela thanked all those whose prayers had kept him alive during the long years in prison, and he told us how God had given him and his fellow prisoners strength to continue the struggle even in the darkest hours. I was reminded of the words of the lady in the Norwegian Seamen's Mission Church.

The history of the Norwegian Churches' attitude towards the struggle for freedom and democracy in Southern Africa embraces both the radical and ANC-friendly missionary and the Christian lady in Durban who gave the impression of supporting the policy of apartheid. It is also a story about those who in 1992 were welcoming Mandela to Oslo, singing *Nkosi Sikelel'i Afrika* and praying together with him in the Cathedral. Among them were bishops and prominent church leaders, but most of the congregation were ordinary lay-people. Some of them had been involved in solidarity work for decades, and at last, Mandela was there right in front of them, alive and smiling.[1]

Introduction

The Church of Norway was one of the main protagonists in Norway for the liberation of Namibia and South Africa. The late Foreign Minister Knut Frydenlund put it like this:

> Without the work performed by the (Church of Norway) Council of Ecumenical and International Relations, we would never have been able to win Parliament's approval of the support for the liberation struggle in Southern Africa. The church's attitude has been decisive in forming a favourable opinion.[2]

Almost NOK 250 million (approx. USD 35 million) was given by the Norwegian Ministry of Foreign Affairs to the church who transferred it to anti-apartheid organisations and individuals within Namibia and South Africa. How was this possible? Why did the church act as a channel for government money? Was it on the instructions of the Norwegian government or did the church itself ask to perform this task? If the latter, why was the Church of Norway so concerned about the liberation struggle in such a distant part of the world? This chapter will try to answer these questions. We will describe how the Norwegian churches got involved in Southern Africa and outline their main activities in the region from when the apartheid regime came to power in South Africa in 1948 and up to the elections of 1994.

There are at least four starting-points for a history of church relations between Norway and Southern Africa:

1. Norwegian settlers and white Lutherans

Descendants of Norwegian traders and missionaries make up a small congregation in the Durban area. In 1880 they established the St. Olav church in Durban, a so-called "white" Lutheran church.[3] Many of the members of this church sympathised with the policy of the Nationalist Government after

---

[1] In the interest of objectivity, I wish to state here that I was employed by the Council on Ecumenical and International Relations (CEIR) from 1987–1997, working on Southern African affairs, human rights and development education. I have also been a board member of the Norwegian Ecumenical Council for Southern Africa (NEKSA) and the Norwegian Council for Southern Africa.

[2] *Norsk Utenrikspolitisk Årbok.* Oslo: Norwegian Institute of International Affairs, 1981.

[3] Literature about St. Olav Church and Norwegian settlers: B.J.T. Leverton: *The Natal Norwegian Centenary, 1882–1982.* Latern, 1982; F.M. Lear: *St. Olav Lutheran Church 1880–1980.* Durban, 1980.

1948. When the St. Olav church in 1975 insisted on not joining the newly established national Evangelical Lutheran Church in South Africa (ELCSA), the Church of Norway was presented with a delicate problem, because the bishop of Oslo had for many years been the spiritual supervisor of the St. Olav church. Bishop Andreas Aarflot visited the congregation in 1985 and tried, in vain, to persuade its members to join their fellow black Lutherans.[4] The St. Olav congregation was split a while later, and those in favour of joining ELCSA established the new congregation St. Michael.

The Church of Norway also got involved in the difficulties the Lutheran World Federation (LWF) experienced with the white Lutherans in South Africa and Namibia. The two bishops Gunnar Lislerud and Andreas Aarflot, together with the Church of Norway Council on Ecumenical and International Relations secretary-general Gunnar Stålsett (secretary-general of LWF from 1985–94), were all personally involved in LWF's effort to motivate the white churches to denounce apartheid as a sin, and to merge with the non-racist Lutheran churches in South Africa and Namibia.

2. Norwegian missions and ELCSA

The Norwegian Pentecostals established mission work in Swaziland, Mozambique and South Africa in the early 20th century. The Norwegian Lutheran Mission[5] has for many decades been working in Tanzania and the Methodist Church in Angola and Mozambique. Since these missions got involved in the political liberation struggle, only to a small degree, they will not be further discussed here.

Instead, we will look at the Norwegian Missionary Society (NMS) which started its work in 1844 in the Zulu kingdom, and was active in South Africa to 1997. This society is an independent organisation but defines itself as working on behalf of the Church of Norway. Striking similarities are to be found between the Lutheran missionary practice and the creation of daughter churches according to race by the Dutch Reformed Churches. It is argued that the main reason why the Lutheran churches were not multi-racial was that the missionaries wanted to create national churches (so-called people's churches) which they were familiar with from Europe. But in Africa a 'nation' was understood by the missionaries as an ethnic group living in one limited area, and not a state created by colonial governments. This Lutheran missionary practice differs from that of the English-speaking churches where all converts became members of the same church irrespective of race

---

[4] A. Aarflot's letter to St. Olav Church of 3 July 1986: 'I feel compelled to suspend my relations to St. Olav congregation until you have found a solution regarding your relationship with ELCSA. As I tried to tell you during my visit, it seems odd that as a bishop of the Church of Norway, I shall enjoy full spiritual fellowship with our Lutheran sister church in South Africa, and at the same time keep up a spiritual supervision of a congregation that has virtually backed away from such full spiritual fellowship with the same church.' CEIR-archives.

[5] Norsk Luthersk Misjonssamband.

(due to the colonial government's policy of territorial race segregation, the local congregation however normally consisted of only one ethnic group).

At the end of the 1950s the European missionaries in South Africa took the initiative to try and establish a Lutheran co-operation on a national level between the different mission churches and the white churches. The first (out of five) regional Lutheran churches in South Africa was established in Natal in 1960 (Evangelical Lutheran Church in South Africa–South East Region), and the Norwegian Zulu Synod was integrated in it. None of the white churches in Natal joined the new church. In 1975 the regional churches merged into the national Evangelical Lutheran Church of South Africa (ELCSA). But still no white churches wished to mix with black Lutherans.[6] The role of the Norwegian missionaries in the establishing of Lutheran churches is an interesting subject. Even if the missionaries never intended to create race-segregated churches, this was the result. Unfortunately, the space available does not allow us to elaborate on this subject.

The Lutheran churches' attitude to apartheid is tangled and difficult, both due to the complex church structure, the division between white and black Lutherans, and not least the Lutheran teaching of the Two Kingdoms. Traditionally Lutherans have been very reluctant in involving the Church in politics, holding this should be left in the hands of the secular authorities. In Natal ELCSA had in addition big problems because many church members belonged to Inkatha, and the church was dragged into the violent conflict between Inkatha and ANC.[7]

It has been difficult for both the Norwegian Mission Society and the Church of Norway to relate to ELCSA's unclear relations both to Inkatha and to the government's policy. After 1960 the missionaries were formally employed by ELCSA-SER, and from 1975 by ELCSA, and in loyalty to their church they did not want to speak out in political matters on their own. The Scandinavian missionaries encouraged the church to give an official criticism of apartheid, which ELCSA did, as the first Lutheran church, in 1963. The missionaries, particularly Gunnar Lislerud[8], also tried to stimulate an internal debate in the church on its role in society. But it was not until NMS-missionary Per Anders Nordengen, working for ELCSA in Durban, signed

---

[6] Literature on the Norwegian Mission and the establishing of Lutheran Churches in South Africa: G. Lislerud: "Luthersk kirkedannelse i Sør-Afrika", *Norsk Tidsskrift for Misjon*, no. 2 and 3, 1998; B. Hagen Agøy: "Norske misjonærer, lutherske kirker og apartheid i Sør-Afrika 1948–1963", *Historisk Tidsskrift*, no. 2, 1993.

[7] A.H. Grung: "Den 'svarte' lutherske kirken i Natal/KwaZulu og Inkatha", *Kirke og kultur*, no. 3, 1991.

[8] G. Lislerud was employed by the American Lutheran Mission, Schreuder Mission. This mission was established when the Norwegian missionary pioneer H.P.S. Schreuder in 1873 left the Norwegian Mission Society.

the *Kairos Document* in 1985 that a Norwegian missionary's politically motivated action caused problems in ELCSA.[9]

The Church of Norway tried during the 1980s and 1990s to offer both
moral and financial support to Lutheran pastors and their families who, due
to their political involvement in the struggle against apartheid, got into
trouble either in relation to the government or with church leaders in
ELCSA. The Norwegian church also tried to motivate the leadership of
ELCSA to take up its responsibility to work for peace, justice and human
rights issues.

However, it was the South African Council of Churches (SACC) and not
its sister church ELCSA, that became the Church of Norway's closest church
partner in work against apartheid in South Africa. This is remarkable due to
the fact that missionaries belonging to the Church of Norway have been
working in South Africa for more that 150 years and that they played an important role in the establishing of Lutheran churches in this country.

3. Norwegian Church Aid (NCA)

Norwegian Church Aid is an ecumenical and independent organisation, but
is also regarded as the Church of Norway's international relief organisation.
Norwegian Church Aid co-operates closely with the Lutheran World Federation (LWF) and the World Council of Churches (WCC). It got involved in
these organisations' work among refugees and persons linked to different
liberation movements in Southern Africa in the 1960s. NCA never operated
on its own in these countries, but gave financial support via the LWF, the
WCC and the national and regional church councils. They were responsible
for carrying out the activities that were supported. Some of the money was
forwarded to organisations other than churches.[10] Some Norwegian church
people were also working in the region together with the international ecumenical organisations, for instance Øystein Tveter. During his years in
Africa working for the LWF and the Norwegian Church Aid, Tveter played
an important role in establishing relations between the liberation
movements and the Norwegian church and government.

Ever since the 1960s there has been a very close relationship between
NCA and the Church of Norway in their common effort to support the lib-

---

[9] Nordengen was sharply criticised by ELCSA's leaders in Kwa-Zulu-Natal, and they complained to NMS' leaders in Norway when he joined the Lutheran Confession Fellowship.

[10] In Namibia NCA supported the Legal Assistance Centre in Windhoek, and schools run by
different churches. In Zimbabwe, Zambia and Mozambique NCA gave financial assistance to
LWF's work among refugees. The Ecumenical Development and Information Centre for Eastern
and Southern Africa (EDICESA) in Harare was also partly funded by NCA. In Zambia human
rights groups got support, both women groups and the regional human rights office
(AFRONET). In Botswana NCA supported the church's work with indigenous people and
women and co-operated with the Kgolagano College. In South Africa SACC, Diakonia and
some other church-related organisations received support from NCA. Material about these
matters is to be found in NCA's archives in Oslo.

eration struggle in Southern Africa. But when it comes to the more politically oriented struggle against apartheid, the work of the Church of Norway was clearly the most important.

The scope of this chapter unfortunately does not allow a full discussion of the Norwegian churches' involvement in Southern Africa from all perspectives. This chapter will therefore concentrate on the Church of Norway involvement in Southern Africa, particular in South Africa and Namibia,

4. The Church of Norway

The Church of Norway is the national so-called state church. The Norwegian constitution decrees that Lutheranism is the official religion of the State and that the King is the supreme temporal head of the Church. Church administration is shared between the Ministry for Church, Education and Research centrally and the municipal authorities locally. The Church of Norway embraces 88% of the Norwegian population (1998). Most of them, however, go to church only in connection with church rituals like baptisms, marriages, confirmations and funerals, or during Christmas. Only about 3% turn up at ordinary Sunday services. Nevertheless, the church has a strong position in Norwegian society, not only because it is a so-called state church financed by the taxpayers, but also because it is seen as an accessible people's church for all Norwegians. The Church can be regarded as a Non-Governmental Organisation paid for by the Government, self-contradictory though this may appear. The laity has traditionally held a strong position in the Church of Norway, and the church is a natural partner for other NGOs both in the local communities and when it comes to national organisations or government institutions.

The Church of Norway General Synod (annual assembly) is the highest church authority. Three councils are connected with the General Synod. The responsibility for the Church of Norway's engagement in Southern Africa rests mainly with the Council on Ecumenical and International Relations (CEIR).[11]

---

[11] The secretary-general, the chairman of the Council and its Committee for International Affairs were the main actors. In addition some of the bishops and Norwegian representatives to bodies within the LWF and the WCC played an important role. A group of only 10–15 churchmen—almost all were male—shaped and implemented the Church of Norway's strategies regarding Southern African affairs. As will be seen later, some of them changed posts over the years. One missionary was appointed bishop, another became responsible for the Church's Development Education Service. Two secretary-generals of CEIR became politicians for a period, and several of the more central persons switched between working for CEIR, Norwegian Church Aid, the LWF and other ecclesiastical organisations at different periods. Having this relatively small group of people who knew each other well through different connections was an asset particularly when CEIR's project activities in South Africa were defined and developed, but also when it came to lobbying in Norwegian political circles. Secretary-generals of CEIR: G. Stålsett, C. Traaen , T. Bakkevig, A. Sommerfeldt and S. Utnem. Chairmen of CEIR: Bishop K. Støylen, Bishop A. Aarflot, P. Voksø, S. Møgedal. Other bishops involved in Southern African affairs: G. Lislerud, K. Støylen, P. Lønning.

Partners

CEIR co-operated with a wide range of different institutions and organisations in Norway, both official and private. The struggle against apartheid also created new alliances between the church and groups that traditionally had a distant relationship to the church. These include most of the political Left, including most of the Labour movement. Just as in Southern Africa the work to abolish apartheid not only strengthened ecumenical relations but also brought together groups that did not usually meet. This happened both at the national level and, not least, in local communities. The church's strong commitment on the apartheid issue clearly strengthened its credibility among political radicals. In this sense the church's work against racism in South Africa became a part of its preaching of the Gospel.

When the anti-apartheid work outside the ecumenical movement was established in Norway in the early 1960s (see chapter 1), church people played an active role. Many (if not all) of those who were most active in CEIR's anti-apartheid work had personally been involved in the Norwegian Council on Southern Africa and the Namibian Association both as members and leading activists. On the other hand, Christians who got involved in the struggle against apartheid through the Council or the Namibian Association often became useful resource people for the church.

The World campaign against military collaboration with South Africa was led by Abdul Minty who was a close friend of CEIR. The information, which this organisation provided for CEIR, was highly appreciated. CEIR's project work in South Africa and Namibia led to close co-operation with the two other main "channels" for governmental funds, the Norwegian Confederation of Trade Unions (LO) and the Students' and Academics' International Assistance Fund.

When it comes to the Church of Norway's partners abroad the Nordic Lutheran churches, LWF, WCC and churches and church councils in Southern Africa were the most important, in addition to CEIR's project organisations in South Africa and Namibia (listed in the last part of this chapter).

Literature and sources

Some research has been done by historians and theologians on the pioneer days of Norwegian missions in Zululand.[12] The different missionary societies have also published historical accounts, yearbooks and magazines, of their work in Southern Africa. Some few missionaries have published articles on the question of apartheid. A very comprehensive archive may be found at the Norwegian Mission Society's College in Stavanger.

---

[12] Literature on NMS's history in South Africa in the early days: J. Simensen (ed.): *Norsk misjon i afrikanske samfunn, Sør-Afrika ca. 1850–1900*. Trondheim: Tapir, 1984; T. Jørgensen: *Contact and Conflict—Norwegian Missionaries, the Zulu Kingdom and the Gospel, 1850–1870*. Stavanger, 1987.

The only systematic work on the role of the Church of Norway's involvement in the struggle against apartheid, is the book *The Church of Norway and the Struggle against Apartheid*, written by former secretary-general of CEIR, Trond Bakkevig.[13] It is available in English, and gives an overview of CEIR's involvement together with a description of the different projects in South Africa and Namibia.

The secretary-generals of CEIR wrote several articles on the political situation in Southern Africa, and modified versions of their travel reports were occasionally published in magazines or newspapers. The annual report from CEIR and from 1984 on from the Annual Church Assembly also gives an impression on the Church of Norway's involvement in Southern Africa. But we need to look at the unpublished documents in the Church of Norway's archives in Oslo to find the details. The most interesting documents are the official statements on apartheid, travel reports from the secretary-general and other staff persons, internal policy documents written in connection with internal or external meetings, and correspondence with partners both in Norway and abroad. Much of this material, especially the correspondence with the Ministry of Foreign Affairs and the partners in South Africa and Namibia is not publicly available. On request, researchers will however be given permission to use parts of it.

Material on the Church of Norway Aid's involvement with Southern Africa is to be found in Church of the Norway Aid's archives in Oslo. For more thorough studies the archives of the WF and the WCC in Geneva and the ELCSA and SACC in South Africa would be of interest.

Why care about apartheid?

Before we investigate the history of the Norwegian churches' involvement in Southern Africa, we need to ask the question of why the Christian church should care about the region in the first place. It did not commit itself to the same extent to liberation struggles going on in other parts of the world. Why did apartheid in South Africa cause this strong commitment, not only from the Norwegian churches, but first and foremost from the churches in South Africa and from the international church family.

One obvious reason was of course the terrible oppression of the majority of the population in South Africa and Namibia. The racist policy of the Nationalist party deprived all those who did not have a white skin of fundamental human rights. This led to unanimous condemnation from the international community. But what about the equally poor and oppressed people you could find in other parts of the world? Why did they not get the same attention from the Nordic churches? Was it because of the great number of whites in South Africa for instance? Did Western opinion care more in

---

[13] T. Bakkevig: *The Church of Norway and the Struggle against Apartheid*. Oslo: Church of Norway Council on Ecumenical and International Relations, 1996.

cases where whites were involved in conflicts than where civil wars were going on between different African ethnic groups? Or is there another explanation?

Apartheid is heresy

The answer is simple: when the National Party in 1948 introduced the policy of apartheid it declared it to be based on the Bible. God created people of different races, it was asserted, and meant them to develop along their own lines and not mix with each other. Theologians from the Dutch Reformed Churches were among the main architects of the apartheid ideology. This Biblical legitimisation of racism made it into a theological issue, which could not be left to the politicians alone. Therefore the English speaking churches watched the policy of the new government carefully. Every step they took which could be regarded as contrary to the Gospel was condemned by most of the churches, not only in South Africa but later on also by the international church community. This made South Africa a very special case. "It was the Christian foundation of the racial segregation policy, which for the churches made this into a situation with a qualitatively other character than other forms of oppression. It was this which in a special way meant that churches around the world could not be indifferent" according to Trond Bakkevig.[14]

Almost all of the official statements on apartheid-related issues from the Church of Norway during the years 1963–1994 give as a reason for the church's involvement the fact that the policy of apartheid is a charicature of the Gospel. One typical example is a statement in 1975:

> When a state which calls itself Christian, so fundamentally violates basic Christian and humanistic values as the case is with South Africa, this can only call for a unanimous condemnation by Christians in all countries. The Church of Norway Council on Foreign Relations encourages all Christians in South Africa, especially our Lutheran sister Churches, to give a clear and fearless witness against apartheid, and to work for a non-violent change in the society in obedience to the will of God.[15]

In 1977 the General Assembly of the LWF adopted the following resolution, approved by the Norwegian delegates:

> Under normal circumstances Christians may have different opinions in political questions. However, political and social systems may become so perverted and oppressive that it is consistent with the confession to reject them, and work for changes. We especially appeal to our white member churches in Southern Africa to recognise the situation in Southern Africa institutes a status confessionis. This means that, on the basis of faith and in order to manifest the unity of the church,

---

[14] T. Bakkevig, 1996, p. 12.

[15] Statement from CEIR-meeting 20 June 1975, CEIR-archives.

churches would publicly and unequivocally reject the existing apartheid-system.[16]

LWF was the first ecumenical organisation to take such a clear theological stand. Apartheid was no longer just an important issue for the Lutheran churches, it was in fact a matter of "status confessionis" which meant that it affected the very core of the Christian faith. When the LWF General Assembly met again in 1984 the delegates discussed the consequences of the 1977 resolution for the white Lutheran churches in South Africa and Namibia who had not been willing to declare apartheid a sin. When they still refused to do so, two of them were suspended from membership of LWF. All the Norwegian delegates, particularly the bishop of Oslo Andreas Aarflot, were eager to vote for the suspension. This event made it clear that a church which defended apartheid "renounced the church's own nature as a true church. From the pulpit of a Christian church must always be preached a message which implicitly and explicitly condemns all forms of Apartheid ideology", according to CEIR.[17]

When one member of the body suffers ...

But there was also another important reason for the church to take action. The English-speaking churches in Southern Africa were asking for solidarity from fellow Christians belonging to the universal church. The call for prayers and acts of solidarity from the oppressed sisters and brothers was, together with the issue of theological heresy, the main reason for the churches in Norway to involve themselves in the struggle against apartheid.

The outcry from churches and liberation movements decided to a large extent what kind of action the churches in Norway chose to make. As the church saw it, it did not act only for itself, but on behalf of the African Christians. Their wishes were considered very important when choosing which organisations to support. This goes for both the missionaries and for CEIR's more politically oriented work.

The appeal for support was directed to Norwegian churches, but also via LWF and WCC. The numerous international ecumenical conferences were important meeting places where Christians from the North listened to testimonies from the victims of apartheid. To meet these fellow Christians from the South face to face encouraged Norwegian church leaders to get personally involved in the struggle against apartheid. The same happened when African Christians met politicians, school children or members of local congregations in Norway.

---

[16] Bakkevig, 1996, p. 26.

[17] Unpublished note by T. Karlsen Seim (CEIR–Committee for Theological Affairs) of 4 August 1985, ('Teologiske perspektiver i Mellomkirkelig Råds arbeid med menneskerettighets-spørsmål') CEIR-archives.

In October 1977, a special service took place in the Oslo Cathedral. The congregation sent the following message to the South African Council of Churches.

> We, Christians in Norway, have been gathered to a service of worship to give expression to our solidarity with and our intercession for the Church and the oppressed of South Africa.

> We have seen the sufferings which have been brought upon the African population of the land, and we concur with the apostle in ... When one member of the body suffers, the entire body suffers [...] Your sufferings, therefore, are our sufferings. We abide with you in our prayers and in our actions, in our common struggle against injustice and oppression. May God be with you.[18]

The reason for the service was the South African Government's banning of eighteen anti-apartheid organisations. In this way it tried once again to outlaw all internal opposition. Due to the extreme restrictions on any form of political work against the regime, especially after 1960, the churches became one of very few institutions still allowed to speak out and criticise apartheid. This of course gave the churches an important role as a spokesman for the oppressed population. The churches' many and regular links abroad through sister churches and international organisations were extremely important. Through them opposition groups in South Africa and Namibia could share information and also receive financial support from partners in other parts of the world.

1948–1960: "Neutral" missions[19]

The history of the Church of Norway's involvement in Southern Africa begins in 1844 when H.P. Schreuder, sent by the newly-established Norwegian Missionary Society, received, as the first white man ever, royal permission to settle in Zululand. At the time of writing, the last NMS missionary has recently left South Africa. For the NMS, more than 150 years of continuous work in preaching the Gospel, building churches, running schools and providing health services in South Africa has come to an end.

For some years following 1948 the Norwegian missionaries had no clear position on apartheid, but adopted a policy of "wait and see". Prime Minister D.F. Malan and his ministers claimed to be devoted Christians, and the missionaries hoped to continue their traditionally good relations with the South African Government. Like all NMS missionaries they were under instruction'not to take part in the politics or strife of the country they worked in. Nevertheless, as early as 1949 they stated the following:

---

[18] Message to SACC from people gathered at a service in the Cathedral of Oslo 23 October 1977, CEIR-archives.

[19] This section is based on the author's thesis in History: "Den tvetydige protesten", University of Oslo, 1987 (about the Norwegian Mission Society and the Policy of Apartheid 1948–1970).

It is a fundamental principle for the Norwegian Missionary Society and its missionaries, the Zulu Church and its workers that they do not meddle in the political controversies of the country. Our regulations bar us from all actions or protests based solely on politics. On the other hand we are committed to further the edification and general well-being of the people we are working among, and we are called to foster a particular concern for the conservation and growth of the church. Situations may therefore arise where it will be necessary for us to uphold Christian principles vis-à-vis the country's authorities as well. If, for instance, the Bible is wrongly used to support political action or measures which are contrary to a Christian view of life or society, then a church has not only the right, but the obligation to protest in unambiguous terms. To take apartheid (segregation of the races) as a specific example, at the present time when the concept is not yet, as far as we know, satisfactorily defined, we as a mission (church) find it difficult to declare ourselves in favour or against. But we reserve the right to appeal and if necessary also to protest if the freedom of conscience and of religion, other fundamental human rights or clearly established legal norms should be violated by the enactment of an apartheid programme or other plans of vital importance for the future of the different ethnic groups which directly affects the position or the work of the Christian church.[20]

It may be noted that Africans working in the church were also subject to the instructions concerning non-involvement in politics.

During the early 1950s the policy of separate development was put into practice, and the brutal and increasing oppression of the black population led to frustration and anger on the part of the missionaries. They were worried, and in line with the instructions from 1949 they carefully watched every new law and all steps taken by the Government. But their analysis of apartheid was extremely narrow, limited to one question only: what would be the consequences for the work of the mission and the church? The missionaries drew a clear distinction between apartheid as ideology and apartheid as policy. Regarded as *ideology* apartheid was racism and in conflict with a correct understanding of the Bible. The ideology of apartheid was a matter for the church. But as long as the apartheid *policy* did not interfere with internal church matters, it should be left to the secular government. This distinction may be seen as springing from the Lutheran teaching of the two Kingdoms.

This tendency to regard apartheid mostly from an ideological point of view, was intensified by the South African churches' involvement. In 1953/54 representatives from different denominations met at several conferences to discuss the theological implications of apartheid. The debates ended with the Dutch Reformed churches defending apartheid while the English-speaking churches, with whom the NMS missionaries closely identified themselves, harshly criticised the Dutch Reformed churches' understanding of the Bible. These churches protested strongly against the segregation of races within the churches. The missionaries took active part in these debates.

---

[20] Report from NMS annual conference in South Africa 1949, NMS-archives.

To some extent the discussions made the question of apartheid a discussion of Dutch reformed theology, which of course was a matter for the church. The missionaries were on the other hand seldom present at meetings when the political or economic consequences of apartheid were discussed. This was simply not on their agenda.

In the first part of the 1950s the missionaries were preoccupied with the process of making the Norwegian Lutheran Zulu Synod independent, and they saw the gradual transferral of leadership to the Zulus as a way of making the Zulu people more autonomous. The missionaries' dream, like that of liberal South African whites, was of progressively integrating "civilised" and Christian blacks into the white society.

Mission and apartheid in conflict

As long as the apartheid policy did not create *immediate* problems for the mission work, the missionaries wanted to avoid committing themselves. However, the Bantu Education Act of 1953 changed this dramatically. For the first time, apartheid created serious problems for the missionaries. NMS, like many other European missionary societies, had established a large number of schools on different levels. The schools were one of the most efficient ways of introducing children and youngsters to the church. It came as a shock to the missionaries that a Christian government would cause problems for mission schools, and the Education Act more that anything else opened the eyes of the missionaries to the realities behind the policy of Separate Development.

The missions could be allowed to continue running their schools without financial support from the State. They would not, however, be allowed to decide on the curriculum themselves. As the NMS did not have sufficient funds to run the schools on their own, their choice was either to close them or hand them over to the Government. If they were closed, it would mean that the children were left with no chance of ever getting an education. NMS therefore chose to transfer their schools to the Government on certain conditions. The missionaries were sincerely worried about the fact that the ideology of apartheid was now going to be the basis of the education of the black children, but what seems to have worried them even more was what kind of education would now be given in Christianity. Would it be possible to ensure that the children learnt the Lutheran catechism? When the Government assured them that the missionaries would be welcome to continue their religious education, their protest calmed down.[21] This illustrated how the missionarie's narrow concern for the mission work led them to accept co-operation with the apartheid government in introducing the new educational system, even though they strongly objected to the ideology on which the new system was based.

---

[21] Mission secretary J. Skauge's letter to N. Follesøe of 14 April 1954, NMS-archives.

The next major conflict came in 1957, when the Government wanted to forcibly remove all the Zulus living on the mission farms. This was a part of the Bantustans programme. In the early days of NMS the missionaries were given some land on which to build mission stations. Some of these areas were so large that Christian Zulus were allowed to settle there with their cattle and carry out subsistence agriculture. The Land Acts of 1913 and 1936 defined the mission farms as White land and the Government now wanted to get rid of these so-called "black spots" in white areas.

Not surprisingly, the NMS-missionaries once again tried to solve the problem in such a way so as not to harm the mission work. Nils Follesøe, the elderly supervisor of the missionaries, was not so worried about the policy of bantustans, but much more about what would happen to "their" Zulus if they had to leave. Would they be able to remain Lutherans? Maybe the Government could move all the "Norwegian" Zulus to the same place, so that NMS could follow in their footsteps and start a new church there? This could even be an improvement, because the Zulus were currently spread out on several different farms.[22] The matter was not resolved since the Government was unable to find any suitable land for the Zulus.

In 1962, however, the Government repeated that the NMS had to get rid of all Zulus on their farms. But now the missionaries' attitude had changed completely, both because of the dramatic political events of 1960, but also because a new and younger more politically oriented supervisor, Andreas Løken, had replaced the conservative Follesøe in 1961. In 1962 NMS refused to assist the Government in moving the Zulus. The reason was stated as being that the missionaries could not in conscience share in the implementation of the bantustans policy, which they now condemned in principle.

In the second part of the 1950s the missionaries had seen the brutality of apartheid demonstrated. However, they did not protest openly because they wanted to avoid mixing mission work and politics and because they feared that any criticism would bring retaliations from the Government, which would harm both the Mission and the Lutheran churches. Instead of open protest, the missionaries demonstrated their point of view in their friendly social relations with blacks:

> Unlike other whites we bring the blacks into our homes as guests, and we always try to show them a courtesy and respect which they have not been spoilt with. We use the many ways we have to let them understand that we are independent witnesses to everything that happens, on the racial front too. We defend them and try to help them when they are ill-treated, we try to influence the whites of our acquaintance to look at the blacks with less prejudice [...] We have a big obligation as bridge-builders, we create contact and trust across the race borders, to the benefit of the church and the blacks as a people.[23]

---

[22] NMS annual conference in South Africa 1957, NMS-archives.

[23] A. Løken: NMS annual conference in South Africa 1960, NMS-archives.

Norwegian missions and black resistance

Norwegian missionaries were present in South Africa during the 1950s, the years of mass mobilisation of black resistance. They also witnessed the decolonialisation on the African continent in the 1960s. At this time the missionaries had a near monopoly on informing the Norwegian opinion about what was going on in Africa. The picture the missionaries gave of the blacks' struggle for liberation, was adopted by many Norwegians. It is therefore interesting to ask what this picture looked like.

The missionaries seem to have had almost no contact with organised political opposition within South Africa. This is notable because they repeatedly assured their friends back in Norway that they were the black man's friend and defender and that they were on the side of the blacks in their struggle against the racist regime. The missionaries gave the impression of not knowing much about political developments. Supervisor Nils Follesøe reflects on the year 1955 in his annual report: "politically, 1955 was a peaceful year. Beside the usual political party squabbles there has been little evidence of larger upheavals in the sea of people [...] Not much has been heard lately about the apartheid policy."[24] Was he not at all aware of the People's Congress which met this year and adopted the Freedom Charter? Actually, 1955 was one of the most eventful years in the resistance in the 1950s. We must assume that Follesøe had heard about the events that took place, but maybe he did not find them sufficiently important to include in his report.

The reports and letters from the missionaries very rarely contain any information on the black resistance. Instead they describe the blacks' terrible social and economic conditions. The Zulus' paganism and traditional culture is seen as part of the explanation for their poor standard of living. One never finds any black intellectuals in the missionary sources (except for pastors). The missionary relates to the poor heathen in need of evangelisation or to the church-member not engaged in politics. They never mixed with the politically conscious activists.

Albert Luthuli is the only freedom fighter that is given a name in the public reports from the missionaries from the 1950s and 1960s. The missionaries admired him enormously, not primarily in his capacity as the president of ANC, but because of his strong Christian testimony. The missionaries wrote to the Nobel Committee to support his candidature to the Peace Prize:

> Luthuli [is] a nationalist leader beyond the ordinary. Oppression causes hatred, and this often characterises the fight for national liberation. But with Luthuli it is different. He is a Christian and his Christian faith has passed its test in the fight he is now fighting. [...] What could not African nationalism have brought of vio-

---

[24] Report from NMS annual conference in South Africa 1956, NMS archives.

lence and misfortunes if Luthuli had not been there [...] The road to liberty goes by way of the cross, says Chief Luthuli.[25]

The missionaries regarded the black request for real influence in society as a justified one. Gradually the blacks should be given responsibility and the right to vote, according to education and level of spiritual maturity. The decolonisation process was regarded as positive by the missionaries, but at the same time they were sceptical towards the liberation movements and African nationalism. The missionaries worried about what would happen to the churches and Christian missions if the Africans took over power from the Christian colonialists: "National pride, racial pride or an ungovernable desire for self-assertion could make the co-operation between mission and church more difficult."[26]

What the missionaries feared most was Communism, and they were afraid that the black nationalist was under the influence of this atheist ideology. Communism, liberation struggle and nationalism seemed closely linked to each other. During the cold war the missionaries believed that a new battle of Africa was being fought between Communism and Christianity. If the Christians did not stand firm, they would lose this battle, and all the missionaries would be sent back to Europe.[27] The fact that many liberation movement leaders were Christians, Luthuli among them, did not affect the missionaries' general opinion.

1960–1967: NMS commits itself publicly

Towards the end of the 1950s the aims and consequences of apartheid became more readily apparent. The missionaries' dream of progressively integrating the blacks into white society was dashed. As time went by, it seemed obvious that the regime in power deprived the blacks of their basic human rights, and that their policies were clearly contrary to God's will. Did this not mean that the missionaries had not only the right but an obligation to protest? Had the time arrived?

The missionaries' first public criticism of apartheid

Early in 1960 the missionaries met for their annual conference, and apartheid was on the agenda. In his lecture on apartheid, the young missionary Andreas Løken asked: "When shall we speak and when shall we remain silent, when shall we speak carefully, when shall we speak openly, protest or make demonstrations or do something else to influence, if possible, a development which many of us view with grave concern?" The question was no longer whether apartheid was objectionable: "we Norwegian

---

[25] *Norsk Misjonstidende,* no. 36, 1961 (magazine published by NMS).

[26] NMS Year Book 1948–1951, NMS archives.

[27] NMS Year Book 1948–1951, *Norsk Misjonstidende,* no. 12, 1954, NMS-archives.

missionaries to South Africa all look with sorrow and concern upon the apartheid legislation and practice we have witnessed lately. And we recognise that the apartheid ideal is non-Christian and that its roots lie in the prejudices and fears of the whites."[28]

The question was what the missionaries were to do next. They decided to dispatch Løken's lecture back to headquarters in Stavanger as an expression of their collective views on apartheid. The NMS leadership asked for and received permission to make it public. The silence of the missionaries had been noted and criticised from some quarters in Norway, and the NMS leaders hoped to counter this criticism by publishing the statement, which would be the first public protest against apartheid from any Lutheran mission or church in South Africa.

The decision to publish the statement was taken before the shots were fired in Sharpeville on 21 March, 1960. But these tragic events meant that the missionaries' protest was perceived as coming at the right moment and received considerable publicity in Norway. "Thereby the missionaries of the Church of Norway for the first time formally and openly declare themselves opponents of the policy of racial segregation that is being pursued", the daily newspaper *Verdens Gang* declared, and its colleague *Morgenposten* expressed its relief that the missionaries had now clearly and unambiguously declared their condemnation of apartheid.[29] The publication of the lecture did not, however, meet with any reaction from the South African authorities.

The Norwegian bishops sent a letter of support to the missionaries, and in June the same year the NMS General Assembly, too, for the first time passed an official resolution condemning apartheid:

> The Christian faith does not allow discrimination of other races. If we for more than a hundred years have worked for the Gospel of Love in South Africa we would fail both this gospel and our entire missionary effort among the Africans if we did not now object to a racial policy which leads to violence and injustice. [...] In the actual situation which has now arisen for church and mission in South Africa the position of the NMS must be decided in close co-operation with our coloured brethren in the struggle for human dignity and right.[30]

The Church of Norway takes an interest

The Sharpeville massacre followed by the outlawing of the liberation movements and the arrest of several prominent political activists, revealed to the world what was happening in the apartheid state. In May 1960 the WCC invited its eight South African member churches (no Lutheran

---

[28] A. Løken, "NMS annual conference in South Africa 1960". His lecture was published in *Norsk Misjonstidende*, no. 12, 1960.

[29] *Verdens Gang*, 6 April 1960 and *Morgenposten*, 7 April 1960.

[30] *Norsk Misjonstidende*, no. 23, 1960.

churches were members at this time) together with member churches from other parts of the world to meet and discuss the critical political situation.

When they meet at Cottesloe College in Johannesburg in December the same year, the tension between the Dutch Reformed Churches and the English-speaking churches was high. The Dutch churches had supported the policy of apartheid ever since 1948. It therefore came as a great surprise that the delegates from these churches approved the final resolution, recognising "that all racial groups who permanently inhabit our country are part of the total population, and we regard them as indigenous. Members of all these groups have an equal right to make their contribution towards the enrichment of the life of their country and share in the ensuing responsibilities, rewards and privileges". The resolution went on to state, among other things, that all adults should have the same right to own land and to participate in the government of the country.[31] This statement was the clearest rejection of apartheid that had so far been made by such a representative group of South African churches.

But the Dutch Reformed delegates were in big trouble. The Afrikaner nationalists with Prime Minister Hendrik F. Verwoerd at the helm were furious, and even though some of the delegates recanted and issued their own modified statement after the conference, the harm was done. The result was that the annual assemblies of the Dutch Reformed churches in 1961 decided to withdraw from the WCC and thereby also from the international church community and from fellowship with the English-speaking churches in their own country. The outcome of the Cottesloe conference created a deep split between churches in South Africa. Three decades were to pass before they were on speaking terms again and any WCC leaders were allowed to enter South Africa.

The Cottesloe conference, the Sharpeville massacre, and the award of the 1960 Nobel Peace Prize to Albert Luthuli and the subsequent visit by the ANC president to Norway in 1961, all attracted attention from the international church community, including Norwegian bishops and churchmen. From now on, the Church of Norway took a lively interest in developments in South Africa.

In 1962 the LWF invited the leader of CEIR to visit South Africa together with representatives from the secretariat in Geneva to investigate what the LWF could do to change the white Lutheran churches' positive attitude to the apartheid policy. These churches, which counted many people of German extraction among their members, stood close to the Dutch Reformed Churches in this matter.

In 1963 the Norwegian bishops for the first time directly broached the apartheid issue with the Norwegian government. They asserted that apartheid was contrary to Christianity, and they wished "to appeal to the

---

[31] L.A. Hewson (ed.): *Cottesloe Consultation*. Grahamstown, 1961, pp. 74–75.

Government of the South African Federation to let the Christian view of the inherent worth of Man—with the idea of brotherhood and the command meant to love one's neighbour as oneself—lead to a radical change of course and a transformation of its entire racial policy before it is too late."[32]

The involvement of the LWF and the WCC in Southern African affairs in the following years came to be of decisive importance for the Church of Norway. In 1964 several leading representatives of liberation movements in Southern Africa participated at a WCC conference in Zambia, and the WCC conference on Church and Society in Geneva in 1966 strengthened the ties that were established between the ecumenical movement and the liberation movements. For Norwegian church leaders, participation at ecumenical meetings became the gateway to a strong commitment to the anti-apartheid cause.

After the Cottesloe conference there was no debate in Norwegian churches as to whether apartheid could be reconciled with Christian or humanitarian values, but it was still not entirely clear what practical consequences followed. The 1960s was a time of searching for suitable ways and means for the church to combat apartheid. Except for the refugee support from the Norwegian Church, verbal condemnations of apartheid from the missionaries', bishops' and churchmen's growing sympathy for the anti-apartheid movement, nothing much happened.

1968–1973: From why to what

1968 was a turning point. In connection with the 20th anniversary of the UN Declaration of Human Rights, the annual bishops' conference in 1968 issued a lengthy statement on human rights. The bishops on the one hand gave a theological defence of church involvement in social issues and on the other urged the Church of Norway to step up its efforts to promote human rights, peace and justice. This statement, which had been prepared by Per Voksø,[33] served as an important call for commitment in the years to come, even though it was very general in terms and restricted to traditional church activities; humanitarian assistance to suffering people, preaching of the Gospel and prayers. [34]

---

[32] Statement from the Bishops' Meeting, 1963, CEIR archives.

[33] P. Voksø has been one of the most influential lay church members in the Church of Norway after the Second World War. He has played key roles as moderator of both the Church of Norway National Council and CEIR. He has represented the Church of Norway in the WCC and several other international and ecumenical institutions. Working as a journalist, he has also had a great influence on the general public.

[34] Statement from the Bishops' Meeting in 1968, CEIR-archives : "Throughout the entire history of the church women and men have obeyed the command of their Lord and gone forth from their own countries to live and work among other peoples. They have spread knowledge of the Lord for whom there is neither Jew nor Greek, they have eased human suffering and they have through their total efforts created the preconditions both for raising the standard of living and for the liberation of the people which we have experienced in so many places. These efforts must be intensified in the time to come. The Gospel is still fresh and powerful [...] The chief

The debate over the WCC's Programme to Combat Racism

The Church of Norway's step towards more politically oriented work on human rights came as a result of actions taken by WCC and LWF. In 1968 the WCC presented the idea of a new Study Programme to Combat Racism (PCR) at the General Assembly in Uppsala. It was also proposed that the WCC should establish a fund to provide economic support for the liberation struggle. The next year WCC Central Committee at their meeting in Notting Hill decided to establish both the PCR and the Special Fund. The president of FRELIMO, Eduardo Mondlane, was invited to speak at the meeting, but he was killed by a car bomb shortly before. The speech was instead given by Oliver Tambo, the acting president of the ANC. The Norwegian bishop Kåre Støylen was a member of the Central Committee, and voted in favour of both the PCR and the Special Fund.

In 1970 the Executive Committee of the WCC granted USD 200,000 to nineteen different liberation movements of which fourteen operated within Southern Africa.[35] The conditions were clear; the money could only be used for humanitarian purposes, and not in the violent struggle. But at the same time WCC accepted that some liberation movements could be forced to use violence in situations where all other means had been shown to be in vain.

The WCC line met with mixed reactions. In South Africa the government quickly equated the WCC with Communism, and the support to the liberation movements was criticised from several quarters in Europe as well. In Norway, the decisions of the Central Committee sparked an intense debate about the church's relations to the ecumenical organisations. Conservative Christians and several missionary organisations claimed that the Church of Norway through its membership in the WCC was supporting armed liberation struggles and many called for a withdrawal from the WCC and also from LWF which they regarded as closely linked to the WCC. During the 1960s, Norwegian Church Aid had, through the LWF, provided financial assistance to humanitarian relief work among refugees in Southern Africa. Among the refugees were several political activists linked to liberation movements. For this reason the Norwegian Church Aid was also a target for criticism.[36]

This debate led, in 1970, to a momentous statement from the bishops' conference on Church of Norway's relations to the ecumenical organisations. It had been prepared by the young secretary of The Ecumenical Institute (which later on was reorganised into CEIR), Gunnar Stålsett (who in 1985 was appointed secretary-general of LWF and in 1998 bishop of Oslo). The bishops expressed approval of the work the LWF and the WCC were doing to combat racism in South Africa, but they were also concerned about

---

weapon in the struggle is and remains the Word of God. It is to be proclaimed to the people, the powers and the authorities of this time."

[35] WCC, Ecumenical Press Service, October 1979.

[36] P. Voksø: *Utfordringen*. Oslo: Norwegian Church Aid, 1987 (Book about the history of NCA).

WCC being involved in situations of gross human rights violations wherever they occurred. The situation in Eastern Europe was in the bishops' minds. Support given to liberation struggles should never be politically motivated, and the bishops restated the WCC's conditions that the grants from the Special Fund could only be used for humanitarian assistance. [37]

The bishops had now given their go-ahead for a more action oriented human rights effort in the Church of Norway along the lines of the WCC and the LWF. But the Church of Norway did not yet have any office or committee to carry out this work. This was soon to change. When the Church of Norway Council of Ecumenical and International Relations (CEIR) was established in 1970, the Church of Norway was given a more effective instrument for handling the church's international and ecumenical work.

LWF and WCC encourage the Church of Norway to work with human rights

In 1970 the LWF General Assembly, meeting in Evian, encouraged its member churches to work concretely with human rights issues and to report results back to the LWF. In early January 1971 a "post-Evian conference" was held in Oslo; it resulted in a study programme on human rights in the Church of Norway.[38] In 1971 a similar call to work on human rights issues came from the WCC Central Committee. The pressure from the ecumenical organisations was to be an important, not to say decisive, factor in starting CEIR's human rights work. A committee for human rights was set up in 1972, linked to CEIR's Committee for International Affairs. This committee was given the task to make a report on Church of Norway's human rights work which was translated into English and presented at the WCC Human Rights Conference in St. Pölten in 1974.

In 1972 the Church of Norway together with the Nordic Ecumenical Institute and the Norwegian Missionary Society arranged a conference in Oslo, "Mission and Church Aid—in the light of the problems in Southern Africa."[39] This was a follow-up of a similar conference held in Sweden in 1970. Church leaders from the Nordic countries and from abroad were invited, and the meeting was chaired by bishop Per Lønning who "showed a very personal blend of authority and personal concern."[40] The bishop of Oslo, Fridtjov Birkeli, at this time also chairman of the Norwegian Missionary Society, gave the opening address.

---

[37] Statement from the Bishops' Meeting in 1970, CEIR-archives.

[38] *Mellomkirkelig Institutt Nytt* (newsletter from CEIR), no. 3, 1975. Protocol from CEIR-meeting 31 August 1981, CEIR-archives.

[39] The Conference "Our responsibility for Southern Africa today" took place in Oslo 24–26 January 1971. Minutes from the conference are to be found in CEIR-archives. Part of the report was published in *Mellomkirkelig Institutt Nytt*, no. 3b, 1971 and no. 1, 1972.

[40] Lars Thunberg, director of Nordic Ecumenical Institute in the preface of the minutes, CEIR-archives.

The conference, which created more interest for Southern Africa in the Nordic churches, adopted a resolution on Namibia and a programme of action for Rhodesia. The final statement requested both the Nordic churches and governments to intensify their work against apartheid. The Conference expressed strong support for the work of the WCC-PCR:

> We are challenged by the fact that a great number of African churches are engaged in the social, economic and political struggles within their societies as they proclaim human rights and human dignity. We believe that the churches and Christians in our Nordic countries have not yet fully seen their total responsibility in Africa. On the basis of the theology of creation, incarnation and redemption, we maintain that the church must be deeply concerned with justice, welfare and dignity of all people—regardless of colour, race and social status. [...] We express our solidarity with the suffering peoples in Africa who are continually struggling for human dignity and human rights, and we see the World Council of Churches Programme to Combat Racism and its grants to the humanitarian programmes of the liberation movements as a concrete expression of this solidarity.[41]

The conference also introduced a new theme; Critical attention should be given to trade relations and industrial investments of Western Countries in Southern Africa. Although vaguely formulated, this is one of the first appearances of one the major political questions in Norway's policy towards Africa: the question of economic sanctions.

Support for the Christian Institute

In the early 1970s there was a strong wish among Norwegian church leaders to show through specific action that the statements of principle were real commitments. But what kind of action could be taken? After the Cottesloe conference and the withdrawal of the Dutch Reformed churches from the WCC, Beyers Naudé, a former Dutch Reformed minister established the Christian Institute. The Church of Norway knew of this institute through LWF and WCC, and the Norwegian missionaries in South Africa were familiar with it.[42] The institute needed support, its funding was insufficient and the government kept it under constant surveillance because of its outspoken criticism of apartheid. Could this be a worthy cause for the Church of Norway to support?

In the spring of 1971 the secretary-general of CEIR asked missionary Andreas Løken in South Africa along with the former missionaries Odd Kvaal Pedersen and Gunnar Lislerud this very question. Lislerud, who had worked closely with Christian Institute as a "charter member" during his time in South Africa, expressed the view that the "Christian Institute is the

---

[41] Final statement from the conference "Our responsibility for Southern Africa today", Oslo, 24–26 January 1972, CEIR-archives.

[42] Bishop P.G. Parkendorf, the leading Swedish missionary Helge Fosseus, Manas Buthelezi, all working in ELCSA-SER worked closely with the Christian Institute (CI).

most effective ecumenical link in the South African situation", while Løken thought that "supporting the Christian Institute is a much greater service to South Africa—with all its deprived people—than WCC did by supporting liberation movements with political and military objectives alongside the humanitarian ones which received so much attention. [...] Let me mention, just between ourselves, that the NMS has quietly supported the Christian Institute economically these last years, out of sympathy with its aims."[43]

CEIR set up a special committee to investigate how CEIR could best support the Christian Institute. Where would the money come from? After having rejected the idea of a fund-raising campaign, it approached the Norwegian Church Aid, which granted NOK 5,000.[44] This was the first grant for the struggle against apartheid within South Africa to be channelled through the Church of Norway, and the church reported to the WCC that it "participated in the fight against racism in South Africa by supporting the Christian Institute and by trying to keep the public informed about the objectives of the struggle".[45] This initiated a 25 year long effort to provide economic support to South Africa and Namibia. In 1972 Naudé visited Norway for the first time. He was to become one of the chief advisers for the Church of Norway's projects in South Africa through the entire period.

1973–1983: The church of Norway's commitment finds its shape

The early 1970s saw another change in the nature of the Church on Norway's commitment. Not only did economic support begin, the commitment also became more politically oriented. Attention was focused on South Africa's economic relations to other countries. Needless to say, this had to do with the fact that these relations were at this time stressed by the anti-apartheid movements, the UN and the international ecumenical organisations. At this time CEIR also established contact with representatives of the liberation movements. Bakkevig claims that CEIR often helped the liberation movements to get in touch with Norwegian government officials, and that CEIR's wide-ranging network made CEIR an asset in overall Norwegian relations to Southern Africa. It also led to close contact with the Norwegian government.

In 1973 the Ministry of Foreign Affairs approved an application from CEIR for NOK 75,000 to the Christian Institute. A very special relationship between CEIR and the Ministry, which lasted until 1995, had begun. From 1973 onwards the Ministry regularly granted funds to the Church to be transferred to churches and organisations within South Africa. That year

---

[43] G. Lislerud's letter to G. Stålsett of 29 March 1971, A. Løken's letter to G. Stålsett of 22 April 1971, CEIR-archives.

[44] Members of the CI-committee: Kvaal Pedersen, Hestvold, Stålsett, Birkeli and Lislerud. CEIR annual report 1971. Minutes from CI-Committee Meeting 23 April 1971, CEIR-archives. *Mellomkirkelig Institutt Nytt* published many articles about CI in the 1970s.

[45] CEIR-meeting 1971, CEIR-archives.

CEIR also managed to raise NOK 75,000 from the Ministry for the WCC-PCR. Balwin Sjollema, director of the PCR, visited Norway in 1973, in connection with the OAU-UN conference (see chapter 1), and he established further contacts with the church.

The Christian Institute: "The axe has fallen"

The Christian Institute was, as we have seen, CEIR's first partner in South Africa. However, the Institute also received unwelcome attention from the South African Government. In 1973 Prime Minister Johannes B. Vorster appointed a parliamentary commission to investigate the work of the institute and several other organisations which were critical towards the apartheid regime.[46] They were accused of inciting violent revolution and of encouraging socialism. The organisations were suspected of being in league with foreign enemies of the regime, among others the WCC. In December Manas Buthelezi, the Lutheran theologian in charge of the Institute's regional office in Natal was banned when refusing to subject himself to secret interrogation.

The LWF appealed to all its member churches to protest against the banning of Buthelezi, and the acting secretary-general of CEIR, who at that time was the former NMS missionary Andreas Løken, did so in no uncertain terms in an interview with the *Church of Norway News*.

In March 1974 the Chairman of CEIR, bishop Kåre Støylen, wrote to the Foreign Minister, Knut Frydenlund, asking the Norwegian Government to raise the banning of Buthelezi with the South African Government.[47] The secretary-general of the International Commission of Jurists observed the court proceedings against the Christian Institute. The Ministry of Foreign Affairs also granted NOK 50,000 for the Institute's legal defence.

The CEIR was deeply worried about the future of the Christian Institute, and discussed the matter at its meeting in March 1975. Soon after, on 6 June, the Council got this message from Isle Naudé, Beyers' wife: "The axe has fallen. On 30 May 1975 the Government of the Republic of South Africa has declared the Christian Institute an affected organisation". This meant among other things that the Christian Institute could no longer legally receive money from abroad.[48]

SACC and churches all over the world protested strongly against this verdict. At this time, several Norwegians had come to know Naudé and other people at the Christian Institute personally, both because they had visited Norway several times, but also because of the work the Institute had been doing inside South Africa. CEIR published a statement on 20 June,

---

[46] National Union of South African Students, University Student Movement, South African Institute of Race Relations.

[47] Letter from CEIR's moderator K. Støylen to K. Frydenlund of 25 March 1973, CEIR-archives.

[48] Letter from I. Beyers of 3 June 75 to CEIR, CEIR-archives.

stating that the council was shocked by the accusations against the Institute: "We express our wholehearted support for such work and appeal to all Christians in our country to pray for Dr. Beyers Naudé and all the other church leaders in South Africa."[49]

It was no longer possible to support the Christian Institute financially, but the Church of Norway continued to stay in close contact with the Institute, even after the banning in 1977 of the Institute itself and several of its staff, including Naudé. For a few years in the late 1970s the work of the Institute was carried on in exile, and this was supported by the Church of Norway. Two other organisations closely connected with the Institute also received financial support from Norway: the Black Community Programme and the African Independent Churches Association.[50]

Soweto and the banning of anti-apartheid organisations

In South Africa the situation went from bad to worse. The picture of the dead child Hector Peterson, killed by police bullets in Soweto on 16 June 1976, appeared on the front page of newspapers all over the world. Both SACC and the Christian Institute appealed to their friends abroad for support and prayers in this dark hour in the history of South Africa. CEIR made an official statement on 22 June assuring their friends in South Africa of their full support in the continuing struggle against apartheid; "The church asks Norwegian Christians to follow the developments in South Africa alertly. We must stand together in prayer that the freedom and peace which we can enjoy today in our country, must also become reality for those people who in other parts of the world live in bondage."[51]

In October 1977 the Government banned 18 anti-apartheid organisations, among them the Christian Institute. As we have seen, Beyers Naudé and several others were either banned or detained. The government thereby signalled to the world that no internal criticism of apartheid would be tolerated. In CEIR's opinion:

> By this action the South African authorities have shown that they are willing to make use of all conceivable means to ensure the privileged position of the white population [...] After this, the black population has practically no institutions or organisations expressing their views, their needs and their grievous need ... It seems as if the churches are now the only organisations who can plead the case of the black population. This situation calls upon our solidarity and our prayers. For the international community in general and for Norway in particular the development must have as a consequence that all political and economic means are employed to bring the apartheid government to an end.[52]

---

[49] Statement from CEIR-meeting 20 June 1975, CEIR-archives.

[50] CEIR annual report 1973, CEIR-archives.

[51] Statement from CEIR-meeting 22 June 1976, CEIR-archives.

[52] Statement from CEIR's secretary-general and moderator of 19 October 1977, CEIR-archives.

After the banning of the organisations the role of the churches became even more crucial because it seemed that the churches were now the only organisations still able to speak for the black population. This situation called for our solidarity and our prayers, according to CEIR.

New partners in South Africa

In this situation it became even more important for CEIR to support organisations within South Africa that could still work and receive financial assistance from abroad. The most important among the new partners was SACC which got financial support from CEIR from 1978, the same year that Desmond Tutu took over as secretary-general. After the Soweto uprising and the murder of Steve Biko, CEIR also started to support the Black Consciousness Movement, and the Black Parents Associations in Soweto, led by Manas Buthelezi

In 1983 the Ministry of Foreign Affairs granted a large sum to help establish the Ecumenical Centre in Durban. This centre housed several organisations, among others Diakonia and Legal Resources Centre which were to become close partners to CEIR. In 1985 CEIR, in close co-operation with the Norwegian consulate in Cape Town, set up the Social Change Assistance Trust which distributed money to a large number of grassroots organisations in the Cape Town area. These partners will be described in more detail in the second part of the chapter.

The secretary-general of CEIR normally travelled to South Africa twice a year to meet with the partners. CEIR also frequently received South African guests in their Oslo offices. The round table meetings of SACC and other international ecumenical meetings also brought the partners together. This contact was of great importance for the development of CEIR's work. Information was shared and advice given through personal contacts. In the course of the 1980s, the church became the Norwegian organisation with the most extensive and frequent communication with opposition groups within South Africa, and this meant a lot in the church's co-operation with Norwegian government and non-governmental organisations, both when it came to sharing information and to political lobbying. The annual support from the Church of Norway was increased from approximately NOK 230,000 in 1976 to more than NOK 1 million in 1977 and about NOK 3 million in the early 1980s.

1981–1983: SACC's activities are scrutinised

Prime Minister Pieter W. Botha's attack on SACC in 1981 became further proof that the churches had to involve themselves in what was happening in South Africa. Botha wanted to map SACC relations with churches aboard, particularly concerning the large amount of money that was given to SACC by the international church community. The so-called "Eloff Commission" was ordered to investigate the sources of these funds and how they were used. The Botha government hoped that the commission would reveal irregularities in SACC's accounting and generally discredit it.

The official hearings started in 1982. SACC called a large number of representatives from their partner churches abroad as witnesses. The secretary-general of CEIR (from 1978 on Carl Traaen), was present at the hearings as an observer, and bishop Gunnar Lislerud testified to the Commission:

> As a church in another part of the world, we may not always be fully informed of all the projects of SACC, but we are in full agreement as to the principle of social-ethical witness given by the Council. This is a prophetic witness, which is the responsibility of the Church—at all times and in all places [...] Today many churches give a prophetic witness on the same issue—that human rights and human dignity, freedom and justice be given to all peoples of this country regardless of race and colour. It is exactly to this issue, SACC has given its witness and devotes its work. And the churches of the world work to support their witness. That is why we have come the long way back to this country and to this hearing.[53]

The case did not turn out the way Botha had hoped. During the hearing church leaders from all over the world expressed their admiration for SACC's work, and emphasised that it was financially independent of its donors. The hearings demonstrated the considerable support SACC commanded internationally, and the Commission was unable to find any irregularities in its accounts. Instead of discrediting the council, the case brought greater recognition for SACC both within and outside South Africa. The Eloff Commission's report, which exonerated SACC, was handed over to the Parliament in 1984, but no one wanted to follow it up.

The liberation struggle in Mozambique, Angola and Zimbabwe

In 1975 the former Portuguese colonies achieved their freedom at last, and five years later Zimbabwe became independent. The Church of Norway was not so much directly involved in the liberation struggle in these three countries. Apart from the Norwegian Methodist Church's mission work in Angola and Mozambique, there were few links between these countries and the Norwegian churches, until the Norwegian Church Aid, in co-operation with the LWF and the WCC and the churches in the region, started to support the large number of refugees in Southern Africa with humanitarian aid in the 1960s.

CEIR had of course followed the struggle going on in these countries against colonial and settler regimes with great interest, not least through information provided by international ecumenical organisations and the Norwegian Council for Southern Africa. Norwegian church leaders were also present at several ecumenical meetings in the region, and met with

---

[53] G. Lislerud's statement to the Eloff Commission, CEIR-archives.

representatives from the liberation movements in these countries. But the Church of Norway took few initiatives of their own related to their struggle.

We have already mentioned that the Nordic Church conference in Oslo in 1972 adopted a Programme of Action on Rhodesia. Some years later, in 1978, the WCC-PCR's Special Fund gave financial support to the Patriotic Front (ZANU) led by Robert Mugabe. Support was not given to the same extent to ZAPU. This was widely regarded as a politically motivated choice. CEIR were among those who opposed the PCR's decision in an official statement from 1 November 1987:

> We support the provision of aid even to this type of liberation movement when the prerequisite is that the money is used for humanitarian purposes, relief for refugees and so on. [...] The grant to the Patriotic Front was however given a political motivation where one of two parties in the national liberation struggle in Rhodesia was given preference. We think that the World Council of Churches has in this way chosen sides in a conflict between different nationalist movements. In our opinion, this is not in accordance with the premisses and we dissociate ourselves from the way the Rhodesia grant was launched.[54]

CEIR also asked Bishop Per Lønning to make CEIR's opinion on this matter known to WCC's Central Committee, of which he was a member. CEIR's Committee on International Affairs discussed the situation in Rhodesia and CEIR's statement at its meeting later in November, and asked CEIR to be more flexible. The situation in Rhodesia was changing so rapidly that the committee advised Lønning to wait and see before he spoke out against the PCR's support to ZANU.[55]

The only official statement given by CEIR on Mozambique came after a meeting in February 1988 at Gran outside Oslo between representatives from the Nordic churches and churches and liberation movements in Southern Africa. At this meeting African church leaders asked for support in the extremely difficult situation in Mozambique due to the South African aggression and the civil war. The meeting, which CEIR hosted, adopted a resolution that also included a passage on the situation in Mozambique:

> The Churches' delegation from the SADCC countries challenges the Nordic countries to press their governments to provide means of self-defence for the government of Mozambique. Delegates from the Nordic churches appreciate the urgency of this plea from representatives of the churches in the SADCC countries. Nordic church delegates agree to take this plea to their churches, so that they can discuss it and raise the matter with the Nordic public and governments.[56]

When CEIR met soon afterwards it issued an open letter asking Norwegian congregations to pray for the people of Mozambique and requested the

---

[54] Statement from CEIR-meeting 1 November 1987, CEIR-archives.

[55] Statement from CEIR-meeting 28 November 1978, CEIR-archives.

[56] Statement from the conference on co-operation between churches in the SADCC member sates and the Nordic countries at Granavolden, 4–7 February 1988, CEIR-archives.

Norwegian Government to increase its support, both financially and politically, for this country.[57]

On several occasions, both in meetings and in informal talks, CEIR tried to prod the Norwegian Government to continue and also increase Norway's support to the countries in Southern Africa which were suffering because of the South African military and economic destabilisation policy towards its neighbours. CEIR also took part in information and solidarity campaigns and cultural events connected with Angola, Mozambique and Zimbabwe. Most of these were results of initiatives from the Norwegian Council for Southern Africa (see chapter 6).

Namibia

The Norwegian churches' interest in Namibia was mainly a result of the South African occupation, especially after the apartheid regime came to power in 1948. No Norwegian churches or missions have ever been working in Namibia, and there have never been many Norwegian settlers. Nevertheless, the situation in Namibia was given considerable attention first and foremost from the Namibian Association, but also from the Norwegian Council for Southern Africa, the Norwegian Ecumenical Council on Southern Africa, the Norwegian Church Aid and the Church of Norway. This was because concern for Namibia was regarded as part of the struggle against the apartheid regime in South Africa. The churches participated in information and political lobby work vis-à-vis the Norwegian public and the government. CEIR maintained close contacts with the Namibian Communication Centre in London, and also provided financial support for it. Information from this independent agency was distributed to churches, NGOs, media and politicians in Norway. CEIR also had close links with the Namibian Council of Churches (NCC) and representatives of SWAPO.

Several steps were taken to urge the Norwegian government to use its influence internationally for an immediate implementation of the UN plan for independence for Namibia (UN Resolution 435-1978). In 1986–87 Namibian church leaders visited Norway and urged the Norwegian churches to keep up the pressure on their government over this issue. In 1988 CEIR's Committee on Intentional Affairs followed this up by adopting a resolution that asked the churches to continue to focus on Namibia by for instance establishing contacts with local congregations within Namibia. The Committee also criticised the Norwegian government for its lukewarm efforts to work internationally for Namibian independence. The committee "wishes to challenge the Norwegian government to become a more active and consistent protagonist for Namibia's right to freedom."[58]

---

[57] Statement from CEIR-meeting of 28 May 1988, CEIR-archives.

[58] Statement from CEIR– Committee on International affairs (KISP) 7 May 1988, CEIR-archives.

The churches also co-operated with other NGOs, in arranging solidarity campaigns and church services on special occasions like Namibia Day (26 August) and 4 May, the day commemorating the Kassinga massacre in 1978 where 800 Namibian refugees were brutally killed by the South African army in a refugee camp in Angola.

The Church of Norway also became involved in Namibia through LWF's effort to motivate the white Lutheran churches to become more critical towards the South African Government. In 1986 LWF arranged a consultation on this matter in Hannover. The interest shown by LWF also inspired the Church of Norway to work on Namibia. The bishop of Oslo Andreas Aarflot participated in a LWF delegation which in 1989 visited the "white" Namibian churches which at that time had been suspended from membership in the LWF.

Norwegian Church Aid and CEIR had for many years provided financial support for church schools in Namibia, and they both supported the Legal Assistance Centre in Windhoek established by David Smuts. The Norwegian churches were in close contact with the Namibian Council of Churches, and CEIR gave financial support for the Repatriation, Resettlement and Rehabilitation programme. In connection with the elections in Namibia in 1989, Berge Furre[59] representing CEIR, was an observer in the WCC and the Namibian Council of Churches' Information and Monitoring Programme. He followed closely the work on the new constitution and also the human rights situation in Ovamboland and discussed his observations later with the Council of Churches in Windhoek.[60]

The Church of Norway and the liberation movements in the 1980s–1990s

Norwegian church leaders first got in touch with representatives from the liberation movements living in exile, at meetings arranged under the supervision the LWF and the WCC. We have already mentioned some of these occasions. From the late 1980s Norwegian Church Aid also gave financial assistance to ANC in Lusaka for its Human Resources Development Programme. The Church of Norway never gave any financial support directly to the liberation movements themselves. This was left to other organisations in Norway.

Norwegian church representatives also met with representatives from ANC and SWAPO visiting Norway after having been invited by the anti-apartheid groups, trade unions or other organisations. On some occasions, like the Gran conference in 1988, the church was host. CEIR had an advantage (over other Norwegian organisations) because their relations to LWF

---

[59] Berge Furre, a professor of history and theology, has been a member of both CEIR and the General Synod of the Church of Norway. He has also been engaged in international end ecumenical work, particularly in the European Conference of Churches. He has also been a member of the Norwegian Parliament representing the Socialist Left Party.

[60] B. Furre, Report from visit to Namibia 16 November–3 December 1989, CEIR-archives.

and WCC brought the church leaders in contact with the liberation movements "CEIR helped the liberation movements reach Norwegian authorities" according to Trond Bakkevig.[61]

As we know, the WCC Programme to Combat Racism and the financial
support to the liberation movements caused an internal debate in the
Church of Norway in 1969–70. After the WCC-PRC meeting in Lusaka in
1987 the same debate arose again. Both the president of ANC, Oliver Tambo,
and the SWAPO President, Sam Nujoma, addressed the conference, together
with the chairman of PAC, Johnson Mlambo. The Lusaka meeting recognised "that the people of South Africa and Namibia, who are yearning for
justice and peace, have identified the liberation movements of their countries as the authentic vehicles of their aspirations for self-determination."[62]
Even though the WCC only gave humanitarian assistance, the conference
accepted that the liberation movements in critical situations chose to use
violence.

Bishop Gunnar Lislerud took an active part in the drafting of the Lusaka
statement. He was present together with Atle Sommerfelt, at that time acting
secretary-general of CEIR. The conference asked the member churches of
WCC to intensify their moral and financial support for the victims of
apartheid both in South Africa and Namibia, but also all those who were
suffering as a result of South Africa's military aggression towards its neighbouring states. The final statement called for international, binding economic sanctions and several other specific actions which could increase the
international pressure on the South African government to abolish
apartheid.

In Norway the Lusaka statement led to renewed debate on the use of
violence, and CEIR arranged a seminar to discuss this matter. CEIR also
adopted a resolution supporting the Lusaka-statement:

> The statement further acknowledges that the South African and Namibian
> people have designated the liberation movements as their legitimate tools in the
> fight for self-determination, justice and peace. CEIR accepts and affirms these
> movements as representative spokesmen and instruments of the liberation
> struggle in Southern Africa. As representative expressions for the will of the
> people these movements must themselves be responsible for choosing what
> means to employ. It will remain the primary task of our church to help ensure
> that all possibilities for non-violent solutions are explored, while we at the same
> time can understand that the oppressed party finds itself forced to resort to
> armed resistance in the course of the liberation struggle.[63]

The Lusaka statement was also discussed at the conference at Gran where
the Nordic churches and their partner churches in the SADCC region dis-

---

[61] Bakkevig, p. 20.

[62] Final Statement, report on Meeting in Lusaka, 4–8 May 1987, WCC-PCR.

[63] CEIR annual report 1987, Statement from CEIR-meeting 30 November 1987, CEIR-archives.

cussed what kind of concrete actions should be taken to follow up their commitments from Lusaka.

In 1988 ANC opened an office in Oslo. From now on much of the contact between the church and ANC was handled by this office. Contact was frequent between CEIR's secretary-general and ANC's representative in Norway. This helped the church to understand ANC's views on political developments during the negotiation process. CEIR's close relations with the Ministry for Foreign Affairs helped ANC to get access to high rank politicians in Norway.

1984–1989: Popular enthusiasm

In the 1960s and 1970s the apartheid question attracted the interest of a few "specially interested people", mostly those working with international organisations or radicals who took a special interest in liberation movements in Africa or in general. In Norway this changed tremendously in the mid-1980s. Visitors from South Africa was surprised to learn that taxi drivers asked about ANC, and that schoolchildren were familiar with Steve Biko and Nelson Mandela. There were two main reasons for this change of attitude; the question of economic sanctions became a hot political issue and the Nobel Peace Prize was awarded to Desmond Tutu and SACC.

In 1983 a group of Christians from different denominations but with a shared interest for Southern Africa came together and established Norwegian Ecumenical Council for Southern Africa (NEKSA). NEKSA's aim was threefold: to mobilise the Norwegian public, especially active church members, to put pressure on the Government to implement economic sanctions towards South Africa, to distribute information in Norway about political events inside South Africa and Namibia in a situation with strict media restrictions, and to establish links between the churches in Norway and in Southern Africa.[64] This council played an important role in mobilising church people all over Norway to support the struggle going on in Southern Africa.

Former South Africa missionary Per Anders Nordengen, in 1987 appointed leader of the Church of Norway Development Education Service and its twin organisation the Council of free Churches, together with NEKSA carried out extensive information work and helped local congregations and church-related organisations all over Norway to arrange local anti-apartheid seminars, prayer services and to organise campaigns against shops selling South African goods. Nordengen's personal commitment to the struggle against apartheid was an inspiration, not least to many young-

---

[64] Bishop G. Lislerud and Ø. Tveter were among the founding members of NEKSA. Today NEKSA is connected to the Norwegian Church Council, and material relating to NEKSA is to be found in NCC-archives in Oslo.

sters, and he motivated youth organisations linked to the church to run their own anti-apartheid campaigns.

An organisational change in the Church of Norway was also important. In 1984 the General Synod was established. It gave CEIR the responsibility for international and ecumenical issues on behalf of the Church of Norway, and CEIR had to report back to the Synod. CEIR's work with Southern Africa thus became much better known publicly than it had been previously, when only the bishops and a few interested individuals knew what was going on. In 1984 Trond Bakkevig replaced Carl Traaen as secretary-general of CEIR, and his close links to the Foreign Ministry were to be of considerable importance for the Council's work in the late 1980s.

1984: The Nobel Peace Prize

Tuesday 16 October 1984 was a busy day at CEIR's office. The phones rang continuously. Early that morning, the Nobel Committee had announced that the Peace Prize for 1984 was awarded to the secretary-general of SACC, Desmond Tutu. CEIR was the obvious place to call for journalists and others who needed information on SACC and comments on the award. It came as no surprise when the Nobel Committee asked CEIR and NEKSA to put together a programme for Tutu and his companions during their stay in Norway. Among the highlights of their visit was a service in the Oslo Cathedral and an open party which the church arranged in co-operation with the Norwegian Council for Southern Africa, and the Norwegian Confederation of Trade Unions (LO) in the assembly hall of LO. Hundreds had to stay outside, since the hall was overcrowded. The party was broadcast live.

The Nobel Peace Prize ceremony itself was memorable for more than one reason. It was interrupted by a bomb threat. All the guests had to leave the University Hall and wait outside in minus 10 degrees Centigrade. After a while the police reported that no bomb had been found, and everyone could go back inside. In the meantime the orchestra had disappeared. What happened next will not be forgotten in a hurry: all the South Africans present, led by Tutu himself, went up to the podium to sing *Nkosi Sikelel'i Afrika* with raised fists. The audience, among them King Olav V of Norway, all rose in respect for this national anthem. The South Africans were deeply moved to hear that the song was well known to many in the audience.

Tutu had brought with him both family members and colleagues in SACC. At gatherings both in Oslo and in other parts of the country their joyful singing and joking combined with testimonies about the terrifying situation in their home country made an enormous impression both on ordinary churchgoers and on those who normally kept their distance to the church.

"The Moment of Truth has arrived"

In 1985 a state of emergency was declared in Natal (in 1986 nation wide), followed by a wave of new oppression as well as mounting resistance. 1985 was also the year of the *Kairos Document*. This document gave a critical historical and theological analysis of the misuse of the Bible both by churches and politicians in South Africa. It also criticised the English-speaking churches for failing to perceive the serious threat in the political, economic and social crisis in South Africa at that time, and for being reluctant in their criticism of the apartheid government. The *Kairos Document* was studied by theologians and lay people all over the world. It was translated into several languages, Norwegian among them, and was followed by similar documents relating both to South Africa (*The Evangelical Witness*), the global crisis (*The Road to Damascus*) and to the situation in particular countries. The *Kairos Document* helped Christians both in South Africa and abroad to understand the seriousness on the South African crisis;

> The time has come. The moment of Truth has arrived. South Africa has been plunged into a crisis that is shaking the foundations and there is every indication that the crisis has just begun and that it will deepen and become even more threatening in the months to come. It is the Kairos or moment of truth not only for apartheid but also in the Church.[65]

They were right; the crisis had just begun. On the morning of 12 June 1986, Per Anders Nordengen was wakened by a phone call. He was told that armoured cars were surrounding the Ecumenical Centre in Durban. He hurried to the centre. Pretending to be a journalist he started to ask the police questions, but was quickly ordered to leave. The next thing he did was to run into a cafe and phone Trond Bakkevig at CEIR. The Ecumenical Centre had been established three years earlier with money from the Church of Norway, and Paddy Kearney, the leader of Diakonia, was at this time one of CEIR's closest partners in South Africa. Later the same day the news came that Kearney had been arrested. So had tens of thousands of others, among them Francois Bill, connected to the African Scholarship Programme, which was also supported by CEIR. Thousands more went into hiding.

But there were happy moments in 1986, too. On 7 September bishop Desmond Tutu was made Archbishop of the Anglican Church in South Africa. Among the many people present were Trond Bakkevig and the Norwegian bishop Bjørn Bue, both of whom took part in the procession. Soon after Frank Chikane was elected secretary-general of SACC. He visited Norway for the first time in 1987, a visit to be followed by several others in the years to come.

In South Africa the crisis escalated in the last years of the Botha regime. In his desperate attempt to reform apartheid so that the political and eco-

---

[65] *The Kairos Document*, published by WCC-PCR 1985, chapter one. Also translated into Norwegian by CEIR, 'Sannhetens øyeblikk'.

nomic power could still rest in the hands of the white minority, he tried to destroy all internal opposition by using more and more force. CEIR sent the following telex to Botha on 16 March 1987 when the imminent hanging of the Sharpeville Six had been announced: "To execute these young South Africans will be contrary to the most fundamental principles of justice and a crime against humanity".

In February 1988 seventeen anti-apartheid organisations were outlawed. These were organisations that were filling the space after those which were outlawed in 1977. Church leaders who protested were arrested. In Norway church leaders from different denominations decided, in their anger and sorrow, to give a joint statement on the crisis in South Africa: "As leaders in Norwegian churches we wish to declare our strong support for the South African church leaders' courageous testimony in the critical situation the people and the church find themselves in. In a non-violent fight for peace, justice and fundamental human rights they voice a central Biblical concern."[66]

The statement, signed by the Church of Norway, the Council of Free Churches and the Catholic Church, was unique because it was the first time ever that these churches acted together in such a way. In Norway, as in South Africa itself and many other parts of the world, the struggle against apartheid led to closer ecumenical contacts.

In September the same year a new and tragic message came through the fax machine at CEIR's office. The main office of the South African Council of Churches, Khotso House, had been blown up by a bomb. Bjarne Lindstrøm, the Norwegian consul-general in Cape Town, and one of CEIR's closest friends in South Africa, travelled immediately to Johannesburg, and within a few days CEIR had made a deal with the Norwegian Ministry of Foreign Affairs that Norway would contribute to a new office. The Council also appealed to the congregations in Norway to pray for the churches in South Africa.[67] In 1998 it was confirmed at the hearings of the Truth and Reconciliation Commission that the bombing of the Khotso House was instigated by the then Minister of "Law and Order", Adrian Vlok.

The critical situation in South Africa during the State of Emergency was the reason that CEIR took the initiative in 1985 to establish the "West European Church Network on South Africa". This network, whose aim was to share information among West European churches involved in South Africa, was co-ordinated by CEIR. Its meetings also gave opportunities to discuss concerted church efforts to get Western politicians to implement stronger economic sanctions against South Africa.

---

[66] WCC, Ecumenical Statement 2 March 1988.

[67] Statement from CEIR-meeting 2 September 1988, CEIR archives.

Theology from the South

Documents like *The Kairos Document, The Road to Damascus , The Evangelical Witness* and *The Rustenburg Declaration* were translated into Norwegian and used in Bible study groups or studied by individuals. The poems of Zephania Kameta from Namibia were also translated, together with sermons by Desmond Tutu, Allan Boesak, Frank Chikane and others. Music, liturgies and hymns from Southern Africa became well known to many Norwegian church members. Prominent Southern African church leaders were invited to summer camps and national arrangements like the "Norwegian Church Days". The Norwegian Ecumenical Council for Southern Africa (NEKSA) has most of the honour for bringing African theology to the Norwegian churches. Several church and Youth choirs learned to sing African liberation songs, and these songs are perhaps what most ordinary Christians in Norway noticed.

The theological institutions in Norway also have been involved with Southern African Theology. The School of Mission and Theology (Norwegian Mission Society) has ever since the pioneer days of the Norwegian mission been in touch with Lutherans in South Africa. A special co-operation was established with the Lutheran Theological College at Mapumulo in Natal. Norwegian missionaries used to work as teachers at this college. The co-operation with the school in Stavanger involved exchanges of both teachers and student. The Norwegian Lutheran Hospital and College, Oslo, co-operates with Kgolagano College in Botswana and is also involved in co-operation with the Institute for Contextual Theology in South Africa. The Finnmark College in Alta is involved in a programme on Contextual Theology and co-operates with South African theologians.

Exchange-programmes and study tours have also been arranged and have been of great importance in establishing personal relations between Christians in Norway and Southern Africa. In 1988 NEKSA arranged for around 25 church leaders and activists from different denomination to visit several countries in the southern part of Africa. This visit made a great impact, both emotionally and intellectually, and some of them encouraged their own churches to increase their work on Southern Africa. One of the travellers, Jon Magne Lund from the Evangelical Lutheran Free Church, did not know much about this region when he left Norway, but after his return he became an enthusiastic chairman of NEKSA. Øystein Tveter was a key person in facilitating the theological co-operation and the exchange programmes. Tveter encouraged other organisations and institutions to establish contact with partners in Southern Africa. His many personal relations with persons in the region were a great advantage in this matter.

When major crises occurred in South Africa, for instance the massacres in Sharpeville in 1960 and in Soweto in 1976, the banning of organisations in 1977 and 1988 and the bombing of the Khotso House, Norwegian church leaders asked the local congregations and Christians to pray for the people of South Africa. These calls came originally from churches within South Africa or from LWF and WCC. In different parts of Norway local congregations arranged special solidarity services. Christians in South Africa reported back that this kind of support meant very much to them, and encouraged them to continue with the struggle. Calls for prayers were also made in connection with the elections both in Namibia and in South Africa.

On special occasions the churches worked together on an ecumenical and national level. This was done for instance in connection with the Peace Prize to Desmond Tutu and Frederik W. de Klerk and prior to the election in South Africa in 1994. In 1987 the Norwegian churches were responsible for a Nordic arrangement on Namibia Day on 26 August 1998. National information campaigns were initiated by the twin organisations, Church of Norway and the Council of Free Churches' Development and Education Service. A few congregations became "friendships congregations" to churches in Southern Africa.[68]

The NORDIC–SADCC Church Co-operation

Soon after the WCC's conference in Lusaka in 1987, CEIR took an initiative to establish closer co-operation between the Nordic churches and the churches in the SADCC region. In February 1989 church representatives from both regions met at Gran in Norway. This was the first of several conferences arranged by the so-called "NORDIC–SADCC Church Co-operation" in the years to come. The first years CEIR co-ordinated this programme, later on this task was taken over by the Nordic Ecumenical Council, based in Uppsala, Sweden.

The Gran conference took place against the background of "The Joint Declaration on Expanded Economic and Cultural Co-operation between the Nordic countries and the SADCC member states". The aim of the conference was to discuss areas of common ground and to share information, hopes and aspirations. The conference was also seen as a continuation of work on the concerns of the Lusaka statement. The participants agreed to work together on these concerns:

– Eradication of apartheid
– Increased development and transfer of assistance to the SADCC countries
– Sharing of themselves as Christians and human beings.

The last one was a special concern for the conference. The participants wanted to create a new form of church co-operation as an alternative and

---

[68] Examples of such friendship congregations are: Surla congregation and Highfield Church, Zimbabwe, Strømmen congregation and Bulawayo, Zimbabwe, Tromsø congregation and Koichas, Namibia and the Diocese of Oslo and ELCSA, South Africa. Material relating to these matters are to be found in the Church of Norway Development Education Service–archives (National Church Council, Oslo).

corrective to the traditional one created by missionaries when the North "assisted" churches in the South. The conference stated that:

> The churches in the north feel that they are living through a spiritual crisis. Even with peace, increased welfare and democratic rights, they see problems of loneliness, meaninglessness, suicide and crime. They see more people turning away from the churches. The churches of the north see a vitality and richness in the worship, witness and spirit of the growing Southern churches. They hope to share and learn.[69]

This was to be done through sharing of liturgy, theological study and exchange and by bringing together both pastors and church workers and ordinary church members from both regions. It was also discussed what kind of concrete actions should be taken in the Nordic churches to follow up the Lusaka statement.

The Gran conference, which was chaired by archbishop Walter Makulu, was also attended by representatives from the liberation movements. Thabo Mbeki and other ANC representatives dressed in warm traditional woollen sweaters had the chance not only to experience snow, but more importantly to meet with Nordic church people and establish closer relations.

The conference at Gran was followed by a new one in Lesotho in 1991 and another in Denmark in 1992. In addition theme conferences were arranged; for instance a Youth Conference in Namibia in 1990, a "Workshop on concerned women theologians" in Botswana, a conference on "Rightwing Christian groups" in Namibia and a women's conference in Swaziland—all of them in 1991.[70] The governments of the Nordic countries gave financial support.

The debate on economic sanctions

The first signs of a church debate in Norway on the trade between the Western countries and the apartheid regime appear in 1972. Both the Nordic Conference on Southern Africa in Oslo in January this year and the WCC Central Committee meeting in August raised the issue of economic sanctions against South Africa.[71] In 1973 the Church, at the request of WCC, turned to the Norwegian Ministry of Foreign Affairs and protested against Norway's co-operation with South Africa in the Intergovernmental Committee for European Migration. This international committee, of which Norway was a member, worked to recruit European workers to South Africa.[72]

---

[69] Statement from the Gran conference, 4–7 February 1987, CEIR-archives.

[70] Today the Nordic-SADCC church co-operation is connected to the Norwegian Church Council, and material relating to NEKSA is to be found in the NCC-archives in Oslo.

[71] K. Støylen, Report from WCC Central Committee Meeting, Utrecht, 13–23 August 1972. Papers to CEIR-meeting 23 October 1972, CEIR archives. Final statement from the conference "Our responsibility for Southern Africa today", Oslo 24–26 January 1972.

[72] *Church of Norway News*, no. 3, 1973.

In March 1974 for first time the Church of Norway raised the question of Norway's economic co-operation with South Africa in a letter to the Foreign Minister Knut Frydenlund. The letter asked the government to protest against the banning of Manas Buthelezi, but it also mentions the question of economic sanctions. CEIR had been disappointed to learn that Norway's trade with South Africa was increasing in spite of requests from the UN and the OAU to limit economic co-operation with the apartheid state. CEIR asked Frydenlund "to offer initiatives to prevent official participation in any such engagement in the field of commercial policy in South Africa, and that the authorities likewise encourage a reduction of the private trade relations with South Africa."[73]

In November the same year Frydenlund got another letter from the church:

> CEIR [has] discussed the reports in domestic and foreign newspapers that Norway is one of the countries still considering buying the Crotale missile system. The Council does not have access to information allowing it to verify the assertion that there is still a connection between South Africa and France regarding the production of this system. The Council nevertheless finds that it has to take as its basis the fact that leading African politicians, e.g. the Foreign Minister of Tanzania, have expressed the view that there is such a connection, and that purchase of the Crotale missile system will entail support, economic, technic and moral, to South Africa. CEIR herewith turns to the esteemed Foreign Minister and asks that the government must accord weight to the reactions which have appeared concerning the Crotale project and abstains from doing anything that could be construed as support of the apartheid regime in South Africa.[74]

The reason for this letter was that the Norwegian Ministry of Defence was considering buying the Crotale missile system from France. It was developed in co-operation with the South African weapons industry, and even if this co-operation had now ended, both South African and international anti-apartheid groups viewed any purchase of Crotale as an indirect recognition of the apartheid regime. This case caused a heated debate in the Norwegian Parliament, and it was thus a controversial political issue the church got involved in.

CEIR's letter to Frydenlund also caused an intense debate within the church. It was not really about the Crotale system itself (ecclesiastical experts on missile systems were few), but on the church's mandate in concrete political issues.[75] Anyway, Norway never bought the Crotale system, and the debate both in the Parliament and the church calmed down.

---

[73] Letter from CEIR's moderator K. Støylen to K. Frydenlund of 25 March 1974, CEIR archives.

[74] Letter from CEIR's moderator K. Støylen and secretary-general G. Stålsett to K. Frydenlund of 29 November 1974, CEIR-archives.

[75] This matter causes an intense debate both at internal church meetings, but also publicly in several daily papers. Material on this issue is to be found in CEIR-archives.

But from the early 1980s the question of economic sanctions was again on the political agenda in Norway. The import of South Africa goods, especially manganese, which was crucial for the large Norwegian production of aluminium, and the transport of oil on Norwegian ships were both difficult since they affected Norwegian companies and a considerable number of jobs both in Norway and on Norwegian ships. In 1979/80 approximately 18% of all oil to South Africa was transported on Norwegian tankers.

CEIR involved itself in the debate and supported the efforts of the Norwegian Council for Southern Africa to try to make Parliament outlaw all trade between Norway and the racist regime. The church's involvement in the matter of sanctions was, not surprisingly, based on the moral condemnation of apartheid and the call for actions of solidarity from the oppressed. CEIR forwarded calls for sanctions from the churches in the region and from the international ecumenical community. In August 1980, for instance, the Central Committee of the WCC adopted the following resolution that it would "press governments and international organisations to enforce comprehensive sanctions against South Africa, including withdrawal of investments, and end to bank loans, arms embargo and oil sanctions and in general for the isolation of the state of South Africa."[76]

In December the bishop of Oslo received a letter from the WCC, reminding him of this resolution, and informing him that SACC and Desmond Tutu were now asking the churches internationally to work for the implementation of economic sanctions.[77]

This WCC initiative led to a statement from CEIR in February 1981 to the Foreign Minster asking that "Norwegian authorities take action to keep Norway's economic relations at so low a level as possible."[78] The statement went on to politely ask the government to continue working for binding resolutions in the UN Security Council for economic sanctions against South Africa.

In March 1983 CEIR sent a new official letter, repeating the message from 1981 and also informing the government that South African church leaders had been shocked to learn that a significant amount of South Africa's oil imports were transported on Norwegian ships. On behalf of the South African churches, CEIR demanded that the transport be stopped. It also called on the government to work for an international oil embargo.[79]

WCC's General Assembly in July 1983 requested its member churches in countries transferring oil to South Africa to demand that their governments stopped this immediately. The request was followed up by CEIR, which in

---

[76] Statement from WCC-meeting, August 1980.

[77] Letter from WCC to A. Aarflot of 11 December 1980, CEIR-archives.

[78] Statement from CEIR-meeting, 2 February 1981, CEIR-archives.

[79] Statement from CEIR Committee on International Affairs, 12 March 1983, CEIR-archives.

December had a meeting with Asbjørn Haugstvedt, Minister for Trade of the conservative-centre coalition government (1983–1986).

Bishop Gunnar Lislerud, secretary-general Carl Traaen, and Øystein Tveter from the Ecumenical Council on Southern Africa told the Minister that they were well aware of the difficult considerations concerning the Norwegian workers who might lose their jobs as a result of sanctions, but that the moral responsibility to work for the abolishing of apartheid had to be given priority. Norway had to implement an oil embargo at once, even if other countries and close trade partners did not do the same. Haugstvedt listened, but gave no promises.[80]

In March 1984 the three church leaders met the Foreign Minister, Svenn Stray, to repeat their demand for a total stop to Norway's transport of oil. They also asked for intensified efforts from Norway to work for an international oil embargo. Stray, however, informed them that the government did not have any immediate plans to implement a Norwegian oil embargo. After the meeting, Tveter told the newspaper *Vårt Land* that "the Foreign Ministry leadership and the church are obviously very far apart in their conception of what political measures might have a positive effect in the struggle against the racist regime in South Africa."[81] In 1984 (prior to the Peace Prize award to Tutu) CEIR also arranged for Tutu to meet Stray, in the hope that he would manage to convince the reluctant cabinet minister. Even though the church leaders' talks with the government gave no visible results, they were noticed by the media and helped to increase the general pressure from public opinion for more government action.

In 1983 a parliamentary committee was appointed to look into the question of economic sanction towards South Africa in general. CEIR's Committee for International Affairs, after having read its 1984 report, issued a press release expressing "deep disappointment". CEIR criticised the report for only considering economic implications, not the moral ones: "Efforts to isolate the South African regime must not be assessed only on the basis of the expected economic consequences in South Africa. Even if the effect may seem limited and small to start with, it is important to see that such efforts have a moral and opinion-building side both in Norway and in South Africa."[82] In a more substantial comment on the report CEIR also suggested a series of concrete steps that the government could take to make Norwegian trade policy towards South Africa more restrictive.[83]

In addition the bishop of Oslo, Andreas Aarflot, took a personal interest in the question of an oil embargo. In his New Year speech to the pastors in

---

[80] Letter from CEIR to A. Haugstvedt 16 December 1983, unpublished CEIR-note 21 December 1983, CEIR-press statement of 21 December 1983, CEIR-archives.

[81] *Vårt Land*, 2 and 21 March 1984.

[82] Statement from CEIR, 20 December 1984, CEIR-archives. T. Bakkevig, article in *Aftenposten*, 6 April 1984.

[83] Comment from CEIR on the report from the parliamentary committee, CEIR-archives.

his diocese he restated his position, condemning the oil transport to South Africa on Norwegian tankers. This provoked a reaction from the Norwegian Shipowners Association. But the bishop stood his ground and wrote in his answer: "It is an intolerable situation that our country should make money on the transport of oil to the police forces and war machine of the apartheid regime. I am aware that this will impose costs on our society, but these are costs we have to be able to bear". The letter ended by stating:

> The economic considerations and practical problems in this matter must not overshadow the fact that we are, in this case, faced with an essentially moral challenge. We are involved in the fate of the blacks in South Africa. Our choices matter, simply because Norwegian ships are delivering oil to a state at war with its own inhabitants. In this situation I as a bishop in the church of Christ must assert that we have to listen more to the cry of distress from the oppressed than to national economic interests which often receive a more dominant role when policy is to be formed.[84]

In early 1986 the conservative-centre government presented a white paper on its policy towards South Africa. CEIR was disappointed once more and gave the following comment:

> The Church of Norway has for many years urged that Norway as a nation must show a strong commitment to contributing to the ending of the apartheid regime in South Africa. The reason for this is that the case in question is an institutionalised racism for which even a Biblical argument is offered. We consider this argument for a classification system based on race and with corresponding discrimination of everyone not belonging to the white race to be blasphemous. The practical consequences to which this leads are a fundamental violation of human dignity. The commitment which the situation in South Africa invokes in itself is reinforced in that we in this case have sister churches which are in the front line in the struggle against the apartheid system. These churches ask for and need solidarity from churches all over the world. On behalf of the Church of Norway we deem it right that our solidarity with the churches and people of South Africa finds expression in the work for political and economic efforts on Norway's part which can contribute to the termination of the unjust apartheid system. The South African Council of Churches and other black leaders have asked for concrete action from Western nations and financial institutions in order to contribute in this way to the peaceful termination of the apartheid system. On the part of the Church of Norway we feel an obligation towards the views put forward by our brothers and sisters in South Africa.[85]

We may note that both bishop Aarflot and CEIR considered the respect for the victims of apartheid to be decisive.

In March 1987, when a Labour Party government had replaced the conservative-centre one, the Parliament at last agreed on a law on economic

---

[84] Letter from A. Aarflot to the Norwegian Association of Shipowners of 7 February 1986, CEIR-archives.

[85] Statement from CEIR-meeting, 11 March 1986, CEIR-archives; T. Bakkevig, article in *Vårt Land*, 29 April 1986; G. Lislerud, article in *Arbeiderbladet*, 27 August 1986.

sanctions. It outlawed all economic co-operation between Norwegian companies and South Africa, and all transport of oil to South Africa on Norwegian ships. The law had, however, some significant loopholes (see chapter 5). To the disappointment of those who wanted a total embargo, CEIR accepted that this was as far as it was possible to get.

The Norwegian Council for Southern Africa had in the autumn of 1986 launched the international consumer boycott of Shell in Norway. The reason for the boycott was the role the transnational company Shell played as one of the main suppliers of oil to South Africa. This oil was crucial for the apartheid regime's military operations. The WCC Central Committee meeting in August 1988 encouraged "the churches to support the International Campaign to boycott the Shell Oil Corporation."[86] (The WCC PCR meeting in Lusaka in 1987 had also asked the churches to support it.) Several churches in other Western counties, particularly in the "home country" of Shell, the Netherlands, were actively supporting the boycott. This put new pressure on the Church of Norway. The Norwegian Council for Southern Africa therefore hoped for the Church of Norway's support, and was both surprised and disappointed when CEIR in December 1988 declined to recommend the boycott of one specific company. CEIR agreed that it was important to work for an oil embargo in general, and that Shell International ought to withdraw from South Africa, but when it came to the specific question of Shell Norway the majority of CEIR's members concluded:

> In the struggle against the apartheid system, the Church of Norway Council on Foreign Relations [CEIR] holds it to be ethically justifiable to boycott multinational companies supplying oil and other strategic goods to South Africa. As a church body, the Council finds it difficult to encourage boycott of specific companies. A boycott of that kind should primarily be the responsibility of each individual person.[87]

CEIR's handling of the Shell boycott must be understood against the background of the more critical guidelines for its Human Rights Work that were approved earlier in 1988. [88]

A more critical approach to human rights work in CEIR

In 1985 the newly established Church of Norway General Synod discussed the Church of Norway's involvement in South Africa, and the committee

---

[86] Statement from WCC Central Committee meeting in Hannover, August 1988.

[87] Statement from CEIR-meeting 11–12 December 1988. One member voted against the statement , another chose not to vote, CEIR-archives.

[88] Statement from CEIR-meeting 27 May 1988: 'where violations of these norms (human rights) are apparent, there is in principle no limit to how specifically or directly the Council and/or its sub-committees may speak. The practical limit in such cases must be drawn by the Council itself and its sub-committees on the basis of consideration for the best interests of the victims and of the specialist resources of the Council. [...] Appeals to CEIR from other churches and ecumenical organisations in specific human rights cases are a significant criterion for the Council's priorities. But such appeals cannot in themselves be decisive.'

responsible for CEIR's annual report for 1984 had "noted the contacts with the Ministry of Foreign Affairs regarding Southern Africa and human rights work in general. In this connection the committee thinks it important that the Council continues to work on criteria for assessing what conditions both in the East, the West, the North and the South demand the Council's attention". A young theologian, Jan Olav Henriksen, was then asked by CEIR to prepare a comprehensive report on the church's work on human rights issues.[89]

The new debate on human rights work in the Church of Norway from 1985 on must be understood against the background of the political development in Europe, the growing interest for human rights in general and the escalating crisis in Southern Africa in the late 1980s. The renewed debate on theological implications of the use of violence in the liberation struggle, which followed after the meeting between the churches and liberation movements in Lusaka in 1987, also contributed. Henriksen made a 100-page report about church involvement in Human Rights issues both from a critical theological and historical perspective. It also discussed the mandate of the church and the different methods it could use in Human Rights matters.[90] CEIR approved the report at its meeting in May 1988, and in that connection the Council made a resolution summing up the report's conclusions:

> The church must and shall speak clearly where God's law is broken and the dignity of Man, bestowed by God, is violated. It cannot allow political considerations to decide how directly to speak. Consideration for those suffering from human rights abuses and for what serves them best must be the criterion deciding how and at what level it should involve itself. To make these decisions an expert knowledge of international human rights work is necessary, and the Council must take responsibility for developing and collecting this knowledge, which will provide the prerequisites and the limitations for the specific actualisation of our concern in each particular case.[91]

When the Annual Assembly of the Church of Norway met in November, (a few weeks before CEIR decided on the Shell-boycott), it confirmed the conclusions CEIR had drawn from Henriksen's report, and also stressed that "the work for human rights is a divine calling for all of us. Therefore, this cannot be isolated by CEIR, but has to be part of our daily activities at work and in the churches."[92] At the meeting the General Synod also gave its first official statement on apartheid:

> As a church we are called to combat this false doctrine, show care and consideration for the victims of the apartheid system and support all good forces work-

---

[89] Members of advisory committee: P. Voksø, A.G. Eikseth, B. Furre and Ø. Telle.

[90] J.O. Henriksen: *For menneskelivets skyld. Den norske kirkes internasjonale menneskerettighetsengasjement.* Oslo: Kirkens Informasjonstjeneste, 1988.

[91] Statement from CEIR-meeting, 27 May 1988, CEIR-archives.

[92] Protocol from General Synod, 1988, National Church Council-archives.

ing for its abolition. The Church Assembly therefore wishes to express its full support to the high priority CEIR on behalf of the Church of Norway gives the struggle against apartheid, the support for the oppressed and the co-operation with churches and organisations in South Africa.[93]

1988–1994: New partners and other challenges

Talks with "the enemy"

A South African turned up in Oslo one day in 1988. He was not met by warm words of welcome, but by protests from young anti-apartheid activists. Willem Bosman had arrived to open a new South African General Consulate in Oslo. The Norwegian and South African Ministries of Foreign Affairs had agreed that the Norwegian General Consulate in Cape Town should be allowed to continue to function if South Africa were allowed to establish an office in Oslo. CEIR agreed to this because Consul Bjarne Lindstrøm in Cape Town played a key role in organising CEIR's financial support to South African opposition groups. Because of this breach in the diplomatic isolation of the apartheid regime, CEIR was heavily criticised by members of the Norwegian Council for Southern Africa. Some also expressed dislike of the close connection between the Church and the Norwegian government. But after 1994, when CEIR's project work in South Africa and Lindstrøm's crucial role in it became publicly known, it was easier to understand why CEIR had accepted Bosman's arrival in Oslo.

Bosman tried to establish friendly relations with the church and asked for a meeting with Trond Bakkevig. Their first meeting in CEIR's office ended in a disagreement over the Bantustan policy, and after that the contact was polite but lukewarm. Christmas greetings and small presents from the South African Consulate to staff persons in CEIR were not enough to create a warmer atmosphere.

CEIR had for some time been in contact with South African politicians, and supported financially the Institute for a Democratic Alternative in South Africa led by the former members of Parliament Alex Boraine and Frederic van Zyl Slabbert. From 1989 on Bakkevig also had talks both with people working for the Foreign Ministry in Pretoria and with ANC leaders both in exile and within South Africa.

In December 1989 Bakkevig was observing the opening of the CODESA-conference together with Knut Vollebæk, the political secretary to the Foreign Minister. Vollebæk also used the opportunity to meet with colleagues in Pretoria in spite of the fact that Thabo Mbeki in ANC had warned against this. The time for such contact had not yet come, according to Mbeki.[94]

---

[93] Protocol from General Synod, 1988, National Church Council-archives.

[94] Bakkevig, p. 45.

These talks were a sign of a new role the church started to play in the late 1980s. Atle Sommerfeldt reflected on the new situation after a visit to South Africa in 1987:

> While the role of the church in the late 1970s and early 1980s was in many ways the only voice for the majority population in South Africa, this is not the case to-day. The strengthening of the trade union movement, the grass roots organisations and the youth make it possible for the churches to withdraw a little. It is therefore clearer than before that the churches are not the driving force in the upheavals. The problem and debate now is what role the church is to play and more specifically how it can serve the forces which first and foremost will make the changes come about: the liberation movements, the youth, the trade unions and the grass roots organisations. The church's function as a meeting place for and bridge-builder between different groups within the liberation forces was pointed out, but also their role as spokesman for the oppressed, support for the suffering and facilitator for the different organisations.[95]

A new situation for the churches

On 2 February 1990 President P.W. de Klerk in a historic announcement lifted the ban on ANC and PAC dating from 1960. With the release of Nelson Mandela and other political prisoners, old players reappeared on the South African stage. The role of the church now changed from being an active partner to becoming more of a facilitator for others.

Trond Bakkevig travelled to South Africa in May to meet with church leaders and partners who gave him a briefing on the new political situation, the position of ANC and the new role of the churches. His old friend Beyers Naudé, still going strong, now worked as an adviser for ANC even though he had never been an ANC member. Another purpose for Bakkevig's visit was to discuss with the partners whether CEIR, in the new circumstances, should continue to support the same organisations as before.[96] Most of the old partners continued to receive support, but in addition CEIR started to support a new kind of organisation, namely those directly involved in the political changes and the work to prepare for democracy, peace and reconciliation. Examples are SACC and WCCs "Ecumenical Monitoring Programme for South Africa", the Matla Trust and the Truth and Reconciliation Committee.

Sensational things were also happening among the churches themselves. 230 church leaders from approximately 100 churches met in Rustenburg in November 1990. Guests from abroad were invited and bishop Lislerud represented the Nordic churches. This conference was the first opportunity for the Dutch Reformed Churches, the English-speaking Churches and others to meet and discuss apartheid since the Cottesloe conference 30 years earlier.

---

[95] A. Sommerfeldt, Report from visit to Southern Africa, 7 April–3 May 1987, CEIR-archives.

[96] T. Bakkevig and B.H. Agøy, Report from visit to Southern Africa, May 1991, CEIR annual report 1990, CEIR-archives; T. Bakkevig, article in *Vårt Land*, 31 October 1991.

The churches still disagreed on several matters, but on one matter they reached 'full consensus; namely the clear condemnation of apartheid as sin.'[97] This finally ended the debate which had been going on since 1948. After the Rustenburg conference no prominent theologian or church leader would publicly support the apartheid ideology.

In October 1991 SACC was able to have its Round Table Partner Meeting inside South Africa. This had not been possible during the years of cruel political restrictions and oppression. SACC could also welcome secretary-general Emilio Castro from the WCC to this meeting. For the Dutch Reformed Churches, which left WCC after the Cottesloe conference, WCC had been associated with the enemy and had represented a threat of international Communist infiltration in South Africa. For the other churches the attitude had been radically different. Frank Chikane expressed deep gratitude for what the WCC had done for the struggling people of South Africa: "You heard our cries when no one else did. You believed what we told you and stood by our side."[98]

Violence and reconciliation

Henrik W. de Klerk's words about negotiations and political changes inspired hope, but they were almost swept away by the wave of violence that washed over South Africa during the last years of the apartheid regime. The Church of Norway became particularly engaged in the struggle between Inkatha and the ANC in Kwa Zulu-Natal. Some of the partner organisations like Legal Resources Centre and Diakonia in Durban and Crisis Care Committee in Chattsworth, were heavily involved in reconciliation work, and Norway had a special connection to these areas, where Norwegian missionaries had worked for so many years. The Lutheran Church, ELCSA, which was formed with their help, was in a very difficult position because the black Lutherans in Zulu-Natal were to be found on both sides of the conflict. Relatives of Gatsha Buthelezi were members of this church. The close links between ELCSA and members of Inkatha also put the Norwegian Missionary Society in a difficult position, since the missionaries were at this time employed by ELCSA. CEIR was on the other hand free to take a clear stand against Inkatha. CEIR's staff did comprehensive information work in Norway about the violent situation and pointed to Inkatha's and the de Klerk government's responsibility. CEIR also tried to encourage ELCSA to do the same.[99]

---

[97] Bishop G. Lislerud participated at the conference, and wrote both a report (CEIR-archives) and an introduction to the Norwegian translation of the conference statement, *Tidsskrift for Teologi og Kirke*, no. 2, 1991.

[98] T. Bakkevig, article in *Vårt Land*, 31 October 1991.

[99] T. Bakkevig, article in *Dagbladet*, 8 October 1992.

Bishop Gunnar Lislerud had been working as a missionary in this area for many years, he spoke Zulu, and knew all the bishops in ELCSA personally from his previous post as the principal of the theological seminar at Umpumulo. Lislerud enjoyed respect from leaders of both ELCSA and SACC, and due to this unique position, he was called to act as a mediator for peace in the conflict in Kwa Zulu-Natal.

In Norway, Willem Bosman wrote a newspaper article trying to convince the readers that everything was moving in the right direction in South Africa and that de Klerk was honestly toiling for the peaceful transformation of his country into a democracy. Trond Bakkevig was not impressed and wrote a sharp letter blaming Bosman's government for the violence: "Dear Ambassador Bosman: Something else is needed. We need a real conversion and deeds to prove that the conversion is genuine."[100]

In the critical period of 1992 CEIR, after receiving an appeal from SACC, called on the churches in Norway to pray for peace and democracy in South Africa at their different summer conventions in 1992.[101]

Welcome to Norway, Mr. Mandela!

From the day Nelson Mandela walked out of prison as a free man, the Norwegians started waiting for him to come to Norway. He attended the "Conference on Hatred" in September 1990, but it was not until 1992 he appeared in public. On 17 May that year, Norway's Constitution Day, he was welcomed at Oslo Airport by a choir singing freedom songs from South Africa.

Church representatives (from CEIR and NEKSA) were members of the reception committee co-ordinated by the ANC office in Oslo. Mandela took part in the celebration of 17 May, and watched the parade of tens of thousands of children singing and waving their flags to greet the royal family on the palace balcony. Later the same day Mandela was present at the service in Oslo Cathedral. His sermon was his first official appearance in Norway. The congregation was deeply moved by his words, and the police had problems escorting him out of the church due to the large crowd outside waiting to catch a glimpse of a great freedom fighter. On the occasion of the visit the Church of Norway sent Mandela a message:

> Together with churches all over the world, and with our sisters and brothers in the South African Council of Churches, we have through these long years of struggle prayed for your release, and for freedom and justice for the people of South Africa. Through these intense days of negotiations and violence, we continue to pray.

---

[100] W. Bosmann, article in *Dagbladet*, 21 October 92; T. Bakkevig, answer in *Dagbladet*, 22 October 1997.

[101] CEIR and the Norwegian Church Aid, Prayer for Democracy and Reconciliation in South Africa, 29 June 1992, CEIR-archives.

[...] Struggling churches and Christians in South Africa have helped us to understand more of what it means that the church cannot withdraw from society but needs to speak out and act when the will of God and basic human values are violated. Our solidarity and commitment to the cause of justice has been awakened, deepened and sustained through the way your people have ensured access to information, and patiently, clearly and repeatedly have interpreted the situation for us. This has made it possible for us to participate in a number of ways, also with financial support and advocacy.[102]

In December 1993 Mandela was back in Oslo. This time he came together with de Klerk to receive the Nobel Peace Prize. This was the third time the prize was awarded to South Africans. And like the two first times, the church played a central role in organising the festivities in Oslo. CEIR hosted an informal reception at the residence of the bishop of Oslo. Mandela and his companions met with prominent church leaders. "For practical reasons" de Klerk was not invited.[103] Mandela was also invited to a service in Oslo Cathedral, where he took the opportunity to thank the church "While we were in prison Christians did tremendous work to keep up our spirits. Thanks to the church we knew that no matter the suffering, the day of freedom would come. Our hope never died."[104]

At this time, late in 1993 the preparation for elections had already started. The day of freedom arrived at last, and exactly five months after Mandela received the Nobel Peace Prize, on 10 May 1994 he became the new president of South Africa. Secretary-general Atle Sommerfeldt from CEIR was one of the many international guests witnessing this historic moment.

The elections

The Norwegian Council for Southern Africa took the initiative for the campaign "Democracy for South Africa" which CEIR joined in October 1993. The aims of the campaign were to collect money for the election preparations in South Africa, but most of all to inform the Norwegian public about the changes that were going on in South Africa. As part of this campaign, a broad alliance of churches and church-related organisations published information material, arranged several seminars, meetings and facilitated visits by South Africans during Spring 1994. All the congregations in the Church of Norway were asked to pray for the elections on the preceding Sunday. A suggestion for a special prayer was sent from the WCC Central Committee and translated into Norwegian.[105]

CEIR also participated in the Ecumenical Monitoring Programme for South Africa initiated by the WCC, SACC and SACBC in 1992, and fourteen

---

[102] Message to Nelson Mandela from the Church of Norway of 17 May 1992, CEIR-archives.

[103] CEIR annual report 1993.

[104] *Banneret*, (paper of the Methodist Church), 16 December 1993.

[105] Committee members: CEIR, Church of Norway Aid, NEKSA, Church of Norway Development Education Service and Council of Free Churches Development Education Service.

church representatives from Norway went to observe and monitor the election. One of these was Stig Utnem who in 1994 was appointed secretary-general of CEIR when Sommerfeldt left the office to become the secretary-general of Norwegian Church Aid. Bishop Gunnar Lislerud was appointed a member by WCC and SACC of the "Eminent Church Leaders Group" who supervised the elections by keeping contact with both the South African government and with SACC.

On 27 May 1994 a short ceremony was held at the ANC office in Oslo. It was no coincidence that ANC representative Thandie Rankoe had asked Trond Bakkevig if he could say grace and symbolically close the office. Soon after a representative for the majority of the South African population moved into the Embassy in Oslo.

Co-operation with the Ministry of Foreign Affairs: CEIR's project work in South Africa and Namibia

Before we can look into the church's co-operation with the Norwegian Foreign Ministry, a few general comments must be made concerning the relationship between the church and the government in Norway. To some foreigners the, generally speaking, close and trusting relationship between the church and government in Norway is striking. Examples of disagreement may of course be found, but these are exceptions rather than the rule.

South African guests were often astonished to learn that church people in Norway could easily phone or meet with the parliamentary Foreign Affairs Committee or the highest officials in the Ministry to discuss matters of common interest. For them it was a new experience to accompany their Norwegian hosts to Parliament and Government offices and meet friendly politicians. It also surprised them that the church, along with other NGOs, could receive millions of Norwegian kroner from the Government for their anti-apartheid work, seemingly without any problems. It was difficult to understand that the Norwegian government gave money to the Church and NGOs even when these strongly opposed government policy.

From 1973 on all the funds transferred by the church to organisations in South African and Namibia were granted by the Ministry of Foreign Affairs. Sometimes the Ministry in Oslo or the Consulate in Cape Town asked CEIR to transfer money to particular organisations which the Norwegian government wanted to support for political reasons. Did this imply that the Ministry dictated CEIR's involvement? No, CEIR made its own appraisals, in co-operation with trusted individuals and organisations in South Africa or Namibia, before it decided on whether or not to support an organisation financially, and in some cases turned down the Ministry's requests. Usually, however, the Ministry and CEIR agreed who to support.

The Nordic countries have traditionally enjoyed good mutual relations between civil society and the governments, and the smooth relationship between the church, NGOs and the Norwegian government may be seen as one of numerous examples of this. A precondition for the close co-operation on Southern African affairs was of course a common political understanding on the apartheid issue. Even though government power shifted between the Labour party and non-socialist coalition partners between 1948 and 1994, nearly all parties to a large extent agreed on Norway's policy toward the Southern African countries. The broad consensus was made all the easier by the fact that Norway did not have any colonial background in the region and very few economic interests there. The only matters of some importance were the import of manganese from South Africa and the transport of oil on Norwegian ships. As we shall see later on, both these matters caused disagreement in Parliament and between politicians, the church and other anti-apartheid groups.

In other West European countries and in the USA the churches often had a much more contentious relationship with their governments. Great Britain, Germany and Portugal were of course directly involved in the independence wars going on in their colonies. Strong ties, political, economic and emotional, had been forged during the colonial period. This made the question of apartheid and especially the issue of economic sanctions much more complex that in the Nordic countries. Some Western churches had shares in companies that invested in South Africa or funds in banks that gave loans to the apartheid regime. This caused intense debates in these churches. For the Church of Norway such questions did not arise.

The relationship between CEIR and the government was made easy not least because of many personal links. Bishop Per Lønning, active in the Church's relationship with LWF and WCC, was a member of parliament (Conservative party). The secretary-general of CEIR, Gunnar Stålsett had a break from CEIR to work as a Political Secretary to the Minister for Church Affairs and Education and when he left CEIR he became chairman of the Centre Party. Secretary-general Trond Bakkevig also worked a while as Political Secretary to the Ministers of Foreign Affairs Knut Frydenlund and Thorvald Stoltenberg (Labour Party). Berge Furre, one of the main architects behind CEIR's Human Rights work, had for many years been a member of parliament and Chairman of the Socialist Left Party. It is also interesting to note that Knut Vollebæk, Foreign Minister from September 1997, had for many years been one of the key persons in the Ministry of Foreign Affairs' co-operation with CEIR. Hilde Frafjord Johnson, until she in September 1997 was named Minister for Development and Human Rights, was a member of CEIR's Committee on International Affairs. The fact that so many of the central people in CEIR had such close links to political parties both on the conservative and socialistic side, was a great advantage for CEIR's political lobby work.

CEIR's project work in South Africa and Namibia

The Ministry is familiar with the work of Diakonia. In our opinion this organisation performs a very important task in South Africa today which should be allowed to continue. CEIR therefore applies for NOK 300,000 to Diakonia this year. This could be an example of an application sent from CEIR to the Ministry of Foreign Affairs in the late 1980s. And the answer would be: "The Ministry grants NOK 300,000 to CEIR to be forwarded to Diakonia." Nothing else was written down.

The giving away of so much government money with such a lack of bureaucracy cannot have been usual. During the period 1974–1995 a total amount of NOK 250 million was granted by the Ministry to CEIR's partners inside South Africa and Namibia. Up to the mid 1980s the support was moderate, in the range of 1–3 million each year. Then it went up to about 10 million each year in 1985 and 1986. In 1987 it was doubled, and in 1988–90 it was almost 30 million each year. From 1991 on the yearly amount was gradually reduced. Until 1987 the secretary-general handled the projects on his own, but in that year CEIR employed a person, working part time assisting him in the administration of, at that time NOK 20–30 million each year to more than 30 different projects.

How was this possible? The answer can be given in few words: trust, reliable church contacts within South Africa and Namibia and personal relations between a few committed persons in CEIR and the Ministry. And of course, the co-operation was founded on a mutual understanding between the church and the Norwegian government of the importance of assisting the internal opposition. The government itself was unable to give financial support to political opposition within another country. But by co-operating with the church (and other Norwegian organisation) this could be done. The church was free to support whoever they wanted to.

All the money CEIR transferred from 1973 on came from the Ministry, the church never tried to raise any funds for this work from the congregations. The limitation for increasing the number of projects, was the church's capacity to follow them up properly, not the lack of money.

When CEIR started its support to the Christian Institute in 1973, this was a result of Norwegian church people's personal knowledge of and respect for Beyers Naudé. Via this institute CEIR got in contact with other organisations connected with it. Some of these became new partners. The Institute also connected CEIR with the Council of Churches. Through SACC' many relations with other organisations, CEIR got to know of other potential recipients of financial support from Norway. Like a spiders web, new potential partners were to be found all over South Africa, and also in Namibia.

"The Old Boys' Network"

The co-operation between the Ministry and CEIR went in a new direction from 1984. From that year onwards the amount of money and the number of projects increased substantially. The reason was partly a need to support the struggle in South Africa that was felt when Tutu came to Norway to receive the Nobel Peace Prize. But more important: that year Bjarne Lindstrøm was appointed general consul in Cape Town. He did not bother much about the rules of diplomacy, but turned the Consulate into a "secret base" for Norwegian financial support to political opposition groups within South Africa. This was done in mutual understanding with the government back home. However, it was not until after 1994 that the parliament got to know the details of the role the Consulate had played.

In the Ministry of Foreign Affairs in Oslo, Knut Vollebæk, working at the Embassy in Zimbabwe, was in charge of Southern African affairs. And in CEIR's office, some few hundred metres away, Bakkevig was taking over the position as secretary-general. These three men, all of them personally committed to the struggle in South Africa, were the architects of CEIR's project work during the last decade of the apartheid regime. It is fair to say that the Consulate was CEIR's "extended secretariat" responsible for staying in close contact with the South African partners.

Apart from this triangle of men (and their successors later on) only the Chairman of CEIR and the political leadership at the Ministry (and probably the South African secret services) knew what was actually going on. Important decisions—both political and financial—were made during informal meetings in Oslo or in Cape Town. There was an unspoken agreement both in the church and in the parliament not to ask too many questions. It was an absolute necessity not to speak loudly about what organisations or individuals received financial support from abroad. Organisations like SACC and other outspoken groups were publicly known, but CEIR also supported organisations whose identity should not become known.

Criteria for project support

The church did not systematically build up its project work in South Africa. According to Bakkevig:

> CEIR did not build up its project portfolio according to a plan. There was no requirement that the projects should be ecclesiastical. Neither could it be denied that the involvement was somewhat shaped by what popped up by chance. The criteria for choosing projects were not very well thought out. Some rules of thumb were followed. The projects were to be able to present accounts and report their activities. In addition, they were required to have a working plan and a budget.[106]

---

[106] Bakkevig, 1996, p. 49.

Recommendations from people whom CEIR trusted for support to an organisation they were familiar with were crucial. In addition staff at the consulate did some investigating and talked with the leaders of the organisations. The secretary-general of CEIR went to South Africa as least twice a year to meet with old and potential partners. These visits also offered opportunities to discuss plans and reports in detail. As a rule CEIR demanded written reports and audited accounts from the partners, but it did happen that such documents were taken away by the police before they were sent to CEIR. In such cases oral reports were accepted. It was a risky business. CEIR channelled more than NOK 250 million to about 100 different organisations and groups over 25 years. Only one case, Allan Boesak's Foundation for Peace and Justice, created problems when it came to the financial reporting.

In addition, representatives from the partner organisation frequently came to Oslo. In 1988, for instance, CEIR received visitors from 20 different partners. These visitors were invited to take part in seminars, services and other events while they stayed in Oslo or travelled to other parts of Norway. Some gave interviews to the media and met with politicians and the different organisations working on Southern African issues. In some cases this led to new alliances and co-operation on concrete projects. The work of SACC and Diakonia was also supported by Norwegian Church Aid and the International Centre at the Norwegian Lutheran Hospital and College. And the Legal Resources Centre in Durban received funds collected during a campaign organised by law students in Norway.

Even if CEIR never had any specific criteria for what kind of projects should be given support, the overall aim for the financial assistance programme was clear. According to Trond Bakkevig:

> It is not the Church of Norway that has achieved things in South Africa. But hopefully our support has made it possible for others to do much. We had confidence that the black organisations could grow in strength. They were responsible for their own situation. Establishing organisations is the most valuable activity we can participate in. Many Western donors wish to show buildings and electricity lines built with their money. But by supporting organisations you are able instead to create a democratic culture that will carry South Africa into the future. That is our special contribution.[107]

Social Change Assistance Trust (SCAT)

Before we go on to describe some of the projects CEIR supported, we need to say something about SCAT, because this trust was established with the help of the Norwegian Consulate and CEIR. SCAT together with the Council of Churches (SACC) was the partner that received the most money from CEIR. The annual support to each of these was approximately NOK 3–6 million.

---

107 T. Bakkevig: *Sammen for demokrati. Norsk støtte i kampen mot apartheid.* Oslo, 1995.

SCAT was an attempt to give Norwegian support to local low-scale projects in Cape Province, especially in the rural areas. It was the result of an initiative from Bjarne Lindstrøm and some white liberals in Cape Town. Applications from local groups were sent to the board of the Trust (Barry Streek, Gordon Young and Di Bishop) which selected the most relevant ones for further presentation. The church considered them and applied to the Ministry for money. The funds were transferred from the ministry to CEIR and then to the Trust which distributed it to the approved organisations.

The first years SCAT was administrated from Streek's home, and he received the applicants in the morning before he started his ordinary work as a journalist at the *Cape Times*. After some time, SCAT got its own office and also hired some administrative staff. At CEIR's request the Board was expanded to include black members.

Via SCAT CEIR was able to support a wide range of projects. Some were local legal advice offices, others were small groups trying to organise black farm labourers. Some arranged workshops on human rights, democracy and women's situation. Co-operatives were also supported. All these organisations had one thing in common: their aim was to assist the population in organising themselves and to take responsibility for the development of their local communities. They also worked to educate ordinary people on the political situation and their human rights, and prepare them for democracy. This was exactly the kind of work CEIR wanted to give priority. Through SCAT and the Norwegian consulate this was possible. Up to 1994 CEIR was SCAT's only donor.

What kind of work did CEIR support apart from the SCAT projects? Some of the projects were church-related like the Christian Institute, SACC and Diakonia, but most of them did not have formal links to churches. It is not possible to go through all the different projects, CEIR supported during 1973–1995, but we will give a few typical examples.

1. Humanitarian and legal support for victims of apartheid

SACC ran several programmes for supporting the victims of apartheid both with humanitarian aid and by offering legal assistance. SACC had special support-programmes for political prisoners and also scholarship programmes for youths. Through SACC's regional offices and field workers this work reached out to the local communities. The Ecumenical Centre in Durban, where among others Diakonia and the Legal Resources Centre were located, was a shelter for people who had experienced violence, rape or other human rights abuses. The centre provided immediate relief, food and humanitarian aid, but it also offered legal assistance.

2. Legal research, monitoring, advocacy, information

The Legal Resources Centre in Durban made regular reports on the human rights situation in Kwa-Zulu/Natal. The Durban centre also studied Kwa-

Zulu's legislation, and did a major job in trying to mediate in the conflict between Inkatha and UDF/ANC groups, even when the conflicts ended up in court. The Legal Resources Centres and the Human Rights Trust in Port Elizabeth also did a lot of work in informing both the South African and international society about the human rights situation and political developments in South Africa and Namibia.

CEIR also supported the film producer Kevin Harris. He made documentaries on the political situation which were distributed internationally to broadcasting companies. This was a way of getting out alternative information in a situation where South African media were under strict regulations. From London, the Namibia Communication Centre, distributed uncensored information on the development in Namibia to the international community.

3. Sex and identity

CEIR considered it to be of great importance to strengthen the feeling of human dignity among oppressed groups of people. Many blacks, particularly women, had experienced that their language, culture and identity had been trampled on by the racist government. CEIR supported some organisations working on these issues, such as the National Language Project in Cape Town and the Health, Education and Welfare Society of South Africa which was run by Neville Alexander. Also local women groups received support from SCAT.

4. Reconciliation work

This kind of work was supported both on the national level through SACC, the Independent Board of Inquiry and the Commission for Truth and Reconciliation, and on the local level through organisations like Diakonia and Crisis Care Centre in Chatsworth outside Durban. A special contribution was, as already mentioned, made by bishop Gunnar Lislerud who was called upon by ELCSA to assist the churches in Natal in solving the difficult and violent situation in this area.

5. Support for the churches' work on human rights and reconciliation

A relatively small part of CEIR's contribution was given to internal church work. The Christian Institute, Ecumenical Advice Bureau (Beyers Naudé and Wolfram Kistner) SACC and Diakonia are all examples of church-related organisations that tried to mobilise the churches to become more active in the struggle against apartheid. This was done through theological research and reflections, but also by bringing church people together and by supporting the different churches or ecumenical organisations nationally or locally in their own work on social-political issues.

6. Preparations for democracy

Almost all the organisations that CEIR supported were in one way or another involved in democracy building. CEIR contributed to this work by supporting the establishment of local and national democratically run organisations. CEIR also supported organisations working to promote democracy by other means, for instance the Institute for Democratic Alternatives in South Africa (IDASA).

7. Voter education, monitoring and observing elections

CEIR supported the Ecumenical Monitoring Programme of South Africa, organised by SACC and the Catholic Bishops' Conference in cooperation with the WCC. The Namibia Council of Churches' programme "Repatriation, Resettlement and Rehabilitation" also received financial support from CEIR. CEIR sent Norwegian church people to observe elections, both in South Africa and Namibia. CEIR also supported some organisations (for instance the Matla Trust) that in many different ways worked to prepare for elections by teaching voters how a democratic election was going to be arranged.

Outside Southern Africa

CEIR in a few and very special cases offered some South Africans assistance either in Norway or in other countries. This was in cases when individuals (or family members) had to leave South Africa for political reasons, were in need of medical treatment or just needed some rest far away from their home country. CEIR was allowed to use money granted by the government for these purposes as well.

"White Angels"

Almost all the funds from CEIR were sent to recipients in South Africa and Namibia by ordinary bank transfer. This money was openly referred to in CEIR's accounts. However, the name of the account did not always belong to the one who received the money in the end. From 1986, CEIR also started to transfer money in other ways. This money was not accounted for. When Bakkevig and Sommerfeldt travelled to South Africa they brought with them travellers' cheques and cash. The secretary-generals could hide as much as NOK 100,000 in small notes under their clothes. Every ticket, customs or passport control made them pale. All in all, more than NOK 2.2 million (10% of the total transfer) was brought into South Africa this way.

The background for this untraditional and also illegal transfer of money was the critical situation in South Africa during the State of Emergency. The money from the church was given to individuals (and their families) who were in extreme situations, for instance hiding from the police. Some of them needed money immediately to escape from the country. Money was also needed for funerals. The Norwegians did not personally meet these people, but handed the money over to Beyers Naudé whom they trusted a hundred percent. Naudé signed for the money he received and reported to the church how it was used. For security reasons he never gave away any names of the recipients. With the use of small committees, with two or three persons he trusted, in different areas of South Africa, Naudé managed to get the money out to those who needed it most.

When CEIR in 1985 asked the Ministry of Foreign Affairs for permission to use some of the money granted to the church for this purpose, and without accounting for it, Foreign Minster Svenn Stray was at first sceptical to this method, but agreed to approve it. Formally it was the church's own money, even it the Government provided it and accepted the use of it. It therefore was the responsibility of the church to transfer money illegally into South Africa. CEIR's chairman and secretary-general were the only church people who knew about it. The rest of CEIR's staff and council members knew that something was going on, but nobody asked about it.

It was not until after the change of government in South Africa that this became publicly known, when the journalist Tomm Kristiansen wrote a book which made Atle Sommerfeldt and Trond Bakkevig into heroes.[108] The story was also presented in some of the national papers. In 1995 Bakkevig published a book on CEIR's work on South Africa, and he told the story in his own words on television in 1997. For the first time Naudé's name was mentioned, and Bakkevig was now able to reveal some details. The title of the programme was "White Angels". Bakkevig and Sommerfeldt tried to focus on those who really took the risk, their contact persons in South Africa, and most of all those who got the money in the end.

Conclusions—"White Angels" and everyday heroes

> We may safely be proud of the role the Council has played and know that this role is well acknowledged in South Africa.[109]

With these words, secretary-general Atle Sommerfeldt concluded his report from the visit to South Africa in May 1994, when he had been a guest at Mandela's inauguration as President. There is no doubt that he expressed a general feeling among those who had been involved in CEIR's work on Southern Africa. But to what extent does this feeling correspond to reality? This article has not tried to answer that question. CEIR's partners often stated that the support from Norway, both the financial but not least the moral one, was extremely important. They appreciated the urgent action taken by the church and its unbureaucratic and flexible procedures. They

---

[108] Tomm Kristansen: *Mandelas land*. Oslo: Cappelen, 1995.

[109] A. Sommerfeldt, Report from South Africa, 2–12 May 1994, concluding remarks, CEIR-archives.

also appreciated the attitude the Norwegians showed in trusting their partners, and their emphasis on supporting democratic organisations. But to answer the question of the effect of CEIR's support a more comprehensive investigation must be undertaken.

This article has shown that it was for theological and moral reasons the
church involved itself in the question of apartheid. It became an essential
part of the message of the church to reject the racist ideology of apartheid.
The commitment of the international ecumenical movement inspired the
Church of Norway. The combination of requests from both LWF and WCC
for more concrete action on human rights, the call for solidarity from
churches and liberation movements in Southern Africa, initiatives from anti-
apartheid groups in Norway, and the Norwegian churches' own theological
reflection on questions of social ethics shaped their commitment to the
struggle for liberation in Southern Africa. Experiences drawn from the part-
nership with African churches in their turn enriched the liturgy and the
Norwegian churches' understanding of the Gospel.

The churches had important advantages compared to other organisations. Even in extreme political situations, like liberation wars or states of
emergency, the churches were able to work legally. Outspoken church leaders and activist were detained or had to escape from their home country, but
the church itself was never banned. Local congregations were to be found all
over Southern Africa, and no other NGOs had the same access to the international community. This, together with the churches' strong theological
commitment to the rejection of the ideology of apartheid, gave the churches
a unique role. With this background the Norwegian churches were able to
contribute to the struggle against apartheid.

In Norway CEIR transferred the largest part of the money which the
Ministry of Foreign Affairs provided for Norwegian organisations to be
forwarded to opposition groups within South Africa and Namibia. This was
possible due to the general political agreement between the church and government on the policy towards apartheid. It was a also a result of the good
working and personal relationship between the key persons in CEIR, the
Ministry and the Norwegian Consulate in Cape Town. Even though the
church worked closely with the government, it was always conscious of its
role as a church with independent responsibility for its involvement in
apartheid.

The church itself did not wish to exaggerate the effects of its work to
destroy the policy of apartheid. The "White Angels" only assisted the people
of Southern Africa in their own struggle for freedom. By prayers, moral and
financial support and political lobby work, the church gave a contribution to
their struggle. The real heroes were all those, who in spite of the brutal
oppression from the racist regime, believed in freedom and worked for it at
the risk of their own lives.

List of the main projects supported by CEIR

Johannesburg area/national

African Independent Church Association
African Scholarship Programme
Black Community Programmes
Black Consciousness Movement
Black Parents' Association, Soweto
Christian Instate
Ecumenical Advice Bureau
Ecumenical Monitoring Programme of South Africa
Inanda Schools /SAIIR/ Woodmead
Independent Board of Inquiry into Informal Repression
Institute for Democratic Alternatives in South Africa
Institute of Race Relations
Kevin Harris Productions
Matla Trust
Open School Project
South African Council of Churches
The Truth and Reconciliation Committee

Durban area

Crisis Care Centre
Diakonia
Ecumenical Centre Trust
Ecumenical Bursary Fund
Legal Resources Centre
Race Relations Educational Trust

Cape area

Black Sash
Co-ordinated Action for Battered Women
Foundation for Peace and Justice
Grahamstown Rural Committee
Health, Education and Welfare Society of South Africa
Mission of the Churches for Community Development
National Language Project
Social Change Assistance Trust
Vassen & Co
Western Cape Relief Fund
World Council on Religion and Peace

Other areas

AFESIS, East London
Human Rights Trust, Port Elizabeth

Namibia

Diocese of Namibia: St. Georges, St. Mary, Onekwanya School
Legal Assistance Centre
Namibia Communication Centre, London
Namibia Council of Churches

Chapter 8
Trade Union Support to the Struggle Against Apartheid: The Role of the Norwegian Confederation of Trade Unions

Vesla Vetlesen

Introduction

Equal rights, regardless of ethnic origin, represent a corner stone of trade unionism. The apartheid system, built on racism and inhuman suppression of the black population, was bound to be fought by the trade unions—internationally as well as by the individual, national unions world wide.

What first triggered off the direct involvement of LO, the Norwegian Confederation of Trade Unions, was an international consumer boycott of South African goods, initiated in 1959 by ICFTU, the International Confederation of Free Trade Unions. As a First of May slogan LO launched an appeal to the consumers not to buy South African fruit, vegetables, wine or brandy in a four month period from May to August 1960.[1] The effect was remarkable as this import of fruit and vegetables to Norway in the said period went down from NOK 10.7 million in 1959 to 0.5 million in 1960.[2] The other Nordic trade unions carried out similar actions as well as unions in 30 other countries.

Even though LO throughout the following years expressed its condemnation of the apartheid system in resolutions and statements, it was not until the mid-1970s that LO got involved in systematic and continuous anti-apartheid work. At a meeting called by the Nordic Trade Union Council in Oslo in 1974[3] a joint Nordic committee was set up to follow the situation in South Africa closely and to come forward with proposals for action. The same year ICFTU established their Co-ordinating Committee for South Africa. A growing public opinion in Norway against apartheid was reflected in a number of resolutions from local trade unions. When LO in 1976 decided to launch its broad campaign against apartheid, it was based on support from rank and file members as well as on Nordic and international trade union co-operation.

---

[1] *Fri Fagbevegelse*, 1960, issue 4 and 6.

[2] Ole Kristian Eivindson, 1997, *Norge og Sør-Afrika 1945–60*, unpublished thesis, Department of History, University of Oslo.

[3] Minutes from the meeting 12 March 1974, "NFS'arbeidsgruppe for Sør-Afrika."

Together with other unions and co-ordinated by the ICFTU, LO contributed to the economic support of the South African trade unions. As we will see below this financial assistance—as well as the moral and political support—had a significant impact on the rapid growth of the trade union movement in South Africa and thus served to build up one of the most important forces in the fight against apartheid.

Campaigning against apartheid

The campaigns were carried out in close co-operation between LO and the Norwegian labour movement as a whole.[4] The organisations involved beside LO were the Labour Party (DNA), the International Solidarity Committee of the Norwegian Labour Movement (AIS), the Workers Educational Association (AOF), the Norwegian People's Aid (Norsk Folkehjelp), the Norwegian Labour Youth (AUF) and the Young Pioneers (Framfylkingen).

The aims of the campaign as formulated in 1976, were:
- To influence the Norwegian public opinion through information, thereby preparing a platform for stronger economic and political action against South Africa.
- To raise funds in support of the liberation movements and the trade unions in Southern Africa as well as for humanitarian aid to the victims of apartheid.

It was evident from the very start that the campaign would have to be a long term one, and with varying levels of intensity it went on for nearly twenty years. The slogan "Solidarity with Southern Africa" indicates that the campaign was not concentrated on South Africa alone, but included Zimbabwe where the liberation struggle was becoming more and more intense, as well as Namibia which was still occupied by South Africa.

The labour movement utilised all its organisational channels to distribute the information material. Leaflets, posters and other printed matter about apartheid, South Africa and the neighbouring states were in 1976–77 sent to all trade union branches. Together with the leaflets were included appeals for fund-raising: Join us in assisting the victims of apartheid! The answer from the grassroots was thousands of contributions amounting to nearly NOK 1.0 million, the main part granted by trade unions. Alongside the money came resolutions demanding political and economic actions against the apartheid-regime in South Africa.

Another slogan in the campaign was: "Show your solidarity—stop buying South African goods!" Fruits and wines were the main targets for the consumer boycott. The Norwegian Consumers Co-operative stopped all imports from South Africa for a year.

---

[4] Vesla Vetlesen: *Frihet for Sør-Afrika. LO og kampen mot apartheid.* Oslo: Tiden Norsk Forlag, 1998, pp. 14–28.

A trade union boycott was implemented at the Wine Monopoly, the state owned company which in Norway at that time monopolised the import of wine and brandy. The Wine Monopoly workers refused to handle South African goods, and LO together with the relevant unions, formalised the action by informing the Executive Board of the Wine Monopoly about the boycott. A letter of 22 December 1976 to Ko-operative Wijnbrowers Vereiningen van Zuid-Afrika, signed by the treasurer general of LO, Einar Strand, informed the company that the boycott would take effect as from 5 January 1977. This boycott, initiated by the trade unions and accepted by the Board of Directors of the Wine Monopoly, was kept up from 1977 to 1994 in which period no wine or brandy was imported from South Africa to Norway.

The campaign continued in 1978–79 when further material was produced and distributed. A number of meetings focusing on South Africa and the struggle against apartheid and colonialism were held in local branches all over the country. Again the result was hundreds of resolutions from trade unions condemning apartheid and granting funds for the liberation movements and for the black trade unions.

Under the slogan "Freedom to Southern Africa" the campaign was revitalised in 1981. Several new brochures, going deeper into the apartheid question, were produced in addition to leaflets and posters. A full time secretary was employed to run the campaign. However, this time South Africa was overshadowed by the events in Poland where the government clamped down on the trade union Solidarnosc and declared a state of emergency. The secretary of the South Africa campaign was re-directed to deal with relief assistance to Polish workers.

However, the campaigns for South Africa were later to be continued with fundraising and solidarity meetings. LO and the other labour organisations would mostly carry out their separate arrangements without involving "outsiders", but on the occasion of Bishop Desmond Tutu receiving the Nobel Peace Prize in 1984, a large meeting was held together with the Norwegian Council for Southern Africa (Fellesrådet for det sørlige Afrika) and the Norwegian Church Council. A similar joint arrangement conducted by the trade unions, the Church and the Solidarity Council was held in 1986 to mark the visit of Nelson Mandela's daughter, Zenani Dhlamini.

In 1985–86 the campaign was re-launched, this time concentrating on South Africa only, under the slogan "Freedom to South Africa". Again a campaign secretary was engaged, and again several hundred thousand leaflets and posters were spread. Local trade union branches put the apartheid question on the agenda, and an information kit specifically produced for students in secondary school was distributed in great numbers.

The demand for the release of Nelson Mandela, who had at that time been imprisoned for more than twenty years, was emphasised and a postcard action to this end was part of the campaign. 70,000 postcards were to be sent to the prison with the following text: "Dear Nelson Mandela. Please accept from a friend in the Norwegian labour movement the best wishes for your future. I want you to know that I work for your immediate release as well as for release of all other political and trade union prisoners in South Africa. ... Best regards ... " This mail action had however to be postponed. According to a press release from LO of 5 December 1985 the reason was—ironically enough—that an international post and telegraph boycott against South Africa was being carried out at this time. A month later though, the cards were mailed. The campaign coincided with big upheavals in South Africa as the strikes in the mining industry took place at that very time. The unions in Norway sent numerous contributions to a strike fund for the miners, and the fundraising gave more than NOK 1 million.

A special fund raising campaign for Namibia—in support of SWAPO and the National Union of Namibian Workers—was carried out in 1989, the same year in which general elections were held in Namibia, leading to independence the following year.

In addition to the campaigns described above, which were all centrally monitored by LO and the other organisations within the labour movement, there were also numerous initiatives taken by individual unions and local branches.

The campaigns were hardly mentioned by the mass media, except by the labour press. However, the impact was notable in particular on the attitudes of rank and file members of the labour organisations. In this respect the campaigns contributed—together with information activities and actions carried out by other organisations—to building a strong public opinion against apartheid. The Norwegian population at large obtained a fairly high level of knowledge about apartheid, and even more so a hardened emotional attitude against apartheid, which was important as a base for the political and economic actions taken by the Norwegian government against South Africa.

The rise of the South African trade union movement

The period in question—from the early 1970s to the 1990s—saw a tremendous growth in the trade union field in South Africa, as the workers—particularly the black workers—were struggling for their rights to form their organisations and their rights to collective bargaining—in line with international labour standards but incompatible with the apartheid system.

Trade unions as a free and non-racial movement were close to non-existent at the end of the 1960s. Apartheid legislation divided the working class according to race, and a union with members of different "colours" would not be officially recognised. As for black workers they were recommended to join so-called "parallel" unions assigned to white unions which had exclusive bargaining rights on behalf of blacks.

The non-racial union SACTU, South African Trade Union Congress, allied to ANC, suffered harassment and oppression from the apartheid regime since 1960. Although SACTU was never banned, as was the case with the liberation movements ANC and PAC, SACTU could not operate openly and function as a proper trade union any more, and the leadership of SACTU went in exile. Other unions were also persecuted. Figures from 1969 show that only 14 independent unions with a membership of approximately 14,000 black workers survived the suppression.[5]

In protest against inhuman and unfair working conditions a wave of illegal strikes involving 100,000 black workers took place in 1972–73. This marked the starting point of a revitalisation of unionism amongst "non-white" workers. These unions—although unregistered and with no bargaining rights—were nevertheless from time to time able to achieve results, to improve the wages and working conditions through informal negotiations and signing of local agreements with employers. The first non-racial, unregistered union to sign a collective agreement was the National Union of Textile Workers in 1974, covering the workers—mostly blacks—at Smith & Nephew, a subsidiary of the British based company. The employers, however, refused to renew the agreement in 1977. Only after trade union pressure was brought to bear on the mother company by the British and international trade union movement was the agreement renewed in 1978.[6] Other cases of international trade union actions to pressurise multinational companies to respect the workers' rights are described below.

The struggle for recognition of trade union rights was supported by "workers' institutes". About 10 such institutes were established all over the country—Urban Training Centre in Johannesburg, Western Province Workers' Advice Bureau in Cape Town and Trade Union Advisory and Co-ordinating Council in Durban, to mention a few of them. At these centres progressive white students and other resource persons assisted in training and educating a new generation of black workers. The legal advice from experts at these centres also played an important role in supporting black workers to achieve their limited labour rights.

The Black Consciousness Movement (BCM), stimulated by the liberation of Mozambique and Angola in 1975, had an important impact on the attitudes of the black population, including the trade unions. The patience of the suppressed black population was about to run out. When the police massacre of children and young students took place in Soweto in 1976, this triggered off strong reactions all over the world, but, naturally, even more so in South Africa itself. The Soweto massacre marked the beginning of the

---

[5] Vesla Vetlesen: *Sør-afrikanske arbeidere i kamp for sine rettigheter.* Oslo: LO/AIS/Norsk Folke-hjelp, 1981, p. 6.

[6] ICFTU, *African Workers Under Apartheid,* Brussels, 1978, p. 27; Roger Southall: *Imperialism or Solidarity? International Labour and South African Trade Unions.* Cape Town: UCT Press, 1995, p. 247.

end of apartheid, as the militancy of the black population flamed up never to die again. This militancy was strongly reflected in the black trade union movement resulting in strikes, stay-aways and demonstrations. The apartheid regime reacted with increased suppression of trade union organisers and activists, who were arrested, banned and harassed.

Strikes and unrest in the labour force in the late 1970s compelled the government to look for reforms. Not only were the workers struggling for their rights, but even spokesmen of the employers demanded reforms as economic growth was hampered by the rigid apartheid regulations. In addition the international community increased its pressure on the apartheid regime in the aftermath of the Soweto massacre. As a result the government in 1977 appointed a commission under the leadership of professor Nic Wiehahn, The Commission of Inquiry into Labour Legislation, which came up with certain recommendations. Two years later the Industrial Conciliation Amendment Act was adopted. Imperfect as this act still was, it nevertheless gave organisational and bargaining rights to black unions on certain conditions, and the organising of black workers was strongly stimulated.

The time was ripe to unite the many non-racial and black unions in one single federation. However, ideological differences and disagreements on strategies resulted in the formation of two national centres. FOSATU, Federation of South African Trade Unions, was formed in 1979 with 13 affiliated unions representing 60,000 members—mostly black workers, but also white, Indian and coloured. CUSA, Council of Unions of South Africa, was launched in 1980 with 8 affiliates and a membership of some 36,000. CUSA rejected whites in their leadership. Some unions still remained independent of these two national centres.[7]

The major task of organising black workers in the mining industry still remained. In this field organising had previously been prohibited by the employers, The Chamber of Mines, by denying organisers any access to the production premises or dormitories. Continuous labour unrest, however, convinced the employers that it would be better to deal with unions than with unorganised workers. CUSA initiated the formation of NUM, National Union of Mineworkers, in 1982. The Norwegian LO contributed at the very start NOK 100,000, sufficient money to employ an organiser, Cyril Ramaphosa, and provide him with transport. During the first year 20,000 workers already had joined the union, and the next year the membership had increased to 110,000. The miners had started their march in the ranks of organised workers.

As the political situation in South Africa in the mid-1980s was characterised by increasing resistance against apartheid and with the formation of United Democratic Front, UDF, new constellations also developed in the trade union movement. Negotiations took place to try to merge the two

---

[7] Vesla Vetlesen, 1981, op. cit., pp. 7–9.

centres, FOSATU and CUSA, as well as other independent unions which had been formed on community bases rather than along traditional industrial lines. The unions had become increasingly politicised, and in particular within FOSATU the support for ANC became more obvious, as was also the case with the "community unions". However, political and strategic disagreements once again made it impossible to gather all the different unions in one single federation.

COSATU, Congress of South African Trade Unions, was formed in 1985 by FOSATU, a number of "community unions" and the miners' union NUM, which had previously left CUSA. With about 400,000 members right from the start, COSATU soon became the dominant workers' organisation and a decisive force in the fight against apartheid. COSATU developed its connections with ANC and the exile leadership of SACTU[8], and joined the UDF in 1989. When SACTU was dissolved in 1990, COSATU signed a cooperation agreement with ANC and SACP, the South African Communist Party.[9]

NACTU, National Council of Trade Unions, was formed in 1986, by the remains of CUSA and some independent unions, representing 200,000 members. NACTU, which affiliated to ICFTU, sympathised with PAC and the Black Consciousness Movement, although no formalised connections existed.

The years following the reorganisation of the labour movement in 1985–86 were marked by a great number of large strikes, partly political and partly wage conflicts. The strikes in the mining industries, following a breakdown in wages negotiations, were particularly violent and cost many lives. Workers on strike were assaulted and killed by police forces, and there were also incidents of workers killing strike-breakers.[10] Through negotiations and strikes the workers were able to increase their real income in the period 1987–90. While the inflation was close to 14% the rise in the nominal wages exceeded 20%.[11] In other cases millions of workers stayed away in political demonstrations, as was the case in 1986 to celebrate the First of May which at that time was not a public holiday. The largest mobilisation however took place in 1992 when 4 million workers stayed away in protest against the position of the government during the negotiations between the government and ANC. As the negotiations were about to collapse, they were brought back on track by the pressure of mass movements where the trade unions played a decisive role.[12]

---

[8] Communiqué from Meeting between COSATU, SACTU and ANC, Lusaka, 7 March 1986.

[9] Letter from COSATU 24/3/90, "To all friendly organisations." Liv Tørres: *Ny hverdag for sørafrikanske arbeidere*. Oslo: LO, 1995, p. 24.

[10] Jeremy Baskin: *Striking Back. A History of COSATU*. Johannesburg: Ravan Press, 1991, pp. 178, 224–239.

[11] Ibid., p. 307.

[12] Nelson Mandela: *Veien til frihet*. Oslo: Aschehough, 1994, pp. 585–587.

During these turbulent times the government of South Africa declared a state of emergency leading to mass arrests of trade union leaders and activists. The COSATU head office was blown up, and branch offices were exposed to armed attacks. Despite the violent onslaughts and all the obstacles which made normal trade union activities so difficult, the unions continued to grow. The organisations increased their striking power and the membership was in the early 1990s close to two million.

Direct links to the South African trade unions

In the initial phase of LO's co-operation with and support of the South African trade unions, the ICFTU played a key role. LO did not traditionally have close contacts with these unions, and the ICFTU Co-ordinating Committee on South Africa served as an important meeting place. Representatives from the South African unions would usually be present in Brussels during these meetings. Furthermore, clandestine meetings took place in South Africa's neighbouring countries as trade union activists sneaked across the border and met with representatives of LO and other unions.[13]

In the 1970s and early 1980s South African trade unionists kept a very low profile when abroad and their opinions would not be exposed through the media or in public. Their most important task was the organising inside South Africa, not to give statements and declarations from abroad. Yet—as a rule—they were likely to be interrogated or arrested on their return to Johannesburg airport. As the South African trade unions gained strength from the mid 1980s, the representatives increased their travelling and frequently visited Europe, including Norway, as well as USA. The risk of being arrested on their return had not diminished, but nevertheless, they now gave interviews to the various media. In the late 1980s they would even publicly appeal to other countries to impose sanctions on South Africa.[14]

The direct links between LO and the unions in South Africa were hampered by the fact that representatives of LO were never allowed visas to visit the country, that is not until 1986. Even at that time a visa was only obtained by mediation of the ICFTU, as the International Secretary of LO, Kaare Sandegren, then was a member of an ICFTU delegation. It would probably have been possible to obtain a tourist visa, but it was the policy of LO to play with open cards and not to hide the real purpose of a visit. Any type of visit to South Africa was however strongly condemned by spokesmen of some liberation movements. In particular the exile leadership of SACTU, South African Trade Union Congress, used harsh words. Over and over again SACTU warned LO against such visits, which they regarded as tantamount to collaboration with the apartheid regime. SACTU, even though in exile, wanted exclusive rights as spokesmen for the South African

---

[13] Report of the ICFTU/Nordic delegation to Southern Africa, 3–18 November 1978.

[14] *LO-aktuelt*, 1 February 1989. Interview with Cyril Ramaphosa.

workers, and they launched the slogan "Direct links stink!", addressed to overseas unions that wanted to develop contacts with unions inside South Africa.[15]

The Swedish trade unions kept closer direct contacts with the South African unions than the Norwegian LO did. In particular this was the case for the Swedish Metal Workers' Union, a consequence of Swedish companies having subsidiaries in South Africa.[16] Further the International Metal Workers' Federation played an important role in building a contact network, as did also the other International Trade Secretariats together with ICFTU.

After the formation of COSATU in 1985 LO participated in regular meetings with this organisation either in one of the Nordic countries or in the Netherlands as part of the assistance programme. At such meetings COSATU's general secretary would normally be present, and sometimes also the chairman and other leaders. This gave an excellent opportunity to discuss policy questions as well as economic aid, and thus to increase LO's familiarity with the situation in South Africa.

Nordic and international co-ordination

With regard to the policy towards South Africa the Nordic Trade Union Council, NTUC, functioned as a co-ordinating body for the Nordic unions, and in 1974 a special committee for this purpose was, as mentioned above, set up. In March 1977 NTUC adopted a "14-point programme regarding South Africa". The programme was formulated as demands to the Nordic governments to sharpen the sanctions, to stop investments and increase assistance to the liberation movements and to the black trade unions. The "14-point programme" was revised in 1979, it being added that the Nordic governments should work for a UN oil embargo and map the Nordic transport and traffic to South Africa in preparation for sanctions. The programme was again revised and further concretised in 1985.[17] Parallel to this trade union programme the Nordic governments adopted their "Programme of action on South Africa" in 1978. On this basis the unions had a continuous dialogue with the governments. When the Nordic Ministers of Foreign Affairs had their regular meetings representatives for the unions would be allowed to present their views and demands.

Prior to meetings in ICFTU the Nordic unions would often consult each other, and thereafter they would speak with one voice on policy matters in the international fora. The Dutch trade union organisation FNV would usu-

---

[15] LO reports from meetings with SACTU, Geneva 13–16 November 1979, and Zambia 17 October–2 November 1982. SACTU's publication *Workers' Unity*, Issue No. 30, 1982; Issue No. 40, 1984.

[16] Sven Fockstedt: *Facket i Sydafrika*. Stockholm: LO/TCO, 1985, pp. 11–16.

[17] Minutes of NTUC board meetings, 8 March 1977, 24 April 1979, and 29 August 1985.

ally take the same stand as the Nordic ones. This constellation of Dutch and Nordic unions was sometimes in the ICFTU context referred to as "the progressives".[18] The Canadian union CLC would also generally join this constellation—thus forming a group of "like-minded organisations" that would press for a policy of action in the fight against apartheid. On one occasion however, it came to serious confrontations between "the progressives" and some of the other ICFTU affiliates—that was about assistance to COSATU, as described below.

In other international fora, such as ILO, the International Labour Organisation, the Nordic unions would again co-ordinate their positions in the Special Committee on Apartheid. South Africa was on a yearly basis also on the agenda of the ILO plenary meeting, and a representative from one of the Nordic unions would then speak on behalf of them all, some times also including FNV of the Netherlands.

The ICFTU was involved in a broad engagement against apartheid. In the mid-1970s ICFTU started to publish lists of companies with investments in South Africa. The lists were kept updated and used as a means to keep the firms under surveillance and force them to recognise the rights of black workers. When conflicts arose in South African subsidiaries, ICFTU would in co-operation with the International Trade Secretariat in question mobilise world wide support for the South African workers and put pressure on the mother company. Such campaigns were organised against Unilever, Glacier Metal & Co and British Tyre & Rubber Co—to mention a few. Furthermore ICFTU put lots of effort into its work to improve the Codes of Conduct regarding investments in South Africa. Such codes were in the late 1970s adopted by Great Britain, EC, Canada and USA. The codes advised the multinationals to implement equal rights regardless of colour and enjoined the companies to report on wages and working conditions in their South African subsidiaries. However, no penalty was inflicted when the codes were broken. In some cases the codes, nevertheless, could be used to pressurise the companies to respect trade union rights.

Acting as a watchdog ICFTU would immediately inform its affiliates when trade unionists were arrested, with the result that trade unions all over the world would react—particularly so if lives were at risk. The case of Neil Aggett awoke particular strong reactions when he in 1982 after being taken into custody and interrogated was found dead in his cell at the John Vorster Square police headquarters in Johannesburg. The South African unions reacted with a stop work action while protests from unions in other countries were sent in great number to the South African authorities. Among others arrested at that time was the well known trade union organiser Emma Mashinini, who was placed in Aggett's neighbouring cell and also suffered hard interrogation and harassments. After her release she was

---

[18] Anna Oulatar, oral information, November 1996.

treated at the clinic for torture victims in Denmark and then returned to South Africa to continue her trade union work.

The ICFTU Co-ordinating Committee on South Africa functioned as a clearing centre to decide which unions and institutes in South Africa should be entitled to receive economic assistance from ICFTU. Representatives for approximately 10 national trade unions would usually meet in the Committee, as well as representatives of some International Trade Secretariats. The Nordic and Dutch unions were represented on a regular basis. Their influence was considerable, the reason partly being that the main bulk of the money came from these unions which had access to official financing in their respective countries. The members of the Co-ordinating Committee usually agreed on which unions should receive assistance. It has been claimed that the Committee was not sufficiently selective, thus giving—if only minor—assistance to some new unions without a firm membership basis, and which eventually turned out to compete with already established unions.[19] But by and large the assistance was channelled to those unions which later on formed the national centres COSATU and NACTU. Assistance however, was never given to Inkatha Freedom Party unions or to unions in exile such as SACTU and the PAC-connected ATUCC.

Prior to the launching of COSATU in 1985 a rather important meeting took place in the ICFTU Co-ordinating Committee.[20] Present at the meeting to inform about the planned new organisation were representatives of the two main founding unions, Alec Erwin—Secretary General of FOSATU, and Cyril Ramaphosa—Secretary General of NUM. Further the Secretary General of CUSA, Piroshaw Camay, and Tyrone August of MWASA, the Media Workers Association of South Africa, were present. In the ICFTU minutes from the meeting it says: "Arising out of the discussion on COSATU's future relations with the ICFTU, the Committee noted that ICFTU assistance would be welcome on the same principles as in the past."

Contrary to the assumptions of the Committee, the founding congress of COSATU however, took the position that no assistance from ICFTU would be accepted, only bilateral contributions from national unions approved by COSATU. This stand of COSATU, as well as the reactions within ICFTU, has to be seen in the light of—or rather in the shadow of—the cold war. The international trade union movement was divided into two main blocks, the ICFTU and the communist dominated WFTU, World Federation of Trade Unions. Although both organisations had a clear stand against apartheid, there was next to no co-operation between them on the issue. The fight against apartheid was characterised by competition between the two centres, in line with their general competition for influence and recruitment of affiliates, in particular in the third world—including South Africa itself.

---

[19] Roger Southall, 1995, op.cit., p. 178; Jan Teron, oral information, November 1996.

[20] Minutes from the 26th Meeting of the ICFTU Co-ordinating Committee for South Africa, 7–8 November 1985.

The founding unions of COSATU had, as described above, during recent years developed a closer relationship with ANC, SACTU (an affiliate of WFTU) and SACP, the South African Communist Party. On the other hand the American trade union federation AFL/CIO, with its anti-communist traditions and attitudes, had re-affiliated to ICFTU after having withdrawn in the period 1969–1982. Following this re-affiliation the Nordic unions, as well as some other unions, might have been of the opinion that AFL/CIO from time to time had a disproportionally strong influence on ICFTU policies.

After the foundation of COSATU the ICFTU again called a meeting of the Co-ordinating Committee[21] to discuss the new situation. The Secretary General of the ICFTU, Johnny Vanderveken, opened the meeting by saying that COSATU had refused to receive any funding from ICFTU. "The reason given by COSATU", he said, "was that there are 'good' and 'bad' organisations within ICFTU, and money from 'bad' organisations (read: AFL/CIO) cannot be accepted by COSATU." The Secretary General himself stated that he would not accept that an outsider should tell the ICFTU which affiliates were "good" and which were "bad" and thus divide the confederation.

There were speakers at the meeting, among these Patrick O'Farrell, the representative of AFL/CIO, who recommended that ICFTU should not take a stand on the financing issue immediately, but rather wait for some weeks or months: COSATU needs the money, and they will soon beg for it and accept it even if it comes from ICFTU, it was said.

The Nordic unions together with the Dutch however, took the stand that there should not be any delay in their support of COSATU. Even if they disagreed with the reasons given by COSATU, the decision taken by COSATU not to receive money from the ICFTU had to be respected. Any stop or delay in the financing of COSATU at this crucial time of the struggle in South Africa would only be to the benefit of the apartheid regime. This should not be allowed to happen. Adding to the tension at the meeting was the suspicion that AFL/CIO supported the Inkatha union UWUSA. This was denied by the American representative, but the fact remained that the George Meany Prize a couple of years before had been rewarded by AFL/CIO to the leader of Inkatha, Mangosuti Buthelezi. This act was strongly condemned by several representatives at the meeting.

To act bilaterally concerning the assistance was contrary to the policy of the Nordic unions. International co-ordination was necessary to avoid double financing of the various organisations, since considerable amounts of money and a number of donor sources were involved. The solution found was that the Nordic unions together with the Dutch formed a "donors' group" which negotiated directly with COSATU. When agreements were

[21] Handwritten notes by the author from the meeting of the ICFTU Co-ordinating Committee on South Africa, 19 March 1986.

reached on the COSATU budget, it would be presented to the ICFTU Co-ordinating Committee.

It should be added that the relationship between COSATU and ICFTU improved after some time. A definite change for the better occurred with the collapse of the Soviet Union, after which communism was no longer regarded as a threat to the free, democratic labour movement. In 1997 COSATU actually applied for affiliation to the ICFTU, and was accepted with acclamation.

Economic assistance to the unions

Without the substantial economic—and moral—support from abroad it would not have been possible for the South African trade union movement to expand as fast as it did in the 1970s and 1980s and thus become capable of playing such a decisive role in the defeat of the apartheid system. The assistance from abroad should, however, not in any sense be allowed to diminish the role played by the African workers themselves. They were the ones who fought on the barricades and bore the burdens of the battle.

The ICFTU assistance programme for South Africa, established in 1975, grew from a yearly amount of some NOK 2–3 million to NOK 15–20 million in the mid-1980s. The Norwegian contribution to the programme varied in this 10 year period from 12% to 15% of the total amount, the Swedish, Danish and Dutch unions being the other main contributors to the programme. In this period practically all the assistance from LO was channelled through the ICFTU.

After 1986, when the Nordic and Dutch unions transferred some of the assistance directly to COSATU, their share of the ICFTU programme diminished. They still continued, however, to be among the biggest contributors only second to the European Community which by now came up with considerable economic grants to the South African unions, thus keeping the ICFTU programme on the same high level of NOK 15–20 million a year.[22]

The ICFTU followed a rather strict regime regarding reporting and accounting from the recipient institutes and organisations. The South African trade unionists, experiencing urgent needs when the leaders and members were arrested and banned or when other critical situations occurred, may have regarded the ICFTU demand for updated accounting as a bit too rigid. In the ICFTU Co-ordinating Committee too disagreements arose when donor organisations like the Nordic ones urged that the ICFTU should transfer money without delay to the waiting organisations, even if the accounting for the last transfer was not satisfactory. The strict accounting system was, however, a necessity considering the sizeable amounts of money involved, the bulk of which came from official sources.

---

[22] ICFTU, *Report of the Fifteenth World Congress*, Brussels, 1992, pp. 286–289.

All trade union assistance from ICFTU was transferred through banks and accounted for by the recipients.[23] The South African authorities never confiscated such assistance, but from time to time they blocked the bank accounts of the unions for periods, thus delaying or interrupting union activities.

The ICFTU assistance programme for South Africa no doubt is the single largest one in the history of trade unionism. When Roger Southall, the author of *Imperialism or Solidarity*, in 1995 is discussing the assistance at large, his conclusions are: "None the less, what remains the most distinctive and vital aspect of the ICFTU's programme was its early recognition of the democratic unions from the moment that they began to emerge and develop in the 1970s. In contrast to those to its left who called for the total isolation of South Africa and who queried the legitimacy and viability of the new wave of Black trade unionism, the ICFTU stepped in and lent the fledgling movement critical moral and material support during its perhaps most difficult days. Indeed, it can be unambiguously stated that such was the extent of their initial dependence upon this funding, that the emerging unions could scarcely have achieved the extent of their organisational reach without it."[24]

When LO from 1986 onwards transferred the assistance directly to COSATU, it was, as mentioned, still co-ordinated through a "donors' group" consisting of the Danish, Norwegian, Swedish and Dutch unions, later on to be joined by the Finnish. To monitor the assistance to COSATU, whose budget was in 1988–94 amounting to some NOK 20 million a year, the respective unions in the group provided in turn the secretarial functions.

The economic assistance from LO to the South African trade union movement in the period 1975 to 1996 amounted to NOK 85 million, out of which NOK 75 million came from official sources, namely the Norwegian Ministry of Foreign Affairs, while NOK 10 million were raised through solidarity campaigns or granted by LO.[25] The Norwegian contributions peaked in the period 1988–93 with NOK 6–9 million a year, also reflecting the extensive activities of COSATU.

The recipients of the ICFTU and LO assistance were in the mid-1970s to a high degree "workers' institutes", while from the 1980s onward the main bulk of the assistance went to the unions. The two federations, FOSATU and CUSA—later on COSATU and NACTU, were the main recipients. A number of unions and institutes, estimated at between 50 and 60, benefited however from the ICFTU programme for shorter or longer periods during the 20 years in question. While approximately two thirds of the assistance from ICFTU and LO was used to strengthen the organisations and for

[23] Cilly Lehners, oral information, November 1996.

[24] Roger Southall, 1995, op.cit., p. 355.

[25] Vesla Vetlesen, 1998, op. cit., pp. 67–68.

training purposes for the union members, the remaining third was used for humanitarian and legal aid.[26] Humanitarian aid was needed for families of arrested trade unionists, and for leaders who were banned and unable to earn their living . Legal aid was required to assist arrested unionists, the number of whom could amount to hundreds and at times even thousands. In the case of Moses Mayekiso, the Secretary General of Metal and Allied Workers' Union, and his co-defendants, they were accused of high treason and risked capital punishment. Their defence was financed by the International Metalworkers Federation and the ICFTU. The outcome of the trial was that they were acquitted and released. The main bulk of the legal aid was however used in connection with labour disputes and trade union affairs.[27] The complicated laws which regulated the labour market continuously brought the workers into situations where legal assistance was needed to defend their rights. The apartheid industrial relations system created conflicts which more often ended in court than they were solved by arbitration.

Contributions to strike funds were kept apart from ordinary assistance programmes in line with traditional trade union behaviour. Such solidarity contributions were often channelled through the International Trade Secretariats, as was the case under the large miners' strike in 1987 when the Miners' International Federation co-ordinated most of the assistance. Money from official sources was never used for strike funds.

When preparations for the first democratic elections took place in 1993–94, assistance was given to the unions to inform and train their members in their rights as voters. At this time COSATU probably had the most efficient non-governmental organisational apparatus in the country, including transport and communication facilities. This was of great value, not only during the preparations, but also during the carrying out of the election. For instance, COSATU vehicles were often the only available ones to supply the necessary material when a locality ran out of voting papers. Thus the trade unions contributed to a fair election.

It has not been reported that any of the ICFTU or the LO assistance to the unions in South Africa disappeared or was misused.

Relations with the liberation movements

Economic support for the liberation movements was another important part of the solidarity campaigns. While LO itself kept a continuous contact with the liberation movements, the economic assistance however was handled by LO's co-operating bodies—The International Solidarity Committee of the Norwegian Labour Movement and Norwegian People's Aid.

---

[26] ICFTU, 1992, op.cit., p. 288.

[27] Roger Southall, 1995, op.cit. p. 130.

A press release from LO of 28 May 1979 states:

> For 1978 and 1979 the following amounts have been granted:
> ANC, South Africa   NOK 125.000
> PAC, South Africa   25.000
> SWAPO, Namibia   25.000
> Patriotic Front (ZANU and ZAPU) Zimbabwe   135.000

While allocations for PAC ceased after a second grant, the assistance for ANC continued, amounting to some hundred thousand NOK achieved through the International Solidarity Committee's fund raising campaigns over the years. From 1988, when ANC opened an office in Oslo, the support was mainly channelled to this representation.

The main bulk of the labour movement's assistance for ANC was however handled by the humanitarian organisation Norwegian People's Aid, NPA. In the initial phase 1977–82 the co-operation between ANC and NPA was concentrated on first aid training, this being one of NPA's specialities. The first two of a series of first aid courses for health personnel recruited from the ANC refugee camps in Tanzania, Angola, Zambia and Mozambique were carried out in Norway and partly in Denmark. The programme in Norway included training in radio link and emergency operations in disaster situations in co-operation with the Norwegian Defence Forces, partly the military and partly the civil service. Also included were basic lectures on nutrition and sanitation. From 1984 onwards the first aid training took place in the ANC camp in Viana near Lusaka in Angola, also including participants from SWAPO. The duration of the courses was extended to twelve months, thus contributing to better qualified health personnel. The construction of the training centre as well as the activities was initially financed mainly by money raised by NPA, including some assistance from the Nordic sister organisations the Danish People's Aid and Finnaid. For this programme the contributions from official sources, i.e. the Norwegian Ministry of Foreign Affairs, were rather limited until 1985 from which time the allocations from the Ministry were some 2 million NOK a year. Up to 1992 approximately 350 students qualified as primary health personnel, thus improving their work in the refugee camps in Africa, as well as being useful on their return to South Africa itself. Dr. Ralph Mgijima, at that time Secretary of the ANC Health Committee—today Health Inspector in Johannesburg, underlines that in addition to the qualified health personnel several thousand refugees got basic first aid training in the camps as a result of this programme.[28]

In the period 1988–92 NPA was, in addition to its engagement in the health sector, also the main channel for the Norwegian assistance to ANC amounting to some NOK 30–40 million a year. Agreements between the

---

[28] Vesla Vetlesen, 1998, op.cit., pp. 87–94.

three parties, the Norwegian Ministry, ANC and NPA, implied that NPA should have the administrative responsibility for the Norwegian assistance to, among other things, the construction of buildings and infrastructures in the ANC refugee camps Mazimbu and Dakawa in Tanzania, as well as for the operation of the camps.[29] This programme was co-financed by the other Nordic countries. NPA was further the channel for parts of the officially financed Norwegian food programme and scholarships both for ANC and PAC refugees in Africa.

ANC delegations would frequently have meetings with LO during their visits to Norway, and representatives of LO travelling to Zambia would always call on ANC's headquarters in Lusaka.[30] Speakers from ANC were invited to address rallies and other arrangements connected with the solidarity campaigns, and ANC cultural groups also gave performances.

Although there were disagreements between ANC and LO on issues concerning unilateral Norwegian sanctions against South Africa—ANC urging for action—the dialogue was felt to be open and friendly by LO. The mutual confidence was indicated by the fact that LO and the International Solidarity Committee hosted the ANC conference at Gran north of Oslo in March 1989. Maximum security was a must when ANC called its resident representatives from all over the world, this time to discuss the new situation after Frederik de Klerk had taken over the position as President in South Africa.

In the late 1970s ANC would request LO to give economic assistance to SACTU,[31] the exile trade union allied to ANC, rather than channel the assistance to the unions inside South Africa, but after some years ANC dropped the issue. To LO this confirmed the ability of ANC to adapt to realities, as LO had no intention of changing its attitude in this matter and as it was important for ANC to remain on good terms with the trade union movement in the Nordic countries. It was also seen as a sign of ANC recognition of the strength and potentials of the growing trade unions inside South Africa, and that the exile leadership of SACTU was about to be isolated from the main stream in the mobilisation against apartheid.

SACTU, on the other hand, continued to press LO for economic assistance. A grant from any ICFTU affiliate was important to SACTU, maybe more so for symbolic than for economic reasons, and a moderate donation from the Canadian federation CLC was referred to by SACTU and used as an argument to exact contributions also from LO. The conflict between LO and SACTU was, apart from by ideological differences, also nourished by SACTU's old bitterness towards ICFTU, which went back to the 1950s.

---

[29] Agreed Minutes from the Meeting between ANC and the Royal Norwegian Ministry of Foreign Affairs, Lusaka, 19 November 1987.

[30] Reports from meetings with ANC, Lusaka, 5 April 1977, 15 November 1978, and 28 October 1982.

[31] Report from meeting with ANC representative to Scandinavia, 30 November 1976.

ICFTU documents from 1960 thus state: "Three missions (from ICFTU to South Africa, author's addition) since 1957 have all come up against an unsympathetic attitude on the part of SACTU, arising out of its association with WFTU." ICFTU developed, on the other hand, close contacts with a new organisation, the Federation of Free African Trade Unions of South Africa, FOFATUSA, which was founded in 1959 and affiliated to ICFTU the following year.[32] This rivalry for affiliates between WFTU and ICFTU reflected the cold war. By SACTU, however, it was regarded as an attempt by ICFTU to split the labour movement which found itself in a critical situation due to suppression by the apartheid regime and as an act of betrayal which was never forgiven. FOFATUSA, with its sympathies for PAC, was after few years for various reasons dissolved.

The SACTU issue also led to conflicts between LO and the Norwegian Council for Southern Africa, which acted as a spokesman for ANC and thereby also for SACTU. The Council's connections with the South African exile milieu were close, while LO on the other hand gave priority to the direct and indirect links to the trade unions inside South Africa. LO saw no reason to support an exile union when the genuine unions in South Africa were obviously expanding and benefiting from the assistance given. It was also feared that economic assistance to SACTU would give the apartheid regime an excuse to stop the economic support to the unions in South Africa.

LO reacted strongly against SACTU's accusations published in their magazine "Workers' Unity" in the period 1982–84 concerning ICFTU and its alleged "imperialistic activities", including the assistance programme for South African unions to which LO contributed. Most meetings between LO and SACTU thus developed into confrontations, the last one in 1989 arising from a letter sent by SACTU to unions in South Africa, warning them against receiving assistance from the ICFTU.[33] This took place only few months before SACTU was dissolved in March 1990. After a meeting in Lusaka between COSATU and SACTU a joint communiqué was published, stating that SACTU would not re-establish itself inside South Africa.[34] The communiqué also reflects a farewell to the cold war with reference to the new international climate and expresses the wish that one day all workers will be united in one international trade union centre.

LO's relationship with the exile trade union of Namibia, NUNW which was closely linked to SWAPO, was smoother. Even though NUNW, like SACTU, was affiliated to WFTU, the dialogue with NUNW was more relaxed and trusting. When the South African occupation of Namibia was nearing the end, it became possible for NUNW to work openly in the coun-

---

[32] ICFTU document 27EB/5, June 1960; Roger Southall, 1995, op.cit., pp. 53, 104.

[33] Letter from SACTU, Lusaka 22 August 1989, to a number of unions in South Africa.

[34] Declaration by COSATU and SACTU, Lusaka, 19 March 1990.

try. At this stage, that is from 1986, LO supported NUNW economically, in particular the Mineworkers Union of Namibia (MUN). Money from the fund-raising campaign in 1989 was also allocated for the SWAPO election campaign.

Trade union engagement in the Southern African region

Partly as a result of involvement in the anti-apartheid activities LO further developed a broad co-operation with the trade unions in the Front Line States. Specific training programmes for contract workers recruited to the South African mines from the neighbouring states were carried out in Botswana and Lesotho, in co-operation with the national trade union federations in these countries. The programmes included lectures and information on trade unionism, the rights of employees and safety at work according to the international standards of ILO. The financial source for these programmes, as well as other trade union projects in the region outside South Africa, was NORAD, the Norwegian Agency for International Development, i.e. the ordinary source of allocations for development projects run by NGOs.

LO was a strong supporter of the official Norwegian aid to the Front Line States, in particular so with regard to assistance to improve communication, transport and harbour facilities in the region. As early as in 1975 the Norwegian Seamen's Union voiced the opinion that such assistance was needed to secure alternatives to South African harbours in the case of a transport boycott of that country.[35]

Following the establishment in 1980 of the intergovernmental regional organisation Southern African Development and Co-ordination Conference, SADCC, the idea to create a matching regional trade union body was launched. It was the Zambian Congress of Trade Unions, ZCTU, at the time headed by Frederick Chiluba as Chairman and Newstead Zimba as Secretary General, that took the initiative which was supported by the other unions in the region. The good relationship between ZCTU and LO led to involvement by LO from the very start.[36] The Southern African Trade Union Co-ordination Council, SATUCC, was founded in Gaborone in March 1983, by the trade unions of Angola, Botswana, Lesotho, Malawi, Mozambique, Swaziland, Tanzania, Zambia and Zimbabwe. Also included were the exile leaderships of SACTU, ATUCC (the trade union wing of PAC) and NUNW. At the time it was exceptional for trade unions belonging to different international centres to co-operate in a joint body like this, with three of the organisations affiliated to ICFTU, three to WFTU and the remaining ones without any affiliation. LO was, by means of financing from NORAD, the main contributor to the founding conference as well as to the running ex-

---

[35] Letter from Norwegian Seamen's Union to LO, 28 October 1975.

[36] Letter from ZCTU to LO, 12 April 1982.

penses of SATUCC. The economic assistance from LO is still maintained in 1998.

On request from SATUCC LO delivered a paper on the experiences with and the modus operandi of the Nordic Trade Unions Council, which in some ways was seen as a model. SATUCC's main tasks have been educational activities with an emphasise on training women trade unionists and presenting viewpoints on intergovernmental development plans for the region often stressing the necessity of taking employment consequences into consideration.

After the fall of apartheid in 1994 the South African unions COSATU and NACTU have taken their places as members of SATUCC.

Attempted infiltration by BOSS

The much feared South African intelligence service BOSS, Bureau of State Security, operated outside as well as inside the country.[37] Characteristically one of its programmes was named "Operation Long Reach". Not only did South Africa carry out armed attacks on ANC bases, offices and refugee settlements in the neighbouring states, but also in Europe, and several anti-apartheid fighters in exile were assassinated.

It was to be expected that organisations in the Nordic countries, being sources and channels for substantial financial assistance to the anti-apartheid activities, would be subject to infiltration by BOSS agents. LO and its co-operating bodies, NPA (Norwegian People's Aid) and the International Solidarity Committee, were aware of such a possibility and handled their contacts with outsiders and the South Africans in exile with great care. When an attempt was made to infiltrate the labour movement, this was however avoided not because of suspicion against the agent, but due to the restrictive routines followed. LO would stick to its own well known trade union network for assistance to the trade unions in South Africa, and not getting involved in channelling money through other organisations, be they national or international bodies. With regard to contributions to the liberation movements, the assistance would be transferred directly to the organisation in question.

When Craig Williamson, who was later revealed as being a captain of BOSS, visited NPA in January 1978, he was introduced as a member of ANC who had fled South Africa following involvement in student activities against apartheid. He now served as Information Officer of IUEF, the International University Exchange Fund, based in Geneva and well known for its assistance to progressive student organisations.

Following this meeting Craig Williamson on behalf of IUEF applied for assistance to various projects, among these certain administrative costs for ANC, SWAPO and Patriotic Front. The applications were rejected with ref-

---

[37] BOSS was in 1978 changed to DONS, Department of National Security.

erence to decisions taken by LO and NPA only to deal directly with the liberation movements. Craig Williamson would however not take no for an answer and continued to forward applications. Some of the projects seemed to be tailored for trade union assistance, but the applications were nevertheless rejected.

In September 1978 Craig Williamson, who had in the meantime advanced to Vice Director of IUEF, paid a new visit to NPA.[38] Again he presented projects for financing without success. No one had yet ever suspected that Williamson acted as an agent of BOSS. Obviously though, seen in retrospect, he wanted to obtain information about the recipients of trade union assistance inside as well as outside South Africa.

When Craig Williamson in January 1980 was revealed as an agent of South Africa, it came as a hard blow to the anti-apartheid movement. LO and NPA, although shocked by the news, were nevertheless immensely relieved that the agent had not been able to penetrate the trade union assistance programmes.

Economic sanctions against South Africa

Three main issues concerning economic isolation of South Africa were focused in the public debate in Norway: 1) disinvestments regarding Shell, 2) severing trade links with South Africa, and 3) cutting off the oil supplies. LO was strongly involved in the debate on all the three issues which are dealt with below.

In 1977 the Norwegian Government stopped all further investments in South Africa. Very few Norwegian firms were however involved and the blockade was effected without strong objections from the investors. In the mid-1980s the investment question was raised again, this time from a new angle: an international campaign demanded the withdrawal of Shell investments in South Africa. The charges against Shell were bad working conditions and anti-trade union attitudes in the Shell subsidiaries in South Africa. LO was called upon by the Norwegian Council for Southern Africa to support a consumer boycott against Shell to force the company to disinvest. LO decided, however, not to support a consumer boycott, but rather continue the dialogue with Shell Norway urging the company to improve working and wages conditions in South Africa.[39] LO kept simultaneously in touch with the unions organising in these subsidiaries, gathering information from them and thus confronting Shell with facts about the local situation for the workers concerned. To press for improvements rather than campaigning for disinvestments was in line with the policy pursued so far by the international trade union movement to which LO belonged. When the Shell cam-

---

[38] Reports from Craig Williamson's meetings with Norwegian People's Aid, 25 January 1978 and 6 September 1978.

[39] Minutes from meeting of the LO executive board, 24 November 1986.

paign came into focus in 1986–89 however some of the ICFTU affiliates, notably the Dutch FNV and the American AFL/CIO, supported the disinvestment campaign against Shell. ICFTU also engaged itself strongly in this campaign. A consumer boycott was, however, never adopted by the ICFTU. The Nordic trade unions did not involve themselves in boycott actions against Shell, but they supported the pressure put upon the company.[40]

It should be noted that the South African trade union COSATU did not take an unconditional stand in favour of disinvestments. Even though some spokesmen for COSATU supported disinvestment campaigns, the policy of COSATU, as expressed through congress resolutions,[41] was equivocal and contained the reservation that any disinvestment had to be compensated by the company, as the values of the South African subsidiary were a result of the workers' sweat. COSATU argued for "a negotiated, fair disinvestment procedure".

The campaign against Shell, carried out partly through actions and demonstrations by solidarity groups and partly through dialogue and pressure applied by trade unions, may have had an impact in improving the company's attitudes towards their workers in South Africa.

UN sanctions were strongly supported by LO. With regard to unilateral sanctions to be taken by Norway, LO would advocate the stand that the burdens which might result from such sanctions should be shared by the society as a whole, and should not be borne by the workers of the affected industries alone. LO also maintained that the Nordic countries ought to act jointly. This attitude was shared by the other Nordic unions as reflected in the "14-point programme" described above, and the unions pressed the governments in order to jointly employ stronger measures against South Africa. Throughout the years LO would be in touch with the relevant ministers, be it a conservative or a labour government in power, always urging new initiatives to be taken to reduce the trade with South Africa step by step.

The effects of severing all trade with South Africa ware analysed by LO, in particular the consequences for the employment situation. It soon became clear that the most sensitive part of the trade was not losses inflicted on the export, but the dependency on import of South African raw materials for the Norwegian chemical process industry, in particular manganese. The Norwegian Chemical Workers Union together with LO spent considerable time and resources on ways and means to get substitutes for the South African manganese. To cut off import without obtaining the needed quantities and qualities of manganese from elsewhere, would devastate an important industry. More than one thousand workers would immediately lose their jobs, and the stoppage would hit local communities completely dependent

---

[40] Kjeld Aakjær, oral information, 1997.

[41] COSATU congress resolutions 1985, 1987, 1989; Roger Southall, 1995, op. cit., pp. 272–277, 341.

upon the running of these industries.[42] In the mid-1980s the political climate in Norway, also reflecting changed attitudes in USA and EC, indicated that a trade boycott was about to be initiated. LO, although in favour of the boycott, took the position that manganese should for the time being be allowed to be imported on licence.

The question of an oil embargo overshadowed other issues in the Norwegian debate on sanctions (see chapter 5). The export of oil from the Norwegian North Sea wells to South Africa was stopped in the late 1970s, but Norwegian tankers continued to supply South Africa with oil from other sources. LO put the cutting of oil supplies to South Africa on the agenda in 1979. UN documentation had revealed that probably 20% of the oil imported by South Africa was supplied by Norwegian tankers.[43] In the Nordic Trade Union Council the oil issue was brought up by the Danish LO, requesting the matter to be examined. Consequently a demand was directed to the governments to work for UN oil embargo. This demand was included in the "14-point programme" in 1979, and furthermore the same year in the ICFTU resolution against apartheid in accordance with a motion by Danish LO on behalf of the Nordic unions.

In the wake of UN sanctions, the idea that UN should call a special conference of the oil exporting countries to discuss the issue was aired by LO. Many countries declared their willingness not to sell oil to South Africa. But the same countries, in particular the Gulf states, did not in reality care whether their oil ended up in South Africa or elsewhere. The oil might be sold to a company, loaded in the Gulf and be bound for a European harbour, but as soon as the ship was on the open sea, it would be redirected to South Africa. The purpose of a special UN conference would be to discuss how this practice could be prevented. LO's Chairman Tor Halvorsen launched the idea of a UN oil conference at a board meeting of the Nordic Trade Union Council in 1981, which favoured it. To promote the idea LO approached the trade unions in all the oil exporting countries, asking them bring pressure to bear on their governments to support such a conference.[44] Some of these unions were well known to LO as affiliates of the ICFTU, others were affiliated to the WFTU or without international affiliation. Several unions responded positively. From the ICFTU, however, came a rather sour comment, signed by Secretary General Otto Kersten.[45] In a telex to LO he expresses appreciation of the initiative, but continued: "Your contacting also WFTU affiliates is in our view a bilateral question but we would nonetheless draw your attention to the fact that these organisations

---

[42] Vesla Vetlesen, 1998, op.cit., pp. 117–122.

[43] M. Bailey and B. Rivers: *Oil Sanctions against South Africa.* New York: UN's Centre against Apartheid, 1978.

[44] Letter from LO to unions in OPEC and other oil exporting countries, 11 September 1981.

[45] Telex from ICFTU til LO, 28 October 1981.

as well as those friendly towards the WFTU might take advantage of this approach for their proper purposes."

LO presented the idea to the Norwegian Government which took upon itself to launch it at UN meetings where it was well received. However, the Gulf states demanded that it should be a conference of both oil exporting *and* transporting countries, which was accepted. After several years of discussions back and forth the UN seminar on an oil embargo against South Africa was held in Oslo in June 1986. Following the recommendations from this meeting, UN established an Intergovernmental Group to monitor the supply and shipping of oil to South Africa. The Intergovernmental Group would encourage governments to impose an embargo and would also offer to assist the states to enact legislation to this end. It is, however, not reported that these efforts had any effect on the practice of the Gulf states, which let their oil flow to South Africa in spite of their declared policy.

The hot political issue in the early and mid 1980s was however whether Norway should take unilateral action against the transport of oil—Norwegian tankers were in 1982 said to carry 35% of the total South African supply—or wait for international sanctions. The position of LO was that unilateral actions would not prevent the oil from reaching South Africa, and that it would hit the seamen manning the Norwegian fleet disproportionally hard. LO further maintained that at least the Nordic countries would have to act jointly if an embargo through national decisions was to be imposed. This stand was in line with the LO affiliated Norwegian Seamen's Union, which in a letter to LO in 1983 wrote: "Today the situation is that the shipping market possesses an enormous surplus of tonnage competing for orders. What one company rejects, others are queuing up to take on. ... As long as this is a fact it is obvious that a boycott by Norway of this oil transport will lead to Norwegian ships being laid up and loss of jobs. We will not enjoin on our members to take part in an action which would make themselves unemployed."[46]

In particular the tanker fleet registered in "Flag of Convenience" countries, including the African state of Liberia, was eager to take over the market. The registration of ships in countries which were not operating normal taxation practices and which did not respect international standards and pay, was already felt as a threat to the traditional seafaring nations and as a danger to the International Transport Workers' Federation. The Norwegian Seamen's Union was, however, eager to introduce registration of all Norwegian ships calling at South African harbours. In letters to and at meetings with the Ministry of Shipping and Commerce the union again and again from 1983 onwards forwarded this proposal. The union wanted an open register spelling out the name of the ships involved as well as the

---

[46] Letter from Norwegian Seamen's Union to LO, 28 October 1983.

nature of the cargo they carried. On the other hand the ship owners freneti-
cally fought the introduction of such a system.

The heated debate on the oil transport was nourished by the SRB, Shipping Research Bureau, founded in 1980 by Dutch anti-apartheid organisations in co-operation with ANC and based in Amsterdam.[47] (See chapter 5.)
Their disclosures of ships supplying South Africa with oil were impressive.
However, the research was concentrated on the Western European transac-
tions, thus leaving out the involvement of the countries supplying the
greater share of the oil—the Gulf states. At that time it was not obvious that
the biased picture given by the SRB was part of an ANC strategy, as it was
not known how close the links were between ANC and SRB. ANC did not
want to expose certain countries and thereby embarrass their "allies"—the
Arab states, the Soviet Union and the East European countries, which would
always support the ANC views when, for instance, it came to UN resolutions.[48] To ANC it would be more beneficial to put pressure to bear on
Western European countries, not least on the Netherlands and the Nordic
countries which harboured strong public opinion against apartheid. The influence of ANC on which findings by SRB were to be published—and which
were not—has later been disclosed by SRB in the book *Embargo. Apartheid's
Oil Secrets Revealed*.

LO gave economic assistance to the Shipping Research Bureau, but at
the same time repeatedly complained about SRB keeping some 50% of the
oil supplies out of their records. The real reason for this was not made
known to LO and was excused by SRB as lack of detailed information. It is
likely that LO would have taken a different line towards SRB and ANC if
their close connections and strategies had been known. Not until 1986, i.e.
after the oil transport sanctions were about to be adopted by the Nordic
countries, was this practise brought to an end by SRB which by now would
also to a certain degree publish findings about the involvement of the Soviet
Union and the Arab states in the oil trade.[49]

In the mid-1980s the political will to take parallel unilateral economic
actions against South Africa was ripening in all the Nordic countries. First
out was Denmark with sanctions adopted in May 1986. The other Nordic
countries followed suit in 1987. In Norway, however, a change of government preceded this decision. When the Labour Party under the leadership
of Prime Minister Gro Harlem Brundtland took power after a conservative
led coalition in May 1986, preparations for boycott legislation were
immediately started. The sanctions, adopted in March 1987, severed all
trade with South Africa and put an end to the oil transport on Norwegian
ships. However, manganese could still be imported on licence, and only

---

[47] R. Hengevold and J. Rodenburg: *Embargo. Apartheid's Oil Secrets Revealed*. Amsterdam:
Amsterdam University Press, 1995, pp. 97–98, 102.

[48] Ibid., p. 99.

[49] Ibid., p 104.

crude oil was covered by the transport boycott. LO was frequently in touch with the Government during the preparation of the boycott legislation and was largely satisfied with the outcome. In 1989 however LO demanded that the boycott should be extended to cover transport of all types of oil products, a demand which was not met.[50]

The Nordic unions were satisfied that the Nordic countries to a high degree had been able to act in unison on the boycott issue.

The role of the South African unions in the downfall of apartheid

When the apartheid regime was brought to a downfall through negotiations several factors contributed to this end. Of great importance was on the one hand the mass mobilisation inside South Africa and on the other hand the increased pressure from the international community. The mass mobilisation in South Africa included a number of elements—the church, local communities, the Black Consciousness and the liberation movements with ANC as the dominant force, and—not least—the trade unions.

A particular and important part of the contribution of the trade unions was their experience and abilities when it came to negotiations, which in the later stage of the apartheid époque and during the period of transition to democracy, were of decisive importance for peaceful transfer and solutions. The unions possessed a genuine willingness to achieve results through negotiations. The struggle throughout the years for trade union rights—not least for the right to bargain—had created a positive attitude to negotiations as a means to achieve progress and improvements. Furthermore no other mass organisation had a similar tradition and training in democratic decision making. The unions with their elected officers at all levels and with their policy built on majority rule if compromises could not be reached brought an important experience into the picture. Finally the organisational strength and the striking power of the unions were of decisive value. The unions had acquired experience in using the strike weapon as an ultimate means if negotiations were not successful. Strikes as part of the mass mobilisations forced the apartheid regime to sit down at the negotiating table, thus contributing to a peaceful transition to democratic procedures in South Africa.

The assistance from the international free trade union movement, where ICFTU and the Nordic unions played an important role, made it possible for the South African unions to grow and expand at a rapid rate, thus becoming a decisive factor in the overthrow of apartheid. The support from the Nordic unions was based on the rank and file members who backed this policy and identified themselves all the way with the struggle against apartheid. This

---

[50] LO's congress resolution 1989. Letter from LO to the Ministry of Foreign Affairs, 14 November 1989.

was achieved through the solidarity campaigns and information activities, as described above.

The South African workers built their trade unions in spite of tremendous suppression, knowing what was at stake. Not only did this trade union movement play a decisive role in the overthrow of apartheid, but also today it plays an important and constructive role in building the new democratic South Africa.

Chapter 9
Pioneering Local Activism:
The Namibia Association of Norway[1]

Eva Helene Østbye

Why Namibia? Why Elverum?

The Namibia Association of Norway was established in 1980 to provide humanitarian assistance to the Namibian people, with the ambition to also support other oppressed peoples in Southern Africa. From the start as a one week's solidarity campaign in Elverum, a town of 17,000 inhabitants in the south-eastern part of Norway, it became the principal Norwegian non-governmental organisation (NGO) devoted to the independence of Namibia. During the years of the liberation struggle, it co-operated closely with South West Africa People's Organisation (SWAPO) and with the Council of Churches in Namibia (CCN). From the start, the scope of the activities ranged from directly supporting Namibian refugees in Angola through products and projects to giving financial support to CCN—and informing the Norwegian public on the situation in Namibia. The largest single involvement was from 1983 to 1990, when the association was the main contributor in the building and running of SWAPO's first secondary school outside Namibia, the Namibia Secondary Technical School in Loudima, Congo. After the liberation of Namibia in 1990, the activities changed focus, from solidarity work with emphasis on relief aid to more regular development aid projects inside Namibia.

Why Namibia? After the liberation of Angola and Mozambique in 1975, the recent changes in Zimbabwe had left Namibia in 1980 as the only remaining colonised—or rather occupied—country in Southern Africa. There was no sign of a South African agreement to implement the UN Security Council Peace Plan for Namibia (Security Council Resolution 435/78) and the condemnation of the South African occupation was widely shared. At the same time, this did not get much attention in the Norwegian media.

---

[1] This chapter in based on *The Namibia Association Annuals Reports*: 1982–1995, information material from The Namibia Association, newspapers and documents from the Ministry of Foreign Affairs. In addition, interviews have been conducted with Dag Hareide, Steinar Sætervadet, Marit Sætervadet, Bente Pedersen, Uazuvara Katjivena, Hans Dieset and Oddvar Øieren. After this chapter was completed the history of the Namibia Association has been written by Trond Andresen and Steinar Sætervadet (*Fra dugnad til bistand*, Elverum: Namibiaforeningen, 2000).

The point of departure was the church, and through the International League of Christian Socialists and the Lutheran World Federation, political activists within the church were well informed about the oppression Namibia was experiencing through the occupation: war, racism, poverty and exploitation. Two of these activists living in Elverum, Ellinor Hareide and Dag Hareide, knew the Namibian struggle well through their friendship with Namibian church leaders. They were engaged as catechists in the church, and wanted their confirmation courses not just to be theoretical, but also to teach about Christianity in practice.

Having so often been used to legitimise apartheid and other injustice, religion was also a basis for one of the main forces in the anti-apartheid struggle, the churches. The candidates for confirmation were taught about the reasons behind the need for support. By learning about apartheid and imperialism, they were encouraged to see the relationships between people in Southern Africa and Norway: "we need this as much as they do". To avoid falling into the tradition of charity, they were taught about the struggle, led by SWAPO, the only organisation recognised by the OAU and by the UN General Assembly as the authentic representative of the Namibian people. They learnt that more than 80% of all Namibians belonged to churches that were engaged in the fight against the occupation. With SWAPO receiving support from the World Council of Churches, the confirmation course leaders saw SWAPO and the churches as providing readily accessible channels that would make sure that the support would reach the people it was meant for.

The liberation struggle in Namibia was a "good cause" to which the church could contribute, and there was no doubt about its justification. It could also serve as a good example of how lives in Norway and Southern Africa were interconnected—and how a "good Christian" could show responsibility in practice. It could be used to illustrate imperialism—and in the case of Namibia it seemed to be possible to make a contribution that could actually make a difference. Besides, there was no other Norwegian NGO exclusively dedicated to the Namibian struggle.

And why Elverum? In 1980, dean Gunnar Stålsett, central in the anti-apartheid involvement of the Norwegian Church headed the local church in Elverum, and with him worked another prominent anti-apartheid clergyman, curate Finn Huseby.[2] Being dedicated to the anti-apartheid struggle themselves, they supported the untraditional confirmation-courses and the campaigns. The Namibia Association could rely on the strong support of the church.

In addition to this, Elverum was a school centre with a folk high-school, a school of nursing and a teachers' training college, in addition to a number of primary schools and one large junior and one large senior secondary

---

[2] Regarding the role of the churches, see chapter 7.

school. The schools have played a very important role for the Namibia Association.

Being a centre for the forestry industry, the trade unions in Elverum have historically had a position that is atypical for Norwegian rural towns. The Labour Party had a stronghold there, and the Centre Party (with its agrarian roots) was more radical than in rural Norway in general. There was a potential for political mobilisation. Right from the start, the Namibia Association at Elverum received the support of the labour movement, both financially and through practical assistance. The typographers' union, for instance, in 1981 voluntarily printed 10,000 books and 40,000 passports for Namibian refugees.

Norway's own experience of being under foreign rule for centuries, and especially the German occupation during the Second World War, provided a motivation to show solidarity with another small state deprived of its independence. This connection opened up for the inclusion of groups otherwise unfamiliar to the solidarity movements. Elverum was one of the towns in the southern part of Norway that was hardest hit during the war—a great number of houses in the centre of town were destroyed after heavy bombing. Thirty-five years later, in 1980, this was still remembered, as were the more or less mythical stories of the resistance movement—which had a stronghold in the Elverum area. When Norway was invaded on 9 April 1940, the Norwegian Government and King left Oslo. At Elverum, King Haakon received an "offer" to co-operate with the German occupation power, which he declined before going into exile in England. When Sam Nujoma visited Elverum on the Norwegian National Day, 17 May 1983, he laid a wreath by a large monument in the centre of Elverum picturing the king saying "no".

From confirmand training to a broad local community action campaign

From its basis in the church, the concept of *learning* about Namibia by *doing* solidarity work was spread to other institutions. The catechists got in touch with school teachers at various schools in Elverum, and together the schools and the church became the main forces in initiating a "Namibia week". The objective of the campaign was not solely to provide support for the Namibian refugees, but also to promote solidarity in the local community, if not in all of Norway. This was sought through defying indifference by showing that a difference could be made, challenging charity through information about imperialism and the struggle against apartheid, and by using cultural exchange to oppose racism.

It became a remarkable arrangement: in the last week of April 1980, 7,000 persons—almost half of the population of Elverum—devoted 20,000 working days to learning and teaching about Namibia and apartheid and to providing humanitarian assistance to the liberation struggle. In the week of the action campaign, 25 tons of clothes and shoes were collected and sent in containers to SWAPO's refugee camps in Angola. 20,000 notebooks for school pupils were made and sent along with 60 patchwork quilts, almost two tons of medicines, 45,000 protein biscuits, one truck, 27 bicycles, 10 sewing machines, 2,500 blackboards, 200 kilos of paper and hundreds of kilos of toys, sleeping bags, textiles, and other equipment and tools. The money that was collected or earned was given to the Council of Churches in Namibia, representing the majority of Namibian Christians. The Norwegian Ministry of Foreign Affairs agreed to pay the costs for the transportation of the goods, as well as to grant money for the Namibia Association to buy other items requested by SWAPO.[3] Even in 1980, this included more than 10,000 woollen blankets and 800 tents, as well as additional equipment. In the following years, a large number of containers were sent with necessities for the Namibian refugees.

To raise the interest that could yield this kind of result, the initiators of the action campaign saw it as crucial to meet people where they actually were. Instead of arranging meetings for the already interested minority, the strategy was to enter the institutions and rituals of the local society. With the support of the church, the schools and the trade unions, a broad basis was established. This, in turn, led to a great interest, and support, from the local press.

One major principle was that the activities should be based on a combination of theory and practice: not to give help without understanding why, and not to know about the need for help without giving it. If you had learnt something about Namibia, you had an obligation to tell someone else about it. The thought was that if you knew anything at all about Namibia and the struggle, you probably knew more than the person next to you did—so you should teach her. Your knowledge should also form a foundation for the practical solidarity work. Schoolchildren went to old people's homes and told about the occupation and injustice in Namibia, and the residents knitted patches for patchwork quilts. Unemployed youths repaired old bicycles that were sent to the refugee camps in Angola and Zambia. "Begging teams" went around to various workplaces and organisations getting contributions, like requesting the pharmaceutical factory to give medicines. Nurses in the hospital encouraged patients to pay for visiting the toilets, and in the waiting rooms at medical and dental clinics knitting needles and yarn were placed for people to knit patches while they waited to go in. Children in kindergartens baked protein biscuits; the Norwegian Housewives' Association (Norsk Husmorforbund) sewed school uniforms. The schools were turned upside down—with pupils making rough books for schoolchildren in the camps, collecting second-hand clothes and shoes and putting on plays about the struggle.

---

[3] *The Namibia Association Annual Report*, 1981, p. 17.

The establishment of an organisation

It had all started quite spontaneously. After the campaign, on 4 June 1980, "The Namibia Association of Norway" was established as a membership organisation with the dual aim of running continuous solidarity work for Namibia from the base in Elverum and spreading the concept of the local action campaign to other communities in Norway. A group, led by Viktor Nilsen, was established to start the planning of the organisation. In March 1981, the structure was made more formal, when a board was elected, consisting of Dag Hareide, Bente Pedersen, Steinar Sætervadet, Viktor Nilsen and Heidi Nygård. This was a very active board: in 10 months it held 30 meetings. From August 1981 the organisation moved into a house placed at their disposal by the town council, after having been housed until then by the Elverum branch of the Norwegian Confederation of Trade Unions (Elverum Samorganisasjon). In 1985 the town council donated the house to the Namibia Association.

In the "Namibia house" a second-hand shop was opened, which right up to 1998 has been run by volunteers. The shop aimed at being a welcoming place, where people could drop by for a cup of coffee, read and have a chat, in addition to perhaps buying items from developing countries, information material or second-hand clothes, shoes, furniture and toys. The items given to the Namibia Association were sorted out. Some of them were sent to the refugee camps and some sold to finance other activities. The devoted workers Inger Avenstrup and Anette Vetlesen, together with a large number of other volunteers, contributed through the 1980s to a yearly income from the second-hand shop ranging from NOK 50,000 to 80,000 a year.

Filling and sending the containers every year through the 1980s was also done by volunteers. Large quantities were shipped off to Namibian refugees: more than 100 tons in 1981 alone. In 1982, just the books sent included 40,000 English textbooks, produced for Namibian students and printed in Elverum, 26,600 rough books, made by school pupils, 2,500 textbooks in mathematics and 2,500 books on pedagogics. In addition, the containers were filled with hundreds of tons of clothes, bicycles, school equipment, toys, protein-biscuits, pre-fabricated houses, woollen blankets, tents etc. On some occasions, this was done in co-operation with other organisations, such as "Bread and Fishes" in Sweden or local communities in Norway. At the beginning of 1981, before the contact with SWAPO had become close and regular, Bente Pedersen and Oddvar Øieren visited Angola, and were reassured that the containers had actually reached the refugees in the camps.

Even though unpaid work played a crucial role for the organisation, as the activities became increasingly complex, it came to a point where it could no longer be run solely by volunteers. As the Namibia Association moved into its own house in August 1981, four persons were employed—on very low salaries—to work full time with running the activities, marking the change from action campaign to solidarity organisation. It is an expression of stability that one of these four, Marit Sætervadet, has stayed on right up to the present day, 1999, taking care of the day-to-day activities of the organisation.

The Namibia Association in Norway quickly became a central Norwegian humanitarian organisation. Getting the framework settled also facilitated the contact and co-operation with a broad spectrum of organisations, such as trade unions, various church organisations, the Students' and Academics' International Assistance Fund, (SAIH) the Norwegian Housewives' Organisation, the UN Association in Norway, NORAD and the Ministry of Foreign Affairs. The co-operation with the Norwegian Council for Southern Africa was particularly close, and the Namibia Association also became a member of this umbrella organisation.[4] After having co-operated with the Council on an "Action against Apartheid" in the United Nations International Year for Sanctions against Apartheid, 1982, the two organisations entered into an agreement regarding co-operation on information. According to the agreement, the Namibia Association would visit local communities to inspire them to arrange similar action campaigns to the one at Elverum, while the Council was to work more with political questions and develop information material. From 1982, the Namibia Association was represented on the Central Committee of the Council. The "Action against Apartheid" culminated in 1984, when the Council and the Namibia Association through information about apartheid and the solidarity action concept inspired around 70 communities in Norway to arrange local campaigns. The money and items collected during these campaigns were sent to SWAPO's textile project in Zambia and to two of the projects that the Council was responsible for: ANC's school in Tanzania (SOMAFCO), and recruiting Norwegian teachers for work in Zimbabwe.

Right from the start, the Namibia Association also entered into extensive and close co-operation with NORAD and the Norwegian Ministry of Foreign Affairs. This concerned a number of areas, like information and policy discussions, being hosts for Namibian visitors to Norway and the implementation of projects, and it lasted right up to the independence of Namibia in 1990.

Spreading the concept

After the successful one-week campaign in 1980, the activists at Elverum wanted to spread information about their experience in order to inspire other local communities to arrange similar events. Eighteen out of twenty of Norway's counties were in 1981 covered by lecture tours, with the result that in all parts of the country a number of local communities arranged

---

[4] For more about the Norwegian Council for Southern Africa, see chapter 6.

some sort of activities to give support to the Namibian people. It was, however, only in a handful of places that these campaigns involved such a large part of the local community as the one in Elverum. In 1982 more than fifty promotion tours were arranged, and there were more than forty practical/theoretical local campaigns of varying size arranged in fifteen counties.

The main motor for these campaigns was the schools; teachers and pupils working together on learning about imperialism, apartheid and Namibia—and the work that needed to be done—and then making a contribution to this work. In addition, church congregations, humanitarian associations and trade unions played important roles.

Beside inspiring these campaigns, the Namibia Association supported the local committees by participating in the planning, providing of necessary material, giving lectures, arranging visits from SWAPO and helping with the shipment of the collected clothes etc.

Various kinds of material were produced to guide activists who wanted to arrange campaigns. A special "Namibia package" was made for use within the church and do-it-yourself kits describing the methods designed for schools that considered actions for Namibia. A slide-show and two videos portraying the original campaign at Elverum were made and distributed widely and used in combination with the numerous lectures that were held to inspire others to arrange similar campaigns.

To inform others about the action campaign concept, and to create channels for co-operation, the representatives of the Namibia Association visited Sweden, Switzerland, USA and Canada. The organisation also received representatives from solidarity and aid organisations from a number of countries interested in discussing the working methods, principles and strategies that the activities in Elverum were based on.

Visits and visitors

From the start in the spring of 1980, the Namibia Association had regular contacts with SWAPO, and as a close relationship developed between the two organisations, numerous visits were exchanged. Naturally, the contact with the SWAPO office to the Nordic countries in Stockholm was particularly close, and Hadino Hishongwa, Joseph Jimmy and Niilo Taapopi often visited Elverum. Representatives from the SWAPO headquarters in Luanda also visited Elverum on a number of occasions to inform people about the struggle and discuss further co-operation. Likewise, representatives of the Namibia Association visited SWAPO's offices and camps in Angola, Zambia, Congo—as well as the office in Sweden.

President Sam Nujoma made his first in a series of visits to Elverum as early as in 1981, where the Namibia Association arranged a meeting which drew 1300 people. Through the years, a number of prominent SWAPO leaders visited the association. Around half the members of the democratically elected Namibian government that was installed in 1990, had thus been to

Elverum. Regular visits had for instance been made by Andimba Toivo ya Toivo, Moses Garoeb, Nahas Angula, Hidipo Hamutenya and Hendrik Witbooi, in addition to Sam Nujoma.

Namibian students in exile participated in school visits, cultural evenings and solidarity services. In the mid-1980s, Uazuvara Katjivena became closely involved with the work of the association, and took part in the development of the activities, as well as participating in solidarity arrangements with speeches and appeals. With support from the UN Council for Namibia, the Namibia Association in October 1986 arranged a seminar at Elverum, where 60 participants from organisations in Denmark, Sweden, Finland, West Germany and Norway discussed how to strengthen the solidarity work in the Nordic countries.

In 1987, the Namibia Association was one of the organisers of the Nordic celebration of Namibia Day, 26 August, which took place in Oslo. Sam Nujoma was the main speaker and the trade union leader Barnabas Tjizu talked about the work of the unions inside Namibia. Representatives of the Norwegian Ministry of Foreign Affairs and the Norwegian Federation of Trade Unions (LO) participated, giving speeches. The same year, the Namibia Association arranged a tour in Norway for a group of students from the Loudima school.

Representatives of the Namibian and South African churches also made a number of visits. A high point in this connection was when Nobel laureate Desmond Tutu visited Elverum in December 1984. After being met by more than a thousand people with burning torches, Desmond and Leah Tutu were guests of honour at festivities arranged by the Namibia Association. Drums, songs, children, youth and adult choirs together with performing artists and speakers celebrated the Peace Prize laureate in what the local newspaper called "the greatest public rejoicing of the century".

Anti-apartheid work in Norway

The local work of the Namibia Association was not solely concerned with spreading the concept of the action campaign. Seeing racism in South Africa and Norway as two sides of the same coin, the challenge had to be met in a number of areas. A broad spectrum of information and cultural activities complemented the ventures, such as courses for unemployed youth and political lobbying towards the Norwegian government on questions such as imposing sanctions on South Africa. New local campaigns were also arranged: in October 1982, the association initiated "Namibia Days" at Elverum, where all the 14 primary schools at Elverum devoted three days to working against racism. The attention in this campaign was directed as much towards the racism encountered by foreigners in Norway, as it was towards supporting the liberation struggle of Namibia.

While spreading the concept of the action campaign, the Namibia Association also provided information about the political situation in Southern

Africa and Namibia. For this, various material was produced, such as a booklet about "Namibia—a rich country with poor people", which by 1982 had been printed in 8,000 copies. After visiting the camps in Angola in 1981, the Association produced an 8-mm film and slides. In every annual report from the association, the political developments regarding Southern Africa, the status of the negotiations, Norwegian policy etc. were accounted for. Furthermore, the Namibia Association distributed material from SWAPO and other organisations like the Norwegian Church (Kirkens U-landsinformasjon) and the Norwegian Council for Southern Africa.

To reach a wider audience, the Namibia Association also endeavoured to get attention in the mass media—local and national newspapers, TV and radio, by inviting the media to press conferences, setting up public meetings and informing the press of various events.

Exhibitions were also arranged. In the main commercial bank of Elverum, Namibia and the projects of the association were presented in connection with the celebration of Namibia Day, 26 August 1986. In 1988, the Namibia Association arranged an exhibition at the local cinema in Elverum. In 1990, the liberation struggle, independent Namibia and the association were presented in a large exhibition financed by NORAD and prepared by the Namibia Association at Glomdalsmuseet, one of Elverum's main museums. When it was dismantled, it was transferred to the State Museum in Windhoek, and reopened there by President Sam Nujoma in March 1992.

Cultural workshop for Namibia

Cultural activities have played a major role in the work of the Namibia Association, both as an extension of information, and as a source of inspiration. The prime mover behind this work was Oddvar Øieren, teacher at the folk high-school and "house poet" of the association. In a number of plays, the themes were concerned with racism and apartheid—and the situation in Namibia. His play "Et stykke raffinert rasisme" (A piece of refined racism), was performed in Elverum and toured in Norway with students from the folk high-school, drawing a parallel between racism in Namibia and Norway. Namibia's history was the theme in "Svart på Hvitt" (Black on White), which was performed by the high-school in 1982 and printed in 5,000 copies with support from NORAD and distributed to other interested theatre companies. In 1984, Øieren's play "Suverene Namibia" (Sovereign Namibia), had 34 actors from 12 countries showing parts of the rich Namibian culture through dances, drums, four-part African choir-song and other music. Øieren also wrote a play about Nelson and Winnie Mandela, which in 1987 had its opening night in one of Norway's central prisons. In 1989 Toivo ya Toivo was present on the opening night of the musical "Salt of the Earth", and later the same year, Norwegian thoughtless self-righteousness was ridiculed in the farce "Nordboere" (Northerners), which was put on in co-operation with the Theatre of the County of Hedmark.

Cultural exchange was also given strong emphasis. The Namibia Association distributed Namibian music, such as the recordings it made in 1983 of SWAPO's Vice-President Hendrik Witbooi singing Namibian songs. Representatives of the association also taught Namibian dances in schools. An octet at the folk high-school, in co-operation with the Namibia Association collected, arranged, and adjusted songs from Southern Africa for Norwegian conditions. The music was distributed as cassettes and folders to schools, congregations, choirs and others. In the early 1980s, Namibian songs and dances were well known to the school pupils in Elverum.

In 1985, the Namibia Association invited Ndlimani—the cultural group of SWAPO—to Norway for a three-week tour in September. The group performed liberation songs, sketches, drum music, dances and African rhythms at schools and work places, and held open-air concerts in a number of Norwegian towns. Their music was also recorded.

The Namibia Association on a number of occasions co-operated with other organisations in cultural arrangements, such as "Rock against apartheid" with Elverum Rock and Roll Club and SOS Racism in May 1990. Together with the Solidarity Theatre at Elverum folk high-school the liberation of Namibia was celebrated through a theatre tour of Norway.

Liberation had already been thoroughly celebrated in 1989, when the Namibia Association again arranged a Namibia action. During this, the "action radio" informed people about arrangements such as the "freedom concert", which was held with well known Norwegian musicians, the "freedom exhibition", where 25 artists had donated pictures, and the "freedom run" through the streets of Elverum. All of this was to celebrate independent Namibia, but also to collect money for the further work of the association. In 1990, the Namibia Association arranged a grand "freedom parade" in Elverum and a "freedom service" in the Church. The information department of the Namibia Association was also represented at the official independence celebrations in Namibia.

Courses for the unemployed

In 1981, 1982 and 1983 the Namibia Association in co-operation with the local authorities (Sør-Østerdal Arbeidsformidling) arranged courses for young unemployed people in Elverum. The Ministry of Labour (Kommunal og Arbeidsdepartmentet) supported the course, which lasted for around three months, and—naturally—consisted of balancing amounts of theory and practice. The courses were run by Sverre Rimberg and Anne-Marie Rimberg, and the ambition was that the participants on the one hand should learn about imperialism, apartheid and Namibia, and on the other about the reasons behind unemployment and the situation in the labour market. While *learning* about Namibian refugees, the participants were also given the chance of *doing* something for them: they repaired bicycles and produced articles like rucksacks, beds, solar-stoves, toys and educational equipment.

In 1981, the participants also went through courses in English and social science before spending one week in London visiting Namibians in exile and youth organisations in parts of London with a high percentage of immigrants. Lecturers from the Norwegian Refugee Council, the labour movement, the business community and the Namibia Association contributed to a theoretical understanding of the various experiences gained through the course. By arranging meetings, getting attention in the local press and participating in debates on local television, the course managed to focus attention on the situation for young people in the labour market.

Although the results of the courses were positive, the Ministry (KAD) chose to terminate the support on the principled grounds that addressing unemployment should be a public concern.

"Education for a free Namibia"

To rebuild independent Namibia, there was a great need for trained and educated people. At the beginning of the 1980s, SWAPO estimated that around 40,000 Namibians and up to 15,000 non-Namibian "experts" were required to fill key positions.[5] SWAPO, therefore, very strongly emphasised the need for education. The possibilities for receiving education within the country were bleak for black pupils, the apartheid school system was designed to give black children just the necessary education to serve the white minority. These were—together with the strong base in the Elverum schools—the main reasons why the Namibia Association in 1981 started a long-term programme under the heading: "Education for a free Namibia". Since then, the main focus of the project work of the Namibia Association has been on education. The principle of involving both the head and the hands, or combining theoretical training with practical work, which characterised the organisation's own work, has also been the major principle behind all the educational projects that the Namibia association has been involved with.

The components of this programme were from the start collecting, producing and purchasing educational equipment and printing textbooks for the refugee camps, recruiting teachers and establishing a print-shop for the training of Namibian printers. Under this programme, a number of projects were initiated, ranging from production of schoolbooks, developing educational plans, building the Congo school, recruiting teachers for the camps, and exchange courses.

The development of textbooks for primary schools started in 1981, after the two representatives of the Namibia Association that visited Angola noted the lack of suitable books for the refugee camps. Ten students at the

---

[5] *The Namibia Association Annual Report*, 1981, p. 14.

teachers' college were engaged in co-operation with SWAPO's representative to the Nordic Countries, Hadino Hishongwa, and teachers at the college, to write ABC's for Namibians. The typographers' union (Grafisk forening) at Elverum volunteered to print 10,000 copies of the book. An exercise book was later produced at a teachers' training college at Nesna, in the north of Norway.

Through these projects, the Namibia Association became especially involved in the development of language education. English was to become the official language in independent Namibia, but it was also seen as important to be able to give children training in their mother tongue. Rolf Teil Endresen, international expert in linguistics, volunteered in 1982 to work on a project to develop a written language for the Namibian vernacular Sibya, that was only in oral use: study the codification, produce grammars and train teachers for bi-lingual teaching. The Ministry of Foreign Affairs supported the projects by covering the expenses for the experts, and for grants for Namibians studying linguistics.

The Print-Shop Project

In May 1982 the Namibia Association started a project for Namibian students to learn printing in Elverum. Norwegian support for a print-shop had by then been discussed for a couple of years with the Ministry of Foreign Affairs, and also with the Norwegian Confederation of Trade Unions.[6] In 1980, SWAPO also requested the Namibia Association for assistance for this.

The project was sponsored from the start by the unions of Nordic and Norwegian typographers (Nordisk Grafisk Union and Norsk Grafisk Forbund)—in addition to the Ministry of Foreign Affairs. The Ministry remained the main supporter of the project up to independence.

To carry out the first phase of the project, a fairly simple, but functioning, second-hand printing press was bought and eight Namibian refugees who had been selected by SWAPO were invited to Elverum for an eight month course to learn to operate the press. The equipment that the printing students had been trained on was subsequently dismantled, brought to Zambia, rebuilt—and handed over to SWAPO. The project leader, Michael Fotheringham, and the students also travelled with the equipment to continue the course. Eight other printers, who had received training in Lusaka through a Dutch organisation, joined the project. When it restarted in Lusaka in March 1983, it was SWAPO's first fully-fledged print-shop. It immediately started producing educational and information material for

---

[6] Memorandum. Støtte til SWAPO for 1979 og 1980 (Support for SWAPO for 1979 and 1980), Tor Elden, the NORAD resident representative in Lusaka, 7 October 1989; Knut Thommessen to Tor Elden, 15 October 1980; and Lars Glans, Arbeiderpressens Samvirke A/L, 22 October 1980. All documents in MFA 34 9/5 XII.

SWAPO, in combination with the training course. As this proved a very ambitious task, a second teacher was recruited in 1984 by the Namibia Association. In the following years, a number of new printers also joined the print-shop, some of them were highly competent in the craft after having gone through three years of printing training in East Germany.

It was a very successful venture. By continuing the education in Africa and using applied technology, some of the pitfalls that are not uncommon in these kinds of projects were avoided. The Namibian students were taken well care of in the period they stayed in Elverum: a contact group of 11 volunteers was responsible for seeing to their social life. They were also encouraged to participate in the information and solidarity activities in Norway, thereby becoming more closely involved with the work, and the people of the Namibia Association. The printing course was designed especially for this situation. The teaching was conducted in English. And—above all—the Namibian students, both while studying and later in their work as printers, were devoted to achieving the aims of the project.

After a couple of years a need to expand the print-shop arose. The production had increased substantially, more people had joined, and new equipment had been installed. In 1987, the print-shop with 33 employees, many of whom were women, therefore moved into newly built premises in Lusaka. In the late 1980s, new sponsors such as the Swedish aid agency SIDA provided new equipment, and the enterprise started using computer systems. In 1986 and 1987, three students received grants financed by the Norwegian Ministry of Foreign Affairs for further education in England. After having completed this, two returned to the print-shop in Lusaka, while one received an additional grant to study economics and administration to prepare SWAPO for the taking over of the economic and administrative running of the enterprise.

Following the agreement to implement UN Security Council Resolution 435, the printing office was moved to Windhoek in the summer of 1989. Because of the regulations tied to this implementation, the Ministry of Foreign Affairs informed the Namibia Association that it would refund the expenses paid by the organisation in connection with the move to Windhoek. In order not to violate the impartiality clause in connection with the transition period, this would, however, only be disbursed after the elections.[7] In preparation for the elections, it printed millions of mock ballot papers, to make it possible for people all over Namibia to become familiar with the procedures and symbols of the various parties. By then, more than 40 people were engaged at the print-shop, in addition to a consultant from the Namibia Association. Large investments in machinery were made, for example a new computer system, a laser printer and a bookbinding machine.

---

[7] Telex from MFA to the Consulate in Windhoek, 11 November 1989, MFA 34 9/5 XVII. See chapter 3.

It was a modern, relatively well functioning Namib Graphics (Pty) Ltd. that President Nujoma officially opened in March 1990. After an evaluation by a British printing expert the same year, rationalisations were made, the auditing put out to an international firm, administrative routines improved and training courses arranged for the personnel.

The market for printing was favourable in independent Namibia. In 1991, the political party Democratic Turnhalle Alliance (DTA), bought competing businesses, with the result that Namib Graphics became the only major print-shop in Namibia in 1992 that was not owned by the DTA. After the activities had been consolidated in 1990 and 1991, Namib Graphics stood firmly on its own feet. Therefore it did not receive direct support in 1992, although a grant was given to one of the printers for a two-year course in England in management and administration. The co-operation between SWAPO and the Namibia Association throughout the years of the printing project was very good, and when Namib Graphics stopped receiving support, it functioned as an independent self-supporting commercial enterprise.

The Textile Project

In another project—very different from the one regarding the print-shop—the Namibia Association invited Namibian refugees to Elverum for educational courses. It started with a request in the autumn of 1982 to the Namibia Association from SWAPO's Women Council (SWC) to recruit two textile teachers for the Council's school in Kwanza Sul, Angola. For four months, the teachers would give courses in textile and art subjects to women who would then become instructors themselves. The Ministry of Foreign Affairs granted the funding and the Namibia Association recruited the teachers, but at the last minute, SWC requested that the project be changed into a training course in weaving and sewing for women in the Nyango camp in Zambia. The reason for this change of plans, was the insecure situation in Kwanza Sul.

Following a period of planning, equipment such as a container house, looms and materials were sent to Nyango, and in the summer of 1983 two teachers were established in the camp to start the course. Twenty women with small children were chosen by SWC to join the project. The women would under any circumstances have to stay in the camp until their children were two years old, and there was hardly any chance of finding other education or jobs. As they did not have much previous experience with textile work, it soon became clear that the timeframe for the project had to be expanded to two years. With intermissions and reorganisations, the project in fact ended up lasting for more than ten years—it closed down in 1994.

The project proved quite demanding. The situation took some getting used to for all involved. The teachers were the only non-Africans in the camp. A conflict arose in the autumn of 1983 between the teachers and the camp manager, which led to the Norwegians being denied food and transport. They therefore left the camp, and one of the teachers did not wish to return. According to Dag Hareide, the conflict should be seen as a gender conflict reflecting SWAPO's low priority of projects for women, in addition to the camp manager's lack of willingness to co-operate.[8] Despite the good spirits of the trainees, problems again arose regarding responsibilities, housing and communication, which in 1984 led to a break for seven months. In 1985, the project had to close down for three months, because all the inhabitants in the camp were evacuated due to an increased danger of South African attacks. The Norwegian teacher in this period left for Lusaka, then returned to Norway.

When the project was resumed, three women had left. Of those who continued, nine had sewing as their main activity, while eight had weaving. Besides the textile training, they also received lessons in mathematics and English. In addition to the education, the women also produced clothes for the orphanages in the camp, where a hundred children between two and seven lived. For the celebration of Namibian Women's Day in 1984, they made school uniforms for all the children. In 1985, the personnel and children in the kindergarten likewise got new uniforms.

Exams were to be held in Nyango in June 1986, but South African bombing of a refugee camp in Lusaka made this impossible. New, alternative plans were quickly made, and the exams were held in Lusaka—giving the women the first papers in their lives on completed training. The diplomas were—naturally—from the SWAPO print-shop.

The harsh conditions in the camp, combined with the security situation, did, however, make it difficult to recruit teachers, and in 1987 the Namibia Association was unable to find new teachers for the textile project. Despite a very large interest in Nyango in joining the project, it therefore closed in 1988.

In the meantime, however, two projects had emerged as offspring from the textile project in Nyango. Following the exams in 1986, four of the women were given grants by the Namibia Association to receive further education in Elverum. Their course was planned in co-operation with the Elverum senior secondary school and the county of Hedmark. The students were partly integrated in regular classes and partly given training as a special group. After four years, they returned to Namibia, to join the textile project, which had by then moved to Windhoek, as instructors in textile and sewing.

The remaining thirteen women from the textile project set up a production unit in Nyango, producing textiles for the commercial market.

---

[8] As stated at a meeting between the Namibian Association and MFA, 19 March 1984, MFA 34 9/5 C. The same incident was discussed by Bjarne Lindstrøm of MFA and Aaron Mushimba in Lusaka, 3 February 1984, MFA 34 9/5 C VI.

In 1987, SWAPO in co-operation with the Namibia Association also started a production co-operative in Lusaka, where women under the guidance of a Norwegian consultant produced textiles for the commercial market. The aim was to give the women an income, but as it would take some time before the co-operative could become commercially viable, the Namibia Association gave support for buying materials and equipment. The main emphasis was on sewing, as it proved difficult to make weaving profitable. Consultants were also recruited to help the textile workers design commercially interesting products—and to assist in the running of the business. The products were sold at various exhibitions and events, as well as in some of the tourist hotels. In 1989, as the repatriation of Namibian refugees started, the project in Lusaka was terminated and the equipment moved to Windhoek. In co-operation with the Repatriation, Rehabilitation and Rebuilding Committee, the textile project was in 1990 reestablished as Katutura Tailoring Co-operative. With new equipment and a consultant from the Namibia Association, the aim was for the eleven members of the co-operative to run a modern, small textile enterprise. The co-operative did, however, need substantial support until it was closed down in 1994, on account of the fact that it did not become viable. The equipment and materials were given to other organisations, and three of the workers were provided with enough equipment to be able to establish their own businesses in Katutura and Windhoek. The other workers did find new jobs, most of them in the textile industry, due to the qualifications they had achieved during the project.

The Namibia Technical Secondary School in Loudima, Congo

The project that occupied most of the time and resources of the association, was the involvement in the building and running of the Namibia Secondary Technical School in Loudima, Congo. As it was implemented in close co-operation with the Norwegian Ministry of Foreign Affairs, a detailed account of the project is given in chapter 2, which concerns the direct official aid to SWAPO.

The Loudima school commitment strongly influenced the development of the Namibia Association itself. The costs for the construction of the school ran up to around NOK 50 million, while NOK 10 million was spent annually on the running of the school. 8,000 square metres of buildings were erected on an area of 750 square kilometres. 3 kilometres of access roads had to be built in addition to the roads on campus. As well as being in charge of this on behalf of SWAPO, the Namibia Association was also central in developing curricula and syllabi for the school. To SWAPO, this was a most important project, as it in addition to providing Namibian students in exile with a secondary education, also had the function of a pilot project. Through the Loudima school, SWAPO acquired very valuable experience for the building up of a secondary educational system in Namibia after independence. It also proved that it was capable of leading the construction of the buildings, the development of the pedagogics, and the actual running of this significant secondary school.

For the Namibia Association, becoming responsible for such a large, complicated and costly project meant that a lot of attention had to be directed towards its organisational, political and economic aspects. Less time was available for local solidarity campaigns. When the association became more professional in questions regarding education, it became an important co-operation partner to SWAPO, and later the democratically elected Namibian government, in developing the school policy for independent Namibia. As an extension of the work done with the Loudima school, in 1990 the Namibia Association at the request of the Minister of Education and Culture, Nahas Angula, recruited Roger Avenstrup as an adviser to the Namibian government on the development of secondary schools. The Loudima school would serve as a model for schools in independent Namibia, and Avenstrup had been responsible for co-ordinating the curriculum development. He was working with the International Institute for Educational Development in Windhoek until 1997.

The deep involvement in education, and the competence gained through the projects for Namibian refugees, which also included recruitment of teachers to the Nyango camp 1988–1990, paved the way for educational projects inside Namibia. In 1988, the Namibia Association in co-operation with the English Language Unit at CCN started a course in Windhoek, training 35 English teachers in language and new teaching methodology. This was followed up by a six week course in Namibia in 1989, where the Norwegian instructors visited the teachers in the schools where they worked. The course proved useful to the Namibian teachers, it was therefore repeated later in 1989 and then in 1990, with a new group of seventy teachers. From 1990, this project was made more permanent, four Namibian teachers were engaged as instructors, and a Resource Centre was built up at the CCN office in Windhoek. The Norwegian Ministry of Foreign Affairs financed the projects.

In 1988 the Operation Day's Work was arranged in favour of "Education against Apartheid". This is an annual solidarity campaign where students in secondary school devote a day to raising money for educational projects in the Third World. In 1988 the funds raised by the campaign were given to the Norwegian Students' and Academics' International Assistance Fund (SAIH), the Norwegian Council for Southern Africa—and the Namibia Association, which received NOK 8 million. With support from NORAD too, part of this was used to finance the building of a kindergarten centre in Katutura, for the private organisation Children's World Creche. It was opened by President Sam Nujoma in June 1990, and had by the end of the year 25 employees and 220 children enrolled. The plan was to make it into a professional resource centre for smaller kindergartens in Namibia. The Namibia Association and OXFAM co-operated on covering the running expenses.

In 1990, the Namibia Association also arranged English courses for Namibian female teachers, with support from the Norwegian Housewives' Association and the annual campaign supported by the Norwegian Broadcasting Corporation to raise funds for worthy causes. In 1988, this was in favour of a group of women's organisations. Two Norwegian teachers visited 12 primary schools in various places in Namibia, and spent the mornings with the teachers in the classrooms and ran courses for the teachers in the afternoons. The courses were well received by the 160 teachers who were included.

In the 1990s, the Namibia Association has continued to support educational projects in Namibia. In doing this, it has continued the co-operation with CCN and the Ministry of Education, Culture, Youth and Sport, and with various other organisations, such as Namibia Development Trust, Legal Assistance Centre and Unemployment Sewing Group. It has also supported the newspaper "Namibia Today".

Transition from solidarity organisation to development aid organisation: The Namibia Association in independent Namibia

The role played by the Namibia Association in Namibia's liberation struggle was significant. In the ten years from the first campaign in Elverum, the association was instrumental in providing goods and services worth NOK 150 million.[9] On the occasion of SWAPO's official thanks to the Nordic countries for the support in the liberation struggle, the Namibia Association was chosen as host for the ceremony which took place in Norway in the summer of 1990. Among the guests at the local museum (Glomdalsmuseet) in Elverum were SWAPO's Chief Deputy Co-ordinator Festus Naholo, the political adviser to the Norwegian Minister of Foreign Affairs, Norway's ambassador to Namibia, SWAPO's co-operation partners among Norwegian NGOs, political parties, trade unions and others.

With the liberation of Namibia, the Namibia Association changed from being a solidarity organisation with a broad, popular base working closely with SWAPO for the freedom of Namibia, to becoming one of many aid organisations that wanted to run projects in the country after independence. The relative importance of the association's support would thus be less. From relating to a liberation movement, it was now co-operating with an elected government. From having its projects fully financed by the Ministry of Foreign Affairs, it now received most of its funds from NORAD. This implied that the Namibia Association would have to finance 20% of the project costs itself. This, in turn, would force the organisation to use more time and

---

[9] Østlendingen, 19 September 1989.

effort on income bringing activities than before. Instead of providing information about Namibian refugees, the main role of the information department now became to raise funds for the projects. This was an important motivation behind starting the publication "Dugnad" (voluntary communal work), which informed members and other interested people about Namibia and the organisation's work there.

The character of the projects also had to change. Instead of large, technically complicated projects, like the Congo school, the Namibia Association would initiate smaller, educational projects based on previous experience. The character of the association changed towards being a project organisation, although it never gave up the ambition to be a local campaign inspirer. Through the 1990s, a wide variety of events have been initiated, and many new projects started in Namibia. Most of these have been concerned with education and health, and it is a vital and enthusiastic Namibia Association that in 1998 is still engaged in the development of the people of Namibia. This is perhaps most clearly expressed in the co-operation between Elverum and Tsumeb.

The twin towns Tsumeb and Elverum

On his first visit to Elverum in 1981, President Sam Nujoma presented the idea of twinning Elverum with Tsumeb. During the liberation struggle, it was of course not easy to make arrangements between the two towns. The thought of Tsumeb being Elverum's twin town was, however, kept alive, and when in 1989 the Mineworkers Union of Namibia, MUN, contacted the Namibia Association with a request to carry out an independent investigation of the working conditions for miners, the response was immediately positive. The mining companies were very restrictive in providing information on the conditions for the workers, and independent visits to the work places were denied. To avoid reprisals, the investigation was carried out clandestinely. With support from the Ministry of Foreign Affairs, a medical doctor in Elverum, Kristian Vetlesen in co-operation with the International Solidarity Committee of the Norwegian Labour Movement (Arbeidernes Internasjonale Støttekomite), revealed that the workers had been exposed to cadmium, lead and arsenic to an extremely health—hazardous degree. In one case, there were signs of serious brain damage on account of lead poisoning. The results of the investigation were presented at a conference held in Windhoek in 1990, where the theme was the working conditions in the mines.

The two towns were tied closer together after a representative of the Namibia Association visited Tsumeb in 1991 to open the door for a people-to-people engagement. In Elverum and Tsumeb, twin-town groups were established, with members from schools, kindergartens, congregations, trade unions and NGOs. In the following years, the friendship between the towns has been strengthened. Fund-raising campaigns have been arranged, the community chairmen and other officials have exchanged visits, together with representatives of local organisations and newspapers. The Namibia Association is running projects in co-operation with local organisations in Tsumeb, and exchange visits have been arranged with health workers and students from the folk high-school and students from Tsumeb. It is the hope, that on the smaller scale of the twin towns, it will be possible to mobilise for continual solidarity work and exchange, in the same spirit as the one which inspired the first action campaign in Elverum in April 1980.

Chapter 10
An Ambiguous Champion: Some Concluding Remarks[1]

Tore Linné Eriksen

Norway and "the apotheosis of all evil"

"The fact is that for almost four decades South Africa had been a central preoccupation of the Norwegians. Whole generations of Norwegian schoolchildren had been raised on the premise that apartheid was the apotheosis of all evil and that Nelson Mandela and the ANC could do no wrong. Norway was one of the main contributors to the ANC and one of its most vociferous supporters in international campaigns to isolate South Africa."[2]

Although this quote from the autobiography of F.W. de Klerk, former president of South Africa and the recipient of the Nobel Peace Prize (together with Nelson Mandela), might be regarded as somewhat exaggerated, it highlights the fact that the struggle for liberation in Southern Africa has been an important issue in Norway since the late 1950s. In the previous chapters we have attempted to document this process and discuss the forms which the support for the liberation movements has taken over the years. Clearly, as even the largely empirical and narrative chapters show, this process has not been without its conflicts, complexities and contradictions. In the concluding chapter we will select a number of central issues for further exploration and attempt to identify some of the major factors and actors shaping Norwegian policies in the Southern African region. To achieve a broader perspective, our discussion of the most striking features of the Norwegian experience will also integrate the "Southern African voice", as expressed in interviews with a wide range of representatives from the liberation movements themselves.[3] In addition, we will where appropriate employ a Nordic comparative perspective.

---

[1] The title is borrowed from Linda Freeman's perceptive study on Canada and the struggle for liberation in Southern Africa: *The Ambiguous Champion. Canada and South Africa in the Trudeau and Mulroney Years*. Toronto: Toronto University Press, 1997.

[2] F. W. de Klerk: *The Last Trek—A New Beginning. The Autobiography*. London: Macmillan, 1999, p. 297.

[3] Tor Sellström (ed.): *Liberation in Southern Africa. Regional and Swedish Voices*. Uppsala: Nordiska Afrikainstitutet, 1999. See also comments by scholars and representatives from the

Although our study was never meant to be a history of the liberation struggle _per se_, we will attempt to situate the history of the Norwegian involvement within a broader Southern African context. As shown below, the attention given to the Southern Africa issue both among NGOs and at a state level to a large extent reflects the resistance and repression in the region itself: the Sharpeville massacre, the successful struggle of the liberation movements in the Portuguese colonies, the Soweto uprising, the achievement of independence in Zimbabwe and the mounting anti-apartheid resistance in South Africa in the mid-1980s. Such conjunctures provided a new coalescence of forces and prompted new responses.

The uniqueness of the Nordic countries

Most Western countries can boast solidarity movements, churches, trade unions and parties on the left which called for support to the liberation struggle and the imposition of sanctions against the apartheid regime. The Nordic countries, however, are unique in the direct humanitarian assistance and diplomatic support they extended to the liberation movements at the state level. This is also why the chapters 1–4 of this study have focused on this particular aspect of the Norwegian-Southern African relations. While the liberation movements received the major part of their arms from China or the Soviet Union and other East European countries, the impact of the Nordic support for their refugee settlements and their non-military struggle can hardly be overrated. Norway played its part in providing food, clothes, schools, means of transport and equipment for printing textbooks and information material. In the words of Raymond Suttner of ANC: "... (the) Nordic countries literally provided the clothes that people wore, the food they ate, the funds for their basic sustenance, the educational infrastructure and volunteers in the ANC schools and support for the ANC Women's League, as part of their commitment to ensuring gender equality in our democratic development."[4]

Which, then, were the movements benefiting from this assistance during what has aptly been described as the "Thirty Years War" in Southern Africa?[5] Having in mind the public debate about whether or not the liberation movements had a popular following, it is interesting to see that the movements supported by Norway are today the ruling parties in their respective countries. ZANU of Zimbabwe, SWAPO of Namibia and ANC of South Africa received an overwhelming majority of the votes in democratic

liberation movement presented to the conference on "Nordic Solidarity with the Liberation Struggles in Southern Africa, and Challenges for Democratic Partnerships into the 21st Century", organised by the Robben Island Museum, the Mayibuye Centre (University of Western Cape) and the Nordic Africa Institute at Robben Island 11–14 February 1999. The proceedings are referred to later in this chapter as _Conference Report_.

[4] Raymond Suttner, _Conference Report_, op.cit., p. 84.

[5] This is a concept coined by John S. Saul in _Recolonization and Resistance: Southern Africa in the 1990s_. Trenton, NJ: Africa World Press, 1993.

elections at independence. When the first multi-party elections were held in Angola (1992) and Mozambique (1994) after many years of war and desta-bilisation, both FRELIMO and MPLA won the majority of the seats in the national assembly. In the case of Zimbabwe, Norwegian humanitarian assis-tance was also rendered to ZAPU, which after seven years in opposition merged with ZANU in 1987.[6] As the only Nordic country, Norway had during the South African liberation struggle also given regular support, although quite modest in financial terms, to PAC, which did not receive more than 1.7% of the votes in the first democratic elections in 1994.

From 1973 until the demise of the South African apartheid regime in 1994, official humanitarian assistance given by the Norwegian government to Southern Africa amounted to NOK 2 billion (see Statistical Appendix: Table I). Included in this figure are both direct assistance to the liberation movements and grants contributed to various UN funds and other multilat-eral institutions. In addition, the liberation movements have also benefited from support from Norwegian NGOs. However, it was official sources that provided the major part of the funds channelled through NGOs such as the Namibia Committee, the Norwegian People's Aid, the Norwegian Confed-eration of Trade Unions (LO), the Students' and Academics' International Assistance Fund (SAIH) and the Council for Ecumenical and International Relations (Mellomkirkelig Råd).

Seen in a comparative perspective, the Norwegian share of the total Nordic disbursements of humanitarian assistance to Southern Africa is estimated at 23%. According to the statistics, Sweden is in front with 58%, Denmark accounts for 15% while Finland did not provide more than 4%.[7] In addition to extending more assistance than the other three countries put to-gether, Sweden is also commonly seen as having established closer links with the liberation movements—based on a firm political commitment—than the other Nordic countries (see below).[8]

If we look at principles guiding humanitarian assistance to Southern Africa, as well as the volume of aid disbursed, there are parallels between Denmark and Norway. Both the NATO countries made support to the liberation movements a regular feature of their development co-operation in 1972/73, while Sweden had embarked upon its ambitious aid programme in 1969. Denmark, however, never entered into the same direct relationship

---

[6] On one occasion a minor grant was also extended to Abel Muzorewa's UANC in Zimbabwe, an organisation which did not gain any seats in the 1980 elections.

[7] These preliminary figures are provided by Tor Sellström, and may be slightly revised in the light of further research.

[8] This conclusion has emerged from a close reading of Tor Sellström (ed.), op. cit.; Tor Sell-ström: *Sweden and National Liberation in Southern Africa. Vol. I: Formation of a Popular Opinion (1950–1970)*. Uppsala: Nordiska Afrikainstitutet, 1999; Tor Sellström: *Sweden and National Libera-tion in Southern Africa, Vol. II*. Uppsala: Nordiska Afrikainstitutet (forthcoming); Iina Soiri and Pekka Peltola: *Finland and National Liberation in Southern Africa*. Uppsala: Nordiska Afrika-institutet, 1999; Christopher Munthe Morgenstierne: *Denmark: A Flexible Response—Humanitar-ian and Political*. Uppsala: Nordiska Afrikainstitutet, 1999 (Draft).

with the liberation movements as Sweden and Norway, preferring instead to channel all its assistance through the UN system and international and Danish NGOs, World University Service (WUS) in particular.[9] In this regard, the history of Norwegian involvement is more similar to the Swedish experience.

In Finland, the principled decision to extend humanitarian assistance to liberation movements was made in March 1973, but Finland was never seriously involved with the liberation movements in Angola, Mozambique and Zimbabwe. The Finnish contributions were largely confined to SWAPO, a fact which is partly explained by the historical links developed with Namibia through the Finnish Lutheran Mission since the late 19th century. The major part of the assistance to Namibia has been spent on a comprehensive scholarship programme which brought Namibian students to Finland from 1975 onwards. Finland was also significantly involved with the Namibian issue as a member of the UN Namibia Council, and through the role played by Martti Ahtisaari as UN Commissioner for Namibia and, later, as the Special Representative of the UN Secretary General.[10]

Although largely outside the scope of the present study, the substantial Norwegian development co-operation with Tanzania, Zambia, Botswana, Mozambique and Zimbabwe, all core recipients of Norwegian aid, should also be mentioned, as these programmes need to be seen in a wider Southern African context. One of the reasons why they came to occupy such a prominent position in the history of Norwegian aid was that they all suffered from the devastating South African destabilisation and in one way or another were involved in the struggle for liberation in the region as a whole. (For the period 1980–1988 the material damages resulting from South African military and economic aggression were estimated at USD 60 billion, not counting the loss of lives and human suffering).[11] When the regional organisation Southern African Development Co-ordination Conference (SADCC) was set up in 1980, the Nordic countries immediately developed strong links with SADCC and offered substantial assistance.[12] During the

---

[9] Christopher Munthe Morgenstierne, op. cit.

[10] See Iina Soiri and Pekka Peltola, op. cit.

[11] For an extensive review of South African aggression in the region, see Joseph Hanlon: *Beggar your neighbours. Apartheid power in Southern Africa*. London: Catholic Institute for International Relations (CIIR) and James Currey, 1986; Phyllis Johnson/David Martin: *Apartheid Terrorism: The Destabilisation Report*. London: James Currey, 1989.

[12] SADCC changed its name to Southern African Development Community (SADC) in 1992. SADCC and SADCC-Nordic relations in the 1980s are discussed in Bertil Odén and Haroub Othman (eds.): *Regional Co-operation in Southern Africa. A Post-Apartheid Perspective*. Uppsala: Nordiska Afrikainstitutet, 1989; Tom Østergaard: *SADCC. A Political and Economic Survey*. Copenhagen: Danida, 1990; Tore Linné Eriksen: *Det regionale samarbeidet mellom det sørlige Afrika og Norden*. Oslo: Norsk Utenrikspolitisk Institutt, 1988. (Forum for Utviklingsstudier, no. 1–3, 1988.) It could also be argued that the SADCC programme for development co-operation constituted "a soft option" at a time when Norway was faced with calls for comprehensive sanctions and unconditional support for the liberation struggle. In this perspective, the aid has been de-

1980s, the foreign ministers of the Frontline States on two occasions held joint meetings with their Nordic counterparts.

However important the humanitarian assistance has been to the liberation movements, which received little aid of this kind from other countries, the amounts in question should not be exaggerated. Not even in the 1980s, when assistance to ANC, PAC and SWAPO and other anti-apartheid forces in the region recorded its highest levels, did these funds exceed 2% of the total Norwegian allocation for development co-operation. The support did not in any sense constitute an economic burden on the donor country. In a period of increasing aid budgets, it was never difficult for the Norwegian government to find the money for this humanitarian assistance. (The Norwegian budget for development co-operation increased from NOK 263 million in 1970 to NOK 4,9 billion in 1985. In terms of aid as percentage of GNP, the same period saw an increase from 0.33% to 1.0%.)[13]

Another relevant aspect is that of comparing the assistance extended to ANC, PAC and SWAPO in the 1980s to the Norwegian trade with the South African apartheid regime. If we take the year 1985 as an example, trade statistics show that Norway imported South African goods worth NOK 250 million, while the total aid to the three movements in question amounted to NOK 70 million. According to the Norwegian Shipowners Association's own estimates the earnings accruing from shipping links to South Africa (oil, bulk cargo and chemicals) amounted to no less than NOK 800 million on an annual basis in the mid-1980s (see chapter 5).

The evolution of Norwegian support to the liberation struggle

From the early 1970s, the Nordic countries, with Sweden in the lead, took their first steps towards a long-term commitment to the liberation struggle in Southern Africa. However, this was certainly not a foregone conclusion. Looking back one might easily picture a general anti-apartheid consensus in the Nordic countries and a firm commitment to the Southern African movements which today are in power in their respective countries. The fact that everybody wants to be on the winning side should not, however, persuade us that the story of Norwegian involvement was without its contradictions. The Norwegian policies changed over time, and the outcome of the struggle between contending forces was never predetermined. It is worth recalling that, in the words of the Labour Prime Minister Gro Harlem Brundtland, "... in the 1960s the liberation movements were considered of a dubious nature in the Western world, even far into the social democratic

---

scribed as "just like fattening us for the slaughter". (Kenneth Kaunda quoted in Linda Freeman, op. cit., p. 208.)

[13] Tore Linné Eriksen (ed.): *Den vanskelige bistanden. Noen trekk ved norsk utviklingshjelps historie.* Oslo: Universitetsforlaget, 1987, p. 11.

parties".[14] We have, therefore, in the previous chapters attempted to document the main forces shaping the nature of the Norwegian involvement. Seen in retrospect, we are also able to identify three stages through which the Norwegian policies on Southern Africa evolved.

While the 1950s have been described as "the silent years", the turn of the decade witnessed significant changes. The first stage of serious Norwegian involvement coincided with major events at the international level as well as in the Southern African region itself. Compared to the previous decade, the 1960s saw significant increases in the attention given to the apartheid regime in South Africa and the struggles in the Portuguese colonies, a change which was reflected both in mass media and in the parliamentary debates on foreign affairs. The Declaration on the Granting of Independence to Colonial Countries and Peoples, adopted by the UN General Assembly in 1960, was indeed a breakthrough for the principles of decolonisation. As most African states gained their independence, international attention was consequently focused on the remaining obstacles for continent-wide independence and democracy: the South African apartheid regime, the Portuguese colonial power and the white settler regime in Rhodesia/Zimbabwe. In Norway, as well as in all other parts of the world, the Sharpeville massacre also made apartheid a burning international issue.

As is shown in chapter 1, the early 1960s were characterised by the first fund-raising campaigns for the victims of apartheid, the formation of anti-apartheid organisations, consumer boycotts initiated by trade unions and youth/student organisations, and the awarding of the Nobel Peace Prize to the President of ANC, Albert Luthuli. The Afro-Scandinavian Youth Congress in Oslo in 1962 significantly increased the awareness in the Nordic countries of the struggle for liberation in Southern Africa. Being a member of the UN Security Council, in 1963/64 Norway was also for a brief period involved with Southern African issues at an international level. Viewed historically, it should be noted that Norway in particular was instrumental in drafting a Security Council resolution appealing to all UN members to implement a limited arms embargo against South Africa. At the same time, Parliament introduced a special grant to exiled students from Southern Africa, to be administered by a Special Committee on Refugees from Southern Africa. The first grants were also given for legal assistance to prisoners and their families through UN funds and the International Defence and Aid Fund (IDAF). While the support for refugees was stepped up during the 1960s, the sanctions issue was, however, relegated to the background when the Norwegian Parliament in 1963 voted against unilateral sanctions. (This vote was only opposed by the two representatives of the Socialist People's Party.) The first attempt at sanctions had thus been precluded by an "un-

---

[14] "The Scandinavian Perspective on the North-South dialogue", p. 15 in Kofi Buenor Hadjor (ed.): *New Perspectives in North-South Dialogue: Essays in Honour of Olof Palme*. London: I.B. Tauris, 1988.

holy alliance" between the dominant parties, the higher echelons of the civil service and the private business sector. Almost a quarter of a century, the era of "protest and trade", would eventually pass before the Norwegian Parliament adopted a comprehensive sanctions law.

During the six years of the non-socialist coalition (1965–1971) official recognition of the liberation movements as legitimate representatives of their peoples was rare, and spokespersons from the movements were either ignored or received at a junior level in the Ministry of Foreign Affairs. In these years, it was mainly left to the solidarity movements (the Norwegian Council for Southern Africa in particular) and the political left to promote the interests of the liberation movements and to put the Southern African issue on the political agenda. This was in marked contrast to what happened in Sweden in this period, where both the Social Democratic Party and the "middle parties" (the Liberal Party and the Centre Party) developed close links with liberation movements, leading to a decision by the Swedish Parliament in 1969 to extend humanitarian assistance to the liberation movements.[15]

1973: A turning point

The unanimous decision by the Norwegian Parliament in 1973 to endorse a policy of direct, official humanitarian support to the liberation movements is commonly regarded as the opening of a new stage. (Until 1977, however, South African liberation movements were excluded from Norwegian aid programmes.) This principled move to give support to the popular movements in Southern Africa was affirmed by the Parliament before the UN/OAU Conference on Southern Africa was held in Oslo in April 1973. However, it is the conference itself which has been justly described as a pivotal event signifying an international breakthrough for the liberation movements as legitimate representatives of the peoples struggling for independence (see chapter 1). The final report of the conference was later endorsed by the OAU Summit and the UN General Assembly. In the same year the Commonwealth conference in Ottawa in its final communiqué recognised the legitimacy of the struggle. But, as historians never stop telling us, behind all turning points we should be able to identify structural factors as well as individual actors at play.

The role of the liberation movements themselves cannot be overrated in explaining why the Norwegian Parliament eventually came to embrace the principle of extending humanitarian assistance to the peoples fighting against colonialism and apartheid. Frequently invited by the Norwegian Council for Southern Africa in the second half of the 1960s, representatives of the movements addressed public meetings, attracted media attention, and forged links with churches, trade unions, political parties, and student and

---

[15] This story is told in great detail in Tor Sellström, op. cit., Vol. I.

youth organisations. In this regard, the diplomatic skills of the leaders of the liberation movements, Eduardo Mondlane (FRELIMO) and Amilcar Cabral (PAIGC) in particular, were highly significant. Seen from their perspective, the position of the Nordic countries was from the early beginnings considered to be unique in the West. As later expressed by Sergio Vieira of FRELIMO: "The absence of a colonial tradition, the values and culture of social democracy, the ethics of the Lutheran and Protestant Church were factors influencing sympathy for our cause".[16] From an early stage all movements paid serious attention to international diplomacy within and outside the UN system, and in this regard often approached the Nordic countries for support and concerted efforts.

Another contributing factor shaping Norwegian policies was the close links developed with Kenneth Kaunda and Julius Nyerere, based on extensive development co-operation with Zambia and Tanzania. The two highly respected African statesmen had frequently criticised the Western countries for their support for Portugal, South Africa and the settler regime in Rhodesia/Zimbabwe and consistently called for assistance to the liberation movements as legitimate representatives of their peoples. The fact that most movements were able to set up offices in Dar es Salaam and Lusaka also facilitated frequent contacts with the Norwegian "community" of aid officials and diplomats. Recognising the unique position of Tanzania, the newly formed Organisation of African Unity in 1963 decided to locate its OAU Liberation Committee in Dar es Salaam. Kenneth Kaunda and Julius Nyerere were also the main architects behind the Lusaka Manifesto of 1969, which was later endorsed by the Organisation of African Unity as well as the UN General Assembly. The liberation movements were not enthusiastic in their appraisal of the Manifesto, as they had not been consulted on the matter. However, the Manifesto did conclude that "... while peaceful progress is being blocked by actions of those at present in power in the states of Southern Africa, we have no choice but to give the peoples of those territories all the support of which we are capable in their struggle against their oppressors."[17]

Following African decolonisation in the early 1960s, Africa, Asia and Latin-America commanded a two-thirds majority in the UN General Assembly. Consequently the UN was another important arena where Norwegian diplomats and politicians were exposed to the views and interests of the Third World nations. The principle of national self-determination was deeply embedded in the 1960 Decolonisation Declaration. In the same way, the apartheid system, which had been described by the UN as "a crime against humanity ", was seen as a gross violation of basic human rights as stated in the UN Declaration on Human Rights (1948).

---

[16] Sergio Vieira, *Conference Report*, op.cit., p. 56.

[17] Quoted in Tor Sellström, op. cit., Vol. II.

By voting for the UN General Assembly Resolution 2295 (1969) on the Portuguese colonies, Norway had already supported the appeal "to grant the peoples of the territories under Portuguese domination the moral and material assistance necessary for their inalienable rights". In 1972 the UN General Assembly had recognised PAIGC as "the sole and authentic representative of people of the territory of Guinea Bissau". Concerning Namibia, the South African mandate had been revoked by the UN General Assembly as early as in 1966, to be followed by a Security Council Resolution which in March 1969 declared the South African presence in the country illegal. Even more important in our context is the fact that another UN Security Council Resolution later in the same year requested all states to increase their moral and material assistance to the people of Namibia in their struggle against foreign occupation.[18] In 1971 the International Court of Justice had declared South Africa's rule in Namibia illegal under international law, while expressing the opinion that the members of the United Nations were under an obligation to recognise the illegality of South Africa's presence in Namibia.

The domestic scene in Norway had since the late 1960s witnessed a general radicalisation, in particular among young people, which, *inter alia*, expressed itself through an increased awareness of the struggle of the peoples of the Third World against colonialism, imperialism and racism.[19] The crucial 1973 decision to give humanitarian assistance to liberation movements was, therefore, deeply embedded in what is today commonly referred to as "the civil society". We have explored in chapters 6–9 the role played by the youth organisations, the Norwegian Council for Southern Africa, the churches, the trade unions and the Namibia Committee in bringing Southern African issues onto the political agenda and making the liberation struggle known to a broader audience. This is also an issue we will return to at the end of this chapter.

Equally decisive were the changes that took place within the Ministry of Foreign Affairs itself. As shown in chapter 1, due to their social isolation and their conservative background, many diplomats had in the 1960s tended to misread the significance of the events in the Portuguese colonies and in South Africa. A younger generation of diplomats and civil servants was more receptive to the "Third World voices" and more open to issues transcending the Cold War divide. Arne Arnesen, Tom Vraalsen and Thorvald Stoltenberg were prominent among the civil servants-cum-politicians who increasingly questioned the prevailing ignorant—and even hostile—attitude towards the liberation movements.[20]

---

[18] UN Security Council Resolution 269 (1969) of 12 August 1969. The resolution was adopted with 11 votes in favour and 4 abstentions.

[19] This "move to the left" is commonly regarded to last until the late 1970s, see Berge Furre: *Norsk historie 1905–1990: vårt hundreår*. Oslo: Samlaget, 1992.

[20] While trained as diplomats in the Ministry of Foreign Affairs, they all later came to occupy political positions. Arne Arnesen (Labour Party) has, *inter alia*, been State Secretary for Foreign

The changing Norwegian position was also in important respects influenced by the Swedish experience. Sweden had in 1969 embarked upon a programme of humanitarian assistance to the liberation movements. In the case of Guinea-Bissau, PAIGC had already given the Swedish authorities proof of high efficiency with regard to administration, distribution and reporting of the goods received.

1980s: Entering the final battle

The final stage in the history of Norwegian support to the liberation movements is largely a reflection of the fundamental changes taking place in the Southern African region itself. Following the independence of Angola (1975), Mozambique (1975) and Zimbabwe (1980), South Africa and Namibia were the only two remaining white bastions. Encouraged by the successes of the national struggle in their neighbouring countries, the liberation movements and other democratic forces in South Africa and Namibia gained in strength and determination. In the aftermath of the Soweto uprising, as well as the murder of Steve Biko and the resurgence of militant trade unionism, the apartheid regime also attracted much more international attention than in the previous decades.

At the level of what is often referred to as "the international community", the situation was a more complex one. While the new constellation of forces within the region made the Nordic countries—both at state and NGO level—even more determined to contribute to the final demise of the apartheid regime and the end of the occupation of Namibia, the Reagan-inspired "constructive engagement" in the region encouraged the South African apartheid regime to launch attacks on a number of neighbouring states and escalate its occupation of the southern part of Angola. By opposing sanctions and ruling out UN interventions, the major Western powers also allowed South Africa to strengthen its illegal hold on Namibia, in spite of the ruling of the International Court of Justice and numerous UN resolutions. The diplomatic stalemate was further prolonged by the US insistence on a linkage between South Africa's withdrawal from Namibia and the withdrawal of Cuba's troops from Angola. During "the Second Cold War" the Reagan administration openly sided with the Angolan UNITA rebels, who like the Contras in Nicaragua were seen as "freedom fighters" in a world-wide containment of communism.[21] Similarly, the coming to power of Margaret Thatcher in the United Kingdom in 1979 was seen from Pretoria as a positive event. While we have identified a growing recognition of ANC

Affairs and Director-General of NORAD; Tom Vraalsen (Centre Party) has been Minister for Development Co-operation; Thorvald Stoltenberg (Labour Party) has been Minister for Foreign Affairs.

[21] See Fred Halliday: *The Making of the Second Cold War*. London: Verso, 1986. The Western interests in the Southern African region are perceptively discussed by William Minter in *King Solomon's Mines Revisited: Western Interests and the Burdened History of Southern Africa*. New York: Basic Books, 1986.

as "a government-in-waiting" in the Nordic countries, to the British Prime Minister ANC was nothing more than a terrorist organisation. As late as in October 1987 she bluntly stated at the Commonwealth summit in Vancouver that "anyone who thought that the ANC was going to run the government in South Africa was living in a cuckoo land".[22] The new Nordic initiatives for a broader and more committed relationship with ANC and SWAPO in the 1980s can, thus, be said to represent a significant departure from the attitudes prevailing among the major Western allies in this period.

In the mid-1980s mounting resistance inside South Africa itself, led by the churches, trade unions, youth organisations and a wide range of civic organisations joining forces under the umbrella of the United Democratic Front, eventually made the apartheid regime crumble. The final years of the regime also saw a humiliating South African military defeat in Angola against Angolan and Cuban forces as well as the introduction of international sanctions, albeit varying in terms of scope and sufficiency. The fact that the apartheid regime was unable to quell the mass actions, in spite of successive states of emergencies and massive detentions, compelled a number of Western corporations and politicians to reassess their position. The new wave of countrywide protests made large areas of South Africa ungovernable and galvanised international opinion. This time, contrary to the assumptions of the Western countries in the past, the apartheid system was clearly vulnerable. It was increasingly being realised both inside and outside South Africa that the contradictions inherent in the apartheid system could not be resolved by piecemeal reforms, and that apartheid in its orthodox shape had to go if Western economic and strategic interests were to be preserved. It was a sign of this change that the president of ANC, Oliver Tambo, was received by the US and British Foreign Ministers in 1986/87; a quarter of a century had then passed since he had been received by the Norwegian Prime Minister Einar Gerhardsen (Labour Party).

The intensification of the struggles inside South Africa and Namibia also ushered in a new chapter in the history of the relations between the liberation movements and Norway. This was primarily manifested in a significant increase in the funds allocated to ANC and SWAPO. While this support had been initiated under a Labour Party government, the change to a Conservative/Centre coalition (1981–86) did not affect the overall policies pursued. After a slow start in 1977, a comprehensive bilateral co-operation programme was developed with ANC—and to a lesser extent with PAC—in the 1980s, based on annual deliberations not very different in form from what took place in the core programme countries. With more South Africans fleeing their country as a result of military build-up and repression, there was also increased need for humanitarian assistance to refugees under the care of the liberation movements in neighbouring countries While the

---

[22] Quoted in Linda Freeman, op.cit., p. 209.

period 1975–80 had seen somewhat strained relations between Norway and SWAPO, due both to internal conflicts in SWAPO, the move to Angola (where Norway did not have any diplomatic representation) and the lack of approved procedures for allocation and disbursement of funds, the 1980s were characterised by mutual trust, improved personal relations, a much more streamlined administration of funds and a more profound Norwegian commitment to the struggle for national liberation. In preparing for independence in the late 1980s, Norway supported a SWAPO-initiated project to develop a new legal system for an independent Namibia. In the final days of the South African occupation, preparations were also made for the transition to regular development co-operation with an independent Namibia (see chapter 2).

While the major part of the Norwegian assistance to ANC and SWAPO in the 1980s was used for refugee settlements and educational centres, the Solomon Mahlangu Freedom College in Tanzania and the Loudima Secondary Technical School in Congo-Brazzaville in particular, from the mid-1980s Norway increasingly channelled funds to a wide range of organisations and projects inside South Africa itself. Trade unions, churches, women's groups, legal aid and human rights centres, community-based organisations, independent mass media and other organisations and institutions under attack from the apartheid state—many of them co-operating within the framework of the broad anti-apartheid alliance (United Democratic Front)—were the main beneficiaries of this change in policy. Even if ANC was never directly given financial support for building up internal structures, in marked contrast to the Swedish policy, the Norwegian decision to supplement assistance to refugees with a more politically-inclined support to democratic forces inside South Africa was taken in agreement with the ANC leadership in exile. The financial contributions to opposition groups were primarily handled by a Norwegian consulate which—as documented in chapter 3—acted in a manner which in many ways departed from diplomatic etiquette and the principle of non-interference.

In the final days of apartheid in Namibia and South Africa, Norway also took an active part in the preparations for elections and a democratic future. During the liberation struggle itself, however, it has been maintained by recent critics that the donor countries paid too little attention to internal democracy, transparency and accountability. This is one of the points made by two Zimbabwean scholars, J.N. Moyo and A.M. Kambudzi, at the Robben Island Conference in February 1999.[23] This sensitive theme has, regrettably, not been pursued in our research, but is touched upon by Tor Sellström in his prologue to the final volume of the Swedish study. His conclusion also seems to cover the Norwegian experience: "During the libera-

---

[23] See Jonathan N. Moyo: "Future Challenges" and A.M. Kambudzi: "Zimbabwe: Nordic solidarity, national liberation and post-independence problems and prospects in Southern Africa", *Conference Report*, op. cit.

tion wars, both the nationalist movements and their African hosts often sacrificed democratic debate and individual liberties for the sake of unity and purpose towards the principal goal of national independence. Sweden—under Social Democratic or non-socialist governments and whether at the official or at the NGO level—more or less uncritically accepted this situation. In addition to humanitarian concerns, from a political point of view it was the ultimate objective—national liberation and majority rule—that determined the stand of a broad opinion".[24] In the case of South Africa in the late 1980s it can more easily be argued that the funding directed to the civil society was a contribution towards a more democratic post-apartheid society.[25]

Sanctions: A contentious issue

The 1980s also saw the final battle over sanctions. While humanitarian assistance to the liberation movements had been a regular—and rather uncontested—feature of Norwegian aid since 1973, the issue of sanctions soon proved to be a battlefield involving political parties, shipowners, major industrial corporations, trade unions, churches and solidarity organisations. The quite modest measures implemented in the late 1970s were in the following decade far too cautious and out of step with the Norwegian public opinion and the mounting international campaigns for comprehensive sanctions. But, as we have seen in chapter 5, it was far from easy for the Norwegian government to make up its mind.

Both ANC, SWAPO and the worldwide anti-apartheid campaign had singled out oil as a critical issue in the struggle for sanctions, since the supply of oil was of vital importance for the survival of the apartheid economy and the South African war machine. This was also one of the salient points made by Bishop Desmond Tutu when receiving the Nobel Peace Prize in Oslo in 1984. The fact that oil was a commodity "oiling the war machine" had for many years been argued by Abdul Minty, who set up in Oslo his World Campaign against Nuclear and Military Collaboration with South Africa. While the liberation movements' calls for humanitarian assistance and diplomatic support had been favourably received in Norway, their calls for sanctions served to demonstrate that the issues were far more complicated when vital Norwegian economic interests were at stake. In spite of the Norwegian government's professed commitment to the liberation struggle

---

[24] Tor Sellström, op.cit., Vol. II.

[25] This argument has, *inter alia*, been made by Raymond Suttner: "Here again, the Nordic countries were vital. Their funding was directed towards organisations based in communities. By providing funding they contributed towards long-term democratic governance in South Africa. By providing funding for democratic structures they helped root democratic practices, the practices that will be essential if we are to have long-term accountable government, popular participation and continued respect for human rights". *Conference Report*, op. cit., p. 88.

in South Africa and Namibia, solidarity is always more tricky when it comes with a price.

While Norwegian trade in goods was rather modest, and the direct investments in South African industry insignificant, Norwegian shipowners were among the most prominent carriers of oil to South Africa. The government, whether Labour or non-socialist, was caught in the crossfire between commercial interests on the one hand and the calls from the liberation movements and a broad Norwegian anti-apartheid alliance on the other. While the Norwegian Shipowners Association (NSA) was used to having its way through intimate relations with the government, it now had to enter a terrain in which moral and political arguments were effectively used by the strong anti-apartheid alliance.

To cut a long story short: when profits were at risk, the Norwegian government opted for a compromise. While the sanctions law which was introduced by the Labour Party in November 1986 and approved by Parliament in March 1987 eventually prohibited the transport of crude oil to South Africa, transport of refined oil products as well as all other goods was not to be interfered with. Thus, the transport of crude oil was sacrificed in order to maintain the other—and far more profitable—shipping links. Weak as this compromise may appear, Norway was after the all the first major shipping country to impose a legal ban on crude oil transport. The general ban on trade in goods was also open for major exemptions, such as the import of manganese deemed important to the Norwegian metallurgical industry. (This partly explains why the import figures actually increased in 1987/88.) Sanctions on imports from South Africa was an easy proposition when alternative sources of supply were readily available (fresh and canned fruit, liquor etc.), but turned out in practice to be rather selective where other goods were concerned. Having in mind these loopholes in trade and shipping, the claims that Norway imposed total sanctions seem to be rather excessive.[26] In a Nordic perspective, it should also be noted that the Norwegian sanctions law was adopted more or less along the same lines—and at the same time—as in Finland, Denmark and Sweden.

From humanitarian assistance to concerned partnership

In the historical overview presented above, we have seen that the policy formulations guiding the Norwegian support to the liberation movements firmly stated that official funds should be confined to humanitarian assistance. In order to give a more fitting description of Norwegian support to the liberation movements, the concept of *humanitarian assistance* should, however, be understood in a much wider perspective. This is also a point

---

[26] These claims are made by Linda Freeman in her otherwise impressive study on Canada, see Freeman, op. cit., p. 194. She also seems to believe that Denmark and Norway cut their diplomatic ties with South Africa, which was never the case.

often made by representatives of the liberation movements themselves, emphasising that the support was always more political in nature than a strict interpretation of the term "humanitarian" would suggest. The SWAPO Secretary of Finance and Administration, Hifikepunye Pohamba, has summarised his experience in this way: "Of course, they told us: 'We are assisting you on a humanitarian basis and we do not want to give anything that could promote the military struggle'. They made it clear. However, when they gave us food, it went to the camps and the camps were also the reserves of the PLAN[27] cadres. It would therefore not be wrong to say that the people of the Nordic world also assisted PLAN. But they never gave us guns. They fed our people, they educated our people, they clothed our people and they gave shelter to our people, but they never gave us guns".[28] Neither should children, men and women in the refugee centres be regarded as ordinary refugees. As stated by Peter Katjavivi, another prominent SWAPO leader: "We were refugees who were out to prepare ourselves to make a contribution towards the liberation of our country. The idea of being in a refugee camp was not to settle there indefinitely. It was an opportunity to regroup and acquire the necessary skills and competence while we were in exile. It became a training camp, where you acquired skills that might be needed in an independent Namibia. I think that consideration was well understood by the Nordic countries".[29]

The representatives of the liberation movements came to accept the reality that arms and other forms of military equipment were excluded from the Norwegian aid budgets, and almost without exceptions asked for the kind of assistance that they thought was obtainable. ("We knew where to go for the arms, that was not the problem. The problem was to build a strong solidarity support for the cause".)[30] In spite of the reservations concerning the armed struggle, the Nordic countries have often been described as "people who at heart support our liberation struggle".[31] Not least important is the fact that the aid relationship opened up a channel for discussions and laid the foundation for mutual trust and exchange of political views. The assistance extended was, thus, increasingly seen as a sign of political commitment and recognition of the legitimacy of the struggle in all areas.

In the diplomatic arena, it was also generally accepted that the Nordic countries did not vote in favour of UN resolutions that made reference to

---

[27] PLAN (People's Liberation Army of Namibia) was the armed wing of SWAPO.

[28] Interview in Tor Sellström (ed.), p. 96.

[29] Ibid., p. 71.

[30] Ibid., p. 73.

[31] Interview with Dumiso Dabengwa (ZAPU) in Tor Sellström (ed.), pp. 211–212: "I think that we to a very large extent felt at ease with the Nordic countries in all our relations. We got the impression that they were (...) people who at heart supported our liberation struggle, but on the other hand found themselves in an embarrassing situation, where—because of their membership in NATO—they could not come out openly to support it".

the armed struggle, although some of the movements, FRELIMO in particular, wanted "the humanitarian position" to be expanded to include an understanding of the nature of their struggle. In an interview with Marcelino dos Santos this was expressed in this way: "I would like to underline that the principal form of struggle that history imposed on Mozambique was the armed struggle. If we had not waged an armed struggle we would never have come to power. Humanitarian assistance alone was not sufficient to assume real power."[32] This perspective was shared by the solidarity movements and many youth organisations in Norway, which—as seen in chapters 1 and 6—argued that official support should be given unconditionally.

The liberation struggle waged in the Portuguese colonies was in Norway widely regarded as the only avenue left for peoples confronting a fascist regime which vehemently opposed all international calls for decolonisation. In the case of ANC of South Africa and SWAPO of Namibia the relationship—especially in the 1980s—was firmly based on the recognition of their struggle to overthrow the South African apartheid regime and its quisling regime installed in occupied Namibia. In retrospect, Lindiwe Mabuza, former ANC representative to the Nordic countries, has expressed her view that "It was important to us that this support was "solidarity", and was not to be confused with "charity". Our supporters and the ANC had a common interest in the overthrow of the apartheid regime and, therefore financial, material support towards attaining this common goal was an imperative."[33]

Transcending the Cold War divide

In our attempt to identify some of the unique features of the Norwegian support to the liberation movements, the Cold War aspects spring naturally to mind. In the wide range of interviews conducted for the Nordic study, many representatives of the liberation movements themselves have also commented upon the fact that humanitarian assistance was given by a member country of NATO. There can be no doubt that this support served to legitimise the movements at a time when they were generally dismissed by the major Western powers as belonging the "the wrong side" of the overriding Cold War divide. It has, thus, been maintained by Ben Amathila (SWAPO) that "the significance of this co-operation lies in the solidarity rendered and recognition given to us when the rest of the Western world was shying away from us, even calling us by the name of terrorists". [34] In a similar vein, Raymond Suttner (ANC) has argued that: "Of major significance in Nordic support was that it broke the Cold War mould, that Nordic countries were prepared to recognise liberation struggles as having merit in

---

[32] Ibid., p. 49.

[33] Lindiwe Mabuza, *Conference Report*, op.cit., p. 95.

[34] *Conference Report*, op.cit., p. 80.

their own right. It was vital for us not to have our aspirations reduced to a battlefield between contending Cold War powers and the Nordic countries, as countries of the West, were vital in breaking this paradigm."[35] In this way, the strong links with the Nordic countries would eventually broaden the international support of the movements and pave the way for humanitarian assistance from other Western countries.

In a Cold War context it is also remarkable that the majority of the movements supported by Norway belonged to the group of "six authentic" movements recognised by the Soviet Union: ANC, SWAPO, ZAPU, FRELIMO, MPLA and PAIGC.[36] In the case of the Portuguese colonies the movements were deeply engaged in an armed struggle against a colonial power aligned with Norway in NATO. The fact that they all received their arms from the Soviet Union and other countries belonging to the Warsaw Pact in fact never eroded their position as the movements favoured by the Norwegian government, the solidarity movements and the churches. In addition, humanitarian assistance was also extended to ZANU and PAC, which generally were regarded to be closer to China.

Especially in a Cold War perspective it has been stressed that the links to the Nordic countries enlarged the political space for the liberation movements. According to their own views, as expressed in recent interviews, they were consistently looking for support outside the Cold War polarisation, but soon realised that few countries other than the Nordic countries made this support available.

As is shown in chapter 1, the principle of extending assistance to the liberation movements was unanimously adopted by the Norwegian Parliament in 1973. This decision was at the time a significant departure from the policies followed by Norway's major allies in NATO and EFTA. The Norwegian position was particularly in striking contrast to the comprehensive review of US policies towards Southern Africa which, known as the "Kissinger report", in 1969 had been commissioned by the Nixon administration. (The confidential *National Security Memorandum 39* was later leaked and appeared as a book in 1975.)[37] According to this study the only way to achieve constructive changes in the region was to co-operate with the white regimes. Framed in an overriding Cold War phraseology, the report concluded that "there is no hope for the blacks to gain the political rights they seek through violence, which will only lead to chaos and increased opportunities for the Communists".[38] At the same time the fascist regime in Por-

---

[35] Ibid., p. 86.

[36] These movements are also known as the "Khartoum alliance", emerging from a conference in Khartoum in 1966. The co-operation was based on longstanding affinities between the six movements and existing relations with the Soviet Union, as explained in Tor Sellström, op.cit., Vol. I.

[37] *The Kissinger Study on Southern Africa*. Nottingham: Spokesman Books, 1975.

[38] Ibid., p. 66.

tugal greatly benefited from economic and military co-operation with its major Western partners in NATO and EFTA. Portugal was a founding member of NATO (1949) and EFTA (1960), and was mainly invited to join NATO because of the strategic Azores Islands.

If we turn to the illegal Ian Smith regime in Rhodesia/Zimbabwe, there were in the early 1970s few signs of a serious British commitment to the struggle for majority rule. (In this case, there were hardly any differences between the two major British political parties.) In South Africa itself, the apartheid regime had during the 1960s effectively crushed the internal opposition in the 1960s, and could witness an unprecedented inflow of foreign capital and arms technology. Within the UN system, the calls for international sanctions were consistently blocked by the major Western powers. The liberation movements were generally regarded as "terrorists" and "communists", and it should not have come as a surprise to the Norwegian hosts that the governments of USA, the United Kingdom, West Germany and France declined the invitation to the 1973 UN/OAU Conference in Oslo (see chapter 1).

While the standard texts on Norwegian foreign policy in the 1950s and 1960s are uniform in stressing the tension between the principles of decolonisation and loyalty to Norway's partners in NATO, it became increasingly difficult to straddle these two worlds. In the Southern African context, this conflict was finally resolved in favour of the principles of national self-determination.[39] As shown in chapter 1, this development did not take place without a struggle within the political establishment and—in particular—in the Ministry of Foreign Affairs. The breakthrough took place with the humanitarian assistance extended to the liberation movements in the Portuguese colonies in the early 1970s, which were struggling against an intransigent colonial power in the era of decolonisation. On the other hand, it was totally unacceptable to a Norwegian government to support UN resolutions that implied a NATO responsibility for the colonial wars or called for a military embargo. South Africa itself was for many years a more complicated issue, involving an independent state and a fellow member of the UN with close economic and strategic links with the major Western powers. Eventually the universal values of human rights, democracy and non-racialism took precedence over the principle of "non-interference", and from 1977 humanitarian assistance was rendered to ANC and, to a lesser extent, to PAC, which were both recognised by the Organisation of African Unity as legitimate liberation movements.

In addition to the preference given to the principles of decolonisation and human rights, the fact that the struggle in Southern African did not constitute a threat to the main geo-strategic interests of Norway, and that

---

[39] Knut Einar Eriksen and Helge Øystein Pharo: *Kald krig og internasjonalisering 1945–1965. Norsk utenrikspolitikks historie, bind 5.* Oslo: Universitetsforlaget, 1997; and Rolf Tamnes: *Oljealder, 1965–1995. Norsk utenrikspolitikks historie, bind 6.* Oslo: Universitetsforlaget, 1997.

few economic interests were at stake, helps in explaining the Norwegian change of course. The Norwegian policy unquestionably also had the effect that the West was not regarded as being a monolithic bloc, and that the support—as seen from the liberation movements themselves—served "to educate our people that the West was not so bad".[40] As shown in chapter 1, when the Norwegian Minister of Foreign Affairs in 1971 voiced his opinion against the Portuguese colonial wars at the NATO Council meeting in Lisbon, it was argued from the Norwegian government that the wars could jeopardise the support for NATO in Norway and damage the standing of the Western powers in the Third World in general. Similarly, in preparing for the UN/OAU Conference in Oslo in 1973, the point was made that such a conference was important for the Western governments not to lose legitimacy in Africa, while at the same time attempting to influence and moderate African countries.

Although it is widely recognised by the representatives of the liberation movements that Norwegian aid was extended without any political conditions, regardless of the ideological persuasion of the various nationalist forces, the issue might in reality be somewhat less straightforward. From the perspectives of the liberation movements, particularly in the former Portuguese colonies, a distinction was often made between the non-aligned Sweden and Denmark/Norway as NATO members.[41] Even if it was never explicitly formulated, one has also to assume that an intended effect of the assistance and the accompanying cordial relations with the liberation movements was to introduce the "Nordic model" and to demonstrate that there were in fact more attractive alternatives outside the Soviet Union and the other East European countries. ("By and large what the Nordic support meant to us is that it distinguished those countries from the rest of the Western world. It was a lesson to us").[42] In his extensive treatment of the Swedish experience, Tor Sellström on more than one occasion shows how Olof Palme engaged in ideological discussions with heads of the liberation movements, arguing the case for social democracy.[43] It would also be rather naive to assume that the invitations to representatives of the liberation movements to address meetings held by the (social democratic) Socialist International (SI) were completely devoid of ideological aspirations.

At least in the South African context, there can be no doubt that anti-apartheid forces with a more liberal than socialist perspective looked to the Nordic countries as "an alternative model". A case in point is the support given by the Norwegian consulate in Cape Town to the Institute for Demo-

---

[40] Interview with Jorge Rebelo (MPLA) in Tor Sellström (ed.), op. cit., p. 46.

[41] See, for instance, the interview with Joaquim Chissano (FRELIMO) in Tor Sellström (ed.), op. cit., p. 38: "It appeared to me that the Swedes already had a full vision about the whole issue, because Sweden did not belong to NATO. For Norway, things were a lot different".

[42] Interview with Peter Katjavivi (SWAPO) in Tor Sellström (ed.), op. cit., p. 75.

[43] Tor Sellström , Vol. I and II, op. cit.

cratic Alternatives in South Africa (IDASA), established by Alex Boraine
with initial Norwegian funding in 1987.[44] When he later was asked whether
he thought that the Nordic support to ANC had an influence on the political
course followed by the government in a post-apartheid South Africa, his
answer was straightforward: "No doubt. I have no doubt about that. In
terms of economics, the whole question of democracy, accountability, the
gentle use of power instead of sweeping away everything and demanding
total power. I sense that the Nordic countries have possibly been the
strongest influence on ANC in making it less of a far left party and more left
of centre. I think that is tremendous. My personal view is that it has been
extremely helpful".[45]

Norway and Sweden: A comparative perspective

Even if Norway in important respects departed from the policies pursued
by its major allies, it does not, of course, mean that the Cold War considerations did not reduce the freedom to manoeuvre as defined by the ruling
governments. Although more comparative research is needed to allow a
firmer conclusion, it is tempting to explain some of the differences between
Norway and Sweden in this light. Within the framework of Nordic co-operation Sweden often assumed a leading role, based on its traditional brand of
neutrality and a deeper political commitment to the liberation struggle. This
is a fact often underscored by representatives of the movements themselves:
"Sweden, the most important of the Nordic countries, maintained its neutrality during the Second World War, and is not a member of NATO. During the liberation struggles in Southern Africa it could therefore consistently
pursue a policy based on the principles of self-determination and democratic rule, enshrined in the United Nations Charter, without submitting to
the constraints imposed by Portugal and South Africa on the NATO members".[46]

Under the leadership of Olof Palme, the Swedish Social Democratic
Party—whether in government or in opposition—developed unique relations with the leaders of the liberation struggles, such as Eduardo Mondlane, Amilcar Cabral, Agostinho Neto and Oliver Tambo. As is emphasised
in the volume containing interviews with representatives from the liberation
movements, the bonds of friendship were based on an expressed ideological
affinity, the principle of national self-determination and a high degree of
mutual trust. It is also beyond doubt that Olof Palme played a more prominent role as a proponent for the liberation struggle at the UN, in the Socialist
International and in other international fora than his Norwegian counterparts. It should also be noted that from the mid-1960s prominent Liberal

---

[44] See the interview with Alex Boraine in Tor Sellström (ed.), op. cit., pp. 107–111.

[45] Ibid., p. 111.

[46] Alberto Ribeiro-Kabulu, *Conference Report*, op.cit., p. 43.

Party and Centre Party politicians in Sweden were close to the liberation movements, and that in opposition they often called for increased support. This is in marked contrast to the Norwegian non-socialist coalition in the 1965–1971 period. Under the non-socialist coalition in Sweden, following the 1976 general elections, the government of Thorbjörn Fälldin not only followed in the footsteps of the Palme government, but embarked upon an even more ambitious aid programme in favour of ZAPU, ZANU, ANC and SWAPO.

In the case of Zimbabwe, Norway and Sweden more or less followed the same course, except for the fact the Swedish humanitarian assistance to ZANU was accompanied by a more explicit political commitment.[47] As shown in chapter 5, Norway had also been much slower than Sweden in severing the economic and diplomatic links with the illegal Ian Smith regime. It should, furthermore, be noted that in 1979, the State of Secretary for Foreign Affairs, Johan Jørgen Holst, argued in a memorandum that Norway had to choose Great Britain over the liberation movements if the Lancaster House talks were to collapse (see chapter 5).

In the history of the liberation struggle in Southern Africa, the Cold War overtones were most clearly evident in the case of Angola. As is shown in chapter 1, there are striking differences between the course chosen by the Swedish and Norwegian governments. In marked contrast to Norway, the assistance from Sweden to MPLA was never suspended during the crucial year of 1975 (see chapter 1). While the Norwegian Labour Party government was reluctant even to acknowledge the receipt of a Christmas card from José Eduardo dos Santos, the Angolan Foreign Minister himself was received in January 1976 by his Swedish counterpart during an important visit to Stockholm. Olof Palme also vigorously intervened in the public Swedish debate on behalf of MPLA, and explicitly argued that the Angolan issue and the support rendered to Angola by Cuban forces should not be seen in a Cold War perspective.[48] The Swedish commitment to MPLA eventually paved the way for a substantial aid programme for Angola from 1977, launched under a Centre/Conservative coalition, which over the years would make Sweden the most significant donor country. On the other hand, in spite of its professed commitment to the Frontline States suffering from South African war and destabilisation, the Norwegian Labour party government desisted from entering any bilateral aid agreements (see chapter 1).

---

[47] The strong links between Sweden and ZANU in the late 1970s are convincingly documented in Tor Sellström, op.cit., Vol. II.

[48] "It is important to remember that the war waged in Angola is not between the 'Free World' and 'Communism' (and that) it must not in a prejudiced way be viewed on the basis of the clichés of the Cold War or from the perspective of the conflicts between the superpowers. It is fundamentally a continuation of the long liberation struggle that was embarked upon one and a half decades ago and which in its final phase has had a tragic course due to internal divisions and foreign intervention", *Dagens Nyheter*, 4 February 1976.

It should also be noted that Swedish support to ANC allowed for a substantial part (up to one third in the period 1978–89) to be spent inside South Africa itself without any strings attached, in what was in the budget allocations described as 'The Home Front'. As judged by the present South African ambassador to Sweden, this had a tremendous impact on the reorganisation of the internal structures of ANC in terms of communication, information and political work.[49] Norway, on the other hand, restricted its support for ANC to humanitarian assistance in the neighbouring countries. For reasons more fully discussed in chapter 3, Norway also departed from its Nordic neighbours in giving support to PAC as well as to ANC.[50]

It is also difficult to avoid the conclusion that to a certain degree Cold War sentiments were also influencing the attitudes of the Norwegian Confederation of Trade Unions (LO). The ANC-affiliated trade union SACTU was, for reasons explained by Vesla Vetlesen (see chapter 8), never recognised by LO, and had always to leave empty-handed when its representatives requested support from LO. This dispute had its origins largely in the bitter Cold War struggle between two competing international trade unions, the International Confederation of Free Trade Unions (to which LO and most other Western trade unions belonged) and the World Federation of Trade Unions (based in Eastern Europe). The non-recognition of SACTU was also one of the reasons why relations between LO and the Norwegian Council for Southern Africa were at times rather strained. (This divide is explained—and reflected—in chapters 6 and 8). It is in this regard also of interest to note that the non-socialist Swedish government from 1977 granted direct support to SACTU. Under the social democratic government the grant to SACTU was eventually to be included within the Swedish regular allocation to ANC.[51]

The role of the civil society

It is not possible to conclude this brief discussion of the unique Norwegian experience without some comments on the role played by the churches, the trade unions and the solidarity movements. While it is often asserted that the impact of civil society is marginal in shaping foreign policy, the case of the Southern African issue seems to prove otherwise (see chapters 6–9). It is

---

[49] Raymond Suttner, *Conference Report*, op. cit., pp. 87–88.

[50] ANC was aligned with the South African Communist Party, and was—in a Cold War perspective—widely regarded to be rather close to Moscow. Interestingly, a recent study on the ANC-Moscow relations by Vladimir Shubin provides a complex picture with many nuances and contradictions. In *ANC: A view from Moscow* (Cape Town: Mayibuye Publishers, 1999) it is argued that parts of the Soviet state apparatus had little sympathy for ANC, that a socialist South Africa was not on the agenda, that the Soviet Union encouraged negotiations with the Nationalist Party at an early stage, that the USSR maintain cordial relations with De Beers for the sale of its own diamonds and that internal developments of the struggle inside South Africa were far more important than the external support received by ANC.

[51] This issue is treated in great detail in Tor Sellström, op.cit., Vol. II.

also a fact that the decision-making process in the Ministry of Foreign Affairs from the 1970s became more attentive to public opinion than had previously been the case, while North/South issues at the same time came to the forefront in the—rather brief—era of North/South dialogue and calls for a "New Economic World Order".[52] The influences of a vocal opinion concerned with Southern Africa also go a long way in explaining why the diplomatic support and the humanitarian aid rendered to the liberation movements was to a great extent independent of the political colours of the governments in power. On the other side of the political spectrum, rightwing and proto-racist forces were quite weak, and the occasional outburst in journals like *Morgenbladet* and *Farmand* against aiding "terrorists" did not have any great impact.

The importance of non-governmental organisations is indeed a recurrent theme in the interviews which have been conducted with representatives from the movements themselves. Just to give one example, Alberto Ribeira-Kabulu of MPLA has stated that: "In countries like Sweden, Denmark and Norway we had direct contacts with the civil society at the level of students and support committees. When I recall my personal ties with the Nordic countries (...) the support always began through the people, students, workers and trade unionists. It was the civil society in those countries that channelled the message to their governments. In other cases, for instance in the socialist countries, the support comes straight from the governments and from parties in one-party states. In the case of the Nordic countries, it first came through contacts from people to people. It was the civil society that was in touch with us. It made a big difference in relation to the support".[53]

Compared to many other Western countries, Norway was very fortunate in having after 1967 a solidarity movement like the Norwegian Council for Southern Africa, which could carry on where the Norwegian Action against Apartheid (NAMA) and the Crisis Fund for South Africa had started in the early 1960s. Embracing large sections of the Norwegian society, NOCOSA largely succeeded in combining grassroots activism with a formal structure based on more than 40 member organisations across the political spectrum. Even if the core of the activists were recruited from the political left and from the Christian community, the fact remains that the Norwegian

---

[52] The "democratisation" of Norwegian foreign policies is commonly associated with Knut Frydenlund, who was Foreign Minister from 1973 to 1981. See Edgeir Benum: *Aschehougs Norges historie, bind 12*. Oslo: Aschehoug, 1998; and Rolf Tamnes, op.cit.

[53] Interview in Tor Sellström (ed.), op.cit., p. 29. A similar view has been expressed by Lindiwe Mabuza of ANC: "As important as official government support was for the ANC it would never be as dynamic in its mobilisation effect as assistance and co-operation from non-governmental organisations (NGOs). Even the governments recognised and greatly encouraged this kind of help", see *Conference Report*, op.cit., p. 96.

Council for Southern Africa always managed to pursue a non-sectarian line.[54]

NOCOSA was in its early years instrumental in establishing the first connections between the liberation movements and the Norwegian government, political parties and youth organisations. Having in mind the close links developed over the years, it is sometimes easy to forget that the liberation movements were not exactly received with open arms in the 1960s. Somebody had to knock on office doors, attract the attention of mass media, host public meetings and put up visitors for the night. Through large-scale hearings on South Africa and its aggression against neighbouring states in 1977 and 1984, NOCOSA managed to reach a broader audience. The cultural dimension of the solidarity work was also strongly emphasised. By organising tours and festivals for African artists, musicians, dancers, actors and poets, both NOCOSA and the Namibia Committee succeeded in conveying African culture directly to the Norwegian public.

Many battles have been fought over the years between the solidarity movements and the Norwegian authorities, as is vividly described in chapter 6. It should not come as a surprise that solidarity activists close to the liberation movements argued for much larger official grants to the peoples struggling for independence and majority rule, and that they took exception to what was seen as a Norwegian "betrayal" of MPLA in 1974–1976. The most contentious issue, however, was the questions of sanctions and the heavy Norwegian involvement in the transport of oil to South Africa. It is in this regard interesting to note that when the Norwegian sanctions law was eventually adopted in 1987, NOCOSA had already been instrumental in establishing "sanctions from below" through municipal boycotts. (Close to 80% of all Norwegian municipalities had—at the initiative of NOCOSA— declared "apartheid-free zones" at the local level.)

On other occasions, however, the government and the solidarity movements acted as partners, exchanging information and consulting each other. Especially in the 1980s, the Ministry of Foreign Affairs was increasingly generous in providing funds for information purposes. NOCOSA also worked hand in hand with prominent members of the Norwegian Parliament forming a parliamentary "contact group", and was widely regarded by the Norwegian mass media as a reliable source with far more to offer than slogans. In this respect it certainly helped that the academic and research community concerned with Southern Africa issues included area specialists with close bonds to NOCOSA, providing what is in the present-day jargon often referred to as a "counter-hegemonic discourse". Although not to the same extent as in Sweden, activists from the solidarity movements later turned up as journalists, researchers, aid officials, diplomats and members of parliament.

---

[54] The role of NOCOSA is treated in chapter 6. See also Nina Drolsum: *For et fritt Afrika*. Oslo: Fellesrådet for Afrika/Solidaritet Forlag, 1999.

The unique experience of the Namibia Association in Elverum, which is discussed in chapter 9, has graphically demonstrated that it is possible to mobilise entire communities through education combined with extending support to peoples struggling for national independence. This concept of *learning* about Namibia by *doing* solidarity work was also spread to other parts of the country. Furthermore, the Elverum story illustrates the fact that the campaigns have only yielded results when they have been planned and executed in close co-operation with the liberation movement itself and other progressive forces. In the case of the Namibia Association strong links were forged with SWAPO and the Council of Churches in Namibia. In terms of practical assistance, from 1983 until the independence of Namibia in 1990 the Namibia Association was the main contributor to the Loudima Technical Secondary School in Congo (Brazzaville).

Together with churches and solidarity movements, the trade unions also formed a main pillar of the broad anti-apartheid alliance. After a brief spell of activism related to consumer boycotts in the early 1960s, the Norwegian Confederation of Trade Unions (LO) became involved in systematic and continuous anti-apartheid work from the mid-1970s.[55] In 1976 it launched a broad campaign, embracing all sectors of the Norwegian labour movement —*Solidarity with Southern Africa*. The campaign was relaunched in 1985/86 as *Freedom to South Africa*. Through these solidarity campaigns—based on rank and file members—many ordinary Norwegians came to identify themselves with the struggle of their South African brothers and sisters.

In the 1980s a new constellation developed in the South African trade union movement, with COSATU rapidly becoming the dominant workers' organisation. COSATU was closely associated with the political ideals of the Freedom Charter and the ANC, and signed a co-operation agreement with ANC and the South African Communist Party when these movements were unbanned in 1990. Although COSATU had taken the position that no assistance from the headquarters of the International Confederation of Free Trade Unions (ICFTU) would be accepted, bilateral support from national unions—such as the Norwegian LO—was in fact welcomed. This opened the way for the transfer of substantial funds from 1986 onwards. In 1989, LO also initiated a special fund-raising campaign in favour of the SWAPO-affil-iated National Union of Namibian Workers (NUNW).

From 1975 to 1996 it has been estimated that NOK 85 million was trans-ferred to trade union activities in South Africa. The bulk of this originated from public funds, while LO itself raised NOK 10 million from campaigns (see chapter 8). LO also worked closely with the Norwegian People's Aid, which in 1988–1992 was the main channel for the Norwegian humanitarian assistance to ANC's health and educational projects in Tanzania. The degree of trust and openness was evident when in 1989 ANC chose Norway as the

---

[55] The story is told in chapter 8 and—in greater detail—in Vesla Vetlesen: *Frihet for Sør-Afrika. LO og kampen mot apartheid*. Oslo: Tiden, 1998.

venue for its high-level consultations to discuss the new stage of the struggle opened up by the ascendancy of F.W. de Klerk as President in 1989. The
LO/International Solidarity Committee (AIS) served as hosts, while the conference was mainly paid for by public funds. Through these links the organisational capacity and negotiating skills of South African trade unions and
the liberation movements were developed, a fact which was of critical importance during the transition period of 1990–1994.

The Norwegian trade unions also co-ordinated their efforts with their
Nordic sister organisations. At a meeting in 1976 in Oslo the Nordic Trade
Union Council set up a joint committee to monitor the developments in
Southern Africa and suggest appropriate actions to be taken. The Nordic
Trade Union Council also consistently called for international sanctions, and
used its privileged links to Labour Party governments to press the issue.
Due to the impact on employment, however, certain sections of the Norwe-
gian trade union movement were more reluctant to call for economic sanc-
tions. On the other hand, as is shown in chapter 6, there were also trade
unions both at the national and local levels which worked closely with the
Norwegian Council for Southern Africa.

Chiefly through its Council for Ecumenical and International Relations
(CEIR—Mellomkirkelig Råd), the Church of Norway has since the early
1970s been another main protagonist in Norway for the liberation struggle.[56]
As quoted in chapter 7, the Norwegian Foreign Minister Knut Frydenlund
(Labour Party) went so far as to conclude that without the Church of
Norway the support for the liberation movements in Southern Africa would
not have been adopted by parliament.

While it was important at this early stage that the Church formed part of
the broad alliance arguing the case for humanitarian assistance to the liberation movements, the direct involvement of the CEIR in terms of political
activism and theological reflections was even more significant in the 1980s.
The Nobel Peace Prize to Archbishop Desmond Tutu in particular was a
source of inspiration and commitment. Working closely with the Ministry of
Foreign Affairs and the Norwegian consulate in Cape Town, the church
connections were increasingly used for channelling funds to a wide range of
churches and other groups opposing apartheid in South Africa and foreign
occupation in Namibia. (This intriguing story is told in chapters 3 and 7).
Arguing the case for sanctions, following the calls of the South African
Council of Churches and Archbishop Desmond Tutu, the Bishop of Oslo,

---

[56] As the first Secretary General of the CEIR, Gunnar Stålsett on many occasions raised the issue
of support to the liberation movements. In 1973 he served as one of the two Norwegian delegates to the UN/OAU Conference in Oslo. With a brief spell in the political arena as chairperson of the Centre Party in the mid-1970s, one can only assume that he was instrumental in
moving the party towards a firmer commitment to the liberation cause. Gunnar Stålsett was
deacon in Elverum when the Namibia Committee was established in 1980, and later served as
the Secretary General of the Lutheran World Federation. He was in 1998 appointed Bishop of
Oslo.

Andreas Aarflot, was in the mid-1980s particularly outspoken regarding the Norwegian involvement in the transport of oil to South Africa. ("It is an intolerable situation that our country should make money on the transport of oil to the police forces and the war machine of the apartheid regime".)[57]

It was also in the 1980s that CEIR and the Norwegian Ecumenical Committee for Southern Africa (NEKSA) on more than one occasion joined forces with the trade unions, the Students' and Academics' Assistance Fund and the Norwegian Council for Southern Africa, forming a broad anti-apartheid movement hosting mass rallies and other huge manifestations of solidarity. One such occasion was the official visit to Norway by Nelson Mandela in May 1992, which coincided with the Norwegian Day of the Constitution (17 May). He was warmly welcomed at the airport by a Norwegian cultural group, *Inkululeko*, singing freedom songs from South Africa, and later attended a service at Oslo Cathedral and an evening festival in his honour.

These concerted efforts culminated in the "Democracy for South Africa" campaign in 1993, when Nelson Mandela requested continued international assistance in the period leading up to the first democratic elections ever. The campaign was launched to coincide with the dual award of the Nobel Peace Prize to Nelson Mandela and F.W. de Klerk. On 10 December 1993, a huge crowd took part in a torch-lit parade obviously only in honour of Nelson Mandela. As is indicated by the quote from F.W. de Klerk, opening this concluding chapter, his encounter with the Norwegian people was even more hostile than he had expected. In his biography he bitterly complains that "my reception was reserved in comparison with the effusive and unrestrained welcome that was accorded to Mandela", and that he felt very uncomfortable when he stood on the balcony of Grand Hotel and watched the crowd shouting ANC slogans and singing the ANC national anthem, *Nkosi Sikilel'i Afrika* in praise of Mandela.[58] This should, in the light of the story told in the previous chapters, not have come as a surprise to the last president of apartheid South Africa.

---

[57] See chapters 5 and 7.
[58] F.W. de Klerk, op.cit., chapter 27: "The Nobel Peace Prize", pp. 293–307.

Bibliography

Agøy, Berit Hagen, 1993, "Norske misjonærer, lutherske kirker og apartheid i Sør-Afrika 1948–1963", *Historisk Tidskrift*, No. 2.

Andreassen, Knut and Birgitta Dahl, 1971, *Guinea-Bissau: Rapport om ett land och en befrielsesrörelse*. Stockholm: Prisma.

Andresen, Trond and Steinar Sætervadet, 2000, *Fra dugnad til bistand*. Elverum: Namibiaforeningen (Namibia Committee).

Anglin, Douglas G. et al. (eds.),1978, *Conflict and change in Southern Africa; Papers from a Scandinavian-Canadian Conference*. Washington: University Press of America.

Bakkevig, Trond, 1986, "Refleksjoner omkring kirkens menneskerettighetsengasjement", *Mennesker og rettigheter*, No. 4.

—, 1995, *Den norske kirke og kampen mot apartheid*. Oslo: Mellomkirkelig Råd.

—, 1996, *The Church of Norway and the Struggle against Apartheid*. Oslo: Mellomkirkelig Råd.

Bailey, Martin and B. Rivers, 1978, *Oil Sanctions against South Africa*. New York: UN Centre against Apartheid.

Baskin, Jeremy, 1991, *Striking Back. A History of COSATU*. Johannesburg: Ravan Press.

Bech, Jon, 1978, *Norsk bistand til frigjøringsbevegelsene i det sørlige Afrika*. Oslo: Norsk Utenrikspolitisk Institutt. (*Forum for utviklingsstudier*, No. 10/1978.)

Benum, Edgeir, 1998, *Overflod og fremtidsfrykt, 1970–. Aschehougs Norges historie, bd.* 12. Oslo: Aschehoug.

Birmingham, David, 1991, *Frontline Nationalism in Angola and Mozambique*. London: James Currey.

Brundtland, Gro Harlem, 1988, "The Scandinavian Perspective on the North-South Dialogue" in Kofi Buenor Hadjor (ed.), *New Perspectives in North-South Dialogue: Essays in Honour of Olof Palme*. London: I.B. Tauris.

Cabral, Amilcar, 1973, *Frigjøringskamp i teori og praksis*. Oslo: NOVUS.

Chabal, Patrick, 1983, *Amilcar Cabral: Revolutionary Leadership and People's War*. Cambridge: Cambridge University Press.

Drolsum, Nina, 1999, *For et fritt Afrika*. Oslo: Fellesrådet for Afrika/Solidaritet Forlag.

Eivindson, Ole Kristian, 1997, *Norge og raseproblemene i Sør-Afrika, 1945–1961*. Oslo: University of Oslo, Department of History. (Thesis.)

Eriksen, Knut Einar and Helge Øystein Pharo, 1997, *Kald krig og internasjonalisering 1945–1965. Norsk utenrikspolitikks historie, bind 5*. Oslo: Universitetsforlaget.

Eriksen, Tore Linné, 1970, "FRELIMOs program for utvikling", *Samtiden*, No. 8.

—, 1973, "Amilcar Cabral og Guinea-Bissau: En frigjøringsleder og en utviklingsmodell", *Kirke og Kultur*, No. 2.

—, 1981, *Sanksjoner, Sør-Afrika og Norge*. Oslo: Norsk Utenrikspolitisk Institutt. (NUPI-Notat 239.)

—, 1985, "Det sørlige Afrika", in J.J. Holst/D. Heradstveit (eds.), *Norsk utenrikspolitikk*. Oslo: TANO.

—, 1986, "Norge, sanksjoner og Sør-Afrika", *Norsk Utenrikspolitisk Årbok 1985*. Oslo: Norsk Utenrikspolitisk Institutt.

—, (ed.), 1987, *Den vanskelige bistanden. Noen trekk ved norsk utviklingshjelps historie*. Oslo: Universitetsforlaget.

—, 1988, *Ingen tårer. Vår framtid er lys. Nelson og Winnie Mandela i den sørafrikanske frigjøringskampen*. Oslo: Gyldendal Norsk Forlag/Fellesrådet for det sørlige Afrika.

—, 1988, *Det regionale samarbeidet mellom det sørlige Afrika og Norden*. Oslo: Norsk Utenrikspolitisk Institutt. (*Forum for Utviklingsstudier*, 1–3, 1988.)

Eriksen, Tore Linné and Øystein Gudim, 1979, *Aftenpostens dekning av konflikten i Rhodesia (Zimbabwe) 1997–1979*. Paper presented to the seminar on Nordic mass media reports on the confrontation in Southern Africa, Kungälv, Sweden, May 1979, arranged by Nordiska Afrikainstutet, Uppsala.

Fockstedt, Sven, 1985, *Facket i Sydafrika*. Stockholm: LO/TCO.

Freeman, Linda, 1997, *The Ambiguous Champion. Canada and South Africa in the Trudeau and Mulroney Years*. Toronto: University of Toronto Press.

Furre, Berge, 1992, *Norsk historie 1905–1990: vårt hundreår*. Oslo: Samlaget.

Grung, Anne Hege, 1991, "Den 'svarte' lutherske kirken i Natal/KwaZulu og Inkatha", *Kirke og Kultur*, No. 3.

Gudim, Øystein, 1996, "A Defeat for the Shipping Lobby? The Norwegian experience", in R. Hengevold and J. Rodenburg (eds.), *Embargo*. Amsterdam: Amsterdam University Press.

Grøndahl, Jan E., 1997, *Portugal-saken. Norge og Portugals kolonipolitikk 1961–1974*. Oslo: University of Oslo, Department of History. (Thesis.)

Halliday, Fred, 1986, *The Making of the Second Cold War*. London: Verso.

Hanlon, Joseph, 1986, *Beggar Your Neighbours. Apartheid Power in Southern Africa*. London: CIIR and James Currey.

Heino, Timo-Erkki, 1992, *Politics on Paper. Finland's South Africa Policy 1956–91*. Uppsala: Nordiska Afrikainstitutet. (Research Report No. 90.)

Heldal, Inger (ed.), 1996, *From Cape to Cape against Apartheid*. Cape Town: Mayibuye Books. (Mayibuye History and Literature Series, No. 61.) Norwegian edition: *Sammen for demokrati—Norsk støtte i kampen mot apartheid*. Oslo: Utenriksdepartementet (1995).

Hengevold, Richard and Jaap Rodenburg (eds.), 1996, *Embargo. Apartheid's Oil Secrets Revealed*. Amsterdam: Amsterdam University Press.

Henriksen, Jan Olav, 1988, *For menneskelivets skyld. Den norske kirkes internasjonale menneskerettighetsengasjement*. Oslo: Kirkens Informasjonstjeneste.

Hewson, L.A. (ed.), 1961, *Cottosloe Consultation*. Grahamstown.

ICFTU, 1978, *African Workers Under Apartheid*. Brussels: ICFTU.

—, 1992, *Report of the Fifteenth World Conference*. Brussels: ICFTU.

Isaacman, Allen and Barabra Isaacman, 1983, *Mozambique: From Colonialism to Revolution, 1999–1982*. Boulder, CO: Westview Press.

Johnson, Phyllis and David Martin, 1989, *Apartheid Terrorism: The Destabilization Report*. London: James Currey.

Jørgensen, Torstein, 1987, *Contact and Conflict. Norwegian Missionaries, the Zulu Kingdom and the Gospel, 1850–1870*. Stavanger: Misjonshøgskolen.

Katjavivi, Peter, 1988, *A History of Resistance in Namibia*. London: James Currey/UNESCO Press.

Kirkens Informasjonstjeneste, 1977, *Sør-Afrika og kirken*. Oslo: Kirkens Informasjonstjeneste.

de Klerk, F.W., 1999, *The Last Trek—A New Beginning. The Autoiography*. London: Macmillan.

Kristensen, Anita, 1996, *Norske myndigheter og boikotten av Sør-Afrika*. Oslo: University of Oslo, Department of Economics. (Thesis.)

Kristiansen, Tomm, 1995, *Mandelas land*. Oslo: Cappelen.

Kristiansen, Tomm and Aud-Lise Norheim (eds.), 1999, *Høvdingen*. Oslo: Cappelen.

Lear, F.M., 1980, *St. Olav Lutheran Church 1880–1980*. Durban.

Leverton, B.J.T., 1982, *The Natal Norwegian Centenary 1882–1982*. Latern.

Leys, Colin and John S. Saul, 1995, *Namibia's Liberation Struggle: The Two-Edged Sword*. London/Athens: James Currey/Ohio University Press.

Lislerud, Gunnar, 1979, "Frigjøringsbevegelsene i det sørlige Afrika", *Kirke og Kultur*, No. 5.

—, 1991, "Kirkens vitnesbyrd i et Sør-Afrika under forvandling", *Tidsskrift for Teologi og Kirke*, No. 2.

—, 1998, "Luthersk kirkedannelse i Sør-Afrika", *Norsk Tidsskrift for Misjon*, No. 2–3.

Lodge, Tom, 1983, *Black Politics in South Africa since 1945*. London: Longman.

Luthuli, Albert, 1962, *Let My People Go*. London: Fontana Books.

Løken, Andreas, 1955, "Misjon og kirke i Sør-Afrika—situasjonen i dag", *Norsk Tidsskrift for Misjon*, No. 2.

—, 1961, "Apartheid—noen synspunkter", *Norsk Tidsskrift for Misjon*, No. 1.

MacQueen, Norrie, 1997, *The Decolonisation of Portuguese Empire: Metropolitan Revolution and the Dissolution of Empire*. London: Longman.

Mandela, Nelson, 1964, *Derfor er jeg beredt til å dø*. Oslo: PAX Forlag. (Reprinted in 1989 with a new preface by Tore Linné Eriksen, Halden: Exil.)

—, 1994, *Long Walk to Freedom*. London: Little, Brown and Company. (Norwegian edition: *Veien til frihet*. Oslo: Aschehoug, 1994.)

Maibyue Centre/Robben Island Museum/Nordiska Afrikainstitutet, 1999, *Nordic Solidarity with the Liberation Struggles in Southern Africa, and Challenges for Democratic Partnerships into the 21st Century. Robben Osland 11–14 February 1999, Conference Report*. Cape Town/Uppsala.

Martin, David and Phyllis Johnson, 1981, *The Struggle for Zimbabwe: The Chimurenga War*. London: Faber and Faber.

Minter, William, 1986, *King Solomon's Mines Revisited: Western Interests and the Burdened History of Southern Africa*. New York: Basic Books.

Mondlane, Eduardo, 1970, *Kampen for Mocambique*. Oslo: Gyldendal Norsk Forlag. (With an introduction by Tore Linné Eriksen.)

Morgenstierne, Christopher Munthe, 1999, *Denmark: A Flexible Response—humanitarian and political*. Uppsala: Nordiska Afrikainstitutet. (Draft).

Morrow, Sean, 1998, "Dakawa Development Centre: an African National Congress settlement in Tanzania 1982–1992", *African Affairs*, Vol. 97, No. 389.

Nangolo, Mvula ya and Tor Sellström, 1995, *Kassinga: A Story Untold*. Windhoek: Namibian Book Development Council.

Narum, Ragnhild, 1998, *Norge og rasekonflikten i Sør-Afrika, 1960–1978*. Oslo: University of Oslo, Department of History. (Thesis.)

Nordengen, Per Anders (ed.), 1994, *Det farlige ordet*. Oslo: Verbum.

Odén, Bertil and Haroub Othman (eds.), 1989, *Regional Co-operation in Southern Africa: A Post-Apartheid Perspective*. Uppsala: Nordiska Afrikainstitutet.

Parsons, Neil, 1995, *The New History of Southern Africa*. London: Macmillan.

Ranger, T.O., 1985, *Peasant Consciousness and guerrilla war in Zimbabwe. A comparative study*. London: James Currey.

Sano, Hans-Otto et al., 1991, *Namibia and the Nordic Countries*. Uppsala: Scandinavian Institute of African Studies.

Saul, John S., 1993, *Recolonization and Resistance: Southern Africa in the 1990s*. Trenton, NJ: Africa World Press.

Sellström, Tor, 1999, *Sweden and National Liberation in Southern Africa. Volume I: Formation of a Popular Opinion (1959–1970)*. Uppsala: Nordiska Afrikainstitutet.

—, 1999, *Liberation in Southern Africa. Regional and Swedish voices*. Uppsala: Nordiska Afrikainstitutet.

—, (forthcoming), *Sweden and National Liberation in Southern Africa. Volume II*. Uppsala: Nordiska Afrikainstitutet.

Shubin, Vladimir, 1999, *ANC: A view from Moscow*. Cape Town: Mayibuye Publishers.

Simensen, Jarle (ed.), 1984, *Norsk misjon i afrikanske samfunn, Sør-Afrika ca. 1850–1900*. Trondheim: Tapir.

Soiri, Iina and Pekka Peltola, 1999, *Finland and National Liberation in Southern Africa*. Uppsala: Nordiska Afrikainstitutet.

Sommerfeldt, Atle, 1988, "For menneskelivets skyld: Om Mellomkirkelig Råds menneskerettighetsengasjement", *Kirke og Kultur*, No. 6.

Southall, Roger, 1995, *Imperialism or Solidarity? International Labour and South African Trade Unions*. Cape Town: UCT Press.

Stokke, Olav, 1970, "Utviklingsbistand og frigjøringsbevegelser", *Internasjonal Politikk*, No. 3.

—, 1973, "Norsk støtte til frgjøringsbevegelser", *Norsk Utenrikspolitisk Årbok 1973*. Oslo: Norsk Utenrikspolitisk Institutt.

Stokke, Olav and Carl Widstrand (eds.), 1973, *Southern Africa, The UN-OAU Conference. Part 1: Programme of Action & Conference Proceedings. Part 2: Papers and Documents*. Uppsala: Scandinavian Institute of African Studies.

Stålsett, Gunnar, 1971, "Kirkelig støtte til frigjøringsbevegelser: hva saken gjelder", *Kirke og Kultur*, No. 5.

Tamnes, Rolf, 1997, *Oljealder, 1965–1995. Norsk utenrikspolitikks historie, bind 6*. Oslo: Universitetsforlaget.

Thorud, Johan, 1972, *Geriljasamfunnet. Guinea-Bissaus kamp mot Portugal*. Oslo: Tiden.

Tjønneland, Elling Njål, 1978, *Kampen for frigjering*. Oslo: Norwegian Council for Southern Africa.

Tørres, Liv, 1995, *Ny hverdag for sør-afrikanske arbeidere*. Oslo: LO.

United Nations, 1994, *The United Nations and Apartheid 1948–1994*. New York: United Nations. (The United Nations Blue Book Series, Vol. I, Department of Public Information.)

(US), 1975, *The Kissinger Study on Southern Africa*. Nottingham: Spokesman Books. (The National Security Memorandum 39.)

Vetlesen, Vesla, 1981, *Sør-afrikanske arbeidere i kamp for sine rettigheter*. Oslo: LO/AIS/Norsk Folkehjelp.

—, 1998, *Frihet for Sør-Afrika. LO og kampen mot apartheid*. Oslo: Tiden Norsk Forlag.

Voksø, Per, 1987, *Utfordringen*. Oslo: Norwegian Church Aid.

World Council of Churches, 1985, *The Kairos Document*. Geneva.

Østergaard, Tom, 1990, *SADCC: A Political and Economic Survey*. Copenhagen: Danida.

Official Norwegian support to the struggle for freedom in Southern Africa[2]

Table I   *Total Norwegian support to Southern Africa 1963–1993*[3]

	Current value	Constant 1998 value
1963	500 000	3 820 000
1964	10 000	70 000
1965	680 000	4 720 000
1966	670 000	4 490 000
1967	840 000	5 520 000
1968	1 720 000	10 960 000
1969	2 290 000	14 140 000
1970	2 260 000	12 610 000
1971	4 000 000	21 010 000
1972	4 530 000	22 210 000
1973	4 710 000	21 460 000
1974	11 930 000	49 740 000
1975	7 580 000	28 260 000
1976	12 730 000	43 450 000
1977	35 910 000	112 370 000
1978	45 910 000	133 110 000
1979	44 100 000	121 960 000
1980	49 360 000	123 040 000
1981	42 500 000	93 170 000
1982	42 000 000	82 760 000
1983	74 200 000	134 880 000
1984	82 300 000	140 750 000
1985	90 200 000	145 920 000
1986	108 300 000	163 440 000
1987	158 200 000	219 690 000
1988	164 750 000	214 430 000
1989	179 650 000	223 570 000
1990	147 800 000	176 600 000
1991	141 200 000	163 170 000
1992	123 600 000	139 540 000
1993	98 500 000	108 770 000
TOTAL	1 682 930 000	2 739 630 000

[1] The tables are prepared by Ole Kristian Eivindson and Eva Helene Østbye.

[2] All amounts in this section are in Norwegian kroner (NOK).

[3] Assistance to independent states in the Southern African region and for regional co-operation is not included in these figures.

Humanitarian aid to the liberation movements in Southern Africa

Table II   *Total Norwegian support to the liberation movements in Southern Africa*

	Current value	Constant 1998 value
1969	200 000	1 230 000
1970	–	–
1971	700 000	3 680 000
1972	1 300 000	5 050 000
1973	380 000	1 730 000
1974	5 750 000	23 970 000
1975	1 130 000	4 210 000
1976	770 000	2 630 000
1977	15 100 000	47 250 000
1978	17 000 000	49 290 000
1979	19 500 000	53 930 000
1980	11 500 000	28 670 000
1981	25 400 000	55 680 000
1982	20 900 000	41 190 000
1983	49 450 000	89 890 000
1984	50 100 000	85 680 000
1985	53 400 000	86 390 000
1986	63 800 000	96 280 000
1987	75 000 000	104 150 000
1988	70 300 000	91 500 000
1989	69 400 000	86 370 000
1990	42 500 000	50 780 000
1991	43 300 000	50 040 000
1992	43 300 000	48 870 000
TOTAL	679 100 000	1 108 460 000

Table III   *Official support to the liberation movement in Mozambique*

	FRELIMO
1969	200 000[4]
1970	–
1971	700 000
1972	700 000
1973	–[5]
1974	5 000 000
TOTAL	6 600 000

---

[4] Both the allocation for 1969 and for 1971 was given through The Norwegian Special Committee for Refugees from Southern Africa to the Mozambique Institute, which was run by FRELIMO.

[5] An allocation of 1 500 000 was not used.

Table IV   *Official support to the liberation movement in Angola*

	MPLA
1972	330 000
1973	280 000[6]
1974	250 000[7]
1975	–[8]
TOTAL	860 000

Table V   *Official support to the liberation movement in Namibia*

	SWAPO
1973	100 000
1974	300 000
1975	1 000 000
1976	770 000[9]
1977	4 000 000
1978	7 000 000
1979	8 000 000
1980	8 000 000
1981	21 000 000[10]
1982	15 400 000
1983	16 000 000
1984	18 000 000
1985	20 000 000[11]
1986	23 400 000
1987	27 000 000
1988	26 200 000
1989	28 800 000
1990	–
TOTAL	224 970 000

[6] Of an allocation of 1 250 000.

[7] An allocation of 1 250 000 was granted but 1 000 000 was transferred to UNHCR.

[8] An allocation of 2 500 000 was granted but not disbursed because of the civil war. Instead 1 500 000 was allocated to humanitarian aid in Angola.

[9] 350 000 was disbursed through The Norwegian Special Committee for Refugees from Southern Africa.

[10] The original grant was 10 000 000 but South African attacks on Angola made additional support necessary.

[11] Norway guaranteed for 65 000 000 to build and run the secondary school for Namibian refugees in Congo. This amount is included in the allocations for the forthcoming years.

Table VI   *Official support to the liberation movement and to*
refugees in Zimbabwe

1974	100 000	ZANU
	100 000	ZAPU
1975	130 000	ANC/Z[12]
1976	–	
1977	4 000 000	ZANU
	4 000 000	ZAPU
	450 000	ANC/Z[13]
1978	3 000 000	ZANU
	3 000 000	ZAPU
1979	4 000 000	ZANU
	4 000 000	ZAPU
TOTAL	22 780 000	

Table VII   *Official support to the liberation movements in*
South Africa

	ANC	PAC
1977	2 000 000	650 000
1978	3 000 000	1 000 000
1979	3 000 000	500 000
1980	3 000 000	500 000
1981	3 500 000	900 000
1982	5 000 000	500 000
1983	32 700 000[14]	750 000
1984	28 800 000	3 300 000
1985	32 000 000	1 400 000
1986	39 100 000	1 300 000
1987	46 000 000	2 000 000
1988	41 500 000	2 600 000
1989	38 500 000	2 100 000
1990	40 400 000	2 100 000
1991	41 000 000	2 300 000
1992	41 000 000	2 300 000
TOTAL	400 500 000	24 200 000

[12] African National Council was at the time regarded as an umbrella organisation including ZANU and ZAPU.

[13] United African National Council was the movement led by Abel Muzorewa.

[14] The increase from 1982 to 1983 is due to an extraordinary allocation of 20 700 000 to the ANC settlement in Mazimbu, Tanzania.

Other channels of Norwegian support to the liberation of Southern Africa

Table VIII *The Norwegian Special Committee for Refugees from Southern Africa*[15]

1963	500 000	1973	2 500 000
1964	10 000	1974	3 000 000
1965	500 000	1975	3 600 000
1966	500 000	1976	4 000 000
1967	500 000	1977	5 500 000
1968	1 600 000	1978	7 000 000
1969	1 650 000	1979	7 900 000
1970	1 650 000	1980	8 000 000
1971	2 900 000	1981	6 000 000
1972	2 200 000	1982	9 000 000
TOTAL			72 510 000

Table IX *Support to Southern Africa through NGOs and UNHCR, granted outside the Special Committee*

1971	10 000	1975	300 000
1972	200 000	1976	4 000 000
1973	430 000	1977	8 250 000
1974	1 380 000	1978	10 000 000
TOTAL			24 570 000

Table X *Other support to Rhodesia*

1976	80 000	To authorities in Botswana to transport Rhodesian refugees from Botswana to Zambia
	120 000	Expenses in connection with the liberation movements participation in the Geneva conference
1977	450 000	Botswana Council of Refugees
1978	2 000 000	Botswana Council of Refugees
	2 000 000	Nucleo de Apoio
1979	4 000 000	Botswana Council of Refugees
	4 000 000	Nucleo de Apoio
1980	16 000 000	To refugees and reconstruction
TOTAL	28 650 000	

[15] The Special Committee financed i.a. scholarships through IUEF and UNHCR and support through the Church of Norway Council on Ecumenical and International Relations, the Norwegian People's Aid and the Students' and Academics' International Assistance Fund (SAIH). The Special Committee was closed down 1 January 1983. Instead the MFA increased the support to Southern Africa through NGOs, see table XI.

Table XI   *Support to Southern Africa through NGOs*

		1988	79 400 000
1983	11 000 000	1989	95 200 000
1984	19 000 000	1990	80 700 000
1985	23 000 000	1991	87 000 000
1986	29 900 000	1992	69 400 000
1987	68 000 000	1993	87 600 000
TOTAL			650 200 000

Table XII   *United Nations Educational and Training Programme for Southern Africa (UNETPSA)*[16]

		1979	3 900 000
1965	180 000	1980	4 200 000
1966	100 000	1981	4 200 000
1967	310 000	1982	4 200 000
1968	–	1983	5 000 000
1969	360 000	1984	5 500 000
1970	430 000	1985	5 600 000
1971	540 000	1986	5 800 000
1972	600 000	1987	6 000 000
1973	700 000	1988	6 000 000
1974	1 000 000	1989	6 000 000
1975	1 400 000	1990	6 500 000
1976	1 700 000	1991	6 500 000
1977	2 500 000	1992	6 500 000
1978	3 200 000	1993	6 500 000
TOTAL			95 420 000

Table XIII *United Nations Trust Fund for South Africa*

1966	70 000	1980	1 600 000
1967	–	1981	1 600 000
1968	70 000	1982	1 800 000
1969	140 000	1983	3 100 000
1970	180 000	1984	3 500 000
1971	250 000	1985	3 600 000
1972	300 000	1986	4 000 000
1973	400 000	1987	4 250 000
1974	500 000	1988	4 250 000
1975	650 000	1989	4 250 000
1976	750 000	1990	4 400 000
1977	900 000	1991	4 400 000
1978	1 200 000	1992	4 400 000
1979	1 400 000	1993	4 400 000
TOTAL			56 360 000

[16] The Norwegian allocations for 1965 and 1966 supported the UN Educational and Training Programme for South Africa and South West Africa respectively. UNETPSA was founded in 1967.

Table XIV *United Nations Nationhood Programme for Namibia*

		1984	2 000 000
1978	500 000	1985	2 000 000
1979	–	1986	2 000 000
1980	4 500 000	1987	2 000 000
1981	1 000 000	1988	2 000 000
1982	1 000 000	1989	2 000 000
1983	3 000 000	1990	2 200 000
TOTAL			24 200 000

Table XV *United Nations Institute for Namibia*

		1983	2 500 000
1976	300 000	1984	2 000 000
1977	500 000	1985	2 400 000
1978	750 000	1986	2 600 000
1979	900 000	1987	2 800 000
1980	1 000 000	1988	2 800 000
1981	1 000 000	1989	2 800 000
1982	1 200 000	1990	3 000 000
TOTAL			26 550 000

Table XVI *United Nations Trust Fund for Namibia*

1990	8 500 000

Table XVII *International Defence and Aid Fund (IDAF)*[17]

1967	30 000	1975	500 000
1968	50 000	1976	1 000 000
1969	140 000	1977	2 500 000
1970	–	1978	2 000 000
1971	300 000	1979	2 500 000
1972	200 000	1980	2 500 000
1973	300 000	1981	3 000 000
1974	300 000	1982	3 500 000
TOTAL			18 820 000

[17] The support to IDAF continued also after 1982 but then as part of the support from the Ministry of Foreign Affairs through NGOs, see table XI.

Contributors

Berit Hagen Agøy, b. 1960, cand.philol. (history) from University of Oslo with a thesis on the attitudes towards apartheid among Norwegian missionaries in South Africa. She has worked with Southern African matters in the Church of Norway Council on Ecumenical and International Relations and headed the Church of Norway Development Education Service. She currently teaches at Telemark University College and Bø Upper Secondary School.

Nina Drolsum, b. 1963, is a historian educated at the University of Oslo. She has recently written the history of the Norwegian Council for (Southern) Africa (*For et fritt Afrika*, Oslo, 1999), and is currently writing the history of the Norwegian Students' and Academics' International Assistance Fund.

Tore Linné Eriksen, b. 1945, Associate Professor at Oslo University College, Section for Development Studies. He has taught at the University of Oslo, and has been a research fellow at the Nordic Africa Institute (Uppsala) and the Norwegian Institute of International Affairs, NUPI (Oslo). He is also the author of *The Political Economy of Namibia* (Uppsala, 1989) and several other books on global history, African history and development studies.

Anita Kristensen Krokan, b. 1970 graduated as an economist (cand. polit.) from the University of Oslo in 1996 with a thesis on sanctions against South Africa (*Norske myndigheter og boikotten av Sør-Afrika*). In 1997 she joined the project *Forced Migration: Early Warning as Basis for Preventive Action* at the Norwegian Institute of International Affairs. From 1998 to 1999 she continued as co-ordinator of the project *Training for Peace in Southern Africa*. At present she is working as Higher Executive Officer at the Norwegian Defence Command.

Wolf Lorenz, b. 1968, has studied history, German and journalism at the University of Oslo, and graduated with a history dissertation on Norway and the liberation of Rhodesia/Zimbabwe. He has travelled widely in Southern Africa, and is currently working as a translator for the Norwegian Broadcasting Corporation.

Vesla Vetlesen, b. 1930, textile worker and designer, organisational and information work for Save the Children (1973–75), Norwegian People's Aid (1975–80), Norwegian Confederation of Trade Unions' International Department (1980–94). Minister of Development Co-operation 1986–88 (Labour Party). She has written articles and books concerned with development issues, European politics, apartheid (*Frihet for Sør-Afrika*, Oslo, 1998) and equal rights for women, and is also editor of botanical periodicals and the author of books about orchids.

Eva Helene Østbye, b. 1960, was trained as a historian at the University of Oslo. Besides writing a thesis on Norwegian development aid in Kenya, she has been one of two authors of the history of the Norwegian Refugee Council, and part of a team writing a manual for a course in conflict resolution and peace building. She is presently engaged as a mediator in a municipal council, besides working as a project co-ordinator at the Norwegian Church Aid.

Name Index

www.ingramcontent.com/pod-product-compliance
Lightning Source LLC
Chambersburg PA
CBHW080642270326
41928CB00017B/3161